# Black Markets and Militants

Understanding the political and socio-economic factors which give rise to youth recruitment into militant organizations is at the heart of grasping some of the most important issues that affect the contemporary Middle East and Africa. In this book, Khalid Mustafa Medani explains why youth are attracted to militant organizations, examining the specific role economic globalization, in the form of outmigration and expatriate remittance inflows, plays in determining how and why militant activists emerge. The study challenges existing accounts that rely primarily on ideology to explain militant recruitment. Based on extensive fieldwork, Medani offers an in-depth analysis of the impact of globalization, neoliberal reforms and informal economic networks as a conduit for the rise and evolution of moderate and militant Islamist movements and as an avenue central to the often, violent enterprise of state building and state formation. In an original contribution to the study of Islamist and ethnic politics more broadly, he thereby shows the importance of understanding when and under what conditions religious rather than other forms of identity become politically salient in the context of changes in local conditions. This title is also available as Open Access on Cambridge Core.

Khalid Mustafa Medani is Associate Professor in the Department of Political Science and the Institute of Islamic Studies at McGill University, where he is also Chair of the African Studies Program. He is the recipient of a Carnegie Scholar on Islam award between 2007–2009, and a Woodrow Wilson Scholarship in 2020–2021.

# Black Markets and Militants

## *Informal Networks in the Middle East and Africa*

Khalid Mustafa Medani
*McGill University*

**CAMBRIDGE**
**UNIVERSITY PRESS**

University Printing House, Cambridge CB2 8BS, United Kingdom

One Liberty Plaza, 20th Floor, New York, NY 10006, USA

477 Williamstown Road, Port Melbourne, VIC 3207, Australia

314–321, 3rd Floor, Plot 3, Splendor Forum, Jasola District Centre, New Delhi – 110025, India

103 Penang Road, #05–06/07, Visioncrest Commercial, Singapore 238467

Cambridge University Press & Assessment is part of the University of Cambridge.

It furthers the University's mission by disseminating knowledge in the pursuit of education, learning, and research at the highest international levels of excellence.

www.cambridge.org
Information on this title: www.cambridge.org/9781009257725
DOI: 10.1017/9781009257749



Reissued as Open Access, 2022



First published 2022

*A catalogue record for this publication is available from the British Library.*

ISBN 978-1-009-25772-5 Paperback

*To my Mentor, Teacher, and Beloved Mother, Aida Jamal Mohamed Ahmad*

# Contents

# Figures

# Tables

# Acknowledgments

The theme of trust that represents the overarching concept of this book, and the one that anchors its central argument, poignantly speaks to the remarkable level of "privileged" trust that I have enjoyed in the process of completing this manuscript. The willingness of scores of Egyptians, Sudanese, and Somalis to aid in my research for this book was just that: a Tillian understanding that their participation and work would ultimately contribute to a collective enterprise and an abiding faith that I would not betray their trust. I extend my heartfelt gratitude to all those who spent their time sharing their life experiences and entrusted me with communicating their "voices." But if this book is in most respects an outcome of their generosity, it is also a result of the labor of my research assistants and friends. I am grateful to Tariq Hassabo and Mahmoud Mourad whose assistance was invaluable during my field research in Egypt, and Abdi Musa who guided me through my data collection and work throughout northern Somalia. All three insisted on instilling courage and resolve in me so that the complicated stories of their communities would be told by a trusted source. I am grateful to Elias Fatih Abdelrahman who first guided me through the historic quarters of Imbaba and introduced me to its inspiring and generous denizens.

I have benefited enormously from the guidance and support of many colleagues and friends. I am sincerely grateful to Malek Abisaab, Rula Abisaab, Laila Parsons, and Juliet Johnson at McGill University for their guidance. This book would not have been possible without the generous advice, guidance, and sanctuary that my friend Michelle Hartman provided me. The writing of this book began while I was a visiting professor at Stanford University's Center for International Security and Cooperation (CISAC). I am indebted to Dr. Lynn Eden, former director of CISAC, whose long-standing support of my work is sincerely appreciated. This book would not have been possible without her mentorship. I am grateful to Kate Meagher and to Frances Hasso for supporting this project from its inception and for encouraging me throughout while I was a faculty member at Oberlin College. The completion of this book would not have been possible without the generous support of my friends in Montreal. I extend my deepest and most sincere thanks to Wilson Jacob, Elena Rozagova, Andrew Ivaska, Lara Braitsein, and Shahin Parhami. I am also deeply grateful for the comments and input that I received from anonymous reviewers. I am indebted to Lauri King and Heather Porter for their editorial assistance, which vastly improved this work.

While this book took many years to complete, I was privileged to supervise a number of doctoral students throughout the writing process. I would like to acknowledge my former PhD students Daniel Douek, Merouan Mekouar, Line Khatib, Jeffrey Sachs, Christopher Anzalone, Ibrahim Sanni, Abdurrahman Abdullahi, and Mohamed Sesay as well as the many MA and undergraduate students at McGill who provided great inspiration over the years. I would like to extend my gratitude to McGill University, and especially to Professor Christopher Manfredi, who provided me with the support I required to complete this book.

I am grateful to several academic institutions and foundations that supported my research at various stages. The preliminary research conducted for this book was funded by a Rocco Scholarship in Advanced African Studies from the African Studies Center at the University of California Berkeley, a Ford Foundation Middle East Research Competition Fieldwork Grant, a Hamburg Fellowship from Stanford University's CISAC, and a Humanities Development Grant from McGill University. The greater part of my research in Egypt, Sudan, Somalia, and Kenya would not have been possible without a grant from the Carnegie Corporation of New York. I would like to acknowledge my greatest debt and appreciation for the Carnegie Foundation for awarding me the Carnegie Scholar of Islam Award – a great honor that made the completion of this book possible.

Finally, there is "family." I am extremely grateful to Atif, Alia, Arif, Adil, and the late Asim: my aunts and uncles whose knowledge of the region, inherited from my grandfather Jamal Mohamed Ahmad, required a meticulous truth telling upon which this book is based. I am also grateful and appreciative to Alawiyya Jamal Mohamed Ahmad whose brilliant and compassionate intellect has served as a model for me throughout my life. This project would not have been possible without her constant intellectual inspiration. My thanks go to Donna Murch who has been an intellectual and moral guide throughout my years in graduate school and beyond.

Ultimately, this project was conceived and executed under the constant guidance of my parents and siblings. Brilliant intellectuals all – this book was partially completed so that Amjad, Ahmad, and Hanine could share in its modest accomplishments. My sister Amal played the most central role in guiding this book to its completion. They were always with me as

I traveled to Egypt, Sudan, Somalia, and Kenya – and all places in between – so that together we could do honor to the integrity and intellectual sophistication of our beloved late father, His Excellency Ambassador Mustafa Medani Abbashar. His insistence that intellectual investment always be closely intertwined with public service has guided this study from its inception.

This book is dedicated to Aida Jamal Mohamed Ahmed who more than anyone else taught me the most intricate details of the politics, culture, and history of the Middle East and Africa; mentored me on how to navigate academic and professional life with uncompromising integrity; and nurtured in me her abiding, uncompromising commitment to *al-'adl al-ijtimayi* (social justice).

This title is part of the Cambridge University Press *Flip it Open* Open Access Books program and has been "flipped" from a traditional book to an Open Access book through the program.

*Flip it Open* sells books through regular channels, treating them at the outset in the same way as any other book; they are part of our library collections for Cambridge Core, and sell as hardbacks and ebooks. The one crucial difference is that we make an upfront commitment that when each of these books meets a set revenue threshold we make them available to everyone Open Access via Cambridge Core.

This paperback edition has been released as part of our Open Access commitment and we would like to use this as an opportunity to thank the libraries and other buyers who have helped us flip this and the other titles in the program to Open Access.

To see the full list of libraries that we know have contributed to *Flip it Open*, as well as the other titles in the program please visit www.cambridge.org/fio-acknowledgements

# Preface

*Abundance and scarcity are never far apart; the rich and the poor frequent the same houses.*

— Somali proverb

This Somali proverb expresses the notion of boom-and-bust cycles and captures the precarious relationship among "boom" periods, economic downturns, and their social and political consequences. While it is widely acknowledged that exogenous shocks associated with different phases of the "business cycle" have long characterized the evolution of advanced industrial countries, rarely has this analysis been applied in a systematic fashion to less-developed countries.

The proverb refers specifically to the vicissitudes associated with ecological and climatic changes for what is a predominantly pastoralist and nomadic society. However, it can just as easily serve as a description of the general framework of this book. No society is immune from structural change and the least-developed countries are more vulnerable to economic shocks than the more advanced countries.

Over the last five decades, the boom-and-bust cycles associated with the oil price hikes of the 1970s and the recession a decade later in the Arabian Gulf have resulted in a dramatic transformation of the economic and political landscape of the major labor-exporting countries of the region. Egypt, Sudan, and Somalia, which are the subject of this book, are prime examples of this phenomenon. Along with countries like Yemen, Morocco, Syria, and Jordan, the linkage and hence political influence of the informal economy in Egypt, Sudan, and Somalia is connected to the "boom" and "bust" cycles of the oil-producing states. These external economic factors also played an important role in the evolution of Islamic and ethnic politics. The boom period of the 1970s fueled an expansion of informal foreign currency trade (i.e., the "black market") as a result of a large inflow of remittances from migrant workers in the oil-rich Gulf States who sent billions of dollars back home. The bust period, characterized by "shrinkage" in the size of informal (or "parallel") foreign currency transactions, coupled with the imposition of economic austerity measures resulted in the reconfiguration of informal economic and social organization. This development had an important influence on state capacities, national economic policies, and the transformation of identity politics in all three countries.[1]

During the oil boom, millions of Egyptians, Sudanese, and Somalis migrated to the Gulf in search of employment. These expatriate laborers sent part of their earnings directly to millions back home, through informal, decentralized, and unregulated banking systems that were often, but not always, in contest with the state. As a consequence, these capital inflows resulted in the rise of strong autonomous informal economic sectors and altered the socioeconomic landscape of all three countries in profound, but divergent, ways. The link between the expansion of informal markets and Islamic and ethnic politics, which lies at the heart of this book, is crucially determined in the social content and operation of these informal economic relations. More specifically, in all three cases, "unregulated" informal market transactions came to be dependent on social ties for their effective functioning. Shared cultural identities became increasingly important as a way of generating trust and guaranteeing that local communities could partake from the material benefits accruing from membership in these informal social networks, as well as a form of protection against repressive authoritarian rulers.[2] By contrasting the rise of religious and ethnic politics in these countries, I show in detail the political and economic conditions that have contributed to the rise, popularity, and recruitment success of Islamic and clan networks in Egypt, Sudan, and Somalia.

By focusing on the role of economic globalization in general, and labor remittance inflows in particular, this book not only explains how informal networks have contributed to social mobilization along religious and ethnic ties, but it also explains the variation in the political outcomes in these labor-exporting countries. I explain the variation in political developments generated by the boom in remittances on two general factors. The first has to do with variations in state capacity and repression, and effectiveness of state elites in regulating the economy. The second factor is related to differences in the cultural endowments of the three countries and, specifically, the social and cultural resources available to civil society actors engaged in informal transactions operating under the exigencies and pressures of economic globalization.[3]

My justification in comparing these three cases is based on the fact that all three continue to be major labor exporters in the region. Moreover, capital inflows accruing from labor migration represent the largest source of foreign currency. Consequently, when taken together, Egypt, Sudan, and Somalia provide a fruitful comparative framework with which to understand important aspects of globalization, the diminished economic role of the state, and the emergence of an issue that has preoccupied analysts and scholars the world over – the political and economic roots of Islamist politics and ethnic conflict. My central goal is to demonstrate in detail how and under what conditions religious rather than other forms of cultural cleavages become politicized.

The central argument of this book is that the effects of economic globalization (i.e., the increasing exposure to international economic forces) undermine state institution and lead to the expansion of market forces, and the erosion of prior social bonds of communities that are no longer protected by national-level institutions. However, I emphasize throughout that the effects of internationalization on domestic politics are not uniform; rather, and most importantly, they are mediated by local-level social and political institutions, resulting in different political outcomes. A central conceptual theme throughout this book centers on the political consequences of informal networks. This is because social networks secure control over informal economic transactions and labor, not only by submitting people to market forces but also by insulating them from the full impact of the market. I also stress that these developments are very much dependent on the policies of state elites and leaders and upon the patronage networks underlying their regimes. Based on many years of living and conducting research in Egypt, Sudan, and Somalia, in the narrative that follows I analyze how local communities are coping with wide-scale economic and political changes. I describe the ways in which many Egyptians, Sudanese, and Somalis are establishing a new set of rules of conduct and obligations based on locally specific Islamic and ethnic ties of not only solidarity and cooperation but also exploitation and violence.

The dramatic emergence of conservative and militant Islamic movements and the onset of ethnic conflict in many parts of the world over the last five decades have made the subject of this book a public as well as an academic concern. This book aims to show the global and local political and economic roots of these movements. It examines the ways in which informal networks have influenced the course of ethnic violence and state collapse in Somalia and the rise of conservative and militant forms of Islamism in Egypt and Sudan. This is not to neglect the importance of ideological and cultural factors addressed elsewhere, but rather to explicate causal factors more precisely by highlighting the role of informal social networks both as a measure of the diminished role of the state and as an arena through which domestic and international economies interact.

I am mindful that the choice of comparing three countries is inherently problematic in terms of sorting out rival explanations and testing hypotheses. This is because comparative analysis involves too few cases and many variables to allow for systematic controls. But by focusing on the comparability of Egypt, Sudan, and Somalia in terms of their shared similarity as remittance economies and employing a parsimonious approach that holds a host of variables constant, it is possible to make important analytical assertions based on a combination of qualitative methods. Naturally, parsimony requires modesty, and I emphasize throughout this book that while labor remittance inflows, and economic globalization more generally, provide a context for ongoing political struggles in Egypt, Sudan, and Somalia, these developments are above all a product of stark variations in state capacities and policies, and social structures particular to the cases at hand.

The idea for this book originated in a little-known incident in my own country of Sudan in late 1989, which over the course of a number of years led me to investigate the relationship among globalization, informal markets, and political violence. In December of that year, while residing in Khartoum, I was a witness to the summary trial and execution of a young Sudanese businessman by the name of Majdi Mahjoub Mohammad Ahmad. While the Islamist-backed regime led by the recently ousted Omer Bashir oversaw the killings and imprisonment of scores of Sudanese since its engineering of the military coup of June 1989, Mr. Ahmad's case illustrated the political struggle between the state and civil society over the informal economy. Following the overthrow of the democratically elected government of Prime Minister Sadiq al-Mahdi, Mr. Ahmad was the first of many to be executed under a new presidential decree that charged him with "economic treason" against the state. In reality, Mr. Ahmad was falsely accused and then executed by the Islamist regime in Khartoum because he, like thousands of other Sudanese, was allegedly involved in the flourishing black market trade in the country. In subsequent years, I began to conduct research on the motive behind the state's "wrath" against those Sudanese involved in the informal economy and discovered that the latter's primary interest was to monopolize the informal trade in workers' remittances as a way to finance their own Islamist clientelistic networks.

It was during my research in Sudan that I first realized the great political significance and true weight of labor remittances in terms of their impact on local political and economic dynamics. Following these observations, I traveled to Somalia to investigate the role of labor remittances. In 2000, I resided and worked in Somalia, I discovered that the inflow of labor remittance to the "weak" state of Somalia also represented a source of conflict, albeit of a different sort. Indeed, in the same period that the Bashir regime was attempting to corner the market on remittances to fund "fundamentalism," in Somalia informal transfer agencies (i.e., *sharikat hawwalat*) were financing clan-based guerilla movements in northern Somalia. Organized under the Somalia National Movement (SNM), migrant workers from the northern-based Isaaq clan were sending funds to finance SNM fighters against the dictatorial regime of Siad Barre. In plainer empirical terms, I discovered that while informal financial markets played an important role in facilitating an Islamist coalition in Sudan, in Somalia they hardened and consolidated clan-centered ties.

These observations and subsequent research in Sudan, Somalia, and Egypt inspired the subject of this book. *Black Markets and Militants: Informal Networks in the Middle East and Africa* focuses on the variable ways that informal social and economic networks have played in the rise of new forms of Islamist Politics. However, given the diversity of cultural and religious cleavages throughout the Muslim Middle East and Africa, I do not a priori assume "Islam" as a primary source of political identification. I also analyze in detail when and under what conditions conservative and militant Islamism engender political activism and, in the case of Somalia, why ethnic and kinship ties may serve as the most important resource of political and social life. This analysis also has global policy relevance. Specifically, in order to examine the ways in which variable types of informal institutions serve to finance and organize different forms of Islamist activism, I detail the expansion of informal financial markets (e.g., hawwalat), unregulated Islamic welfare organizations, and the role of the "Ahali" (or private) Mosque in providing important context for the recruitment of young militants. This book then is a modest contribution to ongoing academic and public concerns. My goal is to enhance global understanding about the relationship between political and economic change and Islamist political movements generally, and to broaden knowledge about which specific types of informal mechanisms are (or are not) conducive to the rise of Islamist militancy and recruitment in particular local contexts.

*I*

# The Framework

# Introduction

## Black Markets, Militants, and Clans: Informal Networks, Islamism, and the Politics of Identity

The emergence, and proliferation, of Islamist militant organizations, ranging from the Islamic State of Iraq and Syria (ISIS) and *Al-Shabbaab* in Somalia, to Boko Haram in Nigeria and other parts of West Africa, has once again demonstrated that political Islam is an important global political issue. It has also highlighted a number of challenging, but increasingly crucial analytical questions: How popular a force is militant Islam, and how is it distinguishable from more conservative and moderate forms of Islamist activism? Does the rise of Islamist militancy across many regions of the Muslim world represent a "clash of civilizations," or is its emergence a result of locally embedded, but globally linked, economic and social forces? And, finally, given the considerable diversity of socio-economic formations within Muslim societies when, and under what conditions, do religious rather than ethnic cleavages serve as the most salient source of political identification?

Many arguments advanced in the context of the emergence of Islamist militant organizations across the globe have sought to answer these questions by invoking the economic underdevelopment of the Muslim world. The increasing permeability of state borders has transformed some economic grievances in the Muslim world into mistrust of Westernization and modern capitalism.[1] And it is this hostility that has also brought about the emergence of Islamic banking, the expansion of Islamic charitable associations, and the use of informal banking systems, or hawwalat. These financial systems are used by Islamists not only to finance terrorist operations, but also to pursue a strict campaign of economic and "moral" separatism.[2] In contrast, other analysts continue to downplay the long-term threat of Islamist militancy. They contend that, by and large, most Muslims are supportive of global markets, technological innovation, and capitalism in general.[3]

These interpretations capture important general truths about some of the causes and consequences of militant Islam. However, it would also be futile to address this challenge without understanding the locally specific social, economic, and political factors that help to sustain these movements. *Black Markets and Militants* sheds light on these issues by examining the economic and political conditions that have led to the rise of different forms of mobilization and recruitment of Islamist conservative and militant activists in three predominantly Muslim countries: Egypt, Sudan, and Somalia.

To understand the socioeconomic conditions under which recruitment into Islamist militant organizations occurs, it is imperative to understand when and under what conditions religious rather than other forms of identity become politically salient in the context of changing local conditions. This study centers on the current debate about the role that social and economic conditions play in giving rise to Islamist militancy and recruitment within the context of globalization.[4] However, instead of emphasizing aspects of Islamic doctrine, pan-Islamist ideology, the impact of US foreign policy, or formal political and economic linkages with nation-states,[5] I focus on the informal institutional arrangements that have resulted in the organization of Islamist conservative and militant organizations as well as ethnic-based political coalitions at the level of the community in three comparable countries.

Drawing on the results of over two decades of field research this work focuses on the informal market mechanisms that, under the exigencies of declining state capacity and state repression, have given rise to new forms of Islamist politics. To examine the ways in which different types of informal institutions serve to finance and organize Islamist militancy within the context of "weak" states, I explore the expansion of hawwalat, unregulated Islamic welfare associations, and the role of the *Ahali*, or private, Mosque in providing a conducive environment for the recruitment of young militants. The ultimate goal of this work is to play a modest role in enhancing global understanding about the relationship between political and economic change and Islamist movements generally and to broaden knowledge about which specific types of informal networks are (or are not) conducive to the rise of Islamist militancy and recruitment in particular local contexts.

*Black Markets and Militants* extends the boundaries of knowledge about the emergence of Islamist political activism and extremism by deepening our comparative understanding of the local and regional connections underpinning the evolution of political Islam. In this regard, I build upon the influential work of Judith Scheele and other scholars who have highlighted the crucial role that regional and transnational linkages play in the evolution of social and political life at the level of the community, and the ways in which, in the Middle Eastern and African contexts, Islam is often used to establish law and order even as it is mediated by different levels of state capacity or state repression.[6] I do so by providing an analytical framework linking knowledge about political Islam with several important analytical debates in academic circles, including the literature on weak and fragile states in developing countries in general, and in Africa in particular; the varieties and political implications of informal institutions for overall patterns of social change and conflict; and the debate on terrorist finance and Islamist militant recruitment.

## Global and Local Linkages in Islamist Politics

If this study addresses some important themes related to the long-standing concern among scholars of comparative politics with respect to the dynamics and evolution of Islamist and ethnic politics in African and Middle Eastern societies, it also has much to say with respect to the revived interest among scholars – across the disciplines – in the political and economic linkages between countries like Egypt, Sudan, and Somalia and the Arabian Gulf. In this respect this study has broader significance in that it explains the ways in which structurally similar relationships to the international and regional economy may help to produce very different political outcomes and generate variable forms of identity-based forms of collective action in three "most similar" cases. Egypt, Sudan, and Somalia are all major labor exporters that witnessed a boom in expatriate remittances in the 1970s and early 1980s. By the mid-1980s and into the 1990s, remittances declined dramatically, generating severe recessions and economic austerity policies. These capital inflows produced similar macro-institutional responses: in the boom, they circumvented official financial institutions and had the unintended consequences of undercutting the state's fiscal and regulatory capacities while simultaneously fueling the expansion of informal markets in foreign currency trade, land, and labor. In the prosperous 1970s, these informal markets came to be "regulated" by indigenous Islamic and ethnic networks, which provided cohesion, shared norms, and an economic infrastructure outside the formal economic and political system. In the economic crisis of the 1980s and 1990s, however, the material links between formal and informal institutions eroded with the result that the nature of Islamist and ethnic politics transmuted again, producing three outcomes in Sudan, Somalia, and Egypt: consolidation, disintegration, and fragmentation.

More specifically, and through an in-depth historical analysis of comparable informal institutional arrangements, I demonstrate when, and under what conditions, informal market relations have oriented social and economic networks around religious networks as in Egypt and Sudan, or ethnic affiliations as in Somalia. I locate the rise and fall of an Islamist-authoritarian regime in Sudan, state disintegration in Somalia, and rising divisions and competition between conservative pro-market

Islamist groups and militant Islamist organizations in Egypt in the way that informal financial and labor markets were captured by segments of the state and social groups. The divergent political outcomes in Somalia, Egypt, and the Sudan reflect – as I show in detail – the results of prior political conflicts between state elites and actors in civil society over the monopolization and social regulation (i.e., the creation) of different types of informal markets. My central argument is that the form identity politics evolved in the three cases was greatly dependent on whether Islamist or kinship groups were successful in establishing a monopoly over informal markets and relatively more proficient in utilizing their newly formed political coalition to control competition, albeit through highly coercive and violent means.

## Labor Remittances and Islamist and Ethnic Politics

The larger comparative framework of *Black Markets and Militants* illuminates some pertinent issues related to the relationship between economic globalization, domestic political outcomes, and identity-based forms of collective action. In less-developed countries remittance inflows have a number of indirect impacts on local-level politics and the domestic economy.[7] First, the internationalization of economic transactions in the form of labor remittances (as a percentage of imports) often coincides with the expansion of the informal financial sector and informal employment.[8] Moreover, the vagaries of world market shocks, the boom and bust cycles, disproportionately impact domestic financial markets in the case of the labor exporters. Black markets for foreign currency, which operate on a relatively free market basis, open up the domestic financial markets to international forces.[9] Second, in the context of weak states, increased economic globalization often leads to political conflict over trade and exchange rate policies that in many instances engender, in civil society, mobilization along regional, religious, and ethnic lines. As a consequence, state elites may meet these challenges with brutal reprisals and devastating human rights violations against groups in civil society. Third, the political power of capital, in relation to labor and the state, increases with internationalization, depending on the specific character of the informal economy. That is, whether the type of capital accumulation that results in its expansion accrues to formal state institutions or to private groups in civil society. Finally, the globalization of markets may either undermine state autonomy and the efficacy of its macroeconomic policies or strengthen its hand in terms of resource extraction and distribution.

Indeed, in Sudan, labor remittances from the 1970s until the late 1980s represented not only the most important source of foreign exchange for millions of Sudanese, they also posed a particularly significant threat for a new Islamist regime that sought to corner the market on these lucrative transfers. That most of these remitted funds bypassed official state channels and were essentially delivered directly to individuals and families meant that they had the potential of financing not only economic livelihoods but also altering state-society relations in crucial ways. Specifically, the role of informally channeled labor remittances had the potential of serving as key financing mechanisms of recruitment to groups working in opposition to the state. The newly ensconced Islamist-military junta led by Omer Bashir was particularly wary of this type of opposition and of the potential for the underground informal economy to provide a necessary financial base to the newly mobilized opposition. Moreover, because Bashir and the Islamist leaders inherited a heavily bankrupt and indebted state, they were keen to monopolize as many of these lucrative informal financial transfers as possible in order to strengthen their economic and political control of the country. The Islamists unprecedented violent crack-down on the black market, including numerous executions of people found guilty of economic treason, was also based on the fact that the Islamists of Sudan had themselves monopolized informal currency trade to build a strong financial base for their movement, recruit followers, and eventually capture the levers of state power. Their attack against the informal economy reflected personal experience.

In Somalia, as in Sudan, labor remittances have played a very important role, but the political consequence of these capital inflows resulted in a different political outcome. Here remittances and their transfer through informal hawwalat banking systems have played a major role in both the disintegration of the state and the financing of clan-based militias. Given the particular weak level of state capacity in Somalia and a distinct social structure wherein clan ties have served as the most important social institution in political and social life, informal financial transfers actually strengthened clan ties and helped to finance militias that were responsible for ousting the dictator Siad Barre. Moreover, following the collapse of the state, informal financial flows continue to ferment interclan conflict.

Egypt represents yet another comparative case wherein the oil boom in the Arab Gulf engendered a boom in labor remittance inflows of dramatic proportions. Like Sudan and Somalia, Egypt has long been a labor-exporting country and it counts the inflow of capital from migrant remittances as the most important source of foreign exchange. In the 1970s and 1980s Egypt followed a political economic trajectory similar to both Sudan and Somalia. Egypt was flush with remittances during the oil boom and much of this was funneled informally via black markets, bypassing the state and central banks. In many respects, this was considered a financial boom for the Islamist movement that took the opportunity to finance a host of businesses, social welfare associations, and money-changing institutions to support their movement and recruit followers. But the remittance boom also engendered an expansion of the country's money supply that altered the very nature of Egypt's informal economy. Specifically, remittances resulted in a boom of another sort centered on the rise and expansion of informal housing outside greater Cairo. Far from negligible, these informal settlements house millions of Cairo's denizens and it is here that, in the 1990s, Cairo saw the rise in popularity of militant Islamism at the very heart of the capital.

## The Politics of Informal Markets

This book thus examines the influence of labor remittance (i.e., informal commercial networks) in the evolution of Islamist and ethnic politics in Egypt, Sudan, and Somalia. This is not to neglect the importance of ideological and cultural factors as alternative explanations, but rather to explicate causal factors more precisely by highlighting the role of the informal, or more specifically the parallel, economy both as a measure of the diminished role of the state and as an arena through which domestic and international economies interact. This is because, while the literature on informal institutions has set the stage for dethroning the state as the primary unit of analysis, rarely have these studies advanced a truly political analysis of the informal realm that relates it to concrete patterns of state formation, state dissolution, democratization, and social mobilization in Africa and the Middle East.[10] Fewer still have attempted to posit a linkage between informal financial markets and the global economy. More specifically, the important linkage between external capital flows and the informal market has not been analyzed sufficiently, with the result that its role in domestic political outcomes has been obscured.[11] As Scott Radnitz noted in an important review of the literature on informality, despite important advances in the field, further research is required that takes seriously the role of informal institutions in political outcomes across difference cases, regime types, and levels of development.[12] My comparative analysis of informality in Egypt, Sudan, and Somalia addresses some of these important concerns, and it goes further by focusing on the role of informal networks in the emergence of identity-based forms of collection.

## A Typology of the "Hidden" Economy

Most work on informal markets in particular has remained largely descriptive as a by-product of the treatment of the state and the market as reified entities. Scholars concerned with the disrupting effects of state intervention focus on interventionist policies, while others inspired by the neutrality of the market are concerned primarily with barriers to market entry.[13] Both views neglect the fact that there exists a plurality of state-society relations that structure markets within and across societies. Even those scholars who recognize the intimate link between the state and a particular type of informal market rarely recognize that the latter may function in close social proximity to other parallel, illicit, criminal, or otherwise unofficial markets. In the case of Somalia, for example, the expansion of the parallel market fueled a different type of informal market centered on livestock trade, which in turn facilitated the creation of an informal urban sector. Comprised primarily of family firms, the latter was thus not only dependent on remittance flows; it was forced to struggle to create a social structure to control competition and pricing behavior. That this development centered on extant clan structures in Somalia was due more to the newness of these informal firms and the absence of alternative financial institutions, rather than age-old emotional rivalries. Similarly, the relative success of the Islamists in Egypt and Sudan was in large part due to the Islamists' monopolization of black-market transactions that negotiated an intimate link with official financial markets. Despite the fact that they represented a relatively small group, this strategy enabled the Islamist elite to establish a monopoly over informal finance and credit creating and utilizing their political coalition to control competition.[14]

Not only is it important to distinguish between the various analytical definitions of the hidden economy, it is equally important to treat these fragmented markets in a dynamic fashion. That is, how – and to what extent – are they created, in what manner are they related to state strength and local social structures, and finally on what state-initiated policies do their fortunes depend? For the parallel sector defined as highly organized foreign currency transactions, often denominated by dollars, situating these exchanges within the international as well as national economic context is analytically crucial.

In this respect it is important to differentiate between the official and this second, or hidden, economy and distinguish the various economic activities that can be observed within the latter category (see Figure I.1). Labor remittances accrue directly to millions back home, through informal, decentralized, and unregulated banking systems that are often, but

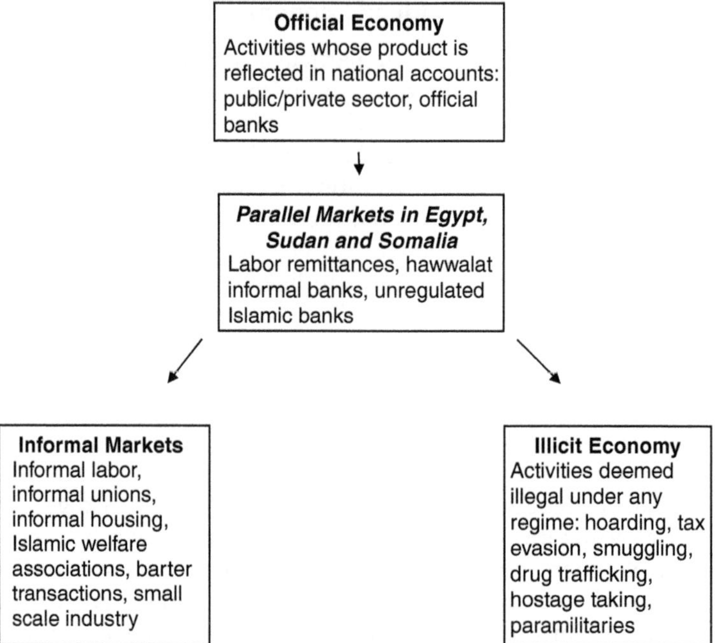


Figure I.1 A typology of informal markets

not always, in contest with the state. As a consequence, one can expect that this type of external capital inflow has in most cases resulted in the rise of strong, autonomous private sectors and altered the socioeconomic landscape in a dramatic fashion.

The link between the expansion and political influence of the parallel market in Egypt, Sudan, and Somalia is critically tied to Gulf economies and consequently highly vulnerable to the vagaries of external economic shocks. The flexibility, efficacy, and the effects of the parallel market as linked to international boom and bust cycles and its relationship with the state have played an important role in political developments and, I argue, the emergence of different religious- and ethnic-based forms of collective action.

## Informal Networks, Islamism, and the Politics of Identity

The question of when, and for what reasons, religious rather than ethnic cleavages serve as the most salient source of political mobilization in predominantly Muslim societies is more urgent than ever following the proliferation of a wide range of Islamist extremist groups and organizations in the Middle East and Africa. After all, the vast majority of Muslims interact without recourse to violence or militancy. Nevertheless, many noted scholars studying the rise of Islamist movements have persuasively pointed out the crucial role Islamic informal institutions play in promoting alternatives to formal political and economic institutions.[15]

However, even within Muslim societies the great bulk of the population is more likely to identify with different forms of Islam like Sufi or popular Islam as opposed to the conservative or extremist variety. Moreover, it is by no means evident that individuals and social groups in Muslim societies perceive "Islam" as the most significant form of political identification over that of family, clan, or ethnic group. This is especially true in the multiethnic societies of Muslim African countries, which until recently have been neglected in the analysis of Islamist movements. In fact, the scholarship on Africa suggests that the link between informal networks and the politicization of Islamist identity remains an open, empirical question since in the context of state failure and repression local actors tend to diversify their social networks to include both kinship and religious networks in order to consolidate efforts at income generation.[16]

In fact, while a large body of work on informal networks has highlighted their role in promoting a shared sense of cultural cohesion that can produce economic efficiency, many scholars have highlighted the "downside" of social networks.[17] These scholars argue that, while social networks can provide an informal framework for greater economic efficiency and the provision of social services in lieu of the state, they can also operate as mechanisms of corruption and even promote clandestine networks, and protection rackets.[18] Indeed, informal networks can be enlisted to support clandestine and militant activities. Moreover, since informal networks are often designed to further the material and ideological interests of individuals and groups, many who participate in an informal network know and trust each other, and these networks can be easily captured by the state or exploited for the purposes of more extremist resistance to state institutions.[19] Consequently, rather than assuming a functionalist understanding of "social networks," this book contributes to this debate by advancing an empirically researched comparative approach that distinguishes between various forms of informal networks and recognizes the ways in which they can form the bases for mobilization and recruitment into Islamist moderate and militant organizations, clan-led militias, and even pro-democracy social forces through the rearticulation of Islamic norms and practice.

This study also breaks with two common explanations of the causes of Islamist militant and terrorist recruitment. The first is largely an economic-centered literature that often downplays the role of Islamic norms in contemporary militancy.[20] The second is the body of work that emphasizes the militant theology of certain aspects of Islamist intellectual traditions to the exclusion of socioeconomic and context-specific factors.[21] *Black Markets and Militants* brings some very important new insights to this debate with respect to the question of why Islamist militants are successful in recruitment that highlight both normative and economic factors. First, from the perspective of their recruits, militant leaders often choose violence in order to improve the lot of their institutions and constituents by resisting state repression and gaining social and economic advancement. Second, the militants' dissemination and enforcement of stringent Islamist norms is based on their own knowledge of the very specific needs of local residents, many of whom are undergoing severe social and economic crisis. Third, it is important to note that while militants may often enjoy a comparative advantage in certain forms of organized violence, their relative "efficiency" in this regard is context specific. That is, Islamist militants almost always come into conflict with other forms of authority including traditional clan and religious leaders (e.g., sectarian) and communities.

Finally, and perhaps most importantly, social and economic factors underpin the process of recruitment in both conservative and extremist organizations. Though conventional scholarship routinely dismisses poverty and other economic and social factors in the analysis of the roots of extremism,[22] I depart strongly from this line of argument. In Egypt the patterns of socioeconomic inequality – social exclusion, economic insecurity, and marginality – are key factors in fostering recruitment.[23] To be sure, the leaders of many of these organizations represent the better educated middle class.[24] However, what is often neglected in this observation is the fact that rank and file members are often younger and far less educated than those in leadership positions. Moreover, the potential pool of recruits more often than not hails from the ranks of the unemployed and underemployed. In this respect, they also represent a segment of the population that is the most vulnerable to socioeconomic crises and economic downturns. Understanding the content of local grievances enables us to gage not only who gets recruited, but also who is susceptible to recruitment in the future.

## Understanding Islamist Activism: Distinguishing Islamism from "Terrorism"

A key problematic of much of the scholarship on violent extremism, much of it generated after the events of 9/11, is that it focuses on militancy or "terrorism" as its primary analytical objective. This obscures the very important fact that radicalization is a *process* and militancy – Islamist or otherwise – is often a militancy of last resort for the vast majority who join these organizations. The result is that this line of analysis suffers from a selection bias that routinely analyzes a small sample of relatively well-educated, middle-class actors engaged in terrorist operations. Moreover, in the case of the study of Islamist movements in particular, there is a scholarly consensus that Islamist activists are, by and large, middle class.[25] This is too narrow of a formulation. Indeed, in order to uncover some of the roots of radicalization, we need to understand recruitment as a process whose success cannot easily be predicted based on a fixed set of motivations, social origins, or even a static Islamist ideological frame. Moreover, while scholars of extremism are correct to note "the poverty paradigm does not seem to prevail among Middle East extremist groups"[26] in general terms, this should not obscure the fact that the lack of economic opportunity, and recessionary economies are often correlated with militancy.[27]

Another key issue related to the war on terrorism in general, and terrorist finance in particular, is the lack of distinction made between terrorism and Islamist forms of collective action. The conflation of Islamist politics with radical extremism in popular discourse and policy circles, in particular, is a major reason why anti-terrorist policies targeting terrorist groups espousing "Islamic" ideology have often proven counter-productive. As Martha Crenshaw has persuasively argued, violent organizations must be analyzed in the same terms as other political or economic organizations and, in this regard, terrorist groups are neither anomalous nor unique.[28] In fact, some of the most recent work on terrorism increasingly focuses on internal dynamics and structures that are common to all terrorist organizations regardless of ideology.[29] A notable example of this strand of scholarship is the work that argues that there is a potential link between the selective distribution of material resources and terrorism. This line of inquiry is useful in that it asks why certain types of groups are able to generate stronger commitment from their members than others. It suggests, in other words, that providing social services or public goods makes it possible for a terrorist or extremist group to ask more of, and demand greater sacrifice from, its followers.

However, a key problematic in this influential work is the lack of distinction made between radical political groups that utilize violence as part of their strategies and tactics, and Islamist forms of collective action that are conservative and often oppositional to domestic states, but are, in all other ways, distinct from radical political organizations such as Boko Haram, ISIS, or al-Qaeda. Indeed, Islamist political mobilization takes a number of forms and requires some analytical refinement. The most prominent include providing social welfare, contesting elections, and engaging in armed violence. As I show in subsequent chapters, the mix of these activities varies; some Islamists engage in only one type of activity, while others pursue two or all three of these activities. Some of the *da'wa* Islamists limit themselves to social welfare provision; the Egyptian Muslim Brotherhood confines itself to social welfare and electoral contestation, while the Egyptian Islamic Group engages in armed violence.

What is important to note, however, is that the major trend of Islamism is nonviolent; it is best understood as an ideology that promotes an active engagement with and cultivation of Islamic beliefs and practices, both in the public sphere and in those activities traditionally considered private. Islamism, therefore, undeniably possesses a "political" component in that it seeks to transform public life in more Islamic directions. In reality, the rise of Islamic Welfare Associations (IWAs) over the last five decades is due in great part to globally induced economic change. More specifically, it is a result of the retreat of state-led social protection policies in the 1980s.[30] The inability of many Muslim countries to fulfill their economic promises following a period of economic prosperity resulting from the oil boom in the Arab Gulf has inadvertently led to the expansion of informal networks and Islamic welfare institutions.[31] In a pattern similar to the majority of less-developed economies, the resulting gap between expectations and reality in Muslim societies fostered among many a sense of disillusionment with both the ideologies and institutions of the secular state.[32] To be sure, in the context of the diminished economic role of the state, there has been a rise of Islamist conservative social movements in many Muslim majority countries. But it would be a mistake to view all Islamists as fundamentally oriented toward overthrowing the political status quo or capturing the state. Such groups do exist, but they represent only a very small minority of a much larger social movement that espouses peaceful and nonviolent social and political change.[33]

In this study I take seriously the popularity of Islamism as representing a larger social movement rather than a militant fringe. This makes it possible to understand why Islamists have become increasingly concerned with supplying social protection to the region's economically and socially vulnerable. Indeed, a major misconception in the anti-terrorist finance campaign pertaining to Islamic charities is the assumption that the latter function only to fulfill the religious obligation of Muslims and thus represent a small part of local economies. In reality, for the last fifty years, IWAs have played an important role in social protection and economic security for thousands in all Muslim countries. Whether by providing health care, education, job training and locating services, loans, or direct payments, IWAs have stepped in to fill many of the gaps created by a retreating welfare state. In addition, many Muslims view these activities as part of a moderate Islamist project of social transformation. In this respect, helping those vulnerable to poverty serves two purposes: it allows pious Muslims to meet their moral duty to aid those less fortunate, and it provides the venues through which they can employ the Islamist *da'wa* (Call to God) to spread their ideology and increase their membership.

Ultimately, however, this book is not exclusively an analysis of Islamist social movements. There is a rich literature on political Islam across the disciplines. These works have offered a sophisticated analysis of the ways in which Islam has been mobilized toward political objectives throughout the Muslim world.[34] Rather, this book rests on the assumption that Islamist militant activism in Muslim societies has elements common to other extremist groups. Specifically, the organizational structures and recruitment methods are similar to other radical organizations in other parts of the world. However, what is specific to Islamist groups is the political and social context within which they operate. Many regimes in the Islamic world rely on political exclusion and repression to maintain rule. Under such conditions, many Muslims are forced to organize through informal networks to coordinate collective action through these channels. In some, but by all means not all, cases, these networks are captured by either conservative or militant Islamists who find themselves in violent confrontations not only with the state but also with many Muslims in their own society.

Finally, it is important to note that a number of scholars of Islamist activism and political extremism have correctly pointed to the role of the state, and in particular government repression, as increasing the propensity of individuals to join militant organizations in countries. However, whether these studies argue that state repression increases the propensity of militant recruitment or decreases the popularity of militancy or political Islam in general,[35] they obscure the important fact that there are important variations of mobilization and that, in multiethnic and multireligious societies, actors may choose to join a host of different Islamist organizations or a variety of different ethnically affiliated insurgencies operating both in contest and parallel to the state.

## Overview

If in the first part of *Black Markets and Militants*, I detail the similar political consequences of remittance inflows in all three of these labor-exporting countries during the boom, the second part of this book details the ways in which the onset of recession and the imposition of economic austerity measures resulted in divergent political developments in the three countries. I show how, in Sudan, Islamists were able to consolidate political power by effectively monopolizing informal financial markets: a development made far easier once they captured the levers of state power. In Egypt, the state imposed effective liberalization policies that undercut the financial power of the middle-class Islamist movement by strategically funneling remittances into official state channels. The unintended consequence of these policies was the further pauperization of millions of Egyptians living in the informal settlements outside the city. While most scholars have assumed that the "poor" in Egypt have not been a force in Islamist movements, I show here that this has not been the case. In fact, the economic insecurity and the economic downturns in the housing market and, by association, informally contracted labor, in Cairo laid the groundwork for militant Islamists to find a fertile ground from which to recruit many of the young men in these neighborhoods. For its part, Somalia, with the very weakest state capacity among all three countries simply disintegrated with the ensuing result of a rise in interclan conflict. In most of Somalia, capital inflows continue to be channeled through informal mechanisms utilizing primarily clan networks. What is interesting to note, however, is that in central Somalia, where no single clan has managed to monopolize the use of force, Islamist militancy has grown both as a response to the continued interclan violence and external actors who have intervened to stamp out militant Islamists and the potential of Islamist terrorism. To be sure, following the rise of militancy in Mogadishu, Somali militants have entered the fray in fighting to control and monopolize some of the hawwalat transfers. However, this has been an outcome rather than the cause of the rise of Islamist militancy in central Somalia. Only after a seismic shift in Islamist politics in the strongly divided central parts of the country have Islamist militants been able to fight for control, albeit unsuccessfully, over the trade in remittances. Ironically, Somali militants have benefited from the war on terrorist finance.

*Black Markets and Militants* then tackles two important questions directly related to the role of what is commonly termed "the black market" in the emergence of Islamist and clan politics in Egypt, Sudan, and Somalia. In contrast to other studies on informal institutions and Islamism I examine rather than assume "Islam" or "Jihadism" as the most salient source of political identity in the context of weakened state capacity. Moreover, rather than comparing "Muslim" societies I take seriously the religious and ethnic heterogeneity of the three countries. My primary aim is to explain when and under what contexts religious loyalties override other social cleavages in terms of their political salience and mode of recruitment. Throughout this volume, I also maintain that economic globalization, and specifically the inflow of remittances before and after the oil boom in the Gulf, has played an important role in delimiting the choices of state elites and thereby influencing domestic politics in Egypt, Sudan, and Somalia.

In these respects, this book departs from some conventional explanations of Islamist movements in three important ways. First, it takes seriously the role of globally induced economy factors in determining the political fortunes of both Islamist and ethnic politics in majority Muslim countries. Second, it differentiates in specific terms the economic factors underpinning conservative middle-class recruitment from its more militant counterpart. Finally, my study offers an explanation of why ethnic (or clan) cleavages may prove a more effective avenue of political organization over religious ties even in countries where many have assumed that Islam is the most "authentic" avenue of cultural identity and opposition to the state.

In this regard, the execution of Mahjoub Mohammed Ahmad for the crime of dealing in black-market transactions reflected a violent conflict between the state and groups in civil society over income generating activities unregulated and uncaptured by formal political authorities. As students of state formation have long noted, state building is crucially dependent on both the promotion and regulation of private economic activity. As a consequence, state builders, old and new, are often preoccupied with the capture of these rents for both the imposition of law and order, and the consolidation of political power. In the case of labor exporters, remittances – as the most important source of foreign exchange and revenue – became a source of economic competition, violent confrontation between state and civil society, and an arena where global economic forces intersected with domestic economies. As I show in the following chapters, the expansion of informal economic activities embedded in variable and locally specific social networks altered state-society relations in dramatic but divergent ways shaping new forms of identity politics. Table I.1 summarizes the expectations and outcomes in all three countries in the remittance boom years (1973–1983), and the recession years (1983–2019). It outlines the specific factors (or variables) highlighted in subsequent chapters that have underpinned variations in state-society relations over this period and thus determined the divergent political trajectories in Egypt, Sudan, and Somalia, respectively.

Table I.1 *Egypt, Sudan, and Somalia: Expectations and Outcomes in Boom Years (1973–1983), and Recession Years (1983–2019).*

| Country | Independent variable | Intervening variables | Expected Relationship | Outcomes in boom years | Outcomes in recession years | Outcomes in terms of new forms of identity politics |
|---|---|---|---|---|---|---|
| **Egypt** | **Parallel Market** (Privately controlled remittances). | High level of state capacity; strong degree of autonomy from civil society. | Strong, autonomous state. | Strong state dependent on remittances and foreign aid. | **Maintenance of bureaucratic-authoritarian regime.** | Islamist activism transformed in socio-economic terms. |
| | External Capital inflow (representing high percentage of national income). | Geo-political constraints-high military spending. | Expansion of informal financial, housing and labor markets. | *Erosion* of fiscal and regulatory capacity.<br>Decline of old public sector. | Financial liberalization accelerates. | Fragmentation of Islamist trend (moderate vs. militant Islamism). |
| | | Socio-cultural cleavages (Religious, sectarian, rural-urban). | Political conflict over trade and exchange rate policies along ascriptive cleavages. | Strong autonomous private and informal sectors represented by **Islamic investment institutions/Islamic welfare associations.**<br>Rise of Islamist commercial bourgeoisie. | Decline of the Islamic economy and financial power of the Islamist bourgeoisie. | State cooptation of Islamist bourgeoisie. |
| | | Structural-economic cleavages (Industrial, commercial, agrarian). | Emergence of stronger civil society vis-à-vis the state. | Expansion of informal housing and labor markets.<br>Exacerbation of class/ religious schisms. | Strong political and ideological conflict between the regime and Islamists over the legitimacy of the state. | Islamist militants rise in power within the context of informal market relations in the recession. |

Table I.1 *(cont.)*

| Country | Independent variable | Intervening variables | Expected Relationship | Outcomes in boom years | Outcomes in recession years | Outcomes in terms of new forms of identity politics |
|---|---|---|---|---|---|---|
| **Sudan** | **Parallel Market** (Privately controlled remittances). | Medium level of state capacity; medium degree of autonomy from civil society. | Relatively weak, non-autonomous state | Relatively weak state dependent on remittances and foreign aid. | **Onset of an Islamist-Authoritarian state.** | Islamist-'Arabist' led transition of state from remittance economy to an oil exporter. |
| | External Capital inflow (representing high percentage of national income). | Geo-political constraints-high level of military spending. | Expansion of informal financial market. | *Decline* of fiscal and regulatory capacity. Decline of old private-commercial sectors. | Informal financial sector captured by the Islamist regime. | Divisions between military and Islamist bourgeoisie. Fragmentation of the Islamist movement. |
| | | Social-cultural cleavages (Religious-sectarian, ethnic, regional). | Political conflict over trade and exchange rate polices along ascriptive cleavages. | Strong autonomous private and informal sectors represented by **Islamic banks.** Rise of Islamist commercial bourgeoise. | Imposition of coercive extractive and regulatory institutions. Overvaluation of domestic currency continues. | Emergence of strong cross-cutting informal networks and unions in opposition to the regime. |
| | | Structural-economic cleavages (Commercial, agrarian). | Emergence of stronger civil society vis-à-vis the state. | Exacerbation of religious, ethnic, regional and class schisms. | State monopolizes export-import trade. | Disintegration and fall of the Islamist-Authoritarian regime. |
| | | | | | Islamism established as primary mode of legitimation | |

Table I.1 *(cont.)*

| Country | Independent variable | Intervening variables | Expected Relationship | Outcomes in boom years | Outcomes in recession years | Outcomes in terms of new forms of identity politics |
|---|---|---|---|---|---|---|
| **Somalia** | **Parallel Market** (Privately controlled remittances). | Low level of state capacity; minimal degree of autonomy from civil society. | Weak, non-autonomous state. | Weak state dependent on remittances and foreign aid. | **State disintegration and collapse**. | Clan and Islamist networks dominate the state building enterprise. |
| | External Capital inflow (representing high percentage of national income). | Geo-political constraints-high military spending. | Expansion of informal financial, and livestock markets. | *Collapse* of all formal financial and regulatory institutions. | Increase in wide scale inter-clan violence. | Clan networks successfully establish a nascent state in Somaliland. |
| | | Social-cultural cleavages (Clan, regional, sectarian). | Political conflict over trade and exchange rate polices along ascriptive cleavages. | Emergence of informal banking agencies (**hawwalat**). Strong informal sector represented by **clan-centered economies.** | Emergence of "warlords" as the primary agents of extraction. | Clan and Islamist networks fail to build a viable state in Puntland. |
| | | Structural-economic cleavages (Pastoralist, agro-pastoralist). | Emergence of stronger civil society vis-à-vis the state. | Proliferation of clan and sub-clan-based militias. | Clan networks dominate the 'unregulated' domestic economy. | Competition between Islamist militants and clans stifles state building in central Somalia. |
| | | | | Exacerbation of inter-clan schisms | Political clannism represents the primary mode of legitimization. | |

*II*

# The Institutional Context in an Era of Abundance

# 1 "The House the Boom Built": The Informal Economy and Islamist Politics in Egypt

In the mid-1970s, the oil boom in the Arab oil-producing states resulted in a dramatic transformation of the economic and political landscape of the major labor-exporting countries of the Arab world, and Egypt is a prime example of this phenomenon. The quadrupling of oil prices in 1973 drastically altered the regional context in which labor emigration took place in the Middle East and North Africa (MENA) region. In contrast to other regions, in MENA, the regional demand for labor was limited until the 1970s oil boom. As oil prices spiked in the aftermath of the 1973 war, huge revenue windfalls accrued to the oil-producing states like Iraq, Libya, and the Gulf States. Using these revenues, oil-producing states launched massive infrastructure and development projects that required more labor than the national states could supply. As a result, oil-producing states sought additional labor from outside to complete their projects. Arab workers spoke Arabic, were geographically close, and were abundant in number, and in the early decades following the oil boom, they proved to be ideal candidates to work in the petrodollar projects.

In Egypt, the combination of the jump in oil prices and the onset of economic reforms in the mid-1970s resulted in a dramatic emigration of Egyptians to the oil-producing states, and what became the largest source of foreign exchange: remittances. By the early 1980s, at the very height of the boom, there were an estimated 3 million Egyptians working in the Arab oil-producing states. Moreover, while in 1970 recorded remittances from migrant workers were estimated at US $30 million, by the early 1980s official government estimates of these capital flows ranged from US $3 billion to US $18 billion.[1] The reason for the discrepancy in official estimates was that workers sent their earnings primarily through informal familial and friendship networks rather than through official banking channels. This was mainly because of the continued overvaluation of the Egyptian pound and the mistrust that many workers had of formal banking institutions back home. As in other labor exporters, the avoidance of official banking channels resulted in the emergence of a large "hidden," or parallel, economy, in remittance inflows that were controlled by a network of currency dealers (*tujjar 'umla*) who effectively institutionalized a "black market" in informal finance.

The economics and demography of transnational migration in the 1970s and 1980s illustrate with dramatic statistical details the larger story of the millions of unskilled and skilled and professional workers who traveled to the Arab oil-producing states to take advantage of new opportunities for work, welfare, and social mobility. However, as demonstrated by the sheer volume of remittances in this period, it is also important to emphasize that the majority of migrants did not cut their individual ties with their families back home.

Magdi Mahmoud Ali is illustrative of the fate of millions of youth (mostly young men) who emigrated during the oil boom in order to seek better opportunities in the oil-producing Arab states of the Gulf, Iraq, and Libya. Mr. Ali migrated to Libya in 1974 at the very beginning of the oil boom. He returned to Egypt nine years later because he lost his job as a result of the regional recession which led to the drying up of opportunities for labor migrants throughout the Arab region. Mr. Ali, a plumber by profession, departed his hometown of *Marsa Matruh* (in the Delta) in 1974. He first traveled to Libya, which he said at the time offered better opportunities for Egyptian labor migrants than the Gulf region. Like so many young men in the 1970s and early 1980s, Mr. Ali traveled illegally to Libya because, as he put it, "he had heard everyone [in Libya] could acquire a car and a nice apartment," and added that "in Libya I earned between 5,000 and 6,000 dinars a month at a time when 1 dinar equaled three Egyptian pounds."[2] In 1987, Mr. Ali relocated to Saudi Arabia to work for a Public Water Works factory, worked and resided in Riyadh for two years, and then returned to Egypt in 1989. In the late 1980s, the combination of the effects of the regional recession and perceived domestic security threats compelled Gulf countries to implement new emigration policies that favored Asian over Arab labor. Consequently, Mr. Ali returned to Egypt in 1989 and noted that while he was earning 2,700 riyals a month in Saudi Arabia, he had to eventually leave the country since Asian workers who were brought in "accepted" wages as low as 700 riyals for the same position.

Importantly, like millions of young men working abroad, Mr. Ali did not cut his social ties with family and kin back home in *Marsa Matruh*. By his own estimation, he sent approximately 600 riyals a month to his mother and family, and he utilized two primary means to remit part of his earnings back home. The first method was to simply buy products and give them to Egyptian "suitcase merchants" (*tujar al-shanta*) traveling from the Gulf to Egypt who would deliver the equivalent value of the products in cash to his mother. The second means was more common in the 1970s and 1980s. This entailed the reliance on what Mr. Ali termed "personal contacts" who he would ask to deliver his remittances to his family directly thus evading the official banking system.

Mr. Ali's experience as an expatriate worker, as well as the remarkable regularity with which he remitted part of his earnings back home to his family, illustrates the genuinely transnational social ties created by long-distance migration in the era of the oil boom. Indeed, Mr. Ali's biography nicely dramatizes the direct linkage between the spike in oil prices in the mid-1970s and the central role that the boom in remittance inflows played for individuals and their families. But if Mr. Ali's experience abroad illustrates one facet of the country's (and indeed the region's) political economy, Mr. Ali's experience upon his return to Egypt, and specifically Cairo, exemplifies yet another phenomenon that altered the very nature and social and political fabric of urban life in Cairo: the boom in informal, unregulated, housing largely financed by the earnings of expatriate workers in the Arab oil-producing countries. Upon his return to Egypt in the late 1980s, Mr. Ali invested his earnings in an apartment building in Ezbat al-Mufti, one of the informal housing quarters in Cairo's Imbaba neighborhood. He was not able to pursue his profession as a plumber with any regulatory since he had not only spent many years abroad but was also from the Delta region rather than Cairo and had no reliable social networks to find regular employment in his profession. Consequently, he was compelled to join the ranks of informally contracted workers in the construction sector. "Most of us," he noted, "returned to places like Ezbat al-Mufti and had to work in construction. I do know some men who opened small workshops or a plastic company here but not many."

## The Remittance Boom and the Internationalization of the Economy

As Charles Tilly has noted in another context, the sheer volume of migrant remittances to relatively poor countries underlines the fact that migration flows "are serious business, not only for the individuals and the families involved, but also for whole national economies."[3] Indeed, Mr. Ali's personal experience – his social and economic aspirations, humility, and hopes for success for himself and for his family – is one of the many individual backstories of the internationalization and the informalization of the Egyptian economy that began in earnest in the 1970s. These two interrelated changes in the country's political economy resulted from the coincidence of exogenous economic shocks associated with the jump in oil prices as well as domestic economic reforms. These reforms are generally associated with revisions in laws governing foreign investment, trade liberalization, exchange rate adjustments, and the reorganization of the public sector. Understandably, Mr. Ali's personal narrative focused on the immediate social aspirations and possibilities offered by out-migration, but it would not have been possible if it had not coincided with two important developments: the boom in out-migration and remittance inflows, and the economic opening (*infitah*) that President Anwar Sadat introduced in the mid-1970s.

Egypt's economy was dramatically transformed in the mid-1970s as a result of the boom in oil exports and remittances. In his study of the country's political economy in the era of the oil boom between 1974 and 1982, John Waterbury noted that while the regional labor market and the world petroleum market have always been intimately linked, "no one could have foreseen the exuberant growth in oil-export earnings and remittances after 1976."[4] Indeed, Egyptian international migration has always been affected by the labor market and political conditions in the receiving countries. While out-migration of Egyptians started in the mid-1950s, the real expansion of workers traveling abroad began in earnest after 1973. This was due to the dramatic hikes in oil prices in 1974 and again in 1979 that were accompanied by increasing demand for Egyptian workers in the oil-producing Arab states. In the era of the oil boom, millions of Egyptians migrated abroad in search of employment, but it is important to note that this takeoff in emigration was a result of internal and external factors. On the one hand, the vast wealth of the oil-producing states accelerated ambitious development programs that required increasing flows of labor. On the other hand, Egypt was witnessing high population growth and high levels of unemployment that increased incentives for both unskilled and new graduates to emigrate in search of employment. The combination of these "push" and "pull" factors resulted in a sharp increase in the migration of Egyptians. Only a small number of Egyptians, primarily professionals, had left the country in search of employment before 1974. But by 1980, more than 1 million Egyptians were working abroad, and that number jumped to 3.28 million at the peak of labor migration in 1983.[5] The main destination of migrants was to the Arab Gulf states, followed by other Arab oil-exporting countries. By 1991, 53.3 percent of the total migrants were working in the Gulf countries, 32.9 percent in other Arab countries, and 3.2 percent in the rest of the world.[6]

To be sure, the boom in labor migration served to alleviate some of the pressure on domestic employment, but their departure resulted in an enormous "brain drain" for the country. This is because emigrants tended to be highly educated professionals, including doctors, engineers, and teachers. For example, one study that compared the educational levels of a large sample of nonmigrants and migrants estimated that 61 percent of migrants have secondary or higher education as compared to 53 percent of nonmigrants. This suggests that there is a high level of selectivity of migration by education. Moreover, individuals working in the public sector are less likely to migrate. Less than 8 percent of the migrants used to work in the public sector before leaving Egypt, compared to more than 27 percent of the nonmigrant group.[7]

Nevertheless, while the majority of expatriate workers tended to be generally more educated, their social profile reflected a distinct regional bias. Specifically, by the late 1980s, Egyptians living in the poorer and more rural parts of the country tended to migrate to the Arab Gulf in greater numbers than their urban counterparts. By 1991, migrants from rural areas represented 62.8 percent of those who migrated as compared to 37.2 percent of urban residents. However, it is important to note that these migrants represented both educated and illiterate Egyptians. Up to 1991, 30.3 percent were illiterate while 20.6 percent had a university degree and above.[8] Moreover, since Egyptian migrants were often married males from rural areas who tended to work abroad in order to send support to their dependents in Egypt, the heads of households receiving remittances were less likely to be wage workers and more likely to be inactive or unpaid family workers.[9] Understandably, millions of Egyptian households came to depend on remittances from family members. A study conducted in 1986/1987 in Minya government showed that remittances accounted for 14.7 percent of the total household income of recipients. Another study found that 74 percent of households receiving remittances use the money on daily household expenses, 7.3 percent use this money to build or buy a home, and 3.9 percent use remittances for the education of a family member.[10]

As millions of Egyptians came to rely on remittances from their expatriate relatives to invest in their family members' education, welfare, and economic livelihoods, the cumulative effect of these capital inflows emerged as a central component of the national economy. Indeed, throughout the 1970s and 1980s, four major items represented the backbone of the national economy: oil, receipts from the Suez Canal, tourism, and workers' remittances. Their share in total resources (gross domestic product [GDP] plus net imports) rose from 6 percent in 1974 to approximately 45 percent by the early 1980s. However, more significantly, by the mid-1980s remittances became undeniably the country's major source of foreign currency. In 1984, for example, they amounted to US $4 billion equivalent to Egypt's "combined revenue from cotton exports, Suez Canal receipts, transit fees and tourism."[11] Table 1.1 summarizes the

Table 1.1 *Summary of Egypt's balance of payments, selected years, 1979–1985 (in millions of US dollars)*

| | 1979 | 1985 |
|---|---|---|
| Current account | 602 | 409 |
| Exports of goods and services | 589 | 897 |
| Tourism | 4,210 | 7,405 |
| Suez Canal | 5,401 | 8,711 |
| Other | **2,445** | **3,496** |
| Total | n.a. | 26 |
| Net current transfers | n.a. | 3,522 |
| Workers' remittances | −1,915 | −4,735 |
| Other | −19.8 | −14.3 |
| Total | −11.2 | −13.6 |
| Current account balance | | |
| Trade balance as percentage of GDP | | |
| Current account balance as percentage of GDP | | |

*Source: World Bank, World Debt Tables, for selected years.*

balance of payments in the boom period between 1979 and 1985 and shows clearly the magnitude of remittances in the context of other sources of revenue. However, the volume of remittance inflows was far larger than those reported by official local and international sources represented in the table.[12] This is because, as noted earlier, expatriate workers remitted part of their earnings back home, through informal, decentralized, and unregulated banking systems that were often, but not always, in contest with the state.

It is important to emphasize that since all four main sources of revenue, remittances included, were exogenous sources (i.e., they had little relation to labor productivity in the country), they were highly vulnerable to external market forces, and engendered dramatic social and political changes beyond the control and purview of the state.

## Infitah and the Politics of Economic Reform

There is a clear consensus that Egypt's economy was dramatically altered in the mid-1970s as a result of the coincidence of two related developments: the oil price hikes that precipitated a boom in remittance inflows and economic liberalization initiated by President Sadat in the mid-1970s. Following the October 1973 war, domestic socioeconomic crises, as well as foreign policy considerations, led President Sadat to liberalize the Egyptian economy under a new policy of *al-infitah al-iqtisadi* (economic opening). John Waterbury has neatly summarized the main objects of the liberalization process in the 1970s: (1) to attract Arab investment capital from the oil-rich Arab states; (2) to encourage Western technology and investment through joint ventures with state-owned and private enterprises; (3) to promote Egyptian exports and privatization; (4) to liberalize trade through currency devaluation; and (5) to promote the "competitiveness" of public sector enterprises.[13]

In the 1970s and 1980s, however, the most important components of economic liberalization were based on the introduction of Law 43 in 1974, and its revision by Law 32 in 1977, and had to do with the desire on the part of the Sadat regime to attract foreign finance, particularly from neighboring oil-rich Arab states, and the need for providing financial facilities to foreign investors to attract them. Accordingly, among the key measures implemented by the Sadat regime was the invitation of foreign backs, incentive rates for the conversion of currency consisting of multiple (or periodically adjusted) exchange rates, moves toward the reorganization of the public sector, and tax exemptions and other privileges to foreign investors as well as the Egyptian private sector.[14] Importantly, in order to offer incentive rates for currency conversion, the regime introduced the "own exchange" system to finance private sector imports. In sum, as Galal Amin has noted, "these laws provided for the opening up of the Egyptian economy to foreign investment, tax exemption for new investment, and the recognition that private companies would not be subject to legislation or regulations covering public sector enterprises and their employees."[15] Moreover, when Hosni Mubarak assumed power in 1981, he continued to promote these policies and further extended the liberalization of the national economy by taking steps to reduce the budget and external account deficits, thereby further reducing barriers to domestic and international trade.

It is important, however, to highlight two essential aspects associated with economic liberalization that reflect the overwhelming reliance and dependence on regional and capital markets resulting from the oil boom and the inflow of remittances. First, the country experienced far higher growth rates than in the etatist era of the 1960s under Gamal Abdel Nasser, but this was primarily due to revenue generated from exogenous sources rather than a result of an influx of private investment. Between 1972 and 1980, for example, the proportion of exports and imports of GDP rose from 14.6 to 43.8 and 21.0 to 53.0, respectively, and the average annual growth of GDP was 8 percent over this period. However, this growth was a result of the revenues from oil exports, Suez Canal receipts, tourism, and workers' remittances. Revenues from these sources rose from $600 million in 1974 to an estimated $7.5 billion by 1983.[16] Importantly, this growth was only partially accounted for by the influx of private investment, which registered only minimal growth in this period from 5.2 to 9.4 percent of GDP.[17] Consequently, although Egypt experienced high rates of economic growth after the early 1970s, rapid rates of economic growth were dependent on "such sectors as housing and workers' remittances which were temporary relief."[18] Indeed, by the latter part of 1981 the assassination of Sadat, the oil glut and global recession, and a high and growing level of imports placed Egypt in severe straits in its foreign exchange balances. In great part this was because worker remittances, tourism receipts, and earnings from oil and Suez Canal receipts fell sharply. By 1984, declining exports and rising imports led to a 30 percent increase in the trade deficit, ballooning to more than $5 billion.[19]

The second and related aspect of infitah is that as a result of the boom in remittances the state was able to retain significant authority over its national economy. As Waterbury has noted, the foreign exchange cushion afforded by remittance inflows and oil rents delayed further implementation of economic reforms until the 1990s and allowed Sadat to essentially maintain the Nasserist social contract and refrain from restructuring the national economy in this period. Indeed, the state was able to retain substantial capacity over its formal economy. In 1982, public expenditures stood at 60 percent, public revenues 40 percent, and the public deficit 20 percent of GDP. In addition, in 1978 the total fixed investment in public sector companies was LE 7.4 billion, the value of public sector production stood at LE 5.3 billion, and public sector value added at LE 2.3 billion. Three hundred and sixty companies employed more than 1.2 million workers. Thus, in the boom period the state was still the dominant actor in the economy in that it was essentially in control of public sector earnings, the marketing of agricultural commodities, petroleum exports, and the greater part of the formal banking system.[20] The state also retained regulatory control over formal financial institutions. In 1983, the Egyptian public banking sector held its own against the onslaught of joint venture and private investment banks. "The four public sector banks in 1983, for example, had financial resources on the order of LE 14.5 billion as opposed to LE 5.1 billion in the private sector."[21]

Indeed, despite the dominant discourse of infitah and economic liberalization that the Egyptian state followed, the regime pursued a gradualist approach to economic liberalization throughout the 1970s and 1980s. This approach characterized both the Sadat and Mubarak eras. As Eva Bellin has noted there were three primary reasons for this approach, which, in many respects, demonstrated the continued strength of the state and its autonomy from social forces during the early phases of economic reform. First, the very idea that economic reforms will produce economic growth and stimulate positive changes in society was weak among state elites and policy makers. Second, the government was intent on protecting fragile sectors of the economy such as the textile industry and agriculture against foreign competition. Finally, and most importantly, the fact that state-owned enterprises had served as a means of state patronage, that is, as an avenue to provide jobs for the masses and lucrative posts for the elite, the government was generally reluctant to privatize public sector companies. As Bellin has noted, "policies that seem economically irrational are crucial to the political logic of these regimes (providing patronage, sustaining coalitions, endowing discretionary power). As a result, a government would not be willing to undertake reform unless pressed by crisis; even then it is likely to hedge its bet and embrace, at best, only partial reform."[22]

Throughout the 1970s and 1980s, the state followed a gradualist strategy that entailed reducing political tensions through a partial liberalization of the economy. As Harik has noted in a comprehensive study of infitah policies in this period, "the decision making power remained authoritarian and centralized,"[23] and despite the emphasis on privatization, the bureaucratic apparatus expanded; many necessary goods continued to be subsidized by the government; and the public sector remained responsible for 70 percent of investment, 80 percent of banking, 95 percent of insurance, and 65 percent of valued added until the early 1990s.[24] Moreover, not only did the state continue to dominate the industrial sector, by the end of the 1980s, the stated object of financial and trade liberalization of the economy was only partially achieved. There were still large price distortions of foodstuff, the foreign exchange rates remained unified, the Central Bank rate was still administratively controlled, and the nominal interest rates were far below the inflation rate.[25] The government successfully resisted orthodox reforms by avoiding negotiations with the IMF and the agreements eventually reached with the IMF were only partly implemented.[26]

Indeed, rent seeking, or the diversion of state resources into private sector activities in return for political loyalty, constituted a major source of opposition to liberalization in the 1980s because bureaucratic elites were intent on "collecting rents on behalf of more highly placed patrons."[27] However, the reason state elites were able to maintain their patronage networks without little disruption had to do with weak capacity on the part of the Egyptian middle classes to decisively affect economic policy. A high level of fragmentation and ambivalence in society aided this autonomy of the Egyptian state from civil society. Indeed, the opposition

Liberal party and Nasserist and Leftist parties in this period were not only weak and divided; they did not endorse wholesale liberalization and concurred with the ruling National Democratic Party (NDP) in the belief that major components of state capitalism must be retained and this view was not opposed by the major opposition parties.[28] For its part, the Muslim Brotherhood organization, the strongest opposition movement in civil society, while hostile to state's involvement in the economy, was "ill-disposed towards reforms proposed by Western financial agencies."[29] A more important reason is that by the 1980s, the Muslim Brotherhood had established a number of Islamic economic enterprises and financial institutions and benefited greatly from the government's economic reforms.

## The Remittance Boom and the Informalization of Financial, Housing, and Labor Markets

A key consequence of Egypt's greater integration into the international capitalist economy in the 1970s, which played an important role in altering state-society relations, had to do with the increasing informalization of the national economy financed primarily by the boom in remittance inflows. To be sure it is important to note that as a result of the country's centrally planned economy in the 1950s and 1960s, the "traditional" informal economy represented a key feature of the national economy. This "traditional" informal economy included a number of key components including smuggling, tax evasion, corruption, illegal transactions, a wide range of barter (i.e., nonmonetized) transactions, and small micro-enterprises that operated outside the purview of the state. As early as 1970, government estimates estimated that this informal sector represented between 25 and 30 percent of total industrial output in the formal sector.[30]

Nevertheless, there is no question that both the nature and volume of the informal economy expanded exponentially in the mid-1970s and that this was a result of both out-migration and particular aspects of economic reform. In one of the most commonly cited studies on the subject, Abdel-Fadil and Daib estimated various economic activities in the informal sector (or what they termed "black economy"), in 1980 at LE 2.1 billion, which at the time constituted more than 17 percent of GDP (see Table 1.2). Understandably, however, there are no agreed-upon estimates of the size of the informal economy in the 1980s. Indeed, other studies on the informal economy in the 1980s estimated that its value ranged from 35 to 55 percent of the total gross national product (GNP).[31]

Table 1.2 *Values of transactions in Egypt's "Black Economy," 1980*

| | |
|---|---|
| Moonlighting | LE 514 million |
| Tax evasion | 250 million |
| Hashish trade | 128 million |
| Profits on real estate speculation | 328 million |
| Customs evasion | 109 million |
| Informal housing construction | 260 million |
| Smuggling | 177 million |
| All sources total | LE 2.1 billion |

*Source*: Mahmoud Abdel-Fadil and Jihan Diab, "The Black Economy and National Accounts in LDC's: The Case of Egypt," draft paper, American University in Cairo, Department of Economics, August 1983, cited in John Waterbury, "The 'Soft State' and the Open Door: Egypt's Experience with Economic Liberalization, 1974–1985," *Comparative Politics* 18, no. 1 (1985): 76.

However, there is little question that the dramatic growth of the informal economy was the direct result of the migration of Egyptian labor and that it was primarily financed by the large volume of remittances that stemmed from out-migration. Indeed, the problem with estimates of the size of the informal economy at the time had to do with the fact that the financing of a wide range of informal economic activities flowed from remittances and these were impossible to estimate in a reliable fashion because these capital flows were transferred through informal means that evaded state regulation and official records.

As a consequence, two interrelated developments greatly accelerated, what I term, the informalization of financial, labor, and housing markets. The first, and most important, stemmed from the boom in remittances, the source of capital for much of the parallel economy and the institutional means by which remittances were transmitted, by the money dealers and Islamic financial and banking institutions. Moreover, like Mr. Ali's personal story noted earlier illustrated, millions of Egyptian workers chose to evade official banks and financial institutions and sent their money back home to their family through intermediary moneylenders. This resulted in a dramatic expansion of a parallel market in financial transfers that evaded the regulation of the state. Moreover, while formal government records estimated the value of remittances at US $3 billion in the early 1980s, this vastly underestimated the true value of these capital flows precisely because they were sent via informal, decentralized, and unregulated channels. From the mid-1970s to the mid-1980s remittances continued to rise, and by 1986 one study estimated that remittances from both official and informal sources stood at US $12 billion.[32]

The second by-product of the huge volume of remittances in this period was the expansion and informalization of the markets in housing and labor. Informal housing, defined as the construction of housing in formerly agricultural land without bureaucratic regulation, enjoyed a boom in urban and rural areas. This lasted until the mid-1980s when the regional recession resulted in the drying up of opportunities for migrant workers in the Arab oil-producing states. Between 1974 and 1985, for example, an estimated 80 percent of all new housing stock was built on formerly agricultural land and outside the purview of state regulation attesting to the central role that remittance earnings, unrecorded by official government figures, played in the expansion of informal housing.[33]

This boom in informal housing, financed largely by expatriate remittances, was due to the effects of economic reform as well as demography. Economic liberalization led to speculative land practices that resulted in the rise in the cost and demand for affordable housing, especially since housing that was provided by the public sector was neither sufficient nor desirable. More specifically, as one important study on the subject noted, the high value of the formal real estate market and the scarce opportunities for rents due to rent control laws, which left many apartments out of the market, meant that young people had no choice but to seek housing in the informal market.[34] Nevertheless, it is also important to note that both the regimes of Sadat and Mubarak actively promoted this boom in informal housing for reasons of political and economic expedience in the context of economic reform. Indeed, it was not until the late 1980s that the state began to regulate new housing stock more vigorously. As I show in Chapter 4, this change in policy had much to do with what the state perceived as an Islamist "terrorist" threat emanating from these informal "slums."

Nevertheless, what is noteworthy during the boom period is that growth in informal housing led to a dramatic rise in the number of informally contracted laborers, who entered the market in order to benefit from increased employment opportunities in the construction of informal housing financed largely by expatriate remittances. Informal, or casual, labor can be defined as work that is unregulated by formal institutions and regulations of society such as labor laws, registration, and taxation. Moreover, in the case of Egypt, the lack of a job contract and social insurance is how informal work is most usefully identified.[35] There are no reliable official figures of informal workers in construction for the period. Nevertheless, there is strong consensus that informal laborers in the construction sector grew dramatically to meet the demand for housing in the informal areas (*manatiq 'ashway'iyya*) in Cairo as well as in the rural parts of the country.

It is important to note that just as economic reform played a key role in the informalization of financial and housing markets, economic reform policies initiated by Sadat in 1973 resulted in the decline of public sector industries and opportunities available to workers in the formal economy. As McCormick and Wahba have noted in an important study, in the period of economic reforms the informal sector played an important role in job creation, and "new entrants to the labor market seemed to bear the brunt whereby by the 1990s, some 69 percent of new entrants to the labor market managed to only secure informal jobs."[36] Moreover, as one study noted, a great many informal workers reside in informal settlements because formal housing is not only unaffordable for low-income families but also too far from job opportunities for persons who rely on informal work for their livelihoods.[37]

What is important to note, however, is that while these markets are not regulated by the bureaucratic institutions of the state, they are nevertheless regulated by informal social networks embedded in local communities. Whether these social ties are organized around religious, regional, or ethnic ties, or served as avenues for nascent class formation depended on two elements: the type of market and the social character of the local community, and the state's linkage and policy toward these informal networks in civil society. In the case of informal financial markets, these came to be organized and dominated by a network of currency dealers that entered into a battle with the state for control over this market. Moreover, while in the boom period informal housing was not registered or regulated by the state, these informal housing settlements were embedded in local social networks and affective ties. Finally, while informal labor is commonly defined in efficiency terms as a form of labor segmentation that is unregulated by formal political or social institutions, they are nevertheless regulated by social ties such as kinship networks, region, and sect.

Consequently, as I discuss in chapters 4 and 7, all three of these informal markets (i.e., finance, housing, and labor) came to serve as important avenues for social and political organization with important consequences in terms of altering state-society relations. This is because not only are these markets embedded in local communities and informal social networks, they are also intimately linked with formal state institutions in ways that resulted in very significant political developments at the level of both the state and civil society. In this respect, these informal markets represented different forms of commercial networks that played a key role in political developments in the country. Indeed, as Charles

Tilly observed in his classical discussion of the political significance of informal commercial trust networks, even the most coercive rulers (i.e., rulers with high levels of state capacity in terms of their repressive apparatus and power to regulate the national economy) are routinely forced to both accommodate and attempt to regulate commercial networks in order to buttress their political power and legitimate their rule.[38]

A final dimension associated with economic reform is that it played an important role in the rise of a new phenomenon: namely a parallel economy in the provision of social, medical, health, and education services provided by Islamist groups in the country. These unregulated and largely unregistered Islamic Welfare Associations (IWAs) played an important role in mobilizing support among the urban middle classes. Along with the emergence of Islamic banking, IWAs came to represent a key component of a growing Islamic economy which, in turn, owed its growth to the dramatic increase in the volume of remittance inflows in the era of the oil boom.

The impetus behind the growth of IWAs had to do with the rapid deterioration in government-provided services. Government efforts to address this issue did not succeed but there is little question that the issue of welfare provisioning became a key concern on the part of state elites. This is clearly evidenced by the fact that the regime announced a five-year plan for 1978–82 that was supposed to establish priorities associated with welfare provisioning. However, the document did not effectively specify how this was to be achieved. This was designed to publicize the state's commitment to the Nassserist social contract. In retrospect, however, it is clear that while the document falsely described Egypt as being in the "forefront of the welfare societies of the world,"[39] the document was nothing more than an attempt to ward off popular discontent following the historic 1977 food rights precipitated by the withdrawal of subsidies on basic food items under the rubric of infitah. Moreover, production inefficiencies and administrative weakness lead to a deepening economic crisis in the 1980s with the result that the parallel and Islamic economy in Egypt emerged in the country and came to play an increasingly important role in the economy and helped to increase the popularity of Islamist groups.

## Informal Finance and Islamist Politics: New Capital Flows and Islamic Management Companies

As noted earlier, etatist policies under the Nasser regime did encourage a wide range of informal economic activities. However, what made the 1970s different from previous decades is that the state's capacity to regulate important sectors of the economy was greatly weakened. This was evident in two important and interrelated developments. First, the rentier effect of external sources of revenue resulted in a "dutch disease" element and led to the neglect of productivity issues mostly centered on formal public sector enterprises. Second, as the informal sector witnessed booming growth, financed by remittances, it had little capacity to siphon these capital flows into official state coffers.

Thus, economic reform policies in this period came to represent a paradox in Egypt's political economy and, over time, greatly altered state-society relations. On the one hand, the state retained authoritative control over the formal economy and relative autonomy from societal forces. That is, the social contract whereby the state was committed to providing goods and services to the public in exchange for political quiescence was maintained. The state continued to control public sector earnings, the marketing of agricultural commodities, oil exports, and a substantial part of the banking system. The regime maintained its capacity over the mobilization of investment capital through the nationalization of private assets and the taxation of public sector enterprise. On the other hand, the country's integration into the global economy, especially capital and labor markets in the Arab oil-producing states, narrowed its options and forced the regime to adopt policies that accommodated and even promoted the informal economy. More specifically, the internationalization of the economy led to a loss of state control over informal financial flows and created new paths for new capital (generated by remittances) to accumulate great wealth.

Indeed, as noted earlier, the primary goal of infitah was to lure Arab Gulf capital and Western development assistance into the country rather than internationalize the formal economy or privatize public sector industries. The primary goal was to apply selective economic reforms in order to encourage financial inflows without disrupting the state sector companies established under Nasser. A key example had to do with the state's policies toward the dramatic expansion of the booming informal financial market stemming from remittance inflows.

The boom in out-migration and remittances provided a foreign currency cushion and acted as a social safety valve for unemployment. This, in turn, enabled the state to delay key economic reforms while simultaneously encouraging the inflow of financial inflows into the national economy. To be sure it enabled the regime to expand the private sector and begin to decentralize the country's economic system. Nevertheless, it is important to note that while the policy of infitah resulted in some opening of the formal sector, private capitals flows were meager and were of a short-term nature and they were primarily directed into joint-venture banks, largely to finance imports. More significantly, the windfall rents accruing from remittances and oil exports enabled the regime to liberalize the banking sector, allow foreign banks to operate in foreign currencies, and relax foreign exchange regulations to stimulate a foreign capital influx. This led to the further internationalization of the economy in that it afforded Egyptians new opportunities to invest, speculate, and transact with the global economy without being forced either to deposit in public sector banks or to abide by the government's overvalued exchange rates. There are many examples that demonstrate the ways in which millions of Egyptians took advantage of these opportunities. A man who owned a block of flats would rent one to an international bank, ask that the bank pay only one-third of the rent to him in domestic currency, and request that the remaining two-thirds be deposited outside the country in dollars.[40]

This in turn resulted in the erosion of the regime's capacity to regulate a greater part of informal financial transactions. Much of Egypt's new private capital, accumulated in the form of remittances from professionals, and laborers working in the Gulf States, might have siphoned into Egypt's official banking, intensifying commercial competition, and strengthening a broad spectrum of infitah banks. However, various government restrictions in the official foreign exchange market, the overvalued exchange rate of the pound, and the incapability of the formal financial sector to cope with the requirements of emigrants meant that emigrants preferred to deal in the parallel ("black") market because the latter offered a more favorable exchange rate than the formal banks. As a consequence, while the state retained control over capital accumulation in the formal economy, it lost control of large swaths of capital generated by informal financial circuits. Infitah, designed to attract foreign capital to invest in Egypt, became an open door for capital flight.

## "Black Marketeers," Islamic Banks, and the Rise of an Islamist Bourgeoisie

The combination of the expansion of informal financial markets as a result of the oil boom and economic reforms (i.e., infitah) resulted in the emergence of Islamic-oriented financial institutions in ways that greatly increased the economic prominence and political influence of a new generation of Islamist activists. Two institutions played a central role in these developments: the emergence of Islamic Investment Companies (IICs) and Islamic banks. In the 1980s, these Islamic financial institutions represented the rise and increasing prominence of a new Islamic economy, which in turn had a strong impact in altering the country's political economy and ultimately expanding the scope and popularity of the Islamist movement in the country. More specifically, it reflected two interrelated dynamics in the country's political economy: the erosion of the state's capacity to regulate informal financial flows, and its struggle to retain its monopoly over the public sector while simultaneously seeking to encourage financial inflows and foreign investment, especially from the wealthy Arab oil countries.

The rise of the IICs, known at the time as *Sharikat Tawzif al-Amwal* (money management companies), was directly linked to the vast number of expatriate workers that migrated to the Arab oil-producing countries during the oil boom. As noted earlier, these workers faced the problem of sending a portion of their earnings to their families and so they quickly turned to foreign exchange dealers operating in the "black market" to channel their remittances. Since throughout the 1970s and 1980s the state maintained an artificially overvalued exchange rate, most expatriate workers chose to avoid using official banking channels since these "black marketeers" offered a rate far more favorable than the official exchange rate. By the late 1970s this informal, or parallel, market in foreign exchange reached an unprecedented volume, and it resulted in a broad organizational informal network that connected households in Egypt with the broader regional economy that consisted of banks and commercial networks in the Gulf. For their part, the currency dealers made enormous profits in two ways: by extracting a commission for their services and by profiting from the time lag in delivering the funds in local currency in order to make short-term interest profits. As in a number of other Arab labor exporters in the region, the boom in remittances combined with the heavy demand for the dollar back home resulted in a veritable bonanza for "black market" currency dealers who essentially came to monopolize the informal financial market.

As the expansion of this parallel market in remittance flows grew, it took on an institutional form in ways that eventually threatened the state's capacity to regulate the financial sector of the economy. As the currency dealers grew in wealth, they established Islamic Investment Companies (IICs) in order to both continue to monopolize the inflow of remittances from expatriate workers and to invest these funds in commercial enterprises. These were "Islamic" investment houses in that they accepted deposits from expatriate workers, and they did so along the lines of Islamic principles in that they did so without going against the Islamic prohibition on interest dealing (*riba*). They also employed religious rhetoric to defend their activities and to encourage depositors working abroad to invest in these financial institutions. Nevertheless, it was clear from the onset that the largest of these companies were indeed established by prominent currency speculators. Two of the directors of the largest

ICCs, *al-Rayyan*, as an important example, were well-known currency dealers in the late 1970s and early 1980s and were formerly listed by the Ministry of Interior as prominent currency dealers.

The rise of these IICs, which gained particular prominence in the mid-1980s, illustrates the importance of the parallel market in the country's economy. This is because while these firms accepted a huge volume of deposits, they operated outside the system of state regulation, and they were not subject to the controls to which other banks had to submit. Indeed, they escaped any form of regulation and did not come under the monetary authority's supervision or even company laws. In addition, their practices fell under parallel and often illicit black-market activities in the informal economy, for example, tax evasion, bribery, theft of state land, violation of import restrictions, and illegal foreign exchange dealings.

## The Parallel Market and the Erosion of State Capacity: Informal and Formal Linkages

The continued resilience of the black market in foreign exchange and the prominence of the IICs in capturing the savings of expatriate workers led to two important developments. First, it further eroded the capacity of the state to regulate financial markets. Indeed, by the late 1980s informal finance was such a grave source of concern for the regime that the state-run media reported that, by escaping state regulation, IICs "dangerously" threatened the economic sovereignty of the state and undermined Egypt's entire financial system.[41] Second, these developments ultimately encouraged and promoted powerful elites within the Mubarak regime as well as a newly ascendant Islamist commercial bourgeoisie in civil society. What is most noteworthy is that in the late 1970s and throughout most of the 1980s informal financial institutions were not necessarily in contest or competition with the interest of state elites. Indeed, the linkage between the network of black marketeers that established the IICs and the state was evident in a number of ways.

First, a number of currency dealers operating in the parallel market were actually awarded significant loans in foreign currency from formal banking institutions, which they reinvested in their IICs. These loans were denominated in dollars, and the black-market dealers utilized these funds to import or smuggle goods into the country. Second, and perhaps most important, is the fact that the political influence of the black-market dealers became so dominant in the financial sector that they were able to strike back successfully against government efforts to reestablish Central Bank control over the financial sector. In 1984, as one key example, the Minister of the Economy, Mustafa al-Said, attempted to push through parliament legislation that would increase import restrictions, and give greater authority for the Ministry of the Economy and the Central Bank to regulate the private and joint venture banks that had been given special privileges, including tax exemptions and, most importantly, crackdown on the currency dealers. Subsequently, a number of the prominent black-market dealers were put on trial and charged with smuggling $3 billion out of the country.[42] However, a week prior to the trial the network of black marketeers raised the price of the dollar 10 percent and openly called for the then Minister of the Economy, Mustafa al-Said, to resign from office. In essence, the black marketeers were able to raise the real price of foreign exchange a full 20 percent higher than the official rate and threaten the national economy. The monopoly of the black marketeers over the financial sector was so dominant vis-à-vis the power of the state that in April 1985, Mustafa al-Said was actually forced to resign after both the black marketeers and other business groups protested against new currency and banking regulations.[43] Importantly, leading Islamists at the time also opposed the crackdown on the currency dealers and argued that al-Said's crackdown was not waged in the public interest, but rather because his own business interests (and that of members of his family) were in competition with the informal financial market dealings dominated by the currency dealers.[44] This incident not only illustrated the economic clout of the currency dealers, it also highlighted the fact that influential state elites were themselves profiting from black-market dealings at the time. Moreover, it also clearly showed that the state's capacity to regulate the parallel market in remittances was crucially weakened. As an important study conducted at the time noted, this development clearly showed that the government's goal of regaining control over the financial system in this period was more elusive than ever.[45]

By the mid-1980s the largest seven *Sharikat Tawzif al-Amwal* (al-Rayyan, al-Sharif, al-Sa'd, al-Huda, Badr, al-Hilal, and al-Hijaz) were in operation largely outside the purview of state regulation, and they had cornered the lucrative market on remittances from migrant workers. One study estimated that at their peak in 1985–86, deposits from expatriate workers to these firms stood at $7 billion. Yet another survey of the IICs, based on 1988 figures of the 52 IICs in operation, showed that the volume of remittances they attracted ranged from 3.4 to 8 billion Egyptian pounds, and this represented half a million depositors.[46] Together with the Islamic banks such as the Faisal Islamic Bank and Al-Baraka Group, which were also promoted by the government to attract remittances, by the late 1980s, the Islamic sector had captured 30 to 40 percent of the market for household deposits and informal investments, and the informal Islamic economy was rivaling and possibly surpassing the formal sector of the formal Islamic banks and their branches.[47] As the Egyptian economist Abd al-Fadil put it, "the struggle over the future of the Islamic money management companies was not simply a struggle over the future of the financial system and the means of mobilizing and investing remittances but a struggle over the very future of [Egypt's] political and economic system."[48]

## Transnational Trust Networks and Legitimizing an "Islamic" Economy

An important reason for the great success of the IICs in attracting deposits from migrants in this period was simply because they distributed high rates of return, almost double of the official rate to their depositors. Indeed, as a number of studies have argued, the high interest offered by the IICs and the overvalued official exchange rate compelled millions of workers to channel their hard-won earnings into these unregulated financial institutions. Indeed, there is little doubt that rationalist and profit-maximizing calculations played a principle role in motivating depositors to invest in the IICs. Indeed, some of these companies offered high rates of return that stood at 24 percent per year, and some of the richest depositors received yearly rates of return nearing 40 percent.[49] Nevertheless, it is also important to note that another reason for the IICs' success is that they claimed to accept deposits along the lines of Islamic principles by claiming to prohibit usury (*riba*) in their transactions and by offering contracts based on Islamic precepts. As a result these firms came to play an important symbolic role in fueling the Islamicization of the economy in this period. Indeed, the prominence of these firms was also linked to the increasing popularity of the Islamist movement that was partially associated with the expansion of Islamic-oriented commercial networks and the rise and popularity of a new Islamic economy.

Indeed, what is often obscured in the studies on the IICs of the time is that it was not only Islamic rhetoric alone (i.e., the banning of interest in their operations) that facilitated the initial success of these firms; it was also due to the unregulated nature of these institutions. Depositors had to be sure that their earnings and investment would be secure and there could be no better "security" than in turning to the prevailing standards of interpersonal trust grounded in a shared commitment to Islam. To be sure, as Abdel-Fadil has aptly noted, the desire to generate windfall profits from their hard-earned savings was a key motivation for depositors to channel their remittances to the IICs. But if the economic incentive to generate wealth was an important consideration for depositors in choosing to transfer their remittances to the IICs, norms also played a role. Specifically, Islamic norms of interpersonal trust and trust worthiness, strongly promoted in the IICs' media campaigns gave depositors a firm sense that their hard-earned earnings would not be squandered or misused by ostensibly like-minded pious Muslims operating these firms. In other words, while the transactions and deposits responsible for the growth of the IICs were unregulated by formal bureaucratic procedures and contracts, they were nevertheless socially regulated by Islamic norms and services that popularized these institutions and, as one scholar put it, made the "economic insecure seek a vehicle for forming [Islamic] networks based on trust."[50]

Put in more economic terms, in the remittance boom decade of the 1980s, the IICs managed to foster notions of interpersonal trust that encouraged individual depositors to do business with these unregulated institutions in ways that reduced the costs of monitoring and enforcing agreements. This was necessary because the IICs essentially offered informal agreements that relied on religious affinities rather than on formal contractual obligations. Indeed, the important role of interpersonal trust in channeling remitted earnings to the IICs had to do with the "contracts" offered by these firms that were ostensibly based on Islamic precepts. The most common method was to simply inform the depositors that their invested funds would be utilized based on the principle of *Mudaraba*. In this case, the company would act as the *Wakil* (i.e., the trusted agent) of the depositor in the investment of his (or her) capital, and profit and loss was to be shared equally between the two partners. The depositor therefore had to essentially trust that the company would follow the guidelines of *Mudaraba* absent a formal contract since he was simply given a paper stating that the money would be invested along the lines of Islamic principles but any formal contract or government authority was dispensed with. Indeed, this was an important reason why despite the absence of formal guarantees and absent oversight and regulations, hundreds of thousands of expatriate workers deposited their remitted earnings into these investment companies.

It is important to note that the heads of these IICs were hardly operating in the interest of the depositors. By the late 1980s it was discovered that these firms had been running pyramid schemes. That is, they were paying investors high dividends on their deposits primarily by drawing on a growing deposit base rather than generating these funds from real assets. Nevertheless, throughout most of the 1980s these firms inadvertently played a role in fostering a transnational commercial network partially linked upon Islamic principles and ideals and thus they helped to popularize the idea of a new Islamic moral economy.

The IICs profited from their relationship to prominent leaders of the Muslim Brotherhood at the time in both economic and political terms. The Brotherhood's networks in the Gulf and long-standing relations with Saudi Arabia at the time facilitated the operations of a number of the IICs, and there is evidence that some owners of the companies gave financial and political support to Islamist candidates in parliamentary elections.[51] Moreover, in the context of rebuilding their organization, the Brotherhood was keenly aware of the need to adapt its internal structure to meet the opportunity of the internationalization of the economy accelerated by the liberalization of financial markets. Indeed, as early as 1973 the general guide (*al-Murshid al-'Am*) of the organization, Hassan al-Hudaybi, began to promote and emphasize the international aspect of the organization as a way of asserting the Brotherhood's leadership both inside and outside the country. In a general meeting of the organization convened in that year, Hudaybi reconstituted the Shura (Consultative) Council. He set up six membership committees in the Gulf region: three in Saudi Arabia, and one each in Kuwait, Qatar, and the United Arab Emirates. These committees functioned mainly to ensure the Brotherhood's "moral" presence and to secure allegiance to it, among Egyptians as well as the general populace of those countries. This reorganization proved to be instrumental in attracting strong financial backing for the Muslim Brotherhood by allowing them to serve as intermediaries between investment from the Gulf and domestic financial institutions. This period of wealth accumulation, *'ahd tajmee al-tharwat* as members of the organization termed it, made possible the promotion, expansion, and success of the Islamists recruitment campaigns.

The investment houses also fostered political linkages in order to solicit support from some leading individuals with close associations to the Brotherhood. A number of the big IICs including Al-Rayan and Sherif appointed leading Muslim Brotherhood individuals and Islamist preachers to serve on their executive boards as a way to legitimize the Islamic credentials of these companies. Some notable Islamist figures included the preacher Mitwalli al-Sha'rawi who joined the Al-Huda Company; Dr. Abd al-Sabur Shahin, a professor at Al-Azhar University, served on the board of al-Rayyan; and a leading Islamist, Salah Abu Isma'il, who was both an investor in and board member of the Hilal Company. Isma'il was a leading Muslim Brotherhood leader who was also elected to the People's Assembly in 1984. Second, when in 1988 the government proposed legislation to regulate the IICs, prominent Muslim Brotherhood leaders, such as Shaykh Mohammad al-Ghazzali, not so much defended the IICs as institutions but rather the very idea of an Islamic economy. Ghazali, for example, argued that regulating these firms would force religious-minded citizens to deposit their savings in *riba* (i.e., interest) bearing accounts, while the respected Islamist intellectual, Tariq al-Bishri, noted that the campaign against the companies was a thinly veiled attempt by the Mubarak regime to undermine an emerging Islamist elite that represents a popular force in civil society.[52]

The more lasting and important link between the IICs and the Islamist movement had to do with the fact that the success of the IICs popularized the idea, in symbolic and practical terms, of building an "Islamic sector" of the economy to parallel and rival the state-dominated official sector. This idea became a key objective for a new Islamist bourgeoisie, which was not confined to the Islamic financial sector. It included investment in education and social welfare services all of which came to compete with the formal sector of the economy.[53] The IICs, for example, invested in Islamic publishing, private education, hospitals, and medical clinics. This was clearly an effort to forge strong links between these institutions and important social groups in civil society, most notably the Muslim Brotherhood, and increase their legitimacy among the public.[54] The funding of these activities was derived from two sources: profits derived from the "Islamic" economy that included the IICs and from voluntary donations in the form of *zakat* (religiously obligatory dues), which helped to finance a significant number of IWAs. The investments associated with the IICs also demonstrated a clear bias toward the commercial and service sectors of the economy and they demonstrated the role these investments played in promoting a middle-class commercial bourgeoisie. As Abdel Fadil has demonstrated in the most cited study on the subject, 49 percent of the IICs' investments went to the tourism sector, 24 into housing, and focused on middle and upper classes. In contrast, only 4 percent went into industry and 9 percent into agriculture.[55] Thus, the IICs did not only not make a contribution to development; they also buttressed and promoted the upper echelon of the Islamist commercial networks.

It is important to highlight, however, that most Islamist leaders defended the IICs on a number of religious and social grounds including the fact that they operated based on Islamic norms of trust and that they improved the livelihoods of millions of Egyptians abroad and at home. Throughout the 1980s prominent Islamist leaders were opposed to the regulation of the informal financial market. This was clearly evident by their position vis-à-vis the exchange rate. When, by the end of the decade, the IMF argued for the floating of the exchange rate and removing the multiple exchange rates system in place, Islamists leaders such as 'Abd al-Hamid al-Ghazali of the Muslim Brotherhood and Magdi Husayn, both of whom were in favor of liberalizing other sectors of the economy, argued for the continued regulation of the currency. Ghazali, who in later years criticized the investment companies for their corrupt practices, in the early 1980s defended them and argued that removing currency controls would not eliminate the black market because Egyptians who engaged in activities such as tourism, the import of goods, and the haj would still resort to the black market since the "official" market would only sell foreign currency for certain purposes.[56] What is significant, however, is that this call for the state to control the demand for foreign currency and foreign goods stood in stark contrast to the Islamists' promotion of pro-market reforms, which included support for liberalized trade and investment that would remove any obstacles to Arab investments.

However, beyond the fact that Islamists supported the IICs at the time, there was a broader and more important issue. The investment houses represented the resurgence of civil society actors operating in the informal economy and as such represented the erosion of state capacity and the legitimacy of the regime in the context of newly resurgent social forces in society. Some of these forces were certainly linked to the Islamist movement but they also represented a wide range of groups in civil society (including millions of expatriate workers) who sought to challenge the state's overwhelming dominance over society. For many, and not just Islamists, the parallel market represented a powerful economic alternative, which broke down the state's monopoly over financial resources and allocation and could even help to usher in political pluralism.

## Islamic Banking and the Dilemma of State Capacity

Another important factor that resulted in the increasing popularity of the Islamist movement and its legitimacy across a broad segment of civil society had to do with the rise and growth of Islamic banking in the 1970s and early 1980s. Islamic banks can be defined in similar terms as the IICs in that they pursued activities that they stated were in conformity with Islamic law (*shari'a*). More specifically, *riba*, the paying or receiving of a fixed interest rate, was replaced with the principle of *musharaka*, that is a partnership in profit or loss. Also, like the IICs the rise of Islamic banks was directly linked to the oil hikes and remittance boom.

The first Islamic bank to be established in Egypt was the Faisal Islamic Bank in 1979. Three other major Islamic banks followed: the Egyptian Saudi Investment Bank (ESIB), the Islamic International Bank for Investment and Development (IIBID), and Al-Baraka Group. As was the case with the IICs, the Islamic Banks were hugely successful in attracting deposits from expatriate depositors as well as financing from the Gulf. The success of these banks in attracting deposits was so significant that by 1995 other commercial banks opened an estimated seventy-five Islamic branches of their own institutions throughout the country.[57] Between 1979 and 1986, the growth rate in the deposits to the major Islamic banks totaled an impressive 82 percent, which represented 9.8 of the total savings in the entire banking system. The Islamic banks were able to channel savings by offering higher interest rates on deposits than conventional banks, but they were also adept at encouraging deposits from migrant workers in the Gulf by offering accounts held in foreign currency. Consequently, by distributing returns quoted in foreign currencies rather than the deteriorated local Egyptian pound Islamic banks were able to encourage deposits from the millions of workers in the Arab oil-producing countries who were remitting part of their savings back home.

The success of the Islamic banking experiment represented the state's somewhat contradictory relationship to the Islamist movement and, in particular, to the increasingly powerful Muslim Brotherhood. Moreover, in terms of the country's larger political economy, Islamic banking represented the regime's paradoxical relationship to the informalization of large segments of the national economy. Indeed, the state was intent on the liberalization of the financial sector and deregulating Islamic financial institutions in order to attract external finance and remittance inflows from expatriate workers, but as Soliman noted in one of the best studies on the subject (and in contrast to the case of Sudan addressed in the next chapter), the state retained considerable capacity to regulate these banks since the "visible hand of the state was behind [both] the foundation and promotion of Islamic banking in the 1970s."[58]

On the one hand, the state was clearly intent on empowering the Islamists in the Islamic economic sphere. To be sure, the establishment of the FIB and other Islamic banks was part of the state's infitah policy and was intended to encourage Gulf Arab investment. Indeed, state policy afforded Islamic banks special advantages over other state and private banks that played a key role in their expansion and success. In the case of the FIB, which served as the model for the other Islamic banks, for example, the regime enacted legislation that stated its assets could not be nationalized or confiscated, exempted the bank from official audits, and a series of taxes and custom and import duties, and it was not subject to the laws that controlled foreign currencies.[59] The unintended consequence of this policy was to empower the role of the Islamists in the economy. Through their contacts in the Gulf, prominent members of the Muslim Brotherhood played a key role in establishing the FIB and they used their influence to ensure that prominent members such as Youssef Nada, Yusuf Qardawi, and Abdel Latif al-Sherif served on the board of directors of the bank.[60] Another example is that of Abdel Hamid al-Ghazali. Ghazali, the Muslim Brotherhood's chief economic thinker, was instrumental in establishing the IIBID. The strong involvement of prominent members of the Muslim Brotherhood in the initial phase of Islamic banking represented a honeymoon period between the state and their empowerment of Islamic finance and, by extension, the economic and symbolic influence of the Muslim Brotherhood.

On the other hand, what is noteworthy with respect to the role of the state and Islamic banking is that, in contrast to its permissive policy toward the IICs, the regime retained strong capacity in terms of regulating these Islamic banks. This can be discerned clearly in terms of the formal institutional linkages between the state and the Islamic banks, and the high degree of oversight that the regime retained over the banking system. Specifically, as of 1983 the Egyptian public banking system held its own against the joint-venture and private investment Islamic banks, and the four public sector banks had financial resources estimated at LE 14.5 billion as opposed to LE 5.1 billion in the private sector.[61]

In addition, the Central Bank and the Ministry of the Economy supervised the commercial activities associated with these banks. More importantly, the Minister of Interior kept a close watch over the role of the Islamists in these banks in case they posed a political threat to state "security." In the 1980s out of fear of the strength of the Muslim Brotherhood, the then director of security, Fouad Allam, expelled members of the Brotherhood from the board of the directors of the Islamic banks.[62] Moreover, just as the regime continued to regulate the expansion of Islamic banking to ward off both economic and security threats, the regime sought to retain an ideological stronghold over the very idea of "Islamic banking." For example, it was the state-appointed Minister of Religious Affairs (*Awqaf*), Sheikh al-Sha'rawi, who submitted the legislation to parliament that sanctioned the establishment of the Islamic banks along with the privileges they enjoyed throughout most of the 1980s. Moreover, the Mubarak regime appointed a number of scholars from Al-Azhar University to preside over the administrative boards of the Islamic banks, and it established a number of government-funded institutions for the study of Islamic Economics. These efforts were all clear attempts on the part of the state to promote Islam as the legitimizing ideology of the state. The aim of these polices was to undermine the increasing popularity of the Muslim Brotherhood who by this time had generated a great deal of legitimacy in civil society.

## The Emergence of an Islamist Bourgeoisie

There is a strong consensus that beginning in the 1970s the leadership of the Muslim Brotherhood in particular experienced strong upward social mobility resulting from their success in private commercial business primarily because, under Nasser, they were barred from the public sector. Instead, they had to focus on the private sector once they were afforded the opportunity under Sadat's open-door policies. By the 1980s, a number of Brothers were wealthy businessmen, and they had important connections to a score of others, many of these, like the construction Tycoon Osman Ahmad Osman, were connected to the organization. Osman was selected to lead the Engineers Syndicate once they took over that professional association. It is this commercial-business element that influenced the Muslim Brotherhood's position with respect to pro-market reforms, black-market financial transactions, and the Islamic institutions more generally. Indeed, Omar al-Tilmasani, the leader of the organization, also supported infitah in his writings strongly and demanded more room for *ras mal al-Islami* (Islamic capital), which, in his view, included Islamic banks, the IICs, and the wide range of Islamic financial institutions of the Gulf countries.[63] However, it is important to emphasize that Telmasani as well as other prominent Brotherhood leaders such as Yusuf Kamal and al-Ghazali defended this position in economic terms. Specifically, they argued that the debt crisis facing the country was due to "the corrupt centralized planning practices" initiated under Nasser, which created grave problems in the vast public sector, leading in turn to capital flight and currency speculation.[64]

Nevertheless, the spread of both informal financial houses and private Islamic banks helped to lay the foundation for the emergence of an Islamist wing of the infitah bourgeoisie, and they also financed the emergence of Islamist patronage networks that promoted the political profile of members of the Muslim Brotherhood. However, the growth in the Brotherhood's financial and political clout in this period was crucially aided by the state's promotion of a new Islamic economy. As noted earlier, from the perspective of state elites this policy was designed to fulfill two important goals: to lure investment from the Islamic countries of the Gulf and to build new clientelistic linkages with the Islamist movement in the country primarily so as to rival and outflank remnants of the Leftists and Nasserites in civil society. Indeed, just as Sadat cultivated the political support from the Islamists in the 1970s, in the 1980s the Mubarak regime encouraged the expansion of Islamic banking and, in doing so, effectively delegitimized the usury-operating formal banks.

This, along with the initial success of the IICs, helped raise the popularity of the Muslim Brotherhood at precisely the time that they had embarked on a vigorous grassroots campaign to expand their popularity and constituency in civil society.

As Soliman aptly put it, the unintended consequence of these policies on the part of the regime was that the state, at least in this period, "empowered its own gladiator." Indeed, along with the success of the IICs, the spread of Islamic banks and informal financial houses laid the foundation for the emergence of an Islamist-oriented middle class. The sectoral composition of the Islamic bank's investment is one indication of this. On the whole the clients of Islamic banks tended to be urban merchants, as opposed to villagers. In addition, the banks showed no inclination to favor labor-intensive firms or investment in industry or agriculture. As one study noted, this was primarily because it was easier to follow Islamic prohibition on usury in the financial sector by simply claiming to abide by noninterest dealing rather than persuade investors of the efficiency and productivity of their investment in other sectors of the economy.[65]

Nevertheless, there are two reasons that an Islamist bourgeoisie emerged as a strong threat in the context of the infitah policies. The first, as described earlier, was directly linked to the opportunity afforded them by the influx of remittance inflows, their close ties to the Arab-Gulf economies and networks, and their prominent role, at least at the time, in establishing Islamic banks. The second reason for their relative success was rooted in the fact that the state, in its efforts to consolidate authoritarian rule, continued to heavily regulate other business groups as well as labor. The other business groups were relatively weak because they were small, heterogeneous, and represented corporatist associations linked to the state. Thus, while new groups such as the Commercial Employee's Syndicate and the Engineers Syndicate emerged in the context of economic reforms, the state frequently intervened to curb any opposition by appointing ruling party stalwarts as the heads of these organizations.[66] Similarly, autonomous labor unions were largely stifled from political opposition through coercive incentives. Specifically, in return for political quietism unions were allowed to utilize their pension funds to establish their own enterprises and enter into joint ventures with foreign capital.[67]

Indeed, under Sadat, and especially Mubarak, state policy reflected a paradox with respect to its changing economic and political strategies in the context of economic reform. On the one hand, it was intent on preserving its dominance over the economy and society by forging a strong alliance between the state, and foreign and private capital both to promote private investment in manufacturing and export sectors as well as to reassert its authoritarian rule over society. Mubarak did this by integrating local business groups such as the new professional syndicates and the Egyptian Businessmen's Association as part of its development strategy.[68] On the other hand, while the state remained in control over the formal economy and generally regulated business and labor groups, this resulted in the fact that the Islamist bourgeoisie emerged as a relatively strong force in civil society precisely because the business community remained weak and divided, and labor organization was forced to renounce demands for autonomous political expression since they became increasingly placed under the power of bureaucratic authority.

As a consequence, since business and labor represented corporatist groups linked to the state, newly emergent private and voluntary business organizations emerged. These were essentially the Egyptian Businessmen's Association and the network of black-market money dealers. Bianchi has noted that these came to "represent important organizational responses of powerful segments of the business community in the context of the Mubarak government's efforts to reorient Egypt's open-door policy in the context of economic liberalization." Business groups, organized around Islamist networks, came to have a great deal of economic clout in civil society.[69]

By the end of the 1980s the political and economic ascendancy of the Islamist wing of the bourgeoisie, centered on the financial sector, had grown so strong that President Mubarak declared: "[T]he citizens are richer than the government."[70] The statement reflected an acknowledgement that the regime had lost significant control over the informal financial sector and that it could no longer meet the needs of job creation and social welfare for the growing population. The combination of an increasingly impoverished formal economy and private wealth centered around informal and deregulated financial markets meant that the Islamist commercial bourgeoisie came to have strong political leverage. Moreover, since foreign direct investment was relatively meager, as noted earlier, this compelled the state to essentially promote and legalize the informal financial market (i.e., the IICs) and to deregulate Islamic banking in the hope of luring more remittance inflows and deposits from expatriate workers. In the 1980s the financial clout of the Islamist bourgeoisie with close international linkages with the oil-rich Gulf States underpinned the state's interest in satisfying this aspiring commercial Islamist class. This is one of the key reasons why the Muslim Brotherhood members were allowed to run in elections in 1984, and in parliament they proved strong advocates for the promotion of pro-market reforms. It was clearly evident however that the NDP was less interested in supporting the Islamists' calls for a new constitutional framework than it was in eliciting their support in its efforts focused on deregulating financial markets in order to lure foreign investment from the Gulf.

The emergence of an Islamist-oriented bourgeoisie and a concurrent rise in the political clout of Islamist movements driven by the oil boom in the Arab oil producers were not unique to Egypt. By the late 1980s, for example, Islamic banks based in the Arab world, which included the two largest groups of Islamic Banks (*Al-Baraka* and *Dar al-Mal al-Islami*), were capitalized at around $2.6 billion, and they held assets worth $22.9 billion. Moreover, during the decade of the 1980s, the assets of these banks grew by 18.8 percent a year reflecting the emergence of a genuinely transnational Islamic-oriented economy. In Egypt, alone, by the late 1980s Islamic banks managed to attract around 20 percent of all the bank deposits and competed with conventional formal banks.[71]

However, what distinguished Egypt from other "weaker" labor-exporting states such as Sudan (Chapter 2) is that the Mubarak regime was able to preserve much of its autonomy from civil society and keep control over much of the formal economy. This is because the flow of Western aid and oil-related earnings channeled into state coffers relieved the regime of the pressure to pursue economic reforms more thoroughly and, as a result, retained much of its capacity not only to suppress dissent but to monopolize formal economic institutions. As scholars of Egypt's political economy have noted, this was primarily because under Mubarak, the state (even in the context of economic reform) represented a "hybrid" system combining the etatist legacies of Nasser with Sadat's open-door policies.[72] Indeed, throughout this period, the bureaucracy that employed much of the salaried middle class expanded, food subsidies increased, and public enterprises remained the dominant sector for government investment as well as employment.

To be sure, the Muslim Brotherhood emerged as a key constituency favoring reforms, and the NDP co-opted their support in the context of economic reform policies. However, it is also important to note that there were important divisions within the organization around economic reform policies that enabled the state to curb their economic influence as well as political activism. Doubtless Islamists businessmen who had made their fortunes in the Gulf were particularly supportive of the state's pro-market orientation. But some leading Islamist members clearly understood that the expansion of the informal market and their monopoly over it necessitated regulation in ways that would continue to channel remittances into a variety of Islamist-supported institutions. This debate over the parallel (i.e., black) market pitted Gulf-connected Islamists, such as Khairat al-Shater, against 'Issam al-Eryan and Adil Husayn who called for wholesale deregulation of the economy. It was this lack of consensus between the Islamist bourgeoisie that allowed the state to keep them divided and prevented this class from truly consolidating their class position vis-à-vis the state.

Nevertheless, it is important to note that businessmen belonging to the Muslim Brotherhood wielded great power and influence over the economic policies of the organization in this period. These businessmen, or *Ikhwan al-Manfa* (Brothers of Exile) as they were commonly labeled, built strong economic networks and became rich in the Gulf in the 1950s and 1960s. Later, in the oil boom era, they built on this foundation and accumulated greater wealth from a large network of commercial enterprises as well as astute investments in Islamic financial institutions. The influence of these businessmen was evident by the positions the organization took with respect to economic reform as well as the boom in informal financial transactions (i.e., the parallel market). Indeed, another indication of the great power of this Islamist commercial elite is that it became a source of great division within the organization. Many prominent *Ikwhan* heading the professional syndicates in the 1980s and, notably, the influential leader, 'Issam al-Eryan (later the spokesperson of the organization), openly criticized what they saw as a monopoly of the wealthy Islamist businessmen over the economic planning of the organization.[73] In addition to their influence over the organization's economic policies, some of these wealthy businessmen built and supported the financial administration that underpinned and sustained the patron-client networks linking the Brotherhood's national-level leadership with the local branches of the organization. Under the leadership of Khairat al-Shater and Hassan Malik (two prominent Brotherhood businessmen and partners in a number of commercial enterprises) the organization's leadership established a decentralized system of administration (reportedly consisting of approximately twenty-five local administrative offices). Khairat was put in charge of overseeing the sources of revenue for this administration, and the directors of administrative affairs (*Mudir al-Idara al-'Ama*) and staff of these branches were charged with a number of financial and administrative tasks. These included collecting monthly fees and regular zakat (alms) donations from official members, allocating funds to some activities associated with the professional syndicates headed by the Brotherhood, mobilizing campaign funds for electoral candidates and financing the recruitment (*tajneed*) and spiritual education (*tarbiyya*) efforts at the local level.[74]

It is vital to highlight that political opportunity as well as a strong economic base worked in tandem to increase the power of the Islamist movement and that of the Muslim Brotherhood in particular. The movement's financial base built, in great part, on the foundations of Islamic financial institutions coincided with the rebuilding of the Brotherhood's organizational capacity and hence political influence under the regime of Anwar Sadat. In order to rival Marxist and Leftist forces loyal to his predecessor Gamal Abdel al-Nasser, Sadat implemented policies designed to forge new patron-client linkages among Islamists in civil society so as to build a constituency loyal to his regime. Sadat released members of the Brotherhood from prison, supported Islamist activists on the University campuses, and allowed them to publish their influential newsletter al-Da'wa (the Call). This "thaw" in relations continued into the early years of the Mubarak regime. While the organization remained illegal, Mubarak afforded the Brotherhood increasing autonomy to organize in civil society, finance welfare associations, and eventually to enter into alliance with other legal parties so that Islamist candidates could enter the political arena. In the 1970s and 1980s, under the General Guide (*al-Murshid al-'Am*) Omar al-Telmasani, the Muslim Brotherhood took advantage of this opportunity and, as El-Ghobashy, has demonstrated in great detail, embarked on pursuing a moderate agenda, mobilized their membership at the grassroots, and carefully prepared their electoral strategies.[75]

## Neoliberal Economic Reforms, Informal Institutions, and Middle-Class Mobilization

By the late 1980s the political and strategic sophistication of the Muslim Brotherhood presented the most formidable social and ideological opposition to the state. As a mass movement the Brotherhood came from diverse backgrounds, ranging from segments of the business community to lower classes, with old, young, male, and female members. An important mainstay of support, reflected in electoral results in the 1980s, could be found among two social segments in civil society: educated groups with a secondary education, particularly the urban lower middle class who filled the ranks of the vast public sector and bureaucracy and who were hit hard by economic downturns; and small- and medium-sized businesses entrepreneurs in the private sector.

The widening scope and influence of the Islamist movement in civil society was most certainly aided by the emergence of strong Islamist commercial networks and institutions. In this period of what one Islamist termed the "era of wealth accumulation" (*'ahd tajmee' al-tharwat*), these informal economic and social networks provided avenues for upward mobility, and employment, and in so doing fostered Islamic sentiment and sympathy in society generally while also increasing the profile and prestige of the Muslim Brotherhood organization. As noted earlier, informal financial houses engendered a transitional Islamist network of primarily middle-class depositors and investors, and prior to their regulation in the 1990s, Islamic banks fostered strong linkages to high-ranking members of the Muslim Brotherhood and provided initial capitalization to a wide range of commercial enterprises in both the urban and rural areas. However, beyond the rise in the prominence of Islamist commercial networks and the rebuilding and reorganization of the Muslim Brotherhood two additional factors broadened the scope of the Islamist movement and consolidated its urban *lower* middle-class base in ways that generated deep loyalty to the organization. The first factor was the rise of informal (i.e., unregulated) Islamic welfare institutions which increased the organization's financial resources and hence its popularity in civil society. The second factor that strengthened the commitment to the movement on the part of its members was the methods of recruitment and mobilization, the organization's local leaders skillfully and effectively utilized in the context of no small measure of state repression and surveillance.

If the policies of infitah facilitated the informalization of financial markets and led to the rise of a strong Islamic sector and the rise of an Islamist bourgeoisie, the state's inability to maintain adequate social welfare provisioning was a key factor in the rise of IWAs and nongovernment (*ahali*) mosques. These two institutions greatly expanded the scale of the Islamist movement at the level of the grassroots. Indeed, Egypt in this period provides a stark example of how the retreat of the welfare state in the context of economic reform, the rise of Islamism, and the growth of a socially frustrated middle class gave birth to a vibrant network of informal Islamic welfare institutions. By the late 1970s, it was possible to discern the coalescence of a broad network of Islamic organizations that together formed what one scholar has termed the "parallel Islamic sector."[76] These are social organizations – many of them charitable in purpose – that operated on the peripheries of the state and fulfilled many of its traditional functions. As the state continued to shrink in scope under the weight of neoliberal economic reforms, the periphery grew larger and the parallel Islamic sector began taking on increasing responsibility for servicing the needs of Egypt's citizens. This Islamic sector would probably have emerged regardless of regime rhetoric, but the statements of Anwar Sadat (the self-styled "Believer President") encouraged the public activities of Egypt's Islamists. Sadat promoted the formation of Islamic student associations, permitted the limited political participation of the theretofore-repressed Muslim Brotherhood, and loosened press laws that had, till then, hindered the ability of Islamist groups to advertise their ideology.

Meanwhile, economic liberalization and the oil boom created vast reserves of private wealth capable of being directed toward charitable organizations. Islamic banking institutions appealed to many in the growing middle class eager to invest their wealth in companies' compatible with Islamic morality. Likewise, much of the money sent back to Egypt in the form of foreign remittances found its way into the Islamic "moral economy." Through the twin systems of Islamic banking and zakat, Muslims could now channel a portion of their profits into religious education, publishing, mutual aid societies, and a wide range of commercial enterprises. According to some estimates, as much as 1 million Egyptians invested in Islamic banking institutions between 1974 and 1984.[77] The resulting wealth supplied Egypt's IWAs with the vast pool of financial resources necessary to provide an alternative to Nasser's welfare state. Thus, the informal Islamic sector, comprised of Islamic Banks, IICs, and IWAs, provided career opportunities for relatively pious youth who were otherwise barred from the state-run sectors of the economy, and whose cultural and class backgrounds might otherwise have kept them out of the corporate world.

When Sadat was assassinated in 1981 and Hosni Mubarak became president, all the pieces were in place for the ascension of the parallel Islamic sector. The collapse of oil prices seriously undermined the economic security of a broad swath of the Egyptian middle and lower classes. Meanwhile, the Islamic charitable organizations that had emerged in the 1970s as a moral alternative to the secular state became in the 1980s an essential means of avoiding or alleviating the effects of poverty. Though they had their origins in times of relative economic plenty, by the late 1980s Islamic charities and voluntary organizations were providing social protection to millions of Egyptians suddenly made vulnerable. These informal Islamic institutions were thus an integral part of the internationalization of Egypt's economy in that they were an outgrowth of regional economic processes combined with the implementation of economic (i.e., infitah) policies.

It is impossible to accurately estimate the number of Islamic charitable organizations active in Egypt in the 1980s and into the 1990s, since so many had overlapping and ambiguous purposes. Citing a variety of sources, Wickham has pegged the number of Islamic organizations in Egypt in the early 1990s at anywhere from 25 percent to 60 percent of the 15,000 or so registered private voluntary organizations.[78] Another study has gauged their number to be about 20 percent at end of the 1990s.[79] This wide differentiation in statistics can be explained by noting the difficulty scholars face in distinguishing an "Islamic" organization from, for instance, a secular organization that occasionally makes reference to religion. Moreover, many self-conscious Islamic voluntary organizations provide services that would not fit into commonly accepted definitions of social welfare: Qur'anic study groups, for instance. Moreover, while the state in later decades exerted much energy into taking legislative and administrative control over these institutions (discussed further in Chapter 4) in the 1980s many avoided governmental regulation. Indeed, by late 2000s, as state repression increased, directors and staff of IWAs had become increasingly concerned over state regulation. Staff members of a number of IWAs in Matiriyya, Cairo, informed me that in contrast to the 1980s where they had relative autonomy, they were now concerned over having to pay taxes and were understandably anxious that the state sought to increasingly curtail any form of peaceful Islamist opposition.[80] Their concern over state regulation and taxation is warranted. After all, one of the main reasons that the IWAs were largely successful in the 1980s and early 1990s was that the Islamic voluntary organizations that provided services like low-interest loans, job training, or health care did so only intermittently or on an *ad hoc* basis. The actual number of Islamic organizations in Egypt that provide services that meet classical definitions of social welfare, therefore, is difficult to estimate with any degree of accuracy. All of the empirical and anecdotal evidence suggests, however, that they have played an enormous role in meeting the needs of Egypt's citizens from the 1980s forward.

Moreover, beginning in the 1980s, IWAs began to receive a great deal of financial support from private and governmental benefactors in the Arab Gulf. Islamic banks and other religious financial institutions represent an important source of income. Much of the money necessary to carry out day-to-day operations, however, stems from their association with mosques and various profit-making businesses. By being formally associated with a particular mosque, many IWAs receive a portion of the zakat (religious tithe) made there. They were also exempt from government taxation, due to a law that prohibited the taxing of mosques and other "religious buildings." Many IWAs also charge for their services (usually a nominal fee applicable only to those who can afford it) or run ancillary businesses (e.g., religious bookstores) that supply them with a modest income. While the poor certainly receive many benefits from Islamic charitable organizations, they are not the organizations' primary clienteles. Clark has shown that in Egypt (as well as in Jordan and Yemen), IWAs are predominantly run by and for the middle class. The study suffers from "selection bias" in that it does not take account of poorer populations; it is clear IWAs supplying the best services are invariably in wealthier neighborhoods to which the poor do not have easy access. Rather than distribute the best doctors and supplies evenly across the area, most resources are concentrated in certain points where they can be easily distributed to the middle class. This reflects the fact that middle-class Islamists were relatively effective in forging strong patron-client linkages with other members of the middle class. Since the poor are less likely to join an Islamist movement, they are less likely to be targets of IWAs generosity. This combination of local charity, tax exemption, and profit, when combined with support from Gulf benefactors and Islamic banks, has allowed Islamic social institutions to provide avenues of not only welfare provisioning but genuine social protection as well as social mobility for millions of Egypt's aspiring middle class. These developments greatly promoted the financial and political clout of the conservative middle class–based Islamist movement in the country.

Nevertheless, it is important to highlight that the success of the Islamist movement was related to ideational (i.e., religious) as well as socioeconomic factors. As scholars have shown, leaders of the Muslim Brotherhood not only provided selective material incentives to prospective members, they also forged a strong sense of collective identity and solidarity embedded in informal social networks.[81] Moreover, this strategy of mobilization is particularly important under state repression, wherein the strategies of mobilization and the ideological vision of Islamist activists rely upon informal, personal networks as well as cultural and religious "associability" to build movements.[82] Indeed, in addition to the stupendous growth of IWAs, throughout the 1970s and 1980s, the Muslim Brotherhood and their supporters were largely responsible for the dramatic increase in the number of privately run Mosques (*ahali*). Between 1981 and 1989, for example, the number of nongovernmental mosques rose from 40,000 to 70,000. Many of these mosques often served as places of dissenting political and religious messages. Taking advantage of their newly found financial affluence and the state's withdrawal from its social welfare role, the Muslim Brotherhood rapidly came to dominate Egypt's (and especially Cairo's) associational life.

By the end of the 1980s it was clearly evident that as a result of these structural and political changes a dramatic shift had occurred in the social profile of both the leadership of the Brotherhood and its rank and file. Whereas the social base of the "first generation" of the Society of the Muslim Brothers led by Hassan al-Banna was made up of lower-level public servants, students, and artisans, the "second-generation" under the leadership of Telmasani was dominated by a commercially minded Islamist elite, private infitah entrepreneurs, and medium and small-sized business owners. In the early 1990s, as a result of these developments, the Brotherhood further consolidated their middle-class social base by taking control of Egypt's professional syndicates – doctors, engineers, pharmacists, lawyers, dentists, commerce, college professors, and student unions. In addition, the Islamic coalition made up of the Muslim Brotherhood and the Labor Party made considerable headway in local and national elections. They gained twelve seats in parliament in 1984 and as many as thirty-eight seats in 1987.[83]

## Informal Networks and the "Golden Age" of Islamist Mobilization under Authoritarian Rule

The strong and violent conflict that characterizes the current relationship between the regime and the Muslim Brotherhood stands in stark contrast to the 1970s and 1980s, which, as one Brotherhood leader put it, represented "a Golden Age" (*al-'ahd al-Thahiba*) of mobilization for the organization.[84] As detailed earlier this golden age was made possible through a tacit accommodation between the state and the Muslim Brotherhood. First, came the emergent, albeit instrumental, alliance in the economic sphere, which coincided with the boom in remittance inflows and infitah policies, which enabled Islamist elites to push toward Islamicizing the informal financial sectors of the economy (to the benefit of their economic and political clout) and to aid in financing IWAs. Second, the Brotherhood made the most of the Mubarak regime's narrow liberalization of the political system. They took this opportunity to enter the political arena and, under the leadership of the General Guide, entered into alliances with other opposition parties: first with the Wafd Party in 1984, and then in 1987 with the Islamist-oriented Labor Party. From the perspective of the Brotherhood leaders, this was a period of relative "freedom."[85] Taken together the combination of these developments played an important role in engendering broad middle-class appeal, support, and legitimacy for the Islamist movement generally and in expanding the membership base of the *Ikhwan* in particular.

Nevertheless, it is important to note that the actual rank-and-file membership in the Muslim Brotherhood was, and continues to be, something different than the popular base built up through personal and economic and political institutional linkages. Indeed, as Singerman has keenly observed, in the context of an increasingly pious public the "vague call of *Islam is the Solution* (*al-Islam huwa al-hal*) influenced multiple forms of identity."[86] Moreover, it is important to highlight that despite the "thaw" in state-Islamist relations in this period state repression continued: that is, the Brotherhood was still deemed an illegal organization, grassroots Islamist mobilization carefully monitored (if not repressed), and electoral participation circumscribed and limited. Consequently, what form of Islamist activism that emerged as more politically salient was not only grounded in religious interpretation; it was crucially determined by the manner in which locally embedded social networks effectively mobilized rank-and-file members while simultaneously making legitimate new forms of social control and discipline.

The modes of mobilization of the middle class and elite leadership of the Muslim Brotherhood differed from those associated with the informal social networks that underpinned the organizational structure at the grassroots, and which facilitated the recruitment and mobilization of the urban lower middle class. Predictably, at the level of the leadership, the Muslim Brotherhood reorganized its structure to accommodate itself to changes in the regime's policy. Similarly, at the level of the grassroots, rank-and-file members also had to adjust and devise ways of generating high levels of commitment. Indeed, as scholars of social movements in authoritarian contexts (including in Egypt) have shown, in the context of relatively meager resources and high-cost activism, leaders are often compelled to narrowly target individuals based on how much they can offer the movement.[87] In my own research among leaders and rank-and-file Brotherhood members in Helwan, Cairo, what emerged from my findings is that not only did local leaders select prospective members in narrow ways, they also noted that as early as the 1980s (and even more at present) they faced the challenge of generating high levels of commitment in the context of state surveillance and repression. Moreover, the unintended consequence of meeting the challenges of evading state security, selecting new members carefully, and generating trust in the organization among the rank and file was twofold: The Brotherhood increasingly consolidated its lower middle-class urban base in neighborhoods such as Helwan, Cairo, where there resided a mix of working-class workers, lower-middle-class professionals, and urban poor. Importantly, however and as predicted by social movement theorists, in my research I found that it was preexisting networks of trust (and particularly friendship networks) rather than merely an affinity toward the Muslim Brotherhood's ideological program that determined whether or not residents in these neighborhoods decided to join the organization.

Accordingly, the examination of why and how rank and files are recruited and mobilized at the local branches of the organization sheds light on two issues that are at the heart of this comparative study: why individuals choose a particular form of Islamist activism to express their political and social ideals as opposed to other forms of sociopolitical cleavages, and why they pursue such activism at such high personal cost and risk. This is not to deny that religious appeals play a key role in the latter. But as theorists have shown at the point of recruitment (i.e., the point where individuals activate informal networks) ideological congruity plays a far less crucial role than preexisting trust networks and, in the case of the Brotherhood, social and class affinity. Moreover, understanding the recruitment methods of rank-and-file members helps us understand how these social networks respond to shifts in the larger political economy and variations in state repression. I address the latter issue in Chapter 7.

My focus group discussions and interviews with both local leaders and rank-and-file members in the quarters of Helwan, Cairo, revealed that without exception the men (most of whom joined in their early and mid-twenties) were introduced to the organization through either close friends in the neighborhood or relatives. Interestingly, however, those who joined in the 1980s and 1990s did so for decidedly "secular" reasons. Specifically, they initially joined the organization because they were deeply concerned about issues of social justice, inequality, government corruption and what they saw as social decay. But importantly, those who joined in the 1980s (now in their forties) acknowledged that they also had "heard" that the *Ikwhan* offered access and connections (*wasta*) to career and financial opportunities although they insisted that they had no other avenue to express their deep political and social discontent about a reality that, in the context of the high cost of living, was increasingly defined by a limited horizon of opportunities both for themselves and for others. Indeed, by offering opportunities for upward mobility for educated professionals and (certain) skilled workers while also expressing political criticism of state policy the Muslim Brotherhood then (as now) were uniquely poised to mobilize the lower, urban middle class as well as more affluent middle-class supporters.

There is little doubt that the boom period associated with the economic prominence of the Islamists represented the "heyday" of the Muslim Brotherhood recruitment drives and great success in mobilizing followers. This is the reason why one Brotherhood leader termed this era the "golden age" of *tarbiyya*, (spiritual education and growth) for the Islamist movement throughout the country. There is, moreover, little question that, as Carrie Rosefky Wickham's pioneering work has shown, ideas as well as economic interests underpinned the growth in the support for the Brotherhood. Specifically, in the context of an authoritarian state, the leaders of the Brotherhood inspired high-risk activism by framing the Islamist cause as a religious obligation as well as relying on preexisting trust networks (i.e., family and friendship ties).[88] Indeed, unsurprisingly, Islamist leaders routinely privilege the role of Islam in their explanation of why young men and women join the movement. 'Issam al-Eryan, the official spokesperson of the Brotherhood, for example, pointed out that religious sentiments have always been the driving force behind the success of the Brotherhood's mobilization campaign (*hamlet al-tarbiyya*): "It is the reason why Egyptians wish to join the *Ikhwan.* [It is also] why the organization has difficulty absorbing all those who want to join the cause of Islam in Egypt."[89]

However, it is also important to note that those actually responsible for recruiting new members at the district levels of Cairo such as Helwan point to a host of nonreligious factors. This is not in itself surprising since social movement theorists have documented across cases that new participants to social movements activate social networks often for social and economic reasons rather than due to inherent ideological congruity with the organization or its leadership.[90] In any case, in the Golden Age of Tarbiyya of the 1980s, the leader of the Brotherhood branch in Helwan noted that, while the general thrust behind their recruitment campaigns is naturally based on Islamic principles, the real Bab (*door*) is through politics. This is not to suggest that religious motivation and the role of ideas do not form the basis for sustained support and loyalty to social movements including the Brotherhood, but to highlight that religious interpretation evolves over time to meet the political and social challenges that the leaders understand to resonate most deeply among the community and prospective participants.

In the view of the recruiters, the real challenge is to impress on the potential recruit that Islam, or more specifically the Brotherhood organization, can overcome the challenges of social injustice, government corruption, and, not insignificantly, the spiraling cost of living. These are the causes that they most often cite as underpinning their motivation for joining the Brotherhood. Consequently, in order to maintain their relevancy as an attractive option in the context of state repression in the 1980s (and even more importantly in later decades), local activist leaders stated that they alter the curriculum and educational content of their program to suit changing conditions. For example, the writings of the Brotherhood's founder, Hassan al-Banna, are carefully selected to stress their educational aspects, and the history of Islamic Andalusia is incorporated as important evidence of religious tolerance for more "liberal"-minded youth. In Helwan, which contains a large proportion of working-class residents, the local leaders of the Brotherhood also have long attempted to mobilize working-class members, albeit with little success. It is for this reason that, for example, at least in Helwan, the local leaders of the organization have reinterpreted the early years of *Hassan al-Banna's* and, in particular, the social profile of the first generation of the Ikhwan. For example, in contrast to members of the national leadership I interviewed, Helwan's *Ikwan* emphasize to potential participants that, in the first generation of the Society of the Muslim Brotherhood, its founder, *Sheikh al-Banna*, enjoyed great popularity and support among the working-class laborers in the province of Ismai'iliyya. These examples demonstrate clearly that ideological flexibility, often obscured in static analysis of the Brotherhood's ideology, has long been the hallmark of its great success at the grassroots. However, it also demonstrates some of the organization's constraints in terms of connecting with the working classes. The Islamist activist leaders in Helwan view their social distance from the working classes as a limitation. In Helwan industrial public sector workers have traditionally been reluctant to join the solidly middle-class movement of the Brotherhood and it is for this reason that Islamist activists have attempted to promulgate the notion that the role of labor in the movement has a long history as one important way to make inroads into this segment of the local community.

This limitation in mobilizing working-class workers reflects two important dimensions of the Brotherhood's organization that helps to explain who joins the organization and why, particularly at the local level: the social exclusivity associated with recruiting and mobilizing new members, and the fact that many new members join the Brotherhood in order to access patronage and achieve some measure of social mobility. To be sure, it is state repression and social and economic crisis that often compel activist leaders to recruit those most helpful to the organization, but it is also important to highlight that activist leaders put great effort in providing both material incentives and spiritual guidance (*tarbiyya*) to those who are afforded the privilege of membership. This is not to say that preexisting trust networks are not a key avenue of entry to the movement, but rather that these trust networks are socially embedded in ways that over time have consolidated the urban lower-class profile of the Brotherhood's membership in neighborhoods such as Helwan as well as in many neighborhoods of Cairo.

In practice the recruitment process of the Muslim Brotherhood is elaborate and potential members are recruited in painstaking fashion. Individuals are chosen according to a number of criteria including preexisting educational attainment, social class, and "talents" in the skilled (as opposed to the unskilled) labor market. Moreover, as the leaders in Helwan informed me, and rank-and-file members confirmed, once an individual becomes a full member of the organization, the leadership takes responsibility for furthering his career through activating the organizations' networks to the best of their ability. Thus, an unemployed poet is tasked with and paid to write religious songs at a wedding of a fellow member or relative; a trained mathematician is employed by the organization to provide private lessons (*durus khususiyya*) to the children of a member; a merchant is encouraged to work in one of the Islamist-run commercial enterprises in what leaders term the "informal market" (*al-suq al-hur*); a craftsmen hired in the building trade; and a professor paid to teach. Moreover, these members are not only helped with connections (*wastas*). As one leader put it: "[W]e help them in these endeavors with supplies of investment capital, regular salaries, and jobs through the organization's social networks. We even help them with marriage."

However, it is important to emphasize that prior to having access to these patronage and economic networks, the organization selects recruits very narrowly. In fact, each potential member is carefully interviewed prior to the recruitment process in order to make a decision as to his (or her) aptitude and potential in the long-term success and efficient running of the organization. As one Brotherhood leader in Helwan district put it: "[T]he poor are not a big part of our recruitment efforts. They simply want *lugmat al-aysh* (bread), and have no education and consciousness that would enable them to understand the *Da'wa* (Islamic Call)."

Other *Ikhwan* members were more detailed (and nuanced) in their explanation of why the organization has not been able to mobilize working-class members in large numbers. Indeed, while the spokesperson at the national level informed me that the organization accepts members from all segments of society, at the district level leaders of the organization acknowledged a "shortcoming" with respect to their ability to mobilize both working-class residents and the urban poor. This is most noticeable in working-class neighborhoods such as *helwan* and *hadayiq helwan* where I conducted my research and where formal workers represent a large proportion of residents. As one activist leader in Helwan who joined the Brotherhood in the 1980s said:

> We try to help *'umaal* [workers] on an individual basis. But we have to acknowledge our shortcomings with respect to making recruitment inroads among laborers. We have much more luck with *hirfiyyin*, than we do with the workers. It is also difficult to have a [Muslim] Brother with a suit going to the poor *shabbab* [youth] in informal areas.

This corroborates the statement of young men in the poorer informal quarters of Imbaba who informed me that they are rarely afforded the opportunity to join the more mainstream Muslim Brotherhood organization. This exclusivist aspect of the *Ikhwan* in terms of mobilization partially explains the popularity of more militant organizations that emerged in the informal settlements in Cairo, which I discuss in Chapter 7. To be sure, the militant Islamic Group in Imbaba also selected members along class lines. However, the latter's "pool" of recruits was comprised of a combination of informal and casual laborers and newly urbanized migrants who constituted much of their membership during their most active recruitment drives in the late 1980s and early 1990s in Imbaba and other informally settled quarters of Cairo. In other words, the "barriers to entry" into the middle-class *Ikhwan* organization had the unintended consequences of driving many poorer and younger Egyptian youth into more militant organizations like the *al-Jama'a al-Islamiyya*.

This is not to suggest that the framing of Islam as a religion of equality and social justice does not resonate across social groups even in Helwan, and one *Ikwhan* leader emphasized that the organization routinely assists workers and the poor on an "individual" bases. Nevertheless, as a result of state repression and resource constraints in less-affluent districts such as Helwan, the leaders of the Brotherhood have always been compelled to select new members along relatively strict class and occupational lines. As I discuss in Chapter 2 this is also the case in the Sudan. Indeed, it is important to note that clear social divisions also exist between lower middle-class members and the middle and upper middle-class strata of the organization. In other words the form that the recruitment and mobilization take even within the organization is effective to the extent that it is specific to the local social and economic context. As one *Ikhwan* leader put it:

> It was always easier to recruit from the *hirfiyiin* [craftsmen] without higher degrees. These are true men (*ruggal*) who do not equivocate. They see things in black and white. [For their part], educated university students are always easily seduced by non-Islamic entertainment and other things.

Importantly, these internal social and class divisions between more affluent Islamists and those lower down on the social ladder do not always generate conflict. This is not only because of the importance of deeply shared religious values and a strong sense of a collective religious identity; it is also due to a key motivation that induced scores of lower middle-class men into joining the Islamist movement: the perceived and, in the 1980s and through the 1990s, real possibility of upward social mobility. As one resident of Helwan told me after he was denied membership by *Ikhwan* recruiters ostensibly due to his lack of education: "I only dream that I could be rich like the *Ikhwan*. They are a role model for me (*al-mathal al-'ala*); being wealthy like many of the *Ikhwan* means being able to get married and raise a family, afford the funds to help my brothers and friends to get married, and attain a good job."[91]

It is important to highlight that even in an era where the authoritarian regime pursued a relative permissive attitude toward the middle-class strata of the Islamist movement, at the level of the grassroots the Brotherhood was compelled to devise methods of mobilization to avoid state repression and surveillance and simultaneously generate high levels of commitment among the members of the organization. As noted earlier, one key method of mobilization utilized was to motivate participants through the provision of selective incentives and carefully select the right kind of member to the organization. However, given the general popularity of the Islamist movement the Muslim Brotherhood attracted deeply committed individuals dedicated to the cause of the organization and willing to make sacrifices and engage in high-risk behavior, as well as low commitment individuals who acted as "consumers" rather than "investors" in the organization and desired short-term gains from participation.[92] Consequently, in the context of continued state repression and the "clandestine" nature of their mobilization efforts, the leadership of the organization designed a method of mobilization (*tarbiyya*) in a way that would facilitate loyalty to the organization and engender genuine long-term investment to its religious, social, and political objectives. One leader who played a crucial role in this regard was Khairat al-Shater. Shater was not only primarily responsible for introducing an innovative way of financing the patronage networks linking national and local-level elements of the Brotherhood; he also outlined a process of mobilizing rank-and-file members in ways that ensured trust and fealty to the movement.

In 2012, in the brief period of freedom afforded the Brotherhood when the organization's political party (the Freedom and Justice Party) headed a civilian government following the Tahrir uprisings of 2011, Shater candidly revealed the vision behind the mobilization campaigns of the organization:

> We are groups, families, branches, and regions and officials, the form of the structure may change from one era to another, but the idea is that there must be an organization. There must be work and, in this system, there must remain certain degrees of commitment. So it is not possible for us to call any gathering a *Gama'a*, as in the technical term of the Islamic movement, where each can do what he wants or one with an idea different from that of the majority . . . not every existing gathering is a Gama'a, even if it were a group of good people who are committed to Islam; they are not a Gama'a as such with their structures and officials, without system, commitment, and obedience.[93]

And further:

> The *Gama'a* thus requires the strength of psychological construction and the strength of organizational construction. The organizational construction needs structures, officials, and relationships that bind them together. The Ulama classified these relationships into brotherhood, trust and obedience.[94]

A close examination of the process of mobilization devised by the Brotherhood, and the duties and obligations associated with different levels of membership in particular, demonstrates how these challenges and objectives noted by Shater were met. In this regard, two important elements associated with the process of mobilization of rank-and-file activists determined the relative strength of the organization even in an era where the state pursued a relative permissive attitude toward the movement. First, while the distribution of material resources provided an important incentive for individuals to join the organization, this factor was hardly sufficient in generating deep loyalty to the organization. Indeed, the primary reason the Brotherhood was able to enjoy strong commitment from its new recruits and long standing members had more to do with a multistage socialization process which, over time, facilitated two important benefits for those who joined the *Ikhwan*: that is, the real possibility of upward social mobility for members in the lower ranks of the organization, and the more spiritual benefit of being shepherded through a process of growth, or *tarbiyya* (literally, guidance and nurturance). Moreover, the latter was underpinned by an adherence to social discipline and the enforcement of strict guidelines associated with proper personal comportment which, taken together, generated not only a strong sense of community in a broad sense, but also the privileged position of participating as a respected member in a select and exclusive brotherhood.

Second, and in more theoretical terms, the process of vetting recruits highlights the construction of a particular type of Islamist *political* identity that is clearly important in the view of the leaders of the Muslim Brotherhood. Indeed, the diversity of Islamist politics in Egypt captured by the popular term the "Islamist trend" (*al-Tayyar al-Islami*) warrants a closer examination of why some individuals join moderate middle-class Islamist organizations, while others either remain apolitical pious citizens or participate in more militant forms of activism. As Shater's statement mentioned earlier clearly captures, for the Muslim Brotherhood the process of *tarbiyya* not only plays a key role in guiding individual participants along the lines of a particularly Islamist political trajectory, it is also open to change in the context of changing political and economic circumstances.

There is little question that the boom period of the 1980s and up to the early 1990s represented the "heyday" of the Muslim Brotherhood's recruitment and mobilization campaigns. It was, in the words of one activist leader in Helwan, the "golden age" of *tarbiyya* (education) for the Islamist movement. Nevertheless, activist leaders maintained that they have long had to address two challenges: to impress on potential members that Islam or, more specifically the Brotherhood organization, can overcome the deep social, political, and moral challenges facing the country; and to generate trust and loyalty to the Brotherhood in particular.

Consequently, joining the Muslim Brotherhood is predicated on a lengthy process that is comprised of three distinct phases: identification, training, and, finally, full membership status. The process is necessarily hierarchical and until 2007 it consisted of as many as five stages of participation from the initial period of identification to full membership. Each level bears with it duties and obligations designed to determine the recruit's level of commitment to the organization. This in turn is measured in accordance with the potential member's attendance of the weekly programs, regular financial contributions, and full participation in the Muslim Brotherhood organization's activities. Moreover, the ranking system (to be described later) has great influence on the decision-making and long-term organizational behavior of the movement. The primary reason for this is that the level of rank qualifies members to elect and to be elected to the higher bodies of the organization.

The first stage is a process characterized by *Da'wa* in which potential recruits are identified through Islamic activities such as local Mosques, schools, and universities. As in other similar organizations preexisting trust plays a key role. Not surprisingly, the easiest recruitment opportunity is one in which recruiters become acquainted with and befriend potential members through informal social networks, most notably relatives, classmate connections, friends, and neighbors. The basic criterion of recruitment is to select individuals in terms of their behavior (*suluuk*). At this early stage, the evaluation or assessment of a potential recruit is based on the extent to which the individual adheres to public morality and distinguishes himself in aptitude with respect to Islamic education. For instance, activist leaders informed me that this includes the individual being dedicated to prayer in the Mosque, and great importance is paid to the dawn (*fajr*) prayer in particular. In addition, the individual must become an active participant in charitable works and have a "good" reputation among residents of his neighborhood. Moreover, in addition to issues of morality, the potential recruit must demonstrate interest and commitment to political issues. As one activist leader put it: "[H]e must be interested in larger public policies associated with the larger Arab community and the Islamic Umma." For example, active sympathy to the Palestinian cause is viewed by the leadership as an important component of the recruit's commitment to the organization, and activist work opposing the regimes in Arab countries, including Egypt, is of paramount importance as a key litmus test of this political commitment. In this instance, the *Da'wa* is viewed in political and not just religious terms. This stage of initial membership or vetting of potential recruits is termed "the stage of general adherence" or *marhalat al rabt al-'am*. What distinguishes the Muslim Brotherhood from more militant organizations, however, is that the age of the individual acquiring membership should not be less than eighteen years. In the 1980s and 1990s, as I discuss in Chapter 7, the more militant Islamic Group (*al-jama'a al-Islamiyya*), for example, routinely recruited adolescents rather than young adults.

Following the identification phase is the socialization or formal training stage. Upon selection, the recruit graduates to the stage of the *muhib*, a "devoted" or aspirant member of the movement. At this stage the individual enters the circle (*khaliyya*) of the Muslim Brotherhood. In order to engender greater commitment, the recruit is educated in the basics of Islamic knowledge (*al-adab al-Islami*) and the principles of the Islamist movement. In this stage, the leadership monitors closely the attendance of the individual to prayers, and the commitment of the members of the cell is evaluated through practical activities. These include *Da'wa* responsibilities and the payment of monthly financial contributions. In addition, the recruit is socialized to follow a specific set of social morays *(adab usuul al-khaliyya)* that range from obedience to parents and elders to adherence to norms of hygiene. The latter includes the proper process of ablution and prayer and related matters designed to impart a strict moral education conducive to disciplined behavior. In the context of state crackdowns against the Muslim Brotherhood, these *khaliyyas* assume a clandestine orientation in which only members of each cell know each other at least until they advance further through the recruitment process. However, communication is achieved across these organizations because leaders of a group of cells, with a relatively longer history of membership, know the others up to the highest hierarchy of the leadership.

It is, however, in the third stage where the formal training phase of the recruit begins in earnest. At this stage the recruit is considered an effective member, or *Udu al-Muaid*, with entry determinant on effectively "vetting" the recruit in the previous stages. According to members of the Muslim Brotherhood's leadership I interviewed in 2008 and 2009, it is at this stage where the process of selecting a future '*udu*, or member, begins. The genuine testing of the recruit, however, occurs in the fourth stage where the recruit is considered an "associate" member, '*Udu al-Muntassib*. Following passage of the first three phases, the recruit is compelled to swear an oath of allegiance (*al-bayi'ah*) to the organization. The leadership then places the individual through several tests to insure his commitment, verify his solidarity to the movement, and develop the recruit's endurance, *sabrihi*. As one recruiter informed me, this is considered a crucial stage precisely because it tests the potential recruit's resolve and "stability to act well" in sensitive situations. Passing this stage makes the member a full-fledged "brother and one step away from full membership."[95] By the fifth stage, the recruit is considered a full member of the organization and is designated as *'Udu al-Multazim*, a "committed member." This is the stage when the member is assigned organizational tasks and is afforded the right to identify and select new members, to monitor and evaluate lower-ranking members (i.e., *al-muhib and muaid*–ranked recruits).

Thus, in practice the vetting process of the Muslim Brotherhood is elaborate and potential members are recruited in painstaking fashion and socialized into the organization as part of a relatively lengthy process. It is important to emphasize that religion clearly plays an important part in the process of *tarbiyya* and rank-and-file members I interviewed are deeply motivated by their understanding of Islam as a religion of equality and justice. However, as noted earlier, the Muslim Brotherhood's activist leaders are also clearly aware of the political and organizational dictates necessary to generate deep commitment, trust, loyalty, and, as Shater put it, "obedience" to the organization. Moreover, it is important to reiterate that while activist leaders are necessarily concerned with building and strengthening the structure of the organization in the context of a strong authoritarian regime, for their part, prospective participants and rank-and-file members are understandably motivated to join the movement out of a desire to achieve a better and higher socio-economic status in life. The challenge for the leaders of the organization came when the state clamped down on the Islamic economy and its financial base beginning in the early 1990s. As the Brotherhood suffered dramatic financial loses as a result of both state policy and economic crisis, the organization's leaders sought ways to adapt so as to continue to provide resources to their rank and file and, even more importantly, to maintain the latter's strong commitment to the organization. It is therefore understandable that, as Shater himself noted, while the structure of the Brotherhood needs a "structure" and "relationships" to function, it is also an organization that changes from "one era to another." In Chapter 4 I address how the Brotherhood was compelled to alter the process of mobilization (*tarbiyya*) in the context of increasing levels of state repression and dwindling resources resulting from the two related factors: the onset of economic recession and the state's concerted attack against informal Islamic institutions ranging from Islamic finance to Islamic welfare institutions.

## Informal Labor and the Foundation for Militancy in Imbaba's Informal Settlements

If Egypt's integration into regional and labor and capital markets resulted in the informalization of financial markets in ways that advanced the economic and political fortunes of the middle-class Islamist movement, it also led to the dramatic expansion of informal housing and labor markets, which laid the foundation for the rise in popularity of a more militant form of Islamist activism in some of Cairo's booming informal settlements. By the late 1980s and early 1990s the militant *al-Jama'a al-Islamiyya* (Islamic Group), which originally emerged in the rural governances of rural Egypt, found significant popularity in Cairo's booming informal housing settlements. Indeed, by the end of the 1970s the deep structural and political changes generated by the internationalization of the economy resulted in the emergence of two segments of Islamic radicalism. The first consisted of newly urbanized, middle-class university students and educated white-collar professionals.[96] The second social group was poorer and more impoverished, and it consisted of rural workers who migrated to the city and found employment in the informal construction sector, which had witnessed dramatic expansion during the oil boom. This section discusses the ways in which the internationalization of Egypt's economy in the 1970s and 1980s led to a boom in informal housing and casualized forms of labor in construction in ways that paved the way for a new politics of ascription based on more militant forms of Islamist activism.

To a large extent, Sadat's shift toward a period of "hyper-liberalism" mirrored global economic trends in this period as Egypt entered a phase of "flexible specialization," characterized by increased capital mobility, and decreased protection of wage earners. That is, the old Nasserite economic system rooted in a "social contract" between large firms and a stable unionized industrial labor force gave way to a new regime based on the dominance of service occupations and a dramatic reorganization of labor markets and wage structures.[97] As the state continued to deregulate the economy, one important result was the expansion of informal markets in housing and labor.[98]

In terms of Cairo's housing market, this had the effect of leading to an explosion in land prices, which skyrocketed thirty-fold in Imbaba and other informal areas in the 1980s. Indeed, the increase in demand for housing was directly connected to Egypt's integration into the new international division of labor. Beginning in 1973–74 as a result of the combination of the oil boom in the Arab oil-producing countries and economic reforms, which opened the country to foreign investments and permitted Egyptians to travel more freely, Cairo witnessed the dramatic expansion of informal housing. The savings and remittances of expatriate workers provided the main source of capital for a boom in the construction of informal housing. This growth was so dramatic that by 1978, only five years after Sadat's infitah policies and the boom in remittances, an estimated 76 percent of new housing units built in Cairo were supplied by the informal sector, and these informal areas (*al-Manatiq al-'Ashwa'iyya)* housed 1.6 million Egyptians or 25 percent of Cairo's population.[99] Nevertheless, despite the large number of residents in these settlements they constituted informal and "illegal" housing because they were built on what was primarily privately held agricultural lands and without official construction licensing and permits.

The boom in remittances and infitah also resulted in two further, albeit related, developments that altered the country's labor market in a crucial way as the boom in informal housing became intimately linked to the expansion of informal labor, especially in the building trade. First, the demand for affordable housing and the speculation in land was accompanied by a dramatic shortage of labor in the construction sector due to the drain caused by emigration. This is because the bulk of the labor that was bid away from the domestic economy originated from construction. This process led to the loss of as much as 60 percent of construction workers during the boom in out-migration.[100] Second, workers in rural villages migrated to the cities in larger numbers to replace emigrant workers as informal laborers in the construction sector. As Assaad has shown, and I observed from my own research, labor in the construction sector in particular is almost exclusively procured on a casual basis. These casual workers have none of the employment benefits guaranteed by law, have no provisions for retirement or disability, and have no formal legal recourse in case of disputes. Moreover, 90 percent of all construction workers throughout the country are hired as casual workers. The precarious nature of their situation is further compounded by the fact that a total of 70 percent have no attachment to a single "boss" and thus must move frequently among employers (i.e., the subcontractors who hire them).[101] By and large the vast majority are compelled to rely on personal contacts, rural-based kinship networks, and their stock of social networks to find jobs.

For their part, these ex-village workers were attracted to the city both because of the increasing diminished availability of agricultural land and the promise of better services in Cairo. Consequently, the general investment boom associated with remittance inflows was translated rapidly into rapid growth in the construction sector, whose share of the total labor force almost doubled from 2.8 percent to 5.2 percent between 1973 and 1982.[102] Moreover, the expansion of informal labor markets and informal housing in informal neighborhoods in the context of economic liberalization became intimately linked since rarely can wages derived from informal work result in income sufficient for rents in formal housing. Consequently, together with poor Cairenes who also sought work and affordable housing in Cairo, the majority of migrants from rural villages settled primarily in newly established informal settlements such as the poor quarters of Western Mounira (*Mounira al-Gharbiyya*) in the neighborhood of Imbaba.[103] It is important to note, however, that because they were built in contravention of official laws and outside the purview of state regulation, these informal areas were ignored by the state. As a result, they lacked any organized streets, and were deprived of social services such as schools, health clinics, and youth centers. In addition, by and large they had little links with the state in terms of political representation or formal law and order institutions. Importantly, it is also here that the militant *al-Jama'a al-Islamiyya* (Islamic Group) came to enjoy the greatest amount of influence among local residents in the early 1990s and early 2000s.

## The Islamic Group in Western Mounira, Imbaba

The informalization of Egypt's labor and housing markets, associated with the remittance boom and infitah policies, is closely linked to the development of more militant Islamist activism that came to be centered on some of Cairo's informal settlements. Indeed, the fact that by the early 1990s leaders of the Islamic Group enjoyed the greatest influence in the newly settled sections of Western Mounira (i.e., al-Waraq, Ezbat al-Mufti, and Beshteel), and none at all in the original areas of Imbaba, suggests a strong affinity between the cultural and political objectives of the Islamist militants and the economic and social aspirations of an increasingly pauperized community of informal laborers.

The transformation of the Mounira sections of Imbaba where I conducted my research represents a larger story of the shift toward the informalization of labor and social relations for Mounira's residents. It is a transformation that has coincided with the displacement of the Egyptian Left and formal labor by both middle-class and moderate Islamists (i.e., Muslim Brotherhood) and the militant *al-Jama'a al-Islamiyya.* This is a particularly important point since conventional analysis has explained the rise of Islamic militancy in Imbaba as the response of an undifferentiated urban poor to their miserable social conditions or exclusively as a result of state repression and neglect. The fact is that of the twenty-eight informal settlements in Cairo none have witnessed the penetration of Islamists to the same degree as the Western Mounira sections of Imbaba. Indeed, despite the acute stress of urban life, most informal settlements still possess viable informal institutions to settle local disputes and, in many cases, generate a viable and supportive social fabric. As in Imbaba generally, most informal settlements lack basic services, but while they do appear extremely disordered on the surface they are nevertheless characterized by an underlying order, which produces a high level of safety, security, and collective notions trust.

Why then should Western Mounira, in particular, experience a high degree of social conflict and prove, ultimately, "fertile" ground for more militant forms of Islamist militancy? What are the underlying causes of these developments, which not only further fragmented the Islamist trend in Egypt but also crucially altered the state's relationship to Islamist forms of activism with lasting reverberations to the present?

## The Social and Economic History of Imbaba

The social and economic history of Imbaba provides a key analytical window into some of the root causes behind the rise of the Islamist trend in the area. *Mounira al-Jadida* – whose Western sections came to contain a strong Islamist militant presence – is an informal settlement, which grew up just beyond Imbaba, which was then the edge of Urban Cairo beginning in the late 1950s and 1960s. Remarkably, what is one of the densest areas in Cairo was, prior to the mid-1950s, part of the cultivated land of Giza Governorate, producing vegetables for the urban market; the urban agglomeration ended at Midan Kitkat, across the Nile from the upper-class neighborhood of Zamalek. Villages were scattered across the land. They had begun to urbanize slowly since the establishment of bridge links to the Cairo side of the Nile via Zamalek in 1913, but the population growth remained slow for many years until the introduction of state-led industrialization policies under the Gamal Abdel Nasser regime. In the 1940s and 1950s, the original area of Imbaba included only Gezirat Imbaba and the surrounding Medinat Taq al-Duwal and Kit Kat.

It is a historical irony that a neighborhood that has become synonymous with state neglect and lack of state provisioning in the 1990s was, in the Nasser period, the beneficiary of a disproportionate amount of state patronage. Indeed, Imbaba originally enjoyed distinct state largesse under Nasser in its early phase of development. It was, in the words of a longtime resident, the "envy" of other municipalities and Governorates as a result of the sheer volume of state investment in the area.[104] In the 1960s Nasser built public housing for workers in *Medinat al-'Umaal* (City of Workers) alongside housing first built by the Wafd government in Medinat al-Tahrir to the north. Since the 1950s, the expansion of the city into agricultural land in the Imbaba direction has proceeded apace, with population growth at the fringe of the urban agglomeration rather than centered on existing villages.

Much of the growth in Imbaba and the larger community in *Mounira Gharbiyya* during the 1950s and 1960s was the result of government programs to provide housing for workers needed to operate the textile factories introduced under Nasser's Import Substitution Industrialization (ISI) policies of the 1960s. The first such development in the area was the City of Workers immediately adjacent to Mounira Gedida, which was established by boat builders just prior to the revolution. The "City of Workers" also housed workers employed with the Egyptian Textile Manufacturing Company (*al-Sharika al-Misriyya li Intaj al-Nasij*) and the General Printing Authority (*al-Haya al-'Ama li Shiuun al-Matabi'*). Eventually, the government also built a substantial number of schools, social clubs, and hospitals in *Gezirat Imbaba*, *Medinat al-'Umaal*, and *Medinat al-Tahrir*. Several substantial factories had also located in this area by the early 1960s, including a match factory and a clothing factory. Public housing projects were later established in *Mounira al-Sharqiyya*, a formal settlement to the east of *Mounira al-Gedida*, and several other public housing projects were built in Imbaba proper.

Not surprisingly, during this period, Leftist and labor union activism centered on the industrial factories and public housing projects in *Medinat Tahrir* and *Medinat al-'Umaal*. The Arab nationalist Left's strongest presence was in the latter, however; an area in Imbaba appropriately named in honor of the "Egyptian worker" – *Medinat al-'Umaal*. Any candidate fielded by the Left in local elections during this period would run in *Medinat al-'Umaal*. In the 1960s and 1970s this Leftist- and socialist-oriented movement was closely linked to the ruling Arab Socialist Union (*al-Itihad al-Ishtiraki*) Party. Later, after 1976, this movement organized around the then newly formed *Taggamu* Party, which sought representation, at the national level, in the Egyptian parliament (*Maglis al-Sha'ab*). Thus, the Leftist movement, so strong at the time, represented an amalgamation of workers, formerly organized, housed in state-built housing, and whose social and political fortunes depended on Nasser's etatist policies, rather than on the neoliberal reforms associated with Sadat's "Open Door" policy introduced in the 1970s.

At the community level Leftist organizing centered on a host of civil associations such as *Munazamat Shabbab Imbaba* (Imbaba Youth Association) and *Nadi al-Riyadah* (the Imbaba Athletic Club). The Imbaba Youth Association in particular played an important role in the recruitment of young men and women to the Arab Socialist movement at the time. They provided a number of services to local residents including academic tutorial classes (*Fusuul al-Taqwiah*). They also convened conferences (*Nadawat*) in "Summer Clubs" (*Nawadi al-Saif*) to discuss and resolve social problems that may exist in the community. In ideological terms, Left of center civil associations represented the voice of Arab Socialists, Marxists, and Radicals during the Nasser era. Of particular significance is that, up to the 1970s, industrial labor in the textile factories formed the most important social base of the Left in the neighborhood.

Naturally, industrial labor in Imbaba was even more intimately linked to the Nasser regime since they were the prime beneficiaries in terms of disbursement of subsidized housing and employment in the state-controlled factories. Of great significance is the fact that these, hitherto, influential Nasserite civil associations were, by the 1980s, completely supplanted by a host of Islamic charitable associations, private mosques, and health clinics linked to the increasingly ascendant and confident Islamist movement. It is important to note that this change did not simply reflect the change in the ideational commitment of former Leftist supporters. Few of the rank and file and leadership associated with the Left in Imbaba "converted" to the Islamist trend. Rather, the Islamist "takeover" of parts of Imbaba is due to the ascendancy of new social groupings associated with the state's neoliberal orientation and who owe their fortunes to the informalization of both housing and labor markets – a phenomenon that itself came to be linked with the large-scale migration of Egyptian workers following the oil boom in the 1970s.

During the 1970s and through the 1980s, Imbaba, and particularly the section of Western Mounira, witnessed an accelerated pace of in-migrants first from rural provinces such as Assiut and Sohag, and in more recent decades, from Fayoum. In the 1970s there was a spectacular rise in migration from the *Saeed* (Upper Egypt) to Imbaba as well as to other informal areas in Cairo. The migration itself had begun as early as the 1960s. At that time it was fueled by increasing population growth and subdivisions of medium plots in Upper Egypt resulting from customary, Islamic laws of inheritance. Initially, male members of one family or clan would travel to Cairo while the rest would remain to cultivate agricultural lands. This in-migration was motivated by the search for *rizq*, or wealth, and most of the migrants settled in what was then agricultural land around Imbaba and *Ain Shams* out of two main considerations. The first consideration stemmed from a desire to find affordable dwellings, and second, to find employment nearby. The most feasible location was along the border between agricultural and urban land since the middle-class neighborhoods of *Dokki* and *Zamalik* were out of reach in terms of affordability.

Associated with these developments – and in the context of the informal labor and housing boom – new informal settlements west of the original communities of *Gezirat Imbaba* and *Medinat al-'Umaal* were spontaneously built to accommodate rural-urban migrants and lower-class Caireens responding to the demand for labor in the construction trade. As a result of in-migration from Upper Egypt, by the late 1980s greater Imbaba came to be spatially divided in social and occupation terms. More specifically, middle-class professionals and government civil servants continued to reside in the older sections of *Medinat al-'Umaal* and *Tahrir*, while Western Mounira became home to a large number of informal laborers spread across the poorer quarters of Western Mounira such as *Oseem*, *Ezbat al-Mufti*, and *Bestheel*. Thus, whereas under Nasser, the industrial workforce represented the dominant form of employment in Imbaba, by the 1980s informal labor in construction represented the most important source of work in the neighborhood. This is true of all of Imbaba, but particularly in Western Mounira.

It is also significant that these social and occupational divisions reflected marked differences along ideological lines. More specifically, as Imbaba shifted from a neighborhood dominated by Leftist and labor union members to one that became densely penetrated by Islamist activists the latter were also divided in socio-spatial and ideological terms. The Muslim Brotherhood found their greatest popularity in the middle-class sections of *al-Waraq* and *al-Arab*, while the *Jama'a al-Islamiyya* and the more Salafist trend of Islamist activists came to be concentrated in the lower-class neighborhoods of *Ezbat al-Mufti*, *Bestheel*, and *Oseem*. However, this transformation associated with the eclipse of the left by the Islamists in the neighborhood did not occur without wrenching political and social conflict.

As in Egypt generally, the displacement of the Nasserist Left by the Islamists in Imbaba was a result of state policy as well as socioeconomic change. According to Imbaba's residents, the most important political turning point in this transformation was related directly to the historic Food Roots of 1977. On January 18 and 19 of that year scores of working class and poor Egyptians throughout the country spontaneously protested in reaction to the government's decision to increase prices of some essential commodities as part of infitah economic austerity measures implemented by Sadat under pressure from the International Monetary Fund (IMF). Ultimately, in the face of overwhelming popular opposition, the regime was forced to rescind its decision to cut food subsidies. Nevertheless, the riots accelerated Sadat's policy of promoting the Islamists in order to undercut the influence of Nasser's socialists (*isthirakuun*) and Arab nationalists (*qawmuun*), which at the time posed a grave threat to the stability of the Sadat regime.

What its supporters called the *"intifada"* (popular uprising) of 1977 was spearheaded by the supporters of the Left in Imbaba, and in fact, began with demonstrations organized by the residents of the public housing projects in the area. Immediately following the food riots, Sadat's security forces cracked down against Leftist and other "pro-Nasserist" forces in Imbaba and elsewhere that it blamed for instigating and organizing the nationwide riots. Members of the *Taggamu* Party in particular were singled out for retaliation and thousands of the organization's members, including many residents in Imbaba, were detained. Subsequently, the influence of Leftists in Imbaba, organized around the *Taggamu* Party, effectively ended.

In addition, following the riots, state authorities supported the Islamists in important ways. First, the regime turned a blind eye to the expansion of informal settlements. To be sure this was a consequence of the withdrawal of the state from the production of subsidized housing for middle- and lower-class Egyptians as part of infitah policy meant to rationalize the public sector. But another reason was to diffuse Leftist political mobilization by altering the demographic composition of the local population and indirectly support a new Islamist-oriented constituency in the informal areas. Second, in the 1970s and early 1980s just as Sadat supported Islamist activists in the universities to outflank Nasserist forces, the regime actively supported moderate as well as militant wings of the Islamist movement in informal areas.[105] This was evident in two important ways. The then ruling NDP promoted and supported members of candidates belonging to the Muslim Brotherhood in local council elections throughout the 1970s and 1980s.[106] Moreover, in contrast to the 1990s when state security forces sought to monitor Islamist religious institutions, in the 1970s and 1980s the regime promoted a key element that brought militants together: the proliferation of *Ahali* mosques in Imbaba and other informal areas. The Islamist resurgence and the displacement of the Leftist forces were thus accompanied by an increase of both private mosques and independent preachers in the neighborhood.[107]

The history of the state's policy of tacitly supporting the Islamists is one reason that despite the 1992 siege of Imbaba by state security forces, Islamists are still active in the neighborhood. To be sure, throughout the Mubarak era state security forces monitored Islamist activists closely, but Islamist preachers affiliated with the Brotherhood (*Ikwhan*) and the Islamic Group (*Jama'a*) continued to be permitted to deliver sermons – within certain security restrictions. However, as the voting patterns of the parliamentary elections following the 2011 uprisings clearly demonstrated, the persistent dismal social conditions in Imbaba is another major reason why there continues to be significant popular support for both the recently banned Muslim Brotherhood Freedom and Justice

Party (FJP) and the Salafist Nour Party and even the Islamic Group across the different quarters of the neighborhood.[108]

Most studies of Cairo's informal settlements have correctly shown that most of these settlements are heterogeneous in that they generally consist of rural-urban migrants, long-time residents of Cairo who were forced to relocate in search of affordable houses, and a mix of poor, working-class and middle-class residents. This is certainly true in terms of the general profile of these areas. However, a closer examination of the different quarters *within* these informally settled neighborhoods reveals a far more socially stratified profile of local residents that is often obscured in the general surveys conducted of "informal Cairo." The poor quarters of the Western Mounira section of Imbaba is a prime example of this phenomenon. Like other informal areas in greater Cairo the district of Imbaba is crowded and poorer than the more affluent middle- and upper-class neighborhoods in the city. Imbaba is also similar to other informal settlements in that the district is home to residents from rural and urban parts of the country and they hail from a variety of social groups. However, what is noteworthy is that the residents in newly settled sections of Western Mounira are primarily from the working class and working poor, and as such they live in worse living conditions than their counterparts in other parts of the district, which has a substantial proportion of middle-class residents.

The residents of the newly settled quarters of Western Mounira make up approximately 65,000, which represents over half (51 percent) of Imbaba's total 1.3 million inhabitants. Furthermore, since this area comprises only 10 percent of the total district, this means that, according to one important study on the neighborhood, Western Mounira is the most densely populated area in all of the Governorate of Giza with a population density of 325000 people/km$^2$.[109] In addition, while there is no available data on the occupational and socioreligious composition of Western Mounira's residents for the 1970s and 1980s, one rare household survey was conducted on the area in 1995. It found that as many as 43.1 percent of residents were either construction workers or described themselves as "unemployed." The proportion of the remaining occupations included 20.5 percent state bureaucrats, 15.7 percent professionals (lawyers, doctors, teachers, engineers), 15.7 percent housewives, and 5 percent businessmen. Equally significant is the relatively young age of the residents. 20.5 percent were found to be thirty years of age and younger, and a large proportion (62 percent) between thirty and forty. Only a small percentage, 17.5 percent, was forty-five or older.[110]

Naturally, these figures cannot fully capture the dismal social and economic conditions of the residents in Western Mounira. However, in important respects they are corroborated by my own ethnographic research in the middle-class areas of Imbaba (i.e., *Waraq al-Bandar* and *al-Arab*) and in the newly settled and poorer sections of *Ezbat al-Mufti*, *Oseem*, and *Bestheel*. The social and economic plight of residents of the newly settled areas stands in stark contrast to that of the original and more solidly middle-class areas of Imbaba. As the youth arrive from Upper Egypt to Imbaba, they search for housing (as well as employment) that is cheaper than that of the older settled sections of the neighborhood. Upon arrival these youth are quickly absorbed into the informal economy mostly in Western Mounira, and they rely primarily on rural-based kinship associations (*Rawabit Iqlimiyya*) to acquire some measure of social services and procure employment. These new migrants live in the worst conditions in all of Imbaba. In the quarter of *Bestheel*, for example, I observed some living quarters with no roof, no sanitation, and no running water. It is not uncommon to visit dwellings housing eight or more individuals in one room, and in the majority of cases (and in *Ezbat al-Mufti* and *Beshteel* in particular) two or three related families reside in the same dilapidated housing structure.

It is significant that older residents refer to these new arrivals to the area as '"*Umaal Taraheel*" (migrant workers). It is a term that commonly refers to agricultural seasonal migrant laborers. In fact, this designation points not only to the rural origin of many of the new arrivals to Mounira, but also to an important similarity between their former and present occupations. Indeed, the *'umaal taraheel* share similar characteristics with informal laborers in construction. Both occupations are vulnerable to seasonal fluctuations and, rarely, can either afford to settle in one place. In fact, just as '"*umaal taraheel*" worked on large agricultural lands (*Taftish* lands) that required seasonal wage laborers, workers in *Ta'ifat al-Mi'maar* (Construction Sector), while residing in Western Mounira, relocate frequently, and many travel as far as Sinai, in addition to different sections of Cairo, to find employment.

## Paving the Way for Islamist Militancy: The Ruralization of the Urban Fringe and the Decline of Traditional Authority

The foundation of the Islamic Group's success in Imbaba lay in its ingenuity in supplanting the traditional authority of local notables while, simultaneously, replicating the neighborhood and family-based Islamic norms familiar to the "rural"-minded residents living on Imbaba's urban fringe. The leaders of the Islamic Group (most of whom are of rural origin) were aided in this effort by stark class divisions between local notables (*kibaar al-mantiqah*) and the majority of Imbaba's newly arrived denizens. The most prominent notables of Imbaba had made their fortunes in the period of land speculation often by coercive means,[111] and this, in combination with other close ties to the state, delegitimized their authority in the eyes of many residents and eroded their traditional status. At the same time, the very density of informal, traditional institutions enabled the Islamic Group to forge close links with rural migrants and lower-class residents of Imbaba who had previously relied on traditional social networks and informal institutions for employment, social cohesion, and to arbitrate disputes among individuals and families in the neighborhood.

The political and social upheavals that culminated in an Islamist militant rebellion in the 1990s had their roots in the expansion of markets and, more specifically, in the ways that this process disrupted traditional rural ways of life, undermining local institutions and, ultimately, the economic livelihoods of many of the residents in the newly settled informal areas. Naturally, there is no smooth evolutionary passage from feudalism to capitalism, and as Mitchell has keenly observed in the context of rural Egypt, the transition to the market cannot be described as a "seamless web" whereby ex-rural workers came to be incorporated into the larger urban capitalist economy.[112] Nevertheless, as studies of market transitions in the context of authoritarian regimes have demonstrated, historically the transition from central planning and regulation to the widespread introduction of private property is often associated with different levels of violence primarily because it is rarely accompanied by the prior establishment of clearly defined property rights, a legitimate legal system, or credible law and order institutions that deter crimes. In addition, since there is a great increase in property and economic transactions there is more opportunity to engage in illicit if not criminal activities such as theft, robbery, land speculation, and the confiscation of property.[113] In the case of Imbaba these changes were accompanied by two related forms of coercion: the manipulation of political patronage and local kinship ties by local notables and merchants intent on amassing greater resources and power, and the emergence of semi-private protection of public order, carried out by local strongmen (*baltagiyya*) under the sponsorship of the newly enriched notables and endorsed by officials of the state.[114]

The erosion of the authority and status of Imbaba's notable families was directly linked to their collusion in profiteering from land speculation associated with rapid rates of urbanization. Prior to the establishment of *Mounira al-Jadida*, five families owned most of the land in the area of *Kafr al-Salmaneya*, *Waraq al-Arab*, *Waraq al-Hadar*, and *Beshteel*, all village communities in the immediate vicinity. These families began to sell their lands in the 1930s, during the early phase of village urbanization, retaining some land for their own use. By 1955, city sprawl had reached the edge of the area, so that the land of *Mounira al-Jadida* began to have increased value as building sites, and subdivisions intensified. The rate of conversion from agricultural to residential usage grew more rapid in the 1960s with tremendous in-migration to Cairo from the countryside and consequent pressures on city boundaries.

As the demand for affordable housing sped apace in the mid-1970s, local notables found themselves well positioned to profit from this boom, and they essentially traded their previous legitimate social and political authority for wealth. Former village agriculturalists found themselves de jure and de facto owners of prime real estate. In Imbaba, a number of village notables were able to take advantage of their right to "prescriptive ownership" – having occupied the plot for an uninterrupted period of fifteen years. Others took advantage of the sudden departure of the owners and were able to buy large areas of land at low prices – the shrewdest forged contracts of sale and engaged in claims against those departed owners who had left without registering the transaction. In the new informal settlements of *al-Waraq* and *Bestheel* none of the families that profited from the boom in land speculation started out with de jure ownership of large plots of land. Almost without exception, the village notables (*Omdas*), the sedentary Bedouin and other category of squatters who succeeded in regularizing their situation, did so by deception, taking advantage of legal ambiguities, and corrupt government authorities.

Ali Morgaan, one of the first of the large land speculators in Imbaba, is illustrative of this process associated with real estate profiteering. At the height of the housing crisis, Morgaan forcibly seized lands close to the juridically designated urban area. If the owner refused to sell the whole plot at below market prices, Morgaan often resorted to hiring local strongmen (*baltagiyya*) to coerce the landowners to sell their land. His tactics went as far as ruining the landowner's soil and the burning and stealing of harvested crops. Morgaan would often use, what one resident termed, "covert terror" tactics.[115] He would buy more land, refuse to cultivate it, and after a while use government assistance to legally convert the land to "residential" rather than agricultural land. He then used his links with the government's Local Council in *al-Waraq* to license this land as residential and then sold it at a much higher price. In one instance, he bought one feddan for 150,000 pounds, only to sell it by the meter for housing construction for a price of 1,000 pounds a meter. In this way he, and others in his position, earned a windfall, which allowed him to buy more land.[116]

Consequently, social conflict was embedded in spatial terms and expressed in local politics. During the 1980s, the notables also enjoyed considerable protection and patronage from state authorities. It was at this juncture that the state cemented its clientelist links with the newly rich land speculators who themselves were often associated with the large clan families such as the family of *Awlad Beni Adiyya* (from Sohag). In Ezbat al-Mufti, where Ali Morgaan made his fortune, his son, Mahmoud Morgaan, is head of the village's local council and, arguably, the wealthiest man in the neighborhood. Not surprisingly, the new social and economic position of these notables translated into political influence, and at present, one finds them in control of local council elections throughout Imbaba. In the latter part of the Mubarak era, a few even gained seats in parliament (*Majlis al-Shaab*).[117]

Local grievances thus resulted not only from frustration over the state's general neglect of the neighborhood, but they also reflected deep structural conflicts between local political and economic interests. Specifically, they represented conflicts over juridical boundaries, resource allocation (i.e., budget outlays), and generally a form of social conflict embedded in spatial terms. This conflict was spatially determined because the degree and level of state patronage came to largely depend on where you lived in Imbaba. Thus, residents of *al-Waraq* as represented by local council members jealousy guard their relatively advantageous legal status as a *Medina* (a city) rather than a *Qaryah* (village) against poorer enclaves such as *Ezbat al-Mufti* and *Oseem*. The latter are neighborhoods that are financially dependent on their neighbors in ways that appear unjust to many local residents.[118]

The attempt on the part of the notables to derive greater profit from land also had the consequences of producing a greater demand for, and competition over, private forms of protection to forcibly settle disputes and enforce "cooperation" in a context where local notables managed to establish a system of patronage that institutionalized extortion. These new rich class of notables emerged as local patrons providing employment and protection for local strongmen (*baltagiyya*), local property owners, as well as petty criminals in the neighborhood. As property owners these land speculators had no interest in crime, though they had interest in maintaining a broad army of followers for coercive purposes. The retainers, on the other hand, had to be allowed pickings and a certain scope for private enterprise. Following the erosion of the power of these notables, the Islamists recruited from a similar base. That is, just as the new rich made use of the *baltagiyya* to reinforce their local monopoly and made fortunes out of informal, and illicit, land dealings, the *Jama'a* utilized the same cadres to institutionalize extortion. In the absence of the central state machinery, this type of criminality could not be eliminated and only increased with social crisis.

However, what distinguished the group of land speculators from the Islamists was the latter's military character. The military formations of the "Mafia" show the same mixture of *baltagiyya* (retainers) and other criminal elements interest in profit. The *baltagiyya*, in particular, proved vital to the *Jama'a's* military campaigns. These *baltagiyya* would join the *Jama'a's* "defense" (i.e., military) wing, partly to follow their religious patrons, partly to raise their personal prestige by the only way open to them – acts of "toughness" and violence, but also because conflict meant profit. This profit incentive derived from the "pickings" they obtained from both forced tax collection (zakat), wages for work conducted on behalf of the organization, and the procurement of construction job contracts though coercive means.

In great part the demand and competition over the services of the *baltagiyya* emerged because of the presence of low levels of interpersonal trust in Imbaba's newly settled areas resulting from the social upheavals associated with the era of land speculation and state corruption. However, what is noteworthy is that both the newly enriched notables and militant activist leaders were perplexed and deeply challenged by the heterogeneity and social complexity of Imbaba's residents. Indeed, contrary to conventional explanations that contend that high levels of urbanization uniformly result in the breakdown of kinship ties and weakened communal solidarities (i.e., low levels of interpersonal trust), residents of Imbaba responded creatively to the economic marginality imposed on them by the larger political economy. Social relationships were cemented not only through real kin, but also through fictive kin, creating a dense network of overlapping networks and informal institutions that provided mutual aid and, for a time, were effective in responding to the residents' desire for social control.[119] Importantly, however, while kinship and familial ties continued to be important they coexisted, and often competed, with more sparsely knit and spatially disbursed social networks. The latter emerged as a result of two important factors that had important consequences for identity-based politics: the high levels of rural-urban migration, which weakened existing social ties and retarded new ones, and the separation of residence and workplace that necessarily involved Imbaba's residents in multiple social networks with weak solidarity attachments.

Significantly, this period saw a form of local politics that reproduced, and made more pronounced, the reliance on clan (*Qabiliyat*) and familial (*'Assabiyyat*) solidarity among local residents. While these traditional norms of fealty served as instruments for social cohesion and ordering in rural Egypt, in the context of informal settlements such as Western Mounira, they came to be associated with class conflict, regionally based schisms, corruption, and intermittent violence. Indeed, institutions such as the *Ghafir*, an individual assigned the role of protecting cultivated agricultural plots, came to be used by Ali Morgaan and other speculators as a bodyguard in charge of protecting him from dissent, opposition, and retaliation by local residents.

At the same time as notables co-opted traditional institutions to preserve their own power, however, other rural-based social institutions earned greater legitimacy among Imbaba's residents precisely because they served the rural migrants' social and economic needs. Upon arrival in Imbaba, migrants from Upper Egypt utilized social networks organized around Clan (*Rawabit Qabaliyya*) and Regional Associations (*Rawabit Iqlimiyya*). These informal institutions provided new migrants a place to "stand together" and helped them in finding housing and jobs in the city. In Imbaba, these associations include the Associations of the Sons of Sohag (*Rabitat abna-Sohag*), and the Association of the People of Assiut (*Rabitat ahl-Assiut*), each named for the region or social group (clan family) that it serves. While these associations can still be observed in Imbaba, they are far less significant in the social life of the neighborhood than they were at the height of the migration from Upper Egypt. This is because, over time, larger and more spatially disbursed social ties became more important for residents in terms of gaining access to employment, more differentiated sources of information, resources, and services than those provided through a small number of kin and familial contacts.[120] Nevertheless, these associations have played an important role in the social and economic life of the neighborhood. The Association of the People of Assiut, for example, continues to play an important role in finding work in the construction sector for new in-migrants from the rural governorate of Assiut. It was this regionally based group that established the first coffee house (*Qahwat al-Assayta*) where informal and casual laborers could meet, and acquire information from local contractors about jobs in the building trade. *Qahwat al-Assayta* served as a model for similar coffee houses that presently dot the unpaved roads of Western Mounira, Imbaba.

In contrast to many other parts of greater Cairo, in the newly settled areas of Imbaba, regional and kin-based identities continued to wield social significance and authority as a result of the arrival of large numbers of rural migrants. Whereas, in the 1960s and 1970s, the majority of local residents were from the northern Delta and lower-class urbanites from

Cairo's Giza Governorate, in the 1980s more than 30 percent of the areas' residents hailed from Upper Egypt. Indeed, the fading era of the social Arab nationalist presence in Imbaba represented what common discourse in Egypt would consider a more "modern," if not more sophisticated, strata of urbanites and farmers (*Fellaheen*) from the Delta, rather than the "ignorant" Sa'aedah hailing from Upper Egypt. Seemingly insignificant in the 1960s and early 1970s, regional cleavages in the area would become more pronounced beginning in the mid-1970s as rural migrants from Upper Egypt flocked to Imbaba and other urban areas in search of employment and affordable housing.

As the demand for affordable housing increased it required the labor to construct it. *Sa'edah* (Upper Egyptians) replaced workers from the northern Delta who had dominated the labor market. Indeed, during the boom years in particular, many labor contractors based in Imbaba traveled to Upper Egypt to look for workers all of which helped to support the construction boom in the informal settlements. This resulted in marked conflict and competition between *sa'aedah* (southerners) and *fellaheen* (northerners) over scarce public resources, housing, and jobs that were often reflected in cultural schisms. Presently, *sa'aedah* and *fellaheen* do not cooperate well and each harbors resentment toward the other. These tensions are particularly acute in sections of Imbaba such as *Waraq al-Arab*, *Bestheel* and *Ezbat al-Mufti* where regional and class divisions stand in clear tension. The *fellaheen* and older residents perceive Upper Egyptians as "backward, illiterate, and prone to spontaneous acts of violence." As one long-time resident of *Waraq al-Arab* put it: "[T]hese sa'aedah of *Mounira al-Gharbiyya* (Western Mounira) are from the past (*al-maadi*)." For their part, the *sa'aedah* speak of the former pejoratively as "*Awlad al-Bandar*" (boys of the city) and accuse them of having been corrupted by modern and decadent secular values.[121] In the late 1990s and early 2000s, I observed the leaders and preachers of the Islamic Group regularly exploit this rift in a complicated and often contradictory fashion. On the one hand, they often preached against the ills of conspicuous consumption in their sermons as a way of drawing in the alienated youth of Western Mounira (*Ezbat al-Mufti* and *Bashteel*) who find themselves outside the circuits of old money and the more diffuse metropolitan social networks. On the other hand, the Islamists also clearly helped to mitigate against social conflict between communities in the quarters of *Ezbat al-Mufti* and *Beshteel*, areas where lower- and middle-class residents from Cairo live and work side by side with rural in-migrants of *sa'aedi* background. In part, they have done this by universalizing certain modes of conduct and by arbitrating between disputes in summary and, often, coercive fashion.

Not surprisingly, the persistent, albeit precarious, significance of kinship and familial ties in the socioeconomic life of Imbaba is reflected in the culture of the neighborhood. Rural-urban migrants have clearly left their cultural imprint in the life of *Ezbat al-Mufti*, *Beshteel*, and to a lesser degree *al-Waraq* (all informal settlements in Western Mounira). In particular, they have brought with them their conservative and patriarchal culture from Upper Egypt and reproduced many of these norms among local residents. Significantly, many of these norms approximate those espoused by the Islamic Group. For example, Sheikh Jabir and preachers belonging to the *Jama'a al-Islamiyya* routinely utilized traditional norms, first introduced by the rural migrants in Imbaba, to recruit followers. During the 1980s, for example, when some of the Regional Associations where attempting to enforce their own dress code for women in the neighborhood (eschewing jeans, skirts, and other forms of "western" dress), Sheikh Jabir appropriated this campaign as part of the Islamist's struggle (*kifah*) against moral degeneration (*tagheer al-Munkar*). *Tagheer al-Munkar*, reinterpreted as a campaign to radically change "degenerate" moral practices, spearheaded by the Islamic Group in Imbaba proved to be a close fit to the cultural orientation of a conservative community in transition. Moreover, the Islamic Group's campaign distinguished its message from the more moderate Muslim Brotherhood whose middle- and lower middle-class profile, education and social aspirations, alienated them from the poorer and less-educated residents of Western Mounira.

However, while the phenomenon of in-migration contributed to the ruralization of Imbaba as a result of the growth of semi-rural settlements, drastic demographic change also paved the way for a neighborhood that became marked by less social homogeneity and cohesion. That is, while traditional kinship networks still played an important role in securing jobs, housing, and providing for the social needs for rural migrants, acute forms of social distress emerged as a result of the combination of the spatialization of class divisions as well as changes in the social composition of the residents of the informal areas. By the late 1980s, and even more so in the 1990s, residents reflected an increasingly heterogeneous population living in close proximity. Throughout the peripheral areas of greater Cairo, including Imbaba, the number of residents, approximately half, were migrants relocating from within the Greater Cairo agglomeration to find affordable housing.[122] In Western Mounira, the stronghold of the Islamic Group in the 1980s and 1990s, the age profile of the residents was another contributing factor that gradually undermined social cohesion and more traditional social ties. In 1992, at the time of the state's crackdown against the Islamic militants in Mounira, about 65 percent of the population were married couples between twenty and forty years old, with at least four children. At least 73 percent of the children were under twenty years of age; 87,000 young boys between the ages of ten and fifteen, 125,000 under fifteen; and 77,000 above twenty years old.[123]

This combination of a highly diverse neighborhood, a relatively young population, and rural migrants has meant a relatively high rate in the incidence of social conflict that often resulted in violence. It is quite common, for example, to see young men using knives in conflict situations and settle even relatively minor disputes by force, and these confrontations often escalate as friends or family members of the injured party are compelled to retaliate. In the context of weakened familial and informal social institutions and networks that are able to maintain "law and order," the Islamic Group filled this void, albeit sporadically.

However, contrary to conventional accounts, the Islamic Group did not wield a hegemonic hold on Imbaba. The heterogeneous nature of the neighborhood and the presence of gangs *('isabaat)* and a significant number of clan-oriented groupings stand in constant tension with the authority of the Islamists in the neighborhood. In fact, rank-and-file members of the Islamic Group are often involved in violent skirmishes with clans such as the Beni Mohamed, and with residents of the neighborhood who saw in their Islamic tax (zakat) collection methods a "protection racket" reminiscent of the era of land speculation in the area rather than a sincere faith-based "moral" campaign.

Many local residents see the work of the Islamic Group in the neighborhood as akin to that of the *baltagiyya*. An institution itself, *baltagiyya* refers to a band of local strongmen who utilize strict coercive norms of reciprocity (shorn of a clear moral or ideological message) to resolve disputes and safeguard the interests of their naturally select membership. Not surprisingly, given the informal nature of social and economic relations in Western Mounira, the *baltagiyya* play an important role in establishing some semblance of social predictability. As a result, residents are careful to distinguish between the "baltagi" who resolves disputes and one who is nothing more than a thug or "troublemaker." Thus, the term itself has earned an honorable connotation, at least among some of the young men in *Ezbat al-Mufti* and *Bestheel*, a point of view little understood outside the local community. For their part, the leaders of the Islamic Group recruited heavily from these *baltagiyya* for their rank-and-file membership and were careful to work with, rather than against, them.

The migration streams from both rural Egypt and Cairo's middle- and lower-class neighborhoods have also put pressure on the already sparse social services in Imbaba. In *Ezbat al-Mufti*, for example, there existed only one school and one private clinic as late as 1998 – a full six years after the government of Mubarak ostensibly recognized the link between "poverty" and Islamic "terrorism." Within this context the dense networks of Islamic Charitable Associations (*Jamiyyat Shari'a*) and private storefront Mosques play a more important role in the social life of residence than they do in other areas of Cairo where formal institutions compete more effectively with Islamic institutions in providing social services.

Yet there is no such thing as a stable state of affairs in Western Mounira. The Islamists are not always successful in resolving conflicts and they themselves have been drawn into violent skirmishes with Upper Egyptian clans in the neighborhood. Indeed, attempts by the Islamists to usurp the traditional authority of clan elders was, according to residents, one of the most common sources of conflict in the neighborhood.

## Conclusion

Out of the structural and political conditions of the 1970s there emerged two distinct tendencies within the Islamist movement in Egypt: a movement organized around the Muslim Brotherhood, which reemerged under a new generation of a more moderate and politically accommodationist cadre of activists, and a second, more radical minority, which considered it an obligation, and a sacred duty, to launch an all-out Jihad against the regime using military force if necessary. The rank-and-file members, albeit not necessarily the leadership, of these two trends could be distinguished to a significant degree by their social and regional divisions. The Muslim Brotherhood were increasingly comprised of middle- and lower-class members while the bulk of the members of the militant groups came from the ranks of the rural population, new migrants to the city, and the working-class, informal workers, and the unemployed or underemployed.

Rather than focusing on "Islamism" as the outcome to be explained, my account of these developments has distinguished Islamism as a sociopolitical phenomenon from the related but wider phenomenon of Islamic revival, which has been the subject of some important works on the subject. The two cases of the Muslim Brotherhood and the Islamic Group illustrate not only the diversity within the larger Islamist movement in Egypt, but also how, in the context of larger structural change, different socioeconomic factors make for diverse political and social outcomes.

More specifically, I have shown how the oil and remittance boom era crucially affected state-society relations in ways that greatly influenced the organizational character, social basis, and ideological orientation of the moderate as well as the militant trends of the Islamist movement. To be sure, ideational factors are important in explaining why individuals join the Islamist movement in such large numbers. However, and without reducing politics to economics, it is clear that in order to grasp why Islamists diverge, and why, in some cases, kinship networks continue to compete with Islamist loyalties at the community level, it is important not only to examine the contentious relationship between the state and Islamist activism, but also to examine precisely how broader shifts in the political economy result in variations in terms of identity-based forms of political mobilization in civil society.

However, it is important to note that despite the country's relative economic openness under infitah, the state retained a relatively strong level of state capacity over the economy and social control over society. This was due to two key factors. First, and most important, the regime continued to dominate the formal economy and the huge state bureaucracy continued to supervise and direct economic life and amass substantial wealth in the context of limited economic liberalization. Moreover, strong sectoral interests represented by both management and formally organized labor continued to wield significant political influence. This, in turn, mitigated the full exposure of the public sector to the market and international economic competition. Second, liberalization of labor migration enabled Egypt to reap considerable benefits from the oil boom of the 1970s and early 1980s. This meant that the country's financial situation was sufficiently strong in ways that allowed the regime to enjoy a short reprieve from the unemployment problem and provide a rudimentary level of basic services for the population, thereby preserving social peace. The overall result is that, despite the great expansion in the informal economy as a result of external economic forces, the regime not only retained significant capacity over regulating the national economy, it also maintained considerable power over society in terms of applying sanctions against groups it perceived to threaten its interests. Figure 1.1. illustrates the relationship between informal transfers and Islamist activism during this remittance boom era.

What is noteworthy is that in the era of the remittance boom and infitah, and in contrast to the state of affairs in later decades associated with the deepening economic crisis and characterized by increasing levels of state repression, the regime did not perceive the Islamists as particularly dangerous and, as noted earlier, often accommodated them into the state's financial and political structures. This was particularly true in the early years of infitah when Sadat supported and forged selective clientelistic linkages with Islamist activists and businessmen as a way to outflank groups and individuals perceived to be still loyal to the anciene regime of Nasser.

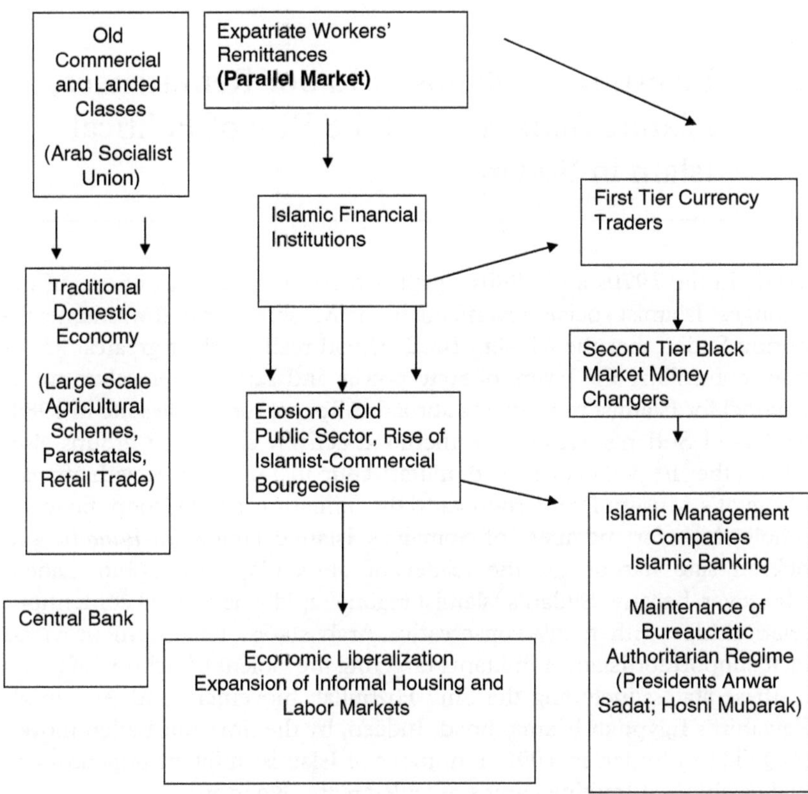


Figure 1.1 Informal transfers and Islamist activism in the remittance boom in Egypt

# 2 Investing in Islamism: Labor Remittances, Islamic Banking, and the Rise of Political Islam in Sudan

While in the 1970s and 1980s Egypt witnessed the growth of one of the strongest Islamist social movements in the Muslim world, it was in neighboring Sudan that the Muslim Brotherhood realized their greatest ambition: controlling the levers of state power and setting themselves up as a model for Islamist movements abroad. After capturing the state in 1989, leaders of Sudan's Muslim Brotherhood actively supported groups elsewhere; they helped plan a failed military coup in Tunisia, met with officials of Egypt's Muslim Brotherhood and the militant Islamic Group, financed scholarships for members of Somalia's Islamic Union (*al-Ittihad*), and offered safe harbor for the leader of al-Qa'ida, Osama bin Laden. Moreover, because Sudan's Islamist regime rapidly developed contentious relationships with many conservative Arab states, Khartoum provided tacit support for Islamist militants targeting the violent overthrow of rulers in these states, including the Shi'i Hizbullah movement and Ayman al-Zawahiri's Egyptian Islamic Jihad. Indeed, by the time Bin Laden moved al-Qa'ida to Sudan in 1992, a number of Islamist militant organizations had established training camps outside greater Khartoum.[1]

## The Puzzle of the Sudanese Islamists' Success

Sudan's Muslim Brotherhood, through its political party, the National Islamic Front (NIF), was buttressed by a formidable economic base and supported by a particularly advantaged social group, making it well placed to assume power. In 1989, on the eve of the disintegration of the state in Somalia and the violent conflict between the Egyptian state and Islamic militants in that country, Sudan experienced an Islamist military coup. The members of the military junta that seized power on June 30 were practically unknown to the public, but from the outset, their ties to the NIF were evident.

The fact that the Muslim Brotherhood was able to enjoy such success in Sudan presents a puzzle. One of the largest countries in Africa, Sudan has more than 500 different tribes speaking as many as 100 different languages, making it perhaps the most heterogeneous country in both Africa and the Arab world. In Sudan, religious cleavages are as pronounced as ethnic ones. Prior to its partition in 2011, the archetypical division was one between an Arab Muslim population in the north and a southern population that subscribes to Christianity and indigenous African religions. In reality, the picture is even more complex. Historically, northern Muslims have tended to identify themselves along Sufi sectarian cleavages, while southerners harbor strong tribal affinities. These cultural, ethnic, and religious cleavages are further compounded by the long-standing hostility of southerners to Muslim Arab domination. Moreover, orthodox and more literal, "fundamentalist" Islamic doctrines have played a limited role as sources of political mobilization or ideological inspiration. In the wake of the coup, many Sudanese asked the same question famously posed by the country's most prominent writer, the late al-Tayyib Salih: "[F]rom where have these [Muslims] hailed?"[2]

Solving this puzzle requires examining the historical and economic factors that enabled the Muslim Brotherhood to achieve political dominance. It also requires examining why it was the Muslim Brotherhood, rather than other movements such as the Communist Party, that gained a foothold in politics. While some scholars have attributed the rise of Islamist politics to the increased attractiveness of Islamist ideas to a newly urbanized, frustrated, and alienated civil society, in the case of Sudan this analysis fails to explain the decline of other forms of religious identity, such as popular Sufi Islam, as the basis of political mobilization.[3]

The story of the Muslim Brotherhood's assumption of state power in 1989 begins in large part with the monopolization of informal financial markets and Islamic banks by a coalition of a newly emergent Islamist commercial class and mid-ranking military officers. This monopoly endowed the Muslim Brotherhood with the financial assets needed to recruit new adherents from an important segment of the military establishment and from civil society more generally. In the process, and in a tactical alliance with the then dictator, Ja'afar al-Nimeiri, the Brotherhood managed to exclude rival groups and to establish a monopoly of violence in the country. This allowed the Islamists, under the leadership of Hassan al-Turabi, to provide a wide range of material incentives to many middle-class Sudanese. Moreover, following the Islamist-backed military coup of 1989, the ruling NIF used coercion and violence to implement a new set of property rights that maximized the revenue of its Islamist coalition and served to consolidate its political power.[4]

## Sudan and Egypt's Divergent Political Paths

Economic and political developments in Sudan originally paralleled those of its northern neighbor. As in Egypt, the surge of labor remittances in the wake of the 1970s oil boom circumvented official financial institutions and fueled the expansion of an informal currency trade. The Muslim Brotherhood successfully monopolized the remittance inflows sent by Sudanese working abroad and quickly established a host of Islamic banks, and Sudanese currency traders used their knowledge of the informal market in foreign currency to channel expatriate funds to the new banks. These business relations became particularly profitable after the state lifted most import restrictions, allowing merchants to import goods with their own sources of foreign exchange. The Muslim Brotherhood's monopolization of informal banking and finance led, as it did in Egypt, to the rise of a distinct and self-consciously Islamist commercial class.

It was in Sudan, however, that the Muslim Brotherhood was first able to transfer this economic leverage into formidable political clout, taking hold of the levers of state power and eventually, under the leadership of Hassan al-Turabi, successfully pressing for the full application of Islamic law (*shari'a*). This contrast to Egypt reflects the relative weakness of Sudan's state capacity and formal banking system. In Sudan, the financial power of the Muslim Brotherhood, whose profits from lucrative speculation in informal market transactions and advantageous access to import licenses further aided by an uninterrupted overvaluation of the Sudanese pound, continued to increase in relationship to the state. It was this financial power vis-à-vis an increasingly bankrupt state that enabled the Muslim Brotherhood to cultivate a constituency far stronger in influence than their rivals in civil society. By the 1980s they successfully utilized this economic leverage to build and expand a well-organized coalition of supporters among segments of the urban middle class, students, and a mid-ranking tier of the military establishment.

## A Weak State and a Divided Society: Colonialism's Dual Legacies

British colonial rule in Sudan left the aspiring state builders of the post-colonial era the dual legacies of a weak state and institutionalized ethnic and religious divisions. In the 1920s the British, partially in response to the threat of the emergence of nationalism in Egypt, inaugurated a strategy of "indirect rule." This policy devolved administrative and political powers to tribal sheikhs. More importantly, Sufi religious leaders were given greater room to organize in the hopes that a reinvigorated Sufi sectarianism would divide a population that might otherwise unite around national politicians. This British political and financial patronage, combined with the hasty manner in which London negotiated the independence of Sudan in 1956, greatly boosted the fortunes of certain Sufi sectarian and tribal leaders in the north as a result of the pursuit of a "separate development" policy vis-à-vis the south. As an Arab-Islamic identity consolidated in the north, in the south, the influence of Christian missionaries, who under British sponsorship provided educational, social, and religious services, resulted in the development of a Christian and African identity that came into conflict with the political elite in Khartoum. In combination with uneven economic development, and Islamicization policies by northern political leaders vis-à-vis the south, this triggered the four-decade-long civil war in the country.[5] They also laid the groundwork for the eventual political success of the Islamist movement in the country.

British economic development focused on cotton production, which was concentrated in the north-central portion of the country – primarily in the fertile lands between the Blue Nile and White Nile south of Khartoum, but also in central Kurdufan to the west and Kassala province in the east. Economic transformations brought three distinct social groups – tribal leaders, merchants, and Sufi religious movements – into positions of economic strength. The latter, organized in the form of "modern" political parties, would dominate civilian politics in the post-independence era as representatives of the economic and political elite.

In the hope of indirectly administering the colonial state and effectively governing the general Sudanese population, British administrators were authorized, in the words of the governor general Lord Kitchener, "to be in touch with the better class of native," which they accomplished through the distribution of land and assets.[6] Most prominent among such beneficiaries were the families of 'Abd al-Rahman al-Mahdi, leader of the Ansar Sufi order (*tariqa*, plural *turuq*), and 'Ali al-Mirghani, leader of the Khatmiyya Sufi order.[7] British patronage enabled the Ansar to monopolize productive agricultural lands and develop large-scale pump and mechanized agricultural schemes.[8] Similarly, it enabled the Khatmiyya to consolidate its economic power in the urban areas of the northern and eastern regions, where its control of retail trade was the basis for the formation of a commercial bourgeoisie. Because these Sufi orders wielded substantial economic power, a large segment of Sudan's intelligentsia and wealthier merchants organized politically around the al-Mahdi and al-Mirghani families.[9] The Ansar sect – which organized under the banner of the Umma Party in 1945 – drew its support mainly from the subsistence agricultural sector and from tribes in the western and central regions of northern Sudan. The Khatmiyya sect – which later organized under the banner of the Democratic Unionist Party (DUP) – dominated Sudan's merchant community and especially the increasingly lucrative export-import trade in gum Arabic, livestock, and oilseed, drawing support from tribes along the Nile in the north and around Kassala in the east.

In Sudan the structure of the Ansar and the Khatmiyya orders allowed them to take full advantage of British financial support. Both were highly centralized with all contributions and dues flowing to a single leader or family (in contrast, e.g., to the decentralized Qadiriyya and Shadhiliyya orders). Moreover, leaders of both the Ansar and Khatmiyya were involved in the economy (in contrast to the Shadhiliyya leaders, who viewed their role primarily in terms of spiritual and doctrinal services).[10] Perhaps most importantly, members of both orders resided in areas where incomes were rising and so they could afford to make significant contributions: the members of the Ansar sect lived in the fertile Gezira plain while followers of the Khatmiyya resided mostly in the semi-arid eastern regions of the country.

By the late 1920s, Ansar leader 'Abd al Rahman al-Mahdi was enjoying an income of more than 30,000 British pounds annually and, furthermore, had begun to establish wider contacts among educated Sudanese, hence translating his impressive economic weight into political leverage.[11] Khatmiyya leader 'Ali al-Mirghani responded to al-Mahdi's tactics by patronizing another segment of the Sudanese educated classes in a similar manner. Both families hoped to use these recruitment mechanisms to shape the postindependence political objectives of the university graduates and urban middle class in Khartoum and other urban towns. Having emerged as a central part of the Sudanese commercial establishment, they moved quickly to acquire an equally strong impact on any future political power-brokering in the country and in so doing, to safeguard and further promote their economic prestige.

Ultimately, British colonial policies resulted in deep ethnic and religious divisions in Sudanese society and the emergence of a relatively weak central state in terms of its rulers' ability to maintain (and sustain) political order, pursue policy autonomous from social forces in civil society, exert legitimate authority over the entirety of its territories and diverse population, and extract revenue from the domestic economy.[12] In particular, the ways in which colonial and postcolonial rulers have sought to generate state revenue have had important implications for the way that Sudanese society has made demands on the state and the capacity of the state to exert control over society. That Sudan possessed a weak state was clearly evident by the fact that, since colonial times, a leading feature of the economy was the extensive role of the state in shaping production and generating revenue. Specifically, through the establishment of the Gezira Cotton Irrigation Scheme in the 1920s, the colonial government was able to significantly alter agrarian activities toward cotton exports and essentially build the fiscal basis of the state on financial linkages to international commodity markets. As in other African countries, the British also established a government marketing board that held a legal monopsony on the procurement and export of cotton. In this process of indirect taxation, the board (as the sole buyer) obtained cotton from Sudanese farmers at prices below open market rates and retained the surplus realized upon export. Consequently, as a result of the global demand for cotton at the time, the colonial state enjoyed a healthy budgetary surplus that belied its underlying vulnerability and economic dependence.[13] In 1956, on the eve of independence, the Sudanese state generated almost 40 percent of its total revenue from nontax sources. The modern industrial and commercial sector contributed 43.6 percent of the country's gross domestic product (GDP), and the traditional sector, 56.4 percent. Nevertheless, the state's extractive capacities, and consequently fiscal health, were almost exclusively based on direct government intervention based on the state-run commodity board, and not taxes on non-state industry or private enterprise.[14] Moreover, although these funds were ostensibly intended to promote rural incomes and development in the outlying, economically marginalized, regions in the country, there were commonly diverted to the state bureaucracy and administration or urban infrastructure as a key source of political patronage for incumbent rulers.

## The Rise and Durability of Sufi Politics

While colonial policies were formative in influencing the trajectory of state-society relations in Sudan following independence, the unique dynamics of Islamic politics in the country are deeply rooted in the precolonial as well as the colonial history of Sufism in the country. The dynamic of Sufi support for regime politics and the state's patronage of Sufi orders reemerged in the colonial and postcolonial period as one of the important features of Sudanese political life. Indeed, it goes some way toward explaining the durability of Sufism in Sudanese politics, even as they lapsed into obscurity in other Arab countries. Michael Gilsenan, for example, has noted the sharp decline of Egyptian Sufism (at both the spiritual and political level) since its height in the late eighteenth century. He attributes this to the orders' inability to respond to a centralized Egyptian state. As he has carefully observed, many of the social functions the Sufi orders used to perform (i.e., charity, job placement, education) were taken up instead by various government agencies. Unable to offer any material goods or services beyond what the state was making available, nor to articulate a unique ideology that would distinguish them from other Muslim groups, they were pushed into retreat. In contrast to Sudan where, thanks to the policies of successive governments, Sufi orders were allowed to assume social functions, in Egypt the traditional functions of the Sufi orders were taken over by other groups and agencies, whether of the state, other voluntary associations, or the religious and intellectual elites.[15] Indeed, whereas by the late eighteenth century Sufism in Egypt declined as a result of the Sufi orders' inability to respond sufficiently to the rise of a strong centralized state, in Sudan Sufi orders survived (and thrived) precisely because of the patronage of local rulers.

Since the nineteenth century, Islam in Sudan has been of an eclectic, diverse, and highly popular variety. Muslim missionaries who came to Sudan from Egypt, the Hijaz, and the Maghrib in the twelfth and thirteenth centuries brought with them the Sufi orders. By the early 1800s, these orders had become the most profound and pervasive form of religious – and political – influence in the country. It was Sufism, rather than the more orthodox Islam of the "ulama," that was institutionalized. Moreover, prior to independence, leaders of the more influential orders were key agents of social change, engineering a number of revolts, first against Turco-Egyptian rule and later against the British colonizers.

The great influence of Sufi Islam across the centuries made for the relatively slow growth of the orthodox Islamist movement in the 1940s, 1950s, and 1960s. Indeed, until the 1970s, the processes associated with modernization did not engender recourse to a fundamentalist doctrine among the majority of Sudanese. Previously the public, cognizant of the harmful effects of colonialism and the corruption of postcolonial leaders, had sought political refuge within their varied sectarian identities vis-à-vis the different Sufi orders. Perhaps more importantly, as noted earlier, the dominance of Sufi political parties until the ascendancy of the Islamists in Sudan in the 1970s can, to a large extent be attributed to the relative weakness of the Sudanese state. During both the Turco-Egyptian period and the British colonial government, the state was heavily dependent on the institutional capacity and popular legitimacy of the Sufi orders, in particular the Ansar and the Khatmiyya. This is a dynamic that would carry over into the postcolonial period and partially explains the swift rise to power of the Islamists.

This is not to say that orthodox Islam had no institutional foundation in Sudan until the Islamist movement emerged ascendant. The Turco-Egyptian conquest of the country in 1820–1821 had brought the shari'a, which previously had played only a minor role in Sudanese life, although nominally the people adhered to the Maliki School of Islamic jurisprudence (*madhhab*). Tribal and popular Islamic custom was in most respects the effective law. The Egyptian administration established a formal hierarchy of qadis and muftis within the context of a system of religious courts designed to administer shari'a according to the Hanafi school. They also built a number of mosques and facilitated the education of a significant number of Sudanese "ulama."

The remote and legalistic religion of the "ulama," however, could not easily constitute a living creed for the majority of the population and especially not for the rural Sudanese, distant as they were from the big mosques of the great cities. By putting forward "paths" (*turuq*) whereby individuals could attain an experience of God, Sufism, named after the simple wool (*suf*) clothing worn by traveling holy men, filled an important human need. And as more than one historian has noted, the intellectual austerity of orthodox teaching in Sudan seems pale compared to the emotional vigor and vitality of the Sufi orders.[16]

The popularity of Sufism throughout northern Sudanese history repudiates the contention that Islamism offers a unifying indigenous identity for many Muslims who, in feeling slighted by Western domination and cultural penetration, have increasingly sought in it a moral, political, and even economic refuge. What is clear, at least in the Sudanese case, is that throughout the periods of Turco-Egyptian rule and British colonialism, orthodox Islam did not play a formative role in determining the nation's economic and political fortunes. What factors, then, contributed to the ascendancy of the Muslim Brotherhood and enabled it to usurp the political authority of the hitherto dominant sectarian Sufi leaders?

## The Conflict over Sudanese Islam: Recruiting "Modern" Muslims

By the 1940s, and in the context of the emergence of Sudan's anticolonial nationalist movement, a number of educated Sudanese youth had begun to seek alternatives to the political dominance of the two most powerful Sufi-backed political parties in the country, the Ansar-led Umma Party and the Khatmiyya-led Ashiqqa' Party (later the DUP). These youths understood that the leadership of both these orders had been opposed to the anticolonial movement in the country and that they had greatly profited from British patronage.[17] The established leadership, in the view of the politicized youths, pursued self-aggrandizing economic interests rather than nationalist objectives.

Two alternatives for political organizing emerged at this time: the Communist Party of Sudan (CPS) and the Muslim Brotherhood.

Although the Muslim Brotherhood has been active in Sudan since the mid-1940s, when a number of students influenced by the Islamist movement in Egypt were returning to the country, the movement's leadership had yet to offer a concrete blueprint for a modern Islamist movement. When in 1949 the leadership of the nascent Islamist movement decided to form a political party, this was done primarily as a reaction to the influence of the Communists in the nationalist student movement. In March of that year, a schoolteacher, Babikir Karrar, formed the Islamic Movement for Liberation (IML), which espoused vague notions of Islamic socialism based on shari'a. The IML's main concern at this time as in later years was the rejection of the CPS, which was then the dominant political organization at University College Khartoum.[18]

In 1954, a divergence erupted within the IML over the primacy of political objectives, with Babikir Karrar and his supporters maintaining that the organization's emphasis should be on the spiritual awakening of the people prior to attempting political activism. It was this point of debate that led to the creation of two separate organizations: the Islamic Group, led by Babikir Karrar, and the Muslim Brotherhood, led initially by Rashid al-Tahir and later in 1964 by Hassan al-Turabi, who received his doctoral degree in law from the Sorbonne in Paris and whose father was a respected *shaykh* from a small town north of Khartoum.

Gifted with a high level of political sophistication, which often prevailed over his professed religious scruples, al-Turabi was able to make the Muslim Brotherhood a crucial part of Sudanese politics. By al-Turabi's own admission, the social base of the movement in its first nine years was limited to students and recent graduates in order to retain the intellectual quality of the movement.[19] Al-Turabi and other leaders of the movement had long known that they made up a new and unique phenomenon in Sudanese politics, and for this reason they thought it "undesirable to dilute the intellectual content of the movement by a large-scale absorption of the masses."[20] They were quite aware that the dominance of Sufi religiosity in the country precluded their particular fundamentalist and more militant brand of Islam from developing into a mass movement. At best, particularly in the formative period of their movement, they hoped to recruit people away from the sects and to give them an alternative to their sectarian identities. Yet they also believed that in order to succeed they must at all costs do away with any other alternatives put before the people, which until the 1970s was the CPS.

The growing influence of the Communists under the regime of Ibrahim 'Abbud (1958–1964), and particularly their dominant role in the October 1964 revolution ousting that regime and in the subsequent transitional government, necessitated a change in the Muslim

Brotherhood's tactics. Specifically, the Brotherhood decided to begin, for the first time, some kind of mass organization in order to participate in the upcoming elections.[21] In 1964, they formed the Islamic Charter Front – the forerunner of the NIF – with Hassan al-Turabi as its chairman. Al-Turabi's strategy was to form political alliances with other traditional forces, which more often than not was the Umma Party, with a view toward achieving two objectives: first, to isolate politically and then to ban the CPS; and second, to utilize the Islamic sentiments of the people to campaign for an Islamic constitution based on shari'a.[22] These objectives were obstructed in May 1969 by the imposition of a pro-Communist regime led by J'afar al-Nimairi. Predictably, the Muslim Brotherhood opposed the regime and along with its frequent ally, the Umma Party, formed an opposition front in exile.

Al-Nimairi's suppression of the CPS following a Communist-backed coup attempt in 1971 greatly enhanced the fortunes of the Islamists' newly named National Islamic Front (NIF) which, along with the Umma party, had by July 1977 entered into a "marriage of convenience" with the Sudanese dictator. In that year, al-Nimairi had embarked on a process of reconciliation whereby he restored to the traditional parties as well as to the Muslim Brotherhood the right to participate in the political process – provided, of course, that they exercised this right within the existing one-party system. More specifically, Nimeiri allowed the two parties to field individual candidates but only as members of the regime's ruling party. In return, the Umma Party and the Muslim Brotherhood agreed to dissolve their opposition front.

The political benefits of this compromising approach became unmistakably evident as time passed. By the autumn of 1980, the NIF was sufficiently well organized to gain a substantial number of seats in the elections for a new people's assembly, and al-Turabi himself was appointed the country's attorney general.[23] The motivation behind al-Nimairi's open co-optation of the Brotherhood at this time stemmed primarily from his perceived need to outflank the Sufi-led political movements, which continued to hold the allegiance of the majority of northern Sudanese. For its part, the Muslim Brotherhood naturally welcomed these developments as an opportunity to enhance its political and organizational strength. Indeed, during this time its membership greatly increased not only in prestige but also in sheer numbers, so much so that by the early 1980s it was no longer the marginal movement it had been during the first twenty years following independence. The political ascendancy of the Islamists quickly brought them into political conflict with the Sufi orders. This clash between Sufism and Islamism, however, is due to political and sociological differences rather than deep cultural animosity. More specifically, Sufis and Islamists in Sudan came to represent different social constituencies jockeying for control over the state and its institutions. Whereas the Sufi brotherhoods span multiple classes and geographic regions, the Muslim Brotherhood's core support is in the urban areas and among people with higher-than-average education.

## Labor Remittances and Islamic Finance in the Boom

During the post-1973 period, international factors greatly influenced the development of Islamic business in Sudan spearheaded by the Muslim Brotherhood opening the way for its rising power in Sudanese political and social life. The Muslim Brotherhood's greatest strength lay in the two sections of Sudanese society that formed its support base. The first was its constituency of secondary school and university students, particularly in the capital and the more urbanized towns. During the 1970s, a large number of its supporters became teachers in the western and eastern provinces, which fostered major support for the movement there. When these students went on to universities in Khartoum, they came to dominate student politics to such an extent that Brotherhood candidates, until 2008, routinely swept student union elections. The second and perhaps more important base was drawn from the urban-based small traders, industrialists, and new commercial elite. They opposed the traditionally powerful Sufi-dominated merchant families primarily because the latter stood in the way of their own economic aspirations.

The Muslim Brotherhood's influence in civil society did not, however, translate into the ability to capture state power until global economic factors altered Sudan's political economy in particular ways. The oil boom in 1973, which saw a corollary boom in both the inflow of labor remittances from Sudanese workers in the Gulf and investment capital from Arab oil-producing states, aided the fortunes of the new Islamist commercial class, which ingeniously translated the economic opportunity into political clout. As the prestige and popularity of the prominent Sufi families declined, an increasing number of youths joined "al-Turabi's Revolution." Fueled by incoming remittance capital, the informal foreign currency trade expanded. This expansion simultaneously helped to dismantle the extractive institutions of the state and to erode the last vestiges of traditional sectarian authority in the private sector.

As the Arab oil-producing states, aided by the Organization of the Petroleum Exporting Countries (OPEC) price hikes in the mid-1970s, accumulated enormous profits in the oil boom, Sudan came to figure prominently in their long-term development plans. More specifically, they became extremely interested in overcoming their reliance on the outside world for food, and they identified Sudan as the potential "breadbasket" of the Arab world. Initially large amounts of foreign assistance from the Gulf enabled the Sudanese state to fill external and internal resource gaps and strengthen formal institutions. Between 1973 and 1977, for example, over USD 3 billion in foreign loans were committed, and the government's development expenditure rose from SDG 17 million in 1970 to SDG 186 million in 1978.[24]

During this period, the state, envisaging large inflows of foreign capital from Arab countries, liberalized key sectors of the economy to lure foreign investment. This took the form of privatization of certain areas of foreign trade and the financial sector. Far from improving Sudan's formal economy, however, the flurry of development in the mid- and late-1970s deepened economic woes and regional and ethnic grievances. Deficient planning, a rising import bill resulting from escalating fuel costs, and pervasive government corruption characterized by prebendal policies trapped Sudan in a vicious cycle of increasing debt and declining production. Between 1978 and 1982, foreign debt rose from USD 3 billion to USD 5.2 billion. In 1985, when al-Nimairi was ousted, the debt stood at USD 9 billion, and by 1989 it had grown to an astronomical USD 13 billion. While this debt is not overly large by international standards, Sudan's debt-service ratio amounted to 100 percent of export earnings – making Sudan one of the most heavily indebted countries in the world.[25]

Equally ominous was the fact that regional inequalities, institutionalized during the colonial era, were now dangerously politicized. Between 1971 and 1980, more than 80 percent of all government expenditure was centered on pump irrigation schemes in Khartoum, the Blue Nile, and Kassala provinces, with little distributed in other regions and almost none going to the south. Moreover, by 1983, only 5 of the 180 branches of the country's government and private commercial banks could be found in the three southern regions of Bahr al-Ghazal, the Upper Nile, and Equatoria.[26] It was within this context that Khartoum's imposition of shari'a in 1983 and its desperate efforts to secure revenue from the discovery of oil in the southern town of Bentiu precipitated the rebellion of the southerners of the Sudanese People's Liberation Movement (SPLM), ushering in the second phase of civil war. Under the leadership of John Garang, the SPLM rejected the imposition of Islamic law at the federal level and accused the Arab-dominated regime of Nimeiri of seeking to monopolize the oil resources of the south.

By the late 1970s, external capital inflow, and Arab finance in particular, declined rapidly. Government revenues plummeted, forcing the state to increasingly resort to central bank lending. To make matters worse, as the economy began to experience severe inflation and balance-of-payments problems, the economic crisis was compounded by a decline in exports from 16 percent of the GDP in 1970–1971 to 8 percent of the GDP by the late 1970s.[27] This was also a period of industrial decline. The large capital inflows that financed a 50-percent increase in public sector investment caused inflationary pressures that hiked the price of imports leading to a sharp decline in the supply of essential goods and inputs from abroad. This, combined with the lack of changes in Sudan's production system and worsening income distribution patterns, resulted in a stagnating industrial sector.[28] Moreover, breadbasket plans favored large-scale and capital-intensive industrial ventures at the expense of the small- and medium-scale firms.

With the formal economy in shambles, a boom of another sort mushroomed, concentrated almost exclusively in the parallel market and fed by remittances from the millions (3 million by 1990 estimates) of Sudanese who, beginning in the mid-1970s, had for economic reasons migrated to the Gulf states. These largely skilled and semi-skilled migrants maximized their own income working in oil-rich states, and moreover, they greatly contributed to the welfare of key segments of the population back home.[29] As late as 1985, formal remittances represented more than 70 percent of the value of Sudan's exports and over more than 35 percent of the value of its imports.[30] Labor had become Sudan's primary export.

As in Egypt during this same period, the capital accruing from remittances came to represent a financial as well as a political threat to state elites primarily because it came to rest in private hands. The formal record vastly under-represents the true magnitude of these external capital flows because most transactions took place in the flourishing but hidden parallel market (Table 2.1). The balance of payment statistics from the International Monetary Fund, for example, accounts for less than 15 percent of the earnings reported by the migrant workers themselves. Some estimates set the value of fixed and liquid assets of workers in the Gulf close to USD 10 billion – most of it channeled through informal networks.[31] Between 1978 and 1987, capital flight from Sudan amounted to USD 11 billion, roughly equivalent to Sudan's entire foreign debt.[32]

Approximately 73 percent of this capital inflow was channeled through informal financial intermediaries or relatives, 18 percent through state-run banks and foreign currency exchange agencies, and 8 percent through foreign banks (see Table 2.1). Most of these remittance (73 percent of the total remittance capital inflow) assets were quickly monopolized by the small but highly organized Islamist commercial class, which organized under the NIF, captured huge "scarcity rents" in foreign exchange through the manipulation of parallel market mechanisms – that is, through control of the black market, speculation in grain, smuggling,

Table 2.1 *Channels of remittance inflows from expatriate Sudanese to Sudanese financial markets, 1988*

| Channel of inflow | Percentage of total remittances |
|---|---|
| *Official economy* | |
| Sudanese banks | 5.3 |
| Foreign banks | 8.4 |
| Foreign exchange agencies | 13.1 |
| *Parallel economy* | |
| Hand delivered | 41.2 |
| Delivered through friends and relatives | 31.3 |
| Other means | .7 |
| Total | 100 |

*Source*: "Akbar hijra fi Tarikh al-Sudan," [The Largest Migration in Sudanese History]. *Al-Majalla*, March 3, 1992, 8.
*Note*: In 1986 it was estimated that the total value of expatriate remittances was as high as USD 2 billion. Assuming a similar value for 1988, it can be approximated that USD 1.5 billion entered Sudan through the parallel market that year. "Qimat Tahwilat al-Sudaneen fi al-Khalij ithnayn miliar dollar amriki," [The Value of Remittances of Sudanese in the Gulf is Worth 2 US Billion Dollars], *Al-Majalla*, June 11, 1986, 31.

and hoarding.[33] Since at the time many Islamists had access to state office under the Nimeiri regime, they were able to use state institutions to monopolize the inflow of remittances. Indeed, by bridging the divide between illicit, parallel, and formal markets, the Islamists gained preferential access to foreign exchange, bank credits, and import licenses.

The transactions in the burgeoning parallel market were centered in urban areas. This naturally meant that capital flowed into the private sector in a manner that compensated many urbanites for declining income-earning opportunities. More importantly for Sudan's political economy, however, these transactions weakened the state's ability to extract revenue in the form of foreign exchange. In particular, the state's capacity to tax greatly diminished, and the state came to rely more and more on custom duties and other forms of indirect taxation. This was especially true in the agricultural sector. The ability of the state to extract revenue from this potentially lucrative sector of the formal economy had been substantial prior to the mid-1970s, averaging 20 percent of the state's annual revenue. But by the mid-1970s, direct taxation declined considerably, averaging less than 10 percent per year before dropping to 4 percent by 1987–1989. As early as 1975, indirect taxation accounted for five times that of direct taxation. The extent of indirect taxation, in the form of customs and import duties, increased steadily from less than

20 percent of total state revenue (excluding grants) in 1973 to 55 percent in 1980.[34] The effects of such a dramatic boom in informal capital inflows in eroding the capacity of weak states to generate taxes and regulate domestic economies are common among the labor-exporting countries in the Arab world. As one scholar of remittance economies has noted in the case of Yemen, for example, "the narrow basis of state revenues cultivated in the boom ensures that state coffers are depleted in the recession period as expendable income and imports and customs duties drop."[35] In Sudan, the political battle over foreign currency and the monopolization of rents garnered from the parallel market and import licenses came to occupy the energies of both state elites and groups in civil society. Various actors vied for the economic and political spoils that they correctly perceived would accrue to the "victor." Disputes among state elites over monetary policy fostered a factionalism that caused many a cabinet reshuffle.

The structural transformation engendered by the parallel market also drastically altered the country's social structure. The traditional private sector, which consisted primarily of the landed Ansar elite and the Khatmiyya of the *suq* (traditional market), was devastated by the state's "shrinkage" since it had in large part relied on the state's largesse, particularly in the early part of the Nimairi regime. Consequently, whereas in the first two decades of the postcolonial state, Sudanese civil society was dominated by the sectarian patrons and their clients, by the late 1970s Sudan's private sector was separated into two social groups: those who profited from transactions in the parallel market and state elites and bureaucrats whose survival was contingent on capturing as much hard currency as possible before it was absorbed by this hidden economy.

The first group included the workers who had migrated to the Gulf. Their remittances, in turn, produced the economic clout enjoyed by financial intermediaries known as suitcase merchants (*tujjar al-shanta*) who bought and sold hard currency in the parallel market. A broad spectrum of the Sudanese petit bourgeoisie, cutting across ethnic and sectarian cleavages, engaged in these transactions, but the industry was effectively monopolized by five powerful foreign currency traders with close ties to Islamist elites.[36] The second group consisted of the central bank and other governmental authorities responsible for official monetary policy. Their priority was to attract private foreign capital from nationals abroad. Commercial banks likewise depended on attracting this business, and it was to them that al-Nimairi looked to for his political survival.

## Islamic Banks as Bridges: Linking Informal and Formal Markets in a Regional Context

By the late 1970s, in search of political legitimacy and the funds with which to finance it, al-Nimairi sought to involve the state in the increasingly autonomous private sector. He saw the Islamic banks, even more than non-Islamic Arab development institutions as the best way to attract more capital from the Gulf while simultaneously garnering much-needed political allegiance of the Muslim Brotherhood. This is because most inter-Arab development funds established by the Arab oil exporters after 1973 stressed less-risky investments in public sector enterprises over private investment. In contrast the more ideologically driven Islamic banks based in the Gulf – created in "accordance to the provisions of shari'a" – were interested (and mandated) to invest in private enterprises outside the purview of domestic states and state-run banks.[37]

Established in 1977 by a special Act of Parliament, the Faisal Islamic Bank of Sudan (FIBS) was the first financial institution in Sudan to operate on an Islamic formula. In theory, this meant that all its banking activities must adhere to the principles of Shari'a law in which *riba* (interest or usury) is prohibited and the time value of money is respected. In practice the lending activities of Islamic banks consist of a contract whereby the bank provides funds to an entrepreneur in return for a share of the profits or losses. For his part, in order to encourage the growth of the FIB, and the Islamicization of the financial sector more generally, al-Nimairi altered property rights in a way that afforded the Islamic financial institutions a special advantage over other commercial and government banks, exempting them from taxes and effective state control. Equally important, the Islamic banks enjoyed complete freedom in the transfer and use of their foreign exchange deposits, which meant that they were able to attract a lion's share of remittance from Sudanese working in the Gulf.[38] Under the Faisal Islamic Bank of Sudan Act, Faisal Islamic Bank (FIB) enjoyed unprecedented privileges, none of which was afforded to other commercial banks. The FIB was the model upon which all the other Islamic banks in the country were established and operated. It was composed of the general assembly of shareholders, a board of directors, and a supervisory board to ensure that the bank would operate according to shari'a. FIB was the first of many Islamic banks to be exempted from the Auditor General Act and from provisions of the Central Bank Act concerning the determination of bank rates, reserve requirements, and restrictions of credit activities. Moreover, the bank's property, profits, and deposits were exempted from all types of taxation. The salaries, wages, and pensions of all bank employees and members of the board of directors and shari'a supervisory board were likewise exempted.

In December 1983, a presidential committee went further and converted the entire banking system, including foreign banks, to an Islamic formula. Al-Nimairi timed this to outflank the traditional religious and political leaders and secure the allegiance of the Muslim Brotherhood – the only group left that supported him. In short, state intervention and selective financial deregulation transformed Islamic banks into secure, unregulated havens for the deposit of foreign currency earned by Sudanese operating within the parallel market. In this regard, the informalization, or rather deregulation, of these informal financial markets could not have been possible without the patronage and policies of the Nimairi regime who, in the wake of declining legitimacy, was desperately striving to rebuild strong patron-client networks in civil society.

The linkage between the Islamic banks and currency dealers operating in the parallel market became increasingly sophisticated and profitable as the market expanded. The informal currency traders fell into essentially two groups. The first comprised five powerful currency traders, each earning a profit of SDG 1 million annually, who advanced the start-up capital for a second group of approximately 100 mid-ranking financial intermediaries. This latter group, each earning between SDG 200–500 daily, served as direct intermediaries between the expatriate sellers and their families.[39] But it was the first-tier currency traders that, owing to their established credibility and knowledge of the urban parallel market, helped channel expatriate funds to the Islamic financial institutions. More importantly, a number of the large currency traders were closely associated with the Islamist movement and members of the NIF.[40]

These business relations became particularly profitable after the state lifted most import restrictions, which allowed merchants to import goods with their own sources of foreign exchange. This meant that to start a business in Sudan, expatriates and their families had to exchange their US dollars or dinars for local currency. Islamic banks were particularly well placed to buy up these dollars, which they did through dealings with, and at the recommendation of, the big currency traders.[41] These Islamic banks had the additional advantage of pursuing an ideological agenda attractive to many wealthy Gulf Arabs, who supported them with large capital deposits. As a result, Islamic banks enjoyed spectacular growth. Faisal Islamic Bank's paid-up capital, for example, rose from SDG 3.6 million in 1979 to as much as SDG 57.6 million in 1983. Over the same period, FIB's net profits rose from SDG 1.1 million to SDG 24.7 million, while its assets, both at home and abroad, increased from SDG 31.1 million to SDG 441.3 million.[42]

As Table 2.2 demonstrates, growth was particularly strong during the oil boom that began in the mid-1970s and lasted through to the early 1980s. Clearly the phenomenal growth of Islamic finance reflected developments in the Gulf, and the tremendous increase in oil prices in the early 1970s, which produced enormous private fortunes in the Gulf countries and provided entrepreneurs with the required capital to invest in Islamic banking. This boom in the Arab Gulf (especially Saudi) financial investment coincided with the sharp rise in the capital stock of Faisal Islamic Bank. In 1980–1981, for example, growth averaged more than 100 percent per annum, almost three times the growth of the other commercial banks. What these figures illustrate is that the financial profile of the Islamist movement, closely linked to its monopoly over the Islamic banks, rose sharply in relation to not only the state-run banks but also other private financial institutions in the country. Moreover, just as al-Nimairi was increasingly starved for funds with which to finance his regime's patronage networks, the Islamists were able to utilize their new-found wealth to provide economic and financial incentives to an increasingly greater number of supporters among the country's urban middle class.

The success of the FIB and its organizational structure was a key model for all the other Islamic banks in the Sudan and it triggered a veritable boom in the proliferation of other Islamic banks in the country. For

Table 2.2 *Comparison of the magnitude and growth of private deposits in Sudan's Commercial Banks (CB) and Faisal Islamic Bank (FIB), in SDG 1,000*

| Year | CB deposits | Annual growth rate (%) | FIB deposits | Annual growth rate (%) | FIB deposits as (%) of CB deposits |
|---|---|---|---|---|---|
| 1979 | 528,805 | – | 21,774 | – | 4.0 |
| 1980 | 694,824 | 31 | 49,512 | 127 | 7.0 |
| 1981 | 856,789 | – | 102,319 | 107 | 12.0 |
| 1982 | 1,305,0444 | – | 202,372 | 98 | 15.0 |
| 1983 | 1,709,015 | 31 | 257,000 | 27 | 19.7 |
| 1984 | 1,964,073 | 15 | 276,000 | 7 | 14.1 |
| 1986 | 3,280,817 | 67 | 293,000 | 6 | 8.9 |
| 1987 | 4,243,712 | 36 | 308,905 | 5 | 7.3 |
| 1988 | 5,786,160 | 36 | 352,310 | 14 | 6.0 |
| 1989 | 7,200,314 | 32 | 493,754 | 40 | 6.0 |

*Source*: Faisal Islamic Bank, "Faisal Islamic Bank Annual Reports: 1980–1988" (Khartoum: Faisal Islamic Bank, 1998).

example, following the FIB model, in 1984 Saudi businessman Shaykh Salih al-Kamil, a shareholder in the Gulf-based al-Baraka Islamic bank, established a branch of this bank in Sudan as a public joint-stock company. Its paid-up capital, provided by al-Kamil, the Faisal Islamic Bank, and other private investors, was USD 40 million. Moreover, the Sudan branch of al-Baraka established two subsidiary companies in Khartoum: al-Baraka Company for Services and al-Baraka Company for Agricultural Development. This process went on as a number of other Islamic banks were established throughout the 1980s, including the Sudanese Islamic Bank and the Islamic Bank for Western Sudan, which like the FIB, specialized in loans to aspiring borrowers looking to start-up small- and medium-sized firms primarily in services and retail businesses.

The Sudanese Muslim Brotherhood saw in the success of the Islamic banking sector an important vehicle from which to achieve its political and economic objectives and outflank its rivals in civil society. Indeed, a striking feature of this growth is the extent to which the majority of the Islamic banks had links with the Brotherhood, and how much the Umma and DUP were left out in the financial wilderness. For its part, the Faisal Islamic Bank was controlled by the Muslim Brotherhood and in particular its leader, the increasingly powerful Hassan al-Turabi.[43] This same bank also entered into a joint venture with Osama Bin Laden, creating the Islamic Al-Shamal Bank.[44] Al-Turabi utilized much of the FIB's profits to help finance the Islamist movement. The Tadamun Islamic Bank also had very close links with the Muslim Brotherhood which established a financial empire that included subsidiary companies in services, trade and investment and real estate. The Al-Baraka Investment and Development Company – also, established in 1983 – was completely controlled by a Saudi family; however, the managing director was a leading member of the Muslim Brotherhood. Notably, the Umma Party did not have its own bank.

The establishment of Faisal Islamic Bank, Tadamun, al-Baraka and other Islamic financial institutions also signaled the unprecedented integration of Sudan's financial markets with those of the Gulf and particularly Saudi Arabia.[45] This was clearly evident in the banks' structure and ownership profile. Indeed, the Faisal Islamic Bank was from the beginning designed to have a broad ownership structure that privileged foreign Muslim shareholders and as such it forged very close links between Sudan's Muslim Brotherhood and Gulf financiers sympathetic to their political objectives.[46] In this context, it is important to note that the exiled members of the Sudanese Muslim Brotherhood belonged to the circle around Prince Muhammad Al-Faisal, and it is because of their influence that he decided to invest in the Sudan and help establish the FIB. The

FIB, like other Islamic banks, established an office in Jedda, which accepted deposits from expatriates living in the Gulf; 40 percent of FIB's capital was provided by Saudi citizens, Sudanese citizens provided another 40 percent, while the remaining 20 percent came from Muslims from other countries, primarily residing in the Gulf states.[47]

By the mid-1980s, Sudan's once relatively closed economy had become closely integrated with the global economy. Both state elites and Islamist financiers benefited from their relationship to the expansion of Islamic banking linked to Gulf. Prior to converting the entire banking system in the country to an Islamic formula, the Nimairi regime had invested heavily in this sector. It established state-run banks including the Development Cooperative Islamic Bank (DCIB) and the National Cooperative Union (NCU). Both these banks were financed from funds coming from the Ministry of Finance. Initially state law mandated that all the shareholders in the DCIB and NCU must be Sudanese nationals. However, the regime promulgated the Bank Act of 1982, which, in order to lure Gulf capital, authorized foreign investment in the banking sector including what were hitherto state-controlled national banks. Sudan's Islamic banks were closely linked not only to prominent government officials, but also to one another. For example, Faisal Islamic Bank and al-Baraka acquired shares in the North Islamic Bank, established in 1990; and the government, together with Arab and other private Sudanese investors, also owned shares in the North Islamic Bank.

Two other key Islamic institutions with global reach established during this time were the Islamic Finance House (IFM) and the Islamic Cooperative Bank of Sudan (ICB). As was the case with most of the other Islamic banks, the IFM and ICB's ownership was linked to a transnational network of Islamist financiers and investors. Based in Geneva, the IFM continues to have institutions and branches all over the world. Like Faisal Islamic Bank, the IFM was founded by Prince Muhammad al-Faisal of Saudi Arabia, who was also the chairman of the International Association of Islamic Banks.[48] It is important to note that the main shareholders of the IFM, besides members of the Saudi royal family, included al-Nimairi and Hassan al-Turabi.[49] The ICB was established in the early 1980s and represented the close integration between Sudan's domestic banking sector and global Islamic financial interests. In addition to its banking activities, ICB owned shares in the Islamic Development Company (Sudan), Islamic Banking System (Luxembourg), and the Islamic Bank for Western Sudan. Its main shareholders were Faisal Islamic Bank, Kuwait Finance House, Dubai Islamic Bank, Bahrain Islamic Bank, and other Arab private investors.

## Inclusion *through* Exclusion: Financing an Islamic Commercial Class

According to FIB officials, a primary purpose of Islamic banks is to provide interest-free personal loans to the general population – in their words, "to ameliorate the suffering of the masses and to present an alternative to interest-based banks, which provide for the 'haves' and give little care to the 'have-nots.'"[50] However, the investment pattern of these banks (see Table 2.3) did not translate into a more equitable distribution of income, as many proponents of the Islamic banks claimed. The credit policy of the Islamic banks was clearly designed to build and enhance the fortunes of an Islamist commercial class, and by the 1980s the latter became far more powerful than the hitherto dominant groups in civil society (particularly the Khatmiyya sect, which had dominated the traditional export-import sector in the urban areas) as well as the state. In this context, it is important to note that the Khatmiyya established the Sudanese Islamic Bank in 1983 to compete with the Muslim Brotherhood–dominated banks and the all-important commercial sector. However, since by the late 1970s, the Khatmiyya had fallen out of favor with the Nimeiri regime they were not able to establish any other financial institutions in the country and revive their social and economic base in urban commerce.

As a study of the entire Sudanese Islamic financial system noted, only 6 percent of all lending is allocated to personal loans with the remaining going entirely to commercial enterprises. Furthermore, Islamic banking is characterized by "low lending capacity, regional inequality in the distribution of banking branches, and sectoral concentration of investment and the bias toward the high profitable institutions in the modern sector at the expense of the small sector."[51] The largest Islamic Bank, FIB, for example, made an explicit policy decision to minimize risk and realize profits in "the shortest possible time" by concentrating lending in export-

Table 2.3 *Faisal Islamic Bank (FIB) lending for trade, 1978–1983*

| Trade sector | Value, USD ml | No. of clients | Percentage |
|---|---|---|---|
| Export | 168 | 96 | 48 |
| Import | 119 | 528 | 40 |
| Domestic Trade | – | 298 | – |

*Source*: Faisal Islamic Bank, "Faisal Islamic Bank Annual Reports, 1983" (Khartoum: Faisal Islamic Bank, 1998).

import trade and the "financing [of] small businessmen."[52] By 1983, more than 90 percent of FIB's investments were allocated to export-import trade and industry and only 0.5 percent to agriculture, thereby ensuring strong support for the Islamists among the middle- and lower-class entrepreneurs.[53] Indeed, the declared policy of FIB was "to promote the interests of Sudan's growing class of small capitalists whose past development has been effectively retarded and frustrated by the dominance and monopolization of commercial banks' credit in the private sector by traditionally powerful merchants."[54]

By concentrating on trade financing, Islamic banks did little to achieve their stated aims of alleviating social and economic inequities. On the contrary, they were widely criticized for profiteering from hoarding and speculation in sorghum (*dura*) and other basic foodstuffs and, moreover, were accused of exacerbating the famine of 1984–1985. Faisal Islamic Bank in particular came under criticism for hoarding more than 30 percent of the 1983–1984 sorghum crop in the Kurdufan region and, when Kurdufan was hit by drought and famine, selling it at very high prices.[55]

Moreover, the branches of the Islamic banks, like those of the conventional banks, were located primarily in urban areas and the predominantly Arab and Muslim regions of the country. Despite claims to serve localities neglected by conventional Western-style banks, Islamic banks were no better than conventional banks, whether national or foreign, in breaking the pattern of urban and regional bias established during the colonial period (Table 2.4).

As the figures in Table 2.4 show, more than 80 percent of Islamic banks were concentrated in the urban centers of the Khartoum, east, and the northwestern regions. Moreover, out of 183 branches in operation, as many as 78 (43 percent) were situated in Khartoum. This is more than the total banking facilities found in the five regions whose population overwhelmingly comprises the subsistence sector of the economy and more than

Table 2.4 *Branch distribution of the Islamic commercial banking network in Sudan by region, 1988*

| | Central/ Khartoum | Eastern | Kurdufan | Darfur | Northern | Southern | Total |
|---|---|---|---|---|---|---|---|
| **No. of bank branches** | 78 | 31 | 30 | 15 | 7 | 11 | 183 |

*Source*: Faisal Islamic Bank, "Faisal Islamic Bank Annual Reports: 1980–1988," (Khartoum: Faisal Islamic Bank, 1998).

90 percent of the country. Indeed, as of 1988, not one Islamic bank had been established in the south and only one was in the western province of Darfur – the most underdeveloped parts of the country (see Table 2.5).

Table 2.5 *Regional branch distribution by type of bank in Sudan with percentage of type of network, 1988*

| | National | (%) | Islamic | (%) | Foreign | (%) | Total |
|---|---|---|---|---|---|---|---|
| Khartoum | 44 | *37* | 20 | *46* | 14 | *67* | 78 |
| Central | 24 | *20* | 6 | *14* | 1 | *5* | 31 |
| Eastern | 16 | *14* | 9 | *21* | 5 | *23* | 30 |
| Kurdufan | 12 | *10* | 2 | *5* | 0 | *5* | 29 |
| Darfur | 6 | *5* | 1 | *2* | 0 | *0* | 7 |
| Northern | 6 | *5* | 5 | *12* | 0 | *0* | 11 |
| Southern | 11 | *9* | 0 | *0* | 0 | *0* | 11 |
| Total | 119 | *100* | 43 | *100* | 21 | *100* | 198 |

*Source*: Faisal Islamic Bank, "Faisal Islamic Bank Annual reports: 1980–1988," (Khartoum: Faisal Islamic Bank, 1998).

The Islamic bankers' claim that they give priority to rural financing and rural development is belied by the absence, or at best minimal presence, of Islamic banks in the southern and western (i.e., Darfur) regions of the country. These banks were from the beginning driven by business rather than social or religious considerations: Their absence in the south and west can be explained by the absence of appropriate infrastructure and the low prospects of profitability in these regions due to their relative underdevelopment and political instability. In addition, religious and ethnic factors have played an important role: The fact that the south is neither Muslim nor Arab is a key reason why the Islamic financiers have shown both a neglect of – and even a great hostility toward – providing credit to its rural communities.

However, it is just as important to point out that Islamist financiers also targeted a particularly small segment *within* the Arab-Muslim population in the northern regions of the country. They recruited bank staff and managers based on their support for the movement, and at the level of civil society, they extended credit and financial support to those who had prior links to the Muslim Brotherhood's Islamist movement.

## The Business of Islamist Recruitment

Since the founding of the Islamic banks, there has been a mutual interest between their shareholders and the Muslim Brotherhood. The largest shareholders were primarily merchants of the Gulf who sought religiously committed individuals ready to support the Islamic banks both materially and ideologically. They thus favored well-known Islamist activists and individuals recommended by the leaders of the Muslim Brotherhood.

The recruitment of bank staff is designed to ensure commitment and trust within and across these financial institutions. Faisal Islamic Bank's general manager outlined the pattern of recruitment in the following manner:

> The personnel needed by Islamic banks should not only be well qualified and competent but should also be committed to the cause of Islam. They should have a high degree of integrity and sense of duty in dealing with all the operations of the bank. Therefore, their performance and sincerity should not only come from the built-in controls of the system, but also from their religious conscious and sentiment.[56]

This bias toward Islamist activists for staff recruitment and in matters of distribution and lending meant that Islamic bank beneficiaries were largely urban supporters of the Muslim Brotherhood. It has also meant that credit activities became concentrated on a small part of the domestic economy to the exclusion of other segments even of the urban population.

The evidence that the Muslim Brotherhood focused their efforts on providing economic incentives to build an aspirant middle class is clear from the Islamic banks' lending practices and the use of Islamic financial proscriptions to bolster their patronage links to newly mobilized clients in urban Sudan. The investment encouraged the growth of small- and medium-sized businesses, effectively ensuring support for the Muslim Brotherhood from the middle and lower strata of the new urban entrepreneurs.

Islamic banks in Sudan rely on essentially two methods, or contracts, for the utilization of funds: *murabaha* and *musharaka*. *Musharaka* takes the form of an equity participation agreement in which both parties agree on a profit-loss split based on the proportion of capital each provides. If, for example, a trader buys and sells USD 10,000 worth of industrial spare parts, the bank (while not charging interest) takes 25 percent of the profits and the borrower the remaining 75 percent, assuming an equivalent proportion of capital provision. Importantly, if there is any loss, the bank and the customer share the loss in proportion to the capital they both initially provided. *Murabaha*, while similar in terms of representing an equity participation contract, differs from *musharaka* in that the bank provides *all* the capital while the customer provides his labor. Consequently, if there is any loss the bank loses its capital and the customer loses his labor and time. In essence, *murabaha* is a contract whereby the bank provides funds to an entrepreneur in return for a share of the profits, or all of the losses, whereas *musharaka* – participation – is more akin to venture capital financing.

In Sudan, the most common contract has been overwhelmingly *murabaha* and, because clients usually have to enter into a joint venture for a specific project in order receive funds from the bank, the capital comes with political and economic strings.[57] Since the transaction is not based on the formal creditworthiness of the client and there is no requirement of presenting securities against possible losses, the bank officials have a great deal of discretion with respect to whom it lends to. Since the Muslim Brotherhood dominated the staff of the Islamic banks they successfully used credit financing to both support existing members and provide financial incentives for new business-minded adherents to the organization. Thus, for example, an aspiring businessman, to qualify for a loan, must provide a reference from an established businessman with a good record of support for the Muslim Brotherhood.[58] This requirement led to almost comic attempts by many in the urban marketplace to assume the physical as well as religious and political guise of Islamists.

For a society in which Sufism had long occupied the most significant space in social, political, and economic life, the dramatic ideological and cultural shift toward Islamism seemed to occur seemingly overnight. But as Douglas North has observed, individuals alter their ideological perspectives when their everyday experiences are at odds with their ideology. Similarly, many young Sudanese men and women who, being denied the resources and social networks crucial for improving their income position in society because of the alteration of "excludable" property rights, became acutely aware that the "more favorable terms of exchange" were to be found in joining the Islamists' cause.[59] As Timur Kuran has noted poignantly, since the 1970s throughout the Muslim world Islamic banking and a wide range of financial networks have helped newcomers who had hitherto been excluded from the economic mainstream and middle-class life to establish relationships with ambitious Islamic capitalists. Indeed, many social aspirant urban residents in Sudan sought in the Islamic banking boom the opportunity for economic and social mobility.[60] However, as the lending patterns of the Islamic banks in the case of Sudan show these Islamic financial houses were also clearly interested in the promotion of specific ideological and political objectives. The bulk of the lending was directed toward a small segment of the middle class in the urban areas and strict monitoring of *murabaha* contracts was enforced in terms of who was to receive a loan and the conditions for repayment. Moreover, as Stiensen has observed, the battle in the boardrooms of the Islamic banks showed that the Muslim Brotherhood actively sought to monopolize these banking institutions and eliminate potential rivals. Specifically, emboldened by the largesse of the Nimeiri regime, the Muslim Brotherhood used its position to recruit members for the movement by hiring them in the banks, and "colleagues known to be critical or hostile to the movement were forced out."[61] The bias in favor of the Muslim Brotherhood did not go unnoticed. Non-Islamist minded businessmen, some of them shareholders, complained that they did not receive finance from the FIB, and audits by the Bank of Sudan revealed that many banks, members of the board of directors, and/or senior management monopolized borrowing, and the default rate of such loans was in general very high.[62]

If Islamic banking aided the Muslim Brotherhood in building a new Islamist commercial class, the organization also attempted to supplant the traditional Sufi movements in the realm of social provisioning. Specifically, it broadened its political base by financing numerous philanthropic and social services. The most notable of its ubiquitous and varied charitable organizations included the Islamic Da'wa Organization, the Islamic Relief Agency, and the Women of Islam Charity, which owned a set of clinics and pharmacies in Khartoum. The Muslim Brotherhood also provided scholarships to study abroad to youths who assumed an ardent political posture in its behalf. Moreover, in the context of a very competitive labor market, the Brotherhood actively solicited recent university graduates for employment in Muslim Brotherhood–run businesses. One student from the University of Khartoum rationalized his support for the Muslim Brotherhood in economic rather than ideological terms:

> I am not really interested in politics. In fact, that is why I support the Ikhwan [Brotherhood] in the student elections. I am much more concerned with being able to live in a comfortable house, eat, and hopefully find a reasonable job after I graduate. The fact is that the Ikhwan are the only ones who will help me accomplish that.[63]

Once formally joining the Muslim Brotherhood organization members would also have privileged access to "additional services."[64] Toward this end, Islamic banks and their affiliated companies established a large number of private clinics, private offices, private schools, and mutual aid societies for certain professional groups including medical and legal professionals.[65] For example, Faisal Islamic Bank and al-Baraka financed the Modern Medical Center in Khartoum. In the field of transport and food processing, the Muslim Brotherhood established enterprises like Fajr al-Islam Company, Halal Transport Company, and Anwar al-Imam Transport Company, among many others, and in food retail, they established chains including al-Rahma al-Islamiyya Groceries and al-Jihad Cooperative. Of all the Islamic enterprises doing "business" in the cause of Islam, however, the Islamic banks were the most important and had the greatest effects on the society and the economy. The Muslim Brotherhood's close links with Saudi Arabia and the Gulf states meant that there was almost no shortage of cash, even in a country as poor as Sudan. Figure 2.1 neatly illustrates this linkage between the transformation of Sudan's economy and the ascendancy of the Muslim Brotherhood in the era of the boom in remittances generated from migration to the Arab Gulf.

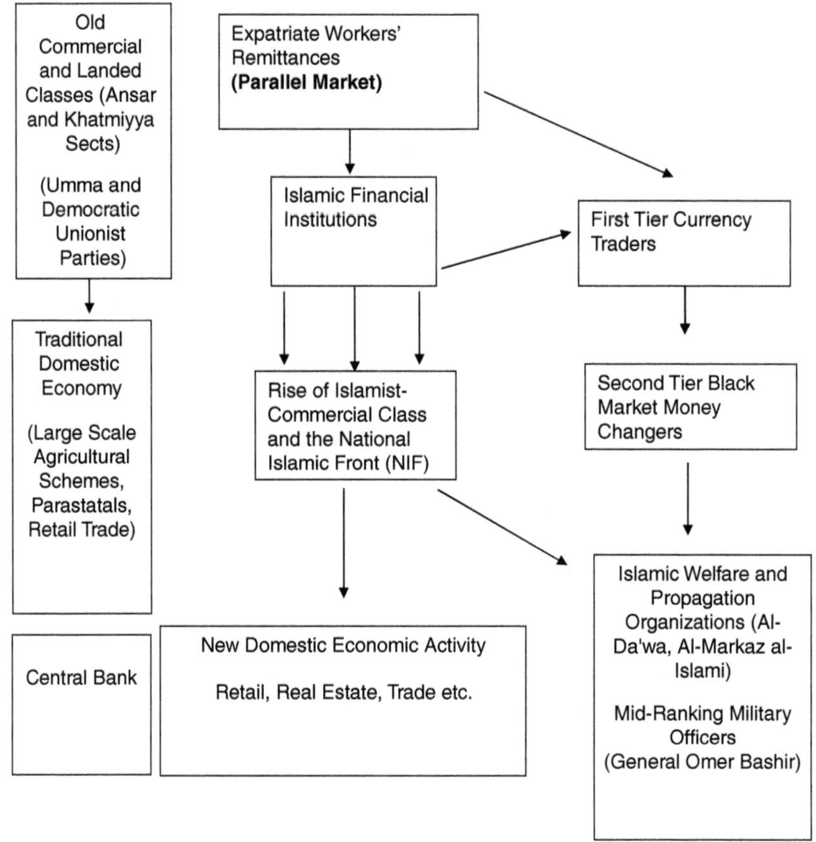


Figure 2.1 Informal transfers and Islamist activism in the remittance boom in Sudan

## Transformation of State Ideology: Nimeiri, Shari'a, and the Muslim Brotherhood (*Ikhwan*)

Although since assuming power in 1969 the Nimairi regime had a strict secularist stance, as a result of its waning political legitimacy and the rise in the economic power of the Muslim Brotherhood, political Islam came to occupy a significant place in Sudanese social, political, and economic life. Indeed, one of the most important factors in explaining the increasing importance of Islam in Sudanese politics was a major change in Nimairi's attitude toward Islam and the great extent to which he incorporated the Brotherhood into state institutions in his illusive search for political legitimacy.

In September 1983, al-Nimairi announced the implementation of shari'a in Sudan, making it the only Arab Muslim country to promulgate a wide range of laws that would completely subsume the secular court system into the Islamic judiciary, which up till then had been limited to hearing matters of personal law.[66] Al-Nimairi's promulgation of the September Laws marked a stunning victory for the Islamists, and particularly for Hassan al-Turabi and the Muslim Brotherhood. More specifically, having established a dominant position in the economy, the September Laws marked the beginning of the Brotherhood's formal consolidation of political power, this time via legal means. In this regard, the political success of Sudan's Islamists was attributable to the weakness of the ruling regime just as it was to the increasing strength of al-Turabi and the Muslim Brotherhood made possible by the rising financial fortunes of the movement. As noted earlier, over the course of the 1970s, al-Nimairi's regime had destroyed or alienated all its former political and ideological allies, leaving it with little option than to court the national opposition movements. At the same time, al-Nimairi was eager to claim for himself the mantle of religious and populist legitimacy. Indeed, in 1982 al-Nimairi, whose political orientation and reputation in the 1960s and 1970s were of a hard-drinking military officer more sympathetic to communism than Islamism, proclaimed himself the people's imam. The promulgation of the September Laws in 1983, therefore, was both an attempt to win support of the Muslim Brotherhood and to establish the religious and populist credentials necessary to shore up a new patron-client network, this time more reliant on the Islamists than the disaffected traditional Sufi-backed political parties of the past.

Interestingly, in many ways, the Sudanese case tracks that of Egypt remarkably closely. Like its northern neighbor, Sudan also experienced major economic upheaval, though somewhat later than Egypt did. While the first half of President Ja'far al-Nimairi's rule (1969–1985) was marked by economic success, the second half was an unmitigated disaster. Large infrastructure projects, including the expansion of the Gezira Scheme and the Kenana Sugar factory, entailed major injections of foreign capital that drove up inflation rates and saddled the country with high levels of debt.[67] Corruption and inefficiencies in the labor market – necessary for al-Nimairi to keep his bureaucracy under control – generated massive amounts of waste at precisely the time when the country was desperate to attract foreign investors. By the mid-1970s, Sudan was saddled with an enormous trade imbalance, largely at the hands of urban elites eager for expensive consumer products from abroad. The problem, according to the noted Sudanese scholar (and former Minister under al-Nimairi) Mansour Khalid, was that al-Nimairi was simply trying to develop the country too quickly.[68] His regime's legitimacy rested in no small part on its aura of competence and effectiveness. The possibility of an economic slowdown, therefore, prompted him to launch an economic program that the country simply could not sustain.

But if in Egypt, the economic crisis of the 1970s created what Rosefsky-Wickham has termed a lumpen intelligentsia sympathetic to Islamist aims, the Sudanese experience is somewhat different.[69] During the 1980s, the Mubarak regime in Egypt broadened its base of support to include the businessmen who had benefited from the country's privatization of industry. Subsequently, Egyptian national politics, before as well as after Tahrir, came to be characterized by a military-business alliance able to successfully split the opposition into unorganized and mutually distrustful camps. In Sudan, by contrast, the opposition has been considerably better organized and stronger by virtue of the relativel weakness of the Sudanese state. Though al-Turabi and many other members of the Muslim Brotherhood were arrested immediately after Nimairi's coup in May 1969, they were able to reconstitute themselves outside the country not long afterward. Turabi joined up with Sadiq al-Mahdi in Libya and began planning an armed uprising, with the possible support of the Khatmiyya as well. Still, having liquidated the communists in 1971 and signed the Addis Ababa accords in March 1972, al-Nimairi enjoyed widespread support both at home and abroad. The uprising of 1973 against the al-Nimairi regime was an unmitigated disaster for the opposition, as was another joint Ikhwan-Ansar uprising in 1976. To most observers at the time al-Nimairi's authoritarian regime appeared unassailable, and the institutional and coercive capacity of the state relatively strong.

Appearances, however, were deceiving. By the mid-1970s, Sudan's economy had begun to stagnate. With economic conditions in Sudan steadily worsening, al-Nimairi sensed that his regime was in peril. Having destroyed the communists some years earlier, he had no choice but reach out to the Brotherhood and the Sufi orders in hopes of achieving some sort of reconciliation. Fortunately, it seems as if the opposition parties were as eager for reconciliation as was Hassan Turabi, who had watched his movement gradually disintegrate over the last decade.[70] Talks with Sadiq al-Mahdi seemed to be progressing as well, but eventually fell apart over disagreements concerning the Ansar's role in government.[71]

It is at this point that the government's alliance with the Brotherhood in 1977 was cemented further as evidenced by the timing of the promulgation of the September Laws in 1983. As Mohammad Bashir Hamid has noted, the reintroduction of *shari'a* in the 1980s was al-Turabi's price for rejoining the government.[72] However, the Brotherhood would not have achieved access to state power if the al-Nimairi regime was not gravely weakened, and he was thus was seeking to rebuild a new, independent base of popular support. This entailed a three-step process. First, the passage of the September Laws allowed al-Nimairi to claim for himself the mantle of religious legitimacy. Beginning in 1972, he had begun regularly attending a minor Sufi order of the Abu Qurun family, which believed that a "second Mahdi" would soon emerge from among its followers and would take up the mantle of leadership for all Muslims.[73] Second, the passage of the September Laws was extremely popular with many northern Sudanese Muslims. Even setting aside the Brotherhood, it is clear that for many Sudanese, the reinstatement of *shari'a* was something worth celebrating. This populist component to the laws is something to which relatively few scholars have given much consideration, preferring instead to focus on their resonance with the country's Islamists. To be sure, the laws' popularity extended to many corners of society, including among followers of the Khatmiyya and Ansar.[74] That appeal was largely a function of the belief that the *shari'a* would deliver "prompt justice" (*al-'Adala al-Najiza*) to the many Sudanese who felt marginalized and abused by the corrupt economic practices of the urban elite.[75]

Lastly, the September Laws presented al-Nimairi with an opportunity to reorganize the federal judiciary in a way that would ensure its subservience to the regime. Earlier that summer, members of the lawyers and judges unions had gone on strike over back wages and poor working conditions.[76] Since this further slowed the delivery of justice to the urban poor and middle class, it risked throwing the stability of the regime into even graver doubt. The secular legal community also constituted an important part of the urban opposition, meaning that the reintroduction of *shari'a* would allow al-Nimairi to stifle one of his primary threats in Khartoum.

Following the passage of the laws and the mass firing of the striking legal personnel, al-Nimairi endowed the religious judiciary with far greater powers than its secular predecessor had ever possessed. At the same time, he sharply curtailed its autonomy, arrogating to himself the discretion to hire and fire as he saw fit. Judges were stripped of their traditional immunity from prosecution for causing unintentional homicide (i.e., by sentencing an innocent party to death), which was a potentially powerful means of influencing judges, since the president retained the right to overturn any conviction he deemed unjust.[77] And the attorney general, who served at the pleasure of the president, was given the right to issue government-endorsed *fatwa*s, turning him into a sort of *mufti*-cum-*muhtasib* capable of wielding enormous political and religious influence.[78]

Another important reason behind the Brotherhood's rise to power prior to their formal take over of the state in the summer of 1989 was the extent to which they infiltrated the politico-bureaucratic and military institutions of the state as a result of Nimairi's own policies in the late 1970s and through the 1980s. Following what Nimairi termed a policy of "national reconciliation" in 1977, and despite strong protestations by the old guard in the regime, Nimairi brought in key members of the Muslim Brotherhood into the ruling Sudan Socialist Union (SSU) party. These new entrants to the SSU party included high-ranking members of the Muslim Brotherhood such as Yassin Omer al-Imam, Suleiman Mustafa, and Musa Ya'qoub. Nimairi also appointed a journalist belonging to the Muslim Brotherhood, Yassin Omer al-Imam, as editor and chief of the most important government-controlled daily newspaper in the country: *Al-Ayyam*. Consequently, the only major daily allowed to be published by the regime quickly become monopolized by some of the most important intellectuals and journalists of the Brotherhood who utilized *Al-Ayyam* to disseminate the message of the Muslim Brotherhood to the general public. Consequently, influential Muslim Brotherhood intellectuals such as Musa Ya'qub, Hassan Mekki, Tijani Abdel-Qader, and Abdel Mahmoud Nur Al-Daim introduced the program and propaganda of the Muslim Brotherhood to a wide range of Sudanese in civil society.

In addition, and by their own admission, the Brotherhood began efforts to infiltrate the Sudanese Armed Forces in 1978 immediately after Nimairi's decision to incorporate Brotherhood supporters into the Sudan Socialist Union (SSU). In that year the Shura Council of the Muslim Brotherhood organization formally requested that the Brotherhoods' executive committee (*al-maktab al-tanfeezi*) take on the task of military operations to be headed by Hassan al-Turabi.[79] The campaign targeted senior and mid-ranking officers already in military service as well as new recruits outside the military establishment. Initially, the operations were clandestine in nature and only members of the committee were privy to the details of recruiting military cadres supportive of the brotherhood. The committee members included Hassan al-Turabi, Awad al-Jaz, Ali Osman Taha, Ali al-Haj, Ibrahim al-Sanussi, and Abdullah Hassan Ahmad. Of these, only al-Turabi, al-Haj and al-Sanussi were permitted direct contact with members of the Armed Forces that had been clandestinely recruited by the Brotherhood's leaders. The latter were the most important leaders of the organization at the time and, not surprisingly, all were appointed influential ministerial portfolios following the Islamist-backed coup of 1989. Moreover, with the exception of al-Turabi himself they all came out of the student movement on the campus of the University of Khartoum. Consequently, they decided that the most reliable way to infiltrate the military establishment was to recruit ardent members of the Brotherhood on the student campuses and to persuade them to enter the military as regular commissioned officers.

By the early 1980s, and primarily as a result of Hassan al-Turabi's appointment as Attorney General in 1979, the Brotherhood's penetration of the military was greatly expedited. Subsequently, a number of other Brotherhood members obtained positions in the judiciary, educational, and financial system as well as in the SSU. Al-Turabi used his influence with Nimairi to put members of the Brotherhood in charge of courses in Islamic ideology (*Da'wa*) for senior and mid-ranking officers. This enabled them to infiltrate into the officers' corps. As one scholar has correctly noted, four members of the military council that ruled Sudan following the June 1989 coup, including Omer Bashir, attended the courses.[80] While it remained a well-kept secret until 1989, by 1982 the implementing committee had formally requested that Omer Bashir supervise the recruitment of Islamists in the military.[81] Following the overthrow of Nimairi in 1985, the NIF was able to strengthen its support within the army further, particularly among mid-ranking military officers.

If the Muslim Brotherhood successfully used the patronage of Nimairi to make inroads into the state bureaucracy, the news media, and the military, the organization also utilized their economic clout to establish and finance key civil society organizations for the recruitment of new cadres. Since, at the time, the Nimairi regime restricted all other civil society organizations the Brotherhood enjoyed a distinctive advantage in building a strong base of support in civil society. This contrasted sharply with the relative weakness of other social and political forces that were still experiencing state repression and surveillance. Indeed, by the early 1980s, and thanks to Nimairi's support at the time, the Brotherhood was able to establish the Authority for the Revitalization of Islamic

Work (*hayat ahya al-nishat al-islami*), the Association for Societal Guidance and Reform (*jamiyyaat al-ri'ayah wa al-islah al-madani*), the Association of the Holy Quran (*jamiyyaat al-quran al-karim*), the Association of the Youth of [Hassan] al-Banna (*jamiyyat shabbab al-Banna*), the Association of Islamic Renaissance (*jamiyyat al-nahda al-islamiyya*), and the General Union of Sudanese Students (*al-ittihad al-'am li al-tulab al-sudaneen*). All these organizations shared the objective of implementing the Muslim Brotherhood's program. More specifically, as one Muslim Brotherhood member acknowledged, these associations had the objective of "attracting new members to the Muslim Brotherhood as well as retaining older members."[82] One of the most important recruitment activities focused on the Brotherhood's oldest and most important source of support: students in the secondary schools and universities. This took the form of what the Brotherhood termed the "summer recruitment program." According to my interviews with rank-and-file members of the Brotherhood, these programs occupied every single summer break. Moreover, the summer program was organized, and the curriculum set, by the directors of the Association of Guidance and Social Reform, the Authority for the Revitalization of Islamic Work, and the Association of the Quran.

These Muslim Brotherhood Associations convened summer camps (*mu'askarat sayfiyya*) in many of the urban areas in Sudan, but particularly in Khartoum. These camps included a variety of religious cultural programs, Islamic book exhibits, and even fashion shows highlighting the proper mode of Islamic dress. The objective was to introduce Sudanese youth from the secondary schools and university campuses to new attitudes toward "Islamic" attire and conduct, and new ways of Islamist thinking that had long been overshadowed by the popularity of Sufi religiosity and practice. In addition, and most importantly, high-ranking members of the Brotherhood would regularly present public lectures as part of the summer camp's curriculum. These lectures included the presentation of the ideas of al-Turabi himself. But the lecture series would also include lectures conducted by Sudanese Brotherhood members on other Islamist modernist thinkers including Abu al-'ala al-Mawdudi, Hassan al-Banna, Abu Hassan al-Nadawi, Yusif al-Qardawi, Mohammed al-Ghazali, and Sayyid Qutb.[83] Following their time at the summer camp, the attendees would be encouraged to return to their schools and universities and recruit others into the Muslim Brotherhood organization.

Of all of the Brotherhood's civil society organizations, the General Union of Sudanese Students (GUSS) was an especially important association for the recruitment of new members. In addition to recruiting students from the university campuses, the GUSS, which was controlled by the Muslim Brotherhood in the 1970s and throughout the 1980s, established strong ties with Islamic movements and associations worldwide. A notable example was the GUSS' convening of an Annual World Muslim Camp which brought to Sudan Muslim Student Associations from all over the Muslim world ranging from the Philippines and Indonesia to Yemen, Saudi Arabia, Jordan, and Egypt. Interestingly, this signaled an unprecedented development wherein some young Sudanese, long isolated from the larger Muslim world, came to increasingly identify as "Muslims" first, drawing closer to a transnational Islamic identity different from the locally centered sectarianism associated with the long history of Sudanese Sufism. As one Sudanese scholar noted, even the recitation of the verses from such writers as the Egyptian Yusuf Qardawi during these annual events reflected a fervent desire to traverse nation-state and ethnic boundaries and make real the ambition for a "global Islamic community" (*al-'Alimiyya al-Islamiyya*):

*My brother from India or Morocco*
*I am of you, you are of me, you are me*
*Do not ask of my country or my kin*
*Islam is my mother and father*
*We are brothers and bonded by love*
*Muslims, Muslims, Muslims*[84]

In other words, in addition to building a formidable financial base that gave them effectively financial hegemony in civil society, the rise of the Islamists to political power in this period was also due to the regime's strategy of co-optation and accommodation, which ultimately failed to revive the state's weak legitimacy. It is unlikely that the Muslim Brotherhood who have always had a smaller constituency than the Sufi movements in Sudan would have been as political successful without the strategic intervention and support of the state. At the same time, al-Nimeiri was clearly trying to break the Sudanese state's long addiction to the support of Sufi and Islamist political movements. Far from capitulating to the wishes of the Brotherhood, the passage of the September Laws marked al-Nimeiri's last attempt to beat Turabi and the two Sayyids at their own game and claim for himself both religious legitimacy and populist support. The Brotherhood's monopolization of informal finance and Islamic banking was a key element in their political ascendancy but the fact that it coincided, and was crucially aided, by the state's very weak institutional capacity and legitimacy is the reason why, by the late 1980s, the Muslim Brotherhood of Sudan were well placed to assume the levers of state power, albeit my violent means.

## Sudan's Muslim Brotherhood and the Revolution for National Salvation

In December 1988, precisely three decades prior to the popular uprising that led to the overthrow of Omer Bashir, widespread strikes and demonstrations erupted in Khartoum, led by a newly revitalized workers' and tenants' union alongside federations of professionals, civil servants, and artisans.[85] These were the social groups that in the 1950s and 1960s had supported the influential Communist Party and were largely responsible for the downfall of the military regimes of Ibrahim 'Abbud in 1964 and Ja'far al-Nimairi in 1985 ushering in two democratic periods in the country.[86] Once again these social groups took to the streets, calling themselves the "Modern Forces" *(al-Quwwat al-Haditha)* to distinguish themselves from the traditional sectarian parties, which dominated civilian electoral politics since independence.

These demonstrations reflected popular frustration with the squabbling between the Umma Party and the Democratic Unionist Party as well as objections to the newly formed alliance between the Umma Party and the NIF to form a majority in parliament. The primary demands of the Modern Forces were a peaceful solution to the civil war between the government and the southern rebel movement, the Sudanese People's Liberation Army (SPLA), and the repeal of the shari'a-based laws implemented in September 1983.[87] Two months later, in February 1989, a group of high-ranking military forces joined the Modern Forces' cause. They submitted a memorandum to the civilian government demanding it seek an immediate solution to the war and calling for a peaceful rather than military solution to the civil war.

These events culminated in a National Memorandum for Peace, subsequently signed by all major parties except the NIF, which opted to leave the government and form an opposition front. This memorandum compelled the prime minister and Umma Party leader, Sadiq al-Mahdi, to form a new coalition incorporating members of the professional, trade, and workers' unions into the government. This coalition recommended that peace talks be based on an agreement signed in Addis Ababa in November 1988 by the SPLA leader at the time, John Garang, and Muhammad 'Uthman al-Mirghani, head of the DUP and spiritual leader of the Khatmiyya order. The agreement called for the repeal of the 1983 September Laws and the postponement of shari'a law until a truly representative constitutional conference (*mu'tamar dusturi*) could be convened following a cease-fire.[88]

In mid-June 1989, al-Mahdi's government announced that a cabinet meeting on July 1 would formally repeal the September Laws, contingent upon the review of a parliamentary committee comprising representatives from all political parties. On July 4, a government delegation and the SPLA were to meet to propose a permanent resolution to the civil war.[89] Twenty-four hours before the July 1 meeting, a group of mid-ranking officers took over the Republican Palace, the parliament, and the national broadcasting station, rounded up top party and union leaders throughout the capital, and announced the Revolutionary Command Council under the leadership of Lt. Gen. ʻUmar Hassan Ahmad al-Bashir.

It quickly became evident that the Muslim Brotherhood and the NIF spearheaded the success of the June 30 coup. Widespread popular support for ending the war by repealing the September 1983 Islamic law as the swiftest way to resolve the country's economic and political problems had threatened to marginalize the Brotherhood. Its twofold aim was to preempt any peace agreement based on repealing shari'a and to reverse the ascendance of the largely secular forces newly incorporated into the government by the then Prime Minster Sadiq al-Mahdi.[90] The junta targeted these forces, dissolving all parties and structures of the constituent assembly and imprisoning a disproportionate number of members of workers' and professional unions. In a swift campaign to consolidate political power, the new regime banned all independent publications, forcibly retired more than 300 senior officers, and replaced hundreds of civil servants with NIF members and sympathizers. But while the Islamists' seizure of state power confirmed that indeed the Islamist commercial class, in collusion with the state, emerged the winners in the "battle" over informal financial markets and Islamic banking, by the late 1980s, as the recession deepened, it would prove to be a pyrrhic victory.

# 3 Islamic versus Clan Networks: Labor Remittances, Hawwala Banking, and the Predatory State in Somalia

One of the most controversial campaigns following the attacks of 9/11 has been the global war on terrorist finance. Initiated under President George W. Bush, US authorities established a wide range of legal mechanisms allegedly targeting the financial sources of supposed militant organizations. The USA Patriot Act[1] and the International Emergency Economic Powers Act (IEEPA)[2] provided Federal officials with the authority to freeze assets of entities and individuals identified as financing terrorist organizations. Launched on October 25, 2001, Operation Green Quest froze more than $34 million in global assets linked to alleged terrorist organizations and individuals. At the time about 142 nations came on board and blocked $70 million worth of assets within their borders and most continue to express open "support" for the American led effort to "choke off" terrorist funding.

This campaign has targeted Islamic welfare associations and a host of informal social institutions in the Muslim world. Included in the Treasury Department's list of entities supporting terrorism are the largely unregulated money transfer agencies known in Somalia as *sharikat hawwalat* or money "transfer agencies." In November 2001, the US government ordered the closure of the US and international offices of what was then Somalia's largest money transfer agency, al-Barakaat, and seized all of its assets, totaling $34 million. They also closed the Somali International Relief Organization and Bank al-Taqwa in the Bahamas.[3]

Despite protests to the contrary from Somali nationals and United Nations (UN) officials, the US administration insisted that there was a clear connection between these Somalia-owned hawwalat and the al-Qaida network. Eventually, however, American and European officials acknowledged that evidence of al-Barakaat's financial backing for terrorism had not materialized. In the years since, only four criminal prosecutions of al-Barakaat officials have been filed but none involved charges of aiding terrorists.[4] US Embassy officials in Nairobi, who had been investigating these linkages since the terrorist bombings in Kenya and Tanzania in 1996, also stated that they "know of no evidence" that al-Qaeda is linked to militant groups in Somalia.[5] Moreover, the FBI agent who led the US delegation, which raided the offices of al-Barakaat, stated that diligent investigation revealed no "smoking gun" evidence – either testimonial or documentary – showing that al-Barakaat was funding al-Qaeda or any other terrorist organization.[6] In August 2006, more than five years after al-Barakaat was designated as a likely financier of terrorism, US authorities finally removed the hawwalat from its terror list.[7] Nevertheless, as late as 2016, the World Bank report acknowledged, that "many banks in the United States, the United Kingdom, Canada and Australia have closed the bank accounts of Somali remittance companies purportedly due to the perceived high risks of money laundering and potential links to terrorism."[8]

In its attempts to set "global standards" for preventing money laundering and counterterrorist financing regimes, US policy makers have also targeted Islamic charities and businesses as part of Operation Green Quest. In 2008, the Financial Action Task Force (FATF) warned: "[T]he misuse of nonprofit organizations for the financing terrorism ... is a crucial weak point in the global struggle to stop such funding at its source."[9] The global nature of the campaign has had significant impact in Muslim countries and in Somalia in particular. One of the major problems has been that not only have governments worldwide regulated the sharikat hawwalat and Islamic charities and designated many as "financing terrorism," states have also used the "war against terrorism" strategically with the result that the campaign has undermined the livelihoods of those most in need of social protection.[10] In countries such as Egypt, Islamic "charities" do not only serve the religious obligations of Muslims, they provide essential goods and services for Islamists and non-Islamists alike.[11] They have filled the social welfare gap in important ways at the very time that states have reduced their role in the provision of social welfare.[12]

It is important to note that there is definitely a connection between the "hidden" economy of remittance inflows and the ascendancy of Islamist groups in the labor-exporting countries of Sudan and Egypt. Since the 1970s, institutions such as the Faisal Islamic Bank, based in Saudi Arabia but with branches in many parts of the Muslim world, have been instrumental in promoting the financial profile of Islamists throughout the Islamic world. Osama bin Laden opened several accounts in these banks, including a number of Sudanese banks while he was residing in that country. Branches of the Faisal Islamic Bank, Baraka, Tadamun Islamic Bank, and the Omdurman Islamic Bank have been an important source of financing for Islamists in Sudan for four decades.[13] In Egypt, Islamic Management Companies, which attracted large deposits from Egyptian workers abroad in the 1980s, helped raise the political profile of a middle-class network of moderate, albeit conservative and nonviolent, Islamic groups by funding a host of commercial enterprises and Islamic welfare associations. These developments coincided with the oil price hikes and the boom in labor migration to the Gulf. Doubtless this connection is part of the reason why US officials have focused their attention on the hawwalat system, with some analysts going so far as to refer to informal transfers as part of an "Islamic banking war."[14]

However, in Somalia, the hawwalat have assumed a quite different role. My own survey research on the hawwalat in Somalia shows that, rather than facilitating the rise of an Islamist coalition encouraged by state elites during the oil boom period, as in Sudan and Egypt, remittance flows have played a large part in the civil conflict in Somalia and reinforced clan divisions rather than reinforcing Islamic ties. Indeed, the unintentional consequence of the war on terrorist finance has been to target the victims of state collapse rather than Islamist militants of the type that engage in transnational terrorism. In reality, informal banking systems (i.e., hawwalat) in Somalia that are commonly used by Somalis to send monies back home to family and kin relations operate largely on the basis of clan networks and do not promote or finance militant Islamist groups. This chapter analyzes how specific types of informal markets in foreign currency (fueled by labor remittances) influenced the development of clan conflict and helped lay the context for state disintegration in Somalia during the remittance boom.

## Targeting Weak and Failed States: Blaming the Victims?

Since the 9/11 attacks a key focus of the war against terrorist finance (i.e., Operation Green Quest) appears to be societies like Somalia that have suffered state disintegration, rather than the formal financial banks and wealthy citizens in the Gulf who have a long history of supporting Islamist groups.[15] As one British parliamentarian put it, "the focus of the campaign should be on states that have very little control within their borders, and where a degree of an invasive military response may be appropriate."[16] In reality, however, the wholesale closure of these informal banks proved counterproductive to the long-term US objective of putting an end to global terrorism. Indeed, rather than "interrupt[ing] the murderers' work,"[17] as George W. Bush put it at the time, shutting down money transfer agencies led to further impoverishment and possible radicalization of average Somalis who rely on these services for their daily survival.

The US campaign against the hawwalat and those who operate them proved overly broad as to defy justification. In addition to shutting down al-Barakaat, the administration froze the US assets of 189 individuals and organizations suspected of supporting terror groups.[18] AT&T and British Telecom's joint venture cut off international services to Somalia's principal telecommunication provider, a subsidiary of al-Barakaat, after the United States claimed that it too was suspected of "financing terror." One of the most vital communication links between Somalia and the outside world – making it possible for millions of Somalis to receive remittances from relatives' abroad – was effectively shut down. Since al-Barakaat was also the largest telecommunications provider, its closure affected all the other hawwalat companies including Dahabshil and Amal, concentrated in northwest and northeast Somalia, respectively. Thus, in addition to exacerbating the humanitarian crisis, the closure of the hawwalat adversely affected all sectors of Somalia's larger economy, which has been heavily dependent on the inflow of remittances for over four decades. Moreover, it is also threatening to upset the fragile state-building efforts that brought peace and stability to the northern parts of Somalia after decades of internecine clan warfare.

Following the attacks of September 11, the most troubling misconception about the hawwalat is that "such operations exist as a sideline within unrelated businesses, such as a grocery store or a jewelry store."[19] In reality, as in other labor-exporting countries, in the case of Somalia, the hawwalat are anything but a sideshow. Not only have these agencies and the cash they send secured countless livelihoods, they have played a major role in political and economic developments for decades. Labor has long been Somalia's principal export, and remittances from Somalis working abroad are the most important source of foreign exchange. As early as 1981, national account figures showed that remittances, most of which escaped state control, equaled almost two-fifths of the country's gross national product.[20] More recent estimates of the total volume of remittances received in Somalia range from a low of $1 billion to $1.6 billion annually. In 2000, for example, more than 40 percent of households in northern Somalia relied on remittances as a supplementary source of income (see Figure 3.1). A more recent study found that remittances to families averaged US$200 per month, compared to the average annual income of US$491 per annum. In other words, the average monthly remittance transfer was more than sufficient to lift people out of poverty in the context of Somali's economic and social crisis.[21]

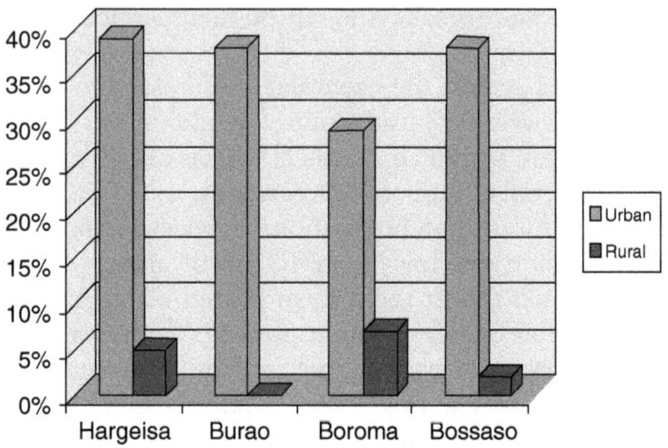


Figure 3.1 Remittance inflows in Northern Somalia
*Source*: Khalid M. Medani, "Report on Internal Migration and Remittance Inflows in Northwest and Northeast Somalia" (Nairobi, Kenya: UN Coordination Unit [UNCU] and Food Security Assessment Unit [FSAU], 2000).

The benefit of these remittance flows accrues to the vast majority, albeit not all, of Somalia's subclans. Among the Isaaq, the clan, which has historically supplied the majority of migrant workers, none of the four subclans has less than 18 percent of its households receiving remittances from abroad. Thirty one percent of the Haber Awal subclan's families, for example, count on transfers (see Figure 3.2). Remittances are usually a supplementary source of income. Typically, in addition to receiving assistance from relatives, Somali families have more than one member involved in informal economic activities. Nevertheless, Somalis rely heavily on support from overseas relatives sent through the hawwalat system, far more than their Egyptian and Sudanese counterparts.[22]

Clearly, family networks are the principal reason why Somalis have been able to secure their livelihoods under harsh economic conditions. Moreover, following the collapse of the Somali state every "family" unit has come to encompass three or more interdependent households.[23] In addition to assisting poorer urban relatives, a large proportion of urban residents support rural kin on a regular basis. While only 2 to 5 percent of rural Somalis receive remittances directly from overseas, Somalia's nomadic population still depends on these capital flows. In northern Somalia, for example, 46 percent of urban households support relations in pastoralist areas with monthly contributions in the range of $10 to $100 a month; of these 46 percent, as many as 40 percent are households which

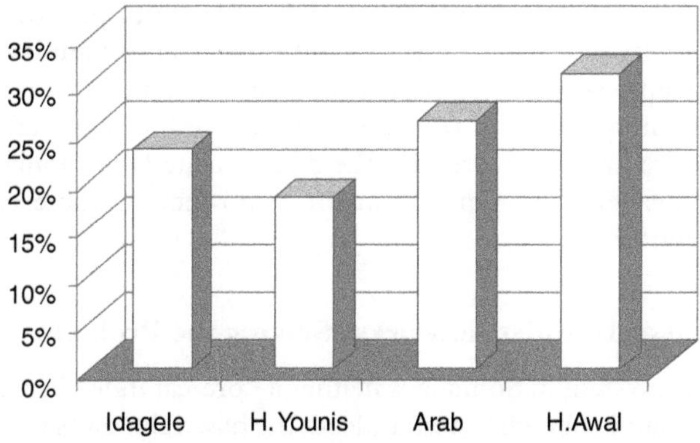


Figure 3.2 Labor remittance recipients by Isaaq subclan, Northwest Somalia
*Source*: Khalid M. Medani, "Report on Internal Migration and Remittance Inflows in Northwest and Northeast Somalia" (Nairobi, Kenya: UN Coordination Unit [UNCU] and Food Security Assessment Unit [FSAU], 2000).

depend on remittances from relatives living abroad (see Figure 3.1). Consequently, even more than Egypt and Sudan, the link between labor migration, urban households, and the larger rural population is a crucial and distinctive element in Somalia's economy.

Most hawwalat transfers represent meager amounts. More than 80 percent of all transfers sent through the largest three of these agencies were no more than an average of $100 a month per household. There is clearly no connection between the vast majority of these transfers and the larger funds associated with terrorist operations.

In this respect, the criminalization of these transfers following the attacks of 9/11 kept more than a billion dollars out of Somalia's economy. Moreover, according to the UN, the closures came at a time when Somalia's second income earner, the livestock sector, was losing an estimated $300 million to $400 million as a result of a ban by its major importer, Saudi Arabia. Coupled with intermittent droughts, the decision to freeze funds in Somalia's network of remittances led to a wide-scale humanitarian disaster. The UN representative for humanitarian affairs for Somalia warned at the time that "Somalia [was] on the precipice of total collapse."[24]

What is noteworthy, however, is that in recent years a number of remittance companies have filled the vacuum left open by the closure of al-Barakaat. Despite compliance with an array of new regulations,

Somalia's remittance companies have continued to multiply providing an array of financial services: regular monthly transfers to families to meet livelihood needs; larger-scale transfers for investment in property and commercial enterprises; and remittances linked to international trade.[25] The question remains, however: Do these unregulated remittance inflows finance Islamist militancy and terrorism or do they promote clan over religious identity?

## Clan or Islamist Networks? Solving the Problem of Trust

The hawwalat system in Somalia is neither a "pre-capitalist" artifact, nor a peculiarly Islamic phenomenon. Indeed, the hawwalat owes very little to the legal or normative principles of zakat or riba. It is, above all, a modern institution resulting from the disintegration of state and formal institutions and the impact of globalization on Somalia's economy. Nor is the hawwalat system synonymous with money laundering, as the US legislation implies. Informal transfers are legitimate financial transfers similar to other international capital flows generally accepted as an inherent part of globalization. Indeed, as a number of scholars have noted, market liberalization has substantially loosened state controls on legal economic flows in recent decades. Indeed, much of this scholarship has tended to assume all "unregulated" cross-border flows as necessarily part of "market criminalization," or "transnational organized crime," including terrorist financial markets.[26] In Somalia, informal transfers are legitimate, and not "illicit," capital flows. The hawwalat system finances the bulk of imports into the country, provides legitimate profits for those engaged in transferring these funds, and makes resources available for investments throughout Somalia.

The first Somali agency, Dahabshil, was formed in the late 1970s prior to the civil war. It developed first in the refugee camps of Ethiopia and was quickly extended to the interior of Northwest Somalia. At the time, Dahabshil was established to meet the demand of Somalia laborers who, like Sudanese and Egyptians, migrated to the Gulf and sought to circumvent foreign exchange controls. But with the onset of the civil war in the late 1980s, the hawwalat system expanded and has come to represent the only avenue for Somali expatriates to send money to support their families.

The poor education of many Somali migrants means that they are often living on the margins in those host societies and it can take time for families to settle, find incomes, and begin to remit significant amounts of money. Somaliland's past, its proximity to the Gulf, the flight from war and repression in the 1980s, and easier immigrant conditions have all been factors that helped to promote the Isaaq clan, in the Northwest in political terms. Isaaq families benefited from remittances before other clans and contributed to interclan divisions.[27] A large proportion of these remittances went to supply arms not to Islamist militants but clan-based guerillas that helped overthrow the Barre regime. In fact, delegates of the Isaaq-led Somalia National Movement (SNM) received between $14 to $25 million in the late 1980s.[28] As with other insurgent groups worldwide, the remittance funded factions in Somalia harbored no specific ideology and depended on the control of domestic territory and local civilian populations to mobilize political support. In this respect Somalia's rebel groups differed markedly from Islamist militants or the *al-Ittihad* organization, which rarely rely on domestic support alone, justify their acts of political violence with religious rhetoric, and advocate and implement terrorist operations across the borders of Somalia.[29]

While hawwalat transfers are not regulated by formal institutions or legal oversight; they are regulated by locally specific norms of reciprocity embedded in clan loyalties and not Islamist extremist ideology. The Islamist *al-Ittihad* organization and the militants of *al-Shabbaab*, the main targets of the global anti-terrorist policy in Somalia, have not been able to monopolize these financial transfers precisely because of the manner in which Somalia's clan networks regulate their distribution in ways that defy discursive and legalistic attributions that have labeled these flows as illicit and clandestine and primarily designed to recruit Jihadist militants.

The hawwalat operate very simply. A customer brings money (cash or cashier's check) to an agent and asks that it be sent to a certain person in Somalia. The remittance agent charges a fee, typically from 5 to 10 percent depending on the destination. Costs may go up to 12 or 15 percent for larger amounts. The remittance agent then contacts a local agent in Mogadishu – via radio, satellite phone, or fax – and instructs him to give the appropriate amount to the person in question. The remittance agent in the United States or elsewhere does not send any money. Instead, both dealers record the transaction and the relative in Somalia receives the money in two or three days.[30] Thus the hawwalat are not as "hidden" or "secret" as US officials have suggested. Remittance companies must maintain detailed, digitized accounting records. One of the factors that makes the Somali hawwalat system different from similar operations elsewhere is that the "address" of the recipient is usually determined by his/her clan or subclan affiliation.

The hawwalat company must be able to pay cash, usually in hard currency, and make sure to resupply the appropriate bank account in due time. For this reason the brokers involved must trust each other absolutely. As a result, recruitment for decisive positions follows clan lines with few exceptions. In Somalia, clan networks, far more than Islamic ties serve the purpose of "privileged trust." That is, in conventional economic terms, informal clan-based networks reduce the costs of contract enforcement in the absence of formal regulatory institutions and engender both trust and cooperation. The customer too must have confidence that the broker, charged with sending the funds, does not disappear with the cash. Not surprisingly, the customer's choice of transfer agency is largely dependent on which clan operates the company.

In the Isaaq-dominated northwest, the Isaaq-run Dahabshil Company enjoys 60 percent of the market. As one competitor from the Amal hawwalat, which is also dominated by the Darod clan, put it: "Dahabshil is a family-owned company."[31] Al-Barakaat, which was primarily operated by the Darod clan, possessed only 15 percent of the market in northwest Somalia (see Figure 3.3), but it did control the lion's share of the business, an estimated 90 percent, in southern and central Somalia.[32] Moreover, following the closure of Al-Barakaat, the latter's market share has been filled by yet another Darod-dominated remittance company, the Amal hawwalat.[33]

Clearly, Somali Islamists are not the prime beneficiaries of this informal currency trade. Many hawwalat agents can be described as religious[34] and

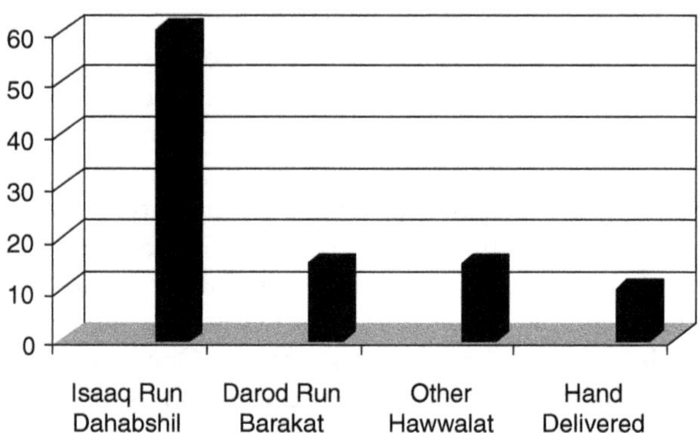


Figure 3.3 Clan networks and remittance transfers in Northern Somalia
*Source*: Khalid M. Medani, "Report on Internal Migration and Remittance Inflows in Northwest and Northeast Somalia" (Nairobi, Kenya: UN Coordination Unit [UNCU] and Food Security Assessment Unit [FSAU], 2000).

are sympathetic to conservative Islamist groups such *al-Ittihad*, but in political terms this "Islamist" influence is more apparent in the northeast and south where for historical reasons solidarity along clan lines is comparatively weak. Moreover, while the managers of some remittance companies share a conservative Islamic agenda similar to Islamist capitalists throughout the Muslim world, they perceive any form of extremism such as that promoted by the *al-Shabbaab* organization as not only "un-Islamic" but "bad for business."[35] In the northwest, *al-Ittihad* and *al-Shabbaab* militants generally do not enjoy the support of the local population. Since the onset of the civil war, *al-Ittihad* has chosen to finance the movement, not through the hawwalat, but by attempting to control the port economies of Bossaso and Merka.

In the early 1990s, *al-Ittihad* did not manage to monopolize the lucrative important-export trade of Bossaso despite a number of military incursions to take over the port by force. Consequently, *al-Ittihad* (which draws members across clan lines) attempted to impose a new form of "Islamic" rule, but this was short-lived. In the early 1990s, after a bitter armed conflict, the Darod-/Majerteen-backed Somali Salvation Democratic Front (SSDF) wrenched political control from *al-Ittihad* forces and has administered the port of Bossaso ever since. Since this defeat, *al-Ittihad* abandoned the few towns and rural outposts it once controlled, and its activists have since integrated into local communities as teachers, health workers, and businessmen. Some members have close links with Islamists in Sudan, primarily in the form of Sudanese-funded educational scholarships. They now represent a mainstream form of conservative Islamist activism, and in recent years they have been primarily interested in expanding their commercial enterprises, providing social services, operating local newspapers, and attaining employment – not global Jihad. This divergence in Somalia's political developments is due to its own particular historical legacy, which played an important role in determining the eventual disintegration of the state and the very nature of clan conflict.

## State Capacity and Social Structure in a Weak State: The Historical Legacy

Somalia is, arguably, the most homogenous country in Africa and the Arab world. All Somalis belong to the same ethnic group (Somali), adhere to Islam, speak the same language, and with minor exceptions trace their ancestry through a single lineage. Moreover, as David Laitin has observed Somalis "have historically harbored a fervent sense of belonging to a distinct national community."[36] Nevertheless, the cultural cleavages in Somalia are equally stark but of a distinct variety. In historical terms clan and regional differences in Somalia marked a highly variable social structure that was belied by Somalia's ethnic and religious homogeneity. The Somali population is divided into economic categories and regions subsumed under a complex of clan networks. The clan system is one that anthropologists' term "acephalous," a segmentary lineage system in which social order is maintained by balancing opposing segments on the same social level, clans and subclans against each other and lineages, families, and individuals against other lineages, families, and individuals. Although members of a family, lineage, or clan may unite against an external threat, the unity is often undermined by internal rivalry precipitated by exogenous developments. The major branches of the Somali lineage system are based on the pastoral clans of the Dir (in the northwest along the Djibouti border), Darod (in the south along the Kenyan border, and the northeast), Isaaq (in the northwest), Hawiye (in the central region around Mogadishu), and the sedentary agricultural clans of the Digil and Rahanwayn in the more fertile regions in southern Somalia (see Clan Chart in Appendix).

In the precolonial period, the delicate balance of power among clan families in Somalia had long been maintained by the traditional authority of Somali elders (Isimo) and the institution of the *Xeer*. The Xeer functioned as a type of social contract, which transcended blood and lineage ties and, informed by Islamic teachings, laid a foundation upon which social conflicts ranging from property disputes to a variety of social transactions could be resolved. Thus, interclan conflict was far from inevitable, for in addition to establishing a delicate and complex web of negotiated agreements, the Xeer stipulated that the leader *(Sultan)* of the ad hoc deliberative assemblies (*Shirs*) that formed the functional basis of the Xeer had to be chosen from one of the outside clans to balance the power of the more dominant clan families.[37] In addition, the decisions of the deliberative assemblies were enforced through a process called the *guddoon.* The guddoon essentially refers to the ratification and sanctioning of consensus decisions reached by elders of the community organized around the deliberative councils. Like other traditional dispute resolution institutions, the guddoon emphasized consensus decision-making. Enforcement of the Isimo's rulings was based on moral authority and the Islamic concept of *'Ijima'* or consent of the people.

During the colonial era in the nineteenth century what Somali nationalists' term "Greater Somalia" became a focus of intense colonial competition that partitioned the territory among British Somaliland in the north, Italian Somaliland in the south, and French Somaliland (present-day Djibouti) in the northwest. The territory of the Ogaden in the west was occupied by imperial Ethiopia. The hitherto resilient Xeer system was disrupted, and the traditional authority of the Isimo gradually eroded, as arbitrary force came to determine the relationship between increasingly centralized colonial states and increasingly fragmented Somali communities. Somali scholar, Abdi Samatar, has argued that it was this development "rather than Somali society or traditions which represents the genesis of contemporary Somali warlordism."[38] To this observation one can add the disruptive development of distinct clan-based economies induced by local and international developments that replaced the institution of the Xeer with new forms of authority based on informal social networks coalescing around clan ties.[39]

The British and Italian colonial traditions left distinctly different imprints in northern and southern Somalia. Considerable variations in education, legal systems, tariffs, customs dues, and patterns of trade distinguished the British administration from that established by the Italians.[40] The Italians, hoping to garner some economic benefit from their colony, introduced large-scale banana plantations in the inter-riverine areas of the south and established more advanced educational and health services, which largely explains the domination of jobs and other privileges by southern bureaucrats in the postindependence era. In the north, the British administration introduced the expansion and commoditization of livestock trade, promoting the fortunes of a handful of northern merchants and state bureaucrats who broke out of precapitalist moral economic ties and began to grow livestock for purposes of trade only. However, most of the surplus (rent) captured by the merchant and the state elite was not invested in productive enterprise; in other words "the state and merchant capital were not progressive forces in terms of laying the foundation for a new and regenerative regime of accumulation."[41] Of great importance in the Somali case is that Somalia's acephalous social structure provided no "native" leadership on which the colonial administration could build state institutions. In neither region of the country was the colonial administration able to incorporate peasant and pastoral production into the capitalist economy.

As a result, the Somali petit bourgeoisie that assumed control of the postcolonial state in 1960 inherited a "weaker" state, which in contrast to Sudan in the same period possessed "weak" extractive capabilities. The fiscal basis of postcolonial Somalia was marked from the beginning by the absence of any form of direct taxation on production as the vast majority of households in the rural areas (the bulk of the Somali population) retained a productive base through their full control of land. Nor did the colonial state establish a marketing board as in Sudan and other parts of Africa to oversee Somalia's most significant source of revenue, livestock trade. In the case of the Italian colony indirect taxes, primarily in the form of custom duties, constituted 73 percent of the state's locally generally revenues by the late 1950s and 80 percent in the British protectorate to the north.[42] These weak regulatory mechanisms would continue throughout modern Somali history with the Siad Barre regime (1969–1990) pursuing similarly indirect avenues of extraction. In political terms, state-society relations would continue to be marked by the exigencies of clientelism, and in economic terms by tributary extractive relations (often imposed by force) focused on consumption rather than productive development.[43] Of course, the Barre regime pursued far more "predatory" policies designed exclusively to maximize revenue for his own clan (Darod) family and eventually his Marehan subclan through unprecedented violence.

Another weakness directly related to the first is Somalia's heavy dependence on foreign assistance for its fiscal health. Both the Italian and the British administration critically depended on the treasury in the home countries and in both cases expenditures consistently outstripped locally generated revenue. The colonial legacy thus set a pattern in which foreign aid would continue to be more significant than domestic production and consequently, the state became the prime focus of not only political authority but accumulation until the critical expansion of the parallel economy in the 1970s. Even at this early date, and owing to the predominance of pastoralism, Somalia showed the beginnings of what a prominent scholar of Africa has termed a "society without a state . . . the latter [sitting] suspended in mid-air over society."[44] Moreover, in Somalia, associational life in the rural areas was governed by clan loyalties, based on informal networks of mutual obligations. These reciprocal relations, however, were drastically eroded leading to the rise of the politics of ascription and violence. This resulted not *because* of increasing state penetration as many scholars have argued, but rather due to the *manner* in which this intervention occurred.[45] The legacy of a weak financial extractive base and dependence on foreign aid would in the context of the international economy result in the gradual disintegration of the Somali state.

## Origins of State Disintegration: Labor Remittances and "Clan Economies"

As in Egypt and Sudan, in Somalia remittances from expatriate labor in the Arab Gulf states were also the primary source of foreign currency for fueling the expansion of the parallel market and signaled a boom for domestic importers and private entrepreneurs. Here too the weight of these capital inflows where not reflected in the few aggregate national income figures available for those years: the importance of repatriated monies in creating and expanding the parallel economy during the boom, and the predominance of Somalia's pastoral economy wherein a great part of internal trade is in livestock escaped official control. Indeed, the greater part of the national income derived not from domestic activities as such, but from remittances of Somali workers abroad, sent through informal channels; the majority of exports and imports were transacted in the parallel economy at free-market exchange rates. Still, national account figures as early as 1981 estimated that remittances equaled almost two-fifths of Somalia's GNP.[46]

The important variant in the Somali case is that unlike in the more urbanized labor exporters, there are no clear-cut divisions along occupation lines such as, for example, wage earners and traders. That is, whereas Egypt and Sudan possess a politically influential "modern commercial sector" and more resilient horizontal social formations along the civil society divide, Somalia's most distinctive characteristic is that over half of its population is dependent on nomadic pastoralism for its livelihood, a proportion not exceeded in any other country in the world.[47] It is within this context that one can speak of the development of two intertwined fragmented markets.

Thus, it is crucial to avoid reification of the "parallel market." Somalia's distinctive socioeconomic structures necessitate highlighting two parallel markets: one centered around foreign currency exchanges (the parallel market) and the other related to livestock trade which played an important role in fueling the expansion of informal financial networks as we shall see later. Moreover, what is equally significant is the fact that operating together these parallel markets fragmented further resulting in the expansion of a thriving urban informal sector. Operating strictly on the basis of familial relations this sector included a host of enterprises ranging from food processing, construction, and carpentry to tailoring and retail trade (commerce).[48]

Predictably, the growth of the parallel market coincided with the increasingly diminishing economic role of the state. As one Somali economist has observed, "while throughout the 1970s wages had stagnated particularly in the public sector [which accounted for the bulk of employment]; inflation had doubled in eight years, 1970–78." Moreover, despite the "shrinkage" of the state's extractive and distributive capacity in this period "no poverty was in evidence and shops were full of imported goods."[49]

Under the Siad Barre regime the Somali state made a special effort during the 1970s to attract Arab capital. In 1974 it joined the Arab league in recognition that the explosion of oil prices meant hefty payoffs for those identifying themselves as Arabs. As Somalia became more dependent on Arab finance, more Somalis engaged in trade with Arab middleman, worked for aid projects funded by Arab funding institutions, and an increasing number spent a great part of their working lives in the Arab states. But while the private sector prospered as a quarter of a million Somali merchants took advantage of the massive oil profits of the Arab oil exporters, the state continued to be hampered by debt and regression. Somalia's debt, which stood at 230 million US dollars in 1975, rose to more than 1 billion by the end of the decade.[50] By 1981, Somalia, now more closely allied with the West, reached an agreement with the IMF and was compelled to decrease the state's role in the hitherto excessively regulated economy and devaluate the Somali shilling in exchange for much-needed hard currency.[51]

The parallel economy was flourishing, as it had been in Sudan over the same period, and its size and relative efficacy in capital accumulation, particularly in relation to the declining extractive capabilities of the state, forced a response from the latter. One can note with great interest that Siad Barre felt compelled to intervene in the parallel sector for the same reasons that drove Nimeiri to encourage Islamic banks in Sudan which themselves were aided by the Gulf countries' "breadbasket" development plans that were later aborted. In Somalia too the formal economy was in shambles as a result of the external capital inflows in the form of labor remittances, a costly war with Ethiopia over the Ogaden in 1977–1978, and the decline of assistance from the Gulf. As a consequence, Barre was left with a narrow political base centered by the late 1980s around his own Marehan subclan. He thus sought to attract revenue from the private sector, which was of course inextricably linked to the parallel market. Whereas Nimeiri's shrinking political and economic base led him to promote Islamic financial institutions and indirectly tap into the lucrative parallel market, no such option was available to Barre. Instead, Barre simply "legalized" the black-market economy by introducing what is known as the franco valuta (f.v.) system in the late 1970s. Barre did this in the hope of generating more indirect taxes (i.e., custom duties) from the booming import-export trade that resulted from the boom in remittance inflow to the domestic economy.

Under this system the government allowed traders virtual freedom to import goods with their own sources of foreign exchange – that is, through parallel market transactions.[52] For their part, the money dealers (the Somali version of *Tujjar al-Shanta*) remitted the proceeds of the foreign exchange purchased from Somali workers abroad to their relatives back home. These proceeds were remitted at the free-market rate. In essence then, the f.v. system fully circumvented the state in procuring imported goods for Somali consumers – brought by Somali dealers, from money earned by Somali workers abroad and purchased by the workers' relatives at home.

The effect these developments had in displacing old state sectors and strengthening an autonomous private sector organized around clan families was enormous. It was estimated in 1980 that 150,000 to 175,000 Somalis worked in the Gulf countries, mostly in Saudi Arabia, earning five to six times the average Somali wage. A great part of this was repatriated to the mother country, especially after the late 1970s, because of the attractive exchange rates offered by the hawwalat currency dealers. This repatriated money, which continued to evade official bureaucratic institutions, nearly equaled two-thirds of the GNP in the urban areas.[53]

Labor, however, was not the only export: of equal importance is the effect the burgeoning parallel market had on livestock exports, traditionally Somalia's foremost foreign exchange earner. Remitted earnings were invested in livestock production and trade with the result that the livestock sector boomed. Like banana production, centered in the south, livestock production remained in private hands. But unlike banana exports, which as a share of total export value declined from 26 percent in 1972 to just 8 percent in 1978, the livestock trade rose from 40 percent of total export value in 1972 to 70 percent by the end of the decade.[54] The livestock traders prospered greatly, taking advantage of the difference between the officially set producer price and the market price in Saudi Arabia, which was under constant inflationary pressure.

The Barre government allowed the livestock traders to import goods from their own personal earnings without tariff restrictions. The state took its share by charging a livestock export tax of 10 percent.[55] In 1978, livestock exports amounted to 589 million shillings. The traders based in Saudi Arabia earned a windfall profit of $93.5 million most of which was recycled back into the parallel market in Somalia.[56] As one study noted "efforts by the [state] to mobilize resources [were] met by increased reliance on parallel markets, thereby further eroding the economic base of government and making coercion appear the only viable means of maintaining control."[57] As a result Somalia's industrial base, always relatively small both in terms of Gross Domestic Product (GDP) and in relation to the overwhelming contribution of the livestock sector and remittances from abroad, deteriorated further after the late 1970s. By the mid-1980s it accounted for only 5 percent of GDP.[58]

Remitted earnings from the large-scale movement of Somalis for wage employment in the Gulf were invested in the livestock sector, the part of the economy perceived to have the best comparative advantage. This had a dramatic effect on socioeconomic structures, particularly in northwest Somalia where the Isaaq clan monopolizes the trade in livestock. The expansion of the livestock market, the investment in wells and water tanks (birkets) caused the beginning of interclan strife. Due to their close proximity to Saudi Arabia and its intimate links with the Gulf Arabs, the Isaaq clan benefited the most from this livestock trade and came to dominate this sector in the boom period. In particular, the Isaaq made inroads into the Haud, a rich grazing plateau stretching from the heart of Isaaq territory in the north to the Ogaden region along the Ethiopian border. Thus, not only did the Isaaq come into economic conflict with the Ogaden clan but through them with the state. The Ogadenis (a subclan of Siad Barre's Darod clan) comprised the overwhelming majority in the military. The aggravation of these ascriptive cleavages by linkages with the Gulf and the doomed war with Ethiopia over the Ogaden (1977–1978) precipitated increased competition over scarcities in the recession.

What the f.v. system meant in terms of the state's extractive capacity is the virtual cessation of the government's attempt to control incomes in the country. Up to 1977 the government still retained a semblance of regulatory institutions based on nationalization of banking and plantations, nationalization and control of wholesale trade, and control over the importation and pricing of foodstuffs, rents, and wages. The state hoped to capture revenue from the parallel market via the f.v. system by maintaining control over wholesale trade and pricing policies of essential commodities, but this ensured only partial control over the income of traders. The f.v. system beginning in 1978 meant traders could import anything so long as they did so with their own foreign exchange leading to the rise of wealthy traders or commercial entrepreneurs at the expense of wage earners employed by the shrinking state bureaucracy. These increasingly wealthy traders were well placed to finance the various rebel organizations and "warlords" that would dominate Somali politics following the collapse of the state.

In contrast to Egypt and Sudan, where new middle classes arose aided by labor migration and the income-generating opportunity this provided, in Somalia the diminution of the formal economy and labor remittances determined a new pattern of clan conflict. This was because as the formal economy diminished giving way to a veritable boom in the parallel sector, two overwhelming factors emerged. First, many urbanites were members of trading firms (both in livestock and commodities) that were increasingly organized around clans, but most often subclans. Second, most families relied on monies received from family members residing abroad for their livelihood.

By the mid-1980s, 93 percent of all capital investment in informal enterprises in Mogadishu was personal savings (derived mainly from remittance) and loans from relatives and friends. Formal lending from commercial banks was no more than 2.3 percent of the total and credit allocation from governmental sources was nonexistent (see Table 3.1). In addition, as a study by the International Labor Organization discovered there were "no specific structures to meet the needs of the informal sector and to mediate between the artisans and informal financial institutions so as to facilitate the former's access to credit."[59]

Consequently, the scramble over control of foreign exchange led to widening schisms between clan, subclan, and family households. It is with the rise of these clan-centered economies that one can trace the development of clanism, which was reinforced during the recession period and

Table 3.1 *Sources of finance for various informal microenterprises in Mogadishu, Somalia: 1987 (in percent)*

| Activity | Personal savings | Kin relations | Joint contribution | Commercial banks | Government lending | Total |
|---|---|---|---|---|---|---|
| Food processing | 53 | 28.2 | 18.0 | – | – | 100 |
| Shoe making | 40.0 | 56.7 | – | 3.1 | – | 100 |
| Tailoring | 53.2 | 39.4 | 3.2 | 4.2 | – | 100 |
| Construction | 85.7 | 14.3 | – | – | – | 100 |
| Carpentry | 56.0 | 40.0 | 4.0 | – | – | 100 |
| Metal work | 67.2 | 24.6 | 6.6 | 1.6 | – | 100 |
| Garages | 54.6 | 37.1 | 5.2 | 3.1 | – | 100 |
| Service repair | 48.2 | 48.2 | 3.6 | – | – | 100 |
| General services | 62.1 | 33.7 | 2.1 | 2.1 | – | 100 |
| Handicraft | 53.2 | 40.4 | – | 6.4 | – | 100 |
| Retail trade | 59.5 | 38.1 | 2.4 | – | – | 100 |
| Other informal work | 56.5 | 37.0 | 4.2 | 2.3 | – | 100 |

*Source:* Aboagye, A. A. *The Informal Sector in Mogadishu: An Analysis of a Survey*. Addis Ababa: International Labour Organisation/Jobs and Skills Programme for Africa, 1988. The average US dollar value of initial capital investment in informal sector enterprises was $490 by the late 1980s. The average wage of all informal workers (80 percent of whom range from 25 to 54 years of age) was 3,100 Somali Shillings, five times the average wage in the formal sector prior to the state's collapse.

solidified to the greatest degree in what one notable Somali scholar termed "*Dad Cunkii*," the era of cannibalism.[60] While in Egypt and Sudan a distinct formation of an Islamist business coalition was "reproduced" organized around privileged financial institutions operating more or less privately, albeit with state patronage, the development of distinct class formation within Somalia's large parallel sector did not occur. This key difference was due to two factors: first, the very dearth of private, formally organized institutions (i.e., official banks and publicly registered enterprises) necessitated the reliance on household economies; second, Barre not only pitted one clan against another in his elusive search for legitimacy as has been widely noted, but once he ran out of external funds he intervened in the economy in order to finance the important patronage system that kept key social constituencies (clans and individuals) wedded to participation in the government. However, with the expansion of the parallel economy, the prebendalist system quickly became irrelevant in Somali politics. The typical wage earner was more likely than not to belong to a trading household and while the incomes of some members of an extended family fell, those of others increased. In other words, few Somalis of any clan could afford to rely on state patronage for their well-being. As Jamal writes:

> The overwhelming fact during this boom period is that apart from government employees whose salaries [were] regulated, everybody else in the urban economy operated in the parallel economy, which unlike the formal economy, is essentially a free-market economy. This economy is, moreover, characterized by the vast network of inter-familial relationships that exist in Somali society.[61]

However, despite the liberal orientation of the Somalia economy engendered by its informalization this did not lead to a pattern of equalization in terms of income distribution as some scholars have maintained.[62] In fact, while the income of families increased dramatically in this period this in itself depended on the proximity and connections the various clans had in terms of access to informal financial networks and livestock trade. For example, while the Isaaq clan of the northwest managed to accumulate capital in a manner that allowed them to carve out an independent financial base for themselves, at the other end of the scale the Rahenwein, Digil, and the "Bantus" of the south emerged the losers in the battle over foreign exchange. The Bantus in particular suffered as a result of declining productivity in the agricultural sector. Under Italian colonial rule they had become dependent on wages earned from the planting and harvesting of export crops (especially bananas) along the Shebelle river.[63] Moreover, since along with the Digil and Rahenwein the Bantus did not share the lineage systems of the major nomadic clan families, they had little financial resources they could mobilize to exercise their "exit" option in the informal realm. In 1992 and 1993 these three clans, located in what came to be known as the "triangle of death," were disproportionately affected by the war-driven famine in the area.

By the early 1980s, at the height of the boom period, the parallel market, while clearly encouraged by the state via the f.v. system, had so weakened formal regulatory mechanisms that the IMF found itself in the ironic position of arguing *against* the sector of Somalia's economy that was functioning on a free-market basis:

> [The franco voluta system has] generated distortions and contributed to inflationary pressures, deprived the authorities of the foreign exchange that would otherwise have been channeled through the banking system and of control over consumption-investment mix of imports.[64]

The economic crises in the 1970s and 1980s were significantly compounded by decades of poor financial management and high levels of corruption wherein, as one Somali economist observed, the banking system was largely a financial tool for Siad Barre and a small group of elites with political influence.[65] Indeed, by the end of the decade there was little question that Somalia's formal economy was in shambles. In 1987 and 1989, the public sector deficit stood at 34 percent and 37 percent of GDP; foreign-debt service over exports and total foreign debt in relation to the gross domestic product (GDP) reached 240 percent and 277 percent in 1988 and 1990, respectively, and state expenditure on social services, including health and education, declined steeply to less than 1 percent of GDP by 1989.[66] Figure 3.2 illustrates the ways in which the parallel market altered state-society relations and thereby ethnic politics during the remittance boom.

## Explaining Somali's Divergent Path

In Somalia, during the boom, institutional links between state and society were destroyed and replaced with regional and clan affiliations that due to the type of parallel economy and Somalia's social structure were adept at capital accumulation. This same general process occurred in Egypt and Sudan. But whereas, in Somalia clan-centered economies operating as a form of embryonic trade unionism dominated the parallel market in that the household was best suited to capture remittance inflows, in Egypt and Sudan by contrast, historical, structural, and cultural conjectures led to the emergence of strong private sectors affiliated with Islamic financial institutions that served as mediators between the state and those segments of civil society engaged in "black market" activities.

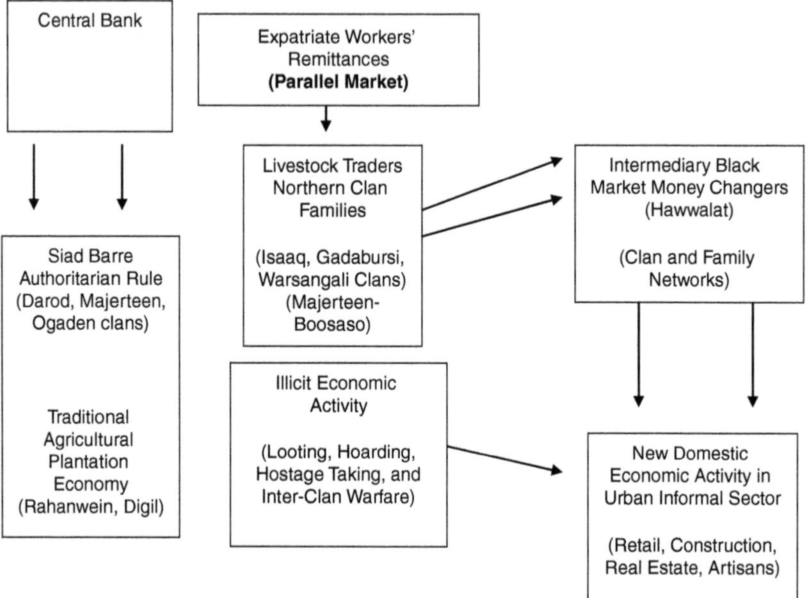


Figure 3.4 Informal transfers and ethnic politics in the remittance boom in Somalia

In Egypt and Sudan, an Islamist-commercial class based in the urban areas was, through the bridging of the official-parallel market divide and the cooperation of the state, not only able to 'reproduce' itself but also to consolidate its political base. This development accompanied a major weakening of the state's extractive institutions as result of decreasing sources of official assistance, the decline in general productivity, and, in the case of Sudan, the resurgence of civil war in 1983. Utilizing the parallel market as their springboard and their privileged relationship to the Sadat and al-Nimeiri regimes, respectively, Egyptian and Sudanese Islamists were well positioned to expand their recruitment drives and popularize their movements.

Sadat and Nimeiri's strategies in Egypt and Sudan, respectively, confirm Tilly's observation that even the strongest formal state administration relies on its relationship with people and their networks (including informal economic networks) to channel and control resources and to benefit from the legitimacy of these relationships.[67] But while in Egypt the stability of the state persisted despite the strong emergence of Islamists in civil society, in Sudan the new partners in this reconfigured hegemonic group ended up swallowing their original state patrons and succeeded in forming their own hegemonic alliance. This alliance, between political and commercial networks is what ushered in the onset and consolidation of the Islamist authoritarian regime of Omer Bashir.

By contrast, in Somalia, the expansion of the parallel economy facilitated the rise of violent, centrifugal tendencies. Unlike Egypt and Sudan, in Somalia no single coalition in civil society emerged as dominant precisely because of a lack of strong horizontal cleavages, and distinct class formations. Moreover, the informal channels utilized to transfer remittances played an important role in the construction of new identity-based politics in that they reinforced the importance of clan, even more than "Islam," as the most important social and political institution in Somali life. That is, with the expansion of the parallel economy, the politics of ethnicity and clan-based commercial networks eclipsed the power of the state. This is because ties of kinship remained crucial to the risky commercial transactions associated with the burgeoning parallel economy. Indeed, far from dissolving previously existing social ties in the Weberian sense, in Somalia market expansion crucially depended on the creation and recreation of far more extensive interpersonal relations of trust embedded in clan networks.

Thus, in contrast to Egypt and Sudan, in Somalia, informal economic activities in the context of far weaker state capacity coalesced around clan cleavages setting the stage for the complete disintegration of the state. As noted earlier, in the early 1980s, the IMF cautioned Barre against his continued promotion of the parallel market in Somalia, but this warning came too late and went unheeded. The recession of the 1980s would not only lead to increasing predatory and violent state behavior, but it would also galvanize an opposition organized around clan families that had enjoyed relative growth and economic autonomy in the boom. Not surprisingly, as discussed in Chapter 6, the unraveling of the Somali state would begin with the insurrection of the Isaaq, the most important beneficiaries of the fading era of abundance.

*III*

# Globalization and Institutional Change in an Era of Scarcity

# 4 Economic Crisis, Informal Institutions, and the Transformation of Islamist Politics in Egypt

If the oil boom of the 1970s was a distinct era of abundance for the labor-exporting states of the region in terms of remittance inflows and financial assistance from Gulf States, the bust in oil revenues that deepened by 1985/86 resulted in a dramatic recessionary downturn that had important long-term consequences for domestic politics. After 1986, in particular, economic austerity measures and shrinkage in the size of the parallel market in terms of the volume of foreign currency transactions reconfigured informal economic and social arrangements in profound albeit different ways in Egypt, Sudan, and Somalia. In all three countries, as the financial and political power of groups engaged in the informal economy rose, state elites struck back – almost at the same time. Only in Egypt was this effort partially successful.

In the case of Egypt, the boom period, lasting from 1975 to 1985, afforded the state extraordinary access to foreign exchange as a result of oil exports, Suez Canal receipts, tourism, and expatriate remittances. These "big four" provided the country 75 percent of its hard currency, and all these sources were linked to the price of oil since expatriate workers mostly worked in the Gulf. Moreover, upward of 50 percent of tourists were from the oil-rich Arab countries, and much of the trade through the Suez Canal consisted of oil shipments (or Western goods) headed to the Gulf countries.[1] Consequently, when the oil price fell in 1985/86 the country suffered a drastic and steady decline in revenue from remittances through the 2000s as well as the other main sources of revenue affecting the entire economy adversely. GDP fell from 7.4 percent in 1984/85 to 4.2 percent in 1986/87 and to as low as 2.1 percent by 1990/91 (see Figure 4.1).[2] Coupled with a soaring external debt the regime was forced to turn to the multilateral lending institution, the International Monetary Fund (IMF), for debt relief and to implement further economic reforms that included the unification of exchange rates, trade liberalization, and to limit imports.[3]

Throughout the 1990s low oil prices resulted in a consistent and dramatic decline in rents flowing into state coffers from oil exports, foreign aid, and Suez Canal fees. Oil revenues declined from 11 percent

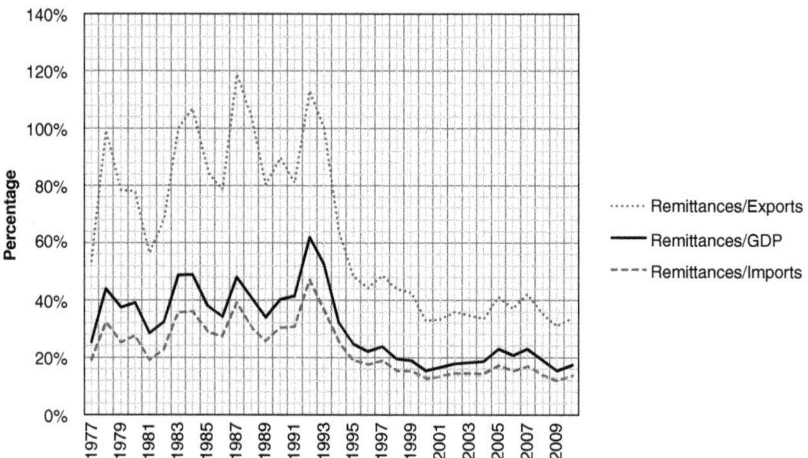


Figure 4.1 Remittances as a proportion of exports/GDP/imports in Egypt
*Source*: World Bank, World Development Indicators (World Bank, Washington, DC). https://datacatalog.worldbank.org/dataset/world-development-indicators.

of total revenues in 1990 to just 2 percent in 2000, and whereas they represented almost 50 percent of total exports in the 1980–2005 period, after the 1986 glut, international crude oil prices did not exceed the 1982 level ($31.55) until 2004 ($37.41), hitting a historical low in 1998 ($11.9).[4] This decline in external rents in the 1990s took its toll on state revenues and total exports which declined roughly from 30 percent in 1990 to 20 percent in 2004. As late as 2008/09, the ratio of revenues to GDP had not surpassed that of the early 1990s.[5]

The post-1986 period accented problems that had already emerged in the 1970s during the remittance boom and the early years of *infitah*. By the early 1980s, under Mubarak, economists generally recognized that infitah had favored the trade and finance sectors of the economy and encouraged the expansion of the black market (i.e., foreign exchange speculative dealings) and that, ultimately, the regime was compelled to implement economic reforms. But it is also clear that these reform measures also sought to curb the power of what the regime considered an Islamist economic and political threat. Consequently, in 1991 the Egyptian government liberalized the exchange rate in order to discourage foreign currency speculation in the black market and redirect labor remittances into formal institutions and away from parallel market transactions. As intended, financial liberalization – coupled with new regulatory measures – undercut the short-lived Islamist monopolization of informal finance.[6] However, rather than eliminate informal economic activities altogether, these policies only altered the social composition of the important segment of the informal economy and in so doing, the organizational structure, material incentives, and normative orientation of both the moderate and Islamist trends of the Islamist movement in the country.

It is important to emphasize that in contrast to other labor exporters with weaker state capacities (e.g., Sudan and Somalia) the regime in Egypt did not forfeit all its autonomy over the economy and it maintained great control over the degree and pace of economic reforms. Moreover, as many scholars have noted, its geopolitical position against radicalism and its peace agreement with Israel won the country generous debt relief throughout the recession period. Nevertheless, the general thrust was to free the local market from state intervention and not surprisingly this had important social and political consequences. Naturally, the recession affected all segments of society and particularly public sector workers whose salaries went into steep decline. But two important segments of society were also affected in ways that had important consequences for Islamist politics in the country: the middle-class Muslim Brotherhood movement and a poorer segment of Egyptian society working in the hitherto booming informal building trade such as those in the poorer quarters of Imbaba discussed in Chapter 7.

## Back to the Future

The violent crackdown by the regime of Abdel Fattah al-Sisi, which overthrew the government of the Muslim Brotherhood's elected Prime Minister Mohamed Mursi in July 2013, is unprecedented in terms of the scale of violence used against opposition groups and individuals. Between July 2013 and May 2014, less than a year after Sisi assumed power, an estimated 40,000 individuals had been arrested, more than 100 members of the Muslim Brotherhood sentenced to death, and both secular as well as Islamist groups banned, including the April 6 youth-led organization that spearheaded the historic Tahrir uprisings of January 25, 2011. However, it is important to note that the state's confrontation with the Islamists dates back to the 1990s and that the ongoing Islamist insurgencies across Cairo and in northern Sinai, which began in earnest in September 2013 against the military and security forces of the Sisi regime, have been routinely and understandably compared to the confrontation between the Egyptian State and the *Jama'a al-Islamiyya* (the Islamic Group) militant group in the 1990s in the neighborhood of Imbaba.[7] Indeed, the 1990s were a watershed in the relationship between the state and the moderate as well as the militant wings of the Islamist movement with important consequences for the present.

In December 1992 the Egyptian state entered the informal housing sections of Imbaba in Cairo. As many as 16,000 paramilitary troops, led by 2,000 military officers, state security personnel, and local police joined forces in the largest campaign against Islamist militancy in Cairo since the assassination of President Anwar Sadat in October 1981. Over the course of one week, 1,700 people were imprisoned, local residents arbitrarily arrested and tortured, and a small number killed. For several days, residents of Imbaba were prevented from leaving their homes for work, and all commercial activity in the neighborhood was prohibited. In addition, security forces forcibly shut down a number of storefront (*ahali*) mosques in the neighborhood. These mosques had served as important institutions through which Islamists activists belonging to the Islamic Group (*al-Jama'a al-Islamiyya*) had mobilized their supporters and rank and file cadres. Among the mosques closed down by security forces were *Masjid Said al-Mursileen*, *Masjid al-Nasr*, and *Masjid al-Rahman*.[8] All three mosques served as important meeting places for the supporters of the Islamists, and it was from their pulpits that Islamist preachers spread their message to local residents.

As Diane Singerman has noted, the reason behind the unprecedented crackdown was the increasing power and popularity of the *Jama'a al-Islamiyya*.[9] To many in Cairo the ascendancy of the Islamic Group at the heart of the city was a surprising development since the bulk of radical political violence during the 1980s was largely confined to the rural and less-developed provinces of Upper Egypt. It was in Upper Egypt that clashes between militants and security forces had left more than 900 dead and tens of thousands of Islamist militants in jail by the late 1980s.[10] But it now appeared that, for several years, members of the Islamic Group had slowly filled the vacuum left by the state's neglect of the Western Munira sections of Imbaba. By the mid-1990s militants in these quarters had become active in providing food to the poor, running health clinics, mediating disputes, collecting taxes, and reinstating a severe form of "law and order" among local residents.

The direct catalyst of the siege was the convening of a press conference by the *Jama'a* in Imbaba in late 1992. At that time Sheikh Jabir Mohammed Ali, the leader of the Islamic Group in the Neighborhood, invited foreign journalists to "celebrate" the anniversary of Sadat's assassination.[11] Sheikh Jabir, commonly referred to as the "ruler of the State of Imbaba" (*hakim dawlat Imbaba*), used this opportunity to announce the establishment of an independent state within a state, the Emirate of Imbaba.[12]

At the same time the regime also broadened its repression of the Muslim Brotherhood by cracking down on what Egyptians commonly refer to as *al-Iqtisaad al-Ikhwani* (the Brotherhood Economy). Beginning in 1991 the Mubarak regime targeted informal financial networks and institutions it perceived to pose a direct economic and political threat to its authoritarian rule. The regime imprisoned and put on trial prominent black-market traders, liberalized the financial sector to undercut the parallel economy, and began to strongly regulate informal welfare institutions in a process that lasted into the latter part of the Mubarak regime and has continued with even greater force under the present regime of Abdel Fattah al-Sisi. In 2007 and again in 2009 the Mubarak regime went further in its campaign of attacking the Brotherhood's business interests. Its military court detained and put on trial two prominent members of the Muslim Brotherhood: Khairat al-Shater and Hassan Malik.[13] The two men stood accused of economic treason against the state and engaging in money laundering and "illicit" commercial activities. In April 2008, the military court dismissed the money-laundering charges. Nevertheless, in what the popular press termed a game of *al-Ker wa al-Fer* ("hit and run"), on April 15, 2008, the military court dismissed money-laundering charges against those arrested, acquitted fifteen, and reduced the prison sentences of the remaining defendants but confiscated the assets of the most prominent Brotherhood businessmen. These included substantial capital investments in a wide range of enterprises including pharmaceuticals, tourism agencies, construction firms, educational institutions, publishing houses,[14] and land reclamation companies.[15]

Consequently, while in its relationship with the Brotherhood the regime continued its policy of strategic cooptation (most notably, permitting the organization a small measure of representation in parliament), it nevertheless marshaled its economic coercive power to regulate and undermine the movement's financial assets built during the boom years. In this regard, what made the arrest of Malik and al-Shater a subject of national debate was that they are known to be the two most prominent Brotherhood businessmen. Al-Shater the then former deputy head of the Muslim Brotherhood, and Hassan Malik, his long-time business associate, had long been significant funders of the Islamist movement in Egypt during *'ahd tajmee' al-tharwat* (the era of wealth accumulation).

In the 1970s and 1980s they were primarily responsible for institutionalizing two important aspects of the Muslim Brotherhood's commercial network: They established a host of successful business enterprises in domestic markets, and they also established links with other Islamists abroad in ways that capitalized on the transnationalization of Islamist commercial networks and investments in global stock markets, particularly in the Arab Gulf and the United States. Moreover, Khairat al-Shater gained further prominence following the fall of Hosni Mubarak's regime. He was released from detention just one month after the toppling of Mubrak's regime by the Tahrir uprising, and he quickly resumed his post as deputy to the Muslim Brotherhood Supreme Guide, Mohammed Badi. However, along with scores of other Muslim Brotherhood leaders, al-Shater was arrested on July 25, 2013, and subsequently sentenced to life imprisonment by a military court following Sisi's military coup against the Brotherhood-led government of Mohamed Mursi.

The successive arrests of al-Shater under the rule of Hosni Mubarak and again under the regime of Abdel Fatah al-Sisi reflect an enduring strategy aimed toward undermining the institutional and financial administrative capacity of the Brotherhood: a capacity that had in previous decades financed the salaries of the organization's employees and cadres, supported Islamist candidates during electoral campaigns in the country, and provided material incentives to new members to the organization.

## The Battle over Informal Finance and Islamic Banks

Two important facets of the Islamic Economy that grew out of the boom period and which benefited from state patronage saw their fortunes come to an end in the 1990s in great part as a result of increasing state regulation and an assault on Islamic economic institutions: the black-market trade responsible for the growth of the unregulated Islamic Investment Companies (IICs) and Islamic banks. In 1988 the Mubarak regime intervened to regulate the IICs. On June 7, 1998, the People's Assembly pushed through Law No. 146 that limited the right to collect capital to joint stock companies and gave wider powers to the Capital Market Authority (*hay'at suq al-mal*) and the Central Auditing Agency (*al-jihaz al-markazi lil-muhasabat*) to regulate and shut down the IICs. Most significantly, the Capital Market Authority was given the right to refuse or revoke existing licensing of any IIC based on a report from the Minister of Interior indicating that its activity was a threat to "national security" or "public (*'amm*) economic interest."[16]

It is important to note that prominent Islamists altered their attitudes toward the IICs and become more critical in the context of the state's attack against these unregulated investment houses.[17] However, the IICs also generated significant investment from members of the Muslim Brothers as well as large sections of Egyptian society during their heyday.

One member of the Muslim Brothers, Ahmed 'Alawi, informed me that like many members of the brotherhood at the time he was strongly in favor of the economic reforms that made the IICs possible for a time and that he, along with other members of the *Ikwhan*, heavily invested in the IICs. He acknowledged that the Muslim Brothers did in fact support these institutions and that they received funding for their organization from them. He noted that al-Rayan in particular helped to finance the movement at the time. As he put it: "*al-Sharikat* were an example of how the state could not control the 'freedom' unleashed by *Infitah*."[18] Nevertheless, while 'Alawi continued to defend the *sharikat* in principle, he acknowledged somewhat bitterly that their leaders suffered from greed. "In the early years they offered depositors 24 percent return from their investment, but by the time they were shut down by the state, this had reached 30 to 40 percent."

Importantly, 'Alawi noted a trend that obtained across the labor exporting countries in the region during the remittance boom. That is, that Egyptian migrants irrespective of whether they harbored sympathies for the Muslim Brotherhood deposited part of their wages in the *sharikat* not, in his view, because they trusted in the Islamic credentials and legitimacy of these financial institutions, but rather because expatriates had little choice owing to high rates of inflation that resulted from the boom in the influx of remittances in the 1980s. Migrants found depositing their hard currency in what were hitherto informal financial institutions more profitable than in the heavily regulated formal banks. This is because, as 'Alawi observed in Imbaba where he resides as elsewhere, when "land prices shot up as a result of migrant money, so did the price of residential apartments. People had to put money into the *sharikat* so as to make their money meet the 'real' [i.e. inflationary] prices of real estate."[19] To be sure, and particularly in the early years of the *sharikat's* establishment, many Egyptians were also encouraged to invest in the *sharikat* out of trust in the religiously garbed and seemingly pious financiers that operated them. The leaders of these companies were careful to patronize public prayers and donate to mosques and Islamic Welfare Associations (IWAs).

The experiment of the IICs was a dramatic and amply documented financial scandal in Egypt. By the late 1980s depositors and the general public became aware that the IICs operated on the basis of a pyramid scheme that swindled thousands of depositors from their hard-won earnings. For its part, the regime's attack against the IICs had more to do with state's fear of a parallel economy in finance that posed a grave economic and political threat to its authority over society. The IICs posed two essential dangers to the regime: the erosion of state capacity in the economic, and particularly financial, sphere and the resurgence and rising power of new economic actors in civil society operating outside the purview of the state. Moreover, irrespective of who benefited most from the profits of the IICs at the time, in the context of economic reform, and since these companies attracted savings ostensibly based on Islamic principles, they came to represent what the economist Abdel Fadil famously noted as "a force that would possibly splinter the dominance of the state over the society."[20] Moreover, when the IICs crashed in the late 1980s they had an important political consequence since their fall discredited all economic projects working under the banner of Islam.

In contrast to the Islamic Investment Houses, the threat to the regime of the Islamic banks was relatively modest. This was primarily due to the strength of the state over the Islamic banking experiment: a state of affairs that stood in stark contrast to the Islamic banks in neighboring Sudan (see Chapter 5). To be sure, as in other Muslim countries, the spread of Islamic banking in Egypt raised the political profile of the Islamist movement in symbolic terms, but from the beginning the regime made sure that these banks would not come to be dominated by the Muslim Brotherhood. In contrast to Sudan, Islamic banking in Egypt has not been the monopoly of the Islamist movement primarily owing to the Egyptian regime's stronger capacity to both regulate the financial sector and exert political, and coercive influence over groups in civil society. More specifically, in the 1980s state security forces intervened repeatedly to expel Muslim Brothers from the banks' board of directors. In addition, in order to ensure that those Islamic banks established by influential Brotherhood leaders did not attract more deposits than the public sector banks, the regime enlisted the government appointed Mufti of al-Azhar's assistance in this objective. In the late 1980s and up to the late 1990s through the issuance of a series of *fatwas* (Islamic legal rulings) the Mufti conferred religious legitimacy on interest taken and dispensed by conventional banks.[21] Equally important is that the recession of the 1980s served to usher in the demise of the Islamic banking experiment in significant ways. An important reason for the decline in the influence of private Islamic banks is simply that the regime established Islamic branches of conventional banks throughout the country in a relatively successful effort to attract more savings. By 1996 Bank Misr, for example, had thirty Islamic branches, and by 1998 deposits in Islamic banks as a percentage of deposits in the conventional banks represented only 3.1 percent.[22]

Economic as well as political factors combined to herald the demise of Islamic banking in the country. In the mid-1980s, at the start of the recession, and up to 1993 the growth rate in the deposits of Islamic banks began to decline dramatically. This was clear in terms of the shrinkage of Egyptian savings kept in Islamic banks, which represented

4.8 percent in 1994 down from 9.8 percent in 1986.[23] One important reason had to do with the decline in remittance inflows associated with the oil slump in the Arab oil-producing countries where thousands of Egyptians had made their living. However, it is important to note that as in Sudan the crisis of Islamic banking can be explained by political factors, and internal mismanagement as well as the decline in deposits of remittances in the recession. Another key decisive factor had to do with the fact that the Islamic banks' share of total deposits plummeted because the rate of return to depositors awarded by these banks was below the interest rates of the conventional banks. This was a result of successive devaluations of the national currency resulting from financial liberalization and the fact that the regime maintained higher rates of interest in its public sector banks in order to, in the elegant formulation of Soliman, "make the price of conformity with Islamic law high and the temptation toward 'sin' of receiving interest stronger."[24] What is noteworthy about the state's role in Islamic banking is that, in contrast to Sudan where these financial institutions came to represent a powerful political and economic force in civil society propelling the Islamist movement to power, in Egypt the state retained great capacity to regulate and curtail the strength of the power of the Muslim Brotherhood in these banks and to undermine their autonomy and popularity in terms of attracting depositors.

Importantly, the assumption to power of the Muslim Brotherhood and the election of President Mohamed Mursi reignited the deep political and economic conflict over the role of Islamic banking as a central pillar of contestation with profound political consequences pitting Islamists versus remnants of the Mubarak regime and, more recently, those supportive of the military regime of Abdel-Fatah al-Sisi. Indeed, almost immediately following Egypt's historic parliamentary elections of November 2011, the Brotherhood's Freedom and Justice Party (JFP) began drafting a series of laws that would modify the role of the Central Bank of Egypt (CBE) and regulate the offering of Islamic financial services across the entire sector. Moreover, by making the registration of Islamic banks easier, the proposed regulations were primarily designed to achieve a long-standing objective of Brotherhood leaders of increasing the market share of Islamic banks vis-à-vis the traditional or conventional banks.

Indeed, what is noteworthy is that these legislative proposals sought to reverse the policies of the Mubarak regime that strongly regulated Islamic banking after the latter's strong growth in the oil boom years. Specifically, they called for Shari'a boards (*Lijan al-Shari'a*) to monitor compliance with Islamic law,[25] the strengthening of Islamic *sukuk* law that governs the issuing of bonds, and the creation of an Islamic banking department at the Central Bank that would regulate the sector.

President Mohamed Mursi and representatives of his party argued that these regulations would make the banking sector more competitive and attract a huge volume of capital inflows from the global Islamic economy estimated in 2012 at more than a trillion US dollars. Mohammed Gouda, a member of the FJP's committee on the economy, predicted that with these new modifications to the Central Bank law the Islamic financial sector would grow from 7.5 percent to 35 percent of the total banking industry over a five-year period. This optimistic target was based on two key assumptions on the part of the Brotherhood: the fact that Egypt, with its predominantly conservative Muslim population of around 90 million, represents an untapped demand for Islamic financial services and that the Brotherhood's long-standing transnational financial linkages represent a strong demand for Islamic banking and source of capital inflows, especially from the Gulf states. As Gouda put it: "They [Arabs in the Gulf] would like to invest here but prefer to do it through Islamic or Shari'a-compliant banks."[26]

However, opponents of these measures insisted that rather than liberalizing the banking sector and enhancing the autonomy of the CBE, these measures were aimed primarily at strengthening the economic and political clout of the Muslim Brotherhood affording them distinct advantage over the money supply in the country. Three important provisions of the draft law presented by JFP delegates to the economic committee of *Majlis al-Sha'ab* (Popular Council) in June 2012 sparked these fears. These included articles 1 and 2 which proposed that the governor of the CBE and his deputy be granted immunity from dismissal by the CBE's Board of Governors and granted authority to the Islamic banks to generate capital from individuals and private and external sources without having to acquire permission from the Ministry of Finance. More controversial, from the point of view of opponents of the draft law, were articles 137 and 138.[27] These articles compelled the CBE to appoint three experts on Shari'a, to be appointed by the prime minister, and charged with overseeing and monitoring all financial operations of the Islamic and conventional banks in order to ensure transactions, investments, and lending policies do not contradict Islamic law. Furthermore, the members of this Shari'a board were entrusted with developing new rules and regulations that would introduce binding guidelines having to do with the appointment of managerial staff of CBE as well as the Islamic and conventional banks.

The perception that Brotherhood leaders were intent on the Islamicization of the financial sector increased on December 8, 2012, when Mursi issued a modification of two important articles governing the Central Bank. Taken together these new regulations granted Mursi more political and administrative authority over the most important financial institution in the country. The modifications reduced the number of board members from 12 to 6 and awarded the president the right to unilaterally nominate the CBE governor without the usual recommendations and oversight from the cabinet. These legislative measures were never implemented as a consequence of the removal of Mursi and the JFP from power by the military, but they would have meant a dramatic departure for an industry that had been carefully regulated under the regime of Hosni Mubarak.[28] Indeed, the debate over the draft law regulating the Central bank reignited the bitter conflict over Islamic banking, which is an enduring legacy of the Mubarak regime, pitting Islamists leaders and activists against their opponents in the military establishment as well as in civil society.

## Confronting the Authoritarian State from Below: The Politics of Patronage in a "Weakened" State

The fiscal crisis of the state and the Mubarak regime's efforts to contain the Islamist "threat" in combination with the increasing bureaucratic and legal regulation of what where previously largely informal financial and welfare institutions dramatically altered the strategies and tactics of the middle-class-based movement of the Muslim Brotherhood. Indeed, while in the 1970s and 1980s the Muslim Brotherhood enjoyed great success in mobilizing thousands to their cause as a result of both financial success and greater political opportunity, in the 1990s and 2000s they faced severe political as well as economic restrictions, which were keenly felt at the local level.

But while the Mubarak regime managed to deepen its authoritarian rule in what is commonly called the era of political de-liberalization (i.e., imposing political restrictions in the context of political liberalization) it showed little interest and ultimately enjoyed far weaker capacity and legitimacy in forging patron-client linkages with communities residing in the vast informal settlements of greater Cairo. The 1992 uprising in Western Munira was certainly an important factor in the state's increasing, albeit minimal, involvement in Imbaba, but the starting point of the government's efforts to forge clientelistic linkages with local leaders originated in the rise in popularity of opposition parties in local elections.

Since the early 1970s, Imbaba was a district where the ruling National Party (NP) always won in all of the government-run elections. However, in 1984 the opposition obtained seats in parliament, which local NP officials saw as a "dangerous trend" and one that increased in the elections of 1987 and in the early 1990s. As a local National Party official in Imbaba informed me, the increasing competition between political parties motivated the National Party to focus on Imbaba, especially since some top opposition leaders were candidates in the area, which increased the level of competition and electoral campaigning.[29]

Moreover, at a time when the National Party was complacent about Imbaba since, as one of its official's noted, "the national party is not interested in any coordination [with other parties] because it has abundant resources,"[30] the opposition parties in Imbaba were engaging in an unprecedented level of coordination. In particular, candidates belonging to the Labor Party and the Brotherhood politicians coordinated closely in the 1995 elections across thirty-nine districts where each of the parties had one candidate, but in the other districts they agreed that the two parties would support an agreed-upon candidate running under the banner of the Labor Party. Interestingly, similar attempts to coordinate between the secular leftist Tagammu and Nasserist candidates, who were successful in other parts of Giza, failed in Imbaba.[31] This was primarily because they could not compete with the high level of coordination and popularity of the Islamist coalition in the area.

There were two primary reasons that Islamist enjoyed popularity among local residents in Imbaba, but it is important to note that, at the local level, this reflected socioeconomic and political factors far more than religious concerns.[32] First, Islamist leaders generated a great deal of legitimacy by signaling to residents a deep knowledge and sympathy with the local context and the social and economic crisis affecting Imbaba's residents. This was clearly evident both by their attempts to alleviate the unemployment problem and offer social services. However, in the context of the state's increasing restrictions on the *al-Iqtisaad al-Ikhwani* (the Brotherhood Economy) these services were minimal and so Islamist leaders also used a particular brand of discourse that resonated with the local community. The combination of material assistance and normative framing evidenced in the sermons was an important reason they were able to mobilize a great deal of support.

## All Politics Is Local: Mobilizing Islamist or Kinship Networks?

Most significantly, Islamist leaders, and those belonging to the Muslim Brothers in particular, were able to derive strong legitimacy through their involvement in local elections. This is illustrated by the nature of the candidates that competed in the 1995 elections in Imbaba. The candidates running included politicians from the ruling National Party, and the opposition Wafd, Tagammu, Nasserite, Labor, and Omma parties, with members of the Muslim Brotherhood running as independents. The most important candidates in the 1995 Imbaba elections included Abdel Hamid Barakat (Labor Party), Ismail Hilal (National Party), No'man Joma'a (Wafd), and the female candidate Fathiya 'Assal (Tagammu). Of these candidates only the pro–Islamist Labor candidate had the legitimacy that earned him great support. Hilal was accused in the context of the local campaign of corruption and inaction, and Joma'a was perceived as out of touch with Imbaba since he resided in the nearby upper-class neighborhood of Zamalak and branded as one of the "Al-Zamak riches" that, as one local newspaper noted, "knows nothing about Imbaba's problems."[33]

Similarly, while government newspapers and the well-funded campaign of the NP candidate, Ismail Hilal, went to great lengths to inform residents that he was an executive with the Ministry of Electricity and that his plan to install electricity in poor areas and fight illiteracy earned him their votes,[34] the NP's historical absence and seeming disinterest in providing even a modicum of social services in Imbaba did not resonate favorably with local residents.[35] But the primary problems with the NP candidates, clearly outlined in the opposition papers at the time, had to do with the corruption of the NP and the state's distance from the local problems facing Imbaba's residents. Al Wafd, for example, ran a number of stories accusing the Ministry of Interior of "modifying" the list of eligible voters, the privatization of municipal services, and the allocation of budget outlays to the district without any consultation with representatives of the local residents.[36] For her part, 'Assal's candidacy on the Tagammu' ticket was based, in her own words, on her awareness of the "poor conditions of Egyptian women, especially in Imbaba,"[37] but her campaign did not reflect a deep knowledge of the social and economic conditions of the population and as such her candidacy did not resonate with more conservative Muslim residents. Perhaps more importantly, 'Assal ran her campaign against Islamic "terrorism" thus further alienating supporters of both the Muslim Brothers and the Islamic Group in Imbaba.[38]

In contrast, an important reason that the Islamists running under the banner of the Labor Party at the time were more popular with Imbaba residents had to do with their social linkages with the local community and, more importantly, their candidate's understanding of its social makeup and concerns. Indeed, the relative success of the candidates depended on the extent to which their respective campaigns focused on primarily economic and social issues and on whether the candidates enjoyed familial and kinship connections in the district.[39] The Labor candidate in 1995, Abdel Hamid Barakat, ran a relatively more successful campaign in Imbaba because his campaign paid closer attention to the poorer quarters in Imbaba. In addition, the Labor Party's *al-Sha'ab* newspaper correctly pointed out that as someone from a rural and agricultural background, he had a great deal in common with the newly urbanized residents of the neighborhood. Specifically, the newspaper noted that he belonged to the Beni 'Adi clan in Manfalout, Assiut in Upper Egypt, and it reminded voters that he was the president of the Ben 'Adi Regional Association (*Rabita Iqlimiyya*) and further noted that security forces had banned his campaign appearances and prevented him from distributing campaign advertisements in their efforts to curtail Muslim (i.e., Islamist) candidates.[40]

Abdel Hamid Barakat's candidacy is illustrative of the reasons why Islamist candidates or those running on an Islamist platform continued to enjoy significant support in the neighborhood. In his campaign Barakat emphasized that he was running in Imbaba for a number of reasons all of which resonated deeply with local residents. First, it was because he is from Imbaba and it is where his parents moved to from Assiut. Second, his electoral platform included two important components. The notion that "Islam is the solution," and that he wanted to establish new laws and regulations in Imbaba. His campaign statements cited Imam Hassan al-Banna regarding the importance of working toward applying Islamic law on all matters and building an Islamic state in Egypt.

But Barakat's real legitimacy, as evidenced by the survey of voters in the neighborhood as well as my interviews with local residents,[41] had to do with his own social profile. In his campaign he focused on the fact that he was from the small village of Mafalout in Assiut, that he was a second-generation migrant to Imbaba like thousands of other families in Western Munira in Imbaba, and he openly acknowledged his involvement in the political branch of the Muslim Brothers as well as his position as secretary general of the Labor Party at the time. He declared often that education was the key solution for all troubles and that the problems associated with the lack of education in Imbaba resulted in other problems such as unemployment, "moral disease," and "fanaticism." Moreover, while the other candidates focused on the issue of "terrorism," promoted by the regime's official discourse, Barakat appealed to the simple, everyday concerns of local residents and what he termed creating a "new spirit in the citizen" based on the principles of self-reliance, and an appreciation of the importance of education, raising awareness of environment degradation, and encouraging donations among Muslims in order to encourage religiously sanctioned private initiatives.[42] In contrast, candidates running on the Tagammu ticket such as Fekri Taha Bedeir chose to appeal to larger national-level concerns which, for Imbaba's residents, appeared to be intangible ideas far removed from pressing and more immediate concerns associated with the problems of poverty, infrastructural development, employment, and education in Imbaba. More specifically, the latter stated that they were running in the elections in order to make a difference in changing laws in parliament and to provide services to Imbaba such as health, employment, and "serve the public through parliament."[43]

## Political Centralization and the Changing Strategy of the Muslim Brotherhood

At a time when much of the focus was on national-level politics and the contest between Islamist elites and the regime, the ramifications associated with the policies of state centralization were deeply felt at the local level. Moreover, they played an important role in altering the electoral strategy of Islamist activists at the municipal level as well as the very nature and the methods of recruitment. Importantly, by the late 1990s the most important constraint, which Brotherhood members in Imbaba cited, had to do with the increasing restrictions imposed by the Mubarak regime on political participation, which limited individual members' path toward social mobility and hence the organization's ability to expand its movement.

"Under Sadat," as one Brother in al-Waraq noted, "there were only four political parties, but there was more democracy during that time, more room to maneuver than under Hosni Mubarak although there are many more parties registered." Both leaders and rank and file members interviewed offered a critical appraisal of their activism in the 1980s and 1990s. According to Wagi Abdel-Raziq, "We did not take advantage of the events in 1977 (i.e. bread riots), and the 1981 crisis (i.e. Sadat's assassination). We should not have kept a low profile at that time. We were overly ambitious." Rather than the accommodationist stance that the organization's leadership assumed vis-à-vis the regime, members of the Brotherhood, citing the regimes suppression of the Brotherhood's political activity and its assault on the organization's commercial enterprises, openly voiced regret that they did not take advantage of instability to wage a more radical opposition to the regime when it was "at its weakest."[44] The rank and file members in particular openly criticized the general guide (*al-Murshid al-'Am*) Telmasani's historic decision to accommodate the movement's objectives and strategies to the state with the view toward garnering more representation in parliament.

According to Wagih Abdel-Raziq Abu-Rawash, a leading member of the Muslim Brotherhood branch in al-Waraq, Imbaba, the strategy of the organization in the 1990s changed as the movement came under more restrictions. "We tried to reform the system from the outside; now we are trying to reform it from the inside."[45]

This change in strategy was a direct result of the state's decision to alter the electoral system for elections to the People's Assembly (*Majlis al-Sha'ab*). Whereas in the past candidates belonging to the Muslim Brotherhood were allowed to form a coalition with small opposition parties such as the Labor Party (*Hizb al-Sha'ab*), the newly implemented winner takes all system essentially guaranteed that the ruling party would not only win the most seats but also that there would be a limited chance for independents to gain seats in the People's Assembly. In the older system, at least "we had a chance even if we were allocated five percent of the seats like we had when we allied with *Hizb al-Sha'ab* in the elections." Sayed Farouk Kamel, another brotherhood member complained that "at present if the Labor Party wins the majority of seats as they often did in the local council elections in Osim, Imbaba, the government simply cancels the elections – so there is no way to win except to infiltrate the ranks of the weak National Party."[46] Consequently, the organization attempted to get their members to join the ruling National Party and run for local elections with the view toward promoting members to run in elections at the level of the *Muhafaza* (governate) rather than at the national level for seats in the People's Assembly. "Our real objective," according to another Brotherhood member, "is to get our people at the Governate, not the National level," and the most effective way to do this was to recruit independents with no "past history" of activism within the Muslim Brotherhood in order to evade state surveillance and corruption.

However, it is important to note that this strategy represented a tacit alliance among a large cross section of residents in Imbaba rather than a strict ideological and political divide. Indeed, members of the Muslim Brotherhood in Imbaba, as well as government-appointed local council leaders and supporters of the Tagammu Party, bitterly complained about the increasing lack of political participation and voice afforded their community. Indeed, just as Brotherhood members complained of government corruption insisting it was not Mubarak, who, in the words of one Brother, "is a nice guy," but rather his cronies Yusif Wali and Kamal al-Shadli, respectively, the deputy chairman of the ruling NDP and the minister of Parliamentary Affairs at the time, who were "running the country." Staff members of the local council in al-Waraq, Imbaba, also bitterly complained of the increasing authoritarianism of the regime. This is because in contrast to other more affluent neighborhoods wherein local council members have closer clientelistic linkages with the state, this is not the case in the poorer quarters of Imbaba.

Indeed, for both the Muslim Brotherhood, and particularly for the government-appointed local officials, the main problem was that, by the late 1990s and into the 2000s, state centralization reduced political participation and eroded previous informal clientelistic networks and linkages to such an extent that it prevented them from providing the type of services needed to their community. "I had a cousin," Farouk Kamel noted,

> who won a seat in *Majlis al-Sha'ab*, and he was able to use his *wasta* (connections) to help people – he was able to exert pressure to get funds from the government and build additional classrooms for our elementary and secondary school students, fund additional teachers, and even install fourteen additional electricity poles in al-Waraq. I was able to get funding for a new paved road after extensive lobbying to the Local Council of the Governante [but] it is a continuous battle." He continued, "the social affairs unit [the governmental welfare association] is closed, and so is *Mirkaz al-Shabbaab* (Youth Center) in al-Waraq, because of the bureaucracy and simply lack of interest on the part of the government. At this point our budget relies on local members who donate much of our money; acquiring official [government] funds for our work is a very laborious process.[47]

Not surprisingly political centralization resulted in an increasingly confrontational stance on the part of the Brotherhood vis-à-vis those institutions of the state that had the greatest impact at the local level. In my interviews with leaders and rank and file members of the Muslim Brothers in Imbaba, and particularly in al-Waraq where the Brothers enjoy support to this day, *Ikhwan* members cited a number of elements associated with political as well as social issues as reasons for joining and remaining loyal to the organization. These include the promise of upward mobility, grievances having to do with the long repressive arm of the state, restrictions on political participation, and genuine anger against the corruption at the level of local government. Naturally, as the Tahrir uprising demonstrated, this anger resonated among much of the population but it is also true that responses vary. The anger on the part of the Brother's leadership, however, is genuinely vitriolic. As one Brother said of the governor of Giza, the primary official authority over communities in Imbaba, "he is a son of a Dog." He also harshly criticized the deputy chairman of the National Democratic Party and the Ministry of Parliament under Mubarak, which he noted act as "watchdogs" in the local elections.[48]

## The Islamists and *Fariq Al-Kura* (the Soccer Club)

This profound disillusionment with politics on the part of the Brotherhood represented both a constraint and opportunity for the organization at the local level. On the one hand, the coercive arm of the regime constrained the organization's efforts at mobilization requiring a change of strategy and vision. On the other, the ruling party's persistent authoritarianism and corruption ensured that Islamist activists continued to enjoy significant popularity, particularly in the middle- and lower middle-class quarters such as al-Waraq, Imbaba. Indeed, if the political and social ambitions of the Brotherhood were increasingly undermined by a newer, more restrictive political arena generating deep anger against the regime and a new strategy among local activists in neighborhoods such as Imbaba, state repression and surveillance of the Islamist movement also altered the strategy of recruitment of new members.

More specifically, the methods of recruitment built on trust networks composed of close relatives, friends and neighbors that were so successful in the 1970s and 1980s (Chapter 1) were greatly undermined by state intervention. According to leading Brotherhood members in al-Waraq, a number of key constraints limited efforts at recruitment. Most notable was the lack of education and high rates of literacy in Imbaba generally, and the persistent divisive policies on the part of the representatives of the NDP in the area. "We cannot," as one Brother put it, "count on the support of family members or even friends since they [the NDP] intervenes and gives money to your cousin or brother to turn against each other." Indeed, by the late 1990s, the state's curtailment of the Brotherhood's was so severe that members of the Muslim Brotherhood took to calling their organization our "soccer club" (*Fareeq al-Kura*) rather than our "movement" (*Haraka*) in public conversations and in locations in Imbaba and other neighborhoods such as Matariyya where the Brothers enjoyed significant support from local residents and where informants and security forces were ubiquitous.

> We are like a football team but a small one, like Arsenal. [For example] I support the Tersani club instead of the Al-Ahly club. This is because it is best to support a small team that is very selective in terms of its membership, one that is more lethal, more effective.

## The Political Economy of Middle-Class Islamist Activism and Recruitment

As with social movements more generally, the Brotherhood's recruitment process involves two essential challenges: motivating participation by offering the type of incentives that are likely to induce individuals to join and attempting to attract the right kind of recruit to the organization. But if, for the Muslim Brotherhood, the 1980s and much of the 1990s was *al-ahd al-thahabi* (the golden age)of recruitment and popular mobilization, by the late 2000s when I returned to conduct further research, local members of the movement explained that this "Golden Age" ended due to a number of developments that obtained in the latter part of Mubarak's regime. These included the imposition of state laws restricting union organization and activity for professional syndicates, the prohibitions of freely run student elections, the regulation of the mosques of Ansar al-Fiqh, the closure of the Brotherhood's Mosques or their replacement by the state-sponsored mosques. Moreover, in a development that prefigured the seemingly surprising popularity of Salafists in the aftermath of the Tahrir uprisings, the Mubarak regime promoted the rise of Islamist groups in order to diminish the popularity and threat posed by the Brotherhood. "The state," as one Brotherhood leader explained bitterly, "has taken to closing our Mosques, putting others under al-Azhar's jurisdiction, and they have established other Salafi Mosques to moderate the Islamists and provide competition between us."[49]

However, a key factor the *Ikwhan* noted is the persistent war against the "Islamic economy" of the country which targeted the financial base of the movement. They suggested that a profound blow in this campaign was the trial in April 2008 against two of the movements' most important businessmen and financiers. Taken together these developments led to serious divisions among members of the Brotherhood, and most notably, between the younger and older generation. However, this conflict does not seem to stem from major doctrinal differences. In fact, few of the younger generation of the Islamists I interviewed expressed a radical departure from the *Ikwhan*'s doctrinal orthodoxy. However, what this intergenerational tension does demonstrate is a genuine disillusionment on the part of members, and a potential pool of recruits, with the inner workings and organizational structure of the Brotherhood. In addition, younger members speak openly about the movement's increasing inability to adequately address their social and political grievances and aspirations. How deep and consequential these intergenerational divisions are was demonstrated following the January 25th Tahrir uprisings. Only a few months after the establishment of the Muslim Brotherhood's Freedom and Justice Party (FJP) the organization not only witnessed major splits in its leadership, the party dismissed many young members who had played a role during the uprisings and who subsequently formed a new party: the Egyptian current.[50]

This factor is clearly evident in the crisis over recruitment that emerged in the years prior to the ouster of Mubarak by the Tahrir uprising. By the late 2000s the Muslim Brotherhood had to shorten the lengthy *taribiyya* (recruitment) process from seven to five stages in order to meet these challenges and make it less arduous for potential recruits to join the organization, albeit at the cost of risking lower levels of commitment and loyalty to the organization. Leaders of the Brotherhood such as ‘Issam al-‘Eryan, the official spokesperson of the Brotherhood (who was imprisoned and sentenced to a life sentence by the regime of Abdel Fatah al-Sisi) cited state repression as the primary culprit and argued that this curtailed the recruitment of laborers and the poor, limited dissemination of the *Da'wa* via the Ahali mosques, and restricted their capacity to provide social welfare services.[51] No doubt, this is one reason why the Brotherhood organization began to lose recruits to other *Da'was* by the late 2000s. Their leadership at the local level resorted to rural recruitment for the first time, forming short-lived coalitions with leftists and liberals at the grassroots level and even attempting to work with Sufi-run mosques. In what at the time was an unprecedented effort, Brotherhood leaders also attempted to make inroads in government mosques in order to seek out potential recruits. “We know,” one *Ikhwan* recruiter in Helwan said, “that we have to focus on the Mosque itself rather than the individual Imam or the content of the *khutbah* [sermon] in these government Mosques.” The heightened level of state repression and the regulation and monitoring of Ahali mosques led to adaptation signaling a relatively new crisis in recruitment for the country's Islamist movement that did not obtain during the boom's “Golden Age.”

But while the role of the state is an important factor in this crisis for the organization, it is also clear that larger economic as well as political changes circumscribed and altered the recruitment process of the Muslim Brotherhood in Egypt. While the state continued its repression of key members of the organization, equally important was the state's role in attacking the financial assets of the movement, a policy that has continued under the present regime of Abdel Fatah Sisi. Moreover, the changing political economy associated with the rise of the service and financial sectors, and deindustrialization meant that the Brotherhood no longer concentrated its recruitment drives on semi-skilled workers where previously professional syndicates were the locus of recruitment. Political repression has led to decentralization of welfare provisions, and Ahali mosques are often driven underground where *zawyas* are now the place where the Muslim Brotherhood attempts to disseminate their message to members. Nevertheless, in informal settlements in Imbaba, Ahali mosques are still prevalent in these largely “ungoverned” areas of greater Cairo wherein one finds a paucity of law and order and educational institutions, a high number and expansion in unregulated housing and informal rather than formal workers in greater numbers. Students – once the central constituency of the *Ikhwan* – now join nonpoliticized *salafi* organizations or charismatic evangelists.[52] One leader of the *Ikhwan* in

Helwan explained the nature of these dynamics of recruitment and mobilization in terms of two important developments: a change of focus *with respect to* the social profile of new entrants to the Brotherhood, and the impact on the organization of new competing *Da'was* and organizations:

> It is easier to recruit from the middle class (*hirfiyiin*) without higher degrees. They are real *regaal* (strongmen), who do not equivocate. They see things in black and white; non-Islamic entertainment and other things easily seduce educated university students. Recently, we organized a protest about Gaza, which was not well attended at all. The University of Helwan and the University of Cairo, hastily organized music festivals at the same time and this drew more students than our protests.[53]

It is important to note that leaders of the Muslim Brotherhood at both the national and local levels have long harbored contradictory perspectives on the role of material incentives in particular, and changes in the larger political economy generally, in inducing men and women to join their movement. On the one hand, leaders and rank and file members of the Brotherhood in Imbaba repeatedly emphasized that economic issues associated with poverty or social inequality had little to do with why young men and women joined the Brotherhood. "Egyptians," one prominent leader of the Brotherhood in al-Waraq insisted, are not "mobilized" by class rhetoric and "you can see rich and poor side by side with no conflict between them. This was never an important element in drawing new members." As he put it: "I mean I was aware of poverty, but it had little influence on me at the time I joined the *Ikhwan*."[54] Moreover, from the point of view of prominent leaders of the Muslim Brotherhood, economic reforms introduced by Sadat's open-door policy and the imposition of further neo-liberal policies under Mubarak did not influence the Islamist movement since, as Abdel-Hamid al-Ghazali, a scholar of economics and economic advisor to the general guide of the movement observed, it "has been very slow to have any concrete effect." In any case, "most Egyptians," he noted, "have become used to working in informal activities or moon lighting to supplement their incomes, or even relying on *rashwa* (bribes), rather than relying on the state for anything."[55]

On the other hand, local leaders of the *Ikhwan* in the quarter of Al-Waraq in Imbaba and in the working-class neighborhood of Helwan interviewed acknowledged that the persistent war against *al-iqtisad al-Islami* (Islamic economy) of the country, which has targeted the financial base of the movement, in combination with the state centralization policies of the "ruling gang" (*al-'isaba al-hakma*), compelled the organization to alter its electoral strategy and methods of recruitment and mobilization.[56] According to Wagih Abdel-Raziq Abu-Rawash, in the

1970s both economic and political opportunities expanded the base and popularity of the Muslim Brotherhood. "During the Sadat era we were let out of prison, while thousands of others went to the Gulf. They came back from the Arab countries after Sadat's death and ran in the 1983 general elections with great financial backing. They financed their run in 1983 with the help of rich businessman and voluntary contributions spanning a large network. They also encountered other Brothers while they were in the Gulf establishing businesses and raising money in the 1960s and 1970s for the movement. They [also] established networks to help others in Egypt travel to the Gulf were many became wealthy."[57]

Indeed, the opportunity of upward social mobility in particular during the boom years played a central role in the popularity of the movement. Following his time in prison, for example, one Brotherhood leader bitterly noted that he lost "most of his life" and was never able to make money and pursue a successful career and that he could only afford to get married late in his life in his forties. This social frustration associated with the increasing constraints on economic and political aspirations is shared widely among the rank and file members of the Brotherhood. Significantly, a number of *Ikhwan* not only criticized the socialist and the, often, violent anti-Brotherhood policies of Nasser's regime, but also the paternalistic, albeit not necessarily patriarchal, nature of Egyptian society. Many leveled a sharp critique against their fathers for "putting limitations" on their ambitions. While the "sons of most families join traditional political parties or follow in their father's line," another Brother stated, "we want political independence." Indeed, for many Brothers it was politics and not anti-state forms of activism that served as a primary avenue of upward mobility and career success. The grave disappointment shared by leaders and rank and file alike by the late 1990s and 2000s is that in the 1980s, many *Ikhwan* prospered in the context of the openness of the Sadat regime and in the early years of Mubarak. When one younger member confessed that he preferred to "stay out of politics," a senior Brother quickly but gently reprimanded him and reminded him that he could do both simultaneously. That is, "pursue politics and still make a good living."[58]

Nevertheless, in the years immediately prior to the ouster of Hosni Mubarak it was evident that an unspoken class conflict had emerged within the Muslim Brotherhood. In great part this was driven by the attack on Islamic business and finance, compounded by generational divisions and schisms represented by youth openly critical of the leadership's authoritarian organizational structure; the lack of transparency with respect to the manner in which Islamist candidates chosen to run in local elections are selected; the persistent discrimination against women in decision-making positions; the leadership's short-lived cooperation with the Mubarak regime in the period before the Tahrir uprisings;[59] and the militant and markedly divisive statements promulgated by the *Wahhabist* wing of the Brothers.[60] Consequently, Brotherhood leaders acknowledged, albeit privately, the limitations they encounter in terms of recruitment based on a number of criteria. These include arguably subjective criteria such as the psychological, emotional, and professional attributes of the individual as well as more objective ones based on the middle-class nature of the movement, the generational divide and social distance between the leadership and the rank and file, the restrictions delimited by continuing government repression, and the drying up of funds for their social welfare programs and commercial enterprises, which was once an important source of financing and recruitment of the middle-ranking cadres of the movement.

## Moderates versus Militants and Sufis

In the 1990s and 2000s, in great part as a result of a dramatic shift in the political economy following the recession, the Muslim Brotherhood witnessed an increasingly marked social and generational divide within what was a hitherto relatively cohesive movement. This period also saw a greater class as well as ideological divide emerge between the moderate and militant wings of the Islamist trend, which has continued to play a central role in contemporary Egyptian politics. Indeed, while Brotherhood members acknowledged that their movement joined with the more radical *Jama'at* (Groups) in the elections on the university campuses in Cairo and Upper Egypt in the 1980s, by the mid-1990s leaders in the Brotherhood openly cooperated with the Mubarak regime's policy, which at the time was aimed at subduing the threat from Islamist militants through a combination of political repression and a policy of dividing the Islamist opposition in the country.

Understandably, leaders in the Brotherhood repeatedly distinguished their movement from that of the radical Islamist activists in terms of what they insisted is a more moderate ideology and accommodationist stance vis-à-vis the state. But even as Brotherhood members minimized the role of economic and social issues in inducing young men and women to join Islamist organizations, they nevertheless described the division between moderate and radical Islamists in terms that highlighted the stark social distance between the two wings of the Islamist trend. Importantly, rather than emphasizing a "natural" and seamless doctrinal divide among the different Islamists, the *Ikwhan* most often pointed to a combination of emotional, psychological, and professional attributes to explain why individuals may join radical rather than moderate organizations. As one member of the Brothers explained: "The *Ikhwan* [Brothers] are more subtle than the *Takfiris*. We represent those with ambitions. A *Muslim Brother must have a profession to join the movement, the militants are the violent ones . . . they are those who failed in school and are often psychologically unbalanced*." Another leader, reflecting what remains a popular view of the *Jama'a al-Islamiyya* and other militant organizations, classified those who joined the group as "victims of their own innocence."[61]

Importantly, and similar to Sudan, for their part Sufi orders in Egypt have historically opposed both the Muslim Brotherhood and Salafist movements on political and ideational grounds. But in stark contrast to Sudan where they have long played a central role in political mobilization and pro-democracy mobilization, in Egypt Sufi orders have generally been subordinate to state authority or been used as instruments of political and economic control.[62] This was demonstrated again in the 2012 presidential election whereby the Sufis threw their complete support behind Mubarak's last prime minister, Ahmad Shafiq, and did not support candidates from any Islamic party.[63] Predictably, and owing in great part to a long history of co-optation by political authorities, the main Sufi party formed, following the Tahrir uprisings, *Hizb al-Masryiin al-Ahrar* (Free Egyptians Party), registered a poor showing in the 2012 elections.[64]

## Islamic Militancy and the "Satanic Settlements"

It is safe to say that the rise of Militancy in Imbaba shocked and perplexed middle-class Cairo as the state came to be threatened by a new, more radical, form of Islamist activism centered in the informal housing areas or spontaneous unplanned areas on the fringes of the City. Indeed, until the unprecedented Tahrir protests of 2011, the militant rebellion in Imbaba in 1992 was the most dramatic uprising in the capital. None of the major civil disorders in urban Cairo required the level of state emergency response or exacted such a toll in terms of life, injuries, and property damage and loss comparable to the Imbaba siege. The state-run media in particular was marshaled in an unprecedented fashion to cover what it termed the "satanic settlements" (*manatiq shaytaniyyah*).[65] Informal housing came to symbolize the problem of the existence and persistence of endemic forms of poverty, and by 1992, a fertile "breeding ground" for a new form of Islamist radicalism.[66] The fact that Cairo witnessed a rise in incidents of violence by militants in this period, coinciding with the phenomenal growth of informal settlements (or shanty towns) on the outskirt of the city, immediately led to speculation that these two developments were somehow linked.[67] However, given the great size, density of population, and social diversity of Cairo's twenty-eight informal settlements the claim, promoted by the media and state officials, that they somehow engendered recourse to Islamist militancy said more about the social distance between middle-class Caireans and the socially marginalized residents of informal quarters such as those in Western Munira than about the root causes underlying the rise of Islamic radicalism. Indeed, far from a marginal phenomenon, by the late 1990s informal settlements housed half of Greater Cairo's twelve million.[68] Yet it was chiefly in the poorest quarters of Imbaba that militant Islamists gained a stronghold in Cairo. In contrast to older, more socially cohesive informal settlements, the quarters of Western Munira are distinguished by their relative poverty and social marginalization as well as their close proximity to more affluent areas of urban Cairo.

However, clearly this new, more militant Islamist movement was not ubiquitous among Egypt's poor. In Chapter 7 I address the important question of what led to the surprising popularity and increasing numbers of Islamic Group supporters in the Western Munira sections of Imbaba. Indeed, in the 1970s and 1980s the Muslim Brotherhood spearheaded the most dominant trend of Islamist activism in urban Cairo. It was in this period that they managed to establish a wide range of civil society institutions through a successful social movement that was, unlike the *al-Jama'a*, largely nonviolent. Why then did Islamist activism in informal Cairo assume an increasingly militant form beginning in the late 1980s and 1990s? And, equally important, why has it continued to enjoy significant support in recent decades?

# 5 From Remittance Economy to Rentier State: The Rise and Fall of an Islamist Authoritarian Regime in Sudan

When on June 30, 1989, a group of middle-ranking army officers led by Brigadier Omer Hassan al-Bashir overthrew the civilian government of Prime Minister Sadiq al-Mahdi in a coup d'etat, it was clear to most Sudanese that the coup leaders were ardent members of the Muslim Brotherhood. The new military regime was organized under the umbrella of the Revolutionary Command Council (RCC) but the planning and decision-making were spearheaded by what was then a clandestine organization that was known as the Council of Defenders of the Revolution, known at time among many Sudanese as the Council of Forty *(al-majlis al-arbeen)*. What was most noteworthy about the council was that it was headed by the influential Ali Osman Taha, the then president of the National Islamic Front (NIF) and well known to be the disciple of Hassan Turabi.

There is little question that in its first decade in power the Bashir regime pursued radical measures in domestic politics as well as foreign affairs. The regime's Islamist-radical credentials became evident as early as December 1990 when the RCC formally announced a more comprehensive array of shari'a laws and promised to implement them by force. The expansion of Islamic penal codes included more stringent laws against apostasy, the enforcement of Islamic dress for women, and the exclusion of non-Muslims from holding high positions in the state bureaucracy. Moreover, with more stringent Islamicization policies came greater militarization. Under pressure from the leadership of the NIF, the RCC almost immediately created a paramilitary force, the Popular Defense Forces (PDF), to secure the Islamic revolution, "expand the faith," and combat the non-Muslim rebellion in the south.[1]

In some respects the officers who made up the RCC followed in the pattern of the many other coups d'etats that have occurred throughout the African continent.[2] However, it quickly became clear that the coup in the summer of 1989 in Sudan was different from the pattern of the two previous coups that the country witnessed in 1958 and 1969. Indeed, while Francois Bayart has observed that in many weak African states the construction of a hegemonic (authoritarian) ruling elite is often forged out of a tacit agreement between a diverse group of power brokers, intermediaries, and local authorities, the Islamist-backed coup in Sudan represented (at least in its first decade in power) the first time in the country's history where an ideological party bureaucracy has sought total dominance over both state institutions and the entire population. Indeed, following the coup of 1989, the Bashir regime quickly outlawed all political parties, professional organizations, trade unions, and civil society organizations. Furthermore, backed by the NIF, the Bashir regime expanded its dominance over the banking system, monopolized the transport and building industries, and took control of the national media. In addition, for the first time, a ruling regime in Khartoum waged a concerted campaign to destroy the economic base and religious popularity of the two most powerful religious sects: the Ansar but particularly the Khatmiyya and its supporters.[3]

In the 1990s radical politics at home was matched with a new form of Islamist radicalism in foreign affairs under the leadership of the leaders of the NIF. In 1991, less than two years after coming to power and under the leadership of the late Hassan Turabi, Khartoum established the Popular Arab and Islamic Congress (PAIC), *al-mutamar al-arabi al-shabi al-islami* with the ambitious goal of coordinating Islamic anti-imperialist movements in fifty Muslim states. It was at this juncture that the Khartoum regime welcomed Osama bin Laden. Bin Laden not only opened accounts in al-Shamal, Tadamun, and Faisal Islamic Banks as a way to assist the regime financially, he also provided funds for al-Qa'ida camps on the outskirts of Khartoum.

But if the 1990s witnessed a strident form of Islamist radical politics, by the end of the decade Khartoum turned to more pragmatic policies withdrawing its support for Islamist radical organizations beyond its national borders. The turning point in Sudan's support for international terrorism came in June 1995, when the Egyptian Islamic Jihad, assisted by the Sudanese intelligence service, carried out an assassination attempt against the Egyptian president Hosni Mubarak in Addis Adaba. In September, the African Union condemned Sudan for supporting terrorism, and by April 1996 the United Nations voted to impose diplomatic sanctions. Shortly after the sanctions were introduced, Sudan offered to turn Osama bin Laden over to the Saudi and US governments. Al-Qa'ida's ouster from Sudan represented a strategic break. The Islamist regime recognized that it was a losing proposition to support terrorists without considering their targets. Three years later, Sudan made peace with most of its neighbors and initiated regular counterterrorism talks with the United States. Following the September 11 attacks, the regime made a tactical choice to cooperate aggressively with US counterterrorism efforts as a way to reduce its international isolation.[4]

To be sure the increasing cost of sanctions did compel the Bashir regime to withdraw support for radical Islam. But the ideological evolution and the shift from radicalism to pragmatism on the part of Khartoum is better explained by domestic factors and, specifically, in the Bashir regime's attempt to consolidate political power in the context of dramatic external and internal economic pressures. Indeed, in the first instance, the rise to power of Islamist politics in the 1990s represented a victory in the long-standing rivalry between Islamist radicalism, traditional Sufism, and ethnicity. Indeed, Sufism and ethnic loyalties have long provided a bulwark against the ideological appeal of Islamist radicalism of the type pursued by the Bashir regime. Nevertheless, under the leadership of the NIF, the Islamists (until recently) were able to prevail primarily because they were able to capitalize on a series of economic changes in the 1970s and 1980s. The NIF in particular developed a great deal of clout through its monopolization of informal financial markets as well as control of much of Sudan's Islamic banking system.

## The Islamists in Power and the Conflict over the "Black Market"

The recession of the mid-1980s triggered the turbulent politics that saw the passing of two regimes in less than a decade and the capture of the state by an Islamist military junta in the summer of 1989. As formal financing from the Gulf (as well as Western bilateral and multilateral assistance) dried up, giving way to the dominance of the parallel market, President Ja'far al-Nimairi was forced to implement an IMF austerity program, removing price controls on basic consumer items. These measures sparked the popular uprising (*intifada*) that resulted in his ouster in 1985 and the election of a democratic government a year later. The civilian government, once again dominated by the old sectarian elites and characterized by interparty squabbling between the Umma Party and the Democratic Unionist Party (DUP), proved ineffectual in the face of Sudan's severe economic crisis. Blocked from formal assistance due to a dispute with the IMF, the civilian government attempted to capture the all-important remittance flows from Sudanese nationals abroad by instituting a two-tier foreign exchange system in the latter part of 1988, but this attempt met with little success.[5]

Not surprisingly the very weakness of the civilian government led to significant progress in peace negotiations with the south based on a potential agreement that called for the repeal of the shari'a-based laws implemented in 1983. These efforts were forestalled, however, by the 1989 military coup, which was backed by the newly ascendant Islamist commercial class. Al-Bashir and the other members of the coup's military cadre had been recruited by the Muslim Brotherhood, who during the 1980s made use of their newfound wealth and access to petrodollar funding to establish a host of tax-exempted Islamic welfare and propagation organizations offering generous stipends and scholarships to a select group of mid-ranking officers.[6]

As discussed in Chapter 2, in the 1970s and 1980s the role of Islamic banks and the monopolization of informal financial transactions played a key role in the rise of the Islamists, organized under the umbrella of the NIF as an instrument of political authority. Nevertheless, the military coup of 1989 radicalized the Islamicization process in Sudan, and the new government gave immediate attention to the financial sector. Throughout the 1990s, the NIF consolidated their power through coercive extractive regulatory mechanisms, most notably the formation of a tax police to intimidate tax evaders, and the execution of black marketeers belonging to politically marginal groups. The state's weakening resulted in more predatory and rent-seeking interventions. In addition to extracting revenue from local taxes, licensing fees, and bank loans, the state tried to capture a share of the informal urban market, exacting taxes on a percentage of the rental value on all shops, sheds, specialized markets, special services, and local development schemes.[7]

Whereas the parallel economy had been a source of strength for the Islamists in their rise to power, once they captured the state, and property rights were thus reassigned to their benefit, the parallel economy became a threat. One of the first measures of the Islamist state was to "declare war on black marketeers, hoarders, smugglers, and traders who 'overcharge,' threatening them with execution."[8] Sudanese expatriates working in Arab states were ordered to declare their money at the Khartoum airport; traders were directed to post official price lists in their shops; and many street vendors were imprisoned. Most significantly, the al-Bashir regime ordered the issuing of a new Sudanese currency and gave Sudanese only two weeks to exchange the hard currency in their possession at the free-market rate. Although this ruling initially enabled Islamic banks to garner a significant amount of hard currency in the short term, government policy did not address the underlying production problem that made black marketeering and hoarding an endemic part of Sudan's economy. Moreover, most merchants simply closed their shops or completely withdrew certain goods from the market. The general result was the exacerbation of the scarcity problem and hyperinflation averaging more than 2,000 percent per annum.[9]

The NIF's Islamist regime's preoccupation with, and even fear of, the parallel market was warranted, given its potential in terms of capital accumulation – a potential that members of the Islamist commercial class utilized to great effect during the boom. In an interesting historical twist of fate, just as al-Nimairi was beholden to a private sector dominated by the Islamists in the 1970s and early 1980s, the latter found themselves with the unenviable position of fighting over rents in the parallel market while promoting liberal macro-economic policies designed to lure external assistance to replenish the depleted coffers of the state and revitalize the commercial sector of the economy. These polices included the transfer of assets to Islamist clients as opposed to privatization in a competitive sense.

Meanwhile, most earnings of Sudanese living in the Gulf continued to be remitted home via the parallel channels. Although the recession reduced the total volume of remittance flows (Figure 5.1), the bankrupt Sudanese economy meant that a broad spectrum of Sudan's middle class relied more and more on informal finances from the Gulf. The parallel market in foreign exchange circumvented both the national banks and the Islamic financial institutions, thereby contributing to the virtual merger of these former rivals attempting to reverse their losses in the "battle for hard

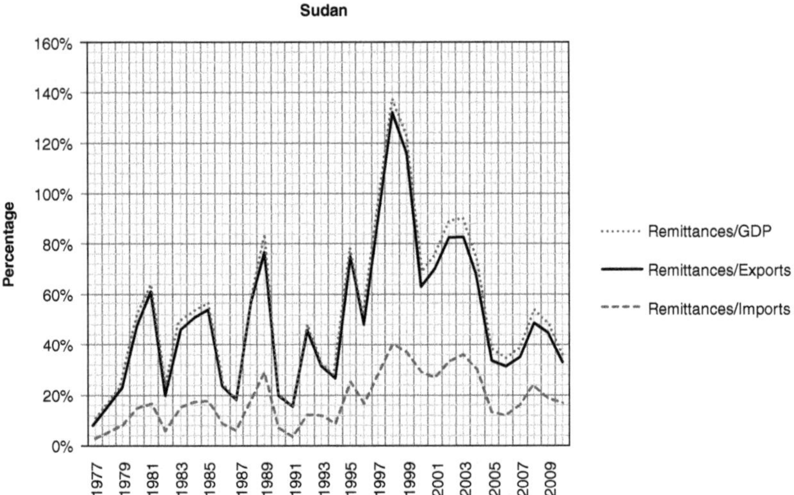


Figure 5.1 Trends in remittances as proportion of GDP, exports, and imports in Sudan
*Source*: World Bank, World Development Indicators (World Bank, Washington, DC). https://datacatalog.worldbank.org/dataset/world-development-indicators.

currency." In essence then, the crackdown on the black market in the 1990s represented an alliance between the faction of the Islamist commercial class (organized under the banner of the NIF) dominating the commercial banks and their supporters in the state bureaucracy to try to capture a significant portion of the earnings of Sudanese working in the Arab countries of the Gulf.

Interestingly, conventional understandings of informal institutions commonly restrict informal markets to those not "officially" sanctioned by the state and assume, erroneously, that informal economic activities are generated exclusively as a direct result of excessive state intervention.[10] In reality, and particularly in weak states, the expansion and operation of informal economic institutions are often produced by the actions and policies of the state elites themselves. In the case of Sudan after 1989, Islamist elites simultaneously countered and cultivated the expansion of black-market currency trade once they took over state institutions. Indeed, as in previous decades, the links between the formal institutions of the state and informal financial markets (i.e., black market) remained interdependent. But what changed after 1989 was that a shift occurred in the social and economic relations of power between a newly ensconced NIF-dominated state and rival sectarian and ethnic groups in civil society.

The crackdown against black-market dealers, for example, targeted only those black-market dealers who did not have links with the now Islamist-dominated state. Indeed, revenue generated from the black market continued to benefit key Islamist state officeholders. So despite the takeover of the state by the Muslim Brotherhood this did not curtail black-market transactions. Nor did it end the pattern of state collusion in parallel markets. Many of the black marketeers before and after the coup of 1989 were Brotherhood supporters. Important NIF bankers, such as Shaykh 'Abd al-Basri and Tayyib al-Nus, and the well-known currency dealer Salah Karrar, having become members of the Revolutionary Command Council's Economic Commission, continued to speculate in grain deals, monopolize export licenses, and hoarded commodities in an effort to capture as much foreign exchange as possible. Moreover, while the Bashir regime implemented a "privatization" program this policy amounted to no more than the large-scale transfer of government-run public property into the "private" hands of Islamists. What is most notable is that Islamist financiers bought these assets with money made from currency speculation associated with remittance deposits.[11]

Having managed to gain control of the state, the Islamist-backed Bashir regime went about the task of consolidating power as quickly as possible. But while the NIF had built a strong middle class of Islamist-minded supporters they hardly had a hegemonic control of civil society. This was clear as early as the general elections of 1986 wherein the NIF managed to win approximately 20 percent of the vote but fell behind the two more popular Sufi-based parties: the UMMA and Democratic Unionist Party. Indeed, financial clout did not immediately translate into hegemonic control in civil society for the Islamists. As a result, following the coup of 1989, the Bashir regime considered it vital to marginalize rival factions of the middle class, while continuing to expand their urban base, built in the 1970s and 1980s, among a new commercial Islamist class. Since the informal economy represented an important source of revenue generation for a wide range of social groups the NIF-backed regime immediately targeted this important avenue of revenue generation. It is in this context, and in order to intimidate the big business families, which did not have any links with the Islamist movement or the NIF party in particular, that the junta accused several members of these rival business families with "illegal" black-market currency dealing and summarily executed them.

If the Islamist regime sought to take complete control of informal finance, they simultaneously went about consolidating their hold on the formal financial institutions of the state. The appointment of 'Abd al-Rahim Hamdi and Sabri Muhammad Hassan, two of the most renowned individuals among Sudan's Islamist financiers, as minister of finance and governor of the Central Bank, respectively, left little doubt as to the Muslim Brotherhood's overwhelming dominance of the state's financial institutions. This monopoly did not go unnoticed. In protests coordinated primarily by students, workers, and professional associations belonging to the Modern Forces (*al-Quwwat al-Haditha*) in 1993 and 1994, it was Islamic Banks, rather than public offices, that were stoned, ransacked, and burned.

The regime's relationship with the IMF was particularly contentious. In 1986 the IMF declared Sudan ineligible for fresh credits because of its failure to enforce economic reforms. In 1990, the IMF went further, declaring Sudan "non-cooperative" due to the fact that it owed more than USD 2 billion in arrears and, in an unprecedented move, it threatened Sudan with expulsion. The government openly sought to improve its relations with the IMF, and under the guidance of Hamdi, floated the Sudanese pound (resulting in a six-fold rise in the value of the US dollar in relation to local currency), liberalized prices of key commodities, and reduced subsidies on a number of consumer commodities. But as the IMF continued to withhold assistance – as did most of the Gulf countries in reprisal for Khartoum's support of Iraq during the 1991 Gulf War and its support of Islamist movements in the region – the al-Bashir regime was forced to reinstate subsidies in order to avert unrest in the urban areas.[12]

As the cost of living soared with the implementation of a wide-scale liberalization program, fears of potential social unrest prompted al-Bashir to dismiss Hamdi, a prominent advocate of the neoliberal economic policies. Hamdi's removal was a sign of the state elites' disenchantment with an economic liberalization program that was designed, but ultimately failed, to lure foreign assistance. But it was a cosmetic change: Hamdi's successor as finance minister, 'Abd Allah Hassan Ahmad, a former manager of Faisal Islamic Bank with strong ties to Europe- and Southeast Asia-based Islamist financiers, continued the neoliberal reforms. With the appointment of Sabir Muhammad al-Hassan, a high-ranking member of the Muslim Brotherhood, and former head of the Bank of Khartoum, as director of the Central Bank of Sudan, the Muslim Brotherhood continued to dominate fiscal and monetary policy. And members of the Muslim Brotherhood's supporters continued to benefit from preferential allocations of bank loans, customs exemptions, and foreign currency for imports. The most important Islamist businessmen enjoyed lucrative asset transfers from the privatization of textiles, agribusiness, telecommunications, and mineral rights. Meanwhile, economic austerity measures, compounded by massive inflation, impoverished the majority of the Sudanese population, including civil servants and those engaged in the private sector but not affiliated with the Brotherhood. Only two sectors of society could meet the prohibitive cost of living: families receiving expatriate remittances and NIF members and their supporters.

While the Islamists demonstrated great willingness to liberalize practically every sector of the economy, they singled out the financial sector – the basis of their support – for regulation. In December 1994, the Transitional National Assembly (TNA) amended the Foreign Currency Dealing Act. The new amendment to the law closely regulated foreign exchange transactions, prohibiting the acquisition of foreign currency without official documents, and recommended that foreign exchange payable to the government be exempt from customs. This was designed to provide a strong incentive for expatriate Sudanese to deposit their remittances in state banks – a clear indication of the state's foreign exchange shortage.[13] The amended law also reduced the penalty for currency violations and called for the confiscation of currency instead of previous punishments, which ranged from twenty years' imprisonment to hanging, and also recommended that a distinction be made between legitimate "possession of" and illicit "dealing in" foreign currency.[14] The changes demonstrated the extent to which the state was willing to specify property rights in ways that would maximize revenue accruing to a small elite rather than to rival constituents in civil society. But these changes were too little and came too late to capture the gains from remittances. The regime's brutal crackdown of black marketeering, as well as the onset of the Iraq war, saw a steep decline in expatriate remittances from the Gulf that fed the parallel market sent to the formal banks of the state. Moreover, Sudan's deep economic crisis in the 1990s led to increasing migrations abroad with the result that remittances continued to fuel the parallel (informal) market and, from the perspective of the regime, took away a significant amount of the hard currency earnings that could have, otherwise, been deposited in the coffers of the state. Interestingly, state institutions became so starved for remittance-based financing that the regime often solicited the support from some of the wealthiest black-market traders in the country in return for allowing the latter to continue operations in contravention of the state's own laws against black-market currency dealings. When the country's most powerful currency trader, Waled al-Jabel, was incarcerated for black marketeering, the National Bank of Sudan (then headed by a prominent Islamist technocrat) intervened on his behalf because he agreed to provide this primary formal financial institution with much-needed capital from his own coffers.[15]

In lieu of a solid fiscal base and a productive formal economy, Khartoum resorted to extreme ideological posturing as its primary mode of legitimation. Specifically, the government formed a tactical alliance with the Islamic regime in Iran in hopes of attaining political support and economic assistance. Iran's chief contribution was to provide arms (worth an estimated USD 300 million) that the regime then utilized to escalate the military campaigns against the southern insurgency, ongoing since 1983, and to establish a repressive security apparatus, parallel to the national army, in northern urban areas. Not only were millions of southerners killed or displaced as a result of an escalation in the civil war, but religious and ethnic cleavages deepened.

The regime further consolidated its rule through a systematic penetration of the civil service, including the monopolization of the important Ministry of Oil and Energy, thereby creating a powerful network throughout the bureaucracy. Immediately following their assumption to power in 1989, the NIF-backed regime pursued a program of dismissals based on ideological and security considerations, targeting supporters of other political parties, secularists, non-Muslims, and members of sectarian organizations, trade and labor unions, and professional associations. The same policy was applied to the armed forces, and officers of anti-Islamist sentiment were dismissed en masse. The Popular Defense Forces (PDF) was established, and its members given extensive ideological and military training befitting the political objectives of the Islamist authoritarian regime. These measures culminated in the formal declaration of an Islamic state in 1991 and in the introduction of a "new" Islamic penal code.

By the mid-1990s the Bashir regime pursued policies abroad as well as at home that reflected a decidedly Islamist radical agenda. In 1991, under the leadership of Hassan Turabi, Khartoum organized the Popular Arab and Islamic Congress (PAIC) hosted gatherings of known militant and terrorist organizations, and Khartoum gave moral, financial, and material support to mujahideen fighting in Bosnia, Albania, Somalia, and Chechnya. Thus, Sudan – one of the Muslim world's most heterogeneous countries – became a center of international jihadism.

## The Demise of "Islamic" Banking and the Struggle for Political Legitimacy

The Islamist elite's continual efforts to consolidate their regime through their "war" against the black marketers, the implementation of a policy of de-statism (rather than privatization on a competitive basis), and their monopolization of import-export trade earned them the unflattering label of *tamasih al-suq* (market crocodiles). More specifically, building on gains made from Islamic finance during the oil boom in the Gulf, once in power, the Islamists continued in their efforts to strengthen the resource base of their movement. Indeed, they essentially took over the import-export sector, previously the territory of merchants belonging to the Khatmiyya sect. Indeed, throughout the 1980s commercial bank lending consisted overwhelmingly of short-term loans and remained focused on foreign and domestic trade rather than agriculture and other sectors (Table 5.1). Importantly, lucrative commodities like sorghum were exported through the subsidiaries of Faisal Islamic Bank and the African Islamic Bank, where Islamist stalwarts were senior executives.

However, the most important reasons for the regime's increasingly predatory rent-seeking behavior was that by the mid-1990s the heyday in which Islamic banks were able to capture upward of 20 percent of the remittances of expatriate Sudanese and benefit from a veritable boom in capital investment from wealthy Gulf Arabs had come to an end. By the end of the decade, there was little question that, at least in economic terms, the Islamic banking experiment in Sudan had proved to be a dismal failure. In 1999, in its review of Sudan's financial sector, the IMF reported that as much as 19 percent of bank credit was nonperforming. Even more devastating, the report further concluded that the Islamic banks had declining deposit bases and credit lending to the private sector (which had risen sharply in the 1980s in relation to other commercial bank lending) had contracted steadily in real terms from 1993 to 1999.[16]

Table 5.1 *Distribution of total commercial bank lending in Sudan by sector and type of commercial loans, 1983–1986, in SDG 1,000*

| | 1983 | 1984 | 1985 | 1986 |
|---|---|---|---|---|
| Short term | 1,002 | 1,155 | 1,348 | 2,003 |
| *Percentage* | *73* | *72* | *76* | *76* |
| Long term | 375 | 454 | 428 | 635 |
| *Percentage* | *27* | *28* | *24* | *24* |
| Agriculture | 4 | 5 | – | – |
| *Percentage* | *0.4* | *0.5* | – | – |
| Foreign trade | 553 | 656 | 573 | 932 |
| *Percentage* | *41.6* | *57* | *43* | *47* |
| Industry | 276 | 286 | 385 | 424 |
| *Percentage* | *28* | *25* | *29* | *21* |
| Domestic trade | 82 | 105 | – | – |
| *Percentage* | *8* | *9* | – | – |
| Other | 86 | 102 | 390 | 647 |
| *Percentage* | *9* | *9* | *29* | *32* |

*Source*: Ministry of Finance and Economic Planning, "Ministry of Finance, Economic Survey, 1984/85, 1986/87" (Khartoum: Ministry of Finance and Economic Planning, 1987).

There were both external as well as domestic political reasons for the failure of Islamic banking in the country. First, the economy in the 1990s was in dire straits as the regional recession deepened and the oil boom in the Gulf ended. The recession in the Gulf resulting from the slump in oil prices in the mid-1980s in particular had vastly reduced the inflow of remittances into the country and officially recorded remittances declined dramatically (Figure 5.1). A chief consequence of the diminution in remittance inflows was that the deposits from expatriate Sudanese into Islamic banks declined resulting in what the IMF observed as a dramatic decline in the capital base of these banks. In addition, the Sudanese domestic economy was in an increasingly weak position. Throughout the 1990s the annual rate of inflation exceeded 50 percent. In the context of a rapidly depreciating currency, commodity prices for cotton also fell just as oil prices were rising. The result was a worsening of the balance of payments and terms of trade. Toward the end of the 1990s, in a last-ditch effort to revitalize the hitherto unregulated financial sector, the Bank of Sudan introduced new restrictions on loans to members of the board of directors and prohibited credit to indebted clients, but this intervention was too little and came too late to save the Islamic banks.

The second reason for the demise of Islamic bank was political. The fact that Islamic banking was essentially utilized by the NIF as a source of finance to expand its patronage network in civil society meant that decisions were often made on political rather than rational-economic grounds. As detailed in Chapter 2, the major shareholders and members of the boards of directors who monopolized the banks' capital resources were linked to the Islamist regime. This was evident in two important ways. First, the major shareholders and members of boards of directors were linked to the Bashir regime and consequently monopolized the capital resources of these banks. In fact, the shareholders also nominated the members of the boards of directors and appointed the senior management, and so they met few restrictions from within the banks themselves.[17]

Second, the clients that were favored in the lending patterns of these banks were chosen for their potential support of the Islamist movement and the Muslim Brotherhood organization in particular. The result of this politicization (and Islamicization) of the entire banking system was that, as one important report on the subject noted, these shareholders met few restrictions from regulatory authorities, and few clients felt any pressure to repay their loans at the agreed time. After all, if a chief objective was to recruit supporters to the Islamist movement there was little incentive to "pay back" the Brotherhood-dominated banks in financial terms. Consequently, not only were the Islamic banks short of capital as a result of the diminishing volume of remittance inflows, by the 1990s these banks suffered from very high default rates. This was primarily because of the unregulated environment in which they were allowed to operate by the regime. The central bank, for example, was simply not able to implement regulations on the financial system to limit corruption because they had to come into conflict with shareholders and bank managers with very close ties to the new NIF-backed regime. By the end of the decade it was clear to most Sudanese that Islamic banking was primarily successful in transferring wealth to a rising middle class and elite of Islamist financiers and businessmen. Indeed, by the late 1990s it was abundantly clear that Sudanese were disillusioned with the Islamicization of the financial sector and they no longer put their trust in depositing their money in the Islamic banking system.

It is important to note that many supporters of the Muslim Brotherhood did claim that the Islamic banking experiment was successful in religious if not financial terms. They argued that, after all, their movement was instrumental in converting national banking laws into those that conformed to the principles of shari'a. In reality, however, the mode of operations of the banks tells a different story in that they did not strictly conform to the shari'a's key prohibition of interest or *riba*. In particular, the overwhelming use and misinterpretation of *murabaha* contracts by the majority of the Islamic banks meant that the latter did indeed derive what is often termed a "hidden form" of interest in their lending practices.[18] Specifically, rather than fix its profit margin to avoid generating interest (*riba*) on a loan the Islamic banks arranged a repayment schedule overtime to determine the cost of the loan. As one study noted, the banks secured these loans against liquid assets rather than the physical commodity that is purchased by the client to start his or her business.[19] In classical *murabaha* contracts the lender is supposed to take physical possession of the commodity in case of default rather than demanding security other than the commodity. In the case of Sudan, the record shows that the Islamic banks were more interested in acquiring profits in cash, which contravened the spirit, if not the law, of shari'a.

Significantly, much of the criticism with respect to the operations of the Islamic banks as well as the great wealth amassed by Islamist financers in a short period of time came from within the membership of the Muslim Brotherhood. This criticism was especially strident among the most ardent members of the organization in the campuses of the universities in the capital of Khartoum. The increasingly ostentatious lifestyles of high-ranking members of the Muslim Brotherhood became a source of great debate primarily because it contradicted the discourse that the movement had utilized to recruit new members. By the late 1980s, the Islamist-dominated financial empire that was built in the boardrooms of the Islamic banks gave rise to a veritable transformation of the urban landscape. In particular, the rise of an Islamist commercial class led to a veritable boom in the establishment and expansion of upper-class neighborhoods of al-Manshiyya, al-Riyyad, and al-Mohandesein. These new neighborhoods came to be labeled *ghabaat al-asmant al-Ikhwaniyya* (the Brotherhoods' cement jungle) because of the high number of wealthy Brotherhood members who built new mansions in these neighborhoods. These new upper-class areas stood in close proximity to the poorer urban settlements; for many Sudanese this represented a stark contradiction between the populist rhetoric of the Brotherhood which often referenced Khomeini's discourse of the dispossessed and underprivileged (*musta'-zafeen*) and the realities of a new Islamist bourgeoisie that appeared more intent on securing a lavish lifestyle rather than the call (Da'wa) of Islam. The rapid transformation of the urban landscape in the capital city represented a highly visible image of the social and ideological contradictions of the ascendancy of the Islamists in the country leading many to label the new mansions of the new Islamist bourgeoisie *hayaat al-mustakbereen*, neighborhoods of the arrogant.

By the mid-1990s just as the Bashir regime had become increasingly unpopular among a wide segment of Sudanese, it was also severally isolated internationally as a result of its support for Islamist militants abroad. The turning point came following Khartoum's role in the assassination attempt against Hosni Mubarak. In January 1996 the UN Security Council passed resolution 1044 imposing sanctions on Sudan for refusing to cooperate fully with the assassination investigation, and in April 1996, at the prodding of the United States, which still accused Sudan of sponsoring terrorism, imposed even harsher sanctions against Khartoum. Indeed, by 1996 the Bashir regime was deemed a pariah in the international community. International isolation, and the imposition of international sanctions in particular, led to a visible rift between the hard-liners and moderates among members of the NIF. Subsequently, following 1996, Turabi's influence declined dramatically as Bashir and his inner circle moved to improve their image abroad. Specifically, the Bashir regime dissolved the PAIC, began to cooperate closely with US intelligence on counter-terrorism information, and saw to it that Osama bin Laden exited the country. For his part, on his departure, Bin Laden complained that he had lost more than $160 million after the Bashir regime terminated all his businesses and froze his bank accounts in Sudan.[20]

In addition, in order to improve its authoritarian image, in 1996 the RCC dissolved itself by passing "Decree 13." Its chairman, Omer al-Bashir, became president of the republic, and power was formally transferred to the civilian Transitional National Assembly (TNA). The TNA approved the "Charter of the Sudanese People" which defined the functions of the president and the national assembly (*majlis watani*) and approved the convening of national elections. Two years later in December 1998 al-Bashir signed into law the Political Associations Act that approved the convening of national elections and supposedly restored Sudan to multiparty politics banned since July 1989. In addition, he reorganized the NIF into his new ruling party: the National Congress Party (NCP). Naturally, this meant that the Islamist of the now defunct NIF maintained their dominance in Bashir's new "civilian" government. The so-called opening up of an electoral process and multiparty politics was no more than a thinly veiled attempt to regain political legitimacy in the face of international isolation and internal dissent. Al-Bashir was elected with more than 75 percent of the vote in the first "elections" in March 1996 and remained in firm control of the military and security apparatus. It was Islamist politics as usual with a government completely dominated by the NIF and its members consisting of primarily young men who had secured the most important positions in the civil service, the military and the government and who did not represent the rest of Sudanese society.

To be sure the introduction of international sanctions against Khartoum in the mid-1990s isolated the Bashir regime both economically and politically, but the crucial shift from a radical to a pragmatic orientation associated with the Khartoum regime's policies is best understood as a result of domestic economic exigencies rather than foreign policy considerations. Specifically, by the end of the 1990s, as a result of a shrinkage in deposits from expatriate Sudanese, the severe economic consequences of the war in the south, and the end of the boom of Islamic Banking, the NIF regime found itself bankrupt. In the 1970s and 1980s the Muslim Brotherhood were, with the aid of the incumbent regime at the time, able to finance their organization through the monopolization of informal financial markets and Islamic banking. But after a decade in power, the NIF leadership, crippled by a heavy debt and a severe balance of payment's crisis, turned to another source of revenue to buttress the patronage networks of the Islamist-backed military regime: oil.

### From Labor Exporter to Rentier State: The Economic Foundations of Islamist Pragmatism

By the 1990s the consequences of the end of the oil boom in the Arab Gulf, and the attendant decline in remittances as well as Arab financial assistance were reflected in Sudan's increasingly deep economic crisis. In terms of remittance, in the 1970s and through the 1980s labor remittances did indeed increase dramatically as a proportion of Sudan's general domestic economy. This is clearly evident in terms of remittance inflows as a proportion of gross domestic product (GDP) as well as exports and imports (Figure 5.1). In 1987, for example, remittances as a proportion of GDP increased dramatically from 20 percent to almost 80 percent. Moreover, between 1997 and 1998, remittances again peaked, this time even more dramatically, from 45 percent to almost 140 percent of GDP. However, following 1998, remittances registered a steady decline and by 2009 declined once again to 45 percent of GDP and 22 percent of imports.

However, while remittances continue to represent an important source of foreign currency their continued relative importance in Sudan's macroeconomy is primarily due to the decline in export revenue over the last four decades. Specifically, what is most notable is the steady deterioration of Sudan's exports over the course of the 1980s and 1990s. Export revenue minus remittances (i.e., "non-remittance current account credits") fell from a high level of US 2 billion dollars in 1981 to a low just below US 500 million dollars in 1993. This is the reason why in the late 1990s (during the period with the broadest sustained gap between exports revenue and import costs) remittances surpassed the financial aid (i.e., "net financial flows") as a source of foreign currency and briefly reached a level equal to total export revenue in 1998 (Figure 5.2). The major economic problem for Sudan in the 1990s was that while the regime was focusing on the financial sector as a source of revenue, commodity exports flattened and dwindled to just above 500 million dollars while imports stayed well above 1 billion dollars for most years. Consequently, as a means of financing these imports, Sudan ran a very high financial debt that, by the early 1990s, had dramatically worsened its balance of payments and crippled the national economy. By the mid-1990s the debt was more than $17 billion, and the annual deficit equaled 25 percent of GDP with hyperinflation running between 80 and 100 percent. A good indicator that showed that the economy was in deep crisis was the steep decline of the Sudanese pound from SL17 to SL500 to the dollar in the summer of 1994, and between 1993 and 2002 there were frequent periods where the country had no foreign currency whatsoever.

In the context of the deep economic crisis in the 1990s, the Bashir regime increasingly sought to hold on to power by developing oil resources in the southern regions of the country. From the perspective of Bashir and his ruling NCP the exploitation of oil in the south was imperative for economic as well as political reasons. On the one hand,

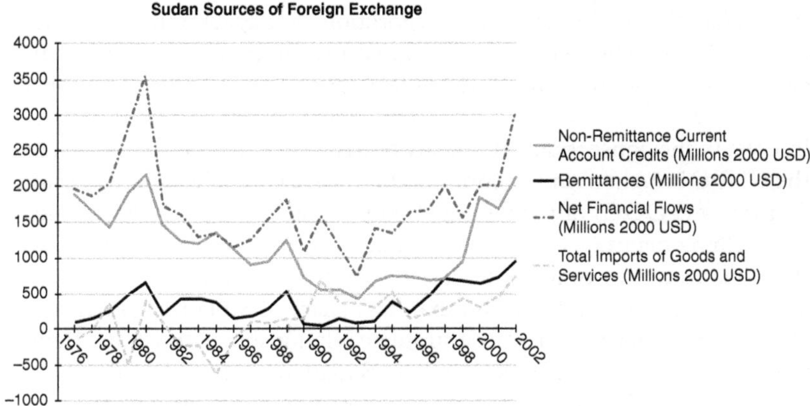


Figure 5.2 Sudan's balance of payments trends with a focus on remittances and deteriorating exports
*Source*: World Bank, World Development Indicators (World Bank, Washington, DC). https://datacatalog.worldbank.org/dataset/world-development-indicators.

within the context of deteriorating exports, a relative decline in remittances, and the diminishing profitability of Islamic banking, Islamist bureaucrats turned their focus increasingly toward the oil sector as a way to sustain their patronage networks. On the other hand, the increasingly fierce southern insurgency was jeopardizing their hold on political power, and most particularly, their hopes of exploiting the oil wealth in the south. Specifically, the NCP understood the need to secure the oilfields and moved toward gaining control of strategic areas in the south by implementing a cordon sanitaire, a task that would be led by proxy jihadist-inspired *Mujahideen* militias.

However, Chevron – which had acquired oil concessions from Khartoum in the 1980s – had by this time grown weary of revolving military and democratic governments in Khartoum throughout the 1980s and was unconvinced that the NIF would do a better job of suppressing the rebellion in the south. In 1992 Chevron sold its production rights to a Sudanese government-owned company (Concorp), and two years later, in May 1994, the small Canadian company, Arakis, acquired Chevron's previous concessions and agreed to construct the 1,000-mile pipeline from Heglig oil field in Southern Sudan to Port Sudan. However, in search of more financing, the Sudanese government and Arakis agreed to enter into a partnership with China and Malaysia. On December 2, 1996, the Greater Nile Operating Petroleum Company (GNOPC) was founded consisting of Arakis holding 25 percent interest, China's CNPC 40 percent, Malaysian Petronas Caragali 30 percent, and the Sudan National Petroleum Corporation (Sudapet) only 5 percent.[21]

It is China, however – with the most urgent energy demands – that continued to dominate the oil sector in Sudan. It was CNPC that took the lead of the GNPOC in 1997 when the Canadian Arakis sold much of its interest in the consortium. It quickly bought the latter's concessions, and the CNPC bought a similar commanding share in the Petrodar Operating Company (PDOC) of Upper Nile State. In each of the CNPC's concessions China maintains the majority share as operator in partnership with the Sudanese government's Sudapet and other foreign oil companies. In addition to giving CNPC a commanding share of Sudanese oilfields, the Bashir regime developed a close strategic relationship with China. Beijing invested in various economic sectors in Sudan, outside of the oil industry, providing soft loans to Islamist businessmen, and giving Khartoum greater access to military arms. On the political stage, China also frustrated and stalled Western efforts at the United Nations Security Council to apply economic and political sanctions against Khartoum for its violations of human rights in its military campaign against the insurgency in Darfur that began in 2003.

In 1999, with China's oil giant CNPC in the lead, Petronas and Sudapet completed the construction of the first oil pipeline in the country transporting oil to the Red Sea port for export. At an export capacity of 250,000 barrels a day, oil exportation enabled Khartoum to enjoy its first trade surplus in 1999–2000 when oil exports first went online. Government oil revenues rose from zero in 1998 to almost 42 percent of total government revenue in 2001. Oil exportation vastly improved the balance of payments situation and the impact of the infusion of petrodollars saw the GDP rising to 6 percent in 2003, thanks primarily to the export of oil. Indeed, between 2002 and 2006, Sudan witnessed a veritable oil boom that had an enormous impact on the national economy (Figure 5.3). While in 2002 Sudan's total revenue amounted to less than USD 2 billion by 2006 the Bashir regime was enjoying upward of USD 8 billion. It was oil, and not remittances, that now financed the bulk of imports into the country and the balance of payments improved dramatically by 2004.

The oil boom enabled the al-Bashir regime to distribute patronage and bring in formerly excluded social groups into the governing coalition. Just as in the 1970s and 1980s the boom in remittance inflows and Islamic banking enabled Islamist elites to mobilize Islamist commercial networks to buttress their movement; during the mid-2000s oil boom, after a decade of austerity, the Bashir regime and his NCP expanded their patronage network to selectively include a wider group of supporters and

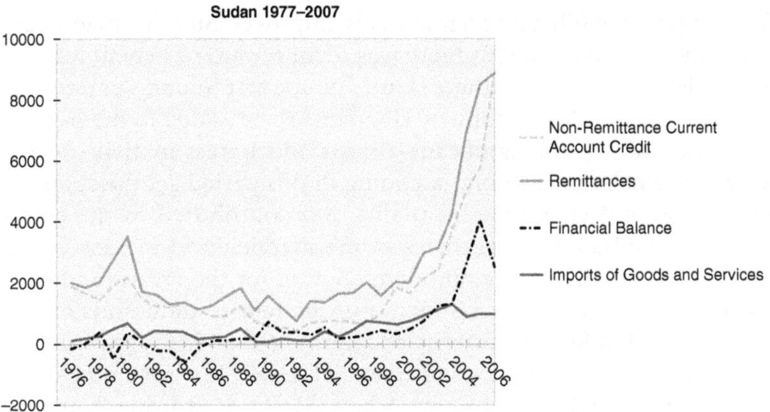


Figure 5.3 Sudan's balance of payments trends reflecting the change in remittances versus non-remittances sources of revenue
*Source*: World Bank, World Development Indicators (World Bank, Washington, DC). https://datacatalog.worldbank.org/dataset/world-development-indicators.

bureaucrats while simultaneously excluding Islamic Sufi social groups and networks.

## Oil: Boom and Curse

Not surprisingly, during the oil boom of the mid-2000s the state quickly conformed to the general patterns of what is commonly called the "resource curse," which uniformly contributes to the weakening of state capacity in many oil-export economies. Specifically, with the exploitation of oil resources, Sudan quickly transformed into a "rentier" state and, as a consequence, the Bashir regime faced two central challenges: the building of legitimate institutions and the exacerbation of the civil conflict in the south where the oil concessions were concentrated. Natural resources greatly weaken the capacity of state institutions because governments are able to extract capital without establishing extensive tax or market infrastructures.[22] Indeed, the case of Sudan following the oil boom conformed closely to the common observation associated with the "resource course": that is, that the profusion of natural resources and the inflow of external rents generated from those resources leads to poor and uneven economic growth, flawed governance practices associated with greater corruption, and an escalation of civil conflict and militarization. Furthermore, these trends occur most visibly in countries like Sudan, which possess heterogeneous societies governed by authoritarian regimes that greatly limit political contestation.[23]

Consequently, while oil revenue vastly improved Sudan's macroeconomic indicators in the 2000s there was scant reward or benefit for civil society at large. To be sure, there is little doubt that Sudan's emergence as an oil producer allowed for new claimants to be added to the patronage systems staving off significant dissent and unrest in civil society. However, the pattern of public spending in this period set the stage for greater social and economic inequality and contributed to the emergence of ethnic-based insurgencies in the marginalized regions of the north. On the one hand, the oil boom allowed for the creation of state governments across northern Sudan, putting tens of thousands on the public payroll. Under the austerity programs of the 1990s, government expenditures were less than 10 percent of GDP, but rose quickly to reach 23 percent in 2006, at a time when GDP was growing from 6 to 10 percent annually.[24] But although the economy grew rapidly and dramatically (Figure 5.3), the benefits were distributed very unequally. The capital city of Khartoum remained a middle-income enclave, while regions such as Darfur and the Red Sea remained extremely poor and underdeveloped. Indeed, the allocation of services, employment, and

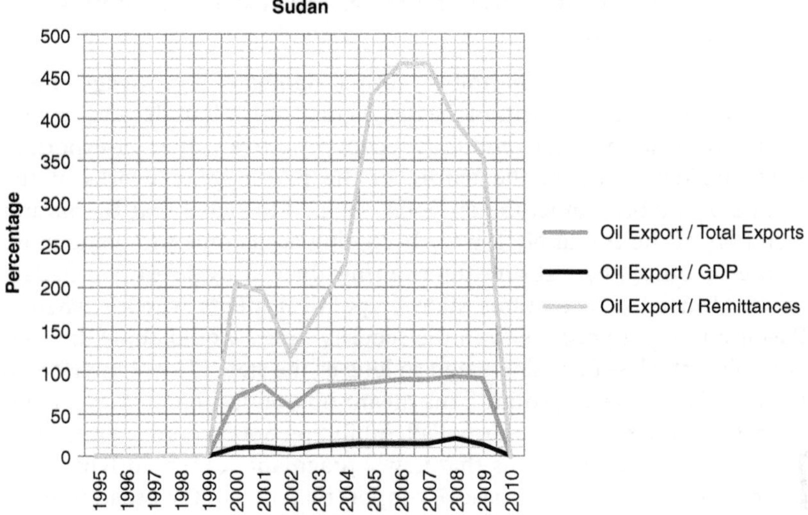


Figure 5.4 Oil exports as share of total exports, GPD, and remittances in Sudan, 1995–2010
*Source*: World Bank, World Development Indicators (World Bank, Washington, DC). https://datacatalog.worldbank.org/dataset/world-development-indicators.

development projects by the Bashir regime did not follow the logic of need, but the logic of political weight. In the early 2000s, almost 90 percent of infrastructure spending occurred in Khartoum state, in response to the political leverage of the urban constituency in Khartoum, and the profits to be made from contracting and import-based commercial enterprises. Following the peace agreement signed with the southern rebels in 2005, about 60 percent of development spending went to five major projects, all of them within the central triangle in the north, notably around the Merowe Dam.[25]

In addition, the lion's share of the revenue from what was to become a short-lived oil boom was spent on the military. In 2001, for example, military spending was estimated at costing USD 349 million. This figure amounted to 60 percent of the 2001 oil revenue generated from exports, which was USD 580.2 million. According to Human Rights Watch, cash military expenditures, which did not include domestic security expenditures, officially rose 45 percent between 1999 and 2001 and this rise reflected the increased government use of helicopter gunships and aerial bombardment against southern insurgents belonging to the Sudanese People's Liberation Movement (SPLM) in the south.

## Oil, Civil Conflict, and the Emergence of the Politics of Ethnicity

By 2005, on the eve of Khartoum's formal signing of a peace agreement with the southern insurgents of the SPLM that ended four decades of war, Sudan's transition from a remittance economy into a rentier oil-exporting state effectively altered the nature of the patronage networks of the regime. For a brief time, the oil boom seemed to signal that Bashir and members of the ruling NCP were becoming accustomed to being more secure in office than at any time during their struggle to consolidate power. Indeed, a precarious state of political affairs was set wherein Bashir and his supporters from the security forces would enjoy the support of a rich class of businessmen so long as the state did not interfere in the latter's pursuit of profits. This meant no political harassment, theological intimidation, and, most of all, inhibiting bureaucratic regulations. The problem, however, was that newly pragmatic leaders in Khartoum came to rely on a narrower base of support than that of the broad Islamist social movements that they cultivated in previous decades. In the context of regional-based rebellions, this development ultimately served to exacerbate the multiple civil conflicts in the country and set the stage for an historic and profound political change: partition.

While the civil war in Sudan has been routinely depicted as rooted in a conflict of national identities between "Arabs" and "Africans," or a religious quarrel between Muslims and Christians,[26] it is best understood as one of several violent disputes between the central state in Khartoum and the regions on the periphery. These include, most notably, the south, the Nuba mountains, the eastern provinces, and the western Darfur region. Indeed, following the Islamist-backed coup of 1989, the Khartoum regime reacted to the various rebellious regional forces with increasing violence, precisely in order to discourage the historically marginalized peripheral regions such as Darfur from rising up in a united front against the central state dominated by a Muslim Arabized riverine elite.[27]

The eruption of the civil conflict between the south and successive central governments in Khartoum began shortly after independence in 1956. Following a brief experiment in parliamentary democracy, in 1958 Sudan witnessed the first of three military authoritarian regimes, that of General Ibrahim 'Abbud. Under 'Abbud, sporadic warfare between the national army and southern guerrillas began in earnest. The fighting outlasted several central governments, both military and civilian. To be sure, the government bureaucracy and the army officer corps have always been dominated by Muslim northerners whose native language is Arabic and who claim Arab lineage, whereas the south is populated by tribes who profess Christianity or animist religions. That is, cultural and religious differences have contributed to the fighting, particularly since Khartoum imposed "Islamic" penal codes in 1983. For its part, the SPLM increasingly defined its identity as African and looked to Sudan's African neighbors for support and patronage during the four-decade-long civil war. What is noteworthy, however, is that having asserted an African identity by resisting what they perceived as Arab domination, the south set an example for other regions, such as Darfur and the eastern provinces, which similarly demanded equality and a more equitable distribution of power and resources.[28]

Despite the SPLM's mobilization of African identity, the core grievances of the south were not only related to issues of cultural identity as such. They also greatly hinged on the issue of the inequitable distribution of economic resources and political power. The promise of oil wealth was a driving force behind the escalation of the conflict and the hardening of interethnic violence in the 1990s.[29] Although the primary cause of Sudan's civil war cannot be attributed to natural resources alone, Sudan's increasing dependence on natural resources determined the conduct of both the civil war and the negotiations that ended military confrontation.[30] Following the discovery of oil, the Bashir regime was keen to ensure that there would be no opposition to its designs to develop the oil economy. In a strategy used later in Darfur to devastating effect, the Sudan Armed Forces (SAF), along with armed militias, conducted devastating aerial bombardments against civilians in the oil-rich areas of the south. In addition, because the regime in Khartoum was unable to find willing recruits to join in what it termed a "jihad" in the south, it encouraged ethnic tensions, in effect using local communities in a proxy war. This it accomplished essentially by arming Misiriyya and Baqqara nomadic tribes and allowing them to pillage and destroy the communities of the Dinka and Nuer pastoralists in the south. In the early 1990s, the Bashir regime had expanded its military campaigns against civilian populations in the south and the Nuba Mountains, and this campaign became more deadly as Khartoum began to profit from increasing oil revenues.[31]

Paradoxically, while the discovery of oil exacerbated the civil conflict in the south it also contributed greatly to the eventual cease-fire and peace agreement between the SPLM and Khartoum. The transformation of Sudan's political economy is the main reason for the emergence of more pragmatic and less radical politics on the part of the Bashir regime in the mid-2000s. It is also the primary reason that Khartoum agreed to sign a peace agreement with its former adversaries in the south and, moreover, oversee the partition of the country. This change, in what was a self-proclaimed "jihadist" military campaign in the 1990s, was mainly due to the fact that the regime's governing system and survival was highly sensitive to cash flow. As the state budget expanded as a result of oil exports, the ruling NCP was able to increase its support base and allow more members of the northern elite to benefit, either directly or through dispensing patronage to them. The national budget, which was less than $1 billion in 1999, increased at a dramatic rate after oil exports began at the end of that year, reaching $11.8 billion in 2007. Even more significant than the expansion of its patronage networks in the north, the Bashir regime now realized that they could afford to bring the SPLM into the government following a peace agreement and thereby gain both economic and political dividends from this pragmatic move. It would open up the opportunity for the exploitation and exploration of more oil fields, and furthermore, it would enhance the potential of improving relations with the United States and the opportunity of receiving US refining technology and other forms of foreign direct investment. Consequently, the signing of the Comprehensive Peace Agreement was a direct result of the oil boom and the ways in which it underpinned the increasing pragmatism of a regime still nominally dominated by Islamist elites.

## Secession and the Evolving Quest for Patronage Networks: Hamdi's Arab-Islamist Triangle

If the Islamist project has in many respects disintegrated, its exacerbation of national divisions had grave consequences for Sudan's national identity and unity.[32] On January 9, 2011, in a referendum in the south on the question of self-determination, the people voted to declare independence. The Bashir regime's willingness (and even eagerness) to oversee the historic partition of Sudan in 2011 remains a puzzle to even some of the most astute analysts of contemporary Sudanese politics. Indeed, South Sudan is the first country in contemporary world history to win independence through peace negotiations, however strife ridden, rather force of arms. There are few governments who would risk such a formidable threat to their sovereignty and political legitimacy as to comply by an internationally supervised agreement that insists on granting an entire swath of territory an "exit option" of this magnitude. In this regard, Khartoum's implementation of the southern referendum in 2011, as stipulated by the Comprehensive Peace Agreement, begs an important question as to why Bashir and his ruling NCP took such a political gamble at the risk of the regime's survival.

Why did the NCP then risk Sudan's partition? The answer lies in the fact that the patronage networks underpinning the Islamist-authoritarian regime changed in tandem with Sudan's evolving economic transition from a labor exporter in the 1970s and 1980s to an aspirant oil exporter in the 1990s and 2000s. Moreover, this structural transformation was accompanied by a marked ideological transformation of the Islamist-backed regime that pragmatically traded in an ideology of global "jihad" in its first decade in power for stability, or rather, for the objective of consolidating political power in the context of increasingly strong insurgencies in the south as well as Darfur. There is, arguably, no individual Islamist who better exemplifies how the state's patronage networks changed over time than Dr. Abdel Rahim Hamdi. As one of the most influential Islamist policy makers and thinkers of Sudan's Islamist movement, Hamdi's own career charts very closely and meaningfully with political, economic, and ideological transformations that have characterized the Islamist-authoritarian evolution of the past four decades. Abdel Rahim Hamdi is a former Islamist financier-turned-investor in an oil company and famously supported southern secession. Hamdi, who, as noted earlier served as Finance Minister throughout most of the 1990s, continued to function as an important economic advisor to the Bashir regime until the latter's ouster in April 2019. Indeed, he continues to represent the overriding economic outlook of the Muslim Brotherhood leadership in economic affairs, which harbors a decidedly favorable view of neoliberal market reform as part and parcel of the Islamicization of the economy. Hamdi has been an ardent member of the Muslim Brotherhood since he was first recruited into the organization as a student at the University of Khartoum in the 1970s. His career reflects the important ways in which Islamic financial institutions and energy production linked up with the state as an important source of financial patronage. Hamdi, a self-proclaimed student of Milton Friedman[33] with a degree from the University of London, was chiefly responsible for accelerating and broadening the country's privatization program that began in earnest in 1992 under what the regime termed the "economic salvation plan." Under his guidance and expertise, the state dramatically and abruptly reduced subsidies on fuel and state-owned enterprises. As Hamdi put it at the time: "We have hit the people with horrendous measures, 500 percent increases in the price of bread, a devaluation of 30 percent and they have accepted it. They have seen the government is working in a very sincere way and, more importantly, in a very uncorrupted way, and, therefore, people have accepted it and endured."[34] Significantly, Hamdi, who is also a long-time executive (and shareholder) with al-Baraka Islamic Bank, insisted on holding on to the position as an al-Baraka's representative in their London-based branch when Bashir appointed him as the Minister of Finance in February 2001. Moreover, in April 1997, he was appointed to the Board of Directors of the Canadian Arakis Energy Corporation (AEC), which was the first to begin oil production in the Sudan following the departure of the American Chevron oil company.

Indeed, Hamdi's career reflects the important ways in which the state sought to finance its patronage networks as Sudan shifted from a remittance to an oil-export economy. But his ideological orientation also presents an important picture of how the Bashir regime sought to consolidate political power through building state-society linkages along exclusivist social networks grounded in very specific cultural, ethnic, and geographic terms. Indeed, as the extractive and military capacity of the state to both generate revenue and prevent insurgents from launching attacks in the capital diminished, Bashir and supporters of his regime emphasized its Arab cultural character in an effort to revitalize the waning ideological legitimacy of the state. In 2006, Hamdi presented a controversial proposal to the ruling NCP conference that became known as "Hamdi Triangle Dialectics." The key moral of his thesis was that the Islamists should begin to turn inward and focus on an Arab-Islamic constituency of the "Riverine North." According to him, this was critical for winning the general elections of 2010 mandated by the CPA and managing its future destiny in the likely event of the partition of the country. In other words, from the perspective of the majority of the Islamists, the division of Sudan should not necessarily be the "natural" outcome of the southern referendum but a result of the Arab-Islamic North's own choice to secede from the rest of the country. It also reflects an important critique of the majority of the Sudanese opposition in the north which has long located the country's primary crises as rooted in an exploitative state that perpetuates the dominance of the center on the peripheries such as Darfur, the east, and southern regions. Indeed, it is this vision of an Arab-Islamic "triangle" that represented the Bashir regime's avenue for political consolidation under the weight of an increasingly bankrupt state battling insurgencies in the outlying regions of the country that guided the high-ranking Islamists in the government before and after the secession of the South Sudan.

## The Resurgence of the Black Market and the "Threat" of Democratization

Nevertheless, by the late 2000s, it was clear that the Bashir regime's efforts to consolidate political power through oil rents following the end of the boom in remittances effectively ended with the secession of South Sudan in summer 2011. Subsequently, the weakened Sudanese pound, high rates of inflation, and rising fuel prices resulted in a resurgence in black-market currency trading that dominated the local economy in the

1970s and 1980s, and this has continued to the present. In a pattern reminiscent of the era of the remittance boom of the 1980s, Sudanese now make regular trips to black-market dealers to buy or sell dollars to take advantage of the difference with the official rate. In response, in a drive to stabilize the exchange rate and curb the expansion of the black market, in May 2012, the central bank licensed some exchange bureaus and banks to trade at a rate closer to the black-market prices. As in previous decades, this was a concerted effort to induce expatriate Sudanese to send more dollars home. But black-market rates stayed higher than the licensed bureaus' prices. In mid-July 2012 the dollar bought 6 pounds on the black market, while in the licensed bureaus it traded at around 3.3. As one Sudanese financial expert pointed out, "when confidence in a currency erodes, it fuels a cycle of speculation and 'dollarization' that makes more depreciation a self-fulfilling prophecy: when you enter this area it is very difficult to escape."[35] In addition to the loss of the all-important oil revenue as a result of the secession of South Sudan, the regime's financial crisis was compounded greatly by the costly rebellions in South Kordofan and Darfur that sapped state finances, and non-oil sectors like agriculture, long neglected by the Bashir regime's economic policies, continue to lag behind their potential.

But the real problem was the Bashir regime's dwindling legitimacy among a cross section of groups and parties in civil society. In June 2012, six years prior to the mass protests that led to Bashir's ouster from power, and at a time when the attention of the international media was focused on the historic victory of the Muslim Brotherhood's presidential candidate in Egypt, street protests of a scale not witnessed for two decades erupted in Khartoum and other major cities in Sudan. They began on June 16 with students protesting the announcement of a 35 percent hike in public transportation fees and calling for the "liberation" of the campus from the presence of the ubiquitous National Intelligence and Security Services (NISS). As was the case with the historic December 2018 popular uprising, the catalyst of the 2012 demonstrations was the Bashir regime's decision to abolish fuel subsidies and the imposition of a wider austerity package that had resulted in a spiraling inflation rate that peaked at more than 30 percent in May 2012.

The June 2012 protests were a direct result of the regime's economic policy decisions linked to the secession of South Sudan in the summer of 2011. Following years of unprecedented oil exports that fueled economic growth, wherein some years featured double-digit growth figures, the financial basis that had served to maintain the resilience and patronage networks of the regime dwindled overnight. In response, and immediately following the south's secession, the Bashir regime placed restrictions on the outflow of foreign currency, banned certain imports, and reduced state subsidies on vital commodities such as sugar and fuel. With a budget deficit estimated at 2.4 billion dollars, on June 18, 2012, Bashir imposed another round of more expansive austerity measures lifting fuel subsidies and announced the stringent enforcement of higher taxes on capital, consumer goods, telecommunications, and a wide range of imports.

At the time the Bashir regime argued that the deep economic crisis was beyond the government's control and that it was, in the words of one NCP member, the result of "malicious traders operating in the informal economy who are smuggling fuel and hard currency at the expense of the Sudanese people." However, the students, and youth activists that confronted the security forces in the streets of Khartoum, and members of the professional syndicates, and the leaders of the NCF (an umbrella group of opposition parties) argued that the roots of the economic crisis are related to the fact that the bulk of the national budget is allocated to the escalating military campaigns in Darfur and the escalating clashes along the borders with South Sudan that began in earnest in April 2012.

Moreover, at the same time that the regime imposed deep austerity measures in the summer of 2012, the NCP announced the expansion in the offices of government no doubt deeply concerned with sustaining its patronage networks and security apparatus in the context of small but persistent protests calling for the removal of the regime. Ironically, the influential vice president at the time, Ali Osman Taha, blamed the economic crisis on the Sudanese themselves who, as he put it, have been "living beyond their means." In a country where the majority of families rely on remitting money from expatriate relatives (i.e., Sudanese workers abroad) for their livelihood, Taha publicly stated that the tendency of Sudanese to maintain extended families – where one individual works and ten others rely on his income – is the real reason that local production and incomes are at such low levels.[36]

To be sure the loss of oil revenue following South Sudan's secession and the imposition of economic austerity policies inspired the protests in the summer of 2012. Nevertheless, the timing of the protests and organizational strategies utilized therein were clearly related to the protests and transitions in the larger Arab world. In the wake of the Arab uprisings that begin in Tunisia in late 2010, observers of Sudanese politics were near unanimous in declaring that the Sudanese government will "not buckle" to popular protests anytime soon. Indeed, following in the lines of scholars of Arab authoritarianism, these analysts noted that Sudan's military establishment was beholden to the government just as they have been since Bashir first took power via a military coup in 1989. That is, that the upper ranks of the military are still loyal to his rule, that the formal political opposition is weak and discredited, and that civil society is even more divided than that of Tunisia and Egypt. As one Sudan analyst aptly put it: "[T]here is certainly discontent with the regime, but it's unclear if enough of the right factors are present to complete the equation in Khartoum [because] protests undertaken thus far have not taken root with a broad section of the population."[37] The influential International Crisis Group similarly argued that "years of subjugation at the hands of the ruling NCP have yielded both political apathy and a weak opposition."[38] Indeed, the wide-scale popular protests of December 2018 came as a surprise to many precisely because the general consensus among analysts was that, in the case of Sudan, the heavy hand of the security services and corresponding fears among the population act to inhibit such a pro-democracy uprising.

The question having to do with whether Sudan will remain resistant democratization then, as now, hinges, on an understanding of factors long associated with the durability of the authoritarian regimes in the Arab world. These include the fact that Arab countries possess weak civil societies, have middle classes beholden to state patronage for their survival, and opposition political parties which are either weak (i.e., Egypt, Sudan) or simply nonexistent. However, as the events in Tunisia and Egypt have shown, none of these conditions precluded the move toward democratization. Indeed, what they have demonstrated is that a weakly organized opposition does not necessarily prevent mass mobilization although it certainly plays a central role as an obstacle to democratic consolidation.

How then can we evaluate the deep popular discontent among Sudanese which resulted in the 2018 popular mobilization calling for yet another period of democracy in Sudan. For the Sudan the answer is relatively straightforward: It lies in the regime's capacity to maintain a monopoly on the means of coercion. As scholars of authoritarianism have persuasively argued, when the state's coercive apparatus remains coherent and effective, it can face down popular disaffection and survive significant illegitimacy. Conversely, where the state's capacity of coercion is weak or lacks the will to crush popular protests, democratic transitions in the Arab world and elsewhere can occur.[39]

Consequently, in the case of the Sudan, the first key question is, how can we best understand the weakening of the Bashir regime's capacity for coercion vis-à-vis a resurgent civil society opposition in the lead up to the December 2018 popular uprising in the country? What the examples of Tunisia and Egypt have demonstrated is that the answer to this question depends on the state's fiscal health, the level of international support, and how entrenched (i.e., institutionalized) the state security sector is in civil society. As in the other Arab countries, taken together, these factors determine whether the level of popular mobilization outweighs the capacity of the coercive apparatus of the regime.

Consequently, the durability of Bashir's authoritarian regime eventually ended due to a number of reasons. First, the level of international support was extremely low. Indeed, only a few months after southern secession the United States reimposed economic sanctions on the Sudan. In combination with the standing ICC's indictment of Bashir issued in July 2010, this increased Bashir's pariah status. More importantly, this diminished any hope on the part of the NCP to generate much needed foreign direct investment and international as well as local legitimacy.

Second, following almost a decade of remarkable growth in GDP (real gross domestic product) averaging 7.7 percent annually, thanks to oil exports, growth declined sharply to 3 percent since 2010.[40] The economic crisis was further compounded by a sharp decline in oil-export revenues as a result of the secession of the oil-rich south, deteriorating terms of trade, and minimal flows of foreign investment outside the oil sector. Consequently, the Bashir regime suffered from an enormous scarcity of foreign currency with which to finance spending to shore up its support base. The financial crisis resulted in the imposition of economic austerity measures leading to cost of living protests beginning as early as 2012. Perhaps more importantly in political terms, it also weakened Khartoum's capacity to suppress dissent since more than 70 percent of oil-export revenue prior to South Sudan's secession was funneled to support the military and PDF in the country. Third, as witnessed by the protests in Khartoum and throughout the north beginning in 2012, a wide cross section of Sudanese already mobilized in opposition to the regime. In addition, protests – which spread to central Sudan in al-Jazira, Kosti, and the Nuba Mountain region as early as 2012 – were accompanied by cyber activism. In a pattern similar to Egypt and Tunisia, this maintained the link between Sudanese in the country and the hundreds of thousands of Sudanese citizens in the diaspora.

Taken together these factors served to further weaken the capacity of the Bashir regime in ways that could not forestall the call for democratization indefinitely. But the most telling and important reason for the Bashir's regime's diminishing authoritarianism was in the fact that the hitherto institutionalized security sector became increasingly fragmented and the top leadership gravely divided. Following the country's partition, political power became centered on Bashir and a close network of loyalists. Moreover, concerned about a coup from within the military establishment, Bashir purposely fragmented the security services, relied increasingly on personal and tribal loyalties, and the formerly strong NCP party no longer had a significant base of social support even among hard-line Islamists.[41] This division was clearly illustrated as early as 2011 by a public dispute between two of the most influential figures in Bashir's government: Nafie Ali Nafie (presidential advisor and head of state security) who along with Bashir represented the hard-line faction opposed to constitutional reforms and Ali Osman Taha (second vice president) who called for inclusion of some opposition parties to help in drafting a new constitution.

In the shifting post-secession landscape Bashir tried to pursue a two-pronged strategy aimed at reviving the state's financial capacity and political legitimacy. On the one hand, the regime imposed economic reforms as part of an effort to strengthen the financial capacity of the state by further reducing the state's role in the economy and already meager public service provisioning. On the other hand, while Omar Bashir routinely insisted on the vigorous reimposition of stricter shari'a legislation, other prominent members of the NCP made strong overtures to the regime's political rivals in a clear bid to revive the state's waning political legitimacy among groups in civil society.

This is largely a result of the fact that civil society opposition grew stronger following the partition of the country. Most notably, in July 2012 after two decades of interparty squabbling, the main opposition parties allied under the National Consensus Forces (NCF) signed the Democratic Alternative Charter (DCA) calling for regime change "through peaceful means." The NCF included the National Umma Party (NUP) of former prime minister Al-Sadiq al-Mahdi and the Popular Congress Party (PCP) led by the late Hassan Turabi, the Sudanese Communist Party, and a coalition of professional associations and labor unions. The NCF agreed on a three-year transition period governed by a caretaker cabinet and a presidential college with rotating chairmanship to rule the country when the NCP's regime is overthrown. In response, and just days after the signing of the DCA, the first vice president, Ali Osman Mohammed Taha, announced that the government was willing to approach the opposition parties for dialogue on the "alternation" of power. What remained to be seen was whether the Bashir regime would extend this accommodationist stance to the rebel coalition of the Sudanese Revolutionary Forces (SRF). The SRF, the most important military insurgent opposition, includes the factions of three groups from Darfur in addition to the Sudan People's Liberation Movement North (SPLM-N), in South Kordofan, who had been fighting to topple the regime through military means. Nevertheless, it was clear, on the eve of the popular uprising of 2018, that the significant divisions in the ruling

NCP party, in combination with the country's international isolation, the deep economic crisis following the south's secession, and persistent levels of popular discontent and mobilization were strong indications that Sudan – a country that witnessed two previous popular revolts that dramatically turned the tide of national politics – would find itself drawing important inspiration from its own history as well as its northern neighbors while following its own path and distinctive "Sudanese" trajectory.

## *Just fall, that is all:* Sudan's 2018 Popular Uprising

Nevertheless, when the wide-scale protests erupted in Sudan in December 2018 and continued unabated calling for President Omer Bashir to step down few would have predicted that this latest iteration of a popular uprising in Sudan would be the first step toward paving the way for a transitional interim period intended to usher in multiparty democracy. This is because, not surprisingly, as with similar protests in the past, the Bashir regime sought a military solution to quell the protests deploying the police and paramilitary security forces against peaceful protestors in Khartoum and throughout the country. By the time Omer Bashir was ousted from power on April 11 the following year more than 200 people had been killed, many as a result of torture in the government's "ghost houses," and more than 2,000 anti-government activists were held in detention despite the regime's repeated insistence at the time that they were intent on releasing political detainees.

Significantly, and despite the government's frequent pronouncements that the protests were relatively small and would therefore have little impact on the regime, or that the demonstrations were essentially sponsored by saboteurs, thugs, or "foreign elements," the popular intifada not only produced significant policy changes on the part of the regime, it clearly undermined the rule of Omer Bashir in ways that led to the overthrow of his thirty-year authoritarian rule. By April 11, 2019, in the wake of continued and sustained demonstrations, strikes and sit-ins across Sudanese civil society, Bashir was compelled to put in place policies to upgrade his authoritarian rule. He was forced to postpone a constitutional amendment that would have allowed him to run for a third term in office, declare a state of emergency in Khartoum, disband the federal government, and replace local governors with senior army officers in a desperate attempt to maintain his power. However, these policies of both appeasement and repression emboldened anti-government protestors further. These policies were designed to give carte blanch to the security forces to use greater violence against the protestors and to further restrict political and civil liberties as well as to crack down on activists and opposition political parties. Immediately following Bashir's announcement of a state of emergency, protestors went back on the streets in more than fifty neighborhoods throughout the country, and particularly in Khartoum and Omdurman, calling once again for Bashir's removal chanting, among other slogans, one of the most uncompromising and popular refrains of the uprising: *Tasqut Bas* (Just fall, that is all).

## The "Periphery" as Catalyst of the Revolution

The protests erupted on December 19, 2018, in the working-class city of Atbara in River Nile state approximately 200 miles north of Khartoum. They were sparked by a three-fold increase in the price of bread. They began with protests led by secondary school students. They were very quickly joined by thousands of the residents in the city of Atbara. Within days anti-government demonstrations expanded across a wide range of cities and towns throughout the northern region and in the capital city of Khartoum. Chanting slogans such as the People Want the Fall of the Regime, inspired from the Arab Uprisings of late 2010 and 2011 in Tunisia and Egypt, respectively, the demonstrators quickly expanded their demands in ways that reflected deep-seated and wide-ranging political as well as economic grievances with the thirty-year authoritarian rule of Omer Bashir and his ruling party, the NCP.

However, despite the fact that political grievances and demands were at the forefront of the uprising, there is little question that these particular protests were first sparked by economic grievances that date back to the consequences of the secession of South Sudan in 2011. This led to the loss of 75 percent of oil revenue for Khartoum since two-thirds of the oil resources are in the south, and consequently approximately 60 percent of its foreign currency earnings. As a result, as noted ealier the Bashir regime implemented austerity measures in 2012 which resulted in similar anti-austerity protests at the time, although these were mostly centered in Khartoum and hence were more centralized than the 2018 protests. Similarly, one of the main factors for the demonstrations was the implementation of IMF-backed austerity measures which led to lifting of the subsidies on bread and fuel and quickly sparked the first of the demonstrations on December 19, 2018. What is important to emphasize, however, is that these protests were not only rooted in opposition to economic austerity measures. They were crucially a result of a widely understood opposition to decades of rampant corruption, including "privatization" policies that transferred assets and wealth to the regime's supporters, and the theft of billions of dollars of profits from the period of the oil boom in the country as well as, in more recent years, the theft of gold.

## A New Pattern of Mobilization and Protest

Following the lead of cities in the periphery, in Khartoum, the demonstrations also began in protest against a deep economic crisis associated with the rise in the prices of bread, fuel, and a severe liquidity crisis. But these demands quickly evolved into calls for the ouster of Bashir from power. Importantly, the Sudanese Professional Association (SPA), which had taken the lead in organizing and scheduling the protests, had initially marched to the Parliament in Khartoum in late December demanding that the government raise wages for public sector workers and for the legalization of informally organized professional and trade unions. However, after security forces used violence against the peaceful protests, these demands quickly escalated into the call for the removal of the ruling NCP, the structural transformation of governance in Sudan, and a transition to democracy.

These demands were similar to those associated with previous popular protests against the regime, including those of 2011, 2012, and 2013. However, what is most important to note with respect to the 2018 protests is that they were unprecedented in terms of their length and sustainability, their geographical spread throughout the entire country, and the remarkable coalition of youth groups, civil society organizations, and opposition political parties that joined in these protests which continued for over six months and ultimately resulted in a power-sharing agreement between a transitional military council and the main opposition coalition the Forces of Freedom and Change (FFC). Equally important is that the coordination of these demonstrations followed a remarkably new, innovative, and sustained process. This is important to highlight because it clearly shows that, just as the authoritarian regime of Omer Bashir had historically implemented policies designed to weaken the opposition in order to prevent any threat to the regime by dismantling labor and trade unions, establishing a wide range of paramilitary militias linked to the state, and putting down armed opposition as well as anti-government activists in civil society, demonstrators also learned from the unsuccessful anti-regime protests of the past. Led by the newly established Sudanese Professional Association, a network of parallel trade and professional unions composed of doctors, engineers, and lawyers among other unions, the demonstrations were coordinated, scheduled, and essentially designed to emphasis sustainability over time rather sheer numbers, spread the protests throughout middle, working class, and poor neighborhoods, and coordinate with protestors in regions far afield from Khartoum, including the Eastern State on the Red Sea to the East, and Darfur to the far west of the country. In addition, the slogans promoted and utilized by the protestors also were purposefully framed to incorporate the grievances of the wider spectrum of Sudanese, including workers in the informal sector, and not just those of the middle class and ethnic and political elites centered in Khartoum and the Northern regions of the country. These slogans were essentially framed in ways designed to mobilize support across ethnic and racial categories, to emphasize that the only way forward is to oust Omer Bashir and the ruling regime from power, and to highlight not only the endemic and unprecedented level of corruption of the regime and its allies but also decades of human rights violations against civilians in the country by a wide range of security forces, and the wars waged by the regime in Darfur, the Blue Nile state on the border of South Sudan, and the Nuba Mountains in South Kordofan.

Indeed, perhaps one of the most notable aspects of the 2018–19 protests requiring closer analytical explication, and which distinguished them greatly from previous uprisings, was not only the sheer regional scale of the demonstrations but the hitherto unprecedented high level of solidarity across class, generational, and regional lines in the country. Youth activists and members of the professional associations not only challenged the political discourse of the state; they played a significant role in engineering cross-class alliances in the context of these demonstrations. Over the course of the six-month-long protests, strikes, work stoppages, and sit-ins were held not only on university campuses and secondary schools, but also among private sector and public sector employees and workers. Among the most important examples were the strikes by workers of Port Sudan on the Red Sea demanding the nullification of the sale of the southern Port to a foreign company, and several work stoppages and protests led by employees of some of the most important telecom providers and other private firms in the country.

## Understanding the Unraveling of Islamist Authoritarianism

Indeed, while many students of Arab and African authoritarianism in general, and Sudanese politics in particular, did not predict the onset of the new mobilization dynamics associated with the 2018 protests that ultimately led to the ouster of Omer Bashir, for more than a decade there were a number of indications that the era of Islamist authoritarianism was unraveling. In addition to the deepening of internal rivalries within the regime and the significant rise in socioeconomic grievances resulting from the economic crises, regime change came to be dependent not only on political opportunity; it was also a result of a number of crucial factors that were in clear evidence during my research prior to the protests of 2018. These included the fragmentation of a previously cohesive Islamist movement, a youth movement which had for a decade forged a new strategy linking formal as well as informal networks of collective action, the emergence in the strength and cohesion of opposition in civil society, and the fragmentation of the NCP's security forces into what Sudanese commonly refer to as *Quwaat al-Dawala al-Muwaaziyyah* (the forces of the parallel state). Taken together these developments explain why, in contrast to previous protests, the popular uprising of 2018 was successful in toppling Omar Bashir's three decades long authoritarian rule.

To be sure, the post–oil boom era played an important role in the disintegration of the regime of Omer Bashir. The decline in oil revenue resulting from the secession of South Sudan on July 9, 2011, led to the deepening of the economic crisis and eroded the authority of the state over the economy. As noted earlier, this, in turn, eroded the patronage networks of the regime, strengthened the rivalry within the NCP leadership, and exacerbated social and economic grievances across a wide spectrum of Sudanese in both urban and rural areas. During the prepartition period, oil accounted for 50 percent of domestic revenue and 95 percent of export earnings. Following the south's secession, Sudan lost 75 percent of its oil reserves and this resulted in a major adjustment to Sudan's fiscal situation.[42] The fiscal crisis of the state also aggravated the already stark imbalance between urban and rural regions in terms of social and economic development. According to the Bashir regime's own Ministry of Welfare and Social Security (MWSS), the loss of oil resulted in cuts to development and federal transfers to the states by 26 and 20 percent, respectively. It also resulted in the depreciation of the Sudanese pound against the US dollar resulting in a dramatic spike in the average inflation rate, which rose to 42 percent in the summer of 2011 up from an average of 13 percent in 2010. Moreover, since most food is imported the rise in inflation worsened poverty levels and impoverished many in the middle class.

As a consequence, the loss of oil revenue dramatically changed the social and economic landscape of the country, and it proved a key element in expanding grievances across the social and geographical spectrum undermining the ruling NCP regime. This is what laid the groundwork for the 2018 popular protests. During the period from 2000 to 2009 real growth in the gross domestic product (GDP) was growing at an average of 8 percent. In addition, and more importantly in terms of the livelihoods of the population, per capita income increased from $US 776 in 2004 to $US 1,570 in 2009.[43] Moreover, the revenue from the oil boom during this period and associated inflows of foreign direct investment (FDI) led to a boom in the service sector. The service sector contributed 40 percent of GDP, surpassing agriculture as the leading sector in the economy. This afforded employment opportunities for thousands of Sudanese, particularly in the urban centers buttressing the resiliency of the regime. It also enabled the NCP to expand its patronage networks in society. During this period, the regime embarked on the creation of state governments across the country and funded the payrolls of thousands of local government bureaucrats. However, although the economy was expanding, the benefits were unequally distributed. The allocation of services, employment and infrastructural projects remained concentrated in Khartoum state and reflected a distinct political logic designed to appease urban constituencies. As one World Bank study noted, during the CPA period, approximately 60 percent of development spending was on five major projects located within the central triangle in the north.[44] Moreover, while FDI expanded during this period it was primarily directed to the oil sector, construction, and services. By contrast, the agriculture sector and other traditional exports were neglected. This further worsened poverty and unemployment in rural areas since upward of 50 percent of the rural labor force is engaged in agricultural activities.

This regional and socioeconomic imbalance was a result of state spending that was disproportionally focused on the center; it reflected a particular strategic political vision on the part of the NCP regime. It was a vision that contended that the ruling elite would be able to survive without the West, East, and other peripheral regions. As noted earlier, this was a vision that promoted a policy of investing development finance in Khartoum and the central part of the country in order to ensure a higher rate of return on capital investment. But this vision also had a political component in that it advocated this policy so as to serve as an insurance strategy against the possibility of the fall of the regime in the context of the insurgencies in the periphery. Significantly, in the context of the secession of the south and the loss of oil revenue, this vision became a de facto reality until the fall of Omer Bashir. Moreover, given the regional imbalance in levels of poverty and other social indicators between Khartoum and other regions this trend exacerbated the economic and social grievances among Sudanese outside the capital city in ways that would lay the groundwork for the peripheral regions sparking the historic protests in December 2018.

## Fragmentation of Islamist Networks: *Al-Sayihoon* (The Wanderers)

Another factor associated with the demise of the Bashir regime had to do with the divisions within the Islamist movement itself and specifically the emergence of a new Islamist oppositional movement that came to be known as the *Sayihoon* or the Wanderers. In fact, some of the causes underlying the power struggles within the NCP regime emerged as a legacy of the evolution and fragmentation of a once-unified Islamist movement that held sway over state and civil society for three decades. The *Sayihoon* represented those who became disillusioned by the financial and political corruption of the regime, its departure from the "Islamic call" (or Da'wa), the partition (or "loss") of South Sudan, and the constant divisions and squabbling among the leaders of the ruling NCP. However, rather than reflecting a unified ideological front, or Islamist political agenda, the *Sayihoon* were composed of three factions, or fragments, of the Islamist movement: supporters of the late Hassan Turabi and other disillusioned Islamists who returned to his fold and joined the PCP; hard-line Islamic militants who, as former members of the PDF militia, had fought in the "Jihadist" wars against the south and the Nuba Mountains in the 1990s; and a younger generation of Islamists who viewed themselves as moderate, democratically inclined "reformers." The latter, in particular, continue to represent the newest trend of the Islamists movement. They are an influential component of the *Sayihoon* in that they have greater legitimacy in Sudanese civil society. These self-proclaimed reformers are led by Ghazi Salih al-Dein al-Atabani, who while a member of the NCP had long been estranged from the upper echelons of the regime, and his former patron, Ali Osman Taha. This reformist group attracted many younger Islamists in the country by acknowledging the mistakes the movement has made in the past, calling for the revitalization of the Islamic Da'wa, an anti-corruption agenda, and grassroots mobilization that would pave the path toward a "peaceful" transition to democracy.

Another important trend in the increasing fragmentation of the Islamist movement is associated with the rise of a militant Salafist group. Consequently, by the time regime Bashir fell, the Islamist movement came to be divided along the lines of Islamist reformers led by Atabani, hard-line Islamists formerly linked to Bashir and the military, and an emergent Salafist movement of a far more militant variety. The emergence of militant Islamists, both tacitly and directly supported by the Bashir regime, deepened grievances among moderate Muslim organizations and women. Salafi militants openly launched attacks on Mosques frequented by members of the more moderate Sufi movements, and they also engaged in a series of violent attacks against unveiled women on the streets of Khartoum.

Importantly, however, the Bashir regime's policy of supporting militant Islamists to divide the Islamists opposition led to the unintended consequence of backfiring against the regime itself. Specifically, militant Islamists vociferously criticized their own patrons within the NCP establishment. On March 5, 2013, for example, the pro-Salafist newspaper, *al Muharir*, ran an editorial in which it described Bashir and other government officials as "engaged in usury, looting and manipulating the nation's faith and religion."[45]

## Linking Informal and Formal Networks: The Youth Movement and Collective Action

Although Sudan witnessed two previous popular protests that succeeded in toppling military authoritarian regimes in 1964 and again in 1985, the wide-scale scope of the December 2018 uprising was unprecedented in the country's history. More specifically, the coordination and linkages forged between informal (i.e., unregistered) trade and labor unions, civil society organizations, and youth activists with the popular and working-class segments of the population who are essentially workers in the informal economy was one of the most important reasons for the durability of the protests. Ultimately, it was the success in organizing across the formal-informal social spectrum that sustained the protests. The idea that informal networks (commonly referred to as *al-Mujtama'at al-Muwazziyyah*) of professional and trade unions should engage more closely with street activists and workers in the informal economy was not one that had been vigorously envisioned or promoted by many political actors involved in previous popular protests. This development played a key role in sustaining the protests and in undermining the Bashir regime in ways that could not easily have been predicted when the uprising first erupted in Atbara, the city in the outlying northern province of River Nile State.

Importantly, in the course of my research on youth activism in 2013, it was clearly evident that leaders of such youth movements as Girifna (We are fed up) and Sudan Change Now (SCN) had carefully begun to craft a new form of opposition to the Islamist authoritarian regime. Like youth movements elsewhere, the Sudanese youth movement can be generally described as a political and social reform movement consisting chiefly of youth between the ages of 15 and 24. However, this common definition of what constitutes "youth" does not accurately reflect the demographic and social changes in Sudan, nor the grievances motivating their political and social activism. As of 2012, labor force participation and the unemployment rates among the young stood at 32.9 percent and 22 percent, respectively, compared to 43 percent and 11 percent for adults.[46] Moreover, Sudan's labor market is highly underdeveloped and heavily dependent on agriculture and the informal sector. These factors, along with Sudan's high birth rate, have resulted in a relatively young population and a high proportion of young people of working age. Indeed, like many countries in Africa and the Arab world, Sudan has struggled to create an adequate number of jobs for new entrants to the labor market and continues to be faced with a bulging youth population with unemployment rising sharply particularly among highly educated young people.

These demographic changes have altered the very structure of family life, as a whole generation of lower- and middle-class Sudanese cannot access regular employment and afford to marry. As one scholar has noted, as a result of these societal changes, "youth" is no longer a fleeting phase between traditional childhood and adulthood; it represents an "extended generational stage that presents both new opportunities and a different set of challenges and responsibilities to young people and the society at large."[47] The Sudanese youth movement which played such an important role in the protests of 2018–2019 emerged from this context. It represents a loose coalition of working, middle-class Sudanese, as well as youth in the informal sector, many in their twenties and thirties, who deftly utilized faster communication and social media to voice both political as well as social grievances against the regime, the older generation of politicians, and even the traditional patriarchal family.

In strategic terms and following in the model of the "Arab Spring" and earlier *intifadas* in Khartoum, the leaders of the youth movement in Sudan engaged in forging links with a broad spectrum of groups in civil society including independent unions, middle and lower segments of businessmen and traders not linked to NCP patronage, some segments of the upper classes, and expatriate Sudanese. Specifically, as early as 2011, they linked up with the informally organized unions of physicians, pharmacists, lawyers, secondary school teachers, and a revitalized bus drivers' union, all of which organized a series of strikes over issues of health care, education, and increases in benefits and wages for public service workers almost a decade prior to 2018. It is important to note that since the early 1990s the regime had co-opted most union activity and repressed independent union activity. However, as early as 2011 "informal" or "parallel" unions emerged. These include not only the unions noted earlier but also new informal associations comprising individuals previously dismissed by the regime such as *Ittihad al-mafsuleen*

(Association of the Dismissed), *Ittihad al-Ma'sheen* (Association of Retirees), and *Tajumu Umaal Qita' al-'Am al-Mafsuleen* (Union of Dismissed Public Factory Workers).

Interestingly, despite some claims by traditional political leaders to the contrary, youth leaders I interviewed in 2012, 2013, 2014, and late 2018 insisted that they were certain of having support among a wide spectrum of Sudanese, which they said comes from their experience and linkage with the evolution of student activism on campus. Specifically, their strategy was to focus on social and economic issues, which unites a wide range of civil society organizations and populations in marginal areas as a key component of political change. They noted that the traditional political parties have lost support because they continue to focus on the mechanics of political change and the distribution of political power rather than on socioeconomic issues relevant to the vast majority of Sudanese. The youth leaders, therefore, tended to dismiss reformist policies such as the 2015 elections orchestrated by Bashir to revive his legitimacy in society; rather, they pursued, in their own terms, a less "institutionalized political agenda" for change.[48]

Equally important, given the role ethnic divisions have played in impeding collective action in Sudan, youth activists were instrumental in bridging the ethnic and racial divide among many in civil society by working toward bridging the social distance between those belonging to Arab ethnic groups residing in the Arabized riverine center and north and Darfurian citizens in the west. An important example in this regard emphasized by a number of youth activists I interviewed occurred in 2012 following the killing of Darfurian students by security forces on the campus of the University of Gezira. In December of that year students protested the dean's decision to compel all students to pay fees including students from Darfur who had previously been exempted because of the war. During two days of strikes and protests the National Security and Intelligence Service (NISS) detained student leaders and killed four students from Darfur placing their corpses in shallow water as a way to deter further protests. In the aftermath, youth organizers mobilized thousands of protestors and forced the police and the NISS to withdraw from campus. In the same month, larger youth-led protests followed in Khartoum calling for solidarity with *Rabitat Awlad Darfur* (the Darfur Student Associations) a large, cross-campus student organization in the capital. In the context of the war in Darfur, and the incendiary racist discourse often utilized by the state, this was considered a breakthrough by the youth movement on issues that bridged a divide between residents from marginalized regions and those from central and north Sudan.

Importantly, and as recent scholarship on informal workers in Africa has observed, in economies where a broad section of workers rely primarily on the informal labor market for employment and income generation, any understanding of the new dynamics of, and potential capacity for, popular mobilization and collective action must take analytical care not to view laborers in the informal economy as "passive targets" for recruitment by formal unions and associations; rather, we should consider people in the informal economy as actors capable of various initiatives, including organizing themselves, despite the many obstacles they face. Indeed, as the historic 2018 popular protests demonstrated, organizing across the formal-informal spectrum should be assessed from the perspective of informal actors and activists and not merely from the vantage point of formal trade and labor unions and institutions.[49]

# 6 State Collapse, Informal Networks, and the Dilemma of State Building in Somalia

It is a central irony in the war on terrorist finance that it has proved counterproductive in the context of Somalia. A key assumption in counterterrorism policy is that weak and collapsed states serve as a breeding ground for terrorist recruitment and a refuge for global terrorist cells. Yet the regulatory constraints imposed on informal financial transfers have had the unintended consequence of potentially undermining state-building efforts in the very region of the world which is in most need of building and strengthening formal institutions. Somalia represents an important example in this regard. The hawwalat system continues to represent the most important conduit of capital accumulation. Moreover, in addition to ensuring the survival of millions of Somalis, the hawwalat have the potential to play an important role in ongoing state-building and consolidation efforts. A key determinant of state formation is the ability to both encourage and tax private economic activity in order to consolidate political control and expand the infrastructural reach and power of the state. The case of northern Somalia has clearly illustrated that achieving success in this sphere both reduces clan-based conflicts and stems the tide of extremism and terrorism.

In the more stable regions of Somalia (i.e., northwest and northeast) where I conducted my field research, political leaders have managed to gain the trust and cooperation of the Somali businessmen operating the hawwalat companies, who have earned windfalls from the lucrative trade in remittances and foreign currency. As a result, state builders, most notably in Somaliland (i.e.,northwest Somalia), have established a high level of peace and stability and revived governance institutions.[1] In November 2017, Somaliland witnessed an unprecedented fourth round of democratic elections with no violent incidence of extremism reported in any parts of the territory.[2] With the financial assistance of the Dahabshil[3] hawwalat and the cooperation of the business community, in northern Somalia, government employees collect revenue; salaried and uniformed police keep law and order; courts administer justice; and ministers dispense public services. In this respect, criminalizing major parts of the informal sector threatens the fragile peace and state building that has been achieved in some parts of Somalia.[4]

## The Origins and Legacy of State Collapse

To understand Somalia's contemporary economic and political dynamics, it is important to examine the underlying reasons for the collapse of the state. As Jamil Mubarak has keenly observed, "most of the resilient features of the post-state-collapse economy, which are attributed to the informal sector, emerged in response to the policies of the [Siad Barre] government."[5] Indeed, in Somalia while the boom in labor remittances in the 1970s and 1980s signaled a resurgent private sector the bulk of the country's labor force was "accommodated mostly as apprentices or family aides in a vast network of shops and workshops" – the informal sector, as distinct from the parallel sector from which the former received its money.[6] Moreover, when the recession period set in, it led to a great deal of unemployment. In fact, as early as 1978, a survey of the urban labor force demonstrated that officially registered wage earners numbered only 90,282 persons out of an estimated labor force of 300–360 thousand.[7]

By the mid-1980s the drop-in oil prices and the consequent slump in the Gulf countries increased unemployment (reaching as high as one-third) and remittances drastically declined. For a society that had for over a decade relied on its livelihood to be financed by remittances from family members outside Somalia the effect was devastating. Moreover, while many relied on supplementary income derived from informal, small-scale businesses financed by remittances, or some support from relatives who were farmers or pastoralists, the 1980s would signal increasing economic competition, pauperization, and social discontent. Moreover, the livestock trade which had always been transacted on the free market and whose profits accrued to private traders operating along fragmented markets that helped to both create and expand the parallel sector also declined drastically in 1983. In that year, Saudi Arabia imposed a ban on cattle imports from all African countries after the discovery of rinderpest. Livestock export earnings plummeted from $106 million in 1982 to $32 million two years later.[8]

This played a large role in Somalia's crisis. By the late 1980s, the overall economic picture for Somalia was grim: manufacturing output, always small, had declined by 5 percent between 1980 and 1987, and exports had decreased by 16.3 percent from 1979 to 1986. According to the World Bank, throughout the 1980s real GNP per person declined by 1.7 percent per year.[9] What was at stake in political terms was control of the exchange rate and hence the parallel market which constituted the financial underpinning of the clientelist system underpinning Barre's dictatorial rule. Eventually, mounting debt forced President Siad Barre to implement economic austerity measures, including currency devaluations, as a way to channel foreign exchange into the central banking system. However, this belated attempt at economic reform, and particularly financial liberalization, failed because Barre could no longer compete with the remittance dealers. The hawwalat continued to offer better rates and safer delivery than the state's extremely weak and corrupt-ridden regulatory and financial institutions could provide. Barre resorted to increasingly predatory and violent behavior, particularly as opposition, organized around clan families, grew. He singled out the Isaaq clan, the main beneficiaries of the remittance boom, for retribution. In Mogadishu and other southern towns, the government attempted to destroy the financial patrons of the Isaaq-led Somali National Movement (SNM) by arresting hundreds of Isaaq merchants and professionals. Generally, Barre's policies against the Isaaq aimed to marginalize them both politically and economically. For example, because the Isaaq enjoyed a monopoly over the livestock trade – a monopoly made possible by their control over the northwestern port of Berbera – Barre placed tariffs on livestock exports from the northern ports. He also outlawed the sale of the mild narcotic qat, a profitable source of revenue for the clan. This policy of economic repression, coupled with Barre's arming of non-Isaaq militias to fight and displace the Isaaq from their lands, further consolidated Isaaq clan identity and solidarity against both the state and neighboring clans, such as the Darod-Ogadenis.[10]

The ensuing civil war naturally exacted a debilitating cost on the economy. A rising import bill (petrol prices rose by 30 percent in 1988 alone) resulted in acute shortages of basic consumer goods and led to hoarding and the circulation of fraudulent checks as a popular form of payment. Barre's lifting of all remaining import restrictions in an effort to stimulate imports had no effect since most of the population were by this time outside government control either because of active opposition or because they were engaged in informal activity. Even Barre's attempts to keep his military alliance intact by raising its pay 50 percent and doubling military rations did not forestall opposition within the ranks as at first the Ogadenis and then other clans went into opposition.[11]

Barre's policies also meant that remittances from the Isaaq diaspora came to play an increasingly key role in financing both clan members' economic livelihoods and the SNM's insurgency against the regime. Prior to the outbreak of civil war in 1990, members of the Isaaq represented more than 50 percent of all Somali migrant workers, partly as a result of their historically close ties to the Gulf and their knowledge of Arabic. A large proportion of their remittances went to supply arms to the rural guerillas. In 1990 delegates of the SNM received USD 14–52 million; and the total remittances transferred to northern Somalia were in the range of USD 200–250 million.[12] The SNM provided crucial financial and logistical support to the Hawiye and other rebel clans, and guerilla warfare spread quickly to the central and southern parts of the country. In January 1991, the Hawiye-based United Somali Congress (USC), led by Gen. Muhammad Farah ‘Aidid and backed by the SNM, ousted Barre from Mogadishu.

By the time Barre's regime fell, the Somali state ceased to exist as reinforced clan identities were asserted in the struggle over territory and increasingly scarce resources. In the North the Somali National Movement dominated. The Somali Salvation Democratic Front (SSDF), consisting mainly of the Majeerteen, a subclan of Barre's own Darod clan, became active once again in the northeast and central regions. Formed as early as 1978, this was the oldest opposition force, but it had little success due to the absence of an autonomous financial base. In the south the Somali Patriotic Movement (SPM) was made up of the Ogadeni, another subclan of the Darod. Between the Juba and Shebelle rivers in the southwest the Rahenwein were represented by the Somali Democratic Movement (SDM) whose weak social position reflects their agro-pastoral base. Possessing the most fertile region in the country, the Rahanwein became the main victims of the war-induced famine and violence as powerful neighboring warlords sought to displace them. Also caught in the fighting in what became known as the "triangle of death" were other riverine populations, namely the Bantus who as descendants of slaves retained an inferior social status. In the center, around the capital of Mogadishu, the epicenter of conflict, was the Hawiye-based United Somali Congress (USC). The USC, founded only one year prior to Barre's ouster, was a relative newcomer to the conflict, but came to occupy a prominent position in 1990 mainly because of its hold over the capital. When the USC broke up the following year into the Hawiye subclans of the Haber Gidir led by Ali Mahdi and the Abgal led by Mohamed Farah Aideed, internecine violence increased dramatically.[13] The fateful decision of southerner Ali Mahdi to declare himself president in a hastily convened 1991 "reconciliation" conference in Djibouti within days after Aideed's forces had driven Barre into exile in Kenya caused an escalation of the violence in Mogadishu. Aideed refused to recognize Mahdi's appointment and attacked his forces in the capital, while years of northern resentment came to the fore resulting in the Isaaq's unilateral declaration of an independent Republic of Somaliland in May 1991.

In ensuing years clan militias emerged to fill the vacuum of the collapsed state. Across the early 1990s, all of Somalia, but particularly the southern and central regions, witnessed a pattern of increasingly violent interclan and intra-subclan fighting. These conflicts broke out largely because of competition over economic resources as well as violent struggles over political authority. Most notably, the USC was divided into two Hawiye sub-subclans: the Hawiye/Habr-Gedir/Abgal clan of ʻAli Mahdi and the Hawiye/Habr-Gedir /Saʻad clan of Gen. ʻAidid.[14] Tension between the two factions arose when in the wake of Barre's ouster, the Abgal faction unilaterally formed an interim government and appointed Mahdi as president.[15] The two opposing movements claimed sovereignty over Mogadishu and utilized their subclan networks and militias to regulate entrance and exit from these areas by demanding payment and protection fees.[16] Initially, this was represented by the division of the city between the north and south, which were controlled by ʻAli Mahdi and Gen. ʻAidid respectively.[17] Eventually, the conflict led to the disintegration of the USC – a harbinger of the heightened level of violence that has plagued southern and central Somalia to the present day.[18]

As newly organized subclan networks rapidly proliferated in a society absent institutions of law and order, the business of protection within Somalia's unregulated economy quickly came to dominate large swaths of southern and central Somalia. The new subclan networks that coalesced over different territories used coercion and violence to extract taxes from village harvests and commercial establishments. They also took hostages for ransom. Indeed, the "economy of war" in Somalia took several forms. Youth gangs began to engage in activities such as robbery and looting as a means to generate income. More profitable, however, were illicit informal economic activities, including the embezzlement of foreign-aid funds; the printing and circulation of counterfeit money; the smuggling and exportation of charcoal, qat, copper, and machinery; and, more recently, piracy.[19] Piracy, in particular, became a sophisticated economic activity primarily because it is facilitated by a very profitable alliance between some members of the business community and clan militias.[20] Writing poignantly in the wake of state collapse, Somali scholar Abdi Samatar noted that the "opportunistic methods with which groups and individuals marshaled support to gain and retain access to public resources finally destroyed the very institution that laid the golden egg."[21]

## Variations in State Building

One of the main legacies of the collapse of the Somalia state was the strong emergence of clan-centered forms of social organization throughout the country. In the wake of the disintegration of the formal institutions of the state, clan solidarity emerged as the primary basis of political, social, and economic organization. However, while interclan and subclan conflict continues to plague much of Somalia, in the northwest state builders have successfully established a relatively stable and democratic state resulting from a highly complex process of negotiation and reconciliation between clans. This included the demobilization of armed militias and the restoration of law and order.[22] Remarkably, since it broke away from the rest of Somalia in 1991, Somaliland has managed to build internal stability without the benefit of international recognition or significant foreign development assistance. Indeed, few international organizations participated in ending internal conflicts or substantially invested in establishing security through disarmament, demobilization, and reintegration or to promote democratization.

Somaliland's remarkable success in transitioning from a clan-based system of governance to multiparty elections was a result of a contentious and often violent process that included the use of traditional mechanisms of conflict resolution. In a constitutional referendum held on May 31, 2001, the vast majority of eligible voters in Somaliland approved a new democratic, multiparty system, thereby eliminating the institutionalization of clan leadership that had existed under the previous system of governance.[23] In 2010 and again in 2017, Somaliland further consolidated its nascent democracy by holding successive rounds of presidential elections, which brought a new political party to power in its capital of Hargeisa. Although Somaliland is now widely recognized as a legitimate state among its population, it has not been granted formal recognition by the international community. Nevertheless, Somaliland has consolidated its state building efforts. Ken Menkhaus, a foremost expert of the politics of the region, has noted that Somaliland has made a relatively successful transition from a clan-based polity to a multiparty democracy by holding local, presidential, and legislative elections and even overseeing a peaceful constitutional transfer of power following the death of the influential president Muhammad Ibrahim Egal in 2002.[24]

In contrast to Somaliland, the semi-autonomous northeastern region of Puntland, once touted as a success of the grassroots approach to reestablishing national stability and widely viewed as one of the most prosperous parts of Somalia, continues to experience high levels of insecurity and political tension. At its root are poor governance, corruption, and a collapse of the intraclan cohesion and pan-Darod solidarity that led to its creation in 1998.[25] In contrast to Somaliland's leaders, none of the four presidents "did what was needed."[26] They did not embark on institution building, establish a proper development and regulatory framework, or build legitimate and efficient security arrangements. Nor has the leadership played a positive role in national reconciliation. In contrast to Somaliland's political elite, they have not managed to forge peace among different clans and subclans within Puntland or with their neighbors. "It was," in the words of one Somalia scholar from the region, "a lost opportunity since civil society was overwhelmingly supportive of the idea of an autonomous Puntland."[27] Indeed, when I returned to conduct further research in 2010 the state of security of the region was profoundly precarious. Residents routinely complained that salaries were not paid on time for public officials; police officers were forced to work on a volunteer basis; and competition over resources, including land, fuel, and fishing rights, led to intermittent conflict between nomads, agro-pastoralists, and fishermen. As one resident of Eyl, in the Nugal province of Puntland, put it: "[W]e have no police force to enforce the law; elders continue to try to intervene to settle disputes since there is an absence of a strong administration and no security. Only mobs and thugs prosper in a community without order."[28]

Standing in starker contrast to both Somaliland and Puntland, Somalia – that is, the southern and central regions of the Republic of Somalia that remain, at least, nominally, a part of that state – has failed to build durable state institutions. It remains beset by continued clan conflict, Islamist extremism, and displacement. Unlike Somaliland, which has benefited from a more united and cohesive clan structure organized under the Isaaq clan family, Somalia is home to a far more diverse and less unified constellation of different clans and subclans. In recent years, the rapid rise of militant Islamist activism has influenced state building efforts in variable ways. In April 2006, the Somali capital city of Mogadishu came under the control of the Union of Islamic Courts (UIC), a cross-clan organization comprising Somalia's Islamist organizations. The UIC seized power from the then increasingly weak clan-based Transitional Federal Government (TFG) in an attempt to establish a system of governance based on shari'a instead of clan loyalty.[29] After sixteen years of intraclan fighting and conflict, the UIC implemented a particularly austere and militant version of shari'a (including *huduud* punishments) to institute law and order. As a consequence, the Islamic courts achieved a short-lived measure of stability in the city before the UIC was ousted in 2007 by an alliance of Ethiopian and US military forces.

Developments in Somaliland, Puntland, and the Republic of Somalia represent alternative approaches to state building that transcend conventional understandings of the role of ethnic and Islamic networks in state formation. Examining these contrasting political trajectories helps illuminate how the transnational character of Somalia's civil war was not only an obstacle to peace building but also, in the case of Somaliland, an opportunity for state formation in the context of an increasingly internationalized economy. Examining the state building projects in Somaliland and Puntland alongside the emergence of Islamist militancy in Somalia also reveals how war, state making, and clan and Islamist networks are related in variable ways.

## State Building in Weak States

Considering the civil conflict underpinning the disintegration of the state in Somalia, a closer analysis of the balance between civil conflict, protection, extraction, and state making is required in order to understand the trajectory of state-building efforts in contemporary Somalia. As scholars of state formation have long observed, historically state building has been ancillary to war making.[30] To support and finance their wars, rulers developed centralized control over private armies, developed institutions to settle disputes, and established rules and courts to control the behavior of the people within their boundaries. Most important, war makers strive to develop fiscal and extractive capacities since success in war depends on the state's ability not only to tax its subjects, but also to generate revenue from domestic and transnational financial sources.[31]

In the case of Somalia, this framework usefully highlights the interaction between war making, state making, and capital accumulation (i.e., extraction). Moreover, this model has important implications for our comparative analysis of state building efforts in Somaliland, Puntland, and Somalia. This is because all the regions have experienced intermittent interclan strife while simultaneously embarking on efforts at state building and state consolidation. Consequently, variations in the way the actors have attempted to collect taxes, make war, and eliminate their local rivals are important and highly unpredictable. Throughout Somalia, the business of "protection" – "the racket" in which a local strong man forces merchants to pay tribute through threats of violence – has indeed determined political developments and the social organization of collective action in various parts of the country. The emergence of regionally based political organizations and initial attempts to establish local currencies, and institute law and order though military and ideological means, are very illustrative here.

Nevertheless, this understanding of the state building process in post-conflict settings falls short in two important ways. The first problem is that this framework's focus on interstate war as the mechanism underpinning state formation obscures the fact that this type of war is a rare occurrence in the developing world and in Africa in particular.[32] Indeed, as a number of scholars have documented, since 1945, *intrastate* wars have dominated armed conflict.[33] This empirical reality associated with the frequency of intrastate wars has led students of state building to refute the applicability of Tilly's model, asserting that in the absence of an external threat and the presence of an internal one, the state can no longer penetrate society to extract resources.[34]

What has not been sufficiently analyzed, however, is this influential model's eurocentrism. According to Charles Tilly, the history of state formation reveals that "states built upon religious organizations were significantly weaker than secular states, as the latter were less fragmented and, therefore, more capable of accumulating capital and means of coercion."[35] But this line of reasoning assumes a priori that a state based on Islamic institutions, or for that matter clan networks, cannot survive in the modern state system. Contrary to this conventional understanding of state formation, state building experiments in Somalia, though based on clan identity and invented tradition, may, depending on the interplay between formal political authorities and identity-based trust networks, represent legitimate alternatives to secular institutions. The fact that Islamist experiments such as the Union of Islamic Courts in central Somalia have failed is due to a combination of external and internal dynamics. This is clearly in evidence when we compare the variations of state building across this Muslim country.

Equally important in the case of Somalia is the fact that developing states are far more vulnerable to regional and international interventions than European states were at the time of their formation. They are also crucially affected by shifts in the global economy. However, what still needs to be explained is the precise manner in which international economic imperatives are interacting with local economic and cultural variations in ways that are decisively shaping political developments in the northwest and northeast. For example, why are clan-based cleavages enjoying greater political salience and popular legitimacy in Somaliland, while Islamist identification is making more inroads in the more homogenous northeast (Puntland)?[36] Indeed, without understanding the impediments as well as opportunities posed by international economic linkages in state-building efforts, any understanding of these developments in Somalia can only be partial. In particular, given the fact that remittance inflows represent the largest source of foreign exchange and are relied upon as a major source of income by 46 percent and 38 percent of all urban households in Somaliland and Puntland, respectively, it is also important to address the latter's complex role in contemporary political developments.

## Clan Networks and State Disintegration

As Charles Tilly famously observed, over most of history, no regime has been able to survive without drawing on resources and the support held by trust networks such as religious or kinship groups. "Rulers' application of various combinations among coercion, capital and commitment in the course of bargaining with subordinate populations produces a variety of regimes."[37] Tilly focused on the threat that contemporary democracies may face if major segments of the population withdraw their trust networks from public politics, but this development has far more profound consequences for weak states like Somalia where it can jeopardize the very foundation of state institutions leading to the collapse of central political authority. In order to properly examine Somalia's civil unrest and its implications for state building we must first turn to precolonial traditions that once regulated the country's social, political, and economic order. In doing so, a clear distinction can be drawn between traditional social organizations and the divisive politicization of clanship that occurred during and after the colonial period.

The nature of precolonial Somali society depended largely on communal interdependence rather than rigid hierarchal authority.[38] Patrilineal kinship ties are derived from one of six clan families – Dir, Isaaq, Hawiye, Darod, Digil, and Rahanwein. Somaliland consists mainly of the Isaaq, Dir, and Darod clans, while southern Somalia is comprised of the Hawiye, Digil, and Rahanwein clans.[39] Subclans known as diya-paying groups (blood compensation groups) were derived from these larger clan families and served to unify kinsmen within a mediating structure. More specifically, kinsmen under these groups are bound by a contractual alliance based on collective payment for wrongs committed by any group member. In effect, this alliance serves as a political as well as a legal entity.[40]

However, beyond patrilineal genealogy and blood ties, cross-clan cooperation was manifested in both the tenets of Islam and customary law or Xeer. According to I. M. Lewis, Islam is "one of the mainsprings of Somali culture," and historically, Somalia's religious leaders have positioned themselves outside of the conflict between clans.[41] Similarly, Xeer served as a unifying structure, which was "socially constructed to safeguard security and social justice within and among Somali communities."[42] This structure, utilized in the ongoing processes of state building in Somalia, thus served as a Somali-wide social contract in that it governed and regulated economic relations as well as social life. In a society that lacked an overarching state structure, where the household was the basic economic unit, and where the means of daily survival were widely distributed, the Xeer prevented the exploitation of one's labor or livestock.[43] Moreover, within precolonial Somalia there did not exist individuals or groups who could monopolize coercive power or economic resources. Clan elders were restricted from exercising such control beyond their households, and their status as political leaders was limited to their role as mediators within and among their clans.[44] In effect, Somali society was regulated by traditional principles of interaction based on clanship, Islam, and Xeer.[45] The Somali scholar Ahmed Yusuf Farah explained the complex interaction of these three aspects of Somali communal life in eloquent terms:

> The sub-clan affiliation is an important one because it represents the most important social group in judicial terms. Known as the Diya paying group, it is at this level of the sub-clan where elders appoint representatives to pay and receive blood compensation as, for example, if someone kills another. It is this group which is charged with negotiating the terms of material value. This is what is known as Xeer: that is, the customary code of conduct which regulates relations between and among groups. It defines the sharing of resources like water, land and blood compensation. [Moreover], in areas where Islamic tradition violates the Xeer the elders just ignore them . . . for them [elders of the subclans] material and class interests and competition override religious strictures.[46]

The introduction of the colonial order, beginning in the early nineteenth century, drastically transformed these traditional networks of the precolonial period. The direct effects of this transformation disrupted the equilibrium of clans and the management and distribution of resources.[47] Although northern and southern Somalis were exposed to different colonial strategies, both regions experienced a high level of intrusion into their social and political systems. Both British and Italian administrative apparatuses politicized the leadership of clan elders. This created a system of chieftainship whereby the role of the clan elder was transformed from regulating clan relations and resources to regulating access to state benefits.[48] In Somaliland, for example, clan chiefs were paid a stipend to enforce diya-paying, thus justifying the British colonial strategy of collective punishment.[49] This practice of chieftainship throughout Somalia undermined the legitimacy of clan elders and their traditional authority by violating the very traditional social structures that had once mitigated against hierarchical authority.

Importantly, however, the colonial experiences of northern and southern Somalia varied in certain respects in ways that illuminate the context of present variations in the success of peace and state building in the different regions of the country. Specifically, the Italian colonialists adopted a method of direct rule, economic intervention, and commercialization of the pastoral economy in southern Somalia. In contrast,

British Somaliland was left economically "undisturbed and governed by indirect rule."[50] The economic effects sustained in southern Somalia undermined the traditional system of "communitarian pastoralism" by producing and distributing agricultural goods according to political motivations rather than household or communal necessity.[51] The commercialization of the economy and direct taxation of livestock produced a nascent class system that privileged merchants and political elite while exploiting the agricultural producers – a process that was previously prevented by the institution of the Xeer.

It is this class system that set the stage for the transformation of clan networks into a hardened clannism under the authoritarian rule of President Siad Barre whereby certain clans enjoyed the political and economic largesse of the state. Upon taking over the presidency in 1969 Siad Barre began an aggressive campaign to eradicate clan loyalties in favor of an irredentist Pan-Somali identity and he went so far as to outlaw any acknowledgment (public or private) of the existence of clans.[52] Contrary to this policy of nationalism, however, Barre engaged heavily in the instrumentalization of clan politics. In order to strengthen his power, he adopted "a divide and rule through blood ties" strategy that pitted one clan or subclan against the other.[53] Through such a policy, he was able to elevate his clan and that of his family members to a level of prominent political and social status. I. M. Lewis has argued that it was the Darod subclans of Barre – the Marehan, Ogaden, and Dulbahante – that dominated representation in parliament.[54] Aside from its supremacy over the political arena, by the 1970s this new political elite controlled most of Somalia's businesses particularly when Barre took over the formal financial sector.[55]

By 1977, Barre had extended his irredentist campaign beyond the territorial boundaries of Somalia, supporting ethnic Somali movements in Kenya, French Somaliland, and Ethiopia. The most significant demonstration of this support was extended to militants from his mother's clan, the Ogadeen in Ethiopia of both the Somalia Abo Liberation Front (SALF) and the Western Somalia Liberation Front (WSLF).[56] This prompted a forceful retaliation by the Ethiopian government, Somalia's long-time rival, thus commencing the Somali-Ethiopia war. Though the war initially engendered national solidarity, Barre's regime came under heavy scrutiny as a result of the influx of hundreds of thousands of Oromo and Ogadeen refugees and Somalia's defeat in 1978.[57] Such scrutiny resulted in an attempted coup by military officers and political opponents of the Darod/Majeerteen clan in 1978. Upon the failure of the coup, many of the perpetrators fled to Ethiopia and, by 1981, had organized under the movement the Somali Salvation Democratic Front (SSDF). Though it was comprised of Darod, Hawiye, and Isaaq clan members, by 1992 it was apparent that the SSDF was a Majeerteen militia.[58] Abdullahi Yusif, the first president of Puntland following the collapse of the state, was among the leading cadres of SSDF throughout the 1980s. Less than thirty years after attempting to overthrow the Barre regime through a clan-based militia and building strong ties with rival Ethiopia, Yusif was made president of Somalia's internationally supported Transitional Federal Government.[59]

Importantly, while Barre's polices institutionalized political preference along the lines of those clans and subclans that were closest to his own, they repressed other clan groups. The Isaaq, in particular, Somaliland's majority clan, were politically and economically marginalized under Barre's predatory regime.[60] The Isaaq were often subject to violent inter-clan violence instigated by the regime directly or by proxy-militias. Barre's tactic was to "militarize the clans be creating militias, giving them weapons, and then implicating them in the repression against a targeted clan segment" in order to fragment potential opposition to his regime.[61] In the early 1980s, for example, Barre resurrected Darod/Ogadeeni-Isaaq clan disputes over access to grazing water in the northern pasturelands. By extending his patronage to Ogadeeni fighters through arms supply, Barre encouraged them to fight the Isaaq and any disloyal Darod subclans.[62] By 1988, Barre's army had destroyed much of Somaliland's two major cities: Hargeisa and Burao. In response to the increasing strength of the Ogadeen and the alienation of the Isaaq clan under Barre's regime, it was at this historical juncture that the Somali National Movement (SNM) was created in 1981 and based in Ethiopia until 1988. Importantly, its origins lay in the strength of the Isaaq diaspora in the Gulf, whose remittances contributed significantly to Somaliland's economy. The creation of the SNM provoked hostile retaliation and further alienation from Barre's regime, which in turn strengthened the legitimacy, popularity, and internal cohesion of the various Isaaq subclans.

The Isaaq SNM movement was a clear example of both the utilization of clan networks for political interests and the increasing need for Somalis to seek political and economic refuge in clan identity from a repressive authoritarian regime. However, it would not have succeeded in producing a coherent and united opposition to Barre if the movement did not benefit from their engagement in informal economic activities in general and labor remittances in particular. Due to the economic alienation and state repression of Somaliland under the Barre regime, northern businessmen sought protection within clan-based credit systems, or *abbans* to manage their business networks and organize informal remittances from overseas.[63] The *abbans* connected local businessmen to the hawwalat, which utilized subclan norms of reciprocity to facilitate the trade.[64] This allowed northern businessmen to finance the armed struggle through remittances and informal networks during the Barre regime.

In addition to the Isaaq-led SNM, a large number of clan-based militant groups emerged in the late 1980s that played a key role in Barre's ouster. The Hawiye clan movement – the United Somali Congress (USC) – was based mostly in central and southern Somalia and formed its own militia in 1989. Indeed, by 1991 the tendency was for "every major Somali clan to form its own militia movement."[65] However, in a development that would be a key factor in future state-building projects in the country, aside from the Isaaq in later years, the general tendency was that most clan-based movements were plagued by intraclan rivalry among subclans in the post-collapse era. To be sure, interclan as well as intraclan feuds had certainly existed in precolonial Somalia, but the violence under Barre and in the civil war period was a drastic deviation from the traditional relations governing clan interaction.[66]

The legacy of the Barre regime was thus one of political, economic as well as societal destruction facilitated through the manipulation of clan networks in an attempt to strengthen his supporters and his increasingly personalized form of authoritarian rule. The result was the emergence of centrifugal movements centered on clan and subclan networks. From within this environment emerged insurgent militias who employed the sentiment of clan in order to rally allegiance, legitimate their authority, and extract resources – a far cry from the role of "traditional" clan elders. But just as these movements such as the SNM, SSDF, and UCM, based on clan networks, challenged and eventually overturned centralized coercive power and extractive capabilities (i.e., the Barre nation state), in the aftermath of the collapse of the state they also embarked on building new state institutions, albeit with varying degrees of success.

## Clan Networks and State Building in Somaliland

Paradoxically, Somaliland, which was devastated by two waves of violent power struggles involving intraclan warfare (in 1992–1993 and 1994–1996), and which has a more heterogeneous population, has achieved better results than Puntland in reviving the basic institutions of governance. The Republic of Somaliland was established in 1991 as a result of the Grand Conference of the Northern Peoples of Burao, where the Somali National Movement joined with clan elders from the various subclans to establish an interim government. The government was given a two-year mandate with the tasks of accommodating non-Isaaq clans into the state structure, drafting a constitution, and preparing the population for presidential elections.[67] Due to its weak revenue base and inability to mediate among intraclan rivals, rather than subverting traditional authority, the government assiduously turned to clan elders to manage local security and reconciliation.

Somaliland's relatively cohesive and united clans, forged in the long and violent struggle against Siad Barre's regime, is certainly one of the root causes of its stability. Nevertheless, it is important to point out that the Isaaq-dominant region was not immune from internal divisions following its unilateral declaration of independence. Fighting erupted in Somaliland among intraclan rivals immediately following the creation of the SNM-led government headed by ʻAbd al-Rahman ʻAli Tur. As in southern and central Somalia during the same period, subclan competition over power and resources fragmented former SNM militia leaders along five major Isaaq subclans. This was followed by fierce violence in March 1992 when the government attempted to gain control over Berbera port and its very lucrative revenue. Indirect taxation at the port at this juncture would have provided crucial resources for state building efforts. Not surprisingly, the other subclans, not wishing to cede their local revenue to the state, rejected the move.[68] Although a peace conference in 1993 reestablished some security, by 1994 intraclan conflicts were resurrected over the issue of resource extraction. Until that time, the airport in the capital of Hargeisa had been controlled by the Idagele subclan of the Isaaq, which enforced its monopoly over air taxes and landing fees. This conflict was sparked when the state, headed by Abdulrahman Ali Tur, tried to take control of the Hargeisa airport away from the Idagele subclan. The conflict led to over a year of violence in Somaliland and the displacement of hundreds of thousands of civilians.[69]

In the wake of intraclan conflicts in 1991 and 1992, Somaliland's elders convened two conferences in Sheikh and Borama. These conferences, referred to by their Somali name *shir beeleed*, made use of the traditional role of clan elders as community mediators, signaling a return to the Xeer system.[70] The 1993 Borama conference was overseen by a *guurti*, or national council of clan elders, and produced both a peace charter and a transnational charter. The former reinstated Somalia's precolonial traditional social order by establishing a Xeer in accordance with the tenets of Islam as a mechanism through which to govern both inter- and intra-clan relations.

The transnational charter established an innovative bicameral legislature, oversaw the transfer of power from interim president ʻAbd al-Rahman ʻAli Tur to the democratically elected President Muhammad Ibrahim Egal, and called for a formal constitutional referendum under

Egal's new government.[71] As such, it struck a balance between traditional Somalian and Western state forms: local clan elders were encouraged to utilize their traditional roles as a way to eradicate interclan enmities while also participating in a temporary power-sharing coalition until a constitutional draft could be agreed upon by the elders of all the clans in Somaliland. Though the *shir beeleed* established the parameters for peace, intraclan violence in Somaliland persisted under the Egal administration. Once again, clan elders convened to mediate among the communities under a second national reconciliation conference held across 1996 and 1997. This pivotal conference successfully ended the war and adopted an interim constitution that called for presidential elections and the establishment of a representative multiparty system of governance.[72] By 1999, a draft constitution was prepared, and on May 31, 2001, it was accepted by 97.9 percent of the population.[73]

But how precisely did the new constitution transcend the clannism forged in the colonial period and that had been so devastating to the country throughout the last decades? First, accredited political parties were obliged to draw at least 20 percent of electoral support from four of Somaliland's six regions, thereby ensuring that no party ran solely on a clan-based platform.[74] Second, to demonstrate the *Guurti*'s adherence to the precolonial era's non-hierarchical clan tradition, the constitution replaced the nonelected council of clan elders with directly elected district councils. Moreover, under the Egal administration, the new government of Somaliland forged mutually beneficial clientelist ties with clan elders. In particular, the Hargeisa government allowed elders of the most prominent clans significant control over a large proportion of the influx of remittances and sufficient autonomy to invest these capital inflows in livestock markets and other sectors of the local economy without imposing heavy taxes. These ties of cooperation have allowed the government to have a degree of social control over clan elders. Moreover, by ensuring that remittance inflows remain unregulated by any formal bureaucratic authorities, officials in Hargeisa have kept them from falling prey to political entrepreneurs. In light of the government's isolation from the global financial system, these connections have been vital for the survival and growth of Somaliland.

The state building model adopted by the government and clan elders of Somaliland represents a viable alternative to a system of top-down patrimonial politics that allows for a certain degree of clan loyalties at the grassroots without imposing a repressive political order from above. In this instance, political order for a society in crisis is rooted in local politics built on clan networks rather than built by the heavy hand of the state. Somaliland serves as an example of how informal social networks and traditional authority can be utilized in the service of peace rather than war. Indeed, the relative success of Somaliland's approach to state building and democratization was crucially underpinned by a lengthy, self-financed, and locally driven interclan reconciliation process through the 1990s, leading to a power-sharing form of government, providing an important base for Somaliland's enduring political stability and for the reconstruction and development in the region. One female community leader from Hargeisa eloquently captured the remarkable, conciliatory, and non-punitive elements, underpinning the indigenous conflict resolution method that played a crucial role in rebuilding trust between previously warring clans and subclans:

> In our tradition when people convene for peace making and peace is accepted in the process of arbitration, whether it is between clans, two people, or two groups, both sides gain some things. Our justice is not about what side is wrong or what side is right; rather it is a win-win situation of mutual benefits for both sides . . . In the case that one side feels like it is the loser and other side believes it is a winner, it would be hard to implement the [peace] agreement unless you had a strong government.[75]

Importantly, a key element in the success of the resolution of clan conflict in Somaliland had to do with settling marital disputes as an important way of addressing the larger, and often violent, conflicts between kinship groups. I personally participated in a high number of deliberative meetings designed to restore marital relations, which I quickly came to understand as a pivotal aspect of the peace-building process. This is because since the clans were intermarried prior to the conflict, deliberations over marital issues were not only common; they were rightly perceived by clan elders and the general community as central to resolving a wide range of social as well as economic disputes between clans and subclans.

## Going It Alone: Building a State in the Absence of International Recognition

Nevertheless, the lack of international recognition has been a mixed blessing for Somaliland. On the one hand, Somaliland has managed to avoid the legacy of aid dependence that bedeviled the postcolonial state under the Barre regime. Indeed, the Republic of Somaliland's existence is in direct violation of UN Resolution 1514 (1960), which forbids any act of self-determination outside the context of former colonial boundaries. Since the African Union upholds the official UN position, it too denies recognition to Somaliland, a neglect that seems to have had positive results for the state.[76]

On the other hand, the lack of international recognition has had grave consequences for the development and strengthening of formal institutions. International commercial law denies certification to Somaliland on the grounds that it would infringe upon the preexisting certification of Somalia, thereby nullifying all contracts made under this certification.[77] Because formal participation in the global economy is impossible, transnational norms and institutions that regulate foreign and trade agreements cannot be enforced in the country. Thus, while Somaliland has succeeded in entering the global economic order through informal financial networks, it remains largely isolated from foreign aid and technical assistance. Somaliland's groundbreaking peace conferences of 1992, 1993, and 1997 were entirely self-financed.[78] While for some scholars this has meant that Somaliland operates in the "shadows" of the global economy, empirically this claim does not hold for two very important reasons. First, this characterization of a Somaliland operating under the radar of the global economy underestimates the importance of remittance inflows. Second, it obscures the importance of the role of locally generated taxes (i.e., direct taxes) in building the kind of state that has proved more stable than its counterparts in Puntland and Somalia.

How, in the face of this neglect and economic exclusion, has the Somaliland state been able to maintain control over its territory and achieve a relatively peaceful state of affairs? Part of the answer lies in the careful crafting of a power-sharing system undergirded by newly revitalized clan networks and traditional authority. As Mark Bradbury, Adan Yusuf Abokor, and Haroon Ahmed Yusuf have asserted, this power-sharing system has proven critical to the process of reconciliation and recovery in Somaliland, succeeding where numerous efforts in Somalia have failed.[79] In addition, the leadership and policies of the late president Muhammad Ibrahim Egal played an important role in laying the groundwork for durable state institutions. Thirdly, the Somaliland state has established a working relationship with hawwalat owners and other members of the business community, which allowed the state to strike a delicate balance, crucial to state formation, of encouraging unregulated remittances flows while taxing other forms of private economic activity. By winning the trust and cooperation of the hawwalat owners, the state managed to establish a system for taxing the largest source of revenue generation and also to encourage private enterprise. Somaliland leaders have done this by substantial structural changes since the early 1990s. Rather than regulating the remittance economy, authorities have dissolved monopolies, done away with rigid economic controls, and pursued a deregulated free market economy that has enlisted the trust and cooperation on the part of the business community.[80] It is in this way that Somaliland authorities have achieved remarkable gains in establishing a delicate balance between taxing and encouraging private economic activity.

Under President Ibrahim Egal's tenure in particular, Somaliland's leaders also managed to reduce clan-based conflicts, most of which were sparked when faction leaders tried to extract revenue from different ports in order to gain political control. The success of both Egal and his successor Dahir Riyale Kahin in these efforts resulted both in a substantial peace and an impressive stability as state builders sought to revive basic institutions of governance.

## Labor Remittances and State Building: Resource Curse or Social Safety Net?

Somaliland's success in state building is even more remarkable given its heavy reliance on remittances in the context of relatively weak formal institutions. Indeed, while work on the political impact of remittances remains sparse, recent scholarship has generally argued that remittances maybe a "resource curse" akin to natural resource rents and foreign financial assistance. This is because, as one important study noted, "they are revenue sources that can be substituted for taxes and serve as a buffer between government performance and citizens."[81] In other words, the informal (or parallel) channels through which remittances are transferred often insulate recipients from local conditions and reduce incentives to participate in politics. However, given the sheer volume of remittance inflows, in the case of Somaliland, remittances have played a very important, albeit indirect, role in generating effective government performance. A closer examination of the popular resistance on the part of hawala bankers to several attempts at regulation, and the response of Somaliland's leaders to this resistance, demonstrates that a bargain was eventually struck between nascent state builders and the most powerful agents of revenue generation in the territory.

In Somalia remittance inflows have the potential to obstruct state building in two key ways: they are difficult to tax by central authorities, and their mode of operation privileges clan networks rather than cross clan or Islamic cleavages. State builders thus face a strong challenge in generating revenue needed for governance and encouraging cross-clan cooperation, which is crucial for peacemaking, national reconciliation, and legitimating political authority. Indeed, we cannot fully understand the path that development has taken in northern Somalia without appreciating how international economic linkages – in the form of remittance inflows – pose impediments as well as opportunities to state building. Labor remittances represent the largest source of foreign exchange, and the majority of urban households in both Somaliland and Puntland rely upon them as a major source of income. Because the average Somali household is composed of eight members whose daily income together totals less than 39 cents, transfers from family members living abroad are crucial for securing a livelihood. Indeed, as much as 40 percent of Somali urban households rely on such funds. Moreover, the benefits of remittance flows are felt across the spectrum of Somali subclans, albeit in unequal terms. For example, only one of the four subclans of the Isaaq, which has historically supplied the majority of migrant workers, revealed 8 percent of its households receiving remittances from abroad, whereas approximately 31 percent of the Habr-Awal subclan's families count on informal transfers (Figure 6.1).

Remittances are usually a supplementary source of income; in addition to receiving assistance from relatives, a Somali family typically has more than one member involved in informal economic activities. Nevertheless, it is important to highlight that Somalis in both Somaliland and Puntland rely heavily on money from overseas relatives sent through the *hawala* agencies. This is clearly evident when one considers the proportion of remittances vis-à-vis other sources of income in both the northwest and northeast (Table 6.1).

Following the collapse of the Somali state, the family unit has come to encompass three or more interdependent households. In addition to assisting poorer urban relatives, a large proportion of urban households support rural kin on a regular basis. While only 2 to 5 percent of rural Somalis receive remittances directly from overseas, Somali's nomadic population still depends on these capital inflows. In northern Somalia, for example, 46 percent of the sampled urban households support relations in pastoralist areas with monthly contributions in the range of USD 10–100 a month; of these 46 percent, as many as 40 percent are households that depend on remittances from relatives living abroad. Consequently, the link between labor migration, urban households, and the larger rural population is a crucial and distinctive element in Somalia's economy.

As the most important source of foreign exchange and a key source of daily income in both Somaliland and Puntland, remittances thus play a pivotal role in the contemporary state-making enterprise. Indeed, state building in Somaliland has been largely successful because the Isaaq-backed leadership has also been able to encourage remittance transfer and gain the cooperation of the wealthy "remittance barons" with whom

Table 6.1 *Main sources of income by percentage of households in Somalia*

| | Hargeisa, Northwest Somalia | | Bossaso, Northeast Somalia | |
|---|---|---|---|---|
| Primary source of income | Resident population | In-migrants | Resident population | In-migrants |
| Remittances | 23% | 5% | 38% | 2% |
| Market activities | 32% | 35% | 26% | 17% |
| Petty trade | 16% | 19% | 20% | 4% |
| Services | 29% | 32% | 16% | 77% |
| Begging | - | 9% | - | - |

Market activities include currency exchangers, market stalls, tea stalls, qat sellers, charcoal and water delivery, and meat sellers. Service jobs include masons, porters, civil servants, waiters, drivers, and unskilled laborers. Trade activities include livestock brokers (*dilaal*), shops/restaurants, import/export traders, and cloth retailers.
*Source*: Khalid M. Medani, "Report on Internal Migration and Remittance Inflows in Northwest and Northeast Somalia" (Nairobi, Kenya: United Nations Coordination Unit [UNCU], 2000).
*Note*: Above figures derived from convenient sample.

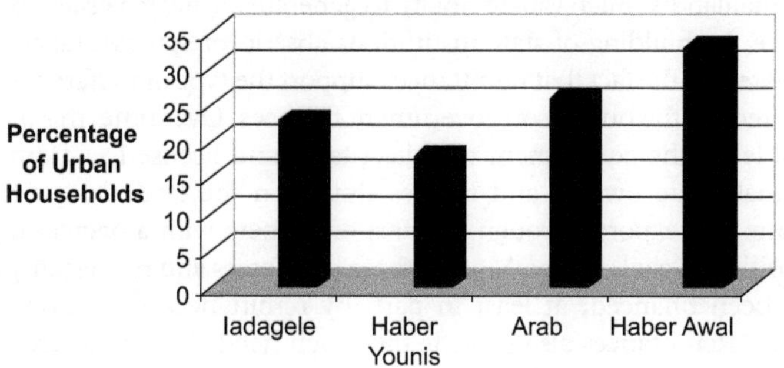


Figure 6.1 Remittance recipients by Isaaq subclans in Somalia
*Source*: Khalid M. Medani, "Report on Internal Migration and Remittance Inflows in Northwest and Northeast Somalia" (Nairobi, Kenya: UN Coordination Unit [UNCU} and Food Security Assessment Unit [FSAU], 2000).

they share a kin relation. Consequently, in Somaliland, the Isaaq largely control revenues accruing from remittances, organized by the private hawala agencies, as well as taxes from the port of Berbera. The

Somaliland government, particularly under Egal's tenure, thus was able to partially finance governmental institutions, including an effective police force, throughout its territory.

Once Somaliland's leaders realized the important role remittances play as a social safety net for the local population, they negotiated a delicate, albeit often contested and conflictual, bargain. This bargain consisted of government authorities ensuring that hawalas remain unregulated by state authorities while the former pursued a more transparent and less-repressive taxation policy.[82] Importantly, the fact that remittances insulated the majority of the population from economic and social deprivation of the kind that would lead to protest and civil conflict greatly facilitated the eventual reduction of taxation in Somaliland thereby bolstering the political legitimacy of the new state among its citizens. In other words, in the case of Somaliland, while remittances remain untaxed by government officials this does not suggest that this engenders a weak link between state institutions and remittance recipients. Indeed, rather than demobilize citizens, the fact that remittances increase incomes dramatically and provide a social safety net for government officials pursuing economic policies means that they have increased civic engagement in ways that not only can be discerned from several protests against government policies deemed unjust or illegitimate, but also in participation in local and presidential elections thereby helping to consolidate democracy.[83]

Somaliland's much touted ability to generate locally generated revenue to finance the building of state institutions absent foreign assistance is greatly facilitated by the fact that remittances support the type of welfare services that often reduce the burden on government finances. Over time, this has made it possible for the government to collect taxes and license fees from business and real-estate owners and impose duties on the trade in qat as well as imports and exports through the port of Berbera with a decreasing level of opposition in civil society. Most of these businesses and real-estate properties have been financed, at least in part, by remittances from Somalis living abroad. Remittances also provide the much-needed hard currency that has led to the expansion of the important livestock trade and even allowed Hargeisa to reduce taxes and fees as, for example, in the elimination of fees for primary and secondary schooling. The success of these policies is related to the important role remittances continue to play in supporting general household expenditures.[84] A rare study on this subject put it succinctly:

> The financial and social contributions and material support of the Somaliland diaspora and their high level of engagement in Somaliland is stimulating the ongoing development in the country and is crucial for sustaining peace. Their engagement comes in the forms of monetary and social remittances, tourism, and economic and social investments. Remittances provide the much-needed hard

currency for trade, support the livelihood of many households, allow some households to establish small businesses, and finance the ongoing construction boom in the country. These business investments in trade, telecommunications, luxury hotels, and light industries do lead to modest job creation and attract a host of other infrastructures. As for social investments, numerous members of the diaspora are either setting up or are actively engaged in local NGOs, medical and educational facilities, and political parties that are positively contributing to the social and political development of the country.[85]

Moreover, while the role of traditional clan elders (*Guurti*) was indeed a critical institution in terms of the success of the series of meetings that focused on putting a stop to hostilities (*Xabad joogi*) and promote reconciliation (*Dibu-heshiisiin*) between the hitherto waring subclans of the Isaaq and non-Isaaq clans, these meetings shared three important characteristics: they were funded largely by Somaliland communities themselves, including those in the diaspora; they involved the voluntary participation of the key figures from each of the clans affected; and decisions were taken by broad consensus among delegates.[86] As I observed by participating in several mediation efforts led by traditional community leaders in both Hargeisa and Bossaso, the process is not only a lengthy one; it is also costly in that it requires the dispatching of carefully selected leaders, deemed legitimate by the local communities, to conflict areas. Since formal law enforcement institutions and local authorities were ill-equipped to provide adequate sources, it was often left to regional and local authorities to solicit funds for these peace-building missions from the community, particularly from notable remittance brokers, livestock traders, and prominent Somalis living abroad. This was especially important, in the rural parts of Somaliland such as Boroma, Burao, and Yirowe where formal authorities lacked adequate financial resources for even basic operational and logistical needs.

If remittances have served as a social safety net enabling the peaceful pursuit of taxation policy, the role of the diaspora has often played an even more direct role in facilitating the success of the state-building enterprise over time. Given that Somaliland has not generally benefited from international recognition or significant foreign development assistance, remittances from the diaspora have played a key role in the state-building enterprise. Indeed, as one Somalilander who was intimately involved in a series of conflict resolution negotiations stressed, "peace building in Somaliland would not have succeeded were it not for the help, resources, and contributions of our diaspora."[87] To be sure the diaspora has not always played a positive role in Somaliland's rebuilding process. During the civil conflicts of 1992 and 1994–1996, they provided funds and other support for their clan militias. Nevertheless, by the late 1990s, remittances sent by members of the Somali diaspora were invested in businesses, and they helped to reestablish basic services that, in serving as a safety valve for Somalilanders, sustained the peace-building and state-making processes. Importantly, and in the context of the absence of international engagement and the relative weakness of its state institutions, Somaliland serves as an important case study in that it shows the importance of international remittances and diasporic communities in the process of rebuilding states in the aftermath of severe civil conflict.

However, this negotiated bargain in pursuit of state building was not achieved without wrenching political conflict. In the early 1990s, as intra-Isaaq clan enmities and divisions between former SMN leaders led to successive rounds of civil conflict, non-Isaaq clans intervened to make peace in the important conference held in Sheikh town. It was at this conference that the most important source of revenue for the state, the port at Hargeisa, reverted to Abdulrahman Tur (the first president of Somaliland). It was also at this conference that the council of elders (Guurti), which became the cornerstone of the hybrid political system bringing together clan networks and the modern institutions of the Somaliland state, was established as a key informal social institution in the state-building project.[88]

Nevertheless, for all of its rightly touted political success, Somaliland remains constrained by limited avenues to generate resources and revenue for the central state. This is because the majority of Somalilanders are nomadic and engaged in the livestock trade which is difficult to tax. Tax revenues are predominately generated from international trade acquired from the port at Berbera. Consequently, throughout the 1990s the nascent state not only expended a large portion of its budget to build a military and police force, under Egal's presidency, patronage politics reemerged that threatened to undermine state-building efforts. Prior to changes in policy, the Somaliland administration faced severe opposition after it imposed financial controls and restrictions, which greatly alienated the private sector including the Hawala bankers and the large livestock traders.

The narrow resource base and weak extractive capacity of the new state compelled the government in Hargeisa to resort to printing money thereby creating inflation.[89] The introduction of new currency by Hargeisa in the mid-1990s also had grave political as well as economic consequences; it was one of the main reasons for the reemergence of conflict between the Isaaq subclans in the mid-1990s. One former SNM member in Burao, in the region of Toghdeer, explained succinctly how and why this policy exacerbated intraclan conflict at the time:

> The main reason for the conflict [1994–1996] was Egal's introduction of the Somaliland shilling. He did this to support his own Haber Awal subclan as a form of patronage. This caused inflationary pressures and to this day most traders here in Burao work with the Somalia shilling although they accept the Somaliland shilling. This is for two reasons: This first is political. Egal's government has yet to be deemed legitimate and so residents here in Buroa and in Yirowe will not legitimate his currency. Economically, since the livestock market is mostly linked to central and eastern Somalia–the Somalia shilling is the real base of the local economy. The purchasing power of the Somalia shilling is stronger. The Somalia shilling is three times less expensive. We can eat and purchase commodities much cheaper in Burao than in Hargeisa.[90]

Importantly, and despite strong resistance against any form of government intervention on the part of many traders I interviewed, the livestock trade, the cornerstone of the domestic economy, was gravely and adversely affected by the unregulated environment in the aftermath of the collapse of the state. This naturally led to mistrust among clans throughout the country. In Somaliland, the livestock trade operates on the basis of a hierarchical structure consisting of a network of brokers who collect livestock from several markets throughout Somalia on behalf of seven or eight large traders. An important source of recurring conflict is that it is difficult to get the traders to cooperate in an unregulated and highly competitive environment. During my time in several livestock market hubs in Somaliland, I observed that the large livestock traders were from the Haber Jalo and Haber Awal Isaaq subclans. The Haber Younis often complained that the Haber Awal not only dominated the trade, but with the assumption to power of Egal at the time they were viewed as dominating the government as well. Livestock brokers routinely cited evidence that since the Haber Awal dominate Berbera and the outlying region where the port is located, they have long dominated the livestock trade.[91] Ultimately, however, the Egal administration was able to provide services and build an association of livestock traders which, over time, introduced a distinct corporate culture to the livestock trade. The result was that the trade recovered and in so doing helped to create more generalizable trust across the clan divide and in the Hargeisa administration itself. Thus, another important reason for Somaliland's success is that governmental authorities in Hargeisa were able not only to cooperate with the hawala brokers soliciting loans and contributions from them; they were also able to negotiate an acceptable and legitimate level of regulation of the all-important livestock trade. Consequently, in this way they were able to built trust among the most important actors in the local economy.

## Puntland and the Struggle to Build a Viable State

In contrast to Somaliland, state building in Puntland has stagnated after making significant inroads in the 1990s. So far, popularly legitimate formal structures of modern governance have played a negligible role in the affairs in northeast Somalia. Ultimately, the relative failure of state building in Puntland has been the result of the ambivalent vision of "statehood" that underpinned the foundation of the state, the predatory behavior of successful leaders, and the failure to pursue economic policies in ways that would generate trust and legitimacy among the different subclans of the Darod, the dominant clan family in the region.

Puntland initially followed a similar pattern of state building to neighboring Somaliland. In May 1998 it was established as a result of the intervention of clan elders of the Darod-Harti subclan in the city of Garowe. The *Isimada*, or clan elders, of the Harti instituted a regional administration that encompassed northeast Somalia, including Sool and Sanag which continue to generate serious tensions between Puntland and Somaliland. Headed by Abdullahi Yusif, the leaders of the Somali Salvation Democratic Front (SSDF) at the time enlisted the cooperation of clan elders in order to establish an autonomous state. Importantly, however, the primary motivation was political survival rather than independence. The Majeerteen, Warsengeli, and Dhulbahante subclans of the Darod in particular felt strongly that they needed to unite in order to avoid emerging as losers in the nation-wide clan struggle for power and territory. In addition, they felt that territorial control would serve as a powerful bargaining chip in their attempts to recreate a central national territory.[92]

Initially, Puntland managed to form a functioning regional state. Clan elders elected Abdullahi Yusif as president, a charter was adopted following a long consultation process among the different subclans of the Darod, and a regional parliament chosen by the clans was established. Yusif also managed to dampen intraclan hostilities by including non-Majeerteen Harti clans in the Garowe Conference that formally established the state of Puntland. In so doing he weakened the political influence of elites of his own Majeerteen subclan, which engendered a significant, albeit short-lived, level of trust in his administration from the other clans in the region.[93] Moreover, in the early years and in a pattern similar to Somaliland's, a relatively more efficient tax and revenue collection system was put in place, and courts and prisons were rebuilt that improved security in most of the major towns. There was, as one study noted, enthusiasm for the new regime and its attempts to create functioning institutions, and a sense of freedom allowed civil liberties and independent media to take root.[94]

However, Puntland's leaders, and Abdullahi Yusif in particular, quickly demonstrated that they were more intent on reestablishing an authoritarian regime rather than embarking on a genuine grassroots peacebuilding process and state-making enterprise. By the early 2000s, infighting between subclans reemerged; the judiciary and civil service became politicized, administrative corruption intensified; and any elections held by Puntland's authorities were tightly managed, manipulated, and controlled.[95] Ominously, and in a pattern similar to that of the ousted Barre regime, cabinet posts and economic privileges were allocated to loyalists drawn mainly from Abdullahi Yusif's Omar Mahmoud sub-subclan, and businessmen, including hawala brokers and livestock traders, were forced to pay large fees to operate or pay bribes for access to export licenses which most of the latter allocated along clan lines. The consequence of these increasingly predatory policies was to erode inter- and intra-clan cohesion and undermine the short-lived security arrangements that had sustained peace in the first years of Puntland's foundation. One resident of Eyfen district explained the state of affairs in Puntland that reflect the authoritarian nature of the Garowe administration, which stands in marked contrast to the situation in Somaliland:

> We ask people to pay taxes, but they say there is no security and no basic services, not even clean water. We don't have a legal framework to tax international non-governmental organizations. [In addition], there is a wide rural-urban divide. As a result, rural areas have no government services or access to remittances from relatives living abroad. The problem is corruption: power is accumulated in the hands of a few powerful clans.[96]

To make matters worse, Puntland's leaders had to contend with a strong local ideological rival represented by the militant Islamist organization, al-Ittihad al-Islami (AIAI). The rise in the popularity of al-Ittihad in the early 1990s was a result of the lack of strong governance structures, and the failure of local leaders to deliver law and order in the aftermath of state collapse. At the height of al-Ittihad's popularity, the forces of the SSDF were simply not able to administer the important port of Bossaso, and consequently AIAI was able to fill the security vacuum and eventually take over the running of the port. It was through their access to the port that they were able to import arms to strengthen their movement and to generate revenue from port taxes which they used as the financial tool with which they recruited followers.[97] During my research in Bossaso and Garowe, it was clear that al-Ittihad's popularity extended beyond Bossaso port. This is because the organization also managed to build strong commercial networks by forging close relationships with influential clan elders in the region and thus were able to wield great economic as well as political influence in civil society. However, this was often accomplished through the use of coercive and violent means. As one resident of Bossaso put it: "[P]eople wanted law and order and better administration, not a religious dictatorship."[98]

## The Political Economy of State Building: Somaliland and Puntland Compared

Compared to Somaliland, the relatively homogenous Puntland, which is populated primarily by the Majeerteen, a subclan of the Darod, should by some conventional accounts be the stronger state. Yet it is Somaliland – devastated by two waves of violent power struggles involving intraclan and interclan warfare and with a heterogeneous population consisting of many rival clans belonging to three large families – that has achieved better results in reviving the basic institutions of governance. What explains the underlying factors for these divergent developments?

An important reason for this divergence has to do with the war-making phase associated with the state-building enterprise. Both de facto states have experienced intermittent ethnic strife, but only Somaliland president Muhammad Egal was able to defeat his military rivals, which he did after a series of violent conflicts centered on control of the port of Berbera. This factor was crucial to Egal's success at state building and his efforts at consolidating political rule. By contrast in Puntland, the conflict between Majeerteen elites and Islamists belonging to al-Ittihad continued, albeit with a modicum of accommodation in recent years. In contrast to Puntland, Somaliland has been able to win the ideological battle over potential Islamist rivals. Clan solidarity among the Isaaq in particular has emerged as a strong element in the success of the state-building enterprise. In Puntland, in the context of persistent intraclan tensions between the subclans of the Darod, Islamist identification continues to make inroads despite the fact that the population is more homogenous in terms of clan affiliation.[99] To be sure by the mid-1990s, Puntland authorities were able to effectively suppress the military wing of al-Ittihad al-Islami. However, following their defeat by the forces of the SSDF and the loss of control over the lucrative Bossaso port, al-Ittihad altered their vision and strategy. They formally stopped advocating violence and turned toward building support in society through peaceful means. Consequently, they increased their social welfare provisioning including building schools, hospitals, and offering humanitarian services, while simultaneously focusing on expanding their business and trade networks with the Gulf.

In Puntland, by the end of the 2000s, the experiment of indigenous state building that combined a system of clan representational side by side with formal parliamentary rule declined.[100] The fragile political system wherein every subclan of the Darod-Harti family would nominate a parliamentarian endorsed by subclan leaders fell apart resulting in the failure to build a viable state in the northeast. An important aspect of this state-building dilemma was that, in addition to facing external threats, the Puntland project's architects had to contend with the influence of a strong Islamist movement that enjoyed more popularity in civil society than the increasing narrow subclan-centered administration. Indeed, one reason Gerowe effectively ended its efforts at genuine electoral reform to usher in a fledgling democracy as occurred in Somaliland is that it feared the strength of the Islamist opposition. But the central problem that explains the failure of state building in Puntland is, as one analyst put it succinctly, an unresolvable conflict "between the ideal of an indigenous, consensual political system underpinned by a mix of traditional and modern governance institutions, and the reality of a top-down repressive system."[101]

Ultimately, variations in economic policies, including the essentially political struggle to create a new currency, shaped state building in Somaliland and Puntland. Currency delimits the economic boundaries of the state and plays a pivotal role in revenue generation. Given the importance of informal financial markets to the Somali economy, aspiring state builders introduced new currencies based on geographic and political, rather than strictly economic, considerations. This is part of an overall strategy to create markets through instituting new currencies, collecting taxes at ports, and establishing militaries and police to oversee these new arrangements. The Isaaq in Somaliland have been more successful in these efforts than the Majeerteen in Puntland, but neither clan has managed to acquire complete monopoly in the legitimate use of force across the various regions under its jurisdiction.

Importantly, in their pursuit of state building, political leaders in Puntland proved the least interventionist in terms of macroeconomic policies. They did not take part in the proliferation of new currencies that were introduced in various clan-based territories following the collapse of the Somali state. Whereas Somaliland authorities (and the two large Hawiye-backed factions controlling the southern and northern parts of Mogadishu) all printed new currencies that are tender in their respective domains, Puntland retained the old Somali shilling as its official currency. The old Somali shilling remains the preferred local currency because of its stability and local convertibility into other currencies. In

Bossaso, the largest market in the northeast uses multiple currencies. In addition to the old Somali shilling, the US dollar, the Gulf countries' various currencies, the Ethiopian birr, and the Kenyan shilling all are freely exchanged. The informalization of financial markets and the proliferation of international money dealers have facilitated the transfer and exchange of money, but they have not yet transformed themselves into formal financial institutions and are unlikely to do so in the near future.

Unlike the Majeerteen leaders of Bossaso, Somaliland's leaders introduced a new local currency, creating inflation and disincentives for merchants, moneychangers, and local consumers to convert their remittances and other income into Somali shillings. This etatist policy has also been the one reason for the intermittent incidents of civil strife, which have slowed down the economy in the decade following the establishment of the state. This is because neighboring clans (the Issa, Warsengeli, and Gadabursi) view Hargeisa's policy of manufacturing money – that is not guaranteed by any bank – as exclusively benefiting the Isaaq clans. Further aggravating clan enmities, during the Egal administration the Somaliland government introduced policies reminiscent of the Barre regime and attempted to heavily tax livestock exports and a wide range of commodity exports. This led to some short-term financial and political gains for Somaliland but undermined interclan cohesion. For a society that is mistrustful of formal institutions of any kind, these policies recalled the "predatory" and authoritarian policies of the previous regime, threatening the hard-won legitimacy garnered by the aspiring state builders.

Puntland, where leaders pursued an essentially "free market" policy, achieved significant economic gains, and its booming economy induced non-Majeerteen clans to migrate and settle in the region. Bossaso residents enjoy a relatively high standard of living: while urban residents of Hargeisa earn, on average, about one US dollar a day, Bossaso residents earn over four.[102] This differential is evident even in comparisons of the more marginalized clans in the two regions. In my survey of non-Isaaq and non-Majeerteen clan families in Hargeisa and Bossaso, respectively, those in Bossaso earned 50 percent higher daily incomes than their counterparts in and around Hargeisa. There are a number of reasons for these variations. First, in Bossaso the Majerteen clan established political stability by defeating al-Ittihad and capturing the port in 1992. Subsequently, a fragile peace was maintained by the good offices of traditional elders (*Isimo*). The Isimo managed to promote social and economic stability, but the periodic bouts of violence, the conflict between Puntland's leaders, and the ultimate failure of the state-building enterprise suggest that clan-based peacekeeping cannot substitute for the law-and-order functions of a modern state. Ultimately,

Majeerteen clan elders failed in their attempts to establish a regional council and to redistribute tax revenue not only for security, but also to neighboring clans of the Bari region. Second, while businessmen in Somaliland have managed to set up a formalized chamber of commerce on a regional level to encourage deposits from livestock merchants and currency dealers, this has not occurred in Puntland.

Ultimately, and particularly following successful indigenous peacebuilding between the region's clans, Somaliland's relative success at state building was aided by the establishment of the Somaliland shilling which, while it led to strong opposition in civil society in the late 1990s and 2000s, proved effective in redirecting revenue from the private sector into state coffers. This, along with Hargeisa's control of tax revenues from Berbera port, and a carefully crafted alliance with the Isaaq business elite, enabled the state to assert some of its fiscal authority. In Puntland, leaders continue to utilize the old Somali shilling and thus have failed to demarcate the economic boundaries of their new state in ways that would generate sufficient revenue to finance strong formal governmental institutions.

Contrasting policies with respect to the informal financial sector also help to explain the divergence in the two regions. As is the case throughout Somalia, in Somaliland and Puntland, the unregulated hawwalat continue to finance the bulk of imports, provide windfall profits for those engaged in transferring these funds, and make resources available for investments throughout the country. However, in contrast to livestock trade, remittances remain unregulated and untaxed and therefore hinder the establishment of formal, reliable, extractive, and regulatory institutions; at the same time, moreover, they promote identity-based modes of collective action. Consequently, remittance inflows, a large component of Somaliland's and Puntland's local economies, have posed a significant challenge to the long-term economic and political objectives of state builders.

In Somaliland an increasingly unified Isaaq business elite emerged as important beneficiaries of the remittance sector. In this regard, it is important to note that while Somaliland is dominated by the subclans of the Isaaq, it is a state that encompasses a number of other clans that have often come into conflict with the Isaaq commercial and political elite. This is clearly reflected in economic terms. The Isaaq leaders of Somaliland benefit from their kin's monopoly on the remittance trade in the region. In fact, 60 percent of remittance-receiving households receive funds via the Isaaq-run Dahabshiil remittance agency. Prior to its closure, al-Barakat, which is largely run by the Darod clan, possessed only 15 percent of the market in Somalia, but controlled the lion's share of the business in the northeast, an estimated 90 percent in Puntland. This is not surprising, given that in Somaliland Dahabshiil enjoys the trust of the majority of the wealthier Isaaq subclans and the political leaders. This mutual trust and cooperation are the reason why businessmen in Somaliland managed to set up a formal regional chamber of commerce to encourage deposits and contributions from livestock merchants, moneychangers, as well as the major commodity importers. Moreover, by 2010 Dahabshiil, the largest hawwalat agency in Somaliland, had invested approximately US 100 million in the Telecom services industry. While this was largely the result of the burgeoning competition in the financial services sector it also reflects the increasingly strong relationship of cooperation that has emerged between the Isaaq business elite and political authorities.

In contrast, while Somaliland's political elite managed to generate revenue from, for example, taxing the major telecommunication companies based in Somaliland such as Hormut and Gulis, Puntland has not been able to do the same with the largest telecom business based in Puntland, Sahal. In Puntland, none of the hawwalat or telecom companies pay taxes to the Gerowe administration. The general manager of the Amal Hawwalat company operating in Puntland explained:

> The Hawalas or Telecom do not trust the politicians in Gerowe. None pay taxes or give any credit or donations to the local administration. The bulk of revenue is derived from direct taxation from Bossaso port. Approximately 90 percent of their budget, an estimated $1 million a month, is still based on the revenue generated from Bossaso. [Moreover], the Puntland administration adjusted the Somali shilling to the US dollar several times beginning in 2008. The result has been a steady rise in inflation and increasing anger against the government on the part of a lot of businessmen.[103]

Given the nature of northern Somalia's economy, political elites in both Somaliland and Puntland also need direct access to the lucrative livestock market. Direct access, in turn, requires regulatory oversight over this trade enforced by an administrative and military power capable of maintaining control over the ports of Berbera and Bossaso, respectively. Somaliland's Isaaq clan established a monopoly on tax revenues from Berbera port, but in Puntland, al-Ittihad's bid to control the port of Bossaso – and thereby pursue its own state building project – failed. In the early 1990s, al-Ittihad's aim to build an Islamist state in Puntland appeared feasible. In 1992, the inability of the political establishment, dominated by the Majerteen subclan's Somali Salvation Democratic Front, to effect political change left a political void that provided al-Ittihad, which already dominated informal finance in the region, the opportunity to gain control over the livestock trade. Initially, al-Ittihad was welcomed in the northeast, where local leaders entrusted it with two urgent tasks: managing the port of Bossaso and maintaining law and order. Consequently, in the formative stages of state formation and at the height of al-Ittihad's popularity, the leaders of Puntland were not able to administer the important port of Bossaso, and al-Ittihad was able to not only fill the security vacuum; they eventually took over the running of the port and controlled the collection of the port's tax revenues.[104]

Al-Ittihad's monopolization of informal finance and the struggle over import/export trade centered around the port of Bossaso hindered Puntland's leaders' efforts at state building by curtailing their attempts to benefit from a veritable economic boom in the region. Historically, successful state building has been associated with the concentration of urban populations and government expenditure. As such it can potentially offer the informal economy invaluable opportunities to capture economies of scale. These economies of scale are most significant in the development of trade and finance. In the livestock sector, opportunities for trade creation and economic specialization also depend upon the central government's ability to establish a tax system that channels rural production (i.e., livestock) into the market. The fact that this advanced further in Somaliland than Puntland is another reason Somaliland's leaders have been more successful in financing their state building efforts.

There is little question that the Isaaq were able to monopolize and regulate livestock trade and remittances to aid the process of state building. However, cooperation *among* the subclans of the Isaaq (Idagelle, Habr-Yunis, Arab, and Habr-Awal) would not have been possible had they not possessed a prior history of uninterrupted resistance to the Barre regime. This historical experience more than some adherence to a fixed notion of clan solidarity facilitated collective action and a shared ideological orientation that has enabled the Isaaq subclans to make significant advances in the process of market and state reconstruction. In contrast, the Majeerteen clan of Bossaso represents a relatively new arrival to northeast Somalia, and its complicated political alliances and kin relations with Siad Barre's Darod clan hampered its ability to undertake collective action and forge politico-ideological cohesion. The Majeerteen have proved to be proficient economic entrepreneurs but have been less adept at political cooperation than their Somaliland counterparts. The relative strength of this moral economy of clannism has determined the nature of political action, social conflict, and the success of negotiated agreements in the two regions. In Puntland (as well as in Mogadishu), where there are more diffuse and fragmented clan networks than in Hargeisa and where neither the Majeerteen nor the Hawiye clan has an institutionalized history of collective action against the previous regime, Islamist activism serves as a moral economy of last resort. It is no coincidence that al-Ittihad enjoys its greatest foothold in Puntland and in the socially fractious regions in and around Mogadishu where clan networks are less cohesive. As one Somali Scholar explained: "[I]n the northwest kinship ties are very strong and serve as the basis for cooperation and economic assistance. The Darod are a more complex clan family like the Hawiye. These are older lineages that are more fluid and flexible in terms of assimilating other clans . . . they rarely cooperate as a clan family."[105]

Somaliland's more unified and stronger Isaaq elite stands in stark contrast to the state of affairs in Puntland. Consequently, another important obstacle to collective action and state building in Puntland is the absence of a distinct and organized economic elite. This is a state of affairs that needs to be explained rather than assumed. Merchants and traders play a central role in the informal trade economy, linking rural producers with local centers of trade, and northern Somalia with external markets in the Gulf. Nevertheless, despite their economic prominence in recent years, local merchants and financiers have not yet developed the ideological makeup or corporate interest that is necessary to establish basic institutions of governance, maintain law and order, lobby for the provision of public (and semi-public) goods, and provide even rudimentary social services like education or health care. In Puntland, and to a lesser extent in Somaliland, local merchants are fiercely competitive individual traders who remain bound above all to their kin groups for the protection of their lives and property and for business opportunities.[106]

A related impediment to collective action across ethnic or religious lines is the fact that while clan networks facilitate economic exchange, they also promote particularistic notions of identification that effectively prevent more broad-based social organization. Consequently, the new, more flexible structure of production and distribution that the clan networks have created is limited in its scope and effectiveness. Moreover, the tendency of ethnic and clan networks to intensify under economic crisis has tended to make many Somalis operating in the largely informal economy vulnerable to the political machinations of more powerful groups among the same clan and subclan affiliation. This combination of both patronage and exploitation has meant that class and economic divisions have been blurred – a common feature of informal relations generally. Dominant and subordinate groups are represented in a multiplicity of forms of interaction, and this has served to nullify basic class divisions. In other words, what appears as ethnic or religious solidarity conceals a mechanism of control and accumulation in which basic antagonisms are ideologically sublimated.

The general tendency of informal institutional arrangements to simultaneously facilitate cooperation and promote modes of social control is the main reason that Islamists are more successful in recruiting new members in Puntland and Mogadishu, where solidarity and shared norms of subordination provided by clan networks are relatively weak. Since the disintegration of the state, al-Ittihad has predictably shown a high degree of ideological cohesiveness and propensity for collective action and "good works." In recent years, these Islamist activists have taken advantage of the divisions among the traditional economic elite in Puntland to provide social services, operate local newspapers, build mosques, and attain employment for their members. They also have close links with Islamists in Sudan, primarily in the form of Sudanese-funded educational scholarships.[107] This is an important reason why, after losing control of the Bossaso port to the Darood-Majeerteen-backed SSDF, al-Ittihad activists successfully integrated into the local community as teachers, health workers, and businessmen.

## Dilemmas of State Building: Networks of Inclusion and Exclusion

The informal finance and export sectors in both Somaliland and Puntland have succeeded remarkably well in feeding local communities in both urban and rural areas, with food imports being exchanged for proceeds from local exports and remittances. Indeed, following the collapse of regulatory and planning institutions in the north, the unregulated markets in many parts of the country have recorded impressive economic dividends for a small, albeit influential, segment of the population. However, it is important to point out that these regional economies have not been able to consolidate these gains across the clan divide or address deep-seated inequality. In Puntland, and to a lesser extent in Somaliland, the largely unregulated economy has spawned an increasing trend of the appropriation and wholesale commercialization of communal and public assets. This development is a logical outcome of attempts by state makers and individuals to establish property rights in order to capture returns from their own entrepreneurial endeavors. In northeast Somalia in particular, this process has resulted in persistent bouts of civil conflict and continues to threaten the most productive base of the local economy. Moreover, alongside the expansion in import/export trade, an extensive market in illicit and criminal trade has developed. This includes the trade in arms, the illegal export of female livestock and wildlife, and piracy (itself spawned by unregulated fishing along the coast of Puntland). In this regard, the flourishing unregulated economy cannot replace the functions of effective formal public and financial institutions. While the booming informal economy has led to the accumulation of wealth by a significant number of Somalis, it has not fulfilled the social needs of the poor and vulnerable, who comprise the vast majority of residents in both Somaliland and Puntland.

In the case of Somalia, and just as economic sociologists and institutional economists would predict, absent formal institutions, wealth accumulation is linked primarily to the networks of contacts that build over time between individuals and communities, and not to income or any other quantitative index of wealth. In other words, it is the density of social networks that determines income generation and helps to secure economic livelihoods. Thus, while clan and familial networks represent the main avenue for the transfer of remittances, who benefits from them is dependent on the possession of previously held social and economic assets. For example, while more than 40 percent of the Isaaq subclans in Somaliland receive remittances from expatriate relatives (Figure 6.1), only 5 percent of the socially and politically marginalized clans (who have enjoyed far more limited access to out-migration in previous decades) in the northwest enjoy the same benefits (Figure 6.2). In addition to their vulnerability stemming from their ethnic and political marginalization, members of the marginalized clan families such as the Gadabursi, Ajuran, and Rahenweyn as well as the Bantu suffer from the lack of access to remittances and consequently have less weight in terms of a voice at the level of the community or government. Moreover, this economic marginalization compounds their relative deprivation and leaves them open to recruitment by Islamist organizations such as al-Ittihad or the more militant al-Shabbaab.[108]

Clearly, as Figure 6.2 demonstrates, the benefits of state building do not accrue to all of the Somaliland's communities and have even exacerbated processes of social and economic exclusion. The Ajuran, Bantu, and other socially excluded minorities, for example, commonly rely on begging and work in the informal sector including a wide range of petty trade activities, handicrafts, domestic work, garbage collection, and the building of latrines. Moreover, while the construction boom in Hargeisa offers opportunities in the building trade, it is a labor market that is segmented along clan lines and favors members of the dominant Isaaq subclans. Consequently, those hailing from minority clans and social groups such as the Bantu, Ajuran, but also non-skilled farmers from the Digil and Rahanwein, find employment only in the lowest, unskilled rung, of the labor market. "We depend on labor in construction if we can find it, or petty trade like selling water or building cement reservoirs. Basically, we

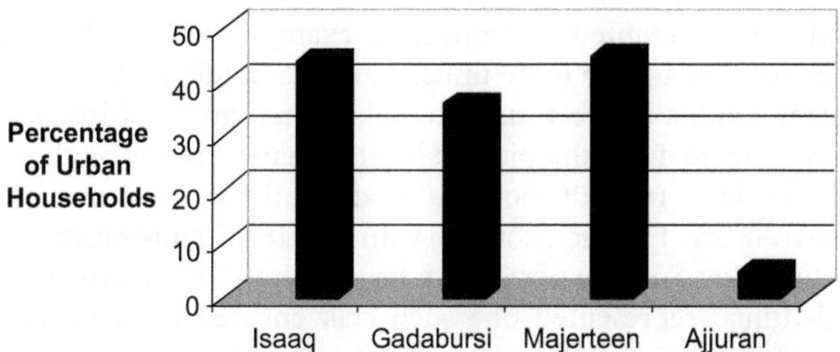


Figure 6.2 Remittances by selected clans in northwest and northeast Somalia
*Source*: Khalid M. Medani, "Report on Internal Migration and Remittance Inflows in Northwest and Northeast Somalia" (Nairobi, Kenya: UN Coordination Unit [UNCU} and Food Security Assessment Unit [FSAU], 2000).

collect gravel and sell it to construction firms in Hargeisa," noted one laborer. Moreover, in contrast to the stronger clans, socially marginalized men and women enjoy minimal access to services offered by the state or social networks of a kind where they are able to benefit from their relatives or kin. As I observed from my research, in both urban and rural areas of Somaliland and Puntland, residents from the socially marginalized groups rarely enjoy financial support from relatives in ways that have secured economic livelihoods for the majority of Somalis. One young man from the Ajuran clan put it simply: "The more relatives you have abroad the more money you receive. We don't have remittances; we don't have relatives outside of Somalia."[109]

## The Challenge of Islamist Recruitment and the Failure of State Building in Southern Somalia

In contrast to the successful state building in Somaliland, southern Somalia has witnessed the emergence of militant Islamist organizations battling for political control. In order to fully understand the Union of Islamic Courts' (UIC) takeover of Mogadishu in 2006, its subsequent attempts at state building, and its ultimate failure at the hands of external actors, we must first place the courts within their historical context. While much attention has been paid to the recent rise of Islamist radicalism in southern Somalia, in reality, Somalia's Islamists are characterized by a lack of internal cohesion, a high level of factionalism, and strong competition between Islamist and clan-based organizations. Consequently, the attempts made by Somalia's Islamic movements and *shari'a* courts to jointly create viable governing administrations to establish security in Mogadishu represented a contrasting example wherein both clan and Islamist networks came to be utilized in state building. As a consequence of violent conflict between the internal militant group al-Ittihad al-Islami on the one hand and Ethiopia and local Somali warlords on the other, the rise of the UIC in 2006 posed a strategic threat to both regional and external powers. This fact, coupled with the US administration's allegation at the time that Somalia served as a haven for al-Qaeda terrorist cells, and that al-Ittihad represented one such cell, ensured the vulnerability and ultimate failure of the UIC's Islamist state building project.

In contrast to the unifying, albeit wrenching conflicts, in Somaliland which ultimately united the various Isaaq subclans, the early civil war period in Somalia resulted in the division of Mogadishu along rival Hawiye "warlords" based on subclan lines. By 1994, Ali Mahdi had been greatly weakened vis-à-vis his local rival General Aideed. In an attempt to establish security, uphold law and order, and restrengthen his position in northern Mogadishu, Mahdi decided to implement the first experiment in *shari'a* courts. The courts managed to do what was thought to be unthinkable for over two decades. Under the charismatic leader Sheikh Ali Dheere, the courts succeeded in establishing security and gaining public support manifest in the recruitment of clan militias and judges during its initial years. These judges and militias, however, were divided into opposing clans and subclans, thereby subjecting the courts to criticism over the validity and neutrality of their judgements. Indeed, as Cedric Barnes and Harun Hassan have observed, during this early period, "the Islamic Courts were part and parcel of clan power in Mogadishu."[110] As such, upon the death of General Aideed in 1996, Sheikh Dheere and the courts came to be viewed as a direct threat to Mahdi's authority and, thus, the courts were dismantled by 1998.

Nevertheless, General Aideed's death presented the opportunity for Islamist organizations to remerge stronger and take root in southern Mogadishu, an area previously hostile to such groups under Aideed. By 1998 the long-standing rivalry between Hawiye subclan militias had failed to provide a secure environment for local businessmen's investments. In 2000 Mogadishu's powerful business elite supported the creation of the Union of Islamic Courts under Hassan Dahir Aweis, the commander of al-Ittihad. Subsequently, the UIC came to serve as an umbrella organization for different clan-based *shari'a* courts to exercise legal authority in particular areas of the city.[111] Though the courts were largely rooted in clan networks, representing the Saleban, Ayr, and Duduble subclans of the Hawiye/Habr-Gedir, the presence of al-Ittihad represented the unifying influence of political Islam.[112] This point is particularly salient, as the UIC's association with al-Ittihad as early as 1998 largely determined its relations with both local and external actors.

The rise of Islamist politics was due to the long, organized presence of Islam in Somalia. A number of the organizations are mainstream Muslim associations of a social, educational, and/or religious nature, and more recently some militants, promulgating a program of coercive and violent expansion with international connections and ambitions emerged. Of the various Islamic associations, the one that laid the roots for modern forms of Islamist militancy, including the Union of Islamic Courts, is al-Ittihad al-Islami. The movement was founded in 1984, bringing together two earlier Islamist organizations: Wahda al-Shabaab al-Islami and, most significantly, the Somali branch of the Ikhwan al-Muslimeen (Muslim Brotherhood). Both these organizations were formed in the 1960s but suppressed by former president Mohamed Siyad Barre. How diverse Islamist politics is in Somalia is reflected by the increasing tension between these modern Islamist organizations and the more traditional, Sufi groups. Most prominent among the latter, is *Ahl al-Sunna wa al-Jama'a* (People of the Sunna and the Community). Ahl al-Sunna was established following the collapse of the Somalia state in 1991. It is self-avowedly opposed to militant and "reformist" Islam and claims to represent traditional, mainstream Muslims in Somalia. They specifically tried to counter Salafist-Wahhabist versions of Islam and thus inevitably became involved in politics. Its efforts to mediate between politics, radical Islam, and Somali Muslim traditions have placed it in a difficult position. In late 2008 it started to form militias to counter the al-Shabaab insurgents.

Of greater political importance has been al-Ittihad al-Islami. Al-Ittihad was first led by the Somaliland Sheikh Ali Warsame, a Saudi-educated Wahhabist cleric. Since the early 1980s it has been a constant presence in Somalia in various forms, both as a social movement with its own services and propagandist-educational activities and as a militant Islamist organization. While al-Ittihad had a social component, it was primarily a political Islamist movement of militants aiming to install an Islamic state in Somalia. It became embroiled in violent disputes and military confrontations with both clan militias and Ethiopian forces along the border with Ethiopia throughout the early 1990s. Its bases in the Gedo region just across the Ethiopian border provoked a campaign by the Ethiopians in 1996–1997 that dislodged the organization and killed many of its leaders. After this defeat, al-Ittihad abandoned its international jihadist ambitions and developed a domestic agenda aimed at creating a semi-legal social network within Somalia society, which was essentially modeled after the National Islamic Front in Sudan before the 1989 coup. Indeed, linkage with al-Ittihad and Sudan is formative and dates back to the early 1970s. In May 1973, five Somali students at Khartoum University who had officially joined the Sudanese Muslim Brotherhood founded the first chapter of the Somali Muslim Brotherhood, the precursor to al-Ittihad.[113]

However, in contrast to the Islamists of Sudan and Egypt where the bulk of rank and file members were recruited from university students and the educated middle class, the Islamists who joined al-Ittihad generally came from a different social segment. Of particular consternation for the leaders of the organization was the fact that potential recruits had a poor knowledge of Arabic and Islam. Consequently, the recruiters of al-Ittihad tried to overcome two important challenges that continue to pose a similar challenge to subsequent militant organizations, including al-Shabbaab. First, leaders had to deal with the low level of education, and particularly rudimentary Islamic learning, and poor Arabic language skills. Second, and most important, they attempted, with varying degrees of success, to overcome the durability of clan and Sufi sectarian loyalties in their efforts to unify Somalis under the broad banner of an Islamist movement. Indeed, their recruitment methods, which owe a great deal to their original influence from the Muslim Brotherhood, follow a familiar methodology but were adapted to meet these challenges which are specific to the Somali context. As with the Muslim Brotherhood in Egypt, potential recruits have to pass through the three stages of identification, training, and recruitment. Similarly, the recruit undergoes a socialization process whereby his commitment and activities are evaluated through the conduct of duties and obligations composed of Da'wa outreach, the payment of monthly contributions, and other activities designed to develop and determine the recruit's level of commitment. Moreover, while potential members of the Brotherhood in Egypt must pass seven stages in this process, al-Ittihad's recruits had to successfully "graduate" through four stages: *Nasir* (aspirant), *Muntasib* (member), *Amil* (effective member), and *Naqib* (full member).[114]

What is noteworthy, however, is that this process of screening and vetting of potential recruits while more efficient in Islamist organizations like that of the Muslim Brotherhood in Egypt is far more precarious in Somalia's more conflict-prone political landscape. Moreover, while clan and sectarian ties may be far less pronounced in Sudan, and even less so in Egypt, in Somalia the competition over identity-based loyalties is far more complex and insecure. Wherein intraclan divisions and Sufi-Islamist conflicts come into confrontation Somali Islamists routinely experience organization vulnerability and internal divisions. In particular, the deaths and displacement which is a common feature in central and southern Somalia routinely undermine the unity and cohesion of al-Ittihad and other Islamist organizations. As the Somali scholar Abdurahman Abdullahi has persuasively argued, while Islamists in Somalia devise a number of innovative strategies to meet these challenges, including shortening the duration of the recruitment process and holding meetings at a "general location," this often leads to a problem of "excessive recruitment" that dilutes the organizational discipline and the religious commitment of the individual to the organization.[115] Consequently, while most scholars have focused on Ethiopia's crackdowns against al-Ittihad forces since the early 1990s to explain the latter's weakness, a more important factor has been the challenges associated with the recruitment process. In other words, al-Ittihad and Islamist militant leaders in general have faced significant political and cultural obstacles in their efforts at recruiting committed, disciplined, and relatively educated, skilled cadres to their organizations. As a result, the recruits of al-Ittihad have been far more susceptible to militant ideologies and strategies than other middle-class-based Islamist movements. Existing in somewhat of a state of ideological ambivalence and unable to forge a stable and cohesive organizational structure, al-Ittihad – like other Islamist militant organizations in south-central Somalia – has simply been unable to monopolize and deploy the "legitimate" use of violence as part of building durable state institutions.

Nevertheless, while it was able to establish an Islamist social movement as in Egypt or Sudan, by the early 1990s, al-Ittihad did emerge as a political force, distinguished from other clan-centered militias by its cross-clan Islamist ideology.[116] In 1991, the group engaged in violent conflict with two local warlords: General Aideed and Colonel Abdullahi Yusuf, whose struggle against the Islamists was backed by Ethiopia. Before joining the Union of Islamic Courts in southern Mogadishu, al-Ittihad was a target of continuous attacks by Ethiopia, which viewed this group as a significant threat to its security. Ethiopia has long been considered an enemy to Somalia, a perception exacerbated by the 1977 Ogaden War, the 1998 Ethiopian-Eritrean War, and now the threat of Islamist militancy along the Somalia-Ethiopia border. In light of the regional and international opposition to the emergence of Islamist militants in Somalia, it came as little surprise that the UIC's emergence as the strongest political and military force in Mogadishu by mid-2005 led to external military intervention and an internal proxy war. Moreover, the

UIC's staunch opposition to the 2004 Transitional Federal Government (TFG) established by Ethiopia and the United States renewed rivalry with certain Hawiye subclan groups and exacerbated suspicions surrounding the courts.

By 2005, the TFG had lost all legitimacy among residents of Mogadishu. The Somali Reconciliation and Rehabilitation Council (SSRC), a loose coalition of Ethiopia-backed and anti-Islamist factions, supported the government and remained as its primary base of support. The TFG-appointed the late president Abdullahi Yusuf who supported Ethiopia and formed an alliance with Addis Ababa against the Islamists of Mogadishu. Perhaps most importantly, unlike the state builders in Hargeisa, the TFG failed to transcend clannism and resolve debilitating interclan conflicts in the region. The 13th Somali Conference, which was held in Kenya under the auspices of the Inter-Governmental Authority on Development (IGAD)[117] and with the support of the UN and European Commission, established a three-phase process to broker peace in Somalia. These were a declaration of cease-fire, resolution of the key conflict issues, and power-sharing in a revived central government. However, Somali delegates were unable to make progress over the second phase and, in order to move ahead with the negotiations, the participants moved on to the final phase without effectively reconciling their differences. Moreover, in stark contrast to Somaliland, the power-sharing arrangement was designed in such a way as to institutionalize rigid clan identity and division, whereby seats were designated to clan-family members, and negotiations over representation took place *within* rather than *between* clans.[118] Indeed, the interventions by external actors also played a significant role in preventing the creation of an indigenous Somali state form as witnessed in Somaliland. As a result, clannism persisted and by mid-2005 the government was incapacitated by deep internal divisions.

In light of the threat posed by Yusuf and the TFG's illegitimacy, by 2005 the UIC was strengthened, allowing it to mobilize its base of support. As a result of an ostensible increase in Islamic "fundamentalist" power, a US-backed coalition of businessmen, militia leaders, and Hawiye "warlords" formed the Alliance for Restoration of Peace and Counter Terrorism in March 2006.[119] Fighting broke out between the UIC and the loosely organized Alliance and, by the first week of April, the UIC had seized most of Mogadishu. By the summer, the UIC gained complete control over the city and ousted the Alliance and warring militants.

The UIC achieved many successes during the first months of its instalment in Mogadishu, not least of which was establishing security and control in the city. It had earned a monopoly over both coercive and extractive power and received high levels of public support. Unlike the

TFG, the UIC attempted to formulate a state structure that eradicated clannism by upholding unifying Islamic traditions and law. For Somalis who had experienced over three decades of interclan warfare, Islamic law interpreted mostly for its "law and order" function proved a viable and attractive option. However, as a new legitimating ideology for a nascent state, shari'a law would not have proven successful were it not for the fact that the UIC's executive apparatus was consistent with traditional Somali clan institutions including the Xeer, and that its leaders refrained from institutionalizing their power at the expense of traditional clan authorities. The representative decision-making body within the UIC effectively bridged clan identity, incorporating subclans of the Hawiye, Rahanweyn, Isaaq, and Darod families. While the executive consisted of a chairman and cabinet, it incorporated such traditional governing bodies as a *shura,* or consultative committee, and its primary governing branch was composed of the independent *shari'a* courts.[120]

Similar to that of Somaliland, the state building approach attempted by the UIC in 2006 sought to combine both clan ties and Islamic norms in ways that would reconcile Mogadishu's rival clans and lay the groundwork for more stable state institutions. Moreover, by the summer of 2006, the UIC provided southern Somalis with an alternative to the TFG's externally driven state building project, incorporating "indigenous" Islamic principles of particular relevance to the Somali context. Much like the experience in Somaliland, and contrary to much writing on state formation, the UIC's approach to state building highlighted the possibility of a state built on local cultural as well as political realities.

This experiment, however, was short-lived. The emergence of UIC authority in Mogadishu was declared by the parliament of Ethiopia as posing a "clear and present danger" to that country. The Ethiopian government, as a result, granted the late prime minister Meles Zenawi the authority to defend the TFG and Ethiopian sovereignty "by any means necessary." As a result, the Ethiopian military supplied the TFG with troops and arms in order to rid Somalia of the UIC. On December 20, 2006, clashes arose between the TFG and UIC. The nascent UIC forces were loosely organized and vastly outnumbered by the Ethiopia-TFG coalition. On December 28, the short-lived Islamist project of the UIC ended as Ethiopian and TFG forces entered Mogadishu unopposed. Not surprisingly, in place of the state-building experiment that sought to combine both Islamist and clan loyalties in what is Somalia's most divided region there emerged a far more radical and militant Islamist organization: al-Shabbaab.

In contrast, to Egypt and Sudan, Islamist activism in Somalia arose precisely due to the strength of political clannism reinforced during the remittance boom. The oil boom era did in fact witness the genesis of the modern Islamist movement in Somalia. However, this development was primarily a result of Somalia's weak state rather than the consolidation of Islamist activism across a broad spectrum of Somali society. Moreover, while both Sudan and Egypt developed a strong middle-class-based Islamist movement, albeit with different levels of success in political terms, this has not been the case in Somalia. Indeed, the factors that have resulted in the proliferation of Islamist militant organizations in south-central Somalia can be attributed to the general absence of an Islamist social movement in the country as well as external interventions.

Also, in contrast to the Islamist movements in Sudan and Egypt, in Somalia clan politics continues to dominate political and social life. Indeed, 'Islamism' in Somalia is fundamentally an externally driven phenomenon; it's ascendance in domestic politics can be traced to the 1970s when thousands of Somalis traveled to find employment in the Arab oil producing states. Moreover, whereas in Egypt and Sudan the political ascendancy of Islamist organizations has been determined by the interplay of state-society relations rather than by external actors, in Somalia the more militant aspects of Islamist mobilization are rooted in Wahhabist influences on some Somalis originating from Saudi Arabia. Al-Ittihad and other Somali Islamist organizations began building the organizational structure of their organizations and constructing the ideological edifice of their movements abroad. Ultimately, however, the real political and ideological battle in south-central Somalia has been the conflict between a small group of Islamist militants and the far more politically salient politics of clannism.

# 7 The Political Economy of Radicalization: Informal Networks and the Rise of an Urban Militant Islamism in Cairo

In Egypt, by the 1990s, both state policy and broader external forces played a role in the rise of Islamist militancy in informal Cairo. To be sure the persistence in the popularity of the *Jama'a al-Islamiyya* following the siege of Imbaba was in great part a response to the blatant abuse of security forces, which incarcerated scores of Islamists and the litany of abuses on the part of state security services, which included the use of local traditional authorities in the monitoring and surveillance of "terrorists." However, the rise in the popularity of militant Islamists in Imbaba was a response to broader external economic forces that had increasingly isolated the quarters of Western Munira, geographically and economically, from the mainstream of Cairean society. These included structural changes in the national and local economy; persistent neglect of the community by state institutions, including local municipal officials, and nearly two decades of authoritarian policies that severely circumscribed avenues of political participation and adversely affected the quality of life of residents of Western Munira and accelerated the decline and deterioration of their neighborhood.[1]

The context for Islamic militancy in this period is closely associated with broader economic and political factors that in the 1970s and early 1980s combined to produce a transformation in terms of the articulation of urban space, social organization, and Islamist political activism. As detailed in Chapter 1, in the Sadat era and the early years of the Mubarak regime expatriate workers heavily invested their earnings in housing stock, which resulted in a dramatic boom in informal housing and, by extension, informal labor (especially labor in the construction sector), concentrated in informal settlements such as Western Munira in Imbaba.

In the post-1986 recession era, the combination of the drying up of remittance inflows from migrant workers and economic reforms in the form of price liberalization effectively undercut black-market currency trading and the power of informal financial institutions. However, it did not result in the demise of all segments of informal economic activity. Economic reforms encouraged the further expansion of informally organized wage earners and the expansion of informally organized production and work. That is, the old Nasserite economic system rooted in a social contract between large firms and a stable, unionized industrial labor force gave way to a new regime based on service occupations and a dramatic reorganization of labor markets and wage structures. By 1995 upward of 62 percent of Egypt's economically active population was engaged in informal sector activities in at least one of their primary, secondary, or tertiary economic activities.[2] Moreover, as in other labor-exporting countries, the general investment boom associated with the internationalization of the Egyptian economy led to an expansion of the informalization of the markets in housing, land, and labor. As a result of the reduction of subsidies and social welfare (as well as the continued increase in the rates in population growth and urbanization), Islamic Welfare Associations (*al-Jam'iyyat al-sharia al-Islamiyya*) and numerous private mosques (*ahali*) expanded dramatically. Taken together these developments altered social relations and political developments at the community level in a dramatic fashion.

As discussed in Chapter 4, by the 1990s, thousands of these Islamic voluntary associations managed to develop a parallel economy and a parallel welfare system. In some instances, these modes of informal organization translated into an Islamist-inspired challenge to the state. Moreover, where radical Islamist activists of the Islamic Group were able to exploit informal financial networks and procure informal labor contracts for their supporters in the informal settlements around Cairo, they used these as bases of power and influence. Using private financial sources that often bypassed the strict regulations of the state to activate social networks and establish and fund a dense network of private mosques, activist leaders of al-Jama'a al-Islamiyya sought to build, literally, a "state within a state." However, contrary to some accounts, this new, more militant Islamist movement was not ubiquitous among Egypt's urban poor. Rather, al-Jama'a's "takeover" of parts of Cairo's informal settlements grew out of the ascendancy of an informal labor force that relied on the expansion of informal markets in housing and labor. In the informal settlements of Cairo, al-Jama'a leaders adapted "traditional" Egyptian rural norms in ways that allowed them to supplant the political power of local notables while institutionalizing extortion practices and implementing their own brand of "law and order."

Al-Jama'a militants exploited the high levels of social and economic uncertainty in Cairo's informal housing areas while simultaneously framing their message in ways that resonated with the conservative norms of many local residents. Indeed, an important reason for the popularity of al-Jama'a in this period among local residents was its ability to settle local disputes, albeit often through highly coercive methods, and to enforce informal labor contracts for its members, while simultaneously preaching against the ills of conspicuous consumption and imposing strict Islamic modes of conduct. The socioeconomic conditions that played a key role in the popularity of Islamist radicalism were made possible by economic change at both the international and domestic level. However, despite its violent confrontation with militant Islam, the Egyptian state, until the historic uprisings of 2011, demonstrated relative political continuity in the context of drastic economic policy transformation.[3]

## A Comprehensive Strategy of Militant Mobilization

The link between these political and economic developments and the rise in the popularity of more militant forms of Islamist activism in the informal quarters of Imbaba is rooted in four factors: First, the social organization of the informal labor market in Imbaba was particularly conducive to drawing the rank and file of adherents to the militants. This, as I argue later, was because it mirrored the structure, organization, and normative framework of al-Jama'a as it developed in the informal quarters. Moreover, while these informal labor markets are characterized by the absence of legal and bureaucratic institutions, they are nevertheless regulated by informal institutions such as customary norms, kinship ties, and in the case of some of these ascriptive ties in Western Munira in the 1980s and 1990s, Islamist networks. As scholars of informal networks have long established, informalization implies that labor control relies less on the associative pattern of social organization (e.g., collective bargaining or corporatist arrangements) and more on authoritarian forms of "indigenous networks" which are knit together by family, friends, kinship, and regional affinities.[4] Naturally, which of these ascriptive ties and networks (i.e., religious, kinship, regional) are mobilized at a particular historical moment requires close examination of locally specific institutional settings.[5]

Second, militant leaders benefited from the weakened role of local traditional leaders and institutions. As detailed in Chapter 1, informal councils (*majalis ʿurfiyya*) and dispute settlement committees (*lijan sulh*) which had traditionally maintained social order saw their traditional authority greatly undermined by the late 1980s as a result of drastic demographic, political, and socioeconomic transformations. But in the 1990s and 2000s the latter's authority in the quarters of Imbaba was further eroded as a result of the regime's persistent "war on terrorism" against militants, which essentially transformed the bulk of local traditional leaders into security agents of the state exacerbating the grievances of local residents against state authorities.

Third, the role of Islamic Welfare Associations, and particularly the dense network of private Mosques in Western Munira, and the dissemination of particular Islamist norms via the congregational sermons provided both the material and normative orientation for young men to join the ranks of the militants. And, finally, an important factor associated with the popularity of the Islamic Group in mobilizing members in Western Munira, and the violent nature of this type of mobilization had to do with the way in which militants established mafia-like "protection rackets." Indeed, the manner in which militants attempted to "build a state within a state" conforms closely to Tilly's description of local strongmen – forcing merchants to pay tribute under threat and actual use of violence. The militants also routinely used intimidation and violence to settle local disputes and procure and enforce labor contracts for new and potential members. One sympathizer of al-Jama'a in Western Munira summarized their strategy succinctly:

> When we have trouble, the Muslims quickly come to help. If someone treats you unfairly, you can go to the Muslims and they speak to him or beat him. If someone tries to flirt with your daughter, they threaten him. If you are in debt, they tell the moneychanger to be patient.[6]

Consequently, the leaders of al-Jama'a utilized a comprehensive strategy, which entailed approximating social relations and normative frames familiar to local residents, enforced strict "Islamic" modes of conduct to safeguard the "Islamic" family, and used coercive as well as noncoercive methods to settle disputes and enforce contracts in a highly competitive, and unstable, informal labor market. As a result of the combination of these factors militant activists in the quarters of Western Munira were able to mobilize a significant number of adherents to their organization and ultimately pose a threat to the state.

## Joining the Militants

The primary reason that the crisis in Imbaba had such dramatic political consequence is that it represented a new phenomenon in the modern history of the Islamist trend in Egypt. In the 1970s and 1980s, in the initial phase of the Islamist trend in urban Cairo, the Muslim Brotherhood primarily spearheaded Islamist activism. In this period the Ikhwan managed to build a wide range of financial and civil society institutions through a successful social movement that was, unlike the Jama'a, largely nonviolent. The siege of Imbaba made it abundantly clear that an important element of the Islamist movement had gone through an important transformation in terms of its social profile in two important respects.

First, many of these militants came from rural backgrounds. But they also drew in segments of Cairo's lower-class residents living in the informal settlements, or shantytowns, lying on the fringes of the city. Of great significance is that by the 1990s there was an unprecedented rise in the recruitment of juveniles by the Islamic Group in Western Munira, Imbaba.[7] Lower-class youth emerged, for the first time, as central players in what was to become a more radical element of Islamist activism. Thus, while the Muslim Brotherhood continued to represent middle-class and lower middle-class aspirations, militant activists reflected a new socioeconomic profile. Specifically, compared to their counterparts in the 1970s and 1980s, by the 1990s, they were younger (ranging from fifteen and twenty old), and less educated.[8]

Second, the fears on the part of the state surrounding the growth of informal settlements represented the regime's anxiety about the informal, or casual, laboring class, which represented a large segment of residents in the poorest quarters of Imbaba. In the quarters of Western Munira, children, fifteen years old or younger, representing the lowest rung of the informal labor force in Imbaba were attracted to the militants in the neighborhood. Moreover, as one study observed, these "youths were often recruited as entry points into households and utilized to recruit additional members of their respective families."[9]

The small "convenient" sample in Table 7.1 collected from interviews with ten leaders of the Jama'at and twelve of its rank and file members in the 1990s is instructive in shedding light on the social and economic profile of the leadership and rank and file members of the organization and it demonstrates the linkage between informal labor and membership in the Islamic Group.[10]

First, it is important to note that while the majority of members of the Jama'a were primarily employed as casual, or informal, laborers in construction and other trades, albeit at different levels of the labor market, there is a distinct social distance between leaders and rank and file members. Indeed, while the majority of the local leaders of the militants are of a higher social class,[11] rank and file members generally represented those in the lower-skilled segment of this labor market. Second, it is evident that the majority of young men (all of whom were in their late teens and early twenties at the time) and who joined in the late 1980s and 1990s were either underemployed or unemployed.

Finally, and of equal significance, in my research among former members of the Islamic Group in Western Munira I found that the bulk of rank and file members in Western Munira were young men, or *Subyan*, often

Table 7.1 *List of select leaders and rank and file members of al-Jama'a al-Islamiyya by profession in Western Munira, Imbaba, Cairo*

| List of Jama'a Sheikhs and leaders by profession in Western Munira, Imbaba | List of rank and file members of the Jama'a by profession in Western Munira, Imbaba |
|---|---|
| Sheikh 'Esam al-Masri – **Physician** | Said Nabil – **Informal laborer** (Bricklayer) |
| (Emir of Imbaba; imprisoned in the late 1990s) | Amgad Gamal – **Informal laborer** in leather workshop |
| Sheikh Gabir Farag – **Drummer** | Abu Hamid – **Informal laborer** in oil factory |
| (Commander, Military Wing; imprisoned in the late 1990s) | Mohamed Hamdi – **Informal laborer** (Furniture weaver) |
| Sheikh Ali Farag – **Pharmacist** | Mohamed Farag – **Unemployed** |
| (Sheikh Gabir's brother) | Yusif Amir – **Unemployed** |
| Mohamed Ibrahim – **Owner of hardware store**, also construction foreman (imprisoned in 1990s) | Mohamed Yusif Hassan Ibrahim – (Bread maker) |
| Shakir Yousef – **Truck driver** | Salah "Karate" – **Karate teacher** |
| Hamd Abu Elias – **Engineer** | Mustafa (Salah's Brother) – **Student** |
| 'Antar al-Din – **Secondary school teacher** | Mohamed Abdel Fattah – **Unemployed** |
| Sheikh Raouf – **Informal laborer** (Plasterer) | Ahmed Abdelwahab – **Student** |
| Mohamed al-Fattah – **Arabic script painter/artist** | Tariq Hassabo – **Informal laborer** (Bricklayer and seller of ceramics) |
| Al-Saed Gabir – **Informal laborer** (Carpenter) | |

*Source:* Data compiled from interviews conducted in the course of the author's field research. Western Munira, Imbaba, Cairo.

the most-exploited laborers in the informal construction firm (*dulab*). Even in the best times, the *subyan* receive the lowest wages of the *dulab*'s employees though they undertake the most strenuous form of work, and due to the high degree of intra-market competition, they are rarely in the position to negotiate terms with the contractor. This concrete, day-to-day exploitation – more than some amorphous sense of alienation or psychological attributes – explains why so many of Imbaba's *subyan* joined the ranks of al-Jama'a. The fact that these *subyan* joined in significant numbers is evidenced by one study, which confirmed the unprecedented increase in the number of juveniles (fifteen and under) in the rank and file membership of al-Jama'a in 'Izbat al-Mufti – the Western Munira quarters of the neighborhood of Imbaba where informal labor is most highly concentrated and where the Islamist militants enjoyed their strongest following.[12]

Tariq Hassabo, a former member of al-Jama'a, represents an illustrative example of the profile of those who joined the Jama'a in the late 1980s and 1990s. In 1998 Tariq was twenty-nine years old, married with one young daughter, and a long-time resident of 'Izbat al-Mufti. He joined the Jama'a when he was twenty-two and noted that most of the members of the Jama'a in the quarter were, like him, in their twenties and worked mostly in the informal labor market. Tariq himself worked as a casual laborer as a wall-fixer and painter on a casual basis. His daughter is of a different mother while his mother and father live in the adjacent apartment. He did have a younger brother whom he described as a "baltagi" and who died in a knife fight in the neighborhood. Like so many in 'Izbat al-Mufti, Tariq Hassabo is off rural origins. His father is originally from al-Munifiyya governorate and an active member of the regional association of *ahl al-Munifiyya*, although he was born in Imbaba.

Tariq was drawn to the Jama'a gradually and for a combination of reasons linked to socioeconomic as well as moral reasons rather than political. Indeed, he rarely mentioned politics, and while many in the leadership stressed politics as the door to recruitment, it is not a factor that was highlighted by Tariq and other former members of the organization. According to his own account, what drew him to the Jama'a was the piety and morality of the leadership, their attention to the social and moral ills of 'Izbat al-Mufti, and what he termed the "passion and fire" of the preachers at the Jama'a mosques. Like many in the quarter, he was particularly drawn to an important leader in the quarter: Sheikh Mohamed Ali. Sheikh Ali, Tariq recollected, gave the poor sheep and meat during festive occasions, assisted the poor and ill with alms, and instructed members of al-Jama'a, including Tariq, to pay visits to the poor in their homes as part of a good-will campaign. Sheikh Ali also organized sessions on "Arab issues" in his apartment where potential members would speak and discuss the politics of the day in the Arab world and, as Tariq put it, discuss the corruption of non-'Muslim' tyrants (*Tagha*). But while "enjoining the good" meant paying visits to the poor, "forbidding evil" was, if certainly more punitive, equally attractive to the young members to the organization. "We often broke up marriages where men and women congregated, closed brothels in the 'Izba, and made sure that people in the neighborhood would inform us (the Jama'a) of where these brothels were. We would then beat the men operating them and cut the hair of the women." At first, he continued, "[T]he residents of the 'Izba appreciated and supported these actions."

He used to pray regularly at Masjid al-Nur in al-'Izba, where he first encountered Sheikh Ali, the brother of Sheikh Gabir who led the uprisings in 1992. Subsequently, he began working and spreading the Da'wa under the instruction and guidance of Sheikh Ali. He was also given a specific task in the organization's recruitment efforts. Specifically, he was charged with the assignment of accompanying a group of fellow "Muslims" to persuade young men "loitering" in the neighborhood's street corners to join in the street prayers (*salat al-masaha*). "We began with only six individual 'Muslims' but our group," he noted with some degree of pride, "increased to thirty within just two months."

## From Boom to Bust: Informal Labor Markets and the Advent of Militant Islam in Informal Cairo

For the young men and boys in Imbaba like Tariq who during the construction boom had come to rely on wages from casual labor, the recession of the mid-1980s struck especially hard. Out of work and destitute, this already demoralized workforce found no social services or social institutions upon which to depend. As the young men of the neighborhood sought out some semblance of social cohesion, stability, and predictability in their daily lives and those of their families, activists from al-Jama'a al-Islamiyya found themselves, in the latter part of the 1980s, well positioned to take advantage of this state of affairs.

During the 1970s, the infitah polices of Anwar Sadat had profoundly restructured the labor market, and lower-skilled labor, such as the non-skilled segment engaged in construction, had paid the highest price for the state's neoliberal economic policy. Because the emerging job market demanded skilled labor a large segment of lower-skilled workers relocated to the informal sector, which meant that they faced higher levels of economic insecurity and lower wages. Semi-skilled craftsmen, in particular, who had learned their trade through many years of apprenticeship, were less flexible about changing their occupations and as result they were particularly hard-hit in terms of finding new employment opportunities.

The key problem is that in Egypt, there is a stark distinction between the nature of the relationship of the state and contractual relations in the formal and informal labor markets. Workers in the formal sector enjoy legal protections that are based on a class-based social organization of production closely linked to the state and thus more favorable to collective action. By contrast labor relations in the informal labor market in informal quarters such as *Western Munira* are essentially locked into dependent contractual relations with jobbers, recruiters, gang bosses, and other intermediaries, often kinsmen or co-villagers, which reduces their capacity to pursue their collective interests. Moreover, this "immobilizing effect" caused by informal work is increased not only by the pressure to invest in informal social ties, it is made more precarious in the context of volatile markets dependent on both the national and world economy.[13]

An important aspect linking informal settlements to the national economy is evidenced by the informal labor markets' vulnerability to boom and bust cycles. In the 1980s procuring work in *ta'ifat al-mi'mar* (construction sector) was crucially dependent on contracts available in the informal housing sector financed by the wages of remittances of migrants working in the Arab oil-producing countries. As informal workers informed me, at that time informal work was not only available in Imbaba but *Masr al-Gadida* and all of the many middle- and upper-class neighborhoods built up by the boom in out-migration. Construction workers often spoke of this time of great opportunity and that even if you lived and worked in *Western Munira* you could find employment as far afield as Sinai and *Sharm al-Sheikh*. One worker recounted how he found a "great" job working on building the Baron Hotel in *Sharm al-Sheikh*, and he proudly noted that an Egyptian rather than a foreign construction firm built it. The fact that many laborers lived in the informal settlements was because it was cheaper and wages for informal work were low and fixed by the subcontractors despite the availability of work. Indeed, it is important to note that workers still expressed frustration because wages were not adjusted upward even when, as one worker put it, "the contractor got more money from a private sector firm." Nevertheless, these social, class, and spatial divisions were greatly subdued during the boom since as one scholar aptly noted, the ethic of group solidarity (both vertical and horizontal) was a key element in procuring gainful employment and of achieving some modest measure of upward mobility for those at the lowest rank of the informal labor market.[14] As one subcontractor noted: "I was responsible for resolving conflict [and] during the boom this was not a crucial problem since work was relatively plentiful and informal housing affordable."[15]

Upon the onset of the recession, however, a severe crisis in the informal labor market emerged as the supply of labor became plentiful as a result not only of the severe economic downturn associated with the slump in oil prices but also because of the increased saturation of the market in affordable land for housing. The real-estate heyday joining land speculators and middle-class Egyptians slowed by the late 1980s. Whereas in 1985 the Egyptian construction industry was touted as the largest construction market in the region,[16] by the end of the decade, rising costs in building materials and falling confidence signaled the end of the era of large-scale infrastructural development that had begun after 1973.[17] The seasonality of the construction business also contributed considerably to the glut of unskilled and semi-skilled informal labor in Imbaba. In general terms, unless the supply of labor is limited, industries that have seasonal peaks of production tend to produce a labor supply in excess of normal needs. During the boom years, when contractors needed a continuous level of employment but faced labor shortages caused by wide-scale out-migration to the Gulf, they heavily recruited workers from Upper Egypt to work in construction throughout greater Cairo. In the case of the neighborhood of Imbaba, workers were most often recruited from the regional associations (*rawabat iqlimiyya*) created from rural-to-urban migrants originating chiefly from the governorates of Assiut and Sohag.

With the recession, construction companies sought to quickly cut down costs, announcing that they would keep labor and material expenses to a minimum.[18] Whereas during the boom, employers kept laborers on salary, in the recession there was little incentive to maintain a continuous level of employment, and contractors targeted semi-skilled and unskilled labor for sharp cutbacks. Subcontractors (i.e., craftsmen) said that by the late 1980s they had to implement a number of strategies to remain competitive and find employment. Under pressure from the big contractors, they had to ration labor or dismiss "redundant" workers, workers had to lower their wages in order to attract contractors, and both had to build a "good reputation" to find work.

While in the past family, kin, or in-law relations mitigated social tensions and served as important networks to find employment, in the recession regular employment was increasingly maintained by a combination of intangible qualities: hard work, a reputation for trustworthiness, and the friendship of an employer or contractor. Skilled and semi-skilled traders who had a reputation for insubordination or tardiness or whose poor health or age was thought to constitute a liability were the workers hit hardest by the downturn in the construction boom. Magdi Mohamed Hussein, a craftsmen specializing in steel support and concrete molding (*Naggar Musalah*) explained the nature and consequences of the bust for informal workers in the building trade in eloquent terms:

> I began work in the early 1970s and in the 1980s there was a real boom in terms of work. There was lots of it for everybody. But there has been a strong recession in our work over the last 5 years in 'Izbat al-Mufti; most of our work went down and "*al-shugl nayim*" (the work fell asleep). 1992 was the beginning of the end. The regulations in terms of informal housing [also] halted our work. Before 1992 people could build here but this is not the case anymore. Now there is more competition. We all have to use our good reputation to get jobs, and the work has to be very clean [of superior quality] because that is the only way we can have an advantage over our competition. I personally cannot do any other work. I am not qualified to do anything else and I am too old to learn.[19]

In the Western Munira quarters of Imbaba, a subcontractor, referred to locally as a *ra'is* or *commanda*, no longer found it profitable, or feasible, to maintain a *dulab* – a full team of building operatives who are contracted informally – and he was forced to ration work in ways that led to the increasing immiseration of semi-skilled and unskilled workers. Employers shortened working hours, adjusted salaries downward, and laid off non-essential workers and apprentices.[20] "As the ra'is," Mr. Hussein explained, "I am responsible for resolving disputes. There is often a problem with six *subyan* (apprentices) because I cannot use them all since the work had disappeared. I try to rotate them, so everyone has a chance."[21] Indeed, as a consequence of the decline in employment opportunities in the building trade, informal laborers were forced to adjust in a number of ways, including simply by living below subsistence.

The severity of the intra-market competition resulting from the recession, and in the construction sector, was gravely compounded by the lack of any social protection or insurance for those who relied on informal work for their livelihood. Kin, familial, and friendship ties served residents well in the boom years, but in the recession these networks lost the material incentives that sustained and secured the economic livelihoods of individuals and families residing in the poorer quarters of *Western Munira*. In the boom years it was sufficient to rely on ties of family, friends, and kin to procure work; in the recession the scarcity of work and the oversupply of labor meant that workers with stronger links to the formal economy and acquaintances outside the neighborhood enjoyed greater access to new information about job opportunities that might otherwise remain unknown.[22] For its part, the state never showed any willingness to insure informal laborers to any degree, introduce legislation to improve work conditions, fix minimum wages, or curb child labor.

Indeed, the great capacity of the state bureaucracy to tightly control product and labor markets stands in stark contrast to its inability to organize and regulate informal labor relations, a fact captured in the official usage of the term *al qita' ghayr al-munazam* to describe this "unorganized sector" of the economy. Moreover, neither public nor private firms, which seek flexibility in the labor market in order to keep wages low, were willing to provide any social benefits to their employees.

Almost overnight, disputes over wages became more common and social tensions intensified in Western Munira, pitting contractor against worker and unskilled laborer against semi-skilled craftsman. Workers began to prefer public construction companies to the previously more lucrative private ones. Informal workers reported that although the public enterprises paid lower wages, they offered stable work. As one worker put it, "at least they [public-sector firms] paid wages in advance, rather than in installments like the corrupt private companies."[23] The recession had proved less of a burden for the large public sector corporations, which, unlike the private firms, operated without the demand for profitability. Because large government-funded projects continued to be the preserve of the large public sector firms, they could offer more stable and reliable contracts for construction workers. Moreover, with the onset of the privatization of the industry in the late 1990s the competition between subcontractors, craftsmen, and unskilled workers for even these shorter-term and less-stable contracts in what emerged as a far more competitive private sector further intensified competition and social tensions between those dependent on the informal labor market for their livelihood in the Imbaba.[24]

What is important to note, however, is that these opportunities continued to be dependent on vertical patron-client ties since employers tend to hire workers they know personally, and workers strive to foster such personal ties to get jobs. In Imbaba procuring employment in the informal labor market is not only dependent on the stock of connections, and access to information and social networks, it is also a function of place of residence. Higher-status workers (i.e., contractors) possess long-standing relations outside the neighborhood and stronger links with the formal economy. As a result they are able to acquire new information about job opportunities that remain unknown to workers lower down the labor market hierarchy. By contrast, subcontractors and lower-status workers residing in Western Munira noted that they simply did not have the connections to procure work in the public sector and, moreover, they could not trust that a contractor (*Muqawil*) from outside Imbaba would meet his contractual obligations. As one worker put it: "On the Sharm El-Sheikh job, the contractor was from outside Imbaba and refused to pay fully after we completed the job. In the 'Izba this would never happen because the contractor has to interact with us face to face." The primary problem for the casual laborer was that no formal contracts regulated these arrangements, and the laborers – and to a lesser degree, the contractors – had to rely on the good reputation of their employers. As one ra'is (head of a dulab) explained:

> Contractors are the ones who find us the jobs. We cannot look for them ourselves. We do not have the tax papers or licenses. This has to come from the contractor in order to bid for the job. [In addition] the contractor works with the public sector and we are in the private [i.e. informal] sector. You have to be connected to the public sector to get job assignments. For example, you have to be approved by someone connected with Sharikat [Osman Ahmad] Osman.[25]

In-migrants who became unemployed waited, despite the recession, in anticipation of further construction work instead of returning to agriculture. As James Toth has noted in a study of workers in rural Egypt, "despite the inflated size of the workforce, both the intermittent nature of construction work and the paternalistic ties to employers made this expectation possible."[26] Indeed, as I witnessed first-hand in the informal settlements of 'Izbat al-Mufti, Beshteel, and al-Waraq, the informal settlements, in Western Munira, the very nature of informal labor lent itself to a particular type of job insecurity in which a large portion of the workforce remained in a casualized limbo, filling short periods of employment by invading an already overfilled, generally unskilled labor market.

To make matters worse, in the context of the recession and increasing land competition in rural Upper Egypt, scores of in-migrants, particularly from Fayoum and Assiut, migrated to Imbaba and came to represent what Egyptian scholars refer to as *al-proleteriat al-ratha* or the lumpenproletariate.[27] These young men possessed little education or skills and they essentially filled the ranks of *Umaal Ugari*, day laborers or odd jobbers, and lived in the worst conditions in the poorest quarters of the neighborhood. In Imbaba, this led to intensified competition reflected in severe and dangerous tensions along regional and sectarian lines. Thus, Muslim "fellahin" (farmers from the Nile delta) stood against "sa'ayida" (upper Egyptians), and the two against Coptic Christians. As one fellahin laborer put it, "The sa'ayida are like Christians. They know how to take care of themselves." In addition, since the cost of living was increasing, the informal labor market also received a steady stream of Cairo denizens ousted from their regular occupations or simply unable to make a living wage in the neighborhoods of middle-class Cairo. This has meant not only that the poorer quarters of Imbaba were assuming a more heterogeneous makeup (similar to the original quarters of the neighborhood and some other informal settlements), but also that there was increasingly stiff competition in the informal labor market between Cairenes and in-migrants.

Another important consequence of the employment crisis that came to be exploited by Islamist militant leaders was the breakdown of the traditional kinship-based patron-client relations through which the *dulab* operated. With the introduction of severe competition, trust became rare and fragile, allowing al-Jama'a members to enter the market as intermediaries between contractors and laborers. Very quickly, leading members of the Jama'a procured the limited number of contracts from the head of the *dulab* for those young men who supported them and, moreover, they acted as guarantors to clients of their choosing guaranteeing to the firm that laborers under their patronage would work for an agreed-upon wage and working hours. In this way, al-Jama'a supplanted the traditional Upper Egyptian patrons in the informal labor market over a short period. The key difference was that al-Jama'a, unlike traditional labor recruiters, often resorted to coercive and violent means to enforce contracts. Selim Hafiz, a long-time resident of 'Izbat al-Mufti, and not affiliated with al-Jama'a observed that prior to the recession "there was no need for the Islamic Group" if you belonged to a "big family" because the big families were able to offer "protection" to their members and find them secure employment. However, he added that with the recession, the big families found it hard to "prevent their sons from joining."[28]

## Mirroring the *Dulab*: Militancy and the Informal Labor Firm

The linkage between the emergence of a radical Islamist social movement that emerged in the 1990s in Imbaba and informal labor markets rests on a empirical affinity between small-scale informal establishments on the one hand and social marginality and the absence of state regulation on the other. Because of their limited start-up costs and the ease with which they enter and exit markets, small firms provide the most appropriate setting for informal practices such as casual labor recruitment. In addition, this informal market is linked to identity-based forms of mobilization as a result of two of its essential features: the segmentation of work conditions (i.e., barriers to entry) along class, kinship, gender, regional and class lines, and the vertical forms of dependency in which the casual laborer is compelled to enter into a contractual relationship with a labor recruiter, subcontractor, and other intermediaries often kinsmen.[29]

In the case of the informal market in construction in Western Munira where I conducted my research two elements stand out. The first is the *dulab*, which structures employment contracts and casual labor relations between individual employers and workers. The *dawaleeb* are also the site of skill acquisition through apprenticeship, which in turn depends on patriarchal forms of social control that prevail in family- or apprentice-based workshops. The second are construction coffee houses, which define the relationship among workers, and between workers as a group, and employers as a group. Since formal trade unions are irrelevant for most construction workers, coffee houses serve as the primary locus of interaction between workers and craftsmen, and it is here where social networks and contacts are made, workers hired and paid, and craftsmen socialized as an "insider" to procure contracts and work.

Al-Jama'a in particular found, to the initial surprise of some of their leaders,[30] that Western Munira (*Munira al-Gharbiyya*) – the poorest section of Imbaba – was fertile ground for recruitment in part because of the similarity of its social organization to that of the *dulab*. The informally organized institution of the *dulab* operates on a system that is hierarchical and built on norms of paternalism, deference, and discipline. For its part, al-Jama'a, at least as it functioned in Western Munira, in many ways mirrored this social institution. The close fit between its own hierarchy, norms, and organization and those of the informal labor market facilitated entry for new recruits. Indeed, newly recruited members easily understood and appreciated the fact that al-Jama'a could serve both as an alternative source of income generation and a source of discipline.

Specifically, what workers in the quarter term *Shuruut al-'Amal*, the rules and conditions of work in the informal labor market, particularly as they applied to day laborers and the *subyan*, closely aligned with the preferences of militant activists in their attempts to draw these laborers to their cause. If subcontractors preferred what one laborer described as "strong, able bodied young men" ranging from eighteen to twenty years old with a reputation for a "strong work ethic, dedication to the job" and less inclined to pursue "frivolous and costly forms of entertainment like the young men of the Bandar (City)," another casual laborer and former member of the Jama'a noted that the organization generally selected recruits for these same attributes and further noted that education for the *sabi* and hence a potential member to the organization was deemed a liability: "[T]o get the job done, you have to have a strong body, not a certificate or diploma."[31]

Moreover, two additional conditions frequently noted by informal workers in 'Izbat al-Mufti facilitated entry in terms of joining the militants in the quarter: a strong belief that class stratification was part of the natural religious and social order as reflected in the frequently cited Quranic injunction of *Wa ja'lnakum foqa ba'dikum darajat* (and we have made of you different classes), and an equally strong perception of the real possibility of upward mobility through *sabr* (patience) and hard work, born out of their own experience with the apprenticeship system of the informal labor firm which in the boom years all but guaranteed reaching a higher position in the informal labor market over time so long as one is "clever, has a strong work ethic and maintains a good reputation for clean work." In addition, the hierarchical and paternalist structure and the rules of conduct and penalties associated with the work conditions of the *sabi* mirrored those enforced by the Jama'a on its rank and file membership. Indeed, just as Jama'a leaders enforced strict modes of conduct and applied penalties against rank and file members for a variety of infractions, the *sabi* in the informal labor firm is under the complete authority and responsibility of his patron or *Mu'alim al-sabi* (teacher). In a similar process utilized and adapted by militant leaders to generate loyalty among its rank and file, a *sabi* who does not complete his assigned work in time, "causes problems" with higher-ranked members of the dulab, or does not abide by *Shurat al-'Amal* of another craftsmen he is assigned to work with, is reported to his *Mu'alim* who decides on the appropriate penalty.

This is an important point because while most analysts of Islamist militancy in Egypt have focused on the role of rural-to-urban migration from Upper Egypt in the transplanting of al-Jama'a's structures and politics to urban Cairo, this in itself is not a sufficient explanation. While the first generation of the leadership of al-Jama'a was, by and large, of rural origin, most of the rank and file of the second generation of leaders, including Shaykh Jabir, were born and raised in the neighborhoods of Imbaba. Shaykh Jabir had originally worked as an informal laborer – he was a plumber by profession.

The social organization of the *dulab* is hierarchical (see Figure 7.1). The firm itself is headed by a subcontractor known as the *ra'is* (head or job boss) whose chief responsibility is to procure work from a contractor (*muqawil*) belonging to one of the large public or private construction firms. Immediately below the *ra'is* is the semi-skilled craftsman (*hirfi* or *sani'*), who serves as the contractor's chief assistant. He is hired by the subcontractor on a causal basis and for this reason he must rely heavily on his own personal contacts and social networks to find employment. Lowest in the *dulab's* hierarchy is the unskilled apprentice, or *sabi* (plural, *subyan*), who is usually no more than fifteen years old but who is, nevertheless, chosen for his strength to withstand the heavy tasks assigned to him. Most often this includes handing out mortar and it is only after many years of apprenticeship as *Musa'id al-sina'iyy* (craftsman's assistant) when he learns the more advanced technical aspects of the *minha*, or profession, that he is allowed to perform the task of the master's trade

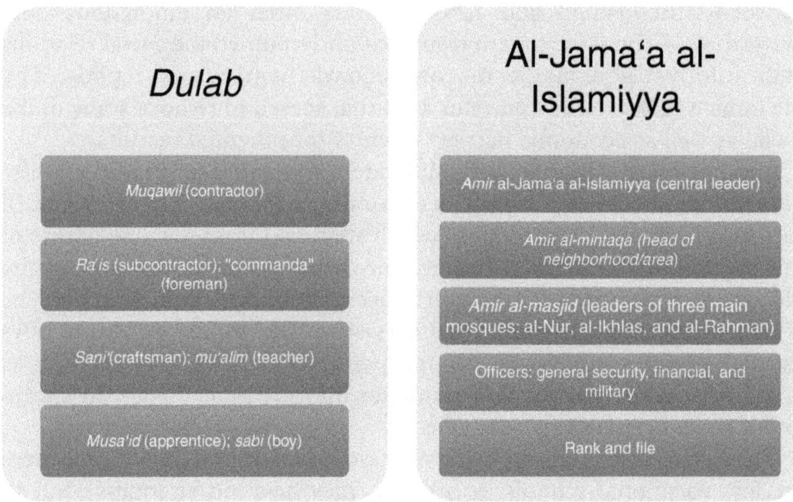


Figure 7.1 Hierarchical structure of the *Dulab* and al-Jama'a al-Islamiyya in Imbaba, Cairo
*Source*: Data compiled from interviews conducted in the course of the author's field research. Western Munira, Imbaba, Cairo.

eventually qualifying him to become a full-fledged assistant. At this point, he may work in the same workshop as his former boss or open his own depending on available resources. In addition, there is a separate market for a common laborer (*'amil*). These workers, known as *'Umaal Ugrah*, day laborers or odd jobbers, are also hired by the subcontractor and are often found outside the coffee houses waiting to be hired on the spot on an impersonal basis. They are often newly arrived small peasant farmers or farm workers.

This hierarchy conforms to strictly paternalist lines and this is reflected in the common reference to the contractor as *commanda*, the subcontractor as *ra'is*, and the apprentice as simply *sabi* (literally, "boy"). The *ra'is* is usually relatively affluent, dressed in an expansively tailored Upper Egyptian *'ibayyah*, and he has the added social privilege of sitting with the *Kibar*, the elders of the clan. Indeed, the nature of this hierarchy and paternalism was one reason why so many youth belonging to the lower rungs of the informal market and the social system joined the Jama'a. While some former members of the Islamic Group stated that a friend or family members recruited them in the quarter, others revealed that subcontractors who had also been recruited by the Group and with whom they had a long-standing relationship recruited them. Naturally, the line between "friendship" and labor boss is often an ambiguous one. Nevertheless, the same paternalism that underpinned the social relations of the informal labor market mirrored and was in many ways replicated by the Jama'a in Western Munira in ways that served to remove some of the social as well as economic barriers to entry for potential recruits.

Another reason Islamic militant leaders were able to recruit successfully among juveniles is simply because they exploited the high levels of social and economic uncertainty which stemmed from the very nature of this informal labor market. Indeed, the demand for "boy" labor, or the *sabi*, is one of the causes of endemic poverty in Imbaba and, moreover, he is one of the most exploited workers since the supply of young boys exceeds demand. Employers use inexpensive *sabi* labor to lower costs as much as possible. As one subcontractor informed me, "You can always find a *sabi* whenever you need one."[32]

The *subyan* are often employed as masons and errand boys. Since there are few vocational schools in Imbaba, they have no alternative but to depend on the apprenticeship system to acquire a higher level of skills – a process that can take up to ten years. Moreover, while the apprenticeship system does provide a *sabi* with the chance for upward mobility over time, in the context of recessionary downturns he faces a higher level of economic insecurity than the more skilled craftsmen who may find employment opportunity in artisan firms outside of the quarters of Western Munira. Those able to work jobs demanding physical strength found regular employment, but most *subyan* simply could not transition into other more skilled forms of work. Nor is pursuing education an option for the majority of boys and young men in the neighborhood: there is one secondary school in Western Munira. By the time they reach adult age, these youths find themselves without any general or special industrial qualifications and little access to a stock of personal contacts that would enable them to find steady work. Thus, a stream of young men from industries that rely upon *sabi* labor continually replenishes the mass pool of the unemployed. Cast adrift, these young *subyan* filled the ranks of al-Jama'a, although many continued to work as informal laborers following their entrance into the organization.

The key point here is that the structure and social organization of the informal labor market resulted in a highly precarious state of affairs in terms of job security for a large segment of the working population in the neighborhood. The increasing reliance on informal social networks and kinship ties means that death of relatives or familial conflict could jeopardize one's chances for work, and the increasing number of bankruptcies of small informal firms working in construction meant that cyclical economic downturns expel a worker into the unskilled labor market at the threshold of adulthood. Indeed, it is difficult to describe the state of frustration, alienation, and depression of these men and their deep resentment against those who, as one worker put it, derive income "*fi al-Bandar* (in the City) from shuffling paper" (i.e., white collar jobs).[33]

This is the reason why the rank and file of the al-Jama'a was increasingly characterized by a younger and less-educated membership composed of essentially two groups: informal laborers who were generally no longer employed in the industry and other workers who continued to find casual employment in the informal market. The latter group benefited from the fact that the leaders of the Islamic Group often served as intermediaries in a tight market securing them work and enforcing their informal contracts.

## Social Networks and *Qahawi Ta'ifat Al-Mi'mar* (Construction Sector Coffee Houses)

The social and political consequences engendered by the severity of intra-market competition in the construction sector that resulted from the nation-wide recession could be discerned at the level of the community from observing the casual laborers in the coffee houses (*qahawi ta'ifat al-mi'mar)* in the poorer quarters of 'Izbat al-Mufti and Beshteel in Imbaba. Since formal trade unions are irrelevant for most construction workers, coffee houses serve as the primary locus of interaction between workers and craftsmen, and it is here where I observed social networks and contacts made, workers hired and paid, and craftsmen socialized as an "insider" to procure contracts and work.[34] Of great significance is that these coffee houses, whose sheer number (upward of forty) in Western Munira suggests that informal labor is the backbone of the local economy, are themselves institutionally differentiated according to the segment of the informal labor market, as well as social and regional lines.

The main lines of social division are between craftsmen who serve as subcontractors for potential employers, lower-skilled apprentices (*subyan*), and common laborers who possess the lowest social status. Thus, one can observe coffee houses for craftsmen such as industrial workers (*qahawi al-sani'un*) and blacksmiths (*qahawi al-haddadeen*), and others frequented primarily by apprentices such as the one for bricklayers (*qahawi al-kharasanjiyya*), and common laborers or day jobbers (*'umal*) congregate in their own coffee houses referred to more generally as *qahawi al-mi'mar* (construction coffee houses). The latter are rarely accepted as social equals and are looked down upon by the craftsmen and the local merchants, shopkeepers, and small businesses owners in the quarter. As a result, they usually congregate in their own separate establishments or simply stand on the nearby streets awaiting recruitment. In addition, there is segmentation in the market along the lines of place of origin as evidenced by several coffee houses established by, and for, rural migrants from *Sohag* and *Assiut.*

It is to these coffee houses, so unlike their social and jovial counterparts in other parts of Cairo that often "provide social ease from anxiety,"[35] that craftsmen as well as lower-skilled laborers arrive in the early morning to acquire information about possible work, and to which they return in the evenings to receive their pay. In Western Munira the workers, mostly in their early to mid-twenties, hardly speak to one another and none play the board game of backgammon popular in Egyptian coffee houses. The only link among the youth is one of a shared social and economic insecurity, which, as one labor explained, is a result of a "very competitive environment; we are all competing in an already tight labor market."[36] New entrants are seen immediately as competition because contractors hire laborers on the spot making sure to keep wages low. The result is that the worker must put in an offer for his pay for a certain job. Consequently, there is great pressure on the laborers to compete with each other by bidding as low possible in order to be hired. In this context, family and kin ties neither mitigate social tensions nor render social relations more palatable; place of residence and friendship do so only minimally.

Moreover, the recession and rise in labor competition in Western Munira meant that the subcontractors and higher-skilled workers lost control of the work process. More specifically, they lost the ability to induce workers to accept their authority and elicit their cooperation in controlling the content, pace, and scope of the work. The division between craftsmen, who relied on their stock of personal contacts to procure contracts, and laborers who most often relied on friends and kin to find work, broke down in the context of increasing competition.

Indeed, in the context of work shortages, laborers were able to find work more efficiently than the craftsmen primarily because more low and menial work was available. As one laborer explained with some pride, "the *Sina'iyyi* (crastmen) or *Mihni* (professional) cannot work without *'amil ugari* (the odd jobber) since no matter how skilled the craftsmen is in measuring, cutting and laying the *bulat* (brick), it is the *'amil* who must mix, pour and carry the cement to the job site."[37] Importantly, since in Western Munira the distinction between subcontractor, usually a craftsmen, and common laborer followed regional lines there emerged a distinct element of cultural competition. As one craftsman noted in frustration, "they [the contractors] only hire Upper Egyptians ... only the ones who can do menial, tough work."[38] During al-Jama'a's reign in

Western Munira, many of these young casual laborers joined its ranks. One of the key advantages of joining the militants, according to former Jama'a members working in construction, was that they no longer had to wait on the streets outside the coffee shops "like slaves." Instead, they typically would congregate in front of the nearby mosque and the contractor would be forced to approach them to give them their wages for the day's work. In the past craftsmen not only distinguished themselves from labors in social terms, they also would not allow the laborers into the Coffee Houses. These members proudly acknowledged that their membership in the organization afforded them special status for their first time in their lives.[39]

### *Ta'amul Ma'a Al-Waqi' Hawlana*: The Erosion of Trust Networks and Social Conflict

In ideological terms the Jama'a distinguished itself from the Muslim Brotherhood and other accommodationist Islamist activists in its reinterpretation of the doctrine of Hisba (*al-amr bi al-ma'ruf wa al-nahy 'an al-munkar*) or commanding the right and forbidding wrong as a collective rather than an individual obligation (*fard kifaya*) designed to establish an Islamic state by force (*bi-al-quwaah*). In this regard the Jama'a laid the ideological foundation for other Islamist militant and Salafist organizations. However, the Islamic Group also laid an important legacy for other clandestine militant organizations in strategic terms. The latter is evident in the manner in which it sought to overcome the central challenge of generating commitment among its rank and file members in order to implement this new responsibility of *al-amr bi al-ma'ruf wa al-nahy 'an al-munkar*. Consequently, after 1984 when the Jama'a first began to make inroads in the informal settlements of greater Cairo a significant change took place in its Islamic program (*al-manhaj al-Islami*) that reflected new strategic considerations. Specifically, its leadership recognized that in order to popularize their movement they had to pursue a course of militant action and a process of recruitment of cadres that was relevant to local social and economic conditions. This is the reason that in the mid-1980s their program stated clearly that the ways in which the organization "interacts with the reality around us" (*ta'amul ma'a al-waqi' hawlana*) and finds "means of changing it" depend on the Imams that are presented by God.[40]

In the case of Imbaba, and Western Munira more specifically, local conditions were influenced in great part by the nature and very structure of the informal labor market associated with the construction sector. This meant that at no time was there a unified, homogenous class pursuing informal work. This is in stark contrast to the unity and class-consciousness associated with industrial labor, which in the Nasser era represented the majority of new migrants to Imbaba. During that period of state-led development, a clear class-consciousness was present among the factory workers residing in Imbaba's government-subsidized housing, but by the late 1980s the great majority of labor in the neighborhood had become informalized. In the 1970s when formal labor organizations waged a short-lived struggle against Sadat's liberalization policies on working-class grounds, a similar brand of class-consciousness did not, and could not, develop among workers living in the informal settlements. Structural inequities had come to be accepted as part of a fatalistic religiosity – in rhetoric if not in practice. This meant that by the late 1980s and 1990s al-Jama'a's discourse sublimating class grievances into issues of morality, the status of the women and the home, and antistate resistance found a much more receptive audience.

This social conflict, reflected along cultural lines, and one that was readily exploited by the Jama'a leaders, had to do with the fluidity of the trust networks that underpinned the organizational and social structure of the informal market. During the boom craftsmen could easily rely on their personal contacts and "friends" to acquire construction contracts. In the recession these trust networks broke down as evidenced by my observations of the Coffee Houses where the competition over any kind of job was a central feature of the increasingly somber cultural life of *Qahawi al-Mi'mar*, and more significantly, the increase in the number of violent conflicts between kin-backed laborers and non-kin-related craftsman. It is in this context that the Jama'a were able to enter the market and recruit from the socially frustrated and downwardly mobile craftsmen as well as the socially elevated common laborer.

The social detachment of these young men was made worse by the fact that in the construction trade, social relations are not oriented around the stable system of reciprocity (*mujamala*) that in other, higher-skilled trades allows for a sense of loyalty and community. Instead, there is a severe form of social stratification between laborer and local contractor or sub-contractor. This is easily observed in mode of dress as well as conduct. Typically, the far more affluent contractor, the *ra'is*, dresses in the Upper Egyptian *'abaya* (robe) and sits across, rather than within, the coffee shop. In contrast to the socially stigmatized casual laborer, the contractor enjoys an elevated status and is held in high esteem by middle-class residents and certainly by the elders of his clan (*kibar al-qabila*). Indeed, class tensions in the neighborhood exacerbate the social exclusion of these underemployed laborers. In spite – or rather, because – of the difficulty of their work, informal laborers are looked down upon by Imbaba's middle-class residents, many of whom own property such as small businesses or retail shops.[41]

An important factor underlying the popularity of the Jama'a in the quarter is that its leadership demonstrated a keen and intimate understanding of these class and cultural tensions, as well as the general economic insecurity faced by casual laborers in Western Munira, and devised its recruitment strategies and offered incentives likely to motivate individual participation.

## *Al-'Umaal Shaylin Al-Balad* (The Workers Are Carrying the Country)

As one local resident who joined the Islamic Group but later left the organization in opposition to their increasing use of violence against their local rivals in the quarter put it, "they [al-Jama'a] recognized that these workers *Shaylin al-Balad* (are carrying the country)."[42] Importantly, al-Jama'a recognized debt payments are a crucial problem in settlements like 'Izbat al-Mufti, Bashteel and Osim where they continue to be a source of a great many disputes, often resulting in violent confrontations. Indeed, it is rare that in the course of one month one does not observe two or three disputes over unpaid debts in 'Izbat al-Mufti. The problem is that daily wages fluctuate arbitrarily while the cost of living steadily increases. Furthermore, because the meager daily wages do not cover household expenditures, to say nothing of allowing for personal savings, most residents live on credit, which is difficult to pay back. Al-Jama'a assisted debtors in settling disputes, repaying or postponing payments on credit, and in general introducing some semblance of stability if not necessarily social peace. Indeed, al-Jama'a regularly utilized coercive means to assist their members and sympathizers to resolve their outstanding debts. Specifically, the Jama'a leaders made use of *baltagiyya*, local strongmen, who through the threat of violence were tasked with extracting compliance from debt collectors. Many of these *baltagiyya* worked as day laborers and a significant number joined the ranks of al-Jama'a.

Al-Jama'a also offered assistance to its members who suffered from a work-related accident. Whereas the subcontractor often refused to pay any form of compensation for on-site injuries and merely dismissed the laborer from the construction site, al-Jama'a would often collect funds for health care provisions and even provide a small pension. They also took care of the family of the injured worker until he could get back on his feet. In instances where the organization was not in a position to actually disburse funds, it would attempt to find the worker a form of employment that was less strenuous than construction work. In cases where the education of the worker (usually very modest) and his skill level are relatively low al-Jama'a neighborhood leaders would assign him the job of collecting the zakat (alms) from local residents.[43]

Al-Jama'a also provided a form of work compensation for casual laborers among their membership who were taken ill for a long period of time in the course of their difficult work in the building trade. In these situations, the al-Jama'a leadership would provide regular payments to the individual and his family generated from contributions collected from other members of the organization. Moreover, since al-Jama'a members were under close surveillance, particularly following the 1992 siege of the neighborhood, the organization would provide less-visible forms of employment within the organization for loyal members released after being incarcerated by state security forces. Since these members were registered as "terrorists" or militants by state security after their release they were unable to find employment in the construction trade as they had often done in the past due to the constant surveillance by the police and state security that stigmatized their reputation among the contractors. Subsequently, the Jama'a would provide these loyal members administrative positions within the organization. Significantly, these members also gained higher social status within the organization. In Western Munira only al-Jama'a members who had been registered after being detained and released by state security wore the Islamist dress (*jalabiyya* and *sirwal*) and grew the customary long beards. These markers were signs of status within the organization; especially among the rank and file, the members who were thus distinguished, and who harbor the greatest loyalty to al-Jama'a, evoked great admiration.

Furthermore, the insecurity of men's labor means women must work to provide the necessary supplementary household income. In Western Munira women often work as fruit-and-vegetable sellers, hawkers, domestic servants, and sex workers. However, the very importance of women's work in Imbaba has resulted in its denigration by some male members of the community, and economic and social hardships among local residents continue to manifest themselves in domestic disputes, a high divorce rate, and absentee husbands. In practical terms al-Jama'a worked to lower the social expectation of women in the neighborhood. In the sermons in Masjid al-Mursileen which I attended in 'Izbat al-Mufti during my research in the quarter, preachers regularly sermonize about the proper place of women as "caretakers of the home" (*Rabuti al-Bayti*) and enjoined men to remember that they are the primary "caretakers of their women." Moreover, two recurring themes of the sermons, which resonated strongly with local residents, pertained to the increasing illicit drug use by the youth in the quarter which was generally understood as a primary reason of juvenile delinquency and the call of a boycott against foreign goods and imports to address the ills associated with conspicuous consumption. Indeed, in contrast to the Muslim Brotherhood which has long maintained a favorable view of foreign investment and economic liberalization policies more generally,[44] the Imam of *Masjid al-Mursileen* called for residents in the quarter to participate in a boycott of imported consumer goods citing, in one sermon, the example of India's Mahatma Gandhi who waged a successful campaign of noneconomic cooperation associated with his campaign of civil disobedience against British colonialism.

## Embedding the "Message": The Relevance of the *Khutba* (Sermon)

That Imbaba, however poor, enjoyed rising social and economic fortunes during the boom in informal housing was a key component of why grievances, exacerbated in the bust, laid the context for the transformation of parts of the neighborhood into a stronghold of militant Islamist activism. However, it is important to note that, as in the case of the Muslim Brotherhood, the recruitment of rank and file members into al-Jama'a was very much a process that involved the provision of both material and normative incentives designed to frame joining the organization as a moral obligation if not as an economic necessity. As Salwa Ismail has noted, there is no seamless web between social and economic immisseration and the turning toward militancy.[45] Indeed, among the important factors that made the difference in the case of al-Jama'a is the careful manner in which the organization's leadership articulated a discourse that simultaneously sought to wage a political and moral campaign against the state, as well as to address the grave social and economic conditions that resulted from the profound economic and social transformations in the quarter. Not surprisingly, an important objective of the sermons was to strengthen the resolve of the organization's members and potential activists against state repression:

> The enemies of Islam know for certain that a confrontation with Muslims in their beliefs will not benefit them. Instead, it will make Muslims even stronger. They know that when a Muslim is challenged in his faith, his beliefs and the Book of his Master and the straight path, this confrontation removes the fog from his brain and makes him leap to defend his nation.[46]

Nevertheless, during my attendance of the highly popular sermons that followed the Friday congregational prayers in Western Munira, the Imams often gave more time to social and economic factors such as the problem of juvenile delinquency, social and moral corruption, and the importance of rehabilitating the patriarchal family which, from the perspective of the Imam's of the Jama'a and many residents, was under threat than to antistate rhetoric. The role of women, in particular, was frequently highlighted in ways that were clearly designed to center the moral reputation of women as both a problem and the potential solution for much of what ails the community. One female resident, critical of al-Jama'a at the time, insisted that the militants were intent on what she termed "lowering the social expectations of women" by insisting on the *Niqab*, calling for anti-consumption behavior and enjoining the men of the family to protect and serve as caretakers for the family.[47]

> The people in this state were divided into three groups: the believers and the unbelievers. These two need no explanation. The third group is the hypocrites. They accuse the Prophet Mohamed's (My God bless him and grant him peace) wife of adultery. You worshipers of Allah, if a man came to you and told you that your wife is an adulteress or if your mother is a whore or if your sister is loose, what would happen to you? Would you be able to sleep for one instant? . . . Worshipers of Allah, it is because of these kind of people that calamity struck the Ummah.[48]

Another regularly reiterated theme of the sermons of particular relevance to residents of Western Munira had to do with what one resident termed *al-Inhyar al-Ijtima'iyy* (societal breakdown); for many, this was the central reason behind the grave social ills and everyday conflicts afflicting the quarter ranging from the rise in thuggery and crime (*baltagiyya*) to juvenile delinquency evidenced by the increasing sale and consumption of drugs by the youth. One sermon, an example of several others, addressed this issue offering both a diagnosis and a not-so subtle critique of the ineptitude of both state institutions as well as traditional male authorities in dealing with the problem.

> Drugs have made their way into children's schools. Those who use have come to me with their parents at the mosque, suffering from their addiction and asking me to recite some verses and invoking some supplications wishing for Allah to wrest the addiction out of their blood. I am not exaggerating if I say that at least two or three come to me each week. These issues cannot be resolved unless people find a religious Islamic consciousness . . . There should be state institutions, which come in aid such as the Ministries of Education, *Awqaf* [The Ministry of Religious Endowment], social services and associations. Above all the responsibility should be with fathers and eminent men and notables.[49]

Indeed, the legitimacy of the content of the sermons of al-Jama'a was effective not only because it was tailored to the lived experience of residents and resonated with their own political orientation; it was also greatly enhanced because it contrasted sharply with the sermons of the government-regulated mosques elsewhere. While Jama'a Imams in Western Munira were preaching against state policy, the ills of conspicuous consumption, and the need to reinvigorate the traditional Islamic family, the government-run mosques promoted an idealized Egypt ruling over compliant and docile citizens and insisted on strict adherence to the laws of what was, from the perspective of al-Jama'a, an unjust and heretical state. Government Imams asserted a notion of the territorial boundaries of national citizenship, stressed the importance of inter-sectarian harmony, and spoke of the need to reform the family structure but only in vague terms. Importantly, rarely did they speak of issues having to do with state corruption. In the government-run mosque in the nearby neighborhood of '*Aguza*, for example, the Imam often repeated these themes:

As long as we have a card of citizenship of the Arab Republic of Egypt, we must obey all its laws and follow its regulations. We must follow the government's laws so long as this does not contradict our main identity as Muslims, and *al-hamdillah* (thank Allah), these [the laws of the State] do not contradict this. For if we do not live in accordance with the state's laws (*Qawaneen al-Nizam*), we lose our ability to live in *Karama* (dignity) and *Salam* (peace). We need *Salam al-Dakhil* (internal peace). [Further], everyone is now a republic unto himself and cares only for his own instrumental and selfish purposes. Allah punishes those who depart from his *Da'wa*; all of the Umma must follow the laws of the book. We must call for *Islah* (reform) between people, and between man and wife. If we live as Shi'a, Sunni or this or that (*hisb*) party, then we live as if we have our own religion without rules. As the verse about Ibrahim says *Lakum dinikum, wa lana dinana*, and so each who lives in Egypt, must live by its laws. We must be united to succeed on this earth and in the hereafter.[50]

## The Politics of *Tarbiyya* (Religious Education)

Other members who joined were simply true believers following a relatively long process of *tarbiyya* or religious education. They fervently and sincerely believed in the message of hell, damnation, and heavenly redemption. The sincerity of these followers should not be underestimated. The sermons that conveyed this message in the storefront mosques of the neighborhood drew thousands of men, young and old alike. These sermons are very attractive to young men who find no temporal explanation for their social conditions and see no prospects for a better life outside the informal settlement. Indeed, the cultivation of piety and a particularly religious form of communal space in the neighborhood played an important role in the success of al-Jama'a in this period. But it is important to note that a primary reason for this success was that the sermons helped make sense of otherwise inexplicable social conditions and, moreover, addressed real-world politics in ways that built on the lived reality of many residents in the quarter.

Religious education (*tarbiyya*) took place in two important ways. The first was through essentially private religious or Quranic lessons, and the second was via the Friday and Tuesday sermons. The religious lessons, attended by Jama'a members, included, most notably, the writings of Ibn Taymiyya and Sayid Qutb, and readings on Islamic Fiqr, as well as Quranic memorization. In addition, members were instructed in the writings and ideas of Sheikh Ahmed Abdel Sattar, an important discipline of Sheikh Omer Abdel-Rahman, the then spiritual guide of the Jama'a. Importantly, members of the Jama'a noted that the oral lessons in particularly were extremely important because "many of us were illiterate at that time, and it was not possible for us to read the Quran and the other writings on our own."[51]

The second method of disseminating the message was achieved through the Khutba or sermon. On the third Friday of every month, all members of the nearby mosques would attend prayers at Masjid al-Ikhlas on Luxor Street in central Cairo, which, at the time, was the headquarters of al-Jama'a. Following the sermon members would discuss not only religious but "political" matters which were the subject of the sermon. Most notably, in addition to the discussion of the writing and ideas of Qutb, Ibn Tayimah, and the "Blind Sheikh" Omer Abdel-Rahman that was certainly noted by former members, what seemed to impress the young men, was the ways in which these religious instructions went hand in hand with the discourse of social welfare and politics.

Naturally, the sermons consisted of the resuscitation of Quranic verses, but they were also accompanied by what members termed "*al-Nashrah*" or the news segment. During al-Nashrah that followed the official sermon members would hear commentary on events in Bosnia, and Afghanistan and other Muslim countries, and would often be shown videos (*al-Manassa* films) on the struggle between the "Nasara" (heathens) and Muslims throughout the world. Importantly, during al-Nashra and often during the screening of the videos the Imam of the al-Jama'a Mosque would collect donations from the organization's members and others in the congregation. As one example, Sheikh Ali Turki in 'Izbat al-Mufti was heavily involved in gathering donations for the cause in Bosnia and for the private (*Ahali*) mosques of al-Jama'a in the neighborhood and for the Ikhwan held in prison and their families.

Nevertheless, there is little evidence that al-Jama'a contributed significantly in terms of providing a wide range of social services to their members or the general resident population. As one member put it, "the Jama'a do not have the means to provide social services. Most of these services are provided by the *Ikwhan* or *al-Da'wa wa al-Tabligh*." Nevertheless, much of the services provided by al-Jama'a had more to do with the religious and moral campaign that was extremely important to religiously minded residents. On Tuesdays after Maghreb (dusk) prayers, the al-Jama'a brought and distributed clothing and some money to the poor all over the neighborhood; on Youm al-Wakfa, banners of al-Jama'a unfurled and children asked to recite Quranic verses in public; and on Eid al-Adha, al-Jama'a members would lead a *masira* (march) bringing cows, sheep, and rice to the poor, and during Ramadan on Shari Luxor they organized a free *iftar* (Ramadan breakfast) for hundreds of poor residents. Most of the members organizing these services would be paid salaries, and the families of members imprisoned by the state security provided with some limited provisions.

Equally significant, according to the members who joined the organization at the time in the neighborhood, was the role of al-Jama'a in terms of assisting in marriages in what is a very poor community. As a member of al-Jama'a members of your family were entitled to an al-Jama'a wedding (*Zawaj al-Jama'a*) wherein food would be provided by the Masjid, the *Mazoun* (officiate) paid for transportation and for his services, and *Wakeel al-Arusa* (the Bride's advocate) would be transported to *katb al-kitab* (wedding ceremony). In addition, the organization would also arrange for the *Masira* (wedding procession), even while women would not be visible and asked to stay at home. It is important to note that these services were often accompanied by far more coercive and unpopular campaigns. Al-Jama'a members, often under the instruction of the leaders of the organization, burned down video stores, broke up marriage celebrations to prevent the mixing of sexes, and beat up any singers, musicians, and artists in the neighborhood that did not conform to proper "Muslim" practices.

Moreover, despite al-Jama'a's relative success in providing a modicum of "services," material as well as symbolic, members also recounted the divisive role of the organization in the neighborhood, particular in terms of exacerbating Muslim-Christian tensions. The role of the Copts was often part of the sermon and it helps in some measure explain the rise of inter-sectarian conflict in Imbaba at that time. Indeed, the conflict between Muslims and Copts in Imbaba is well known and it continues to the present day. The sermons often consisted of allegations that the Copts in the neighborhood were not only *Nasara* (Christian "heathens") but also that they monopolized commerce and trade in the neighborhood. This perception, among many in the quarter, was increasingly popularized on the ground in part due to the sermons of the Imams which alleged that Copts practiced riba (usury), monopolized the Gold and retail markets, and charged exorbitant prices for medicine. This is an important reason why Muslim-Copt attacks became commonplace in this period leading to a dangerous spiral of violence. According to accounts by former members themselves, as the Jama'a mobilized larger numbers to their cause by the early 1990s, the violent clashes between Muslims and Copts in the quarter increased significantly.

The social and economic immiseration of the local population in the context of the recessionary downturn, and particularly those who worked as causal laborers, was an important contributor factor that motivated many young men to join the Jama'a's ranks; it also helps to explain the timing associated with their popularity in the late 1980s and 1990s in particular. The informalization of the economy in Western Munira provided the context for radical mobilization in the quarter and afforded the Jama'a the opportunity to provide selective social, economic, and ideational incentives relevant to many young men in the quarter, which it used to mobilize new cadres. Naturally, however, this was hardly a sufficient condition for *militant* activism. Moreover, while state repression, which was considerable particularly following the 1992 siege of the neighborhood, played a role in the persistent popularity of the militants in Western Munira this factor does not fully explain why individuals in Western Munira joined the militant al-Jama'a rather than the more moderate Muslim Brotherhood Islamist trend and, moreover, why they continued to remain fervently committed to al-Jama'a's cause at very high risk to themselves. Answering the questions of why members chose a militant rather than an accommodationist form of political and social activism and why Jama'a leaders employed particularly radical and often violent modes of collective action requires a closer analysis of the organization itself and the local context in which it thrived in the poorer quarters of Western Munira.

## Mobilizing Militants: The Challenge of Generating Commitment and Trust among the Rank and File

The most important way to understand how militant organizations are able to pursue effective recruitment campaigns and generate commitment is to examine the challenges these organizations face in securing loyalty to the organization and generating trust among their ranks in the context of severe state repression.[52] In the case of the Jama'a al-Islamiyya in Western Munira, three additional elements stand out as key factors that enabled leaders of the organization to accomplish these objectives: the organizational structure of the organization, its methods of recruitment and socialization of new militant activists, and the context-specific Islamist ideology disseminated through the congregational sermon (*Khutbah*) in the unregulated institutions of the private (*Ahali*) mosques.

## The Role of the *Ahali* Mosque

In Imbaba as in many neighborhoods in Cairo, Islamic welfare associations (*al-jami'at al-shar'ia al-Islamiyya*) filled the gap between government services and cost-prohibitive fully privatized social services. In so doing, they presented a "third way" that has proved highly successful particularly among the middle and lower classes. In Western Munira in Imbaba, for example, the sheer density of Islamic charitable associations and the fact that most of the private (*ahali*) mosques in the area had some form of health care unit or clinic indicates the important role Islamists played in providing key social services. However, to say that the Islamic trend in Egypt was invigorated by the spread of Islamic welfare associations does not necessarily implicate them in the rise of al-Jama'a in Imbaba. A far more significant factor was the density of small private mosques in the neighborhood. It is here that Islamist preachers delivered persuasive sermons to the community and youth found the opportunity to fashion a new, more "moral" way of life.

There is no large-scale survey available that accounts for the entire organization and its many branches in the 1990s. Indeed, studying the entire organizational makeup of any clandestine organization is a naturally difficult task. However, my ethnographic research in Imbaba among former members of the *Jama'a* provides an important lens through which to understand how a militant organization, in this case the Jama'a in Western Munira, was able to build their organization in the context of state repression and generate trust networks of the type that generated relatively high levels of commitment to their cause. One of the main arguments I make, building on my interviews with al-Jama'a members and attendance of the organization's sermons, is that while ideology and the framing of the message played an important role in generating high-risk behavior this in itself is not a sufficient explanation to explain the relative efficacy in recruiting and mobilizing new members.

According to former members of the Jama'a, the first Masjid of al-Jama'a al-Islamiyya established in Western Munira was *Masjid al-Rahman li al-'Itimad*, which was established in 1986–1987. At that time, the Amir of the neighborhood of Imbaba was Sheikh Ali Abdel-Bakri, and the Amir of Western Munira was Sheikh Mohamed Za'ar who was born in Aswan in Upper Egypt and migrated to Cairo. It was at this time that the network of mosques of the Jama'a was established. These included *Masjid al-Nur*, *Masjid al-Ikhlas*, and *Masjid al-Rahman*, and each of these was led by an Amir of the respective Masjid. Overseeing all three was Sheikh Hossam al-Rayyan. Importantly, the link between these mosques that made up this network was based on weekly interactions and close coordination between the respective mosques of the organization. Every Tuesday, rather than Friday, primarily to avoid state surveillance, the different branches and groups from the mosques would congregate at the Masjid in Shari Luxor. These meetings included Jama'a members not only from Imbaba but members of the organization residing in other informal settlements including Bulaq al-Daqrur and al-Umraniyya. Imbaba alone brought 7,000 persons from as many as twenty-five different mosques, which, according to one former member, were the "largest groups of *Jama'a* members of any other neighborhood."[53] It was in this period that Sheikh Jabir served as the "military" rather than spiritual or political leader chiefly responsible for military and "jihadist" operations.[54]

In addition to the close coordination among the various mosques, the organizational structure of the *Jama'a* was carefully institutionalized and embedded in the quarter through a strict hierarchical structure. At the level of the executive there were the heads of the area (*Amir al-Mantiqqah*), the mosque (*Amir al-Masjid*), and the organization itself (*Amir al-Jama'a*). Overseeing the operation of these units, was a consultative council (*Majlis al-Shura*), which included all the Amirs and comprised the decision-making body of the organization on the ground. Finally, the day-to-day operations were the responsibility of officers responsible for finance, general security, and military operations.

Importantly, in order to successfully recruit individuals in the quarter, the organization also appointed an official spokesperson (*mutahadith rasmi*) at the level of the community who would speak on behalf of the Jama'a in Imbaba. It was the responsibility of Amir al-Masjid, who possessed intimate knowledge of the local community to personally appoint every one of the local officers of the organization. Masjid al-Nur in Western Munira serves as a good example of this organizational structure. In the late 1980s and 1990s Amir al-Mantiqqa was Sheikh Hossam al-Rayyan, and Amir al-Masjid was Sheikh Ahmed Abdel Wahab. In this period, Amir al-Jama'a of Imbaba was Sheikh Emad Gohar who succeeded Mohamed Za'ar, and the spokesperson for al-Jama'a was Mohamed Abdel Yousef. During the 1992 clashes, it was Abdel Yousef who became Amir al-Jama'a.

In addition to Amir al-Mantiqqah and Amir al-Masjid, these local officers collected dues, organized the military wing, oversaw the security operations, and recruited youth. In Masjid al-Nur, which was the center of recruitment, Amir al-Mantiqqah, Hossam al-Rayyan, was the one chiefly responsible for these aspects of the organization. Significantly, al-Rayyan was a second-generation migrant from Upper Egypt and as such had great legitimacy among local residents. Indeed, in contrast to the

Muslim Brotherhood in this period, al-Jama'a continued to privilege the organization's security and military wings, which included an emphasis on military training and the training of cadres in methods to evade state security forces. Fridays were the days of training wherein selected members were instructed in karate and other martial arts and engaged in role-playing with other members who would play the role of the state's security forces. Sheikh Gabir, the head of the military wing at the peak of the organization's popularity in the neighborhood in the late 1980s and 1990s, personally trained new members in athletics and sports, especially football. Importantly, this training was conducted from early dawn to ten in the morning following which everyone would attend the Friday *khutbah* most often in *Masjid al-Ikhlas* in 'Izbat al-Mufti, a stronghold of al-Jama'a influence at the time.

The congregational prayers in particular offered a social, spiritual, and political outlet and a distinctly congenial and communally oriented cultural space amid the squalor of daily life. These prayers were regularly held on the street (*Salat al-Masaha*) to accommodate the large numbers of devotees who eagerly looked forward to them. Unlike the spatially individuated mosques of middle-class Cairo, which are often built on very expansive grounds and set apart from daily street life, the storefront mosques of Imbaba are integrated into the street. It is here that a particular form of community ethic is fostered and where young children are given microphones and encouraged to introduce the prayers before the multitude of men who make up the congregation. As a consequence, those who joined the ranks of al-Jama'a were rewarded with a profound sense of community and "fellow feeling." Rank and file members often expressed great affection and loyalty for their "brothers" in the movement. When a member is imprisoned by *Amn al-Dawla* (state security), al-Jama'a members often banded together, in collecting the necessary funds in order to employ competent lawyers for their friends "inside" (*fi al-dakhil*) and also to support the families of those incarcerated. This message of brotherhood, which was disseminated frequently by the Imams in their sermons, had particular resonance and appeal to residents in the informal settlements. This is because the majority of them, particularly those residing in the quarters of Western Munira, were living in a context of deeply fractured social relations, difficult and unpredictable forms of work, environmental hazards, and claustrophobic dwellings.

Another important service provided by al-Jama'a was to improve the literacy of those youth who joined its ranks. Most young men in Western Munira, where there was only one elementary school and no secondary school at the time, said that they saw no future in education. Moreover, rarely could families afford to forego the labor of any member, no matter how young. The organization's mosques partially compensated for the limited educational opportunities neighborhood residents faced. Former members of al-Jama'a noted that through the memorization of the Qur'an and weekly religious lessons conducted by the *shaykhs* in the neighborhood mosques, youths learned how to read and write properly. To be sure, these lessons were conducted under strict disciplinary guidelines, and the young men coerced into memorizing verses from the Qur'an under threat of penalties. Nevertheless, these lessons offered the hitherto rare opportunity to receive a modest education at no cost.

## Rules of Conduct and Militant Recruitment

In contrast to the recruitment of Muslim Brothers, but similar to other clandestine militant organizations, al-Jama'a implemented a far more stringent code of conduct designed to secure loyalty and to maintain a high level of commitment among its rank and file. According to former members of the Jama'a, members who do not follow certain obligations are punished in ways that guarantee loyalty to the organization and signal to other members not to stray.[55] A key method of accomplishing this is through *Ta'zeer* or ostracism. Members who do not comply by the rules of conduct and certain obligations in the form of attending prayer meetings and *khutbahs* regularly or dispute the strategic decision or moral positions of leaders faced a number of penalties. Most notably, these include financial penalties that are paid to the Jama'a's leadership directly from their wages, and a form of social ostracism designed to generate discipline among the ranks and strengthen the loyalty of adherents to the cause. In the case of the latter, Jama'a leaders commanded members not to talk to the noncooperative individual and they rescinded the member's privilege of participating in any collective activities of the organization. Former members noted that *Ta'zeer* was a particularly *mulim* (hurtful) form of punishment since by this time they were isolated from their families and other forms of social support and networks. Another punishment utilized is *'Itikaf* (meditative seclusion) whereby the individual is instructed to spend a period of up to one week inside the mosque, eat, sleep there, conduct daily maintenance, and, most importantly, is compelled to conduct additional prayers in isolation.

A number of actions warrant the penalties of *Ta'zeer* and *'Itiqaf*. First, this can occur when individual members conduct certain actions without the supervision of the leadership or amir. One example occurred in 'Izbat al-Mufti when the Beni Hamed clan came into conflict with the Jama'a and Sheikh Ali Gabir attacked the Beni Mohamed without first consulting the leadership, which, in this case, was the amir of a Masgid in Imbaba. Under the guidelines of the Jama'a, any lower-ranking member in the organization must inform the amir prior to any retaliatory action against individuals or groups outside of the Group. Second, if a member is instructed to conduct an operation and he does not fulfill this act the local amir of the mosque reports this infraction to Amir al-Mantiqqa who decides on the punishment for the individual. Former members informed the author of a number of these actions. These included minor and major offenses to the leadership such as when a member is told to clean the Masjid, collect donations, memorize the Quran in its entirety, or spread the *Da'wa* (Islamic call) in the neighborhood to the satisfaction of the emir of the settlement.

Given these stringent codes of conduct the key question is, why do members join in the first place? There are of course those true believers who join for religious reasons and are genuinely inspired by the religious classes and moral message associated with the congregational sermons and the *Da'wa*. As one former member recalled, one amir used to gather us *Shabaab* (youth), read to us the Quran because we couldn't, and give each of us one pound after each lesson.[56] He gave us a "sense of community ... a sense of communal love."[57] Others joined simply for reasons of social security and a sense of solidarity. As one former member put it, "some of us joined so that we could feel stronger ... and to have others stand with us in times of need and trouble."[58]

Doubtless these are factors that induced many to join the middle-class Muslim Brotherhood organization. However, the profound social and economic transformations in Imbaba since the 1970s meant that many who joined the militants did so as a result of reasons unique to the informal settlements of Cairo. As former members acknowledged, some individuals who joined were "criminals" and they made their way into the Jama'a to engage in theft and extortion. A number of others joined to escape blood feuds (*Tar*) in their home villages in Upper Egypt. Indeed, a number of residents noted that those Upper Egyptians that joined, and there were a number who did, arrived to *'Izbat al-Mufti*, *Beshteel* and *Osim* to escape conflict in their town of origin although they also acknowledged that the majority migrated for economic reasons to "make money" in the city.[59]

Finally, it is important to highlight that in the Western Munira sections of Imbaba, a large number of young men and juveniles who joined the militants did so as a second choice when they experienced socioeconomic barriers of entry with respect to their aspiration to join the Muslim Brotherhood. This was evident in both spatial and class terms in two ways. First, the Muslim Brothers in the neighborhood often utilized

Masjid al-Rahman in the more socially and spatially distant middle-class sections of Imbaba "far away from Munira beyond *Shari al-Buiyyi.*" A second important barrier to entry into the Brotherhood for the young men in Western Munira was simply their lack of education, prospects, and general economic and social marginalization. This is the reason why a number of members regularly complained that even when they attempted to join the *Ikhwan* they were not chosen since the Brotherhood required upwardly mobile, middle-class, and lower-middle-class recruits. "They want," one lamented, "those who have *ras maal* (capital) or a university degree so they can make use of them."[60]

## Explaining Militant Violence: *Tagheer Al-Munkar* and the Struggle for Law and Order in a Heterogeneous Community

One of the most important challenges for clandestine organizations and social movements is not only to generate commitment among their rank and file, but also to establish a source of legitimate law and order. Islamists have only been partially successful in this endeavor. In this regard, and in the case of militant organizations in particular, the central principle of *taghher al-munkar*, which serves as a key source of ideational legitimacy, recruitment, and popular mobilization, also functions as a central instrument in securing territorially based political and economic control. However, in the context of a community divided along the lines of sect, class, kinship, and gender militant activists not only faced state repression, they also encountered a daunting challenge in establishing a monopoly over law and order in their efforts at building a "state within a state." This is evidenced in the way militant members clashed with the Copts as well as kin groups and women in the informal settlements of Western Munira.

In this poorer quarter of Imbaba the attraction of many local residents and young men to the principle of *tagheer al-munkar* had very much to do with a perceived moral and social corruption (*al-fasad al-akhlaqi*) in the neighborhood. It is a state of affairs that the Jama'a were intent on remedying, albeit often through coercive and violent means. One incident, which exemplifies the "protection racket" aspect, associated with the Jama'a's methods, inspired Tariq, a long-standing member of the Jama'a at the time, to renounce his membership in the organization. In this instant, a married landlord solicited an unmarried woman living in one of the apartments in the neighborhood for sex, and he threatened to evict her if she did not comply. Subsequently, she sent word to Jama'a members who then forcibly removed the man from his home and physically assaulted him. However, the man eventually donated 1,000 pounds to *Masjid al-Rahman* in *al-'Itimad* street and persuaded the Jama'a to evict the woman from her apartment. When Tariq went to the amir of the Masjid to complain and criticize the expulsion of the woman from her home he was duly punished for insubordination, forced into *'itikaf* (meditative seclusion), and fined a fee of twenty pounds. It was this incident, among others, that led to his withdrawal from the Jama'a.

Yet another example illustrates the way in which the implementation of *tagheer al-munkar* by militant activists in the neighborhood regularly resulted in fueling what emerged as a pattern of inter-sectarian tensions and violence. In this one instance, a coffee shop owner and Coptic Christian in 'Izbat al-Mufti, Abdel Labib was commanded by a well-known member of the Jama'a, Mustafa al-Rayan, to shut down his coffee shop on the grounds that he allowed the consumption of alcohol on his premises despite there being no formal ban against alcohol consumption. A fight quickly ensued between the Copt and al-Rayan and, as al-Rayan informed me, he made a complaint to Amir al-Jama'a at the time, *Amir Mutwali*, but received no response. After four days with no response from any members of the leadership of the organization, al-Rayan organized Jama'a members at a meeting in *Masjid al-Rahman al-'Itimad* and formed what Jama'a members term the *Khamsaat*, a formation of five rows each consisting of five individuals who stand side by side in the Masjid, and refer to themselves as martyrs. In this instance al-Rayan led a *Khamsaat* in military formation to the coffee house of Abdel Labib. By Mustafa al-Rayan's owned admission they "destroyed" the coffee shop, stole the video player and television, and caused what Abdel Labib said was more than seventy pounds worth of damages. In retaliation the Copts in the quarter responded and attacked members of the Jama'a, which escalated into a larger inter-sectarian conflict in the quarter.

To these inter-sectarian tensions, rooted in the marked increase in economic competition and rivalries in the quarter, the Jama'a interjected what proved to be an incendiary message directed toward some of their most ardent and committed followers intended to legitimize anti-Copt violence on "religious" grounds. One example of this message relayed through one of their Imam's sermons cast doubt on the moral intentions and character of *Ahl al-Kitab* (the People of the Book) as well as unbelievers (*Kufar*):

> He who exhibits hostility towards you, you do not need evidence or proof to confirm his enmity . . . The battle against unbelievers is clear since ancient times; listen to what Allah said: those who do not believe, the pagans and the People of the Book, reject the goodness from God and God is merciful with whomever he wants saying: "You believe them but they do not love you." As the saying goes:

"He gives you sweets from the tip of the tongue and deceives you as the cunning fox teases its prey."[61]

If the Jama'a came into frequent conflict with Copts in *'Izbat al-Mufti* resulting in violence, another equally important source of conflict had to do with the organization's relationship to members of the newly urbanized kinship groups. However, the relationship between Islamists and kinship networks is a complicated one. To be sure, far from an archetype of the past, kinship networks in Cairo's informal fringe continue to have great influence among the local population especially among the poorer and more recent migrants from rural areas. Nevertheless, the nature and consequences of violence between the militant activists and clan elders and larger kinship-based associations reflect a pattern of violent conflict as well as tacit cooperation.

One illustrative incident involved a violent conflict between the Beni Mohamed clan, led by Safwat Abdel Ghani,[62] whose members represent new rural migrants from Assiut and Sohag to 'Izbat al-Mufti. When the wife of a member of the Jama'a (wearing the *Niqab*) disposed her garbage in front of the coffee house of Mohamed Ali Magbouli, a member of the Beni Mohamed clan of Assiut, Ali insulted her and she complained to Amir Masjid al-Nur who then organized a Jama'a Khamsaat, marched to Magbouli's coffee shop, and assaulted him. In retaliation, members of the Beni Mohamed clan fired on a number of the Jama'a. Quickly the violence between the Islamists and the Beni Mohamed escalated. Sheikh Gabir organized his own personal security force drawn from Masjid al-Ikhlas and Masjid al-Nur and marched to 'Izbat al-Mufti in a show of force, beat Magbouli, and vandalized his car. In the Friday prayers that followed a group from the Beni Mohamed went to Masjid al-Ikhlas and fired into the mosque killing one person. At a Tuesday Jama'a meeting held at Masjid Sayid al-Mursileen, and after three days of clashes, the Imam, himself from Assiut, resolved the conflict, vouching for the Beni Mohamed as "good Muslims" and persuading the Jama'a to make peace with them. The conflict was resolved when the leader of the Beni Mohamed paid damages to the Masjid and, according to local residents, built a second story for *Masjid al-Ikhlas*. Importantly, in this instance, while traditional conflict resolution mechanisms were used to resolve the dispute the reason that this proved effective was primarily because those members of the Jama'a chiefly responsible for negotiating an end to the conflict with the elders of the Beni Mohamed hailed from the same clan.

Nevertheless, despite frequent conflict between Islamist militants and individuals belonging to local clans in the neighborhood, the notion of *tagheer al-munkar* found a popular resonance among a wide range of local residents. Indeed, a number of former members of the Jama'a as well as local residents not formally aligned with the organization acknowledged that they were deeply attracted to the militants understanding of *tagheer al-munkar*. That is the notion that it was a collective rather than an individual obligation. They felt strongly that this interpretation established both a sense of peace and religious morality in the neighborhood, and this attraction was markedly evident by the hundreds of residents who attended the *khutbahs* on a regular basis and who clearly found the message of morality associated with the idea of commanding the good and forbidding evil an obligation as well as a necessity in their conflict-ridden quarter. They noted that the idea of changing "immoral ways" by hand *(al-yad)* and not just via Jihad was crucially important in that it gave them a sense of authority in the neighborhood and a great deal of *ihtiram* (respect).

Importantly, former members of the Jama'a spoke of *tagheer al-munkar* in very similar terms as their notions of *tar* or blood feud and it was clear in my interviews that the notion of morality, honor, punishment, and justifiable reprisals associated with the tradition of *tar* was perceived as a form of *tagheer al-munkar*. In this respect, *tagheer al-munkar* resonated deeply with Upper Egyptian norms, which despite the fast-paced developments of Imbaba still resonate strongly in certain quarters of the neighborhood. The adherence to, and implementation of, *tagheer al-munkar* also provided militants with an ideological advantage and legitimacy in the neighborhood vis-à-vis the Muslim Brotherhood. According to former members of the Jama'a, the *Ikhwan* not only do not abide by the proper understanding and interpretation of *tagheer al-munkar* as part of their strategy and *Da'wa*; they also "do not hold conferences or *Khutbas* against the government."[63] While this was not always the case even in the late 1990s, it was indeed a time of political accommodation on the part of the Brotherhood's leadership, a state of affairs that the Jama'a routinely exploited in their efforts at popularizing their own brand of Islamist activism and to outbid the Muslim Brotherhood in mobilizing adherents to their cause.

As inter-sectarian violence continued in the neighborhood long-standing socioeconomic as well as religious divisions have deepened. Indeed, as a stronghold of Cairo's Coptic minority, housing five Coptic Churches and four Anglican Churches within a space of only three blocks, Imbaba continues to be a site of inter-sectarian tensions and frequent incidences of violence. This pattern of violence pitting Salafists against Coptic Christians, which emerged in the 1990s, increased in the years just prior to Mubarak's ouster and in the aftermath of the Tahrir uprising. On

May 12, 2011, less than four months after the uprising, the Supreme Court of Prosecution arrested twenty-three Salafists for their alleged involvement in inter-sectarian clashes that followed the burning of Saint Mena Church in Imbaba earlier that month. The Salafists were charged with terrorism and murder as well as vandalism and the destruction of public and private property. The ensuing violence left fifteen Copts dead and injured hundreds of others reigniting dangerous levels of religious violence. In response to the violence, and as a result of a notable absence of a legitimate and impartial police presence in the neighborhood, members of the Coptic community organized small groups of "self-defense" units to protect not only the churches but also small businesses and coffee shops owned by Copts.[64]

### The Role of the Local Strongman: *Baltagiyya Al- 'Ataat* and the "Market" in Coercion

The association of al-Jama'a with the institution of the local strongman, or *Baltagi*, provided the organization with another source of recruitment as well as another important source of conflict. From the point of view of the Jama'a, these strongmen served three important functions in the organization's attempts to expand its popularity among local residents and to build a shadow government under the radar of state authorities: the coercive enforcement of informal contracts, the extraction of "taxes" from local residents and merchants, and as a means of providing material incentives in the form of monetary compensation for some rank and file members, albeit generated from illicit and coercive means.

According to former members in 'Izbat al-Mufti and Beshteel, leaders of the organization preferred "clever people" who were "healthy and physically strong." Some, albeit certainly not all, of these "strong" youth were well known in the neighborhood as *baltagiyya* (strong men) and they were selected to be part of the military wing and to participate in antistate "defense campaigns" (*Hamlaat al-Tameen*). In addition to the strong men recruited by al-Jama'a, young boys (*subyan*), ranging from thirteen to fifteen years old, were also recruited into the organization's *Istihlal* (praise) wing. The latter's primary responsibility was to ride their bicycles and man checkpoints to detect state security personnel, particularly during the Tuesday and Friday prayers and meetings. Leaders, responsible for recruitment at the time, acknowledged that the *baltagiyya* rarely joined for religious reasons and many did not attend prayers regularly. Rather, they joined because, as one former recruiter put it, "street life is dangerous and there is a great deal of competition, rivalries and violence between the *Baltagiyya*." Thus, joining al-Jama'a was not only a good way of joining a large group of like-minded people; it "assured the *Baltagi* the opportunity to earn income."

Indeed, while the *Baltagiyya* phenomenon is commonly associated with general criminality, in its modern manifestation it is closely linked to the increasing levels of wealth and socio-spatial disparity, and most particularly to the great expansion of informal labor concentrated in informal housing areas such as those in Imbaba. To be sure the *baltagiyya* are distinct from informal labors and marginalized youth in the neighborhood in important ways (most notably in their propensity to engage in violence and to participate in the outsourcing of coercion) but because they often must take on informal jobs, it is difficult to separate the two groups in socioeconomic terms. Many of these *baltagiyya* work as day laborers or odd jobbers, and a significant number joined the ranks of al-Jama'a. Importantly, in the case of Western Munira, recruiters acknowledged that most of the *baltagiyya* who joined the al-Jama'a did so not so much for the opportunity of engaging in new forms of racketeering, but simply because they had no other alternative. "There is," as one activist noted, "little work in the informal settlements and no infrastructure or transportation to the City to find work."[65] It is this state of constant economic and social insecurity, rather than simply the poverty or high unemployment, that can quickly transform these youth into "*Baltagiyya*," serving as freelance operators who can, as Adel Iskander has aptly noted, act like an "unofficial urban mercenary force providing services to the highest bidder."

Moreover, local residents in Imbaba distinguish three varieties of *Baltagiyya* with only two categories of urban mercenaries linked to the security arm of the state or militant Islamist activism, albeit in different ways. The first group is known as *Baltagiyya al-Bashawat* (thugs of the elite or aristocracy) and, among local residents, these are considered the "thugs" who are linked to the State Security forces and who do the dirty work of the political and military elite. The second category is *Baltagiyya al-Futuwwa* or the chivalrous *baltagiyya*. Traditionally these young men were revered (and feared) by local residents and generally considered a legitimate segment of social and political life. They served as agents of protection buttressing the legitimacy of traditional authority by aiding in the enforcement of informal social contracts following the resolution of local conflicts via traditional methods. The Jama'a recruited some of these *Futuwwa* into their military wing because of their legitimacy among local residents and also because they are known for their physical prowess and knowledge of the security forces.

Finally, and most importantly, in terms of those considered opportunists and freelance operators of coercion are the *Baltagiyya al-'Ataat* (literally, the enforcers of contracts or "bids"). In the context of the erosion of traditional authority, the *Baltagiyya 'Ataat* emerged as powerful agents of coercion in the neighborhood. Many were enlisted by militant leaders to serve two important functions denoted by their name, *'Ataat*: the enforcement of informal labor contracts, and the extraction of revenue, or "taxes," generated from local residents and commercial establishments. These were the youth who regularly used violence or the threat of violence to extort fees from the *Suq* (market). This included implementation of an informal tax regime on informal street peddlers, on vehicles parking or passing through the neighborhood's narrow alleys, and on formal commercial establishments and retailers.

But if the *baltagiyya* provided an opportunity for the Jama'a leadership, they also presented a key dilemma for the organization. On the one hand, the association of al-Jama'a with the institution of the local strongman provided the organization with an additional source of recruitment and they were an important component of the military wing of the organization. On the other hand, Jama'a leaders experienced great difficulty in generating discipline and ideological commitment from them in a sustained fashion. Initially, the organization's leadership was able to institute a modicum of law and order by recruiting the *baltagiyya* into their ranks, but ultimately they were not able to limit the latter's violent excesses in Western Munira which served as a key constraint in the expansion of their popularity among local residents and resulted in defections of a significant number of rank and file members of the organization. Three key issues were important in this regard: the method of recruitment of the *baltagiyya*, the coercive methods used by strong men to generate revenue for the organization, and the attempt on the part of local leaders of al-Jama'a to sanction the coercive methods of the *baltagiyya* on religious grounds. The latter had the unintended consequence of undermining the ideological legitimacy of the Islamic Group in the quarter.

Importantly, local residents describe the recruitment of *Baltagiyya al-'Ataat* by militants in starkly different and far less selective terms from the one used to generate high levels of commitment from the organization's general rank and file, but one uncannily similar to the process and guidelines (*kuras shuruut*) job recruiters employ in contracting informal workers in the construction firms in the neighborhood. One resident familiar with the process explained: "When there is a demand for them [*Baltagiyya al-'Ataat*], the patron offers a tender ['*ataat*] at competitive prices and whosoever has good reputation in the market wins. Of course, some in the 'Izba have regular clients that they have built over time." The difference of course is that in the heyday of the Jama'a's recruitment drives in Western Munira the "contractor" of *Baltagiyya al-'Ataat* was oftentimes a local resident harboring strong allegiance to the organization in the quarter.

As is the case with the recruitment of cadres, generating revenue is another key challenge for any clandestine organization operating in the shadow of an authoritarian state. In the case of the Jama'a it is important to note that the organization generated funds through noncoercive as well as coercive means. Indeed, the bulk of the funding was locally generated and based on local donations, dues, and fees collected on Tuesdays and Fridays at prayers and meetings where as many as 7,000 to 8,000 individuals were in attendance. The financial system was underpinned by the dense networks of small *Masajid* not registered by the Ministry of Religious Affairs all of which were linked to the memberships and maintained by weekly meetings and prayer groups. That is, while the funding was gathered informally it was done through a highly centralized fashion overseen by the amir of Financial Affairs. Moreover, most of the investment and funding sources of the Jama'a centered on smaller enterprises focused on the domestic market. Retail chains such as *Tawhid al-Nur* and other small shops specialized in selling Islamic dress, clothing, belts and other attire, and income from livestock raising projects (*Nishat Tarbiyyat al-Mawashi*) and the selling of meat from livestock raised in Assiut, al-Minia, and other Upper Egyptian cities provided another source of legitimate revenue. Another source of funding was in the sale of cassettes of sermons of Egyptian as well as Saudi Arabian Wahhabist preachers sold at the mosques in the neighborhood. This was designed not only to generate profit but also to raise the consciousness of followers. At the height of the Jama'a's popularity former members noted that each Masjid sold approximately 250 cassettes that would be collected by the leadership of the organization from all the mosques generating annual revenue of upward of 2 million Egyptian pounds. Since these cassettes were not licensed or taxed by the state, they represented an important source of funding from informal trade for the organization.

A second source of funds generated primarily through coercive means involved the participation of the *Baltagiyya al-'Ataat*. Under the authority and guidance of *Amir Majlis al-Shura* who was responsible for the financing of the organization, many of these *baltagiyya* were put in charge of organizing and staffing "Zakat Committees" and collecting, in the words of one participant, "donations from the street." By their own admission, even some of the most devout members stated that they would keep a small amount to themselves with the tacit approval of the Jama'a leaders in lieu of, or as a supplement to, their regular salaries. However, what distinguished the discursive designation of which individual among the ranks was a *Baltagi Futuwwa* or a *Baltagi 'Ataat* hinged on who joined the organization primarily for opportunistic reasons. To be sure, the Jama'a recruited from both groups, which often resulted in rivalries and conflict among the *baltagiyya* and between the latter and the Jama'a organization.

Nevertheless, a former committed Jama'a member informed me that the *Baltagiyya al-'Ataat* in particular joined because they found it lucrative and that they regularly extorted money form store owners, coffee house owners, housewives, and "anyone they could." Indeed, from the perspective of the Jama'a, as well as many local residents, these were the most divisive variety of *baltagiyya* since they not only extracted *'ataat* (fees) from local residents by force, they were also involved in selling and distributing illicit drugs thus further degrading the moral status of the community. The challenge for the Jama'a leadership was not only that the lines of division between these categories were blurred, but that the rules of conduct and obligations so important to generate commitment and trust did not apply to those recruited but who were more interested in racketeering rather than the ideological program of the Jama'a. The challenge for the Jama'a leadership emerged as the lines of division between *Baltagiyya al-Futuwa* and *Baltagiyya al-'Ataat* blurred, and coercion for opportunistic reasons became indistinguishable from that formerly deployed by al-Jama'a in the service of mobilizing resistance against the authoritarians state. At the heart of the problem was that the rules of conduct and obligations so important in generating commitment, trust, and discipline among the ranks did not apply to those *baltagiyya* more interested in racketeering and personal gain rather than the ideological and political program of the Jama'a.

If the excessive forms of coercion and violence deployed against local residents and commercial interests diminished the organization's popularity among local residents, its legitimacy was further undermined by the efforts of the Jama'a to legitimate the coercive tactics of those *baltagiyya* under their charge in religious terms. Specifically, leaders in the organization referred to the extortion of revenue and "taxes" from local residents and merchants as a form of *Fard al-'Ataat*, that is, a religious duty for those working on behalf of the cause of the organization, and some leaders and some rank and file alike went as far as to promote the idea that stealing from gold shops, groceries and coffee shops owned by Copts (*Kufar*) is *Hallalu al-Sirqa* (a permissible, albeit illicit, form of primitive capital accumulation) and an important aspect of their campaign of *Tagheer al-munkar wa al-amr bi al-Ma'ruf*.

## Economic Crisis and the Erosion of Traditional Authority: Militants versus Kin

If a major objective of any clandestine organization is to build institutions of law and order so as to establish hegemonic control and a monopoly of coercion over local populations, a major challenge in this endeavor for militant activists is how to successfully supplant, or displace, the authority of local rivals. In the case of Imbaba, the most important source of rivalry for al-Jama'a was the customary judicial systems, which underpin traditional kin or regionally based local authorities. Among the most important of these were the regional community associations (*rawabit iqlimiyya*), which traditionally resolved disputes among kin through reconciliation committees (*lijan al-sulh*) of an informal deliberative council (*al-majlis al-'urfi*). A major reason that al-Jama'a were able to establish what their leaders termed the "Emirate of Imbaba" (i.e., "a state within a state") in Western Munira was because they were able to capitalize on the erosion in the legitimacy and social relevance of these institutions to local residents. Moreover, an important source of grievance among local residents that played an important role in many joining the Jama'a had to do with the erosion in the authority of local notables which was greatly diminished as a result of two developments: the economic transformations, predating the rise of al-Jama'a, which profoundly altered the socioeconomic conditions in the quarter, and the increased regulation and co-optation of these informal institutions by state authorities through legal as well as coercive means.

Under traditional law and custom, it was the wealthy and notable family elders, most often possessing an average of 10–20 feddans, that controlled the village and resolved local disputes. Importantly, these local notables also appointed individuals to the *lejan al-sulh* (reconciliation committees), and while strict hierarchies were enforced the latter generally enjoyed the legitimacy of local authority among local residents. In great part this was due to the manner in which the Omdas (village governors) were appointed. The traditional requirements for appointment included three important criteria that ensured their legitimacy among local residents: that he is nominated by the local residents of the village, perceived to hold a "good reputation," and that he be a medium landowner, neither poor nor exceedingly wealthy but sufficiently "comfortable" to ensure a form of evenness. The wealthiest landowners were rarely chosen to be Omdas because of the perceived bias such wealth would necessarily engender.[66]

The legitimacy of these traditional authorities was further enhanced by relatively transparent, if not democratic, process of dispute settlement. Prior to 1992, informal councils (*majalis 'urfiyya*) were presided over by the Omda and the Sheikh, the religious authority of the village who served as the Omda's assistant. The disputants would meet at the Omda's house, deliberate until a decision is made, and, in accordance with custom, the disputant who lost the case would be awarded with a gift by the one who was awarded the favorable decision. Moreover, the proceeding would be presided over by the reconciliation committee (*lajnat al-Musalaha*), which comprises kin elders of two or more clans involved in the dispute. Prior to 1997, when the state formally intervened in the neighborhood, and according to Sheikh Osman Mohamed of Osim village, these committees comprised five large families who would elect a representative to the committee who in turn would be formally approved by the Omda.[67]

However, by the mid-1980s these customary justice systems underwent drastic changes as a result of three interrelated social and economic transformations: the influx of rural-to-urban migration, in-migration from other lower-class sections of Cairo, and the cyclical depression associated with construction trade during the era of the informal housing boom which was an important source of employment for many men and youth in Imbaba. Indeed, what is noteworthy is that, as a consequence of the absence of strong and legitimate state institutions and formalized labor relations, residents of the poorest sections in Western Munira came to increasingly rely on informal social institutions to negotiate their social relations. However, over the years, and prior to the mid-1990s, social and familial conflicts in Western Munira, and Osim, Beshteel, and ʻIzbat al-Mufti in particular, worsened in the context of the economic crisis and increasing competition in the informal labor and housing markets.

The disputes were often over agricultural plots in the home village. In the past these disputes were often mitigated by a brother who came to the city to find work but following the recession in the 1980s in Osim and ʻIzbat al-Mufti, the Omdas I interviewed in Western Munira noted that these brothers often laid claim to their lands back home in upper Egypt, and families were no longer able to resolve the situation on their own. Increasingly, problems of inheritance were referred to the police and the Omda and Sheikh would be asked by the police to appear before the judge to legitimate as well as to formalize the legal decision already reached by state authorities. Indeed, Sheikh Osman recalled that in the past, the majority of disputes he had to resolve had to do with *tar* (blood feuds), killings in addition to disputes over inheritance. By the 1980s and 1990s, however, the most common were inheritance problems, which usually occur among brothers. "We have had very little problems with *ʻunsuriyya* (clannism) or *taifiyya* (sectarianism) here in the past although *tar* (blood feud) was our biggest security problem in the old days."[68]

### "Putting Out Fires": Surveillance and the Securitization of Traditional Authority

However, while dramatic economic and social transformations undermined traditional authorities in ways that provided the context and opportunity for militants and some of their *baltagiyya* emissaries to fill the vacuum of sociopolitical life, this should not obscure the role of state coercion and surveillance that played a crucial role in exacerbating grievances of many residents that enhanced the popularity of al-Jama'a.

The ubiquitous nature of surveillance in authoritarian states is of course a matter of common knowledge and public concern. However, rarely are the consequences of this form of not-so hidden coercion apparent in terms of its consequences at the level of the community. Indeed, a key element associated with authoritarian states is the overlap and linkage between the formal regulatory and coercive arm of the state (whether legal, military, or intelligence), and the informal institutions at the level of the community that, taken together, are intended to simultaneously subdue dissent and expand and consolidate state power. However, the unintended consequences of this are the erosion of traditional authority, the enhanced popularity of antistate organizations, and, in the case of some of Cairo's informal areas, the expansion in the market for informal sources of coercion.

Following the pivotal events of 1992, the Mubarak regime intervened in Imbaba and effectively upended the already weakened authority of the informal councils, Omdas, and Sheiks in the neighborhood. In contrast to previous decades, for example, the Omda is directly appointed by the Ministry of Interior and automatically becomes a member of the ruling party at both the local council and village level. Moreover, he receives funding directly from the state[69] rather than from local residents or from his land, as was the case in the past. Furthermore, while in the past the Omda wielded great influence in selecting the member of the Local Council (the local branch of the National Democratic Party at the time), the latter is now more often chosen from one of the wealthiest families. As one resident in Osim put it, "big families and wealth are [now] the two main means of getting into the Local Council."[70] By the late 1990s, for example, in *al-Waraq* representatives of *Malis al-Sha'ab* were members of the most powerful and largest clans, the *Hamdiyya* and *Amer* clans, and the Local Council, the administrative arm of the National Party in Imbaba, was dominated by the clans of the *Salmaniyya*, *Shawaykha*, and *Ashmuniyya*. These are all families, which while not representing the biggest clans in Imbaba generated great wealth through land speculation (Chapter 1). Consequently, a major reason the government-appointed "leadership" of the local councils lost legitimacy is that they catered almost exclusively to the more affluent members of the local community. Moreover, in the eyes of most residents, local councils stood as a poor substitute for the traditional notables, whose weakened role was exemplified by the shallow reach of informal councils and reconciliation committees. Traditionally, these bodies arbitrated disputes, but the erosion of formerly legitimate institutions of social cohesion and control had rendered them increasingly irrelevant in Western Munira.

In 1997 the state further regulated the traditional institutions in Osim and other satellite villages in ways that transformed them into a veritable security arm of the state. In that year the regime passed *Qarar Ta'ayeen al-Omid* (Law of Appointing Omdas).[71] Thus, by 1992 and formally in 1997, the Omda and Sheikh (Omda's assistant) were appointed by the regime rather than by local residents; the membership of *Lajnat al-Sulh* had to be approved by the security forces; and the police rather than the informal councils took the lead in resolving familial as well as social disputes in the neighborhood. Moreover, the Ministry of Interior now forwarded selected individuals from the community and compelled the Omda to nominate them to the local council and assign them the task of monitoring residents. While the Omda in Osim informed me that the new system was "no problem," it was very clear that the inability of having independence in appointments and the ill reputation it engendered among local residents were a source of great consternation for what are still traditional minded rural migrants with great attachment to their community.

A central function of the government-appointed Omdas became one of security rather than resolving local disputes. The Sheiks and Omdas were essentially transformed from *Ghuffar*, traditional caretakers of plots of land or apartment buildings in Cairo, to what local residents derisively termed *Ghuffar al-Nizam*, caretakers of the regime. "Our two main concerns are criminals in the village and security problems."[72] If the Omda is disconnected from local residents, the Sheikh or Omda's assistant also lacks legitimacy. Residents complained that the Sheikh was not only appointed by the Ministry of Interior but that he had no religious background whatsoever and "comes from a military background: the Omda is paid not by the Minister of Education and the Sheikh but the Minister of Interior."[73] To make matters worse for state-community relations, as one resident, 'Alaa noted, "few government-appointed Imams at the Mosques in Osim are respected by local residents." Indeed, they are treated with open disdain. For example, in the late 1990s, Sheikh Hassan Sa'eed appointed by the Ministry of Religious Endowment and who ran the Masjid in Osim was the only one of the government's appointed Imams that the Omda and Sheikh noted as having any authority.

The responsibility of the Omda and Sheikh is to resolve local disputes, register voting-age residents for elections, issue personal IDs, confirm competency for the military drafts, and oversee issues having to do with security, farming fertilizers, and the irrigation of land from ground wells, and assist orphans. However, the Omda and Sheikh in Osim, Western Munira, acknowledged that by the late 1990s, the "most important duty" is to work with security authorities and "even if the resident is rich and has land to make sure he has moderate, democratic values." They noted that the lieutenant (*liwa*) of the security forces informed the Omda and Sheikhs that their main role is now to build the "new social order" (*bina Ijtima' jadeed*) which is composed of three issues: civil defense, the emergency laws, and to "put out fires."[74] One Omda in Western Munira described succinctly the exact manner in which the former Mubarak regime designed and orchestrated its surveillance through the use of local intermediaries:

> If the terrorists are from among our own residents here in Osim, we immediately tell the state security (*amn*), if they are simply *baltagiyya* than we tell the police (*shurta*) ... if terrorists are from outside, we immediately inform the security forces. If we see Islamists implementing *Da'wa* we do not approach them ourselves, but simply report them to the security forces. We monitor them for the state security (*Amn al-Dawla*) that ask us to do so and see if they are really terrorists ... we don't tell the large families, they have no role in these things.[75]

It is within this context that, and at the peak in their popularity, that militants were able to capitalize on the erosion of traditional authority in very specific ways. Specifically, the militant Islamic Group found it possible to diffuse a particular form of family-based Islamic norms through the establishment of the dense network of unregulated private mosques that provided a wide range of social services. While these social services were minimal, they were nevertheless far more substantial than those provided by kin-based or state institutions such as the local councils (*majalis mahliyya*) and governmental Developmental Associations (*munazamat tanmiyya*). As a consequence, Islamists largely supplemented both the state and the traditional Regional Community Associations (*rawbit 'iqlimiyya*).

Furthermore, Islamist militants used their newfound institutions to legitimize their stringent codes of social control and they intervened to settle disputes in the quarter formerly resolved through customary judicial systems. They routinely imposed a strictly enforced code of behavior and discipline legitimized via the espousal of norms of social justice (*al-'adl al-ijtima'iyy*) and presented local residents an "alternative lifestyle" in the context of very poor and squalid conditions.[76] These norms resonated strongly in the local community since they stood in marked contrast to both the neglect of the state and the ineffective and co-opted traditional kin-based institutions; that is, they approximated the normative outlook and "lived experience" of a large segment of Cairo's urban poor.

Following the 1992 siege, the state did intervene to underwrite some basic infrastructural development. Yet as late as 2000, the rehabilitation of Imbaba's poorest areas was only partial and failed to bolster the legitimacy of the state in the view of local residents. The minimal social services the state provided following Imbaba's siege were largely financed by foreign aid rather than domestic sources. The bulk of these funds were allocated to extending electricity and paving roads – allocations made out of security considerations rather than a sincere interest in improving the material conditions of the community. Members of the local council (the local branch of the then ruling National Democratic Party) remained apprehensive about al-Jama'a's presence in their neighborhood. They expressed great frustration with the government's less-than-sufficient assistance and were well aware that residents held them in low regard in comparison to al-Jama'a.[77] Indeed, when I returned to visit in the summer of 2015 very little State or foreign assistance was in evidence and, by most accounts, the changes following the 1992 siege have been superficial: unemployment remained high, housing scarce, and health problems prevalent. As one resident put it, the Islamists did not spread in Imbaba just because there was sewage or there was not sewage.[78]

## How Poverty Matters

The vast literature on political radicalization and terrorism has reached a somewhat troubling consensus that relegates social and economic conditions to the back burner in terms of explaining the "root causes" of religious, and particularly Islamist, militancy. Scholars such as Alan Krugman and Marc Sagemen, for example, contend that since most militant leaders are generally from a middle- or even upper-class backgrounds, this indicates the lack of correlation between economic status and political radicalization, militancy, and terrorism.[79] In other words, poverty is not an explanatory variable. The problem with this line of analysis is that the attempt to formulate a generalized model of radicalization that presupposes an equally generalized conception of poverty obscures the locally specific economic contexts and networks within which the process of radicalization is deeply embedded. What the case of Egypt demonstrates is that it is not poverty as such that sets the stage for militant recruitment. Rather, it is the condition of economic and social insecurity that is gravely compounded by economic downturns and recessionary cycles. I do not mean to imply that this exacerbated insecurity is both a necessary and sufficient condition for militant recruitment. There is little in the way of a consensus on a generalized theory of political radicalization, and some scholars, most notably Martha Crenshaw, have argued that it is both a process that evolves over time and that it is context specific. In the case of Imbaba, for example, historical contingency and an externally induced economic crisis combined to set the stage, giving young men a motivation to join the militant al-Jama'a al-Islamiyya. Neglected by the state and acutely aware of their social marginality in relation to the more prosperous middle-class quarters, the young men of Imbaba were drawn to a particular discourse that was crafted to accommodate all manner of grievances. Moreover, al-Jama'a promised, however unrealistically, to provide employment, social cohesion, and moral uplift.

While these types of conditions provide an enabling environment for recruitment into social movements generally, they do not adequately address the question of why some join Islamist moderate movements as opposed to militant organization. This requires the difficult task of empirically grounded research. In the case of Egypt, socioeconomic conditions provided the context for recruitment for both moderate and militant organizations. What really made the difference were the opportunity structures that are grounded in class and social dynamics. The most poignant experiences that I had interviewing militants in Imbaba were when I asked why they did not join the Muslim Brotherhood. The response was always immediate and unanimous: "We have tried to join them, but they will not have us." The barriers to entry guarded by the middle-class moderate Islamist movements were insurmountable for the scores of lower-class and poor Egyptians. In Imbaba, the young men wanted desperately to be included in a movement that promised social mobility and political voice. They simply did not have the social and cultural capital to do so. The exacting and complex screening and vetting processes barred them from entry, denied selection, or led to their expulsion at the latter stages of the recruitment process. As a result, many young men who might otherwise have become moderate Islamists were thus left vulnerable to recruiters from militant groups whose history of violent confrontation with the state reflected not simply their protest against its negligence and coercive apparatus, but an extremist project of toppling Arab regimes and promoting jihad worldwide.

# Conclusion

## Informal Markets and the Politics of Identity

### Transnational Linkages and Islamist and Ethnic Mobilization

One of the central arguments of this book is that economic globalization is not a homogenous process. The course of economic and political development, even within the constraints of the international economy, produces a variety of outcomes based on the *type* of transnational economic linkages, the balance between state elites and civil society groups, and locally specific cultural traditions. This comparative study of Egypt, Sudan, and Somalia provides some general conclusions with respect to the relationship between shifts in the international economy, the expansion of informal markets, and the emergence of new identity-based forms of collective action.

First, the increase in "internationalization" (i.e., the increase in capital and labor mobility) in the form of remittance inflows does indeed produce similar macro-institutional responses. In the cases of Egypt, Sudan, and Somalia, in the boom, these capital inflows circumvented official financial institutions and undercut the states' fiscal and regulatory capacities while simultaneously fueling the expansion of the informal market in foreign currency. In each case, the integration of domestic financial sectors with international financial markets increased with the expansion of parallel, or black, market activities. The consequence of this capital mobility was to weaken the effectiveness of capital controls imposed by formal banking institutions. During the era of the boom in labor remittances, this forced state elites in all three countries to forego some control over the allocation of these capital inflows in the hope of capturing at least a fraction of these resources.

Second, absent bureaucratic regulation, these informal markets came to be "regulated" by indigenous religious and ethnic networks. However, while these informal markets expanded in the context of the ineffectiveness of legal and bureaucratic institutions, they did not represent the free interplay of market forces. Moreover, the expansion of informality over the last three decades cannot be attributed merely to globally induced economic changes; it was caused primarily by deliberate state policy including excessive state regulation, cutbacks in social services as part of economic austerity measures, and extreme levels of state repression. In addition, the consequences of these developments have varied depending on the specific socioeconomic features of each country.

Finally, since capital accumulation generated by the monopolization of labor remittances generally accrued to private groups, state elites met this political challenge with brutal reprisals against newly mobilized groups in civil society operating within the informal economy. Ultimately, despite their initial similarities, the divergent outcomes in Egypt, Sudan, and Somalia attest to the crucial role of informal institutional arrangements in explaining political developments, namely identity-based forms of collective action. In this instance, the development of Islamic and ethnic politics in the three countries reflects prior political conflicts between state elites and actors in civil society over the monopolization of informal markets. Informal social networks, particularly religious and ethnic-based trust networks, played a key role in collective mobilization by regulating informal financial and labor markets and controlling entry into lucrative informal economic activities.

## Informal Markets, Collective Action, and the State: Breaking Down the Conventional State-Society Dichotomy

Whereas most scholarship on the state and civil society in Africa and the Middle East has often assumed a falsely dichotomous and antagonistic relationship between state and society in developing countries, the politics of informal markets in Egypt, Sudan, and Somalia has confirmed speculation that they are closely intertwined. In these countries, the state and groups engaged in informal activity have operated both symbiotically and in conflict – the latter at moments when the state has perceived the parallel economy as depriving it of significant revenue; the former when key state agents, who are engaged in currency trading, sought to accumulate wealth and cooperate with informal entrepreneurs. In Egypt and Sudan, state elites not only participated in the burgeoning expansion of black marketeering but also eventually promoted Islamic financial institutions in an attempt to corner the market on these foreign exchanges. Ironically, this development allowed for the consolidation of an Islamist commercial class that facilitated the latter's subsequent capture of state power in Sudan and promoted the political profile of the Islamists in Egypt.

Similarly, over the same period the dictatorial regime of Siad Barre in Somalia encouraged the not-so-"hidden" economy by removing all restrictions on remittance inflows and instituting a system whereby merchants could import goods on a free market basis. Due to historical and institutional conjunctures and the social structure specific to Somalia, these policies aggravated clan cleavages, facilitating the societal collapse that ensued. While the state in all three countries enjoyed a systemic connection with, and even stimulated, informal economic activities as a way to promote political patronage, all three states eventually had to react violently against what Polanyi has termed "market society."[1] As the informalization process continued, all three societies conformed to the dictates of a self-regulated market in the context of weak regulatory institutions. In Egypt and Sudan, the development of Islamic financial institutions offered protection for the few inspired by ideological linkages with political Islam by organizing their access to money supply under an institutionalized market system. In Somalia, no institutional protection was forthcoming and with the collapse of traditional structures a new and unprecedented level of social disintegration set in.[2]

To elaborate on these general propositions in more specific empirical terms, in the first section of the book I provided an analysis of the oil boom years and their effect on state-society relations in ways that resulted in the rise of a new politics of identity in Egypt, Sudan, and Somalia. The subsequent three chapters detailed the relationship between the inflow of labor remittances and its role in Islamic and ethnic politics in the three countries. Chapter 1 on Egypt detailed the ways in which workers' remittances and the flow of petrodollars in the boom provided initially capitalization of Islamic banks and a host of Islamic investment companies that operated outside the system of state regulation. Along with labor migration this new "Islamic economy" resulted in raising the political profile of the middle-class Islamist movement in Egypt. I also argued that the boom in labor export and remittance inflows helped shape Egyptian national economic policy in important ways. In particular, out-migration and the expansion of the informal economy afforded the Egyptian state enough "relative autonomy" to expand the private sector and accelerate the decentralization of the country's economy, which led to the internationalization of the Egyptian economy. However, these policies had two important unintended consequences. First, economic reform policies opened the door for Islamic financial institutions, which helped popularize the Islamic movement in Egypt. Second, it inadvertently facilitated a boom in informal housing and the informalization of the labor market in the poorer sections of Cairo. The latter, in particular, helped set the social and economic conditions that were to provide a fertile ground for the recruitment of Islamist militants.

Chapter 2 chronicled the political economy of Sudan during the same period. As in Egypt, in Sudan the remittance boom produced a similar macro-institutional response as the flood of labor remittances similarly circumvented official financial institutions, undercutting the state's fiscal and regulatory capacity and fueling the expansion of informal foreign currency trade. I showed that these initial developments paralleled those of Sudan's northern neighbor in two interrelated ways. First, as in Egypt, the boom witnessed the rise of a distinct Islamist-commercial class. Second, Islamists activists were able to successfully monopolize both informal finance and the Islamic banking sector. However, in contrast to Egypt, by the summer of 1989 Sudanese Islamists were able to take over the levers of state power via a military coup. I attributed this divergent political development to Sudan's weaker state capacity, the extreme weakness of Sudan's formal banking system, and the uninterrupted overvaluation of the Sudanese pound in this period. Consequently, in contrast to Egypt, the financial power of the Muslim Brethren (*al-Ikhwan al-Muslimeen*) continued to increase in relationship to the state, and the latter continued to profit from the informal financial (i.e., "black") market.

Chapter 3 addressed the impact of remittances on clan politics in Somalia during the boom. In comparison to Egypt and Sudan, Somalia possesses the weakest state capacity with almost no formal financial institutions of any kind. While I showed that the boom in remittances also reduced the Somali state's ability to regulate the economy, I also highlighted the fact that the consequences of this development differed in important ways. Specifically, in contrast to both Egypt and Sudan during the boom, in Somalia informal financial networks facilitated a thriving commercial sector comprised of firms oriented around kinship networks (i.e., clans). It was not religious or class affiliations, but rather ethnic mobilization that became the most politically salient. The Somali case poses the important question: why would a country with an exclusively Muslim population not go the way of Egypt and Sudan? I attributed this difference to two factors: first, the very dearth of private, formally organized institutions necessitated the reliance on household economies; second, the manner in which the informal channels utilized to transfer remittances operated had the consequence of reinforcing the clan and subclan cleavages in economic and political terms.

In the second section of *Black Markets and Militants* I examined changes in state-society relations in the three countries in the context of recession, economic reform, and, in the case of Somalia, state collapse.

I maintained that this period of economic contractions was indeed positively correlated with new levels of political violence, albeit with different consequences for civil society in the three countries. More specifically, I argued that the post-1986 period, characterized by "shrinkage" in the size of informal foreign currency trade and economic reforms, resulted in the reconfiguration of informal economic and social organization with different consequences in each country. In all three countries, as the financial and political power of groups engaged in the informal economy rose, state elites struck back against the informal realm. Beginning with Egypt, in Chapter 4, I showed that only in Egypt was this successful. Specifically, in 1991 the Egyptian government liberalized the exchange rate in order to discourage foreign currency speculation and to re-direct labor remittances into formal institutions. As intended, financial liberalization did undercut the Islamist monopolization of informal finance. However, rather than eliminate informal economic activities altogether, these policies altered the social composition of the informal economy. In particular, as in other labor exporters, a key consequence of the internationalization of the Egyptian economy was the expansion of the informalization of domestic markets in housing and labor. In the third chapter on Egypt (Chapter 7) I showed how this development played an important role in the rise of Islamist militancy in the informal quarters of Imbaba, Cairo. Specifically, I illustrated in detail the ways in which radical Islamist groups were able to exploit new conditions of economic uncertainty to recruit from among the denizens of the some of the informal housing quarters of greater Cairo. An important reason behind the popularity of radical Islamists among the underemployed residents was due to the ways in which their leaders utilized highly coercive methods to settle disputes, enforce scarce labor contracts in the informal labor market, while simultaneously preach against the ills of conspicuous consumption in their sermons. In other words, both material and ideological factors played an important role in the popularity of the militants.

Chapter 5 chronicled the assumption to power of the Islamists in Sudan. In contrast to Egypt, in Sudan the recession and attendant economic reforms resulted in the consolidation of an Islamist-commercial class that forged an alliance with the military and captured the state. Whereas in Egypt the state "won the battle" over the informal economy, and its competition with the Muslim Brotherhood over rents accruing from labor remittances, Sudan witnessed the opposite outcome. In contrast to developments in Egypt, in Sudan the Islamists were successful in monopolizing informal finance and Islamic banking which they used to finance their movement and eventually realize their greatest political ambition by taking over the levers of state power. Moreover, having gained control of the state, the Sudanese Islamists considered it vital to marginalize rival groups in civil society, enact economic reforms geared toward maintaining power, and recruit jihadist elements particularly among the poorer segments of the population. However, I also demonstrated that in the context of Sudan's changing political economy from a labor to an oil exporter, the jihadist experiment of the Islamists declined in political terms as opposition from subnational groups increasingly isolated the regime in Khartoum. Two consequences of this "fall" of Sudan's jihadist policies have been the impending separation of South Sudan, and the remarkable and historic pro-democracy popular uprising, which ultimately led to the fall of the Islamist-Authoritarian regime of Omer al-Bashir in April 2019.

The final chapter on Somalia (Chapter 6) chronicled the fateful and fatal consequences of the collapse of the Somali nation-state. I argued that in the wake of state disintegration Somali politics continues to be greatly influenced by its internationalized economy. Specifically, I showed how the informal economy's relative efficiency in facilitating the transfer of labor remittances, and the extent to which informal social networks in the form of both clan and religious networks control the wages of expatriate Somali labor continues to determine the political fortunes in many parts of the country. Moreover, in northern Somalia in particular, this has led to the emergence of regionally based political organizations and nascent state-building efforts, which have enjoyed varying levels of success. Thus, whereas Egypt and Sudan stand as examples of the shifting fortunes of Islamist activism within the context of economic and political change, Somalia calls into question the very principles and conventional understanding of national "sovereignty" where the modern internationally recognized state has simply ceased to exist.

## Failed States, the Criminalization of Informal Networks, and the Global War on Terrorism

I conclude *Black Markets and Militants* with an analysis of some important lessons my comparative analysis of Somalia, Sudan, and Egypt provides with respect to some of the misconceptions and long-term repercussions associated with the global war against terrorism and Islamist extremism. The cases of Somalia and Sudan in particular help us to tackle two important questions: the first has to do with the linkage between informal hawwalat financial systems and Islamist extremism; the second is the question of whether failed states actually serve as an effective haven for militants and terrorists, as many have assumed. Building on my field research, and contrary to conventional wisdom, I have demonstrated empirically that rather than facilitating the rise of Islamist extremist groups (or financing terrorist organizations), the financial flows sent via these informal banks by Somali migrants have actually reinforced kinship networks as the most important political and social institution in Somalia. This is because these transfers are regulated by norms of reciprocity and trust embedded in clan and familial relations. Moreover, it is for this reason that militant Islamist groups in Somalia have not been able to monopolize these hawwalat transfers to fund their organizations. This is clearly evident by the fact that since the collapse of the Somalia state, Islamist militants have attempted to generate financing, not through the hawwalat, but by attempting to control the port economies of the country. Based on interviews with hawwalat operators, I have also argued that the latter do indeed harbor an Islamist form of political identification. However, I have also shown that this is a form of moderate Islamism that is similar to other Islamist capitalists, which represents a moderate rather than a militant form of Islamist activism. Indeed, rather than focusing on informal banks as an arena of terrorist finance and risking a more militant version of anti-Western sentiment, policy makers should engage more moderate Islamists in Somalia to undermine the efforts of extremists to exploit an increasingly poor, uneducated, and young population in the country.

In addition, the absence of state institutions in much of Somalia does not necessarily provide a safe haven for terrorists. This is because the popularity of militants among local populations is dependent on their own capacity to provide public goods and contract enforcement more effectively than state authorities. In this regard, it is important to note that what made Afghanistan so useful to Al-Qaeda in the mid-1990s was not the failure of the state, but rather the fact that they relied on the state to protect its members from attack and to provide its leadership with important benefits.

Similarly, the "failed states" of the Horn of Africa do not afford global terrorists networks such benefits. This is due to four challenges that confront militant organizations. The first challenge is the lack of government-enforced order that is needed to provide security against local authorities. Second is the unreliability of local allies. As I have shown, clan ties are still the most important source of identification for Somalis, and terrorists cannot depend on the commitment of Somalis for Islamist extremist causes over their strong adherence and loyalty to their clan or subclan. The third challenge is that the better an area is for training militants, the more remote and sparsely populated it is and the harder it is to meet basic sustenance needs. Finally, on the question of terrorism financing, it is important to note that terrorists face the challenge of getting fiscal resources in place. In Somalia financial services continue to be weak. Most importantly, Islamist militants have not been able to effectively use the *hawalaat* to provide key financial services to terrorists in weakly governed areas. This is the reason why Somalia, with its collapsed state, has not served as a fertile breeding ground for global terrorism (i.e., al-Qaeda), despite popular arguments to the contrary. The al-Shabaab organization is indeed a militant organization, but the roots of its extremism are rooted in local and regional factors[3] and not due to the expansion of hawwalat agencies in the country.

By contrast, as I demonstrated in the case study of Sudan, jihadists function more successfully under regimes that are able to provide both, security from external attack, as well as the necessary financing and labor recruitment to organize jihadists. In fact, existing security vacuums have not proven to be a viable base for exporting attacks abroad. From this perspective, policy makers should be concerned with "ungoverned" spaces only so far as they allow terrorists to operate openly. Instead, a greater focus should be paid to states that have promoted militant forms of Islamism and where terrorists have at various times found it useful to operate from. Indeed, what seems to be of the utmost importance to jihadist leaders is not the existence of a security vacuum and "fragile states" as such, but the potential of establishing new functioning state institutions under jihadi control as was the case of the Sudan.

If the cases of Somalia and Sudan demonstrate the pitfalls of locating the roots of terrorism in the absence of state institutions and informal financial markets, the case of Egypt highlights the misconceptions associated with the criminalization of Islamic Welfare Associations. The most important misconception here has been the persistent conflation of Islamic Welfare Associations with Islamist militancy, with little analysis as to the socioeconomic roots of extremism. What is crucial is for policy makers to distinguish clearly between the causes underpinning the rise of the moderate Islamist movement and extremism. On the one hand, I have shown that the rise in popularity of Egypt's Islamist social movement was due to two linked developments. The first is associated with the retreat of the state from its provision of welfare services, and the related "absence" of viable formal state institutions in both the middle class as well as the poor neighborhoods of urban Cairo. The second related trend is the expansion of a host of Islamist Welfare Associations that have essentially filled the gap of welfare and social protection in the context of the diminished economic role of the state.

However, whereas a major assumption in the scholarship of terrorism assumes financial incentives to be primarily responsible for militant or terrorist recruitment, I have shown that Islamist extremism is contingent on locally specific economic, social, and political transformations that are exploited by a minority of militant activists. In other words, to say that the moderate Islamist trend in Egypt has been largely invigorated by the spread of Islamic Welfare Associations does not necessarily implicate them in the support and financing of extremist groups. Based on my research, far more significant has been the role of the density of small private mosques in the neighborhood. It is here that militant preachers deliver persuasive sermons to the community and where young children and youth are recruited via both material and social incentives and the promise of both upward mobility and an elevated social and political status. To be sure, over the last four decades, socioeconomic changes have altered the demography and job prospects of local residents in urban Cairo in important ways. But I have argued that Islamists militants were able to capitalize on these developments in very specific ways that had little to do with the role of Islamic charitable giving financing these groups. Specifically, the militant Islamic Group found it possible to diffuse a particular form of family-based Islamic norms through the establishment of a dense network of unregulated private mosques that provided a wide range of social services. Presently, many of the social services in the poorest sections of Cairo are underwritten by Islamist activists, rather than by state institutions such as the local councils (*Majalis Mahliyya*) and governmental Developmental Associations (*Munazamat Tanmiyya*). As a consequence, Islamists have largely supplemented both the state and the more traditional Regional Community Associations (*Rawbit Iqlimiyya*). This is not a state of affairs that is likely to change with the closure or regulation of these Islamic Welfare Associations. However, policy makers and local authorities can easily focus on the unregulated nature of the store-front Mosques rather than the Islamic Welfare Associations, which by offering social protection to the poor can actually curb any potential of another rise in militant or terrorist recruitment.

Furthermore, Islamist militants used their newfound institutions to legitimize their stringent codes of social control. They routinely imposed a strictly enforced code of behavior and discipline legitimized via the espousal of norms of social justice (*al-'adl al-ijtima'iyy*) and presented local residents an "alternative lifestyle" in the context of very poor and squalid conditions.[4] In my observations, I found that, far more than financial incentives, these norms resonated strongly in the local community since they stood in marked contrast to the neglect of the state; that is, they approximated the normative outlook and "lived experience" of a large segment of Cairo's urban poor.

In this respect, the absence of significant state-funded social programs particularly in poor areas is a contributing (albeit not the only) factor in breeding extremism. Following the 1992 siege, the Egyptian state did intervene to underwrite some basic services in terms of basic infrastructural development. Yet over four decades later the rehabilitation of Cairo's poorest areas is only partial and has so far failed to bolster the legitimacy of the state in the view of local residents. The minimal social services that were provided following the state's self-proclaimed "anti-terrorist campaign" were largely financed by foreign aid, rather than domestic sources. This continues to be the case. The bulk of these funds were allocated toward extending electricity and paving roads out of security considerations, rather than out of a sincere effort to improve the social and economic conditions of the local community. Even members of the Local Council (*Majlis al-Mahli*), the local branch of the former ruling National Party remained apprehensive about the potential of extremism in their neighborhood. They expressed great frustration with the government's less-than-sufficient assistance and were well aware that residents held them in low regard in comparison to the Islamists. Clearly, government policy that promotes domestic sources of economic development and social protection would play an important role in addressing some of the root causes of extremism among some of the most socially vulnerable. This is a category that has, in the past, represented an important source of rank and file recruitment.

The case of Egypt illustrates clearly the dangers of criminalizing informal networks without taking seriously the impact of economic changes in altering local social realities. Moreover, in an ironic development, blaming any facet of terrorism on Islamic Welfare Associations obscures the role (and responsibility) of domestic governments, which have in many ways abdicated their role in social protection and welfare vis-à-vis local communities. Taken together with the failure to liberalize the political system, extremism finds a more fruitful breeding ground. In the case of Egypt, the government-appointed "leadership" of the local councils continues to clearly represent the interests of the state. Moreover, these leaders cater almost exclusively to the more affluent members of the local community rather than the most vulnerable constituency. As a consequence, in the eyes of most poor residents, local government stands as a poor substitute to the weakened role of the traditional authority. This is exemplified by the shallow reach of informal councils (*Majalis 'Urfiyya*) and reconciliation committees (*Lejan Sulh*). These kinship-based institutions, which had traditionally arbitrated disputes, now reflect the erosion of formerly legitimate institutions of social cohesion and control.

What the erosion of traditional authority has meant among the poor is that Islamic Welfare Associations, private Mosques, and zakat Committees will continue to be more popular and relevant to the lives of impoverished communities. This is most certainly the case in many parts of the Muslim world. It is to these social and economic developments that we must look if we are to understand both the social roots of militancy and the attraction of terrorism to a small minority. It is a grave mistake to transform these complicated social and economic conditions into psychological traits and "criminalize" the most vulnerable, as so much analysis having to do with the war on terror has been prone to do.

The larger policy implications of *Black Markets and Militants* are clear. In the short term, the best cost-effective strategy is to monitor ungoverned spaces in failing states more closely but not to assume that they are automatically breeding grounds for militant and terrorist organization. However, in the long term, the international community must devise a more comprehensive solution in order to undercut the popularity of militant Islam, which remains a minority movement in the Muslim world. Rather than waging a war against the "soul of Islam" as some analysts have suggested, it is far more effective to devise effecting measures that examines the "secular" challenges that militant organizations face themselves. In multiethnic societies in the Horn of Africa and Egypt, militants and Islamists have faced a host of overlapping ethnic and sectarian affiliations, insecurity, and a complex array of local political rivals and motivations. Until recently, it was only in the Sudan where militants were able to benefit from a safe haven, robust financial resources, and a regime that utilized functioning, albeit fragile, formal institutions and militias operating in parallel to the state to support and promote a transnational jihadist network.

Finally, *Black Markets and Militants* makes a strong case that social and economic crises do indeed play an important role in the success of Islamist movements. My findings suggest that rather than advising policy makers to be wary of pursuing polices of economic development in poorer states in the hopes of curtailing militant activism as most analysts have advised, it is vital to understand that particular forms of economic insecurity and externally induced recessionary downturns do indeed play a role in expanding the "pool" of militant recruits.

# Appendix A

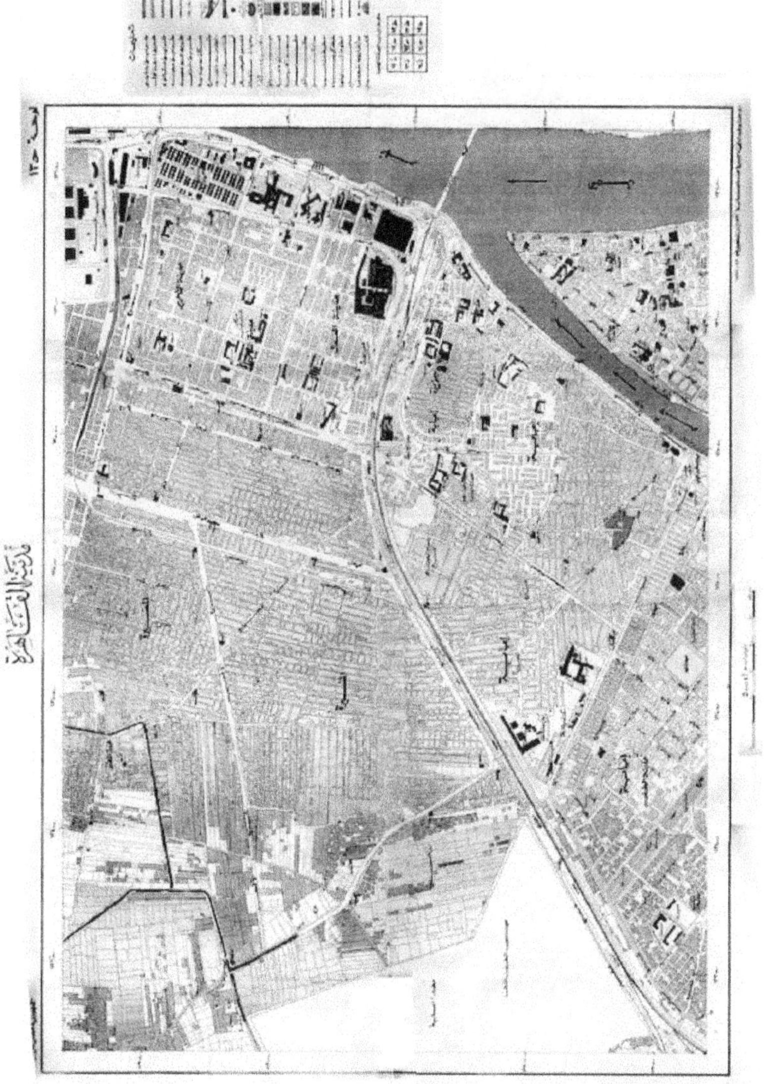

Figure A.1 Map of Imbaba, Cairo
*Source:* Central Agency for Public Mobilization and Statistics (CAPMAS), 2000. Cairo, Egypt

# Appendix B

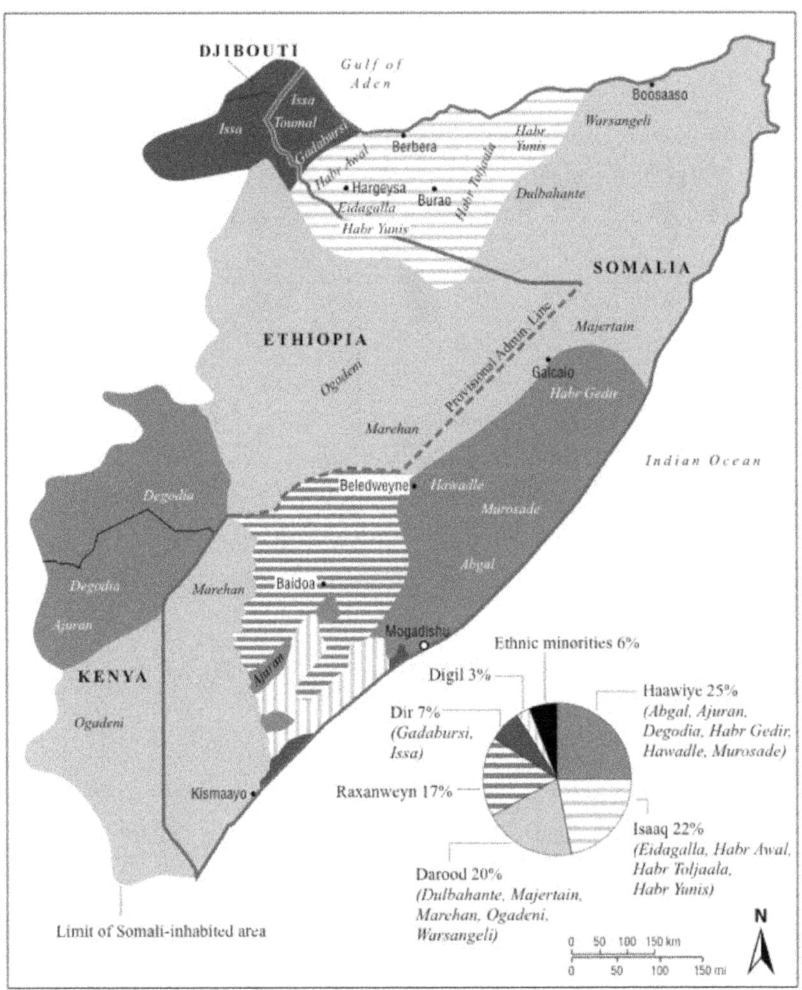


Figure A.2 Map of Somalia

# Notes

## PREFACE

1. Although there are a number of channels that can carry the effects of foreign disturbances to an economy (namely, in the alteration of foreign currency prices of traded goods, quantities of traded commodities demanded or supplied, and credit and capital markets), the focus of this book is on labor and remittance flows. This is because for the remittance economies the latter is the most important in terms of both the nature of the disturbance and the extent of the links between the domestic and global economy. This in turn allows us to draw some causal inferences with regard to the political, social, and economic ramifications of exogenous shocks on domestic politics. For a full discussion on the subject, see Laura D'Andrea Tyson and Peter B. Kenen, "The International Transmission of Disturbances: A Framework of Comparative Analysis," in *The Impact of International Economic Disturbances on the Soviet Union and Eastern Europe: Transmission and Response*, ed. Egon Neuberger and Laura D'Andrea Tyson (New York: Pegamon Press, 1990), 33–62.
2. Indeed, as Charles Tilly famously observed, throughout history, subordinate populations have participated in trust networks including clandestine religious sects and kinship groups as a shield against the repression of rulers and to protect themselves from dispossession and exploitation. Charles Tilly, "Trust and Rule," *Theory and Society* 33, no. 1 (2004): 1.
3. Leanardo A. Villalon, *Islamic Society and State Power in Senegal: Disciples and Citizens in Fatick* (New York: Cambridge University Press, 1995), 36.

## INTRODUCTION

1. Peter Mandaville, *Islam and Politics* (New York: Routledge Press, 2014); Oliver Roy, *Globalized Islam: The Search for a New Ummah* (New York: Columbia University Press, 2004).
2. Millard J. Burr and Robert O. Collings, *Alms for Jihad* (New York: Cambridge University Press, 2006); Hernando De Soto, "The Capitalist Cure for Terrorism," *The Wall Street Journal*, October 10, 2014.
3. John Esposito, *The Islamic Threat: Myth or Reality?* (New York: Oxford University Press, 1992); John Esposito, *Unholy War: Terror in the Name of Islam* (New York: Oxford University Press, 1992); Timor Kuran, *Islam and Mammon: The Economic Predicaments of Islamism* (Princeton, NJ: Princeton

University Press, 2004); Charles Tripp, *Islam and the Moral Economy: The Challenge of Capitalism* (New York: Cambridge University Press, 2006); Vali Nasr, *The Rise of Islamic Capitalism: Why the New Muslim Middle Class Is the Key to Defeating Terrorism* (New York: Council on Foreign Relations Free Press, 2010); Asef Bayat, *Post-Islamism: The Changing Face of Political Islam* (New York: Oxford University Press, 2013).

4. Mark Tessler, "The Origins of Popular Support for Islamist Movements: A Political Economy Analysis," in *Islam, Democracy, and the State in North Africa*, ed. John Entelis (Bloomington: Indiana University Press, 1997), 93–126; Eli Berman and Laurence R. Iannaconne, "Hamas, Taliban and the Jewish Underground: An Economist's View of Radical Religious Militias," *NBER Working Paper*, no. w10004 (2003); Eli Berman and Laurence R. Iannaconne, "Religious Extremism: The Good, the Bad, and the Deadly," *Public Choice* 128, no. 1–2 (2006): 109–129; Anne B. Krueger and J. Maleckova, "Education, Poverty and Terrorism: Is There a Causal Connection?" *National Bureau of Economic Research (NBER) Working Paper*, no. 9074 (July 2003): 1–36; Jacob Shapiro, *The Terrorist's Dilemma: Managing Violent Covert Organizations* (Princeton, NJ: Princeton University Press, 2015).
5. Gilles Keppel, *Jihad: The Trail of Political Islam* (Cambridge, MA: Harvard University Press, 2002); Bernard Lewis, *The Crisis of Islam: Holy War and Unholy Terror* (New York: Random House, 2004); David Cook, *Understanding Jihad* (Oakland: University of California Press, 2005); Robert Pape, *Dying to Win: The Strategic Logic of Suicide Terrorism* (New York: Random House, 2006); Thomas Hegghammer, *Jihad in Saudi Arabia: Violence and Pan-Islamism since 1979* (New York: Cambridge University Press, 2010); Teri Ostebo, "African Salafism: Religious Piety and the Politicization of Purity," *Islamic Africa* 6 (2015): 1–29.
6. Judith Scheele, *Smugglers and Saints of the Sahara: Regional Connectivity in the Twentieth Century* (New York: Cambridge University Press, 2015).
7. It is important to note the significance of international remittances. In 2008, for example, remittances to developing countries reached an estimated $305 billion, registering a growth of 120 percent from 2002. In Africa and the Middle East, workers' remittances are the largest source of development finance, exceeding both official development assistance and foreign direct investment. Moreover, these capital inflows have increased dramatically, up from $0.5 billion in 1975 to over $8 billion in 2005. Over roughly the same period, informal markets increased dramatically in size. A World Bank study estimated that in Africa over 60 percent of the population relied on the informal economy for their livelihood. These trends of international economic transactions and increasing domestic informal economic activity have coincided with the rise of the politics of ascription in African countries most deeply affected by these developments. Samuel M. Miambi and Dilip Ratha, eds., *Global Development Finance* (Washington, DC: World Bank Report, 2007), 14.
8. Most new institutionalist studies on the politics of internationalization take increase in trade as proportion of gross domestic product (GDP) or the ratio

of a country's net foreign investment to its total domestic assets as indicators of internationalization. As a consequence, the least-developed countries have been routinely left out of the analysis. In fact, most conceptualizations of the politics inherent in the process are applicable to Third World countries. Jeffrey Frieden, "Invested Interests: The Politics of National Economic Policies in a World of Global Finance," *International Organization* 45 (Autumn 1991): 425–452; Ronald Rogowski, *Commerce and Coalitions* (Princeton, NJ: Princeton University Press, 1989); Peter J. Katzenstein, *Small States in World Markets: Industrial Policy in Europe* (Ithaca, NY: Cornell University Press, 1985).

9. Tariq Banuri has demonstrated the extent to which the integration of domestic financial sectors with international financial markets increases with the expansion of "black market" activities. Tariq Banuri, *United Nations University World Institute for Development Economics Research (WIDER) Working Paper: Black Markets, Openness and Central Bank Autonomy* (Amherst: University of Massachusetts, 1988), 2–3.
10. Among some notable exceptions that examine the influence of informal networks and political transitions across cases, albeit in the context of Central Asia, is the work of Kathleen Collins, *Clan Politics and Regime Transitions in Central Asia* (New York: Cambridge University Press, 2006).
11. Important research on the relationship between informal institutions and democratization while contributing a great deal toward laying a theoretical foundation for informal institutional analysis does not take into account informal *economic* institutions. Gretchen Helmke and Steven Levitsky, eds., *Informal Institutions and Democracy: Lessons from Latin America* (Baltimore: Johns Hopkins, 2006). The authors acknowledge that they "leave aside economic (e.g., black markets) institutions" in their work. Ibid., 4.
12. Scott Radnitz, "Informal Politics and the State," *Comparative Politics* 43, no. 3 (2011): 351–371.
13. Robert H. Bates, for example, while correctly pointing out that risk averse agents behaving rationally prefer regulated incomes, assumes that market liberalization would summarily shrink informal activities. This ignores the structural underpinnings of how informal markets are created and which historically specific institutions would end their resiliency. Robert H. Bates, *Prosperity and Violence: The Political Economy of Development* (New York: Norton, 2001), 115–132.
14. The scholarship in economic sociology is particularly useful in helping us understand the similarities between different markets and social movements. Neil Fligstein, "Markets as Politics: A Political-Cultural Approach to Market Institutions," *American Sociological Review* 61 (1996): 656–673; Sidney G. Tarrow, *Power in Movement: Social Movements and Contentious Politics* (Cambridge, UK: Cambridge University Press, 1994); Mark Granovetter, "The Old and the New Economic Sociology: A History and an Agenda," in *Beyond the Marketplace*, ed. R. Friedland and A. F. Robertson (New York: Aldine de Gruyter, 1990), 89–112. Granovetter, taking a middle position between new institutionalist and neo-classical economic perspectives, argues that differences in social structure, institutional history and collective action

(i.e., "embedded social relations") in addition to power relations crucially shape future possibilities.

15. Deborah Brautigam, "Substituting for the State: Institutional and Industrial Development in Eastern Nigeria," *World Development* 25, no. 7 (1997): 1063–1080; Asef Bayat, *Making Islam Democratic: Social Movements and the Post-Islamist Turn* (Redwood City, CA:Stanford University Press, 2007); Diane Singerman, "The Networked World of Islamist Social Movements," in *Islamic Activism: A Social Movement Approach*, ed. Quinton Wiktorowicz (Bloomington: Indiana University Press, 2004), 143–163; Janine A. Clark, *Islam, Social Welfare and the Middle Class: Networks, Activism, and Charity in Egypt, Yemen and Jordan* (Bloomington: Indiana University Press, 2004); Jillian Schwedler, "Myth, Menace or Mobilizer?" *SAIS Review* 21, no. 2 (Summer 2001): 1–17; Quinton Wiktorowicz, ed., *Islamic Activism*; Carrie Rosefsky Wickham, *Mobilizing Islam: Religion, Activism and Political Change in Egypt* (New York: Columbia University Press, 2002).
16. Frances Cleaver, "Institutional Bricolage, Conflict and Cooperation in Usangu, Tanzania," *IDS Bulletin* 32, no. 4 (October 2001): 26–43; Janet I. Guyer, *Marginal Gains: Monetary Transactions in Atlantic Africa* (Chicago: University of Chicago Press, 2004); Karen Tranberg Hansen and Mariken Vaa, *Reconsidering Informality: Perspectives from Urban Africa* (Uppsala: Nordiska Afrikainstitute, 2004); Janet MacGaffey, *Entrepreneurs and Parasites: The Struggle for Indigenous Capitalism in Zaire* (New York: Cambridge University Press, 2014) originally published in 1987.
17. Alejandro Portes and Peter Landolt, "The Downside of Social Capital," *The American Prospect* 26 (1996): 18–21; Partha Dasgupta, "Economic Progress and the Idea of Social Capital," in *Social Capital: A Multifaceted Perspective*, ed. Partha Dasgupta and Ismail Serageldin (Washington, DC: World Bank, 2002), 325–399; Sydney Tarrow, "Making Social Science Work across Time and Space: A Critical Reflection on Robert Putman's 'Making Democracy Work'," *American Political Science Review* 2, no. 90 (1996): 389–397.
18. Diego Gambetta, *The Sicilian Mafia: The Business of Private Protection* (Cambridge, MA: Harvard University Press, 1993); Frederic Varese, *The Russian Mafia: Private Protection in a New Market Economy* (New York: Oxford University Press, 2001); Edgar L. Feige and Katarina Ott, eds., *Underground Economies in Transition: Unrecorded Activity, Tax Evasion, Corruption and Organized Crime* (Aldershot, UK: Ashgate, 1999).
19. Kate Meagher, *Identity Economics: Social Networks and the Informal Economy in Nigeria* (London: James Currey,Africa Issues Series, 2010).
20. Ethan Bueno De Mesquita, "The Quality of Terror," *American Journal of Political Science* 49, no. 3 (July 2005): 515–530.
21. Fawaz A. Gerges, *The Far Enemy: Why Jihad Went Global* (Cambridge, UK: Cambridge University Press, 2005).
22. See, for example, the influential work of Krueger and Maleckova. Alan Krueger and Jitka Maleckova, "Education, Poverty and Terrorism: Is There a Causal Connection?" *The Journal of Economic Perspectives* 17, no. 4

(2003): 119–144; Alan B. Krueger, *What Makes a Terrorist: Economics and the Roots of Terrorism* (Princeton, NJ: Princeton University Press, 2007).

23. There is, of course, a long tradition in political science that argues that economic and ideological factors are important determinants of violent mobilization. See, for example, Ted Robert Gurr, *Why Men Rebel* (Princeton, NJ: Princeton University Press, 1970); Mark Irving Lichbach, "An Evaluation of 'Does Economic Inequality Breed Political Conflict?' Studies" *World Politics* 41, no. 4 (1989): 431–470.
24. Marc Sageman, *Understanding Terror Networks* (Philadelphia: University of Pennsylvania Press, 2004).
25. Henry Munson, "Social Movement Theory and the Egyptian Muslim Brotherhood," *Sociological Quarterly* 42, no. 2 (2002): 487–521.
26. Jika Maleckova, "Impoverished Terrorists: Stereotype or Reality," in *Root Causes of Terrorism: Myths, Reality and Ways Forward*, ed. Tore Bjorgo (New York: Routledge, 2005), 35. See also Alan B. Krueger, "Poverty Doesn't Create Terrorists," *The New York Times*, May 29, 2003.
27. The fact that militancy and terrorism have been correlated to economic contraction and deprivation has been documented in both the Middle East context and across regions. See, for example, S. Brock Blomberg, Gregory D. Hess, and Akila Weerapan, "Terrorism from Within: An Economic Model of Terrorism," *Claremont Colleges Working Papers*, no. 2002–14 (2002).
28. Martha Crenshaw, "Theories of Terrorism: Instrumental and Organizational Approaches," *Journal of Strategic Studies* 10, no. 4 (1987): 13–31; and Martha Crenshsaw, "'New' vs. 'Old' Terrorism: A Critical Appraisal," in *Jihad Terrorism and the Radicalization Challenge in Europe*, ed. Rick Coolsaet (Aldershot: Ashgate Publishing, 2008), 25–36.
29. Eli Berman and David D. Laitin, "Religion, Terrorism and Public Goods: Testing the Club Model," *Journal of Public Economics* 92, no. 10–11 (2008): 1942–1968.
30. Hamed El-Said and Jane Harrigan, "Globalization, International Finance, and Political Islam in the Arab World," *The Middle East Journal* 60, no. 3 (2006): 444–466.
31. Zafiris Tzannatos and Iqbal Kaur, "Welfare State Policies in the Middle East and North Africa," in *When Markets Fail: Social Policy and Economic Reform* in Ethan B. Kapstein and Brando Milanovic, eds. (New York: Russel Sage Foundation, 2002), 146–182.
32. Ibid.
33. Dale Eickelman and James Piscatori, *Muslim Politics* (Princeton, NJ: Princeton University Press, 2004).
34. Notable examples include Bayat, *Making Islam Democratic*; Wiktorowicz, *Islamic Activism*.
35. State repression can lead to either increased or decreased mobilization of militant groups. In the contest of Authoritarian regimes in the Middle East, this appears to depend on the timing of government crackdowns and the level of strength of the target group or groups in civil society. Wiktorowicz, *Islamic Activism*.

## "THE HOUSE THE BOOM BUILT": THE INFORMAL ECONOMY AND ISLAMIST POLITICS IN EGYPT

1. Helen Chapin Metz, ed., *Egypt, a Country Study* (Washington, DC: Library of Congress Publication, 1991), 213.
2. Interview with Mr. Magdi Mahmoud Ali. Interview with the author, `Izbat al-Mufti, Imbaba Cairo, Egypt, January 18, 1999. Although economic incentives were clearly the driving force behind his choice to emigrate, Mr. Ali also noted that an important reason why he chose Libya as his first destination was because of the "cultural affinity" between Egyptians and Libyans.
3. Charles Tilly, "Trust Networks in Transnational Migration," *Sociological Forum* 22, no. 1 (March 2007): 3.
4. John Waterbury, "The 'Soft State' and the Open Door: Egypt's Experience with Economic Liberalization, 1974–1985," *Comparative Politics* 18, no. 1 (October 1985): 67.
5. Ragui Assaad, ed., *The Egyptian Labor Market Revisited* (Cairo: American University in Cairo Press, 2009), 8–9.
6. Ragui Assaad and Rania Roushdy, "Job Quality among the Non-Wage Workers in the Agricultural and Non-Agricultural Sectors in Egypt," *Economic Research Forum Working Papers* 386 (2008): 37.
7. Ibid., 18.
8. Ibid., 38.
9. Ibid., 21.
10. Eurostat, "Push and Pull Factors of International Migration, Country Report, Egypt," Eurostat Working Papers, Population and Social Conditions 2/2000/E/N07, 2000.
11. Heba Nasser, "Migration, Transfer and Development in Egypt," Euro-Mediterranean Consortium for Applied Research on International Migration (CARIM) Research Report (Florence: Robert Schuman Centre for Advanced Studies, 2005).
12. Assaad and Roushdy, "Job Quality," 9.
13. Waterbury, "The 'Soft State'," 70.
14. Essam Mitwally, "On the Emerging Industrialization Policies and Practices in the Arab Republic of Egypt," *Journal of Economic Cooperation among Islamic Countries* 20, no. 1 (1999): 22.
15. Galal Amin, "Some Economic and Cultural Aspects of Economic Liberalization in Egypt," *Social Problems* 28, no. 4 (April 1981): 430–441.
16. Waterbury, "The 'Soft State'," 66.
17. MERI Report, *Central Bank of Egypt* (London: The Economist Intelligence Unit Viewswire, 1985), 79.
18. Hamza Ateş, Mehmet Duman, and Yüksel Bayraktar, "A Story of *Infitah*: Egyptian Liberalisation under Stress," *Yapı Kredi Economic Review* 17, no. 1 (2006): 66. https://pdfs.semanticscholar.org/ebe9/0230896a1c71dccfaea def2ed3eb4e763b73.pdf.
19. Ibid., 65.
20. Ibid., 69.
21. Ibid., 79.

22. Eva Bellin, "The Political Economic Conundrum: The Affinity of Economic and Political Reform in the Middle East and North Africa," *Carnegie Papers, Middle East Series*, no. 53 (November 2004): 6–7. https://carnegieendowment.org/2004/11/09/political-economic-conundrum-affinity-of-economic-and-political-reform-in-middle-east-and-north-africa-pub-16051.
23. Ilya Harik, *Economic Policy Reform in Egypt* (Gainesville: University Press of Florida, 1997), 27.
24. Ibid., 37.
25. Hans Löfgren, "Economic Policy in Egypt: A Breakdown in Reform Resistance," *International Journal of Middle Eastern Studies* 25 (August 1993): 407–421.
26. Ibid., 408.
27. Robert Springborg, "Egypt," in *Economic and Political Liberalisation in the Middle East*, ed. Tim Niblock and Emma Murphy (London: British Academic Press, 1993), 161.
28. Löfgren, "Economic Policy."
29. Springborg, "Egypt," 161.
30. Delwin A. Roy, "The Hidden Economy of Egypt," *Middle East Studies* 28, no. 4 (1991): 697.
31. Waterbury, "The 'Soft State'," 69.
32. Roy, "The Hidden Economy om Egypt," 692.
33. Ibid.
34. Eric Denis, "Cairo as Neoliberal Capital? From Walled City to Gated Communities," in *Cairo Cosmopolitan: Politics, Culture, and Urban Space in the New Globalized Middle East*, ed. Diane Singerman and Paul Amar (Cairo: American University in Cairo Press, 2006), 47–72.
35. Jackline Wahba, "Informality in Egypt: A Stepping Stone or a Dead End?" *Cairo, Egypt: Economic Research Forum (ERF), Working Paper*, no. 456 (2009). Informal employment refers to workers in informal enterprises as well as wage employment in formal enterprises, households, or those with no fixed employer, and who are not covered by social security and have no formal contract.
36. B. McCormick and Jackline Wahba, "Migration and Mobility in the Egyptian Labor Market," *Economic Research Forum Research Report*, no. 0401 (2004).
37. David Sims, *Understanding Cairo: The Logic of a City Out of Control* (Cairo: American University in Cairo Press, 2010), 99.
38. Charles Tilly, *Trust and Rule* (New York: Cambridge University Press, 2005).
39. Ministry of Planning, *Five Year Plan for 1978–1982* (Cairo: Ministry of Planning, 1977), cited in Rodney Wilson, "Wither the Egyptian Economy," *British Journal of Middle Eastern Studies* 20, no. 2 (1993): 205.
40. Roy, "The Hidden Economy," 690.
41. "Al-bunuk wa munafasat sharikat tawsif al-amwal" [The Banks and the Competition of the Money Management Companies], *Al-Ahram al-Iqtissadi*, December 2, 1987; "Kayf nawajih tahdiyat sharikat tawsif al-amwal" [How do

We Confront the Challenges of the Money Management Companies], *Al-Ahram al-Iqtissadi*, February 8, 1988.

42. Abdel-Rahman Aql, "Difa' wazir al-iqtisad an tadil qanun al-bunuk" [The Minister of the Economy's Defense of the Amendment of the Banking Law], *Al-Ahram al-iqtisadi*, April 2, 1984, cited in Robert Bianchi, "Businessmen's Association in Egypt and Turkey," *Annals of the American Academy of Political and Social Science* 482, no. 1 (1985): 152.
43. "Ta'idil wizari wasi' wa taraju shamil 'an al-islah al-iqtisadi" [A Broad Cabinet Change and Sweeping Retreat from Economic Reform], *Al-Ahali*, April 3, 1985, cited in Bianchi, "Businessmen's Association," 152.
44. Björn Olav Utvik, *Islamist Economics in Egypt: The Pious Road to Development* (Boulder, CO: Lynn Reinner Press, 2006), 170.
45. Bianchi, "Businessmen's Association," 152.
46. "Islamic Banks Bury the Egyptian Economy," *Middle East Economics Digest (MEED)* (July 7, 1992): 20.
47. Mahmoud 'Abd al-Fadil, *Al-khadi'a al-maliyya al-kubra. Al-iqtisad al-siyasi li-sharikat tawzif al-amwal* [The Great Financial Deception: The Political Economy of the Investment Companies] (Cairo: Dar al-mustaqbal al-'arabi, 1989) cited in Utvik, *Islamist Economics*, 204.
48. Ibid., 66.
49. Ibid.
50. Kuran, "Islamic Economics and the Islamic Subeconomy. 168.
51. Sami Zubaida, "The Politics of Islamic Investment Companies in Egypt," *British Journal of Middle Eastern Studies* 17, no 2 (1990): 158.
52. Zubaida, "The Politics of Islamic," 160.
53. Ibid., 160.
54. Ibid., 76–77, cited in Utvik, *Islamist Economics*, 207.
55. Mahmoud Abdel-Fadil, *Al-iqtisad al-siyassi li sharikat tawzif al-amwal* [The Political Economy of Islamic Investment Companies] (Cairo: Dar al-Mustaqbal al-Arabi, 1989), 64.
56. Dr. Hamid al-Ghazali, interview with the author, November 12, 2008, Cairo, Egypt; Utvik, *Islamist Economics*, 141.
57. Samer Soliman, "The Rise and Decline of the Islamic Banking Model in Egypt," in *The Politics of Islamic Finance*, ed. Clement M. Henry Moore and Rodney Wilson (Edinburgh: Edinburgh University Press, 2004), 21.
58. Ibid., 271.
59. Ibid., 270.
60. Ibid., 274.
61. Waterbury, "The 'Soft State'," 79.
62. Soliman, "The Rise and Decline," 272.
63. See Umar al-Tilmisani, "Idha ja'a al-muslimun fa-la mal li-ahad" [If the Islamists Come There Will be No Money for Anyone], *al-Dawa* 383 (February 1977).
64. Utvik, *Islamist Economics*, 151.
65. Ibid.
66. Bianchi, "Businessmen's Association," 153.

67. Adel al-Mashad, "Al-ghazu al-istithmari lil-niqabat al-mihniya wa al-'ummaliya" [The Entrepreneurial Invasion of the Professional and Labor Syndicates], *Al-Sha'ab*, January 25, 1983.
68. Bianchi, "Businessmen's Association," 156.
69. Ibid.
70. Ibid.
71. Timur Kuran, "Islamic Economics and the Islamic Subeconomy," *Journal of Economic Perspectives* 9, no. 4 (Fall 1995): 155–173.
72. Raymond A. Hinnebusch, "The Politics of Economic Reform in Egypt," *Third World Quarterly* 14, no. 1 (1993): 163.
73. 'Issam al-Eryan (official spokesperson of the Muslim Brotherhood), interview with the author, November 12, 2008, Cairo, Egypt.
74. "Tahweeel al-anshita al-Ikhwaniyyah min al-nizam al-fardi ila al-muassasah" [The Transformation in the Ikhwan's Activities from the Individual Effort (Nizam) to an Institution], 24 *Sa'ah*, August 13, 2007.
75. Mona El-Ghobashy, "The Metamorphosis of the Egyptian Muslim Brothers," *International Journal of Middle East Studies* 37, no. 3 (2005): 373–395. However, as El-Ghobashy noted, there was no question of legalizing the organization, only "de-facto" toleration. 377.
76. Wickham, *Mobilizing Islam*, 95.
77. Ibid.
78. Ibid., 99.
79. Clark, *Islam*, 28.
80. Author interviews with the staff of the Islamic Welfare Association, December 14, 2008, Zamalek, Cairo, Egypt.
81. Singerman, "The Networked World"; Wickham, *Mobilizing Islam.*
82. Singerman, "The Networked World," 149.
83. Ibid.
84. Author interview with activist Islamist leader and rank and file members of the Muslim Brotherhood, November 14, 2008, Helwan, Cairo, Egypt. [Names withheld by request.]
85. Mohamed Asim (Muslim Brotherhood activist leader), interview with the author, October 3, 1999, Western Mounira, Imbaba, Egypt.
86. Singerman, "The Networked World."
87. Janine A. Clark makes this important observation in her review of the literature on how social movements adapt their recruitment methods. Clark, *Islam*, 24.
88. Wickham, *Mobilizing Islam.*
89. 'Issam al-Eryan (official spokesperson of the Muslim Brotherhood), interview with the author, May 14, 2009, Cairo, Egypt.
90. Clark, *Islam*, 67.
91. Author interviews with leaders and rank and file members of the Brotherhood, November 16, 2008, Helwan, Cairo, Egypt.
92. Jeremy M. Weinstein, *Inside Rebellion: The Politics of Insurgent Violence* (New York: Cambridge University Press, 2007), 8–9.
93. Speech given by Khaiter al-Shater, "Mashru'u al-Nahda al-Islamiyya" [The Islamic Renaissance Project], amlalommahtv, April 13, 2011, YouTube

video, 92:03, www.youtube.com/watch?v=JnSshs2qzrM. The importance of Khaiter al-Shater in terms of the Brotherhood's leadership is by now widely acknowledged. Shater was the candidate that was selected by the Brotherhood's General Guide as their party's first presidential candidate following the Tahrir uprisings of January 2011.

94. Ibid.
95. This analysis of the recruitment and mobilization process is based on my interviews with members and recruiters of the Muslim Brotherhood in Helwan, Cairo, in November and December 2008.
96. Gilles Kepel, *Muslim Extremism in Egypt: The Prophet and Pharaoh* (Berkeley: University of California Press, 1984).
97. Michael J. Piore and Charles F. Sabel, *The Second Industrial Divide: Possibilities for Prosperity* (New York: Basic Books, 1984).
98. Saskia Sassen, *A Sociology of Globalization* (New York: W. W. Norton & Company, 2007), 119.
99. Galila El-Kadi, "Market Mechanism and Spontaneous Urbanization in Egypt: The Cairo Case," *International Journal of Urban Regional Research* 12, no. 2 (1988): 22–37. Another often-cited study estimated that by 1982, 84 percent of new units built in Cairo were supplied by the informal sector, and by 2009 approximately 17.3 million of Cairo's residents (an estimated 63.65 percent) lived in informal settlements. Sims, *Understanding Cairo*, 64, 96.
100. Mahmoud Abdel-Fadil, "Egyptian Workers and Gulf Migration" (unpublished manuscript, December 1995); Dr. Mahmoud Abdel-Fadil, interview with the author, December 1998, Cairo, Egypt.
101. Ragui Assaad, *The Egyptian Labor Market Revisited* (Cairo: American University in Cairo Press, 2009).
102. Ibid.
103. James Toth, "Beating Plowshares into Swords: The Relocation of Rural Egyptian Workers and Their Discontent," in *Directions of Change in Rural Egypt*, ed. Nicholas S. Hopkins and Kirsten Westergaard (Cairo: American University in Cairo Press, 1998), 66–87.
104. This historical analysis is based on my interviews with local residents and my own participant observation. I am particularly grateful to colleagues at *Markaz al-Ard* (The Land Center) for guiding me through Imbaba's social and economic history.
105. Indeed, prior to Sadat's assassination by militants in 1981 when the state cracked down on militant activists, Telmasani, the then General Guide of the Brotherhood, argued that the militant *Jama'at* were officially sponsored, and even "created," in order to counterbalance his movement. Interview with Omer Tilmisani, *Al-Ahrar*, February 15, 1982.
106. Author interviews with local residents in Imbaba, Cairo, December 1999.
107. According to one estimate, the number of Ahali Mosques increased from 20,000 in 1970 to 46,000 by 1981. In 1981 only 6,000 of them were under the control of the Ministry of Religious Endowments, *al-Awqaf*, and maintained by 3,000 officially appointed Imams. *Al-Liwa' al-Islami*, February 25, 1982, cited in Hamid Ansari, *Egypt: The Stalled Society* (Albany: State University of New York Press, 1986), 218.

108. There was a markedly low voter turnout in the elections to the parliament (Shura Council) of 2011 in Imbaba most likely due to the population's low education levels as well as poor social and economic conditions. Nevertheless, residents gave their largest support to the two Islamist political parties. The Brotherhood's Freedom and Justice Party (FJP) and Al-Nour registered clear victories. Of the 179,000 validated votes the FJP captured 84,000 and *Al-Nour* 54,000 votes. *Al-Wafd* recorded 18,000 votes, and *al-Wasat* received 10,000 votes. "Al-Misrawi yanshur natayij al-marhalah al-thanyah lil-intikhabat al-barlamaniyiyyah" [Al-Misrawi Publishes the Results of the Second Round of Parliamentary Elections], *al-Misrawi*, August 6, 2011.
109. *Al-Syasi al-Masri*, August 27, 1995.
110. In terms of Western Mounira's religious profile, 92 percent are Muslims and 8 percent Coptic Christians, "Dirasa fi al-intikhabat fi Mounira al-Gharbiyya: Imbaba" [A Study on the Western Mounira Elections: Imbaba], *Al-Ahram*, Cairo: Center for Strategic Studies (unpublished report, 1995): 3–4.
111. The wealthiest families (*'aylat*) in Imbaba such as *al-'Amarna*, *al-Hamayda*, *al-Morgaan*, and *al-Salmaniya* all made their fortunes in land speculations. Other families representing the "medium" rich and who also made their fortunes in land speculation include *al-Hanadwa*, *al-Shwaikhiyya*, and *al-'Atabi*. Still, other families eventually invested capital derived from land speculation into other business ventures ranging from leather, automobile parts, and clothing factories to retail trade in consumer goods and carpet imports. Thus, the *Surur Sabah* family now operates a clothing factory; *Nabil Adawil*, a carpet store; *Abdel-Moneim 'Amara*, a car horn factory; *Mohamed Wagdi*, a leather factory; and *al-Makawi*, a chain of grocery stores.
112. Rather than merely representing a series of self-contained incremental changes or transitional arrangements, the expansion of market forces is characterized by forms of displacement, reformulation, and adaptation of nonmarket systems to market principles. See Timothy Mitchell, "The Market's Place," in *Directions of Change in Rural Egypt*, ed. Nicholas S. Hopkins and Kirsten Westergaard (Cairo: American University in Cairo Press, 1998), 34. In the case of Western Mounira, the relaxing of regulations and controls over housing and labor markets did not lead to a free-market system but cartels and price-fixing, on the one side, and reintroduction of new forms of social control and coerced forms of labor, on the other.
113. Varese, *The Russian Mafia*.
114. Gambetta's influential work on the Sicilian Mafia has shown that the expansion of market capitalism in combination with high levels of societal distrust, and the absence of clearly defined property rights, increases the demand for protection. Importantly, however, the particular form that this protection assumes is dependent on the context and historical timing of the transition to the market. See Gambetta, *The Sicilian Mafia*.

115. Significantly, many long-term residents of Imbaba claim that this period witnessed the first incidents of terrorism (*irhab*). However, this resentment also stems from a clear social conflict between the "new" class of wealthy real estate entrepreneurs and the older, more urbanized, middle-class strata of residents.
116. The severity and violent nature of these tactics came with huge financial rewards. Ali Morgaan, for example, made an estimated 4 to 5 million Egyptian pounds from land speculation in this period.
117. Among the residents of al-Waraq that held seats in the Egyptian parliament were Surur Sabbah, Nabil 'Adawil, and Abdel Moneim 'Amara all of whom represented the ruling National Democratic Party (NDP) in the district's Local Council (*Majlis Mahali*).
118. One can thus observe that the expansion of the market mechanism played an important role in disrupting the social balance of kinship society, first by turning some kin into "rich" and others into "poor" families, and later by disrupting the kinship structure itself. As an example, the traditional institution of blood vengeance (*tar*) became transformed producing a myriad of "modern" feuds into which an element of class conflict was clearly realized if not acknowledged.
119. For one of the rare studies on the persistence of regional and ethnic identities in Cairo, see Catherine Miller, "Upper Egyptian Regionally Based Communities in Cairo: Traditional or Modern Forms of Urbanization?" in *Cairo Cosmopolitan: Politics, Culture, and Urban Space in the New Globalized Middle East*, ed. Diane Singerman and Paul Amar (Cairo: American University in Cairo Press, 2006), 384.
120. Melvin L. Oliver, "The Urban Black Community as Network: Toward a Social Network Perspective," *The Sociological Quarterly* 29, no. 4 (1988): 623–645.
121. Author interviews with local residents in *Waraq al-Arab*, *Beshteel*, and *Ezbat al-Mufti*, Imababa, December 16, 1999.
122. Leila Vignal and Eric Denis, "Cairo as Regional/Global Economic Capital," in *Cairo Cosmopolitan: Politics, Culture, and Urban Space in the New Globalized Middle East*, ed. Diane Singerman and Paul Amar (Cairo: American University in Cairo Press, 2006), 101.
123. Nabil Omar, "Imbaba's Empire of 'Terrorism'," *Al-Ahram*, December 8, 1992, 3.

## INVESTING IN ISLAMISM: LABOR REMITTANCES, ISLAMIC BANKING, AND THE RISE OF POLITICAL ISLAM IN SUDAN

1. Daniel Beyman, *Deadly Connections: States That Sponsor Terrorism* (New York: Cambridge University Press, 2005), 41–43; Jane Perlez, "Sudan Is Seen as Safe Base for Mideast Terror Groups," *New York Times*, January 26, 1992.
2. *Min ayna ja'u hawalahi*?[From where did they come?] *Al-Sudan al-Hadith*, June 12.

3. Samuel Huntington, *The Clash of Civilizations and the Remaking of World Order* (New York: Touchstone, 1996); Francis Fukuyama, *The End of History and the Last Man* (New York: Free Press, 1992); Henry Munson, Jr., *Islam and Revolution in the Middle East* (New Haven: Yale University Press, 1986); Hassan Turabi, "The Islamic State," in *Voices of a Resurgent Islam*, ed. John Esposito (New York: Oxford University Press, 1983), 241–251; Abdelwahab El-Affendi, *Turabi's Revolution: Islam and Power in Sudan* (London: Grey Seal, 1991).
4. For a classic description of state formation see Douglas C. North, *Structure and Change in Economic History* (New York: WW Norton and Company, 1981), 21–22.
5. For a comprehensive account of Sudan's civil war, see Douglas H. Johnson, *The Root Causes of Sudan's Civil Wars* (Bloomington: Indiana University Press, 2003).
6. Riad Ibrahim [Khalid M. Medani], "Factors Contributing to the Political Ascendancy of the Muslim Brethren in Sudan," *Arab Studies Quarterly* 12, no. 3/4 (1990): 33–53: 13.
7. Khalid M. Medani, "Sudan's Human and Political Crisis," *Current History* 92, no. 574 (1993): 204.
8. Ali Salih Karrar, *The Sufi Brotherhoods in the Sudan* (Evanston: Northwestern University Press, 1992). See also Fatima Babiker Mahmoud, *The Sudanese Bourgeoisie: Vanguard of Development?* (London: Zed Books, 1984), 135.
9. Carol Collins, "Colonialism and Class Struggle in Sudan," *Middle East Research and Information Project (MERIP) Reports* 46 (1976): 3–20. See also Muhammad Mahmoud, "Sufism and Islamism in the Sudan," in *African Islam and Islam in Africa*, ed. Eva Rosander and David Westerlund (Athens: Ohio State University Press, 1997), 170–177.
10. Karrar, *The Sufi Brotherhoods*, 40–41.
11. Tim Niblock, *Class and Power in Sudan* (Albany: State University of New York Press, 1987), 51.
12. While political science research often makes use of state capacity to explain a variety of outcomes across cases, there is no clear consensus on the meaning of the term. But as Margaret Levi has noted good analysis requires conceptually differentiating among the features of state capacity in order to assess its importance in comparative analysis. Margaret Levi, "The State of the Study of the State," in *Political Science: The State of the Discipline*, ed. Ira Katznelson and Helen V. Milner (New York: WW Norton, 2002).
13. C. H. Harive and J. G. Kleve, "The National Income of Sudan, 1955/56," Khartoum: Department of Statistics, 1959, cited in Richard P. C. Brown, *Public Debt and Private Wealth: Debt, Capital Flight and the IMF in Sudan* (London: Macmillan 1992), 90.
14. Ibid.
15. Michael Gilsenan, "Some Factors in the Decline of the Sufi Orders in Modern Egypt," *Muslim World* 57, no.1 (1967): 13–14.
16. J. Spencer Trimingham, *The Sufi Orders of Islam* (London: Oxford University Press, 1971).
17. Fatima Babiker Mahmoud, *The Sudanese Bourgeoisie*, 134.

18. "Islam: Blueprint for a New Century," *Sudanow*, November 1979, 11.
19. Hassan al-Turabi, interview with the author, *al-Manshiyya*, December 14, 1997.
20. Hassan al-Turabi, quoted in Peter K. Bechtold, *Politics in Sudan: Parliamentary and Military Rule in an Emerging African Nation* (New York: Praeger, 1976), 89.
21. Ibid.
22. Tijani al-Tayib (deputy chairman of the Communist Party), interview with the author, June 24, 2010, Nairobi, Kenya. For confirmation of these strategic objectives as articulated by Hassan al-Turabi at the time, see Alexander S. Cudsi, "Islam and Politics in the Sudan," *AFRICA* (March 1978): 48.
23. Hassan al-Turabi, interview, "An Equal Place for All," *Sudannow*, February 1980, 12.
24. Brown, *Public Debt and Private Wealth*, 109–110.
25. The World Bank, *World Debt Tables: 1989–1990*, vols. 1 and 2 (Washington DC: World Bank, 1991).
26. For figures on the uneven regional distribution of public expenditures, investment, banks, and educational and health facilities see B. Yongo-Bure, "Prospects for Socioeconomic Development of the South," in *The Search for Peace and Unity in Sudan*, ed. Francis M. Deng and Prosser Gifford (Washington, DC: Wilson Center Press, 1987), 36–55; Ali Abdalla Abbas, "The National Islamic Front and the Politics of Education," *Middle East Report* 21, no. 5 (September–October 1991): 22–25.
27. World Bank, *World Debt Tables*, 111.
28. Dirk Hansohm and Karl Wohlmuth, "Sudan's Small Industry Development: Structures, Failures and Perspectives," in *Industrialization in the Third World: The Need for Alternative Strategies*, ed. Meine Pieter van Dijk and Henrik Secher Marcussen (London: Frank Cass, 1990), 146–155.
29. Ali Abdel Gadir, "A Note on the Brain-Drain in the Sudan," *Sudan Journal of Economic and Social Studies* 2, no. 1 (Summer 1977): 16.
30. Khalid M. Medani, "Funding Fundamentalism: The Political Economy of an Islamist State," in *Political Islam: Essays from Middle East Report*, ed. Joel Beinin and Joe Stork (Berkeley: University of California Press, 1996), 166–177.
31. Nazli Choucri, "The Hidden Economy: A New View of Remittances in the Arab World," *World Development Report* 14, no. 6 (1986): 702–709. See also *Al-Majalla*, "Ithnayn milyar dulaar tahwilat al-sudaneen fi al-khalij" [Two billion dollars worth of remittances from Sudanese in the Gulf], *Al-Majalla*, June 11–17, 1986, 31.
32. Richard P. C. Brown, "The Hidden Economy," *New Internationalist*, June 1991, 12–13; Richard P. C. Brown, "Migrants' Remittances, Capital Flight, and Macroeconomic Imbalance in Sudan's Hidden Economy," *Journal of African Economies* 1, no. 1 (March 1992): 59–85.
33. Mark Duffield makes a similar point in "Where Famine Is Functional: Actual Adjustment and the Politics of Relief in Sudan," *Middle East Report* 21, no. 5 (September–October 1991): 23–30.

34. Ibrahim Elbadawi, "Real Overvaluation, Terms of Trade Shocks, and the Cost to Agriculture in Sub-Saharan Africa: The Case of the Sudan," *Journal of African Economies* 1, no. 1 (March 1992): 79.
35. Kiren Aziz Chaudhry, "The Price of Wealth: Business and State in Labor Remittance and Oil Economies," *International Organization* 43, no. 1 (Winter 1989): 101–145.
36. Interviews with black-market currency traders, Khartoum, December 22, 1998. Names withheld by request.
37. Jeswald W. Salacuse, "Arab Capital and Middle Eastern Development Finance: The Emerging Institutional Framework," *Journal of World Trade Law* 14, no. 1 (1980): 302–303.
38. Elfatih Shaaeldin and Richard C. Brown, "Towards an Understanding of Islamic Banking in Sudan: The Case of the Faisal Islamic Bank," in *Sudan: State, Capital and Transformation*, ed. Abbas Abdelkarim and Tony Barnett (New York: Croom Helm, 1988), 133.
39. Interviews with black-market currency traders. Khartoum, January 15, 2008. Names withheld by request.
40. The Muslim Brotherhood's National Islamic Front party was the first organization to mobilize the savings of expatriate workers through informal channels; by 1985, the year Al-Nimeiri was deposed, 2/3 of the professional and skilled workers were employed outside Sudan. They sought ways to smuggle funds back to Sudan without being taxed. The NIF established a network of currency traders and took the money of the expatriates, and after deducting a percentage, gave it to their families in Sudan. Gabriel R. Warburg. "The Muslim Brotherhood in Sudan: From Reforms to Radicalism," *The Project for the Research of Islamist Movements (PRISM)*. Global Research in International Affairs (GLORIA) Center, Islam in Africa Research Project (August 2006), 4.
41. "Kilmit al-sir baskawit: khamsa tujjar yasaytarun 'ala al-suq al-aswad fi al-Sudan," [Password biscuit: Five merchants dominate the black market in Sudan], *Al-Majalla*, no. 331 (June 11–14, 1986): 30–31. While the expatriate remitting part of his wages can conduct these transactions directly with one of the big currency traders, it is more reliable to get a check drawn on a bank in Sudan, especially when large sums are being transacted.
42. Ibid.
43. Ibrahim Wade, *Islamic Finance in the Global Economy* (Edinburgh: Edinburgh University Press, 2000), 212–213.
44. Henry and Wilson, *The Politics of Islamic Finance*, 41.
45. The six largest Islamic banks in Sudan include Faisal Islamic Bank, Islamic Cooperative Bank, the Sudanese Islamic Bank, the Islamic Bank for Development Cooperation, the Western Sudanese Islamic Bank, Al-Baraka Bank, and Umdurman Islamic Bank. The latter's chairman and CEO is none other than former President Omar al-Bashir. By the end of the remittance boom period in 1987, the share of the total paid-up capital of these Islamic banks to that of the commercial banks was equal to 43 percent. Muhammad Hashim 'Awad, "Al-Bunuk al-Islamiyya: haqa'ik wa arqam" [Sudanese

Islamic Banks: Facts and Figures] (unpublished paper: University of Khartoum, 1987), 11.

46. Mansour Khalid, *The Revolution of Dismay* (London: Kegan Paul International, 1985), 63.
47. Rodney Wilson, *Banking and Finance in the Arab Middle East* (London: St. Martin's Press, 1983), 85. See also 'Awad, "Al-Bunuk al-Islamiyya," 1–18.
48. Mansour Khalid, *Al-Nukhba al-Sudaniyya wa idman al-fashal* [The Sudanese Elite and the Addiction to Failure] (Cairo: Dar al-Amin, 1993).
49. Muhammad 'Umar Khalifa, *Malamih min tajribat al-islah al-iqtisadi fi al-Sudan*, [Characteristics of the experiment in economic reform in Sudan] (Khartoum: The National Center for Media Production, 1995).
50. Abdin Ahmad Salama, "Islamic Banks: Economic Significance and Methods of Control," *Faisal Islamic Bank Sudan Publications*, no. 3 (1984): 18–19.
51. Badr al-Din A. Ibrahim, "Poverty Alleviation via Islamic Banking: Finance to Micro-Enterprises (MEs) in Sudan: Some Lessons for Poor Countries," in *Sudan Economy Research Group Discussion Paper: Institute for World Economics and International Management (IWIM)*, no. 35 (March 2003): 3.
52. Badr al-Din Ibrahim, "Some Aspects of Islamic Banking in LDACs: Reflections on the Faisal Islamic Bank, Sudan," in *The Least Developed and the Oil-Rich Arab Countries*, ed. M. A. Mohamed Salih and Kunibert Raffer (London: Macmillan Press, 1992), 222.
53. Ibid., 224.
54. 'Abd al-Rahim Hamdi, "Islamization of the Banking System in Sudan." Paper presented at the National Assembly, Khartoum, December 1984.
55. The governor of Kurdufan at that time made a public statement saying that Faisal Islamic Bank caused a dramatic rise in the sorghum price in the region because it monopolized the sorghum trade. *Al-Ayyam*, December 1984, 5.
56. Al Bagir Yusif Mudawi, "Islamic Banks Problems and Prospects: Islamic Banking Evaluation of Experience," *Faisal Islamic Bank Publications* (1984): 10.
57. In *Murabaha*, the client applies to the bank for financing his purchase of specific raw materials or assets. The bank buys and resells the raw materials or assets at a price, which covers the expenses and allows the bank a profit margin upon which the two parties agree. The partner usually pays the bank back in agreed installments. Ibrahim, "Poverty Alleviation," 8.
58. Interview with prominent Sudanese journalist, June 17, 1990, Khartoum. Name withheld by request.
59. This observation can be generalized to explain the timing of the Islamist "revolution" in much of the Muslim world in the 1970s and 1980s. North, *Structure and Change in Economic History*, 49–50.
60. Kuran, *Islam and Mammon.*
61. Endre Stiansen, "Interest Politics: Islamic Finance in Sudan, 1977–2001," in *The Politics of Islamic Finance*, ed. Clement M. Henry and Rodney Wilson (Edinburgh: Edinburgh University Press, 2004), 159.
62. Ibid.
63. Interview with black-market trader, June 15, 1989. Name withheld by request.

64. Author interviews with members of the National Islamic Front (NIF), University of Khartoum, Faculty of Medicine, January 10, 1990, Khartoum, Sudan. Names withheld by request.
65. Ahmad al-Batthani, *Economic Transformation and Political Islam in Sudan, 1975–1989* (unpublished paper, University of Khartoum, 1996).
66. For a comprehensive analysis of the Shari'a laws, see Aharon Layish and Gabriel Warburg, *The Reinstatement of Islamic Law in Sudan Under Numayri: An Evaluation of a Legal Experiment in the Light of Its Historical Context, Methodology, and Repercussions* (London: Brill, 2002). See also Kend Benedict Gravelle, "Islamic Law in Sudan: A Comparative Analysis," *Journal of International and Comparative Law* 5, no. 1 (1988): 1–22; Carolyn Fleur-Lobban, "Islamicization in Sudan: A Critical Assessment," *Middle East Journal* 44, no. 4 (1990): 610–623; El-Affendi, *Turabi's Revolution*; and Carolyn Fleur-Lobban, *Islamic Law and Society in Sudan* (London: Frank Cass, 1987).
67. Tim Niblock, "Sudan's Economic Nightmare," *Middle East Research and Information Project (MERIP)* 135 (1985):15–32.
68. Mansour, *The Government They Deserve*, 312–324.
69. Wickham, *Mobilizing Islam.*
70. El-Affendi, *Turabi's Revolution*, 113.
71. Mohammed Bashir Hamid, *The Politics of National Reconciliation in the Sudan: The Numayri Regime and the National Front Opposition, 1956–1985*, Washington DC: Center for Contemporary Arab Studies at Georgetown University (1984).
72. Ibid., 9. Similar arguments are made by Gabriel Warburg. See "The *Sharia* in Sudan: Implementation and Repercussions, 1983–1989," *The Middle East Journal* 44, no. 4 (1990): 624–637. And Layish and Warburg, *The Reinstatement of Islamic Law*, 41–50.
73. Layish and Warburg, *The Reinstatement of Islamic Law*, 35.
74. See, e.g., Abdullahi Ali Ibrahim, *Manichean Delirium: Decolonizing the Judiciary and Islamic Renewal in Sudan, 1898–1985* (Leiden: Brill, 2008), 222; Peter Woodward, *Sudan, 1898–1989: The Unstable State* (London: Lynne Rienner Publishers, 1990), 158; Victoria Bernal, "Islam, Transnational Culture, and Modernity in Rural Sudan," in *Gendered Encounters: Challenging Cultural Boundaries and Social Hierarchies in Africa*, ed. Maria Grosz-Ngate and Omari Kokole (New York: Routledge Press, 1997).
75. Elbadawi, *Islamic Finance*, 221–272.
76. Alex De Waal, ed., *Islamism and Its Enemies in the Horn of Africa* (Bloomington: Indiana University Press, 2004), 80.
77. Layish and Warburg, *The Reinstatement of Islamic Law*, 144–145.
78. Tamir Moustafa, *The Struggle for Constitutional Power: Law, Politics, and Economic Development in Egypt* (Cambridge, UK: Cambridge University Press, 2007).
79. Abdelrahman Omer Moheilddin, *Turabi wa al-inqath* [*Turabi and the 'Salvation'*] (Damascus, Syria: Dar Ekrema Publishing, 2006), 176.
80. Gabriel R. Warburg, *The Muslim Brotherhood in Sudan*, 5.
81. Moheildin, *Turabi and the "Salvation,"* 178.

82. Ibid., 27.
83. Ibid., 28.
84. Ibid., 27.
85. Sudan National Democratic Alliance, "Bayyan min far' al-tadamun al-watani al-dimuqrati bi Washington," [Memorandum from the Branch of the National Democratic Alliance in Washington] *Sudan National Democratic Alliance* (unpublished document, January 5, 1989).
86. Niblock, *Class and Power*, 226.
87. Sudan National Democratic Alliance, "Bayyan min far' al-tadammun al-watani al-dimuqrati bi Washington."
88. Ibid.
89. Ibid.
90. Mubarak al-Fadl (former Sudanese minister of the interior), interview in *Al-Hayat*, /September 2–3, 1989.

## ISLAMIC VERSUS CLAN NETWORKS: LABOR REMITTANCES, HAWWALA BANKING, AND THE PREDATORY STATE IN SOMALIA

1. Title III, USA PATRIOT Act of 2001, 107 P.L. 56, 115 Stat. 272, 2001.
2. Title II of P.L. 95–223 (codified at 50 U.S.C. 1701 et seq).
3. US law enforcement official also shut down al-Barakaat headquarters in Dubai, and its offices in Boston, Minneapolis, Columbus, and Seattle, as well as in Mogadishu and Bossaso, in southern and northeast Somalia, respectively.
4. One senior US official said that the incriminating information came from a single source. As he put it at the time: "This is not normally the way we do things. We needed to make splash. We needed to designate now, and sort it out later." *New York Times*, April 13, 2002.
5. *Reuters*, December 5, 2001.
6. "Chapter 5: Al-Barakaat Case Study," in National Commission on Terrorist Attacks upon the United States, *The 9/11 Commission Report: Final Report of the National Commission on Terrorist Attacks upon the United States.* New York: Norton, 2004.
7. *BBC News*, "US Ends Somali Banking Backlist," *BBC News*, August 28, 2006.
8. The World Bank, *World Bank Makes Progress to Support Remittance Flows to Somalia*, June 10, 2016, accessed August 9, 2019. www.worldbank.org/en/news/press-release/2016/06/10/world-bank-makes-progress-to-support-remittance-flows-to-somalia.
9. "Financial Action Task Force," *Terrorist Financing* (Paris: Organization for Economic Cooperation and Development, 2008), 8. See also the initial report on the subject, *Financial Action Task Force on Money Laundering: Combating the Abuse of Non-Profit Organizations* (Paris: Organization for Economic Cooperation and Development, 2002), 1.
10. For a comprehensive analysis of the effect of the War on Terrorist Finance, see Jennifer Turner, "Blocking Faith, Freezing Charity: Chilling Muslim

Charitable Giving In the 'War on Terrorist Financing'" (New York: American Civil Liberties Union, June 2009).

11. For more on the development of contemporary Muslim pious activism, see Mahmoud, *Politics of Piety*, 3.
12. Jane R. Harrigan and Hamid el-Said, *Economic Liberalisation, Social Capital and Islamic Welfare* (New York: Palgrave MacMillan, 2009).
13. See, e.g., Medani, "Funding Fundamentalism."
14. Charles Tripp, *Islam and the Moral Economy: the Challenge of Capitalism* (Cambridge, New York: Cambridge University Press, 2006).
15. A number of scholars and policy analysts have argued that there is a link between failed states and international terrorism. See, most notably, Stephen D. Krasner and Carlos Pascual, "Addressing State Failure," *Foreign Affairs* (2002): 153–163; Sebastian Mallay, "The Reluctant Imperialist: Terrorism, Failed States, and the Case for American Empire," *Foreign Affairs* (2002): 2–7.
16. Associated Press, November 28, 2001.
17. Kathleen Day, "US Islamic Cash Outlets Investigated as Source for Terror Funds," Washington Post, November 7, 2001. www.unitedstatesaction.com/islam-money-changing.htm.
18. By January 1, 2002, anyone who wants to operate a money transfer agency in the United States must obtain a license from the Department of Commerce. The application must show a net worth of $100,000 and pay upward of $70,000 in licensing fees – the most expensive application for a nonbanking financial institution in the United States. *Financial Times*, January 5, 2002.
19. One Treasury Department investigator admitted that the hawwalat system is an "alien concept" to US authorities. *Financial Times*, January 17, 2002.
20. Vali Jamal, "Somalia: Understanding an Unconventional Economy," *Development and Change* 19, no. 2 (1988): 203–265.
21. Anna Lindley, "Migrant Remittances in the Context of Crisis in Somali Society," (London: Overseas Development Institute, Humanitarian Policy Group, 2006). See also, Mark Bradbury, *Becoming Somaliland* (London: James Currey, 2008).
22. Khalid M. Medani, "Survey on Internal Migration and Remittance Inflows in Northwest and Northeast Somalia" (Nairobi, Kenya: United Nations Coordination Unit (UNCU), 2000).
23. It is worth noting that the average Somali household is composed of eight members.
24. *Reuters*, December 3, 2001.
25. Director of Amal Hawwalat Agency, interview with the author, July 14, 2010, Nairobi, Kenya.
26. For a good review of this literature, see Peter Andreas, "Illicit International Political Economy: The Clandestine side of Globalization," *Review of International Political Economy* 11, no. 3 (2004): 641–652.
27. Mark Bradbury also makes this important point. See Bradbury, *Becoming Somaliland*, 150.
28. *Africa Confidential*, July 12, 1990.

29. For a comprehensive analysis of the distinctive nature and political objectives of insurgent militia organizations, see Weinstein, *Inside Rebellion*.
30. Interviews with Dahabshil Hawalat Brokers, December 14, 2000, Hargeisa, Boroma, and Boosaso, Somalia.
31. Director of Amal Hawwalat, interview with the author, July 14, 2010, Nairobi, Kenya.
32. The above figure is derived from interviews with al-Barakaat and Dahabshil representatives in Hargeisa and Bossaso.
33. Director of Amal Hawwalat, interview with the author, July 14, 2010, Nairobi, Kenya.
34. Hawwalat brokers freely discuss their support of al-Ittihad but firmly deny any interest in Somalia's militants. As one broker informed me: "Why would we support them? They are bad for business." Interview with Amal Hawwalat Broker, June 15, 2010, Nairobi, Kenya.
35. Interviews with manager, and staff, of the Mattawikil Hawwalat, July 20, 2010, Nairobi, Kenya. Remittance brokers stated that young Somalis join the militant al-Shabbaab for two reasons: a decidedly low level of education and poor employment prospects. It is worth noting that *al-Shabbaab* enjoyed unprecedented success in its recruitment drives following the Ethiopian invasion and US air bombing of central Somalia beginning in the summer of 2006 and not due to funds received from the *hawwalat.*
36. David D. Laitin and Said S. Samatar, *Somalia: A Nation in Search of a State* (Boulder, CO: Westview Press, 1987), 45.
37. Ibid., 41–44.
38. Abdi I. Samatar, "Dictators and Warlords Are a Modern Invention," *Africa News*, January 3, 1993, 5.
39. Goran Hyden, *African Politics in Comparative Perspective* (New York: Cambridge University Press, 2008).
40. I. M. Lewis, *A Modern History of Somalia: Nation and State in the Horn of Africa* (Boulder, CO: Westview Press, 1987), 170–171.
41. Abdi I. Samatar, *The State and Rural Transformation in Northern Somalia, 1884–1986* (Madison: University of Wisconsin Press, 1989), 80–81.
42. Ibid., 86.
43. Michael Bratton makes this important general point in his review of Goran Hyden's *No Shortcuts to Progress* (London: Heineman, 1983). Michael Bratton, "Beyond the State: Civil Society and Associational Life in Africa," *World Politics* 41 (April 1989): 413.
44. Goran Hyden, *No Shortcuts to Progress*, 7.
45. Clifford Geertz, *The Interpretation of Cultures* (New York: Basic Book, 1973), 225–310.
46. Jamal, "Somalia: Understanding an Unconventional Economy."
47. Ibid.
48. A. A. Aboagye, *The Informal Sector in Mogadishu: An Analysis of a Survey* (Addis Ababa: International Labour Organisation/Jobs and Skills Programme for Africa, 1988).
49. Ibid., 222.
50. World Bank, *World Debt Tables*.

51. David D. Laitin and Said S. Samatar, "Somalia and the World Economy," *Review of African Political Economy* 11, no. 30 (1984): 71.
52. *African Business*, "Will the Forex Bureaux Close Zongo Lane?" *African Business*, June 1989, 1–2.
53. Jamal, "Somalia: Understanding an Unconventional Economy," 213.
54. Laitian and S. S. Samatar, "Somalia and the World Economy," 45.
55. John Markakis, *National and Class Conflict in the Horn of Africa* (Cambridge, UK: Cambridge University Press, 1987), 222.
56. Jamal, "Somalia: Understanding an Unconventional Economy," 224.
57. *The Somali Social and Institutional Profile: An Executive Summary* (Working Papers, no. 79, African Studies Center, Boston University), 5.
58. Aboagye, "The Informal Sector in Mogadishu," 13.
59. Ibid., 93.
60. Abdi I. Samatar, "Destruction of State and Society in Somalia: Beyond the Tribal Convention," *Journal of Modern African Studies* 30, no. 4 (1992): 625.
61. Vali Jamal, "Somalia: Understanding an Unconventional Economy," 243.
62. Kiren Aziz Chaudhry, "The Price of Wealth: Business and State in Labor Remittance and Oil Economies," *International Organization* 43 (Winter 1989), 112.
63. David D. Laitin and Said S. Samatar, "Somalia and the World Economy," Review of African Political Economy, 58–72.
64. *IMF Adjustment Programs in Africa: 1985 Occasional Paper*, no. 5 (Washington, DC: International Monetary Fund, 1985).
65. By the end of the 1980s, the formal financial sector essentially collapsed. The Commercial and Savings Bank was declared officially bankrupt, and none of the few formal banks in the country were able to provide lending by the end of the decade. Mubarak, "The 'Hidden Hand,'" 2028.
66. To make matters worse for Somalis dependent on the formal economy for their wages, salaries of the civil service drastically declined in 1989 to less than 3 percent compared to their levels in the early 1970s. Ibid., 2028.
67. Charles Tilly, "Trust and Rule," *Theory and Society*, vol. 33, 2004: 1-30.

## ECONOMIC CRISIS, INFORMAL INSTITUTIONS, AND THE TRANSFORMATION OF ISLAMIST POLITICS IN EGYPT

1. Significantly, no reductions in military spending were considered as military spending was drastically increased. Springborg, "Egypt," 47.
2. World Bank, World Bank World Debt Tables.
3. Hinnebusch, "The Politics of Economic Reform," 161.
4. Adly, "When Cheap Is Costly," 295.
5. Ibid.
6. "La li-qanun al-tawari: al-mu'arada tarfud al-qanun 'al-aswad li-tadmir sharikat tawsif al-amwal [No to the Emergency Law: The Opposition Rejects the 'Black Law' Designed to Destroy the Islamic Investment Houses], *Al-Sha'ab*, June 14, 1988.

7. Amira Howeidy, "Matariyya, Egypt's New Theater of Dissent," *Middle East Report Online*, June 4, 2015, https://merip.org/2015/06/matariyya-egypts-new-theater-of-dissent/.
8. *Mudun Masr Taht al-Hisar* [Egyptian Cities under Siege], *Al-Sha'ab*, January 19, 1993.
9. Diane Singerman, "The Siege of Imbaba, Egypt's Internal 'Other,' and the Criminalization of Politics," in *Cairo Contested: Governance, Urban Space, and Global Modernity*, ed. Diane Singerman (Cairo: American University in Cairo Press, 2011).
10. Mamoun Fandy, "Egypt's Islamic Group: Regional Revenge?" *Middle East Journal* 48, no. 4 (1994): 607–625; Hamdi Nasr, *Ta'mulat fi 'Unf wa Tobah al-Jama'a al-Islamiyya* [Reflections on the Violence and Repentance of the Jama'a al-Islamiyya], (Alexandria: Dar al-Ein Publishing, 2010).
11. *Al-Sha'ab*, "The Crisis Continues in Imbaba: Expect More Clashes," *Al-Sha'ab*, December 15, 1992.
12. *Al-Hayat*, "Cairo: Detention of 290 Fundamentalist Militants in a Wide Campaign in Imbaba," *Al-Hayat*, December 9, 1992.
13. Of the twenty-five Brotherhood leaders arrested in 2007 and sentenced in 2008, ten (i.e., 40 percent) were among the most prominent businessmen in the organization residing in Egypt such as Ahmed Abdel 'Ati, and Ahmed Ashraf as well as abroad in the Gulf, Turkey, and Europe including, most notably, Youssef Nada and Himmat Shater Zayat. However, the greatest damage to the group's financial infrastructure was the arrest of the two top businessmen, Shater and Hassan Malek, who funded an estimated one-third of the group's expenses, with another one-third coming from small traders, and the final third from membership dues. *Moneep*, "Natayij al-Ahkam al-'Askariyya 'ala al-Ikhwan al-Muslimeen" [Results of the Military Verdicts against the Muslim Brotherhood], *Moneep*, March 5, 2008.
14. Among some of the most important of these publishing houses are *Dar Ibn Sinna*, *Dar al-Wafaa*, *Dar Jaffa*, *Dar Mecca*, *Dar al-Zahra al-Islamiyya*, and, perhaps most notably, *Dar al-Tawzi' wa al-Nashr al-Islamiyya* which distributed a series of extremely popular pamphlets of the writings of the Muslim Brotherhood.
15. *Moneep, Natayij al-Ahkam al-'Askariyya 'ala al-Ikhwan al-Muslimeen.*
16. Soliman, "The Rise and Decline," 266.
17. Utvik, *Islamist Economics*.
18. Ahmed 'Alawi (member of the Muslim Brotherhood), interview with the author, November 6, 1998, Imbaba, Cairo: Egypt.
19. Ahmed 'Alawi, interview with author, Cairo: Egypt.
20. Abdel-Fadil, 66, cited in Utvik, *Islamist Economics*, 205.
21. Samer Soliman, "The Rise and Decline," 272.
22. Ibid.
23. Ibid., 276.
24. Ibid., 6.
25. Daria Solovieva, "A Trillion Dollars and Counting: How Egypt's New President Will Boost Islamic Banking," *International Business Times*, July 18, 2012. See also Jonathan G. Burns, "The Banking Sector in Post-Revolution Egypt: Is Islam the Solution?" *Banking & Finance Law Review* 319, no. 2 (2014): 319–352.

26. Solovieva, "A Trillion Dollars and Counting: How Egypt's New President Will Boost Islamic Banking,"
27. Ibrahim Nur, *Al-Siyassah al-Iqtisadiyya li-al-Ikhwan*, [The Brotherhood's Economic Policy] (Cairo: Markaz al-Mahrusi Publishing, 2014), 139–140.
28. As of 2015 there were only three Islamic banks operating under an Islamic formula, and eleven other institutions offering Islamic banking services, sharia compliant finance. Solovieva, "A Trillion Dollars and Counting: How Egypt's New President Will Boost Islamic Banking."
29. Ibid.
30. *Al-Syasi al-Masri*, August 27, 1995.
31. *Al-Hayat*, November 15, 1995. The secretary general of the Nasserist Party, Dia al-Din Daoud, stated that they pulled out of their coalition with the Tagammu Party in Imbaba in order to avoid any violent clashes that might take place in an area where the Muslim Brothers and other Islamist groups enjoyed overwhelming popularity. *Al-Ahali*, November 1, 1995.
32. Abdel Hamid Barak, "A Study on the Imbaba Elections," Unpublished Report, Al-Ahram Center for Strategic Studies, Cairo, 1996.
33. *May Newspaper*, November 11, 1995.
34. *Sawt Giza* (Voice of Giza), November 1995.
35. *Al-Masaa*, November 15, 1995.
36. *Al-Wafd*, November 10, 1995; *Al-Wafd*, November 19, 1995; *Al-Wafd*, November 28, 1995.
37. *Al-Ahali*, December 1, 1995.
38. Ibid.
39. E.g., Abdel Hamid Barakat ran in his neighborhood of al-Munira al-Gharbiyya, and Salah al-Maliji in al-Mo'tadadiyya where he had strong kinship ties among local residents.
40. *Al-Sha'ab*, November 31, 1995; *Al-Sha'ab*, November 11, 1995.
41. "A study on the Imbaba Elections," Unpublished Report, Al-Ahram Center for Strategic Studies, Cairo (1996).
42. Ibid.
43. Hala Mustafa ed. *Al-intikhabat al-barlamaniyya fi Misr: 1995* [The 1995 Parliamentary Elections in Egypt] (Cairo: Al-Ahram Center for Political and Strategic Studies, 1995).
44. Ibid.
45. Wagih Abdel-Raziq (member of the Muslim Brotherhood), interview with the author, December 12, 1998, Al-Waraq, Imbaba, Cairo: Egypt.
46. Ibid.
47. Ibid.
48. Wagih Abdel-Raziq (member of the Muslim Brotherhood), interview with the author, December 12, 1998, Al-Waraq, Imbaba, Cairo: Egypt.
49. Author's interview with Muslim Brotherhood local leader, November 19, 2009, Helwan, Cairo: Egypt.
50. Ibrahim El Houdaiby, "Islamism in and after Egypt's Revolution," in *The Arab Spring in Egypt: Revolution and Beyond*, ed. Bahgat Korany and Rabab El-Mahdi (Cairo: American University in Cairo Press, 2012), 125.

51. ‘Issam al-Eryan, interview with the author, December 21, 2009, Cairo, Egypt.
52. I am grateful to Hossam Tamman for this insight. Author’s interview with Hossam Tamman, Cairo, November 14, 2008.
53. Interview with Muslim Brotherhood local leader, Cairo, November 24, 2008.
54. Ibid.
55. Professor Abdel Hamid al-Ghazali, interview with the author, December 18, 2009, Cairo: Egypt.
56. Wagih Abdel-Raziq Abu Rawash (member of the Muslim Brotherhood), interview with the author, December 12, 1998, Al-Waraq, Imbaba, Cairo: Egypt.
57. Ibid.
58. Ibid.
59. Salim Ahmed Omer (Muslim Brotherhood Member), interview with the author, January 20, 2009, Masr al-Gedida (New Cairo): Egypt.
60. Hossam Tamman, *Al-Ikhwan al-Muslimeen: Sanawat Ma Qabl al-Thawra* [The Muslim Brotherhood: The Years before the Revolution] (Cairo: Dar al-Shuruq, 2013), 95–135.
61. Ibid.
62. Tarek Ladjal and Benaouda Bensaid, “Sufism and Politics in Contemporary Egypt: A Study of Sufi Political Engagement in the Pre- and Post-revolutionary Reality of January 2011,” *Journal of Asian and African Studies* 50, no. 4 (2015): 9.
63. A. Al-Asnawi. “The New Face of Sufism: Transformation towards Politics,” *Al-Ahram Numbered Journal* (2011). http://digital.ahram.org.eg/articles.aspx?Serial=715044&eid=15, cited in Ladjal and Bensaid, “Sufism and Politics in Contemporary Egypt,” 9.
64. Ladjal and Bensaid, “Sufism and Politics in Contemporary Egypt,” 1–19.
65. Singerman, “The Siege of Imbaba,” 129–137.
66. Ibid., 111–144.
67. By the mid-1990s radical Islamist groups were responsible for an estimated 221 episodes of violence in Cairo up from 19 from the 1970s, a rise of 163 percent from the 1970s. Nemaat Guenena and Saad Eddin Ibrahim, “The Changing Face of Egypt’s Islamic Activism: 1974–1995,” unpublished manuscript (Cairo: Ibn Khaldun Center for Development Studies, September 1995).
68. Manal El-Batran and Christian Arandel, “A Shelter of Their Own: Informal Settlement Expansion in Greater Cairo and Government Responses,” *Environment and Urbanization* 10, no. 1 (April 1998): 217–232.

## FROM REMITTANCE ECONOMY TO RENTIER STATE: THE RISE AND FALL OF AN ISLAMIST AUTHORITARIAN REGIME IN SUDAN

1. For a detailed history of this period see Robert O. Collins, *A History of Modern Sudan* (Cambridge, UK: Cambridge University Press, 2008), 193.

2. Jean-Francois Bayart, *The State in Africa: The Politics of the Belly* (Cambridge, UK: Polity, 2009).
3. Since upward of 90 percent of the Islamic banks' investments went into import-export businesses, the NIF did succeed in dominating urban commercial enterprises at the expense of the Khatmiyya supporters who had controlled this sector in the past.
4. International Crisis Group, "God, Oil, and Country: Changing the Logic of War in Sudan," Executive Summary Report, no. 39 (January 10, 2004): 24–27.
5. *African Business*, "IMF Awaits Reforms as Aid Donors Hang Back," *African Business*, July 1989, 35.
6. Among the two most notable organizations are the Islamic Relief Agency (al-Da'wa al-Islamiyya) and the Islamic African Center (al-Markaz al-Islami al-Ifriqi). The latter offered USD 100 monthly to military officers who registered for Islamic studies and financial rewards upon completion.
7. Mohamed. O. El Sammani, "Management Problems of Greater Khartoum," in *African Cities in Crisis: Managing Rapid Urban Growth*, ed. Richard. E. Stren and Rodney R. White (Boulder, CO: Westview Press, 1989): 247–275.
8. Ibid.
9. *African Business*, "Technocrats May End Naïve Policies," *African Business*, September 1989, 58.
10. Gretchen Helmke and Steven Levitsky, "Informal Institutions and Comparative Politics: A Research Agenda," *Perspectives on Politics* 2, no. 4 (2004): 725–740.
11. Abdou Maliqalim Simone, *In Whose Image? Political Islam and Urban Practices* (Chicago: University of Chicago Press, 1994), 104.
12. *African Business*, "Subsidies Row Continues," *African Business*, September 1993, 35.
13. *Horn of Africa Bulletin*, "Foreign Currency Dealing Act Amended," *Horn of Africa Bulletin*, January 1994, 35.
14. Ibid.
15. Author's interview with black-market currency trader, April 1994, Khartoum: Sudan. Name withheld by request.
16. Stiansen, "Interest Politics," 164.
17. Ibid.
18. Clement M. Henry and Rodney Wilson, "Introduction," *The Politics of Islamic Finance*, ed. Clement M. Henry and Rodney Wilson (Edinburgh: Edinburgh University Press, 2004), 2–3.
19. Ibid., 166.
20. Collins, *A History of Modern Sudan*, 221.
21. Luke Anthony Patey, "State Rules: Oil Companies and Armed Conflict in Sudan," *Third World Quarterly*, 28, no. 5, (2007): 997–1016.
22. Paul Collier, *The Bottom Million: Why the Poorest Countries Are Failing and What Can Be Done about It* (Oxford: Oxford University Press,

2007); Pauline Luong and Erika Weinthal, "Rethinking the Resource Curse: Ownership Structure, Institutional Capacity, and Domestic Constraints," *Annual Review of Political Science* 9 (2006): 241–263. Michael Ross, "A Closer Look at Oil, Diamonds, and Civil War," *Annual Review of Political Science* 9 (2006): 265–300; Michael Ross, "Does Oil Hinder Democracy?" *World Politics* 53, no. 3 (2001): 325–361.

23. Luong and Weinthal, "Rethinking the Resource Curse," 241.
24. The World Bank, Sudan Public Expenditure Review: Synthesis Report No. 41840-SD (December 2007).
25. Ibid.
26. Francis M. Deng, "Sudan: A Nation in Turbulent Search of Itself," *The ANNALS of the American Academy of Political and Social Science* 603, no. 1 (2006): 155–162; Heather J. Sharkey, "Arab Identity and Ideology in Sudan: The Politics of Language, Ethnicity and Race," *African Affairs* 107, no. 426 (January 2008): 21–43.
27. Deng, "Sudan: A Nation in Turbulent Search of Itself," 159.
28. Ibid.
29. Paul Collier and Anke Hoeffler, "Greed and Grievance in Civil War," *Oxford Economic Papers* 56, no. 4 (2004): 563–595.
30. Macartan Humphreys, "Natural Resources, Conflict, and Resolution: Uncovering the Mechanisms," *The Journal of Conflict Resolution* 49, no. 4 (2005): 508–537.
31. Luke A. Patey, "State Rules: Oil Companies and Armed Conflict in Sudan," *Third World Quarterly* 28, no. 5 (2007): 5.
32. Abdullahi A. Gallab, *The First Islamic Republic: Development and Disintegration of Islamism in Sudan* (London: Ashgate Publishing 2008).
33. Henry and Wilson, *The Politics of Islamic Finance*, 16.
34. Kim Murphy, "Islamic Militants Build Power Base in Sudan: The Regime Vows to Export Beliefs Worrying It's More Secular Arab Neighbors and the West," *The Los Angeles Times*, April 6, 1992, 5.
35. Ibid.
36. Magdi El Gizouli, "Sudan: Khartoum-the Political Economy of Bankruptcy," *Sudan Tribune*, June 23, 2012.
37. Alex Thurston, "Northern Sudan's Protests Sparked by Egypt and Tunisia, But Will They Have the Same Effect?" *Christian Science Monitor*, January 31, 2011.
38. Jeffrey Gettleman, "Young Sudanese Start Movement," *New York Times*, February 2, 2011. For a more cautious analysis that does not directly address Sudan, see Marc Lynch, "Will the Arab Revolutions Spread?" *Foreign Policy*, January 26, 2011.
39. Eva Bellin, "The Robustness of Authoritarianism in the Middle East: Exceptionalism in Comparative Perspective," *Comparative Politics* 36, no.2 (2004): 139–157.
40. Medani M. Ahmed, *Global Financial Crisis Discussion Series Paper 19: Sudan Phase 2* (London: Overseas Development Institute, February 2010), 1–2.

41. International Crisis Group, "Divisions in Sudan's Ruling Party and the Threat to the Country's Future Stability," *Africa Report*, no. 174 (May 4, 2011): 1–34.
42. The National Population Council, Ministry of Social Welfare and Security, "Draft Report: The Millennium Development Goals (MDGs): Status, Challenges and Prospects for Sudan." Khartoum, Sudan, March 2012, 11–22.
43. Ibid.
44. World Bank, Sudan Public Expenditure Review: Synthesis Report. World Bank, Report no. 41840-SD. Washington, DC. December, 2007.
45. "Pro-Salafist Newspaper Blasts Sudan's Bashir, Calls Him a 'Serial Liar.'" *Sudan Tribune*, March 6, 2013. *Al-Muharir* was the mouthpiece of the Salafist group led by Mohamed Abdel-Kareem.
46. Africa Economic Outlook (AEO), 2012.
47. Marwan Bishara, *The Invisible Arab: The Promise and Peril of the Arab Revolutions* (New York: Nation Books, 2012), p.14.
48. Author's interviews with Youth leaders of Girifna and Sudan Change Now. February 2013. Khartoum: Sudan.
49. Ilda Lindell, "Introduction," in *Africa's Informal Workers*, ed. Ilda Lindell (London: Zed Books, 2010), 22–23.

## STATE COLLAPSE, INFORMAL NETWORKS, AND THE DILEMMA OF STATE BUILDING IN SOMALIA

1. Mark Bradbury, *Becoming Somaliland.*
2. Mark Bradbury, Adan Yusuf Abokor, and Haroon Ahmed Yusuf, "Somaliland: Choosing Politics over Violence," *Review of African Political Economy* 30, no. 97 (2003): 455–478; *BBC News*, "Voters Defy Islamist Threats in Somaliland," *BBC News*, September 2001.
3. Dahabshil, which became the model for all other hawwalat in Somalia, was first established in 1971. Originally it was a small retail store established in the town of Burao that sold clothes and food stuff imported primarily from the Gulf. By the early 1980s, it expanded across northern Somalia as a result of both the onset of the civil war and the boom in remittances from expatriate Somalis. Dahabshil staff member, interview with the author, December 7, 1999. Burao, Somaliland.
4. James Cockayne and Liat Shetret, *Capitalizing on Trust: Harnessing Somali Remittances for Counterterrorism, Human Rights and State Building* (Goshen, IN: Center on Global Counterterrorism Cooperation, 2012), 52. www.globalcenter.org/wp-content/uploads/2012/07/CapitalizingOnTrust.pdf.
5. Jamil A. Mubarak, "The 'Hidden Hand,'" 2028.
6. Jamal, "Somalia: Understanding an Unconventional Economy," 235.
7. Ibid.
8. Ibid.

9. Roland Marchal, *Final Report on the Post Civil War Somali Business Class* (Paris: European Commission, Somalia Unit, 1996), 24.
10. I. M. Lewis, "The Ogaden War," 59. Jutta Bakonyi and Kirsti Stuvoy, "Violence and Social Order beyond the State: Somalia and Angola," *Review of African Political Economy* 32, no. 104 (2005): 359–382.
11. "Wounded North, Bruised South," *Africa Confidential*, November 18, 1988, 2–4.
12. *Africa Confidential*, July 12, 1990.
13. See *Africa Watch, Somalia: A Fight to the Death?* (Washington: Human Rights Watch, February 13, 1992).
14. Bakonyi and Stuvoy, "Violence and Social Order," 377.
15. Daniel Compagnon, "Somali Armed Movements: The Interplay of Political Entrepreneurship and Clan-Based Factions," in *African Guerillas*, ed. Christopher Clapham (Bloomington: Indiana University Press, 1998); and I. M. Lewis, "Doing Violence to Ethnography: A Response to Catherine Besteman's 'Representing Violence and "Othering" Somalia,'" *Cultural Anthropology* 13, no. 1 (1994): 100–108.
16. Abdi I. Samatar, "Leadership and Ethnicity in the Making of African State Models: Botswana versus Somalia," *Third World Quarterly* 18, no. 4 (1992): 687–708; and I. M. Lewis, "Doing Violence to Ethnography," 232.
17. Marchal, *Final Report*, 132.
18. A. I. Samatar, "Destruction of State and Society," 625.
19. Ken Menkhaus, "State Collapse in Somalia: Second Thoughts," *Review of African Political Economy* 30, no. 97 (2003): 405–422.
20. Bakonyi and Stuvoy, "Violence and Social Order," 366.
21. A. I. Samatar, "Destruction of State and Society," 640.
22. Jason Peter Pham, "The Somaliland Exception: Lessons on Post-Conflict State Building from the Part of the Former Somalia That Works," *Marine Corps University Journal* 3, no. 1 (2012): 1–33.
23. Mark Bradbury, *Somaliland: CIIR Country Report* (London: CIIR, 2003).
24. Ken Menkhaus, "Governance without Government in Somalia: Spoilers, State Building, and the Politics of Coping," *International Security* 31, no. 3 (Winter 2006–7): 74–106.
25. International Crisis Group, "Somalia: The Trouble with Puntland," *Africa Briefing*, no. 63, (August 12, 2009), 1–15.
26. Waldo Mohamad, interview with the author, January 24, 2010, Nairobi: Kenya.
27. Ibid.
28. Ibid.
29. Ken Menkhaus, "The Crisis in Somalia: Tragedy in Five Acts," *African Affairs* 106, no. 204 (2007): 357–390; and Cedric Barnes and Hamed Hassan, "The Rise and Fall of Mogadishu's Islamic Courts," *Journal of Eastern African Studies* 1, no. 2 (2007): 151–160.
30. Charles Tilly, "War Making and State Making as Organized Crime," in *Bringing the State Back In*, ed. Peter B. Evans, Dietrich Rueschemeir and Theda Skocpol (Cambridge, UK: Cambridge University Press, 1985).

31. Charles Tilly, *Coercion, Capital and European States, AD 990–1990* (Cambridge, UK: Cambridge University Press, 1990), 3.
32. Jeffrey Herbst, *States and Power in Africa: Comparative Lessons in Authority and Control* (Princeton, NJ: Princeton University Press, 1990).
33. Barbara F. Walter, "The Critical Barrier to Civil War Settlement," *International Organization* 51, no. 3 (1997): 335–364; and James D. Fearon and David D. Laitin, "Ethnicity, Insurgency, and Civil War," *Political Science Review* 97, no. 1 (2003): 75–90.
34. Michael C. Desch, "War and Strong States, Peace and Weak States?" *International Organization* 50, no. 4 (1996): 242; and Herbst, *States and Power in Africa*, 26.
35. Tilly, "War Making and State Making," 183.
36. It is important to emphasize that Puntland is more homogenous than neighboring Somaliland.
37. Charles Tilly, "Trust and Rule," 1.
38. Samatar 1997; Lewis, *A Modern History of the Somali.*
39. Lewis 1994; Lewis, *A Modern History of the Somali.*
40. Kibble 2001; Lewis, *A Modern History of the Somali.*
41. Lewis, *A Modern History of the Somali*, 15–16.
42. A. I. Samatar, "Destruction of State and Society," 630.
43. Ibid., 637.
44. Ibid.
45. Ibid.
46. Dr. Ahmad Yusuf Farah, interview with the author, October 2, 1994, Nairobi: Kenya.
47. Steve Kibble. "Somaliland: Surviving without Recognition"; Somalia: Recognized But Failing?" *International Relations* 15, no. 5 (2001): 11.
48. Mark Bradbury, "Somaliland: Changing Minds Changing Lives." *CIIR*, (1997): 1–48; Samatar, "Leadership and Ethnicity."
49. William Reno, "Somalia and Survival in the Shadow of the Global Economy," Queen Elizabeth House (QEH) Working Papers, 2003: 8–12.
50. Ibid., 12.
51. Reno. "Somalia and Survival." Ibid., 15.
52. Lewis, *A Modern History of the Somali.*
53. Samatar 1992: 637.
54. Lewis, *A Modern History of the Somali*, 222.
55. Reno, "Somalia and Survival."
56. Ibid., 15.
57. I. M. Lewis, *Blood and Bone: The Call of Kinship in Somali Society.* Lawrencevill, NJ: Red Sea Press, 1994: 178.
58. Ibid.
59. Bakonyi and Stuvoy, "Violence and Social Order."
60. Catherine L. Besteman, *Unraveling Somalia: Race, Class and the Legacy of Slavery*, University of Pennsylvania Press, 2003; Bakonyi and Stuvoy, "Violence and Social Order."

61. Daniel Campagnon, “Somali Armed Unites: The Interplay of Political Entrepreneurship and Clan-Based Factions,” in Christopher Clapham, ed. *African Guerillas* (Oxford University Press, James Currey, 1998), 76.
62. Lewis, *Blood and Bone*; Reno, “Somalia and Survival.”
63. Reno, “Somalia and Survival.”
64. Ibid.
65. Lewis, *A Modern History of the Somali*, 231.
66. Several scholars of Somalia have emphasized this point. See Samatar, 1992; Compagnon 1998; Reno 2003; Besteman 2003.
67. Bradbury, Abokor, and Yusuf, “Somaliland: Choosing Politics over Violence,” 97.
68. Lewis, *A Modern History of the Somali*; Bradbury, Abokor, and Yusuf, “Somaliland: Choosing Politics over Violence,” 459.
69. Bradbury, Abokor, and Yusuf, “Somaliland: Choosing Politics over Violence,” 97.
70. Lewis, *A Modern History of the Somali*, 476.
71. Ibid., 283.
72. Bradbury, Abokor, and Yusuf, “Somaliland: Choosing Politics over Violence,” 461.
73. Ibid.
74. Kibble, “Somaliland: Surviving.”
75. Hibaaq Osman, interview with author, February 2000, Hargeisa, Somaliland.
76. Ibid., 2.
77. Ibid.
78. Bradbury, Abokor, and Yusuf, “Somaliland: Choosing Politics over Violence,” 462.
79. Ibid.
80. Berouk Mesfin, “The Political Development of Somaliland and Its Conflict with Puntland,” *Institute for Security Studies Papers* 200 (2009): 2.
81. Kim Yi Dionne, Kris L. Inman, and Gabriella R. Montinola, “Another Resource Curse? The Impact of Remittances on Political Participation,” *Afrobarometer Working Papers*, no. 145 (2014): 17.
82. Somali business elites have regularly protested a host of regulatory measures by the state preferring to provide the state authorities loans and contributions rather than “paying sufficient taxes.” Ahmed M. Musa and Cindy Horst. “State Formation and Economic Development in Post-War Somaliland: The Impact of the Private Sector in an Unrecognized State,” *Conflict, Security and Development* 19, no. 1 (2019): 35–53.
83. A cross-country, individual-level analysis across twenty sub-Saharan African countries confirmed that rather than representing a resource curse, remittances may increase political participation. Ibid.
84. Pham, “The Somaliland Exception,” 26.
85. “Somailand’s Investment in Peace: Analysing the Diaspora’s Economic Engagement in Peace Building,” Hargeisa, Somaliland: Interpeace, June 2008: 11.
86. Ibid., 2.

87. Hibaaq Osman, interview with the author, June 2010, Nairobi: Kenya.
88. Mesfin, "The Political Development," 4.
89. In the period between February and March 1996, consumer prices of some basic food tripled, compared to an official rate of 50 per US$ in July 1995; the exchange rate of Somaliland's Shilling was around 5,300–5,600 per US$ in December 1996. Mubarak, "The 'Hidden Hand,'" 2038.
90. Interview with livestock traders. December 7, 1999. Buroa, Toghdeer: Somaliland.
91. Abdi Musa (FSAU team leader), interview with the author, December 1999, Hargeisa: Somaliland.
92. International Crisis Group, "Somalia: The Trouble with Puntland," 3.
93. Ibid.
94. Ibid., 4–5.
95. Ibid., 6
96. Dr. Ahmad Yusif Farah, interview with the author, October 2, 1994, Nairobi: Kenya.
97. Ibid.
98. Ibid.
99. James C. McKinley, "Islamic Movement's Niche: Bringing Order to Somalia's Clans," *New York Times*, August 23, 1996.
100. The hybrid political system established allowed every subclan of the Darod/ Harti family to nominate a parliamentarian endorsed by subclan leaders but when intraclan conflicts resumed the system fell apart resulting in the failure of state building in the northeast region of Somalia.
101. Ibid., 6.
102. Medani, "Report on Internal Migration."
103. General branch manager of Amal Hawwalat, interview with the author, June 14, 2010, Nairobi: Kenya.
104. Control over the port – the lucrative economic lifeline of the northeast – resulted in a desire for political control as well. By the early 1990s, al-Ittihad was in a strong position to impose a new form of "Islamic rule" on a society deeply apprehensive of any form of totalitarianism. The threat posed by al-Ittihad galvanized support for the SSDF, which previously had received only lukewarm support from the local population for anything beyond its military role in instituting measures to promote security. In 1992, a year after al-Ittihad had taken over the port of Bossaso and after a bitter armed conflict, the SSDF wrenched control of Bossaso port from al-Ittihad, and subsequent Puntland government authorities have administered the port ever since.
105. Ibid.
106. Isaaq and Majerteen businessmen, interviews with the author, June 17, 2010, Nairobi: Kenya. Names withheld by request.
107. Al-Ittihad members, interviews with the author, April 2000, Gerowe: Puntland. Names withheld by request.
108. Roland Marchal, "A Tentative Assessment of the Somali Harakat Al-Shabaab," *Journal of Eastern African Studies* 3, no. 3 (2009): 381–404.

109. Al-Ittihad members, interviews with the author, April 2000, Gerowe: Puntland, Names withheld by request.
110. Cedric Barns and H. Hassan, 2007, 150.
111. Andre Le Sage, "Somalia: Sovereign disguise for a Mogadishu Mafia," *Review of African Political Economy*, 29, no. 91 (2001): 475.
112. Cedric Barnes and H. Hassan, 2007, 152.
113. Abdurahman Moalim Abdullahi, *The Historical Evolution of the Islamic Movement in Somalia*. Unpublished PhD diss., McGill University, 2010, 197.
114. Ibid., 198–199.
115. Ibid., 200.
116. Andre Le Sage 2001, 476.
117. IGAD is comprised of the states of Djibouti, Eritrea, Ethiopia, Kenya, Somalia, Sudan, and Uganda.
118. Ken Menkhaus, 2007, 370.
119. Cedric Barnes and H. Hassan 2007, 369.
120. Ibid., pp. 372–373.

## THE POLITICAL ECONOMY OF RADICALIZATION: INFORMAL NETWORKS AND THE RISE OF AN URBAN MILITANT ISLAMISM IN CAIRO

1. Salwa Ismail, "The Politics of Urban Cairo: Informal Communities and the State," *The Arab Studies Journal* 4, no. 2 (Fall 1996): 119–132.
2. Diane Singerman, *Avenues of Participation* (Princeton, NJ: Princeton University Press, 1995), 173.
3. Amr Ismail Ahmed Adly, "When Cheap Is Costly: Rent Decline, Regime Survival and State Reform in Mubarak's Egypt (1900–2009)," *Middle Eastern Studies* 47, no. 2 (2011): 295–313.
4. Enzio Mingione, "Life Strategies and Social Economies in the Postfordist Age," *International Journal of Urban and Regional Research* 18, no.1 (1994): 25. For a more detailed review of Mingione's argument in favor of a social analysis of economic behavior see, Enzio Mingione, *Fragmented Societies: A Sociology of Economic Life beyond the Market Paradigm* (Oxford, UK: Blackwell, 1991).
5. Charles Tilly, "Models and Realities of Popular Collective Action," *Social Research* 52 (Winter 1985): 717–748.
6. Ragab Gabir Mohamed (shop owner), interview with the author, December 18, 1999, Imbaba: Cairo.
7. From data collected about Islamist militants arrested and charged for acts of violence, the average age of members dropped from twenty-seven years in the 1970s, to twenty-one years in the 1990s. Moreover, while in the 1970s as many as 80 percent of militants were college students or graduates, this figure dropped to a mere 20 percent in the 1990s. Guenena and Ibrahim, "The Changing Face of Egypt's Islamic Activism: 1974–1995," 7–8.
8. Ibid., 7–8.

9. The study was conducted in Imbaba by a team from the Ibn Khaldun Center for Development Studies. However, while this study pointed to the increasing recruitment of juveniles it did not survey the occupational profile of rank and file members (or former members) of the Islamic Group. See ibid.
10. Given security constraints this is necessarily a small sample. However, the findings are corroborated by my ethnographic research in Western Munira.
11. For example, a number of these leaders had university degrees such as Sheikh Ali Ryan and Sheikh Essam al-Ginda. Both were imprisoned in the 1990s following the 1992 siege.
12. See, for example, Guenena and Ibrahim, "The Changing Face of Egypt's Islamic Activism: 1974–1995."
13. Patrick Heller, "Social Capital as a Product of Class Mobilization and State Intervention: Industrial Workers in Kerala, India," *World Development* 24, no. 6 (1996): 1055–1071.
14. Ragui Assaad. "Formal and Informal Institutions in the Labor Market, with Applications to the Construction Sector in Egypt." *World Development* 21 (June 1996).
15. Tariq Hassabo, interview with the author, December 18, 1999, 'Izbat al-Mufti, Cairo: Egypt.
16. "Egypt Holds Promise for the Patient," *Middle East Economic Digest (MEED)* (May 1985): 10.
17. The sharp price increases – especially in cement, but also in steel – were the immediate source of the economic downturn for the construction industry. Official prices for cement rose by 50 percent in 1988, and the shortage of cement even at higher prices compounded the problem. "Egypt: Suffering from a Crisis in Confidence," *Middle East Economic Digest* (MEED) (February 23, 1990): 15.
18. Ibid.
19. Magdi Mohamed Hussein, interview with the author, January 14, 1999. 'Izbat al-Mufti, Imbaba, Cairo: Egypt.
20. By the late 1990s subcontractors and heads of the informal labor firms based in Imbaba had little choice but to compete, often with little success, in the far more competitive construction sites dominated by the large private construction firms in the new industrial and housing development areas such as *6 October*, *Toskha*, *Wad al-Gedid*, and farther afield outside Cairo in *Sinai* and *'Arish*.
21. Ibid.
22. James R. Elliot, "Social Isolation and Labor Market Insulation: Network and Neighborhood Effects on Less-Educated Urban Workers," *The Sociological Quarterly* 40, no. 2 (1999): 199–216.
23. Interview with informal construction laborer, March 1999, 'Izbat al-Mufti, Cairo: Egypt.
24. In addition to the well-known private construction firm of Osman Ahmed Osman's Arab Contractors firm, a host of new private sector construction firms emerged that resulted in further competition for contracts and jobs in the industry. Among the most notable of these companies that recruit

subcontractors and laborers from Imbaba are *Nasr al-'Ama li al-Muqawalat, Sharikat Hassan Mukhtar li al-Muqawalat, al-Istishareen li al-Muqawalat*, and *Sharikat Hassan Ismail li al-Muqawalat.*

25. Mohamed Ahmed Gohar, interview with the author, 'Izbat al-Mufti, January 16, 1999, Imbaba, Cairo: Egypt.
26. Toth, "Beating Plowshares," 75.
27. Akram Abdel-Moula, (Director: Land Center), interview with the author, December 20, 1999, Cairo: Egypt.
28. Selim Hafez, interview with the author, December 18, 1999, 'Izbat al-Mufti, Imbaba: Cairo.
29. Heller, "Social Capital."
30. One leader of the Jama'a in Western Munira acknowledged privately that the Group was surprised to find such great success in attracting adherents to their cause when they first introduced their Da'wa to residents in Western Munira in the late 1980s. Ahmed Sabri (former Jama'at Leader), December 24, 1998, Imbaba, Cairo: Egypt.
31. Ibid.
32. Magdi Hussein (subcontractor), interview with the author, December 14, 1998, 'Izbat al-Mufti, Imbaba, Cairo: Egypt.
33. Author's interview with construction workers, December 23, 1998, 'Izbat al-Mufti, Imbaba, Cairo: Egypt.
34. Assaad, "Formal and Informal Institutions," 97–112 and 935.
35. Dr. Galal Amin, interview with the author, September 4, 1999, Cairo: Egypt.
36. Author's interviews with laborers, January 29, 1999, 'Izbat al-Mufti, Western Munira, Imbaba, Cairo: Egypt.
37. Author's interview with laborer in *Dulab Mubayit al-Muhar* (Wall Bricklayer Firm), December 26, 1998, 'Izbat al-Mufti, Imbaba, Cairo: Egypt.
38. Magdi Hussein, interview with the author, January 28, 1999. Cairo: Egypt.
39. Members of al-Jama'a al-Islamiyya, interviews with the author, January 1999, 'Izbat al-Mufti, Imbaba, Cairo: Egypt.
40. Roel Meijer, "Commanding Right and Forbidding Wrong as a Principle of Social Action: The Case of the Egyptian al-Jama'a al-Islamiyya," in *Global Salafism: Islam's New Religious Movement*, ed. Roel Meijer (London: C. Hurst and Co., 2009), 204.
41. Interview with Shopkeeper, January 28, 1999, 'Izbat al-Mufti, Imbaba, Cairo: Egypt.
42. Tariq Hassabo (former member of Jama'at), interview with the author, December 29, 1998, 'Izbat al-Mufti, Imbaba, Cairo: Egypt.
43. Author's interviews with members of al-Jama'a al-Islamiyya in 'Izbat al-Mufti that I conducted between November 1998 and March 1999.
44. The Muslim Brotherhood's long-standing support of the private sector and foreign investment is well known, and it has been repeatedly promoted by leading figures such Khaiter al-Shater, the deputy to the General Guide, as late as 2010. Ray Bush, "Marginality or Objection? The Political Economy of Poverty Reduction in Egypt," in *Marginality and Exclusion in Egypt*, ed. Habib Ayeb and Ray Bush (Cairo: American University in Cairo Press, 2012), 61.

45. Salwa Ismail, "The Politics of Urban Cairo: Informal Communities and the State," *The Arab Studies Journal* 4, no. 2 (1996): 119–132.
46. Ibid.
47. Manal 'Awad, interview with the author, December 24, 1998, Western Munira, Imbaba, Cairo: Egypt.
48. Ibid.
49. Ibid.
50. Sermon at *Masjid al-Nur*, Agouza, Cairo, Egypt, November 1, 1998. It is important to note that the government-run mosques mirrored *salat al-masaha* in Cairo in that the sermons were broadcast via loudspeakers in order to spread the message beyond the congregation to the entire neighborhood.
51. Interview with former members of al-Jama'a, January 4, 1999, 'Izbat al-Mufti, Imbaba, Cairo: Egypt.
52. I am grateful to Martha Crenshaw for this insight.
53. Ibid.
54. Ibid.
55. Tariq Hassabo (former member of the Jama'at), interview with the author, January 4, 1999. Imbaba, Cairo: Egypt.
56. Ibid.
57. Ibid.
58. Author's interview with former Jama'a members, February 7, 1999, Imbaba, Cairo: Egypt.
59. Author's interview with cab driver (former member of Jama'at Al-Waraq), February 6, 1999, Imbaba, Cairo: Egypt.
60. Ibid.
61. Excerpt from Sermon, Masjid al-Nur, March 21, 1999, 'Izbat al-Mufti, Imbaba, Cairo: Egypt.
62. Safwat Abdel Ghani (leader of the Beni Mohamed Regional Association), interview with the author, February 14, 1999, 'Izbat al-Mufti, Imbaba, Cairo: Egypt.
63. Ibid.
64. Ahmed Abdel Latif, Sami Abdel Radi and Ahmed Shalaby, "Twenty-Three Salafis Charged with Terrorism in Imbaba," *Egypt Independent*, May 12, 2011. Ahmad Zaki Osman, "Cairo's Copts Organize Groups for Self-Defense," *Egypt Independent*, May 8, 2011.
65. Author's interview with Imbaba resident, December 14, 1998, 'Izbat al-Mufti, Imbaba, Cairo: Egypt.
66. Sheikh Osman Mohamed, interview with the author, January 2, 1998, Omda of Osim, Imbaba, Cairo: Egypt.
67. Ibid.
68. Ibid.
69. Ahmed Salim, interview with the author, February 14, 1999, Osim, Imbaba, Cairo: Egypt.
70. Ibid.
71. Sayed Abdel Hamid, interview with the author, January 21, 1998, Omda in Osim, Imbaba, Cairo: Egypt.

72. Author's interview with Sayed Abdel Hamid. December 9, 2008. Cairo: Egypt.
73. Ibid.
74. Ibid.
75. Ibid.
76. Author's interviews with members of al-Jama'a al-Islamiyya, January 12–14, 1999, Imbaba, Cairo: Egypt.
77. Author's interviews with local council members, December 15–16, 1998, al-Warraq and 'Izbat al-Mufti, Cairo: Egypt.
78. Author's interview with resident, February 14, 1999, 'Izbat al-Mufti, Imbaba, Cairo: Egypt.
79. Krueger, *What Makes a Terrorist*; Sageman, *Understanding Terror Networks.*

## CONCLUSIONS: INFORMAL MARKETS AND THE POLITICS OF IDENTITY

1. Manuel Castells and Alejandro Portes have made this point in "The World Underneath: The Origins, Dynamics, and Effects of the Informal Economy," in *The Informal Economy: Studies in Advanced and Less Advanced Countries*, ed. Manuel Castells, Alejandro Portes, and Lauren Benton (Baltimore: Johns Hopkins Press, 1989), 33.
2. Karl Polyani makes this point with respect to the social disintegration ("massive suffering") caused by attempts to free economic activity from government regulation in nineteenth-century Europe. Karl Polyani, *The Great Transformation: The Political and Economic Origins of Our Time* (Boston: Beacon Press, 1994), 249–258.
3. Marchal, "A Tentative Assessment."
4. Interviews with members of *al-Jama'a al-Islamiyya*, January 12–14, 1999, Imbaba, Cairo, Egypt.

# Bibliography

## Interviews

Abdel-Fadil, Mahmoud. Interview with the author. December 8, 1999, Cairo.
Abdel-Hamid, Sayed. Interview with the author. January 21, 1998, Omda in Osim, Imbaba, Cairo.
Abdel-Meguid, Ahmad. Interview with the author. January 4, 2013, Cairo.
Abdel-Raziq, Wagih Abu-Rawash (member of the Muslim Brotherhood). Interview with the author. December 12, 1998; December 14, 1998, Al-Waraq, Imbaba, Cairo.
Ahmed, Hanafi. Interview with the author. February 14, 1999, Imbaba, Cairo.
Akram, Abdel-Moula. Interview with the author. December 20, 1999, Helwan, Cairo.
'Alama, Ahmed (member of the Muslim Brotherhood). Interview with the author. November 6, 1998, Imbaba, Cairo.
Asim, Mohamed (Muslim Brotherhood activist leader). Interview with the author. October 3, 1999, Western Mounira, Imbaba, Cairo.
Al-Eryan, 'Issam (official spokesperson of the Muslim Brotherhood). Interview with the author. December 21, 2009, Cairo.
Eldin, Ahmad Gamal (Professor, Faculty of Political Science, University of Khartoum). Interview with the author. January 27, 2013, Khartoum.
Farah, Ahmad Yusif. Interview with the author. October 2, 1994, Nairobi, Kenya.
Amin, Galal. Interview with the author. September 4, 1999, Cairo.
Al-Ghazali, Abdel Hamid. Interview with the author. December 18, 2009, Cairo.
Gohar, Mohamed Ahmed. Interview with the author. January 16, 1999, `Izbat al-Mufti, Imbaba, Cairo.
Hafez, Selim. Interview with the author. December 18, 1999, Cairo.
Harbi, Mohamed (wholesale importer). Interview with the author. December 7, 1999, Yirowe.
Hassabo, Tariq (former member of the *al-Jama'a)*. Interview with the author. December 29, 1998; January 12, 1999; February 4, 1999, Imbaba, Cairo.
Hussein, Magdi Mohamed. Interview with the author. December 14, 1998; January 28, 1999, 'Izbat al-Mufti, Imbaba, Cairo.
Informal Laborers. Interview with the author. December 23, 1998; March 1999, 'Izbat al-Mufti, Imbaba, Cairo.

Mahjoub, Mohamed (Editor, Al-Ayam Newspaper). Interview with the author. February 3, 2013, Khartoum.
Manal, 'Awad. Interview with the author. December 24, 1999, Imbaba, Cairo.
Mohamad, Waldo. Interview with the author. January 24, 2010, Nairobi, Kenya.
Musa, Abdi. Interview with the author. February 2000, Hargeisa, Somaliland.
Osman, Hibaaq. Interview with the author. June 2010, Nairobi, Kenya.
Ragab Gabir, Mohamed. Interview with the author. December 18, 1999, Imbaba, Cairo.
Sabri, Ahmed. Interview with the author. December 24, 1998, Cairo.
Salih, Osman. Interview with the author. January 27, 1999, 'Izbat al-Mufti, Western Munira, Cairo.
Omer, Salim Ahmed (member of the Muslim Brotherhood). Interview with the author. January 20, 2009, Masr al-Gedida (New Cairo).
Sheikh Osman, Mohamed. Interview with the author. January 2, 1998, Omda of Osim, Imbaba, Cairo.
Tamman, Hossam. Interview with the author. November 14, 2008, Cairo, Egypt.
Tijani, Al-Tayib (deputy chairman of the Communist Party). Interview with the author. June 24, 2010, Nairobi, Kenya.

## Newspapers and Periodicals

*African Business*. 1989.
*Africa Confidential*. 1990.
*Africa News*. 1992, 1993.
*Al-Ahali*. 1995.
*Al-Ahram*. 1992, 1995.
*Al-Ayyam*. 1984.
*Al-Hayat*. 1989, 1992, 1995.
*Al-Majalla*. 1986.
*Al-Sha'ab*. 1983, 1988.
*Al-Sha'ab*, November 31, 1995.
*Al-Sha'ab* November 11, 1995.
*Associated Press*. 2001.
*Al-Wafd*, November 10, 1995.
*Al-Wafd*, November 19, 1995.
*Al-Wafd*, November 28, 1995.
*Egypt Independent*. 2011.
*Financial Times*. January 5, 2002.
*Financial Times*. January 17, 2002.
*May Newspaper*. 1995.
*New Internationalist*. 1991.
*New York Times*. 1992, 2002, 2011.
*Reuters*. 2001.
*Sudan Tribune*. 2010, 2012.
*Sudanow*. 1979, 1980.
*The Wall Street Journal*. 2014.

## Secondary Sources

Abbas, Ali Abdalla. "The National Islamic Front and the Politics of Education." *Middle East Report* 21, no. 5 (1991): 22–25.

Abdel Fadil, Mahmoud. *Al-iqtisad al-siyassi li sharikat tawzif al-amwal* [The Political Economy of Islamic Investment Companies] [Arabic]. Cairo: Dar al-Mustaqbal al-Arabi, 1989.

"*Egyptian Workers and Gulf Migration.*" Unpublished manuscript, December 1995.

Aboagye, A. A. *The Informal Sector in Mogadishu: An Analysis of a Survey*. Addis Ababa: International Labour Organisation/Jobs and Skills Programme for Africa, 1988.

Abdullahi, Abdurrahman Moalim. "*The Historical Evolution of the Islamic Movement in Somalia.*" Unpublished PhD dissertation, McGill University, 2010.

Adly, Amr Ismail Ahmed. "When Cheap Is Costly: Rent Decline, Regime Survival and State Reform in Mubarak's Egypt (1900–2009)." *Middle Eastern Studies* 47, no. 2 (2011): 295–313.

Abu al-'ilah, Mohamed Hussein. *Al-'unf al-dini fi Misr* [Religious Violence in Egypt]. Cairo: Al-Ahram Center for Strategic Studies, 1998.

El-Affendi, Abdelwahab. "Studying My Movement: Social Science without Cynicism." *International Journal of Middle East Studies* 23, no. 1 (1991): 83–94.

*Turabi's Revolution: Islam and Power in Sudan*. London: Grey Seal, 1991.

African Business. "Technocrats May End Naïve Policies." *African Business*. September 1989.

"Will the Forex Bureaux Close Zongo Lane?" *African Business*. June 1989.

"Subsidies Row Continues." *African Business*. September 1993.

"Wounded North, Bruised South." *Africa Confidential*. November 18, 1988, 2–4.

"Somalia: Showdown in the North." *Africa Confidential*. July 29, 1988, 1–3.

Africa Economic Outlook (AEO). 2012.

Africa Watch. *Somalia: A Fight to the Death?* Washington: Human Rights Watch, February 13, 1992.

Agati, Mohamed. "Undermining Standards of Good Governance: Egypt's NGO Law and Its Impact on the Transparency and Accountability of CSOs." *The International Journal of Not-for-Profit Law* 9, no. 2 (April 2007): 56–72.

Ahmed, Medani M. *Global Financial Crisis Discussion Series Paper 19: Sudan Phase 2*. London: Overseas Development Institute, February 2010.

Al-Ahrar. Interview with Omer Tilmisani. *Al-Ahrar*. February 15, 1982.

Interview with Dr. Mohammad al-Fangary, Chairman of the Islamic Charity Association. *Al-Ahrar*. June 13, 2002, 3–4, quoted in Agati, Mohamed. "Undermining Standards of Good Governance: Egypt's NGO Law and Its Impact on the Transparency and Accountability of CSOs." *The International Journal of Not-for-Profit Law* 9, no. 2 (April 2007): 56–72.

Al-Ahram Al-Iqtissadi. "Kayf nawajih tahdiyat sharikat tawsif al-amwal" [How do We Confront the Challenge of the Money Management Companies]. *Al-Ahram Al-Iqtissadi*, February 8, 1988.

Aliyev, Huseyn. "Strong Militias, Weak States and Armed Violence: Towards a Theory of 'State-Parallel' Paramilitaries." *Security Dialogue* 47, no. 6 (2016): 498–516.

Amin, Ash and Jerzy Hausner. "Interactive Governance and Social Complexity." In *Beyond Market and Hierarchy: Interactive Governance and Social Complexity*, edited by Ash Hausner, 71–92. Cheltenham: Edward Elgar Publishing, 1997.

Amin, Ash and Nigel Thrift. "What Kind of Theory for What Kind of Economic Geography?" *Antipode* 32, no. 1 (2000): 4–9.

Amin, Galal. "Some Economic and Cultural Aspects of Economic Liberalization in Egypt." *Social Problems* 28, no. 4 (April 1981): 430–441.

Amselle, Jean-Loup. "Globalization and the Future of Anthropology." *African Affairs* 101, no. 403 (2002): 213–229.

Anderson, Gary M., Audrey B. Davidson, Robert B. Ekelund, Robert F. Hébert, and Robert D. Tollison. *Sacred Trust: The Medieval Church as an Economic Firm*. New York: Oxford University Press, 1996.

Andreas, Peter. "Illicit International Political Economy: The Clandestine side of Globalization." *Review of International Political Economy* 11, no. 3 (2004): 641–652.

Ansari, Hamid. *Egypt: The Stalled Society*. Albany: State University of New York Press, 1986.

Aql, Abdel-Rahman. "Difa wazir al-iqtisad an tadil qanun al-bunuk" [The Minister of the Economy's Defense of the Amendment of the Banking Law]. *Al-Ahram al-iqtisadi*. April 2, 1984, 3–9, cited in Bianchi, Robert. "Businessmen's Association in Egypt and Turkey." *Annals of the American Academy of Political and Social Science* 482, no. 1 (1985): 147–159.

Al-Asnawi, A. "The New Face of Sufism: Transformation Towards Politics." *Al-Ahram Numbered Journal* (2011), http://digital.ahram.org.eg/articles.aspx?Serial=715044&eid=15. Accessed January 12, 2013, 3–5, cited in Tarek Ladjal and Benaouda Bensaid. "Sufism and Politics in Contemporary Egypt: A Study of Sufi Political Engagement in the Pre and Post-revolutionary Reality of January 2011." *Journal of Asian and African Studies* 50, no. 4 (2015): 468–485.

AllAfrica.com. "Somalia: Cabinet Minister Resigns in Puntland." *AllAfrica.com*. August 9, 2008, cited in ICG: 7.

Al-Mashad, Adal. "Al-ghazu al-istihmari lil-niqabat al-mihniya wa al-ummaliya" [The Entrepreneurial Invasion of Professional's Labor Syndicates]. *Al-Sha'ab*. January 25, 1983.

Assaad, Ragui. "Formal and Informal Institutions in the Labor Market, with Applications to the Construction Sector in Egypt." *World Development* 21 (June 1996), 925–939.

ed. *The Egyptian Labor Market Revisited*. Cairo: American University in Cairo Press, 2009.

Assaad, Ragui and Rania Roushdy. "Job Quality among the Non-wage Workers in the Agriculture and Non-agricultural Sectors in Egypt." *Economic Research Forum Working Paper* 386 (2008).

Ateş, Hamza, Yüksel Bayraktar, and Mehmet Duman. "A Story of *Infitah*: Egyptian Liberalisation under Stress." *Yapı Kredi Economic Review* 17, no. 1 (2006): 59–77. https://pdfs.semanticscholar.org/ebe9/0230896a1c71dccfaeadef2ed3eb4e763b73.pdf.

'Awad, Muhammad Hashim. "*Al-Bunuk al-Islamiyya: haqa'ik wa arqam*" [Sudanese Islamic Banks: Facts and Figures]. Unpublished paper, University of Khartoum, 1987.

Babou, Cheikh Anta. "Brotherhood Solidarity, Education and Migration: The Role of the Dahiras among the Murid Community of New York." *African Affairs* 101, no. 403 (2002): 151–170.

Baier, S. *An Economic History of Central Niger*. Oxford: Clarendon Press, 1980.

Bakonyi, Jutta and Kirsti Stuvoy, "Violence and Social Order beyond the State: Somalia and Angola." *Review of African Political Economy* 32, no. 104 (2005): 359–382.

Bankston, Amanda. "Somali-American Students Say Hawala Shutdown Hurts Them: Recent Crackdown on Money Transfers to Somalia Affect Those Sending Cash to Relatives." *Minnesota Daily*. January 18, 2012.

Banuri, Tariq. *United Nations University World Institute for Development Economics Research (WIDER) Working Paper: Black Markets, Openness and Central Bank Autonomy*. Amherst: University of Massachusetts, 1988.

"Al-Barakaat Case Study." *National Commission on Terrorist Attacks upon the United States, Chapter Five*. www.9-11commission.gov/staff-statements/index.htm.

Barnes, Cedric and Hamed Hassan. "The Rise and Fall of Mogadishu's Islamic Courts." *Journal of Eastern African Studies* 1, no. 2 (2007): 151–160.

Barr, Abigail. "Do SMEs Network for Growth." In *Enterprise in Africa: Between Poverty and Growth*, edited by Kenneth King and Simon McGrath, 121–131. London: Intermediate Technology Publications, 1999.

Bates, Robert. *Markets and States in Tropical Africa*. Berkeley: University of California Press, 1981.

"Comments on Underground Economies, in Jerome Jenkins." In *Beyond the Informal Sector: Included the Excluded in Developing Countries*, edited by Jerome Jenkins, 14–31. Berkeley: University of California Press, 1988.

*Prosperity and Violence: The Political Economy of Development*. New York: Norton, 2001.

El-Batran, Manal and Christian Arandel. "A Shelter of Their Own: Informal Settlement Expansion in Greater Cairo and Government Responses." *Environment and Urbanization* 10, no. 1 (1998): 217–232.

Al-Batthani, Ahmad. *Economic Transformation and Political Islam in Sudan, 1975–1989*. Unpublished paper, University of Khartoum, 1996.

Bayart, Jean-Francois. "The 'Social Capital' of the Felonious State." In *The Criminalization of the State in Africa*, edited by Jean-Francois Bayart, Stephen Ellis, and Béatrice Hibou, 31–52. Bloomington: James Currey and Indiana University Press, 1999.

"Africa in the World: A History of Extraversion." *African Affairs* 99, no. 395 (April 2000): 217–267.

*The State in Africa: The Politics of the Belly*, 2nd ed. Cambridge, UK: Polity, 2009.

Bayart, Jean-Francois, Stephen Ellis, and Béatrice Hibou. *The Criminalization of the State in Africa*. Bloomington: James Currey and Indiana University Press, 1999.

Bayat, Asef. *Making Islam Democratic: Social Movements and the Post-Islamist Turn*. Redwood City, CA: Stanford University Press, 2007.

"Radical Religion and the Habitus of the Dispossessed: Does Islamic Militancy Have an Urban Ecology." *International Journal of Urban and Regional Research* 31, no. 3 (2007): 579–590.

*Post-Islamism: The Changing Face of Political Islam*. New York: Oxford University Press, 2013.

Bayat, Asef and Eric Denis. "Who Is Afraid of *Ashwaiyyat*? Urban Change and Politics in Egypt." *Environment and Urbanization* 12, no. 2 (2000): 185–199.

BBC News. "South Sudan Reneging on Peace Deal – President Beshir." *BBC News*. October 10, 2010. www.bbc.com/news/world-africa-11510109.

"US Ends Somali Banking Backlist." *BBC News*. August 28, 2006.

"Voters Defy Islamist Threats in Somaliland." *BBC News*. September 2001.

Bechtold, Peter K. *Politics in Sudan: Parliamentary and Military Rule in an Emerging African Nation*. New York: Praeger, 1976.

Becker, Gary S. *The Economic Approach to Human Behavior*. Chicago: University of Chicago Press, 1976.

Bellin, Eva. "The Political Economic Conundrum: The Affinity of Economic and Political Reform in the Middle East and North Africa." *Carnegie Papers, Middle East Series*, no. 53 (November 2004).

"The Robustness of Authoritarianism in the Middle East: Exceptionalism in Comparative Perspective." *Comparative Politics* 36, no. 2 (2004): 139–157.

Berdal, Mats and David Malone. *Greed and Grievance: Economic Agendas in Civil Wars*. Boulder, CO: Lynne Rienner Press, 2000.

Berman, Eli and Laurence R. Iannaconne. "Hamas, Taliban and the Jewish Underground: An Economist's View of Radical Religious Militias." *NBER Working Paper*, no. w10004 (2003).

"Religious Extremism: The Good, the Bad, and the Deadly." *Public Choice* 128, no. 1–2 (2006): 109–129.

Berman, Eli and David D. Laitin. "Religion, Terrorism and Public Goods: Testing the Club Model." *Journal of Public Economics* 92, no. 10–11 (2008): 1942–1968.

Bernal, Victoria. "Islam, Transnational Culture, and Modernity in Rural Sudan." In *Gendered Encounters: Challenging Cultural Boundaries and Social Hierarchies in Africa*, edited by Maria Grosz-Ngate and Omari Kokole, 131–151. New York: Routledge Press, 1997.

Berry, Sara. "Coping with Confusion: African Farmers' Response to Economic Instability in the 1970s and 1980s." In *Hemmed In: Responses to Africa's Economic Decline*, edited by Thomas M. Callaghy and John Ravenhill, 248–278. New York: Columbia University Press, 1993.

Besteman, Catherine L. *Unraveling Somalia: Race, Class and the Legacy of Slavery*. Philadelphia: University of Pennsylvania Press, 2003.

Beyman, Daniel. *Deadly Connections: States That Sponsor Terrorism*. New York: Cambridge University Press, 2005.

Bianchi, Robert. "Businessmen's Association in Egypt and Turkey." *Annals of the American Academy of Political and Social Science* 482, no. 1 (1985): 147–159.

Bishara, Marwan. *The Invisible Arab: The Promise and Peril of the Arab Revolutions*. New York: Nation Books, 2012.

Blokand, Talja and Mike Savage. "Networks, Class and Place." *International Journal of Urban and Regional Research* 25, no. 2 (2001): 221–226.

Blomberg, S. Brock, Gregory D. Hess, and Akila Weerapana. "Terrorism from Within: An Economic Model of Terrorism." *Claremont Colleges Working Papers*, no. 2002–14 (2002).

Bloom, Mia. "Palestinian Suicide Bombing: Public Support, Market Share, and Outbidding." *Political Science Quarterly* 119, no. 1 (2004): 61–88.

Bradach, Jeffrey L. and Robert G. Eccles. "Price, Authority and Trust: From Ideal Types to Plural Forms." In *Markets, Hierarchies and Networks: The Coordination of Social Life*, edited by Jennifer Frances, Rosalind Levacic, Jeremy Mitchell, and Grahame Thompson, 277–292. London: Sage, 1991.

Bradbury, Mark. "Somaliland: Changing Minds Changing Lives." *CIIR*. 1997.

"Somaliland: CIIR Country Report." *CIIR*, London. 2003.

*Becoming Somaliland*. London: James Currey, 2008.

Bradbury, Mark, Adan Yusuf Abokor, and Haroon Ahmed Yusuf. "Somaliland: Choosing Politics over Violence." *Review of African Political Economy* 30, no. 97 (2003): 455–478.

Brand, Laurie A. *Citizens Abroad: Emigration and the State in the Middle East and North Africa*. Cambridge, UK: Cambridge University Press, 2008.

Bratton, Michael. "Beyond the State: Civil Society and Associational Life in Africa." *World Politics* 41 (April 1989): 407–430.

Brautigam, Deborah. "Substituting for the State: Institutional and Industrial Development in Eastern Nigeria." *World Development* 25, no. 7 (1997): 1063–1080.

"Close Encounters: Chinese Business Networks as Industrial Catalyst in Sub-Saharan Africa." *African Affairs* 102, no. 408 (July 2003): 447–467.

Brown, Richard P. C. "Migrant Remittances, Capital Flight and Macroeconomic Imbalance in Sudan's Hidden Economy." *Journal of African Economies* 1, No. 1 (1992): 59–85.

"The Hidden Economy." *New Internationalist* 97, no. 110 (June 1991): 14–31.

"Al-bunuk wa munafasat sharikat tawsif al-amwal" [The Banks and the Competition of the Money Management Companies]. *Al-Ahram al-Iqtissadi*. December 2, 1987.

Burns, Jonathan G. "The Banking Sector in Post-Revolution Egypt: Is Islam the Solution?" *Banking & Finance Law Review* 319, no. 2 (2014): 319–352.

Burr, Millard J. and Robert O. Collins. *Alms for Jihad*. New York: Cambridge University Press, 2006.

Bush, Ray. "Marginality or Objection? The Political Economy of Poverty Reduction in Egypt." In *Marginality and Exclusion in Egypt*, edited by

Ray Bush and Habib Ayeb, 55–71. Cairo: American University in Cairo Press, 2012.

Callaghy, Thomas. "Lost between State and Market: The Politics of Economic Adjustment in Ghana, Zambia, and Nigeria." In *Economic Crisis and Policy Choice*, edited by John Nelson, 258–304. Cambridge, UK: Cambridge University Press, 1992.

Campagnon, Daniel. "Somali Armed Units: The Interplay of Political Entrepreneurship and Clan-Based Factions." In *African Guerillas*, edited by Christopher Clapham, 14–27. Oxford, United Kingdom or Oxford, UK: Oxford University Press and James Currey, 1998.

Castells, Manuel. *The Power of Identity*. Malden, MA: Blackwell, 1997.

Castells, Manuel and Alejandro Portes. "The World Underneath: The Origins, Dynamics, and Effects of the Informal Economy." In *The Informal Economy: Studies in Advanced and Less Advanced Countries*, edited by Manuel Castells, Lauren Benton, and Alejandro Portes, 1–34. Baltimore: Johns Hopkins Press, 1989.

Chaudhry, Kiren Aziz. "The Price of Wealth: Business and State in Labor Remittance and Oil Economies." *International Organization* 43, no. 1 (1989): 101–145.

Cheng, Lu-Lin and Gary Gereffi. "The Informal Economy in East Asian Development." *International Journal of Urban and Regional Studies* 18, no. 2 (1994): 194–219.

Chen, D. "Club Goods and Group Identity: Evidence from Islamic Resurgence during the Indonesian Financial Crisis." *Journal of Political Economy* 118, no. 21 (2010): 300–354.

Choucri, Nazli. "The Hidden Economy: A New View of Remittances in the Arab World." *World Development Report* 14, no. 6 (1986): 697–712.

Christelow, Allan. "Property and Theft in Kano at the Dawn of the Groundnut Boom 1912–1914." *The International Journal of African Historical Studies* 20, no. 2 (1987): 225–243.

Clark, Janine A. *Islam, Social Welfare and the Middle Class: Networks, Activism, and Charity in Egypt, Yemen and Jordan*. Bloomington: Indiana University Press, 2004.

Cleaver, Frances. "Institutional Bricolage, Conflict and Cooperation in Usangu, Tanzania." *Institute of Development Studies (IDS) Bulletin* 32, no. 4 (2001): 26–43.

Cockayne, James and Liat Shetret. *Capitalizing on Trust: Harnessing Somali Remittances for Counterterrorism, Human Rights and State Building*. Goshen, IN: Center on Global Counterterrorism Cooperation, 2012. www.globalcenter.org/wp-content/uploads/2012/07/CapitalizingOnTrust.pdf.

Cohen, Abner. *Custom and Politics in Urban Africa: A Study of Hausa Migrants in Yoruba Towns*. London: Routledge & Kegan Paul, 1969.

Coleman, James S. "Social Capital in the Creation of Human Capital." In *Social Capital: A Multifaceted Perspective*, edited by Partha Dasgupta and Ismail Serageldin, 13–39. Washington, DC: World Bank, 2000.

Collier, David. "*The Comparative Method.*" Paper presented at the Annual Meeting of the American Political Science Association, San Francisco, CA, June 1993.

"Trajectory of a Concept: Corporatism in the Study of Latin American Politics." In *Latin America in Comparative Perspective: New Approaches to Method and Analysis*, edited by Peter H. Smith, 135–162. Boulder, CO: Westview Press, 1995.

Collier, Paul. *The Bottom Million: Why the Poorest Countries Are Failing and What Can Be Done about It.* Oxford, UK: Oxford University Press, 2007.

Collier, Paul and Anke Hoeffler. "Greed and Grievance in Civil War." *Oxford Economic Papers* 56, no. 4 (2004): 563–595.

Collins, Carole. "Colonialism and Class Struggle in Sudan." *Middle East Research and Information Project (MERIP) Reports* 46 (1976): 3–20.

Collins, Kathleen. *Clan Politics and Regime Transitions in Central Asia.* New York: Cambridge University Press, 2006.

Collins, Robert O. *A History of Modern Sudan.* Cambridge, UK: Cambridge University Press, 2008.

Cook, David. *Understanding Jihad.* Oakland: University of California Press, 2005.

Cooper, Frederick. "What Is the Concept of Globalization Good For? An African Historian's Perspective." *African Affairs* 100, no. 399 (2001): 189–213.

Crenshaw, Martha. "Theories of Terrorism: Instrumental and Organizational Approaches." *Journal of Strategic Studies* 10, no. 4 (1987): 13–31.

"'New' vs. 'Old' Terrorism: A Critical Appraisal." In *Jihad Terrorism and Radicalization and the Radicalization Challenge in Europe*, edited by Rick Coolsaet, 25–38. Aldershot, UK: Ashgate Publishing, 2008.

"The Crisis Continues in Imbaba: Expect More Clashes." *Al-Sha'ab.* December 15, 1992.

Cudsi, Alexander S. "Islam and Politics in the Sudan." AFRICA (March 1978): 36–55.

Curtin, Phillip D. "Pre-Colonial Trading Networks and Traders: The Diakhanke." In *The Development of Indigenous Trade Markets in West Africa*, edited by Claude Meillassoux, 3–15. London: Oxford University Press, 1971.

Daniel, Williams and Alaa Shahin, "Egypt Extends Emergency Law, U.S. Call for New Anti-Terror Law." *Bloomberg*, May 11, 2010. Available at: https://www.bloomberg.com/news/articles/2010-05-11/egypt-to-renew-1981-emergency-law-citing-terror-threat-government-says

Dasgupta, Partha. "Economic Progress and the Idea of Social Capital." In *Social Capital: A Multifaceted Perspective*, edited by Partha Dasgupta and Ismail Serageldin, 325–399. Washington, DC: World Bank, 2000.

Al-Tilmisani, Umar. "Idha ja'a al-muslimun fa-la mal li-ahad" [If Muslims Come Then There Will be No Money for Anyone]. *Al-Dawa* 383 (February 1977), 1–7.

Day, Kathleen. "US Islamic Cash Outlets Investigated as Source for Terror Funds." *Washington Post.* November 7, 2001.

De Mesquita, Ethan Bueno. "The Quality of Terror." *American Journal of Political Science* 49, no. 3 (2005): 515–530.

Deng, Francis M. "Sudan: A Nation in Turbulent Search of Itself." *The ANNALS of the American Academy of Political and Social Science* 603, no. 1 (2006): 155–162.

Denis, Eric. "Cairo as Neoliberal Capital? From Walled City to Gated Communities." In *Cairo Cosmopolitan: Politics, Culture, and Urban Space in the New Globalized Middle East*, edited by Paul Amar and Diane Singerman, 47–71. Cairo: American University in Cairo Press, 2006.

De-Soto, Hernardo. *The Other Path*. New York: Harper and Row, 1989.

"The Capitalist Cure for Terrorism," *The Wall Street Journal*. October 10, 2014.

Deyo, Frederic C., Richard F. Doner, and Eric Hershberg, eds. *Economic Governance and the Challenge of Flexibility in East Asia*. Lanham, MD: Rowman and Littlefield Publishers, 2001.

Desch, Michael C. "War and Strong States, Peace and Weak States?" *International Organization* 50, no. 4 (1996): 237–268.

De Waal, Alex, ed. *Islamism and Its Enemies in the Horn of Africa*. Bloomington: Indiana University Press, 2004.

"Who are Sudan's RSF and their Commander Hemeti? *Al Jazeera*. June 5, 2019.

Dike, K. O. and F. I. Ekejiuba. *The Ark of Southeastern Nigeria, 1650–1980: A Study of the Socio- Economic Formation and Transformation of Nigeria*. Ibadan, Nigeria: University Press, 1990.

Dionne, Kim Yi, Kris L. Inman, and Gabriella R. Montinola. "Another Resource Curse? The Impact of Remittances on Political Participation." Afrobarometer Working Papers, no. 145 (2014): 1–28.

"Dirasa fi al-intikhabat fi Mounira al-Gharbiyya: Imbaba" [A Study on the Western Mounira Elections: Imbaba]. *Al-Ahram*. Cairo: Center for Strategic Studies. Unpublished report, 1995.

Duffield, Mark. "Where Famine Is Functional: Actual Adjustment and the Politics of Relief in Sudan." *Middle East Report* 21, no. 5 (1991): 23–30.

The Economist. "Somalia after the Peacekeepers Go." *The Economist*. February 8, 1995.

Elliot, James R. "Social Isolation and Labor Market Insulation: Network and Neighborhood Effects on Less-Educated Urban Workers." *The Sociological Quarterly* 40, no. 2 (1999): 199–216.

El-Said, Hamel and Jane R. Harrigan. "Globalization, International Finance, and Political Islam in the Arab World." *The Middle East Journal* 60, no. 3 (2006): 444–466.

*Economic Liberalisation, Social Capital and Islamic Welfare*. New York: Palgrave MacMillan, 2009.

"Egypt: Anti-Money Laundering/Combating Terrorist Financing Standard." *Report of the Financial Standards Foundation*. www.estandardsforum.org/Egypt/standards/anti-money-laundering-combating-terrorist-finance-standard.pdf.

"Egypt Extends Emergency Law, U.S. Calls for New Anti-Terror Law." In *Muslim Politics*, edited by Dale Eickelman and James Piscatori. Princeton, NJ: Princeton University Press, 2004.

Elbadawi, Ibrahim. "Real Overvaluation, Terms of Trade Shocks, and the Cost to Agriculture in Sub-Saharan Africa: The Case of the Sudan." *Journal of African Economies* 1, no. 1 (1992): 59–85.

Ellickson, Robert C. *Order without Law: How Neighbors Settle Disputes.* Cambridge, MA: Harvard University Press, 1991.

Emirbayer, Mustafa and Jeff Goodwin. "Network Analysis, Culture and the Problem of Agency." *American Journal of Sociology* 99, no.6 (1994): 1411–1454.

Esposito, John. *Islam and Politics.* Syracuse, NY: Syracuse University Press, 1984.

*The Islamic Threat: Myth or Reality?* New York: Oxford University Press, 2003.

*Unholy War: Terror in the Name of Islam.* New York: Oxford University Press, 2003.

Eurostat. "Push and Pull Factors of International Migration, Country Report, Egypt." *Eurostat Working Papers*, Population and Social Conditions, no. 7 (2000).

Evans, Peter. "Government Action, Social Capital and Development: Reviewing the Evidence of Synergy." *World Development* 24, no. 6 (1996): 1119–1132.

Evers, Hans-Dieter. "Large Markets and Small Profits: A Sociological Interpretation of Javanese Petty Trade." In *Traditional Marketing System*, edited by Luder Cammann, 14–48. Munich: German Foundation for International Development, 1992.

Fandy, Mamoun. "Egypt's Islamic Group: Regional Revenge?" *Middle East Journal* 48, no. 4 (1994): 607–625.

Fearon, James D. and David D. Laitin. "Ethnicity, Insurgency, and Civil War." *Political Science Review* 97, no. 1 (2003): 75–90.

Feige, Edgar L. "Defining and Estimating Underground and Informal Economies: The New Institutional Economics Approach." *World Development* 18, no. 7 (1990): 989–1002.

Feige, Edgar L. and Katarina Ott, eds. *Underground Economies in Transition: Unrecorded Activity, Tax Evasion, Corruption and Organized Crime.* Aldershot, UK: Ashgate, 1999.

*Financial Times.* January 5, 2002.

*Financial Times.* January 17, 2002.

Fine, Ben. *Social Capital versus Social Theory: Political Economy and Social Science in the Turn of the Millennium.* London: Routledge, 2001.

Fleur-Lobban, Carolyn. *Islamic Law and Society in Sudan.* London: Frank Cass, 1987.

"Islamicization in Sudan: A Critical Assessment." *Middle East Journal* 44, no. 4 (1990): 610–623.

Fligstein, Neil. "Markets as Politics: A Political-Cultural Approach to Market Institutions." *American Sociological Review* 61 (1996): 656–673.

Freidberg, Suzanne Elizabeth. *Making a Living: A Social History of Market-Garden Work in the Regional Economy of Bobo-Dioulasso, Burkina Faso.* Berkeley: University of California Press, 1996.

Frieden, Jeffrey. "Invested Interests: The Politics of National Economic Policies in a World of Global Finance." *International Organization* 45 (Autumn 1991): 425–451.

Friedland, Roger and Alexander F. Robertson, eds. *Beyond the Marketplace: Rethinking Economy and Society*. New York: Aldine de Gruyter, 1990.

Fukuyama, Francis. *The End of History and the Last Man*. New York: Free Press, 1992.

"Social Capital and the Global Economy." *Foreign Affairs* 74, no. 5 (1995): 89–103.

*Trust: The Social Virtues and the Creation of Prosperity*. London: Hamish Hamilton, 1995.

Gadir, Ali Abdel. "A Note on the Brain-Drain in the Sudan." *Sudan Journal of Economic and Social Studies* 2, no. 1 (1977): 1–26.

Gallab, Abdullahi A. *The First Islamic Republic: Development and Disintegration of Islamism in Sudan*. London: Ashgate Publishing, 2008.

Gambetta, Diego. *The Sicilian Mafia: The Business of Private Protection*. Cambridge, MA: Harvard University Press, 1993.

Garang, Ngor Arol. "SPLM Slams Calls for War by NCP Official." *Sudan Tribune*. October 4, 2010.

Geertz, Clifford. *The Interpretation of Cultures*. New York: Basic Book, 1973.

Gerges, Fawaz A. *The Far Enemy: Why Jihad Went Global*. New York: Cambridge University Press, 2005.

*Journey of the Jihadist: Inside Muslim Militancy*. London: Harcourt Inc, 2007.

Geschiere, Peter and Birgit Meyer. "Globalization and Identity: Dialectics of Flow and Closure." *Development and Change* 29, no. 4 (1998): 601–615.

Gettleman, Jeffrey. "Young Sudanese Start Movement." *New York Times*. February 2, 2011.

El-Ghobashy, Mona. "The Metamorphosis of the Egyptian Muslim Brothers." *International Journal of Middle East Studies* 37, no. 3 (2005): 373–395.

Gibbon, Peter, ed. *Markets, Civil Society and Democracy in Kenya*. Uppsala: Nordiska Africainstitutet, 1995.

"Civil Society, Locality and Globalization in Rural Tanzania: A Forty-Year Perspective." *Development and Change* 32, no. 5 (2001): 819–844.

Gilsenan, Michael. "Some Factors in the Decline of the Sufi Orders in Modern Egypt." *Muslim World* 57, no. 1 (1967): 11–18.

El Gizouli, Magdi. "Sudan: Khartoum-the Political Economy of Bankruptcy." *Sudan Tribune*. June 23, 2012.

Gold, Steven J. "Gender, Class, and Network: Social Structure and Migration Patterns Among Transnational Israelis." *Global Networks* 1, no. 1 (January 2001): 57–78.

Grabher, Gernot and David Stark. "Organizing Diversity: Evolutionary Theory, Network Analysis, and Post-Socialism." In *Restructuring Networks in Post-Socialism: Legacies, Linkages, and Localities*, edited by Gernot Grabher and David Stark, 1–32. Oxford: Oxford University Press, 1997.

Granovetter, Mark. "Economic Action and Social Structure: The Problem of Embeddedness." *American Journal of Sociology* 91, no. 3 (1985): 481–510.

"The Old and the New Economic Sociology: A History and an Agenda." In *Beyond the Marketplace*, edited by Roger Friedland and A. F. Robertson, 89–112. New York: Aldine de Gruyter, 1990.

"The Economic Sociology of Firms and Entrepreneurs." In *The Economic Sociology of Immigration: Essays on Ethnic Entrepreneurship*, edited by Alejandro Portes, 128–165. New York: Russell Sage Foundation, 1995.

Gravelle, Kend Benedict. "Islamic Law in Sudan: A Comparative Analysis." *Journal of International and Comparative Law* 5, no. 1 (1988): 1–22.

Grey-Johnson, Crispin. "The African Informal Sector at the Crossroads: Emerging Policy Options." *Africa Development* 17, no. 1 (1992): 65–91.

Gurr, Ted Robert. *Why Men Rebel*. Princeton, NJ: Princeton University Press, 1970.

Guyer, Janet I. "Introduction: Markets in Africa in a New Era." *Africa* 71, no. 2 (2001): 197–201.

*Marginal Gains: Monetary Transactions in Atlantic Africa*. Chicago: University of Chicago Press, 2004.

Hamdi, Abd al-Rahman. "*Islamization of the Banking System in Sudan*." Paper presented at the National Assembly, Khartoum, December 1984.

Hamid, Mohammed Beshir. *The Politics of National Reconciliation in the Sudan: The Numayri Regime and the National Front Opposition, 1956–1985*. Washington, DC: Center for Contemporary Arab Studies at Georgetown University, 1984.

Hamilton, Gary G. "The Theoretical Significance of Asian Business Networks." In *Asian Business Networks*, edited by Gary G. Hamilton, 283. Berlin: Walter de Gruyter, 1996.

Handoussa, Heba. "*The Role of the State: The Case of Egypt*." Paper presented at the first Annual Conference on Development Economics, Cairo, June 1993. Cited in Utvik, Björn Olav. *Islamist Economics in Egypt: The Pious Road to Development*. Boulder, CO: Lynn Reinner Press, 2006.

*Egypt Human Development Report 2008 – Egypt's Social Contract: The Roll of Civil Society*. New York: United Nations Development Project (UNDP) and Institute of National Planning, 2008.

Hansen, Karen Tranberg and Mariken Vaa, eds. *Reconsidering Informality: Perspectives from Urban Africa*. Uppsala: Nordiska Afrikainstitutet, 2004.

Hansohm, Dirk and Karl Wohlmuth. "Sudan's Small Industry Development: Structures, Failures and Perspectives." In *Industrialization in the Third World: The Need for Alternative Strategies*, edited by Meine Pieter van Dijk and Henrik Secher Marcussen, 14–28. London: Frank Cass, 1990.

Harik, Ilya. *Economic Policy Reform in Egypt*. Gainesville: University Press of Florida, 1997.

Harive, C. H. and J. G. Kleve. "The National Income of Sudan, 1955/56." Khartoum: Department of Statistics, 1959, 23–52, cited in Brown, Richard P. C. *Public Debt and Private Wealth: Debt, Capital Flight and the IMF in Sudan*. London: Macmillan, 1992.

Harris-Jones, Peter. "'Home-boy' Ties and Political Organization in a Copperbelt Township." In *Social Networks in Urban Situations: Analyses of Personal*

*Relationships in Central African Towns*, edited by James Clyde Mitchell, 297–338. Manchester: Manchester University Press, 1969.

Hart, Gillian. "Multiple Trajectories: A Critique of Industrial Restructuring and the New Institutionalism." *Antipode* 30, no. 4 (1998): 333–356.

Hashim, Yahaya and Kate Meagher. *Cross-Border Trade and the Parallel Currency Market: Trade and Finance in the Context of Structural Adjustment: A Case Study from Kano, Nigeria*. Uppsala: Nordiska Afrikainstitutet, 1999.

Al-Hayat. "Cairo: Detention of 290 Fundamentalist Militants in a Wide Campaign in Imbaba." *Al-Hayat*. December 9, 1992.

Mubarak al-Fadl Interview. *Al-Hayat*. September 2–3, 1989.

Al-Hayat. "Terrorism in Cairo's Informal Settlements." Al-Hayat, November 15, 1995.

Hegghammer, Thomas. *Jihad in Saudi Arabia: Violence and Pan-Islamism since 1979*. New York: Cambridge University Press, 2010.

Heller, Patrick. "Social Capital as a Product of Class Mobilization and State Intervention: Industrial Workers in Kerala, India." *World Development* 24, no. 6 (1996): 1055–1071.

Helmke, Gretchen and Steven Levitsky. "Informal Institutions and Comparative Politics: A Research Agenda." *Perspectives on Politics* 2, no. 4 (2004): 725–740.

eds. *Informal Institutions and Democracy: Lessons from Latin America*. Baltimore: Johns Hopkins, 2006.

Henry, Clement M. and Rodney Wilson, eds. *The Politics of Islamic Finance*. Edinburgh: Edinburgh University Press, 2004.

Herbst, Jeffrey. *States and Power in Africa: Comparative Lessons in Authority and Control*. Princeton, NJ: Princeton University Press, 1990.

Hinnebusch, Raymond A. "The Politics of Economic Reform in Egypt." *Third World Quarterly* 14, no. 1 (1993): 159–171.

Horn of Africa Bulletin. "Foreign Currency Dealing Act Amended." *Horn of Africa Bulletin* (January 1994): 35.

"An Overview of Developments in Somaliland." *Horn of Africa Bulletin* 7, no.1 (1995): 23–24.

El Houdaiby, Ibrahim. "Islamism in and after Egypt's Revolution." In *The Arab Spring in Egypt: Revolution and Beyond*, edited by Bahgat Korany and Rabab El-Mahdi, 125–152. Cairo: American University in Cairo Press, 2012.

Howeidy, Amira. "Matariyya, Egypt's New Theater of Dissent." *Middle East Report Online*. June 4, 2015. www.merip.org/2015/06/matariyya-egypts-new-theater-of-dissent/.

Humphreys, Macartan. "Natural Resources, Conflict, and Resolution: Uncovering the Mechanisms." *The Journal of Conflict Resolution* 49, no. 4 (2005): 508–537.

Huntington, Samuel. *The Clash of Civilizations and the Remaking of World Order*. New York: Touchstone, 1996.

Hussein, Sayiid. *Al-qita' gheir al-munazam fi Misr, Al-markaz al-qawmi lil-buhuuth al- ijtima'iyah wa al-jinaiyah* [The Informal Sector in Egypt, the National Center for Social and Criminal Research]. Cairo: Al-Ahram Strategic Center, 1996.

Hyden, Goran. *No Shortcuts to Progress*. London: Heineman, 1983.

*The Changing Context of Institutional Development in Sub-Saharan Africa, The Long-Term Perspective of Sub-Saharan Africa, vol. I*. Washington, DC: World Bank, 1990.

*Comparative Politics in Comparative Perspective*. Cambridge, UK: Cambridge University Press, 2006.

*African Politics in Comparative Perspective*. New York: Cambridge University Press, 2008.

Iannaccone, Laurence R. "Why Strict Churches Are Strong." *American Journal of Sociology* 99, no. 5 (1994): 1180–1211.

Ibrahim, Abdullahi Ali. *Manichean Delirium: Decolonizing the Judiciary and Islamic Renewal in Sudan, 1898–1985*. Leiden: Brill, 2008.

Ibrahim, Badr al-Din A. "Some Aspects of Islamic Banking in LDACs: Reflections on the Faisal Islamic Bank, Sudan." In *The Least Developed and the Oil-Rich Arab Countries*, edited by Kunibert Raffer and M. A. Mohamed Salih, 6–14. London: Macmillan Press, 1992.

"Poverty Alleviation via Islamic Banking: Finance to Micro-Enterprises (MEs) in Sudan: Some Lessons for Poor Countries." *Sudan Economy Research Group Discussion Paper: Institute for World Economics and International Management (IWIM)*, no. 35 (March 2003).

Ibrahim, Saad Eddin and Nemaat Guenena. "The Changing Face of Egypt's Islamic Activism: 1974–1995." Unpublished manuscript. Cairo: Ibn Khaldun Center for Development Studies, September 1995.

International Monetary Fund. IMF Adjustment Programs in Africa: 1985 Occasional Paper, no. 5. Washington, DC: International Monetary Fund, 1985.

"IMF Awaits Reforms as Aid Donors Hang Back." *African Business*. July 1989, 35.

International Crisis Group. "Divisions in Sudan's Ruling Party and the Threat to the Country's Future Stability." Africa Report, no. 174 (2011).

"God, Oil, and Country: Changing the Logic of War in Sudan." Executive Summary Report, no. 39 (2004).

"Somalia: The Trouble with Puntland." Africa Briefing, no. 63 (2009).

International Labor Organization. *Employment, Income and Equality: A Strategy for Increasing Productivity in Kenya*. Geneva: International Labor Organization, 1972.

"Islamic Banks Bury the Egyptian Economy." *Middle East Economics Digest (MEED)* (July 7, 1992).

"Egypt Holds Promise for the Patient." *Middle East Economic Digest (MEED)* (May 1985): 10.

Ismail, Salwa. "The Politics of Urban Cairo: Informal Communities and the State." *The Arab Studies Journal* 4, no. 2 (1996): 119–132.

"Ithnayn milyar dulaar tahwilat as-sudanin fi al-khalij" [Two Billion Dollars' Worth of Remittances from Sudanese in the Gulf]. *Al-Majalla*. June 11–17, 1986.

Jamal, Vali. "Somalia: Understanding an Unconventional Economy." *Development and Change* 19, no. 2 (1988): 203–265.

Johnson, Douglas H. *The Root Causes of Sudan's Civil Wars*. Bloomington: Indiana University Press, 2003.

El-Kadi, Galila. "Market Mechanism and Spontaneous Urbanization in Egypt: The Cairo Case." *International Journal of Urban Regional Research* 12, no. 2 (1988): 22–37.

Kagwanja, Peter Mwangi. "Facing Mount Kenya or Facing Mecca? The Mungiki, Ethnic Violence and the Politics of the Moi Succession in Kenya." *African Affairs* 102 (2003): 25–49.

Kaldor, Mary. *New and Old Wars: Organized Violence in a Global Era*. Redwood City, CA: Stanford University Press, 1999.

Karrar, Ali Salih. *The Sufi Brotherhoods in the Sudan*. Evanston, IL: Northwestern University Press, 1992.

Katzenstein, Peter J. *Small States in World Markets: Industrial Policy in Europe*. Ithaca, NY: Cornell University Press, 1985.

Keppel, Gilles. *Muslim Extremism in Egypt: The Prophet and Pharaoh*. Berkeley: University of California Press, 1984.

"Islamists versus the State in Egypt and Algeria." *Daedalus* 27 (Summer 1995): 109–121.

*Jihad: The Trail of Political Islam*. Cambridge, MA: Harvard University Press, 2002.

Khalid, Mansour. *The Revolution of Dismay*. London: Kegan Paul International, 1985.

*The Government They Deserve: The Role of the Elite in Sudan's Political Evolution*. London: Kegan Paul International, 1990.

*Al-Nukhba al-Sudaniyya wa idman al-fashal*. Cairo: Dar al-Amin, 1993.

Khalifa, Muhammad 'Umar. *Malamih min tajribat al-islah al-iqtisadi fi al-Sudan* [Reflections on the Experiments in Economic Reform in Sudan]. Khartoum: The National Center for Media Production, 1995.

Kibble, Steve. "Somaliland: Surviving without Recognition, Somalia: Recognized but Failing?" *International Relations* 15, no. 5 (2001): 5–25.

"Kilmit al-sir baskawit: khamsat tujjar yasaytarun 'ala al-suq al-aswad fi al-Sudan" [Password Biscuit: Five Merchants Dominate the Black Market in Sudan]. Al-Majalla, no. 331 (June 11–14, 1986): 30–31.

Krasner, Stephen D. and Carlos Pascual. "Addressing State Failure." *Foreign Affairs* 84, no. 4 (2002): 153–163.

Krueger, Alan B. and Jitka Maleckova. "Education, Poverty and Terrorism: Is There a Causal Connection?" *The Journal of Economic Perspectives* 17, no. 4 (2003): 119–144.

"Poverty Doesn't Create Terrorists." *The New York Times*. May 29, 2003.

*What Makes a Terrorist: Economics and the Roots of Terrorism*. Princeton, NJ: Princeton University Press, 2007.

Kuran, Timur. "Islamic Economics and the Islamic Subeconomy." *Journal of Economic Perspectives* 9, no. 4 (Fall 1995): 155–173.

*Islam and Mammon: The Economic Predicaments of Islamism*. Princeton, NJ: Princeton University Press, 2004.

Ladjal, Tarek and Benaouda Bensaid. "Sufism and Politics in Contemporary Egypt: A Study of Sufi Political Engagement in the Pre and Post-revolutionary Reality of January 2011." *Journal of Asian and African Studies* 50, no. 4 (2015): 468–485.

Laitin David D. and Said S. Samata. "Somalia and the World Economy." *Review of African Political Economy* 11, no. 30 (1984): 58–72.

*Somalia: A Nation in Search of a State*. Boulder, CO: Westview Press, 1987.

"La li-qanun al-tawari: al-mu'arada tarfud al-qanun 'al-aswad' li-tadmir sharikat tawsif al-amwal" [No to the Emergency Law: The Opposition Rejects the 'Black Law' Designed to Destroy the Islamic Investment Houses]. *Al-Sha'ab*. June 14, 1988.

Layish, Aharon and Gabriel Warburg. *The Reinstatement of Islamic Law in Sudan under Numayri: An Evaluation of a Legal Experiment in the Light of Its Historical Context, Methodology, and Repercussions*. London: Brill, 2002.

Levi, Margaret. "The State of the Study of the State." In *Political Science: The State of the Discipline*, edited by Ira Katznelson and Helen V. Milner, 33–54. New York: W. W. Norton, 2002.

Le Sage, Andre. "Somalia: Sovereign Disguise for a Mogadishu Mafia." *Review of African Political Economy* 29, no. 91 (2001): 132–138.

Lewis, Bernard. *The Crisis of Islam: Holy War and Unholy Terror*. New York: Random House, 2004.

Lewis, I. M. *A Modern History of the Somali: Nation and State in the Horn of Africa*. Oxford, United Kingdom or Oxford, UK: Oxford University Press and James Currey, 2002.

"The Ogaden War and the Fragility of Somali Segmented Nationalism." *Horn of Africa* 13, no. 1, 2 (1990): 573–579.

*Blood and Bone: The Call of Kinship in Somali Society*. Lawrenceville, NJ: Red Sea Press, 1994, 178.

"Doing Violence to Ethnography: A Response to Catherine Besteman's 'Representing Violence and "Othering" Somalia'." *Cultural Anthropology* 13, no. 1 (1994): 100–108.

Lichbach, Mark Irving. "An Evaluation of 'Does Economic Inequality Breed Political Conflict?' Studies" *World Politics* 41, no. 4 (1989): 431–470.

Lindell, Ilda. "Introduction." In *Africa's Informal Workers*, edited by Ilda Lindell, 1–30. London: Zed Books, 2010.

Lindley, Anna. *Migrant Remittances in the Context of Crisis in Somali Society: A Case Study of Hargesia*. London: Overseas Development Institute, Humanitarian Policy Group, 2006.

*Al-Liwa' al-Islami* [The Islamic Current]. February 25, 1982, cited in Ansari, Hamid. *Egypt: The Stalled Society*. Albany: State University of New York Press, 1986.

Löfgren, Hans. "Economic Policy in Egypt: A Breakdown in Reform Resistance." *International Journal of Middle Eastern Studies* 25 (August 1993): 407–421.

Luong, Pauline and Erika Weinthal. "Rethinking the Resource Curse: Ownership Structure, Institutional Capacity, and Domestic Constraints." *Annual Review of Political Science* 9 (2006): 241–263.

Lynch, Marc. "Will the Arab Revolutions Spread?" *Foreign Policy*. January 26, 2011.

MacGaffey, Janet. *Entrepreneurs and Parasites: The Struggle for Indigenous Capitalism in Zaire*. New York: Cambridge University Press, 2014.

MacGaffey, Janet. and R. Bazenguissa-Ganga. *Congo-Paris: Transnational Traders on the Margins of the Law*. Oxford: James Currey, 2000.

MacGaffey, Janet. and G. Windsperger. *The Endogenous Economy, the Long-Term Perspective Study of Sub-Saharan Africa 1*. Washington, DC: World Bank, 1990.

Mahmoud, 'Abd al-Fadil. *Al-khadi'a al-maliyya al-kubra. Al-iqtisad al-siyasi li-sharikat tawzif al- amwal* [The Great Financial Deception: The Political Economy of the Investment Companies]. Cairo: Dar al-mustaqbal al-'arabi, 1989, 12–30. Cited in Utvik, Björn Olav. *Islamist Economics in Egypt: The Pious Road to Development*. Boulder, CO: Lynn Reinner Press, 2006.

Mahmoud, Fatima Babiker. *The Sudanese Bourgeoisie: Vanguard of Development?* London: Zed Books, 1984.

Mahmoud, Muhammad. "Sufism and Islamism in the Sudan." In *African Islam and Islam in Africa*, edited by Eva Rosander and David Westerlund, 33–64. Athens: Ohio State University Press, 1997.

Mahmoud, Saba. *Politics of Piety: The Islamic Revival and the Feminist Subject*. Princeton, NJ: Princeton University Press, 2005.

Makinda, Samuel M. *Seeking Peace from Chaos: Humanitarian Intervention in Somalia*. Boulder, CO: Lynn Reinner, 1993.

Maleckova, Jika. "Impoverished Terrorists: Stereotype or Reality." In *Root Causes of Terrorism: Myths, Reality and Ways Forward*, edited by Tore Bjorgo, 33–43. New York: Routledge, 2005.

Mallay, Sebastian. "The Reluctant Imperialist: Terrorism, Failed States, and the Case for American Empire." *Foreign Affairs*. 2002, 2–7.

Mandaville, Peter. *Islam and Politics*. New York: Routledge Press, 2014.

Marchal, Roland. "Understanding Somalia." *May Newspaper*. November 11, 1995.

*Final Report on the Post Civil War Somali Business Class*. Paris: European Commission, Somalia Unit, 1996.

"A Tentative Assessment of the Somali Harakat Al-Shabaab." *Journal of Eastern African Studies* 3, no. 3 (2009): 381–404.

Markakis, John. *National and Class Conflict in the Horn of Africa*. Cambridge, UK: Cambridge University Press, 1987.

Marty, Martin E. and R. Scott Appleby, eds. *Fundamentalism Observed*. Chicago: University of Chicago Press, 1991.

McCormick B. and Jackline Wahba. "Migration and Mobility in the Egyptian Labor Market." *Economic Research Forum Research Report*, no. 0401 (2004).

McKinley, James C. "Islamic Movement's Niche: Bringing Order to Somalia's Clans." *New York Times*. August 23, 1996.

Meagher, Kate. *Identity Economics: Social Networks and the Informal Economy in Nigeria*. London: James Currey, 2010.

Medani, Khalid M. "Factors Contributing to the Political Ascendancy of the Muslim Brethren in Sudan." *Arab Studies Quarterly* (Summer 1990): 33–53.

"Sudan's Human and Political Crisis." *Current History* 92, no. 574 (1993): 203–207.

"Funding Fundamentalism: The Political Economy of an Islamist State." In *Political Islam: Essays from Middle East Report*, edited by Joel Beinin and Joe Stork, 166–180. Berkeley: University of California Press, 1996.

"Survey on Internal Migration and Remittance Inflows in Northwest and Northeast Somalia." *United Nations Coordination Unit (UNCU) and Food Security Assessment Unit [FSAU]* (March 2000): 1–78.

"Financing Terrorism or Survival: Informal Finance, State Collapse in Somalia, and the US War on Terror." *Middle East Report* 32, no. 2 (2002): 2–9.

"The Horn of Africa in the Shadow of the Cold War: Understanding the Partition of Sudan from a Regional Perspective." *Journal of North African Studies* 17, no. 2 (2011): 275–294.

"Informal Networks, Economic Livelihoods and the Politics of Social Welfare in Somalia and Egypt: The Political Consequences of the War on Terrorist Finance." *Journal of Near East and Islamic Law* 10, no. 99 (2011): 99–137.

"Sudanese Echoes." *Middle East Report Online*. December 19, 2012.

"Between Grievances and State Violence: Youth and Islamist Activism beyond the Arab Spring." *Middle East Report* 267 (2013): 37–48.

Meijer, Roel. "Commanding Right and Forbidding Wrong as a Principle of Social Action: The Case of the Egyptian al-Jama'a al-Islamiyya." In *Global Salafism: Islam's New Religious Movement*, edited by Roel Meijer, 190–219. London: C. Hurst and Co., 2009.

Menkhaus, Ken and Terrence Lyons. *What Are the Lessons to Be Learned from Somalia?* Washington, DC: Center for Strategic and International Studies (CSIS), January 1993.

"State Collapse in Somalia: Second Thoughts." *Review of African Political Economy* 30, no. 97 (2003): 405–422.

"The Crisis in Somalia: Tragedy in Five Acts." *African Affairs* 106, no. 204 (2007): 357–390.

"Governance without Government in Somalia: Spoilers, State Building, and the Politics of Coping." *International Security* 31, no. 3 (2007): 74–106.

MERI Report. *Central Bank of Egypt*. London: The Economist Intelligence Unit Viewswire, 1985.

Mesfin, Berouk. "The Political Development of Somaliland and Its Conflict with Puntland." *Institute for Security Studies Papers* 200 (2009): 20.

Metz, Helen Chapin, ed. *Egypt, a Country Study*. Washington, DC: Library of Congress Publication, 1991.

Miller, Catherine. "Upper Egyptian Regionally Based Communities in Cairo: Traditional or Modern Forms of Urbanization?" In *Cairo Cosmopolitan: Politics, Culture, and Urban Space in the New Globalized Middle East*, edited by Diane Singerman and Paul Amar, 375–398. Cairo: American University in Cairo Press, 2006.

Mingione, Enzio. *Fragmented Societies: A Sociology of Economic Life beyond the Market Paradigm*. Oxford: Blackwell, 1991.

"Life Strategies and Social Economies in the Postfordist Age." *International Journal of Urban and Regional Research* 18, no. 1 (1994): 24–45.

Ministry of Planning. *Five Year Plan for 1978–1982*. Cairo: Ministry of Planning, 1977. Cited in Wilson, Rodney. "Wither the Egyptian Economy." *British Journal of Middle Eastern Studies* 20, no. 2 (1993): 12–18.

*Al-Misrawi yanshur natayij al-marhalah al-thanyah lil-intikhabat al-barlamaniyiyyah* [Al-Misrawi Publishes the Result of the Second Round of Parliamentary Elections], *al-Misrawi*. August 6, 2011.

Mitchell, Timothy. "The Market's Place." In *Directions of Change in Rural Egypt*, edited by Nicholas S. Hopkins and Kirsten Westergaard, 3–24. Cairo: American University in Cairo Press, 1998.

Mitwally, Essam. "On the Emerging Industrialization Policies and Practices in the Arab Republic of Egypt." *Journal of Economic Cooperation Among Islamic Countries* 20, no. 1 (1999): 22.

Mohamed Ahmad Hassan, Fareed. "Adjustment Policies, Economic Growth, and Income Distribution: The Sudanese Case." *Scandinavian Journal of Development Studies* 13 (May–June 1994): 221–245.

Mohan, Giles and Alfred B. Zack-Williams. "Globalization from Below: Conceptualizing the Role of the African Diaspora in Africa's Development." *Review of African Political Economy* 92, no. 29 (2002): 85–89.

Moheldin, Abdelrahman Omer. *Turabi wa al-inqath* [Turabi and the 'Salvation]. Damascus: Dar Ekrema Publishing, 2006.

Moneep. "Natayij al-Ahkam al-'Askariyya 'ala al-Ikhwan al-Muslimeen" [Results of the Military Verdicts against the Muslim Brotherhood]. *Moneep*. March 5, 2008.

Moustafa, Tamir. *The Struggle for Constitutional Power: Law, Politics, and Economic Development in Egypt*. Cambridge, UK: Cambridge University Press, 2007.

Mubarak, Jamil A. "The 'Hidden Hand' behind the Resilience of the Stateless Economy of Somalia." *World Development* 25, no. 12 (1997): 2027–2041.

Mudawi, Al Bagkir Yusif. "Islamic Banks Problems and Prospects: Islamic Banking Evaluation of Experience." *Faisal Islamic Bank Publications*. 1984, 1–67.

"Mudun Masr Taht al-'Isar" [Egyptian Cities under Siege]. *Al-Sha'ab*. January 19, 1993.

Munson, Henry, Jr. *Islam and Revolution in the Middle East*. New Haven: Yale University Press, 1986.

Munson, Ziad. "Islamic Mobilization: Social Movement Theory and the Egyptian Muslim Brotherhood." *Sociological Quarterly* 42, no. 2 (2002): 487–521.

Murphy, Kim. "Islamic Militants Build Power Base in Sudan: The Regime Vows to Export Beliefs Worrying Its More Secular Arab Neighbors and the West." *The Los Angeles Times*. April 6, 1992.

Musa, Ahmed M. and Cindy Horst. "State Formation and Economic Development in Post-War Somaliland: The Impact of the Private Sector in an Unrecognized State." *Conflict, Security and Development* 19, no. 1 (2019): 35–53.

Musallam, Adnan A. *From Secularism to Jihad: Sayyid Qutb and the Foundations of Radical Islam*. Westport, CT: Praeger Publishers, 2005.

Mustafa, Hala. *Al-intikhabat al-barlamaniyya fi Misr: 1995* [The 1995 Elections in Egypt]. Cairo: Al-Ahram Center for Political and Strategic Studies, 1995.

Narayan, D. *Bonds and Bridges: Social Capital and Poverty*. Washington, DC: World Bank, 1999.

Nasr, Hamdi. *Tamulat fi 'Unf wa Tobah al-Jama'at al-Islamiyya* [Reflections on the Violence and Repentance of the Jama'at al-Islamiyya]. Alexandria: Dar al-Ein Publishing, 2010.

Nasr, Vali. *The Rise of Islamic Capitalism: Why the New Muslim Middle Class Is the Key to Defeating Extremism.* New York: Council on Foreign Relations Free Press, 2010.

Nasser, Heba. "Migration, Transfer and Development in Egypt." *Euro-Mediterranean Consortium for Applied Research on International Migration (CARIM) Research Report.* Florence: Robert Schuman Centre for Advanced Studies, 2005.

The National Commission on Terrorist Attacks upon the United States. *The 9/11 Commission Report: Final Report of the National Commission on Terrorist Attacks Upon the United States.* New York: Norton, 2004.

The National Population Council, Ministry of Social Welfare and Security. "Draft Report: The Millennium Development Goals (MDGs): Status, Challenges and Prospects for Sudan." Khartoum, Sudan, 2012.

Niblock, Tim. "Sudan's Economic Nightmare." *Middle East Research and Information Project (MERIP)* 35 (1985): 15–32.

*Class and Power in Sudan.* Albany: State University of New York Press, 1987.

North, Douglas C. *Structure and Change in Economic History.* New York: W. W. Norton and Company, 1981.

*Institutions, Institutional Change and Economic Performance.* Cambridge, UK: Cambridge University Press, 1990.

Nur, Ibrahim. *Al-Siyassah al-Iqtisadiyya li-al-Ikhwan* [The Brotherhood's Economic Policy]. Cairo: Markaz al-Mahrusi Publishing, 2014.

Oliver, Melvin L. "The Urban Black Community as Network: Toward a Social Network Perspective." *The Sociological Quarterly* 29, no. 4 (1988): 623–645.

Omar, Nabil. "Imbaba's Empire of 'Terrorism'." *Al-Ahram.* December 8, 1992.

Osman, Ahmad Zaki. "Cairo's Copts Organize Groups for Self-Defense." *Egypt Independent.* May 8, 2011.

"Roots of Religious Violence Lie in Both State and Society." *Egypt Independent.* April 13, 2013.

Ostebo, Teri. "African Salafism: Religious Piety and the Politicization of Purity." *Islamic Africa* 6 (2015): 1–29.

Ouchi, William G. "Markets, Bureaucracies and Clans." In *Markets, Hierarchies and Networks the Coordination of Social Life,* edited by Jennifer Frances, Rosalind Levacic, Jeremy Mitchell, and Grahame Thompson, 246–255. London: Sage, 1991.

Pape, Robert. *Dying to Win: The Strategic Logic of Suicide Terrorism.* New York: Random House, 2006.

Patey, Luke A. "State Rules: Oil Companies and Armed Conflict in Sudan." *Third World Quarterly* 28, no. 5 (2007): 997–1016.

Perlez, Jane. "Sudan Is Seen as Safe Base for Mideast Terror Groups." *New York Times.* January 26, 1992.

Pham, Jason Peter. "The Somaliland Exception: Lessons on Post-Conflict State Building from the Part of the Former Somalia that Works." *Marine Corps University Journal* 3, no. 1 (2012): 1–33.

Piore, Michael J. and Charles F. Sabel. *The Second Industrial Divide: Possibilities for Prosperity*. New York: Basic Books, 1984.

Polyani, Karl. *The Great Transformation: The Political and Economic Origins of Our Time*. Boston: Beacon Press, 1944.

Portes, Alejandro. "The Informal Economy and Its Paradoxes." In *The Handbook of Economic Sociology*, edited by N. J. Smelser and R. Swedberg, 426–447. Princeton, NJ: Princeton University Press, 1994.

Portes, Alejandro, Manuel Castells, and Lauren A. Benton. *The Informal Economy: Studies in Advanced and Less Developed Countries*. Baltimore: Johns Hopkins University Press, 1989.

Portes, Alejandro and P. Peter Landolt. "The Downside of Social Capital." *The American Prospect* 26 (1996): 18–21.

Portes, Alejandro and Julia Sensenbrenner. "Embeddedness and Immigration – Notes on the Social Determinants of Economic Action." *American Journal of Sociology* 98, no. 6 (1993): 1320–1350.

Powell, Walter W. "Neither Market Nor Hierarchy: Network Forms of Organization." In *Markets, Hierarchies and Networks. The Coordination of Social Life*, edited by Jennifer Frances, Rosalind Levacic, Jeremy Mitchell, and Grahame Thompson, 265–276. London: Sage, 1991.

Powell, Walter W. and Laurel Smith-Doerr. "Networks and Economic Life." In *The Handbook of Economic Sociology*, edited by Neil J. Smelser and Richard Swedberg, 368–402. Princeton, NJ: Princeton University Press, 1994.

Qandil, Amany. *Civil Society and Social Change*. Cairo: Al-Ahram Center for Political Studies, 1998.

Qardawi, Yusif. *Al-Sahwa' al-Islamiyyah: bayn al-juhuud wa al-tataruuf* [The Islamic Revival: Between Efforts and Extremism]. Cairo: Al-Ahram Strategic Center, 1994.

Qutb, Sayyid. *Al-'Adalah al-ijtima'iyah fi 'l-Islam* [Social Justice in Islam]. Cairo, Egypt: Maktabat Misr, 1953).

Radnitz, Scott. "Informal Politics and the State." *Comparative Politics* 43, no. 3 (2011): 351–371.

Rashid, A. *Jihad: The Rise of Militant Islam in Central Asia*. New Haven, CT: Yale University, 2002.

Reno, William. *Warlord Politics and African States*. Boulder, CO: Lynne Rienner, 1998.

"Clandestine Economies, Violence and States in Africa." *Journal of International Affairs* 53 (February 2000): 433–459.

"Somalia and Survival in the Shadow of the Global Economy." *Queen Elizabeth House (QEH) Working Papers* (2003): 8–12.

Roberts, Bryan. "Informal Economy and Family Strategies." *International Journal of Urban and Regional Networks* 18, no. 1 (1994): 6–23.

Roitman, Janet. *Fiscal Disobedience: An Anthropology of Economic Regulation in Central Africa*. Princeton, NJ: Princeton University Press, 1993.

Rogowski, Ronald. *Commerce and Coalitions*. Princeton, NJ: Princeton University Press, 1989.

Rose, Richard. *Measures of Social Capital in African Surveys*. Strathclyde, UK: University of Strathclyde, 2002.

Ross, Michael. "Does Oil Hinder Democracy?" *World Politics* 53, no. 3 (2001): 325–361.

"A Closer Look at Oil, Diamonds, and Civil War." *Annual Review of Political Science* 9 (2006): 265–300.

Rothchild, Donald. "Ethnic Insecurity, Peace Agreements, and State Building." In *State, Conflict and Democracy in Africa*, edited by Richard Joseph, 319–338. Boulder, CO: Lynne Reinner Press, 1999.

Roy, Delwin A. "The Hidden Economy of Egypt." *Middle East Studies* 28, no. 4 (1991): 689–711.

Roy, Oliver. *Globalized Islam: The Search for a New Ummah*. New York: Columbia University Press, 2004.

Sageman, Marc. *Understanding Terror Networks*. Philadelphia: University of Pennsylvania Press, 2004.

Salacuse, Jeswald W. "Arab Capital and Middle Eastern Development Finance: The Emerging Institutional Framework." *Journal of World Trade Law* 14, no. 1 (1980): 283–309.

Salama, 'Abdin Ahmad. "Islamic Banks: Economic Significance and Methods of Control." Faisal Islamic Bank Sudan Publications, no. 3 (1984): 1–46.

Samatar, Abdi I. *The State and Rural Transformation in Northern Somalia, 1884–1986*. Madison: University of Wisconsin Press, 1989.

"Destruction of State and Society in Somalia: Beyond the Tribal Convention." *Journal of Modern African Studies* 30, no. 4 (1992): 625–641.

"Dictators and Warlords Are a Modern Invention." *Africa News*. December 21, 1992 and January 3, 1993.

"Leadership and Ethnicity in the Making of African State Models: Botswana versus Somalia." *Third World Quarterly* 18, no. 4 (1997): 687–707.

El Sammani, Mohamed O. "Management Problems of Greater Khartoum." In *African Cities in Crisis: Managing Rapid Urban Growth*, edited by Richard. E. Stren and Rodney R. White, 170–200. Boulder, CO: Westview Press, 1989.

Sassen, Saskia. *The Mobility of Labor and Capital: A Study in International Investment and Labor Flow*. New York: Cambridge University Press, 1988.

*A Sociology of Globalization*. New York: W. W. Norton and Company, 2007.

*Sawt Giza* (Voice of Giza), November 1995.

Scheele, Judith. *Smugglers and Saints of the Sahara: Regional Connectivity in the Twentieth Century*. New York: Cambridge University Press, 2015.

Schwedler, Jillian. "Myth, Menace or Mobilizer?" *SAIS Review* 21, no. 2 (2001): 1–17.

Scott, James. *The Moral Economy of the Peasant: Rebellions and Subsistence in Southeast Asia*. New Haven: Yale University Press, 1976.

Shaaeldin, Elfatih and Richard C. Brown. "Towards an Understanding of Islamic Banking in Sudan: The Case of the Faisal Islamic Bank." In *Sudan: State,*

*Capital and Transformation*, edited by Tony Barnett and Abbas Abdelkarim, 4–28. New York: Croom Helm, 1988.

Shalaby, Ahmed, Sami Abdel Radi, and Ahmed Abdel Latif. "Twenty-Three Salafis Charged with Terrorism in Imbaba." *Egypt Independent*. May 12, 2011.

Shapiro, Jacob N. *The Terrorist's Dilemma: Managing Violent Covert Organizations*. Princeton, NJ: Princeton University Press, 2015.

Shapiro, Jacob N. and David A. Siegel. "Underfunding in Terrorist Organizations." *International Studies Quarterly* 51, no. 2 (2008): 415–429.

Sharkey, Heather J. "Arab Identity and Ideology in Sudan: The Politics of Language, Ethnicity and Race." *African Affairs* 107, no. 426 (January 2008): 21–43.

Simone, Abdou Maliqalim. *In Whose Image? Political Islam and Urban Practices in Sudan*. Chicago: University of Chicago Press, 1994.

Sims, David. *Understanding Cairo: The Logic of a City Out of Control*. Cairo: American University in Cairo Press, 2010.

Singerman, Diane. *Avenues of Participation*. Princeton, NJ: Princeton University Press, 1995, 173.

"The Networked World of Islamist Social Movements." In *Islamic Activism: A Social Movements Approach*, edited by Quinton Wiktorowicz, 143–163. Bloomington: Indiana University Press, 2004.

"The Siege of Imbaba, Egypt's Internal 'Other', and the Criminalization of Politics." In *Cairo Contested: Governance, Urban Space, and Global Modernity*, edited by Diane Singerman, 111–144. Cairo: American University in Cairo Press, 2011.

Sissons, Miranda. "Egypt, Margins of Repression: State Limits on Non-Governmental Organization Activism." *Human Rights Watch* 17, no. 8 (2005): 1–43. http://hrw.org/reports/2005/egypt0705

*Somailand's Investment in Peace: Analysing the Diaspora's Economic Engagement in Peace Building*. Hargeisa, Somaliland: Interpeace, June 2008, 11.

Soliman, Samer. "The Rise and Decline of the Islamic Banking Model in Egypt." In *The Politics of Islamic Finance*, edited by Clement M. Henry Moore and Rodney Wilson, 266–284. Edinburgh: Edinburgh University Press, 2004.

"The Somali Social and Institutional Profile: An Executive Summary." *Working Papers*, no. 79, African Studies Center, Boston University, 1983.

Solovieva, Daria. "A Trillion Dollars and Counting: How Egypt's New President Will Boost Islamic Banking." *International Business Times*. July 18, 2012.

Springborg, Robert. "Egypt." In *Economic and Political Liberalisation in the Middle East*, edited by Tim Niblock and Emma Murphy, 145–163. London: British Academic Press, 1993.

Sprinzak, Ehud. "Rational Fanatics." *Foreign Policy* 120 (September–October 2000): 66–73.

Stiansen, Endre. "Interest Politics: Islamic Finance in Sudan, 1977–2001." In *The Politics of Islamic Finance*, edited by Clement M. Henry and Rodney Wilson, 156–165. Edinburgh: Edinburgh University Press, 2004.

Stiglitz, Joseph E. "Formal and Informal Institutions." In *Social Capital: A Multifaceted Perspective*, edited by Partha Dasgupta and Ismail Serageldin, 59–68. Washington, DC: World Bank, 2000.

A Study on the Imbaba Elections, Unpublished Report, 2000.

Sudanow. "An Equal Place for All." *Sudanow*. February 1980.

Sudanow. "Islam: Blueprint for a New Century." *Sudanow*. November 1979, 11.

Sudan Tribune. "Sudanese President Pledges to Protect Southerners Living in the North." *Sudan Tribune*. October 4, 2010.

"Pro-Salafist Newspaper Blasts Sudan's Beshir, Calls Him a 'Serial Liar'." *Sudan Tribune*. March 6, 2013.

Sullivan, Denis J. *Private Voluntary Organizations in Egypt, Islamic Development, Private Initiative, and State Control*. Gainesville: University of Florida Press, 1994.

"A profile of Islamic Banking." *Al-Syasi al-Masri*, August 27, 1995.

"Tadil wizari wasi wa taraju shamil 'an al-islah al-iqtisadi" [A Broad Cabinet Change and Sweeping Retreat from Economic Reform]. *Al-Ahali*. April 3, 1985, 3–4. Cited in Bianchi, Robert. "Businessmen's Association in Egypt and Turkey." *Annals of the American Academy of Political and Social Science* 482, no. 1 (1985): 147–159.

"Tahweeel al-anshita al-Ikhwaniyyah min al-nizam al-fardi ila al-muassasah" [The Transformation in the Ikhwan's Activities from the Individual Effort (Nizam) to an Institution]. 24 *Sa'ah*. August 13, 2007.

Tammam, Hossam. *Al-Ikhwan al-Muslimeen: Sanawat Ma Qabl al-Thawra* [The Muslim Brotherhood: The Years before the Revolution]. Cairo: Dar al-Shuruq, 2013.

Taylor, Michael. "Rationality and Revolutionary Collective Action." In *Rationality and Revolution*, edited by Michael Taylor, 1–38. Cambridge, UK: Cambridge University Press, 1988.

Tarrow, Syndey G. *Power in Movement: Social Movements and Contentious Politics*. London: Cambridge University Press, 1994.

"Making Social Science Work across Time and Space: A Critical Reflection on Robert Putman's Making Democracy Work." *American Political Science Review* 2, no. 90 (1996): 389–339.

Tessler, Mark. "The Origins of Popular Support for Islamist Movements: A Political Economy Analysis." In *Islam, Democracy, and the State in North Africa*, edited by John Entelis, 93–126. Bloomington: Indiana University Press, 1997.

Thurston, Alex. "Northern Sudan's Protests Sparked by Egypt and Tunisia, But Will They Have the Same Effect?" *Christian Science Monitor*. January 31, 2011.

Tilly, Charles. "Models and Realities of Popular Collective Action." *Social Research* 52 (Winter 1985): 717–748.

"War Making and State Making as Organized Crime." In *Bringing the State Back In*, edited by Peter Evans, Dietrich Rueschemeir, and Theda Skocpol, 169–191. Cambridge, UK: Cambridge University Press, 1985.

*Coercion, Capital and European States, AD 990–1990*. Cambridge, UK: Cambridge University Press, 1990.

*The Politics of Collective Violence*. Cambridge, UK: Cambridge University Press, 2003.

"Trust and Rule." *Theory and Society* 33, no. 1 (2004): 1–30.

*Trust and Rule*. New York: Cambridge University Press, 2005.

"Trust Networks in Transnational Migration." *Sociological Forum* 22, no.1 (March 2007): 3–24.

Title III, USA PATRIOT Act of 2001, 107 P.L. 56, 115 Stat. 272, 2001.

Title II of P.L. 95–223 (codified at 50 U.S.C. 1701 et seq).

Toth, James. "Beating Plowshares into Swords: The Relocation of Rural Egyptian Workers and Their Discontent." In *Directions of Change in Rural Egypt*, edited by Nicholas S. Hopkins and Kirsten Westergaard, 51–72. Cairo: American University in Cairo Press, 1998.

Trimingham, Spencer J. *The Sufi Orders of Islam*. London: Oxford University Press, 1971.

Tripp, Charles. *Islam and the Moral Economy: The Challenge of Capitalism*. New York: Cambridge University Press, 2006.

Turabi, Hassan. "The Islamic State." In *Voices of a Resurgent Islam*, edited by John Esposito, 241–251. New York: Oxford University Press, 1983.

*Tajdid al-fikr al-Islami* [Renewal of Islamic Thought]. Khartoum: Dar al-Qarafi, Al- Maghrib, 1993.

*Al-Harakah al-Islamiyya fi al-Sudan* [The Islamic Movement in the Sudan]. Khartoum: Mahad al-buhuuth, wa al-dirasaat al ijtima'iyyah [Institute of Research and Social Studies], 1992.

Turner, Jennifer. *Blocking Faith, Freezing Charity: Chilling Muslim Charitable Giving in the 'War on Terrorist Financing'*. New York: American Civil Liberties Union (ACLU), June 2009.

Tyson, Laura D'Andrea and Peter B. Kenen. "The International Transmission of Disturbances: A Framework of Comparative Analysis." In *The Impact of International Economic Disturbances on the Soviet Union and Eastern Europe: Transmission and Response*, edited by Egon Neuberger and Laura D'Andrea Tyson, 33–62. New York: Pegamon Press, 1990.

Tzannatos, Zafris and Iqbal Kaur. "Welfare State Policies in the Middle East and North Africa." In *When Markets Fail: Social Policy and Economic Reform*, edited by Ethan B. Kapstein and Branko Milanovic, 146–182. New York: Russell Sage Foundation, 2002.

United Nations Development Program. *Human Development Report 2001*. New York: United Nations Development Program, 2001.

Utvik, Björn Olav. *Islamist Economics in Egypt: The Pious Road to Development*. Boulder, CO: Lynn Reinner Press, 2006.

Varese, Frederic. *The Russian Mafia: Private Protection in a New Market Economy*. New York: Oxford University Press, 2001.

Verhoeven, Harry. *Water, Civilization and Power in Sudan: The Political Economy of Military- Islamist State Building*. Cambridge, UK: Cambridge University Press, 2015.

Vignal, Leila and Eric Denis. "Cairo as Regional/Global Economic Capital." In *Cairo Cosmopolitan: Politics, Culture, and Urban Space in the New Globalized*

*Middle East*, edited by Paul Amar and Diane Singerman, 99–152. Cairo: American University in Cairo Press, 2006.

Villalon, Leonardo A. *Islamic Society and State Power in Senegal: Disciplines and Citizens in Fatick*. Cambridge, UK: Cambridge University Press, 2006.

Voice of America. "Sudan President Warns Civil War Could Re-ignite." *Voice of America*. October 10, 2010. www.voanews.com/africa/sudan-president-warns-civil-war-could-re-ignite.

Wade, Ibrahim. *Islamic Finance in the Global Economy*. Edinburgh: Edinburgh University Press, 2000.

Wahba, Jackline. "Informality in Egypt: A Stepping Stone or a Dead End?" *Cairo, Egypt: Economic Research Forum (ERF)*, *Working Paper*, no. 456 (2009).

Waldinger, Roger. "The 'Other Side' of Embeddedness: A Case Study of the Interplay of Economy and Ethnicity." *Ethnic and Racial Studies* 18, no. 3 (1995): 555–580.

Walter, Barbara F. "The Critical Barrier to Civil War Settlement." *International Organization* 51, no. 3 (1997): 335–364.

Warburg, Gabriel R. "The *Sharia* in Sudan: Implementation and Repercussions, 1983–1989." *The Middle East Journal* 44, no. 4 (1990): 624–637.

"The Muslim Brotherhood in Sudan: From Reforms to Radicalism." *The Project for the Research of Islamist Movements (PRISM)*. Global Research in International Affairs (GLORIA) Center, Islam in Africa Research Project, 2006.

Waterbury, John. "The 'Soft State' and the Open Door: Egypt's Experience with Economic Liberalization, 1974–1985." *Comparative Politics* 18, no. 1 (1985): 65–83.

Weinstein, Jeremy M. *Inside Rebellion: The Politics of Insurgent Violence*. New York: Cambridge University Press, 2007.

Weintraub, Sidney. "Disrupting the Financing of Terrorism." *The Washington Quarterly* 25, no. 1 (2002): 53–60.

"Who Governs Sudan" [man yamluk al-sudan]. *Al-Sudan al-Hadith*. June 2, 2010.

Wickham, Carrie Rosefsky. *Mobilizing Islam: Religion, Activism and Political Change in Egypt*. New York: Columbia University Press, 2002.

Wiktorowicz, Quinton. *Islamic Activism: A Social Movement Approach*. Bloomington: Indiana University Press, 2004.

Wilson, Rodney. *Banking and Finance in the Arab Middle East*. London: St. Martin's Press, 1983.

"Wither the Egyptian Economy." *British Journal of Middle Eastern Studies* 20, no. 2 (1993): 204–213.

Wood, Graeme. "What ISIS Really Wants." *The Atlantic Monthly*. March 2015.

Woodward, Peter. *Sudan, 1898–1989: The Unstable State*. Boulder, CO: Lynne Rienner Publishers, 1990.

Woolcock, Michael and Deepa Narayan. "Social Capital: Implications for Development Theory, Research and Policy." *World Bank Research Observer* 15, no. 2 (2000): 225–249.

The World Bank. *Global Development Finance*. Washington, DC: World Bank Reports, 2007.

*Sudan Public Expenditure Review: Synthesis Report no. 41840-SD* (December 2007).

*World Bank Makes Progress to Support Remittance Flows to Somalia*, June 10, 2016. Accessed August 9, 2019. www.worldbank.org/en/news/press-release/2016/06/10/world-bank-makes-progress-to-support-remittance-flows-to-somalia.

The World Bank. *World Debt Tables: 1989–1990*, vols. 1 and 2. Washington, DC: World Bank, 1991.

Yongo-Bure, B. "Prospects for Socioeconomic Development of the South." In *The Search for Peace and Unity in Sudan*, edited by Francis M. Deng and Prosser Gifford, 14–28. Washington, DC: Wilson Center Press, 1987.

Young, John. "Eastern Sudan: Caught in a Web of External Interests." *Review of African Political Economy* 33, no. 109 (2006): 594–601.

Zubaida, Sami. "The Politics of Islamic Investment Companies in Egypt." *British Journal of Middle Eastern Studies* 17, no 2 (1990): 152–161.

Zahran, Farid. "New Civil Associations Law and the Current Political Times." *Al-Ahram*. July 23, 2002.

# Index

For EU product safety concerns, contact us at Calle de José Abascal, 56–1°,
28003 Madrid, Spain or eugpsr@cambridge.org.

www.ingramcontent.com/pod-product-compliance
Ingram Content Group UK Ltd.
Pitfield, Milton Keynes, MK11 3LW, UK
UKHW020403140625
459647UK00020B/2623
* 9 7 8 1 0 0 9 2 5 7 7 2 5 *